THE SPANISH KINGDOMS
1250–1516

Volume I

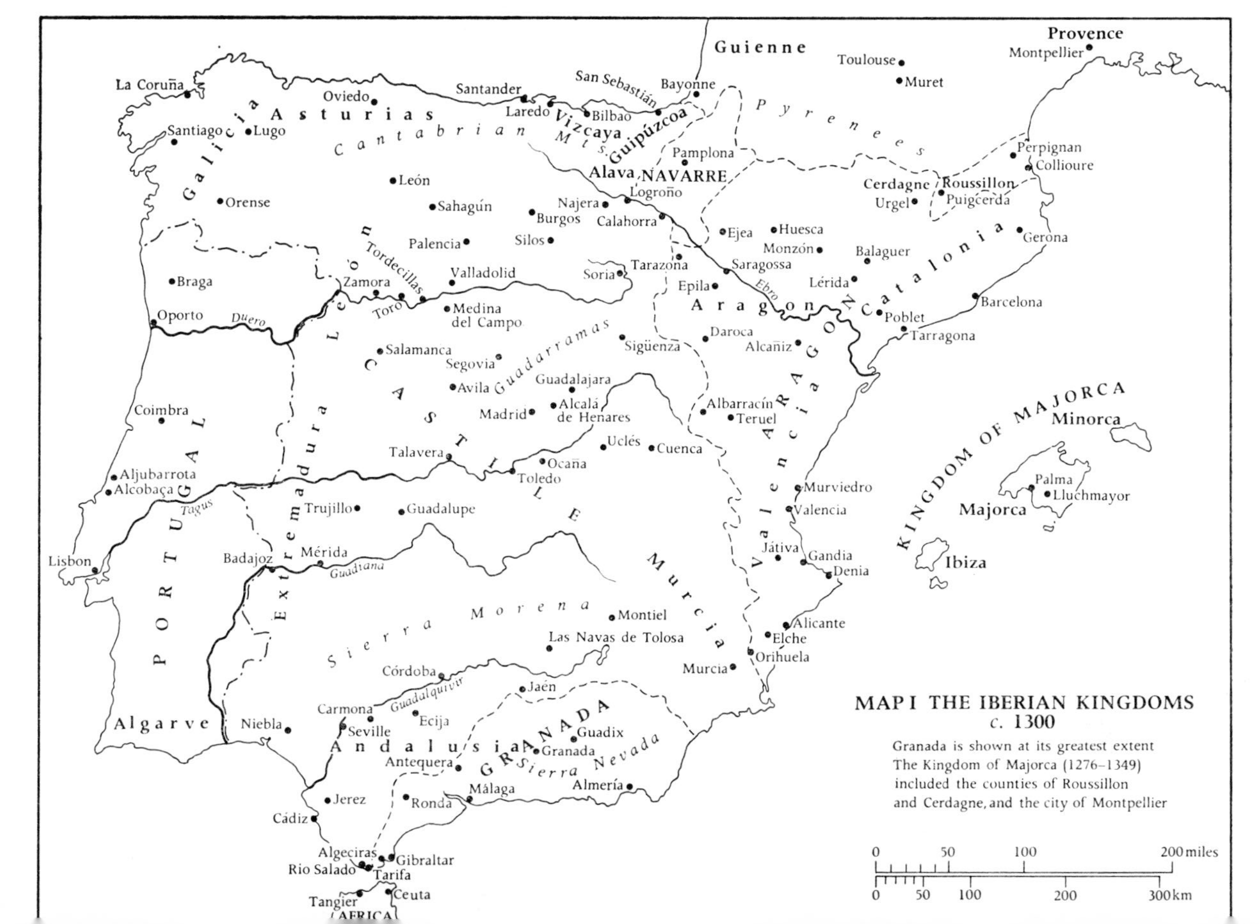
MAP I THE IBERIAN KINGDOMS
c. 1300
Granada is shown at its greatest extent
The Kingdom of Majorca (1276–1349)
included the counties of Roussillon
and Cerdagne, and the city of Montpellier
0 50 100 200 miles
0 50 100 200 300 km
Guienne
Provence
Montpellier
Toulouse
Muret
Pyrenees
Galicia
Asturias
Cantabrian Mts.
Vizcaya
Guipúzcoa
Alava
NAVARRE
Cerdagne
Roussillon
Catalonia
Aragon
ARAGON
León
CASTILE
Extremadura
Valencia
Murcia
PORTUGAL
Algarve
Andalusia
GRANADA
Sierra Morena
Sierra Nevada
Guadarramas
KINGDOM OF MAJORCA
Minorca
Majorca
Ibiza
Palma
Lluchmayor
La Coruña
Santiago
Lugo
Oviedo
Orense
León
Sahagún
Palencia
Santander
Laredo
Bilbao
San Sebastián
Bayonne
Pamplona
Logroño
Najera
Burgos
Calahorra
Silos
Soria
Tarazona
Ejea
Huesca
Monzón
Saragossa
Epila
Ebro
Daroca
Sigüenza
Alcañiz
Balaguer
Lérida
Poblet
Tarragona
Barcelona
Gerona
Perpignan
Collioure
Urgel
Puigcerda
Braga
Oporto
Duero
Zamora
Toro
Tordecillas
Valladolid
Medina del Campo
Salamanca
Segovia
Avila
Guadalajara
Alcalá de Henares
Madrid
Coimbra
Aljubarrota
Alcobaça
Tagus
Lisbon
Talavera
Toledo
Ocaña
Uclés
Cuenca
Albarracín
Teruel
Murviedro
Valencia
Játiva
Gandia
Denia
Trujillo
Guadalupe
Mérida
Badajoz
Guadiana
Montiel
Las Navas de Tolosa
Alicante
Elche
Orihuela
Murcia
Córdoba
Guadalquivir
Jaén
Carmona
Ecija
Seville
Niebla
Antequera
Granada
Guadix
Almería
Málaga
Ronda
Jerez
Cádiz
Algeciras
Gibraltar
Rio Salado
Tarifa
Tangier
Ceuta
AFRICA

THE SPANISH KINGDOMS
1250–1516

by J. N. Hillgarth

VOLUME I
1250–1410
Precarious Balance

CLARENDON PRESS · OXFORD
1976

Oxford University Press, Ely House, London W. 1
GLASGOW NEW YORK TORONTO MELBOURNE WELLINGTON
CAPE TOWN IBADAN NAIROBI DAR ES SALAAM LUSAKA ADDIS ABABA
DELHI BOMBAY CALCUTTA MADRAS KARACHI LAHORE DACCA
KUALA LUMPUR SINGAPORE HONG KONG TOKYO

ISBN 0 19 822530 X

Printed in Great Britain
by Cox & Wyman Ltd
London, Fakenham and Reading

A LA MEMORIA DE

Don Juan Pons y Marqués,
poeta, historiador, mallorquín,
ejemplo de una tradición viva y vivfiicante,
y a otros amigos de España y Portugal

Apud Hispanos ego vitam agere
malo, quam apud alios.
LUCIUS MARINAEUS SICULUS

Preface

THIS is the first volume of a two-volume work in which I have tried to study the Iberian peninsula during the thirteenth, fourteenth, and fifteenth centuries, and, politically, from about 1250 to 1516. I am, of course, aware of the temerity of one scholar trying to encompass the political, social, economic, religious, and intellectual activities of three centuries. I was induced to begin the work by the consciousness that no such general but detailed and documented study existed in English. I have also been led to believe that what I have attempted to provide does not exist in Spanish.

The title of the book was deliberately chosen, 'The Spanish Kingdoms', not 'Spain'. Spain did not exist, even as a geographical expression for what we today call Spain, in 1250, and it can only with many reservations be said to have existed in 1516 as a political, let alone a social or administrative, unity. The (very relative) union of the Spanish kingdoms which was only begun in 1474, through the marriage of Fernando and Isabel, and completed through the conquest of Granada in 1492 and of Spanish Navarre in 1512, was far from inevitable. There were fully as great differences between the territories of the Crown of Aragon and those of Castile as existed between Castile and Portugal. The way the Navarrese fought for the independence of their small kingdom against Enrique II of Castile in 1378 is as revealing as the refusal of Portugal to accept a Castilian ruler in 1383.

In 1250, and still in 1516, the picture is one of diversity and variety. The differences between the Crown of Aragon and Castile and, within these two Crowns, between different regions, with their own life and traditions, Catalonia and Aragon or Galicia and Andalusia, for instance, are as important as the resemblances which make comparison possible—as they would also be possible between Castile or Aragon and medieval France or England. In 1250, and for almost 250 years thereafter, one of the Spanish kingdoms was the Islamic emirate of Granada, another was Navarre, largely French in its rulers and political attachments. The strength of local traditions, grown to maturity in the Middle Ages, has emerged time and again in later Spanish history.

As Soldevila remarked, it is indefensible to separate the history of Portugal before the sixteenth century from that of Spain. My excuse for not saying more about Portugal is that of Soldevila, that the complexity of the evidence for Castile, Aragon, Navarre, and Granada is such that I find it impossible to embrace Portugal also.[1] I have endeavoured, however, to make constant use of comparative Portuguese material and always to remember that Portugal was as much a part of the Iberian pattern as Catalonia—or Old Castile.

While at least half the book is concerned with economic, social, institutional, religious, and cultural history, considerable space is devoted to political developments. Here my point of view can be made clear by reference to the theses of Jaime Vicens Vives and to the recent critique of these views by another great Catalan historian, Ramon d'Abadal i de Vinyals.[2] As Sr. d'Abadal remarked, Vicens renewed the themes and problems of Catalan history by incorporating into it the methods pursued by modern economic historians outside Spain. That his work was of the greatest importance goes without saying. It was so important, and so novel in its effect in Spain, that it appears to have made some younger Spanish historians see history as simply a matter of economic causation. But the limitation of history to economics is as absolutist and one-sided a view as any past historian's concentration on political and diplomatic activity. I agree with a younger Castilian scholar that to apply sociological categories to the Middle Ages and to speak of 'the Castile of the bourgeoisie and of trade', in opposition to 'the Castile of hierarchy and the land' does not get us very close to reality.[3] To make the wool trade, important as it was, the only pivot of late-medieval Castilian history (or, for that matter, the spice trade the only pivot of contemporary Catalan development) is to simplify to the point of distortion.

[1] F. Soldevila, *Historia de España*, I (Barcelona, 1959), p. xi. I have given less space to Navarre than to the other kingdoms because they seem relatively of far greater importance.

[2] R. d'Abadal, in *Moments crucials de la història de Catalunya* (Barcelona, 1962), and his 'Pròleg' to J. Vicens Vives, *Obra dispersa*, i (Barcelona, 1967).

[3] J. Valdeón Baruque, *Hispania*, 28 (1968), 54 f.

I would also agree with Sr. d'Abadal that history is not, as Vicens in his later years implied or stated, created by the masses. The masses are part of history but history is created by privileged minorities, not only, of course, kings, nobles, and prelates, though they bulk large in our centuries, but also by the representatives of the oligarchies that ruled medieval towns. These views may explain why I have paid attention to the leading personalities of the age and to political, military, and diplomatic history. It seems to me important to try to know Pere III of Catalonia–Aragon or Fernando the Catholic, for their effect on history is considerably less disputable than the operation of cycles of economic growth and decline, whose direction and duration are in debate and for whose very existence the evidence is not always compelling.[1]

Much recent Iberian historiography is one-sided, too much concerned, for instance, with Old rather than New Castile, or with Catalonia in isolation, so focused on the supposed 'Catalan decline' of the fifteenth century that it forgets the concomitant rise of the rest of the peninsula, and especially of Castile and Portugal. The Crown of Aragon did not consist only of Catalonia. The contributions of Valencia, Aragon proper, and Majorca are often forgotten, though they are of increasing importance from 1300 onwards. In Castile Vizcaya and Andalusia are at present under intensive study but very little has been done so far on other regions such as Asturias. The Mudejar communities have been far less closely explored in the past than the Jews, and this is still largely true of the Mudejars of Castile and Portugal. One must agree with Professor Gibert that it is essential 'to give the same attention to *all* the parts of Spain . . . to recognize their individual historical value'.[2] Until this is done

[1] Modern scholars like to find rational policies behind diplomacy and wars. The searcher is assisted by the way we speak today of the 'government of Spain' or the 'English government'. But the word 'government' can be misleading when it is applied to 1300 or 1500; it conveys the impression of a modern bureaucratic machine. Even modern governments' decisions are made, in the end, by very few individuals. The personal nature of command was much more evident in the fourteenth century. The motives for decisions made then are often obscure; sometimes they prove startling. While some Iberian kings—e.g. Pere II of Catalonia–Aragon (1276–85) or Enrique II of Castile (1369–79)—appear to have pursued rational and moderately consistent foreign policies, other rulers, such as Fernando I of Portugal (1367–83) or Joan I of Aragon (1387–95), were swayed by beliefs in astrological influences or the advice of visionary hermits.

[2] R. Gibert, *Historia general del derecho español*, i (Granada, 1968), pp. x f.

any general study of the period is bound to be partly unbalanced. The lack, for Castile, of the studies we possess for much of Catalan political and economic history is not solely due to the idiosyncratic preferences of historians but to the nature of the sources. The great German scholar Heinrich Finke remarked many years ago that probably no other country could produce, for the thirteenth and fourteenth centuries, such a rich collection of documents on cultural life as Catalonia.[1] The fact that Castile does not possess a medieval royal archive to rival the Archivo de la Corona de Aragón in Barcelona is bound to influence any comparative account of Aragon and Castile.

'It is only thanks to a great effort of scholarship that we will be able to understand the peninsular world of the Middle Ages, so different from our own, since two of its formative elements have been radically removed—the Jewish and the Muslim.'[2] To understand the past one has to try to see it, as far as possible, through the eyes of its actors. Hence the amount of space devoted in this book to quotations from contemporary authors—most of whom are not available in English translations. Professor Criado de Val has pointed out that the historical sources of the late Iberian Middle Ages are interwoven with literary works and that one can reach reality more objectively through literary documents than through chronicles, which were, one may add, only interested in limited spheres of life and action. The element of propaganda in the chronicles has not always been remembered. I have sought to bear it in mind. Even royal correspondence—so richly preserved in Barcelona, so fragmentarily in Castile—recounts only the official side of the story. The records of Cortes give us more, and so do private documents, but it is through poems, religious literature (especially sermons), philosophy, and novels that one can most surely penetrate the past. These works have to be used (as do chronicles, documents, and the visual arts) with due attention to the conventions and models behind them but to fail to use them is to impoverish one's understanding of any age.[3]

[1] H. Finke, *EUC*, 4 (1910), 75.

[2] M. Criado de Val, *Teoria de Castilla la Nueva* (Madrid, 1960), p. 9.

[3] I would like to make it clear that I am not attempting a general description of Spanish medieval literature (or of architecture or painting) but trying, with what caution I can command, to use literary works, as well as art, etc., as evidence for

One point in the book may need explanation—the use of Catalan names. It is customary, in English works dealing largely or even entirely with Catalan subjects, to render Catalan names either into Castilian or English. I prefer to give men the names they bore in their own time. (I follow the same practice with regard to Italians, Portuguese, Granadans, etc.). The possible inconvenience for English readers of finding 'Pere' or 'Jaume' for a king of Aragon, who, being also count of Barcelona and using Catalan as his first language, normally used this name for himself, rather than the Castilian Pedro or Jaime (let alone Peter or James), is counterbalanced by the advantage of recalling the diversity of the Spanish kingdoms. To be consistent I use the Catalan regnal numbers (e.g. Pere III, not Pedro IV).[1] Place-names, however, are given as they occur on modern maps, a few exceptions, such as Seville or Saragossa, being made for names which have been naturalized in English.

The two volumes are divided politically at 1410, a date which marks the first real triumph of the central plateau of the Iberian peninsula—Castile—over the merchants of Catalonia. In the 1380s Castile had failed to conquer Portugal. In 1410 the native dynasty of the counts of Barcelona came to an end at the death of Martí I. Two years later, after a long and embittered struggle, with the 'Compromiso de Caspe', the Castilian claimant was installed on the thrones of Catalonia–Aragon. The sub-titles for the two volumes, 'Precarious Balance' and 'Castilian Hegemony', are intended to stress this change. To divide the period in other than political terms is more difficult. The most reasonable chronological division here falls about 1350. Part I of this volume embraces Iberian economic, social, and cultural history from about 1200 to about 1350, Part I of Volume ii similar themes from 1350 to about 1500.

• • • • •

[1] For consistency I use the Catalan numbers even when reverting to Castilian for the kings of the House of Trastámara (after 1412), whom it would be absurd (unless writing in Catalan) to describe as Joan II (not Juan II), etc. For Pere III's preferences as to name and regnal number see J. Coroleu, *Documents historichs catalans del sigle XIV* (Barcelona, 1889), pp. 24, 33. Catalan names were also used by contemporary rulers, e.g. the kings of Naples. The practice I follow was adopted by P. E. Russell, *The English Intervention in Spain and Portugal* (Oxford, 1955).

the period. I follow the views of M. Menéndez y Pelayo, expressed, for instance, with regard to the Archpriest of Hita (see below, Part I, Ch. VI, p. 226).

For most of my life I have spent some months every year in Spain and could adapt the phrase used by Antonio Geraldini in the fifteenth century to say 'licet natione sim Anglus, tamen Hispanus sum educatione, quippe qui a teneris annis in Hispania versatus'.[1] Although I have sought to avoid bias, I do not pretend to be free of preferences when writing of Spanish history. Who, one may dare to ask, is? I cannot claim to know Castile to the extent I know Catalonia and Majorca or to have the same (relative) familiarity and deep affection for Castilian history as I have for Catalan. I should also add that I have not felt it necessary to argue my case at length whenever I make a statement that might be disputed. To do so would make the book intolerably long and tedious. The references in my notes are there for those who wish to pursue the question at issue. I have also tried to point out whenever (as is often the case) a problem demands further treatment or a needed monograph is lacking.

The multiplicity of my debts to other scholars will be evident in the notes and bibliography. Any general synthesis must depend on earlier works. Certain specific acknowledgements are necessary. A number of them would be made by the author of any work on this subject. The late Jaime Vicens Vives (d. 1960) renewed the whole history of the later Middle Ages in the Crown of Aragon and especially in Catalonia. The fact that one may differ strongly from him on some main issues is in itself a sign that, again and again, he provided the starting-point from which others can hope to progress. Professor Luís Suárez Fernández and his disciples at Valladolid have begun to achieve the same for late-medieval Castile as Vicens did for Catalonia. To the late Dr. Virgínia Rau (d. 1973), who illuminated the history of late-medieval and early modern Portugal and so all Iberian history, an equal debt is owed.

I would wish—and here I am conscious I would not carry with me all medievalists—to acknowledge also a deep debt to the late Professor Américo Castro (d. 1972), who revealed more clearly than earlier writers the complex, threefold nature of the Iberian peninsula, Christian, but also Jewish and Muslim. I am greatly indebted to other historians of literature, both in Spain and elsewhere, particularly to Dr. Jordi Rubió i Balaguer, Dr.

[1] W. P. Mustard (ed.), *The Eclogues of Antonio Geraldini* (Baltimore, 1924), p. 13.

Pere Bohigas, Professor Martí de Riquer, and Professor David Romano in Barcelona, to Professor Rafael Lapesa in Madrid, and to Professor Stephen Gilman at Harvard. These and other scholars, including Professors Suárez Fernández, Rau and Castro, have clarified problems for me in personal discussion as well as by their writings. At the risk of omitting other friends and colleagues, I should also like to thank Dr. Federico Udina and Dr. Antonio M. Aragó Cabañas, Director and Vice-Director, respectively, of the Archivo de la Corona de Aragón, Professor Emilio Sáez, of the Departamiento de Estudios Medievales of the University of Barcelona, Professor Rafael Gibert of the University of Granada, and Professor Alberto Boscolo, Rector of the University of Cagliari. I owe a special debt to two successive directors of the Archivo Histórico del Reino de Mallorca, in Palma. The present Director, Don Francisco Sevillano Colom, has been unfailingly helpful. To his predecessor, Don Juan Pons y Marqués (d. 1971), together with other Spanish and Portuguese friends, this book is dedicated. Errors are inevitably present. That they are fewer than they might be is due to the labours and kindness of the scholars I have mentioned, and also to the care and patience with which my mother and my wife have toiled in the preparation of the typescript. Much work on the book has been done in the libraries of the British Museum and Widener Library at Harvard. I am grateful to the staffs of these libraries for their assistance.[1]

I would like to conclude by quoting an older historian, of Spanish Muslim descent, 'Admission of one's shortcomings saves from censure. Kindness from colleagues is hoped for'.

[1] The work on this book has been greatly assisted by my appointment as a John Simon Guggenheim Memorial Fellow for 1968–9 and later by a leave of absence from Boston College for part of the academic year 1971–2. I am grateful to Longmans for permission to use material from *The Problems of a Catalan Mediterranean Empire, 1229–1327* (Supplement 8 to the *English Historical Review*), London, 1975, in Part II, Ch. I, below.

Contents

List of Maps

Abbreviations

ACA	Archivo de la Corona de Aragón, Barcelona.
AEM	*Anuario de Estudios Medievales*, Barcelona, 1964– .
AHDE	*Anuario de Historia del Derecho Español*, Madrid, 1924– .
AHES	*Anuario de Historia Económica y Social*, Madrid, 1968– .
AIA	*Archivo Ibero-Americano*, Madrid, 1914– .
AIEC	*Anuari de l'Institut d'Estudis Catalans*, Barcelona, 1907–31.
AIEG	*Anales del Instituto de Estudios Gerundenses*, Gerona, 1946– .
AST	*Analecta Sacra Tarraconensia*, Barcelona, 1926– .
BAE	*Biblioteca de Autores Españoles*, Madrid.
Baer, *Die Juden*	Y. F. Baer, *Die Juden im christlichen Spanien*, 2 vols., Berlin, 1929–36.
Baer, *History*	Idem, *A History of the Jews in Christian Spain*, 2 vols., Philadelphia, 1961–6.
BBC	*Butlletí de la Biblioteca de Catalunya*, Barcelona, 1914–32.
Benavides	A. Benavides, *Memorias de Fernando IV de Castilla*, II, Madrid, 1860.
BRABL	*Boletín de la Real Academia de Buenas Letras de Barcelona*, 1901– .
BRAE	*Boletín de la Real Academia Española*, Madrid, 1914– .
BRAH	*Boletín de la Real Academia de la Historia*, Madrid, 1877– .
BSAL	*Bolletí de la Societat Arqueològica Lul. liana*, Palma, 1885– .
BSCC	*Boletín de la Sociedad Castellonense de Cultura*, Castellón de la Plana, 1920– .
Capmany	A. de Capmany y de Monpalau, *Memorias históricas sobre la marina, comercio y artes de la antigua ciudad de Barcelona* (1st edn., 4 vols., 1779–92; new edn., by E. Giralt y Raventós and C. Batlle y Gallart, 3 vols., Barcelona, 1961–3).
Carini, *Archivi*	I. Carini, *Gli archivi e le biblioteche di Spagna, in*

	rapporto alla storia d'Italia in generale e di Sicilia in particolare, II, Palermo, 1884.
Carini, *De rebus*	Idem, *De rebus regni Siciliae (1282–1283)* (= *Documenti per servire alla storia di Sicilia*, 1st series V), Palermo, 1882.
Carreras Artau	T. and J. Carreras Artau, *Historia de la filosofía española, filosofía cristiana de los siglos XIII al XV*, 2 vols., Madrid, 1939–43.
CDIACA	*Colección de Documentos inéditos del Archivo General de la Corona de Aragón*, 45 vols., Barcelona, 1849–1970.
CDIHE	*Colección de Documentos inéditos para la Historia de España*, 112 vols., Madrid, 1842–95.
CH	*Cuadernos de Historia, anexos de la revista 'Hispania'*, Madrid, 1967– .
CHCA	*Congreso de Historia de la Corona de Aragón* (eight published, 1909–70), Barcelona, etc.
CHE	*Cuadernos de Historia de España*, Buenos Aires, 1944– .
CHEC	*Cuadernos de Historia Económica de Cataluña*, Barcelona, 1968– .
Cortes de Cataluña	*Cortes de los antiguos reinos de Aragón y de Valencia y principado de Cataluña: Cortes de Cataluña*, 26 vols., Madrid, 1896–1922.
Cortes de León	*Cortes de los antiguos reinos de León y de Castilla, publicadas por la Real Academia de la Historia*, 5 vols., Madrid, 1861–1903.
Dufourcq	Ch-E. Dufourcq, *L'Espagne catalane et le Maghrib aux XIIIe et XIVe siècles* (Bibliothèque de l'école des hautes études hispaniques, XXXVII), Paris, 1966 (Catalan transl., Barcelona, 1969).
EEMCA	*Estudios de Edad Media de la Corona de Aragón*, Saragossa, 1946– .
EHMed	*Estudis d'història medieval*, Barcelona, 1969– .
EHMod	*Estudios de historia moderna*, 6 vols., Barcelona, 1953–9.
ENC	*Els Nostres Clàssics*, Barcelona.
ER	*Estudis romànics*, Barcelona, 1947– .
EUC	*Estudis Universitaris Catalans*, 22 vols., Barcelona, 1907–36.
Finke, *Acta*	H. Finke, *Acta Aragonensia*, 3 vols., Berlin–Leipzig, 1908–22.
HE	*Historia de España*, ed. R. Menéndez Pidal,

	Madrid. Relevant vols. are XIV (1966), XV (1964), XVII, 2 parts (1969).
HGLH	*Historia General de las Literaturas Hispánicas*, ed. G. Díaz-Plaja, Barcelona, 1949– .
HM	*Homenaje a Millás-Vallicrosa*, 2 vols., Barcelona, 1954–6.
HV	*Homenaje a Jaime Vicens Vives*, 2 vols., Barcelona, 1965–7.
Huici, *Colección*	A. Huici, *Colección diplomática de Jaime I, el Conquistador*, 3 vols., Valencia, 1916–22.
IHE	*Indice Histórico Español*, Barcelona, 1953– .
MÂ	*Le Moyen Âge*, Paris, 1888– .
MCV	*Mélanges de la Casa de Velázquez*, Madrid, 1965– .
MEAH	*Miscelánea de Estudios Arabes y Hebraicos*, Granada, 1952– .
Menéndez Pelayo, *Antología*	M. Menéndez y Pelayo, *Antología de poetas líricos castellanos*, 10 vols., Santander, 1944–5.
Menéndez Pelayo, *Orígenes*	Idem, *Orígenes de la novela*, 4 vols., Santander, 1943.
MHE	*Memorial Histórico Español*, Madrid, 1851– .
MLR	*Modern Language Review*, Cambridge, 1905– .
NBAE	*Nueva Biblioteca de Autores Españoles*, 26 vols., Madrid, 1905–28.
NRFH	*Nueva Revista de Filología Hispánica*, Mexico, 1947– .
Oliveira Marques, *Daily Life*	A. H. de Oliveira Marques, *Daily Life in Portugal in the Late Middle Ages*, Madison, Wis., 1971.
RABM	*Revista de Archivos, Bibliotecas y Museos*, Madrid, 1871– .
RET	*Revista Española de Teología*, Madrid, 1940– .
RFE	*Revista de Filología Española*, Madrid, 1914– .
RHCM	*Revue d'histoire et de civilisation du Maghrib*, Algiers, 1966– .
Riquer	M. de Riquer, *Història de la literatura catalana*, 3 vols., Barcelona, 1964.
Rubió, *Diplomatari*	A. Rubió i Lluch, *Diplomatari de l'orient català (1301–1409)*, Barcelona, 1947.
Rubió, *Documents*	Idem, *Documents per l'història de la cultura catalana mig-eval*, 2 vols., Barcelona, 1908–21.
Rubió, *Vida*	J. Rubió, *Vida española en la época gótica*, Barcelona, 1943.
Segura, *Aplech*	J. Segura, 'Aplech de Documents curiosos é

inedits fahents per la història de las Costums de Catalunya', *Jochs Florals*, 1883–5, pp. 119–287.

SFG — *Spanische Forschungen der Görresgesellschaft*, I Reihe, *Gesammelte Aufsatze zur Kulturgeschichte Spaniens*, Münster i. W. 1928– .

Tejada y Ramiro — J. Tejada y Ramiro, *Colección de canones de la iglesia española*, 6 vols., Madrid, 1849–59.

Verlinden — Ch. Verlinden, *L'Esclavage dans l'Europe médiévale*, I (Rijksuniversiteit te Gent, Werken uitgegeven door te Faculteit van de Letteren en Wijsbegeerte, 119), Bruges, 1955.

Villanueva — [J.] Villanueva, *Viage literario a las iglesias de España*, 22 vols., Madrid, 1802–52.

Vincke, *Documenta* — J. Vincke, *Documenta selecta mutuas civitatis Arago-Cathalaunicae et ecclesiae relationes illustrantia*, Barcelona, 1936.

Zurita, *Anales* — J. Zurita, *Anales de la Corona de Aragón*, 4 vols., Saragossa, 1610 (cited by book and chapters).

PART I

THE IBERIAN PENINSULA
1200–1350

I

The Plurality of the Peninsula

THE situation of the Iberian peninsula, extending farther south and west than the other great peninsulas of the Mediterranean, contributes to its character as a land of sharp contrasts in geography and climate. The dry climate of the south-east resembles that of North Africa; the north-west is humid, subject to winds from the Atlantic and the British Isles. Both the southern and eastern coasts are in easy reach of the other lands of the western Mediterranean; the west and north tend as naturally to communicate with northern Europe and later with the New World.

Spain is closer to Africa than any other European land—the Straits of Gibraltar only measure 15 kilometres. Men can cross the Straits with almost the same ease as the winds of the Sahara and the plants of Morocco. Communications with western Europe, except by sea, are less easy. Walls of mountains (150 kilometres across in the centre) lead up, on both sides, to the chain of the Pyrenees. At the centre of the peninsula there is a table-land, the Meseta, a platform measuring over 211,000 square kilometres (some 300 miles from north to south), of which the northern border is formed by the Cantabrian mountains, the southern by the Sierra Morena. This platform is divided by the mountains of Toledo—while the northern part of the Meseta is 800 metres high, the southern is only 600—but the Meseta as a whole is fundamentally different from the coastal zones, Portugal, Andalusia, Murcia, Valencia, and Catalonia, and also from the humid mountains of Galicia and Asturias.

The Mediterranean coastal areas and the north and centre have always found themselves in opposition, since the time the south of the peninsula was Iberian and the north Celtic. The Islamic conquest of the south reinforced its links with Africa and separated it from Europe. The conquest broke up completely the superficial unity imposed on the peninsula by the

Visigoths. Nor did the north resist as a unit. Resistance to Islam was local in character. There was hardly any connection between the kingdom of Asturias, that of Navarre, the Pyrenean counties of Aragon and Ribagorza, and the Catalan counts farther east. These local centres of resistance, in particular Asturias and Catalonia, had emerged separately and for very different reasons. In Asturias the vital element was the indigenous tribal resistance to any foreign power operating from the south. The Asturians fought the Muslims as they had fought the Romans and Visigoths. The fact that the Asturians were now (more or less) Christians and that religion entered into the conflict merely gave it a sharper edge. The situation was much the same in the Basque provinces and Navarre. In contrast, the Catalan counts were sustained by the Franks. Their ties to western Europe through the Frankish empire and to the papacy were more important to them than the memories of Gothic Toledo, cultivated by a small élite, were to Asturias–León.[1]

The Christian centres of the north began their lives in independence. They continued to develop in virtual isolation from each other until the eleventh century. That century saw the break-up of the political unity of the Islamic south. The Christian kingdoms came together, usually in conflict, in a struggle for the spoils.

The unity of the south under Islam—though a striking contrast to the fissiparous nature of the Christian north—was always insecure. In the ninth century al-Andalus almost dissolved in a welter of separatist rebellions. In the eleventh century the dissolution was more permanent. Over twenty *Taifas* (party kingdoms) emerged. The successive Almoravid and Almohad attempts to reimpose unity by force, by Berber troops from North Africa, both failed within about fifty years. In the twelfth and again in the thirteenth century new *Taifas* appeared. In the thirteenth century, since the Christians were now stronger and no help came from the Berbers, the post-Almohad *Taifas* were swallowed up by Christian armies, with only Granada surviving. And in Granada one finds, on a miniature scale, the same separatism as in earlier al-Andalus.

The Christian armies were not those of one united state but

[1] See M. Vigil and A. Barbero, *BRAH* 156 (1965), 271–339. A. Cabo, 'Condicionamentos geográficos', in *Historia de España Alfaguara*, i (Madrid, 1973).

of Portugal, León and Castile (united in 1230), and of the federation of Catalonia–Aragon. The main drive was due to Castile (the heir of Asturias) and to Catalonia. These very different societies now extended their distinct conceptions of life to the Islamic south. Castile–León acquired an Islamic area over four times as large as that conquered by Catalans. The Islamic influence on Castile was correspondingly deeper than that exercised on Catalonia. Not satisfied with their gains in the peninsula, Catalans turned to the Mediterranean. Their Mediterranean involvement deepened their ties to western Europe. As Castile became more deeply Islamicized Catalonia grew more European. The process is continuous, from the thirteenth to the sixteenth century.[1]

TEXTS EMPHASIZING UNITY: CASTILE

A number of texts can be cited which show the survival of the concept of 'Hispania'. Reacting to a boast by a German canonist that all men were under the German emperor, Vincentius Hispanus exalts 'Blessed Lady Spain' and the 'Spanish' who 'are acquiring the lordship' over her. The compilations due to Alfonso X of Castile attempt to revive Saint Isidore of Seville's exaltation of the Goths and see the separate *Fueros* of the peninsula as all stemming from Gothic Law; the division came from the Islamic invasion and could presumably be reversed by the Reconquest of Islamic Spain. Another work due to Alfonso, the *Primera Crónica General*, remarks: 'We take our general history of the Spains from all the kings [of the Spains].' A Provençal troubadour speaks of 'four kings of Spain' (Portugal, Aragon, Castile, and León) and prefers them all to the king of France.

CATALAN TEXTS

Catalan chroniclers also pay tribute to this idea of 'Spain'. Pere I of Catalonia–Aragon tells the foreign crusaders who arrive too late for the battle of Las Navas in 1212 that 'the

[1] For the Islamicization of Castile (more disputed than the Europeanization of Catalonia) see below, *passim*, especially Chs. V and VI. It is not without significance that when Fernando and Isabel accepted the surrender of Granada on 2 Jan. 1492 they were both dressed as Moors. See also Vol. ii, Appendix, on coinage.

kings of Spain' have already defeated the Muslim hosts. Desclot sees 'all the hosts of Spain' as symbolically present to defend Catalonia against the French in 1285 although in fact the defending army consisted almost exclusively of Catalans. In 1283 Pere II, asking a Catalan knight to appear with him at Bordeaux in a duel against the French, invoked 'Our honour and yours and that of all Spain'. A little later the most patriotic of Catalan chroniclers, Ramon Muntaner, was to write: 'If those four kings of Spain [Castile, Aragon, Majorca, and Portugal], who are one flesh and blood, hold together, they need fear little any other power in the world.'[1]

Such statements as these are often adduced to show that a consciousness of unity continued to exist in the peninsula which overshadowed the divisions between different kingdoms. No doubt this consciousness did exist, at least among the educated. It was stimulated by the boasts of foreign xenophobes and by crises such as those of 1212 and 1283. But sometimes too much is built on these texts. Muntaner, for one, is an idealist with a very imperfect grasp of the realities even of the Crown of Aragon and its relations to Sicily and Majorca, let alone of the interplay of the peninsular kingdoms. He should not be cited as representing ordinary Catalan sentiment on this question.

Jaume I of Aragon has also been cited as emphasizing the unity of 'Spain'. In his *Book of Deeds* he sets down the reasons why he helped his son-in-law Alfonso X of Castile to put down the Muslim revolt in Murcia in 1265–6. He did so because his daughter asked him for aid, because he feared Castile's revenge if Alfonso extricated himself unaided, and, 'the strongest reason of all: if the king of Castile loses his land I shall hardly be safe in mine'.

A little later more reasons are given: 'for God's sake: to save *Spain*: that I and you [the barons of Aragon] may deserve the great praise and honour of *saving Spain from the Saracens*', but though these reasons no doubt weighed with Jaume self-interest and the preservation of his own lands seem paramount.

[1] Gaines Post, *Studies in Medieval Legal Thought* (Princeton, 1964), pp. 489 f. (the date is after 1234): Alfonso X, *Espéculo*, V.v.l (*Opúsculos legales*, i (Madrid, 1836), 315); *Primera Crónica General*, c. 971, ed. Menéndez Pidal, ii. 653; Desclot, cc. 5, 139 (ed. Coll, ii. 37; v. 132); Carini, *De rebus*, p. 701; Muntaner, c. 102.

Jaume I's grandson, Jaume II, refers, in 1304, to the harm that war between Aragon and Castile might do to 'all Spain' as a reason for accepting less territory from Castile than he had hoped for. This statement is striking but should be interpreted with caution. In 1304 Jaume was in a difficult situation. He was lucky to get the conditions he obtained in his peace with Castile. His idealism may be a cloak for failure. In 1299 he had informed the pope that the only way to expel Muslims from Spain was to divide Castile into two parts.[1]

TEXTS EMPHASIZING DIVERSITY: CATALAN TEXTS

As many texts can be quoted that emphasize diversity or mutual hostility as those that emphasize unity. In 1274, on the death of the last king of Navarre of the House of Champagne, Jaume I of Aragon addressed a manifesto to the Navarrese. He urged them to 'choose rather to come under the fraternal and friendly liberty of Our rule rather than suffer the tyranny of other kings and their many unjust burdens'. Jaume was alluding to the well-known difference between the rule of Castile and the gentler sway of Aragon.

The overbearing pride of Castilians is a recurrent theme in Catalan writers. Describing the Castilian attempt to seize Játiva in 1244 (against the provisions of an earlier treaty) Jaume I remarked: 'You Castilians imagine that your threats can make an impression on me . . . You do everything with such haughtiness and pride; you imagine that everything you wish for should be immediately granted.' Catalan pride answered Castilian. When Alfonso X attempted to assert claims to 'empire' over Spain he was sharply checked by Jaume I. The chronicles and documents of thirteenth- and fourteenth-century Catalonia reflect a high level of self-consciousness, not so much nationalism as royalism. The greatest Catalan writer of that—perhaps of any—day, Ramon Lull (1232–1316) remarked: 'common rule signifies the common *person* of the prince'. Other Catalan writers express an intense loyalty to their native dynasty, the House of Barcelona, a realization of the solid interests binding the Catalan people

[1] On Muntaner, see below, Part II, Ch. I, pp. 234 ff.; Jaume I, *Libre dels feyts*, cc. 382, 392 ; Salavert, *Cerdena*, ii. 141; A. Giménez Soler, *La Corona de Aragón y Granada* (Barcelona, 1908), pp. 55 f.

together in the projection of their power throughout the Mediterranean world. Cerverí de Girona, the leading troubadour of the age, saw the death of the viscount of Cardona as harming all Catalonia.

The expression 'patria' often appears in the Latin *Acts of the Counts of Barcelona* (about 1300). For the author God is on the side of his Count King, Pere II, though he is betrayed by his ally Castile and by the nobles of Aragon, when the French invade Catalonia in 1285.

The sun shone on their shields and the mountains reflected their glory but the strength of the people which trusted in its power was dispelled at last by *our* people, stronger and juster and more strenuous. O Catalonia! You will be glorious through all ages. You will deserve great things and you will rule.

Desclot, in Catalan, voices the same patriotism when he describes Pere II's armada sailing to Tunisia in 1282: 'In all that host there were no Genoese or Pisans or Venetians or Provençals, on sea or land. The whole fleet was of Catalans and Aragonese, all tried and approved in arms.'

Slightly later Muntaner celebrates the 'true Catalans', who 'speak fine Catalan', who were settled in Murcia by Jaume I. The Sicilians Ruggiero di Loria and Corrado Lancia have become 'the most perfect Catalans, speaking the best Catalan'.

Muntaner compares the Count Kings of Catalonia–Aragon with other rulers. They are much more simple, visible, accessible than other kings. They do not oppress their subjects. They appear at the marriages and funerals not only of nobles but of the 'honoured citizens' of the cities.

Let no one think that Catalonia is a small province, for all men should know that Catalonia has a richer population than any other . . . Catalonia does not have so many rich men as other lands but the people in general is the most fortunate in the world and they live better and in greater order than any other.[1]

[1] Soldevila, *Pere el Gran, l'Infant*, i. 2, 269 ff.; i. 3, 467 f.; Jaume I, *Libre dels feyts*, c. 347; see Finke, *Acta* ii. 837; Lull, *Arbre de ciència*, Arbre Imperial, i (*Obres essencials*, i. 664); M. del Treppo, in *Nuove questioni di storia medioevale* (Milan, 1964), p. 262; Cerverí de Girona, *Obras completas*, ed. M. de Riquer (Barcelona, 1947), pp. 111–13; *Gesta comitum Barcinonensium*, ed. Barrau-Dihigo and Massó Torrents, xxviii. 32, p. 78; 47, p. 90; Desclot, c. 89 (ed. Coll, iii. 96); Muntaner, cc. 17 f., 20, 29.

CASTILIAN TEXTS

Castilians were as eager as Catalans to maintain the superiority of their country over the rest of the peninsula. The *Poema de Fernán González*, written about 1250, follows the traditional type of 'praise of Spain' according to the model established by Isidore of Seville in the seventh century. Spain is superior to all other countries by its national riches and (here the *Poema* draws on later sources than Isidore) because, unlike England and France, it has been distinguished by the coming of an Apostle, Santiago.

But of all Spanna Castile is the best. The Creator chose to advance her because she was greater in the beginning than the other [regions] and because she always waited on her Lord and feared Him. In my understanding Old Castile is still better than the rest for it was its foundation.

Or, again: 'Aragon and Navarre are good approved land [as are] León and Portugal. Castile is unique. No such province will be found in the world.'

Any enterprise undertaken in common by Castile and Aragon led to mutual recriminations.

A Catalan naval commander, commanding the squadron guarding the Straits of Gibraltar in 1309 and attempting to assist the siege of Algeciras by Fernando IV of Castile, told his ruler Jaume II: 'You know the people I have to deal with, for, Lord, I never knew what pains, anxiety, and care were until now.'

On the other hand a contemporary Castilian chronicler describing the events of 1309 believed that the king of Aragon was only saved from destruction during his siege of Almería by the fortifications he had built round his camp. 'But the king Don Fernando [IV] had no barricade around his siege of Algeciras, for he did not need one, nor was it ever a custom of *Castilians* to [fortify their camps] when they besieged towns.'

The *Crónica de Alfonso X* evaded having to speak of the way Jaume I of Aragon recovered Murcia for Castile in 1266 by completely ignoring the crucial aid given by Jaume. The *Crónicas* of Sancho IV and Fernando IV ignore the fact that Tarifa was relieved in 1294 and Gibraltar taken in 1309 because of Catalan galleys. Castilian prejudices appear even in a man such as Don Juan Manuel, twice married to princesses of the House of Barcelona. When Jaume II, for diplomatic reasons, repudiated his Castilian bride, Don Juan observed: 'The House of Aragon *always* behaves in this way; before this it has dishonoured Castile.'[1]

Even to such external observers as Ibn Khaldūn or the Arabic geographers it was perfectly clear that the king of Aragon was an entirely separate ruler from the ruler of Castile. He was seen as 'King of Kings of the Franks, known as the Barcelonese . . . called the Catalan' or as 'King of Barcelona.'[2]

ARTISTIC DIVERSITY: BARCELONA AND SEVILLE

The position of Barcelona as capital of the Crown of Aragon was emphasized by Arabic writers because of the importance of the city in Mediterranean trade. The geographical position of Barcelona and the role it played as capital help to explain many other features of Catalonia which distinguished it, and, with it, the whole Crown of Aragon, from Castile. Although Castile had no fixed capital, from 1250 to 1284, and, again, from 1350 to 1369, Seville was the favourite residence of the court. The Trastámaras preferred Valladolid but this change came too late to make much difference. The preference for the Islamic south explains the fact that the only 'national' art and architecture of Castile is Mudejar. The fact that the builders, artisans, and masons of Castile were normally Mudejars is not an accident. The most remarkable Gothic buildings in Castile, the cathedrals of Toledo, Burgos, and León, were planned by foreign architects. They produced relatively little effect on native builders. In the late fourteenth and early fifteenth centuries the finest Gothic paintings in Castile were also the work of Italians or Frenchmen. In contrast, Catalan Gothic architecture and, later, paintings were the work of distinct

[1] *Poema de Fernán González*, vv. 144–57, 57, ed. A. Zamora Vicente (Madrid, 1946), pp. 44–8, 15; Giménez Soler, op. cit., p. 159, n. 1; *Crónica de Fernando IV*, c. 17 (*BAE* lxvi. 163); *Crónica de Alfonso X*, c. 15, *Crónica de Sancho IV*, c. 11 (ibid., pp. 11, 89); see A. Ballesteros-Beretta, *Alfonso X el Sabio*, pp. 386–402; Finke, *SFG* i. 4 (1933), 393; also *BAE* li. 260.

[2] Ibn Khaldūn, *Histoire des berbères*, transl. Slane, i. 162, ii. 398; also in R. Dozy, *Recherches*, 3rd edn., i. 93, 113–16; Abulfeda of Damascus (late 13th cent.), in *Boletín de la Real Sociedad geográfica de Madrid*, 48 (1906), 96 ff. (see p. 102).

native schools, of native builders and artists, with a clear personality of their own. They were not exotic importations into a Mudejar world.

The conquest of Andalusia and especially of Seville plunged Castile into the Islamic past. Barcelona (and, later, Majorca and Valencia) connected the Crown of Aragon to France, Italy, and western Europe in general. Catalonia was enough part of Europe to be able to transform the gifts it received from other European countries and create its own school, not only in art but in lyric poetry, in liturgical drama and in institutions. Catalan poetry developed out of Provençal, as Catalan architecture grew out of southern-French Gothic, but the poems of Ramon Lull or Bernat Metge are as distinct in their excellence from those written by the Provençal troubadours as the cathedrals of Majorca or Gerona are from the churches of Languedoc. In contrast Castile has epic poetry but no lyric poetry in Castilian until the late fourteenth century. Similarly, Catalonia possessed a rich Latin liturgical drama which developed naturally, as in France, out of the Roman rite. Castile only acquired this rite in the eleventh century, too late for such a drama to come into being.[1]

INSTITUTIONAL DIVERSITY

In institutions Catalonia and the areas settled by Catalans—Valencia and Majorca—differed sharply from Castile. Catalan feudalism, imported from France, combining with the early influence of Roman law, affected far more than legal formulas. The whole concept of 'honour' differed fundamentally in Catalonia and Castile. 'In Castile a man considered himself free, *lord* of his own sphere of action, direct avenger of any affront.' The *Fuero de Cuenca* considered a man justified in committing homicide in retaliation for a personal attack, such as a man pulling his beard, because this attack constituted an infringement of his personal 'honour'. This attitude is found in Castilian legal sources down to the *Fuero Real* of Alfonso X.

[1] For art see below, Ch. V, and Vol. II, Part I, Ch. IV. In Spanish Romanesque art, also, there are two clearly distinct styles. See W. M. Whitehill, *Spanish Romanesque Architecture of the Eleventh Century* (Oxford, 1968), and K. J. Conant, *Carolingian and Romanesque Architecture*, 3rd edn. (Penguin Books, 1973), p. 50 etc. On the absence of a lyric poetry in Castilian see R. Lapesa, *ER* 9 (1961), 11–14. For liturgical drama see Ch. IV below.

In Catalonia men were not considered justified if they acted for themselves in this way. A vassal who was attacked had to request his feudal lord to see that justice was done him. Hence, in Castile the most characteristic crime was 'injuria', a personal affront inflicted on a free man, which he is legally justified in avenging himself. In Catalonia the corresponding crime was 'bausia', treason committed by a vassal against his feudal lord.

It has been shown that in Castilian 'desafiar' means to defy, to challenge another man, whereas in Catalonia 'des-fidare' meant to break faith sworn by a vassal to his lord. In Catalonia the Latin 'honor' (*honrra*) meant a fief, not a man's personal dignity. 'Injuria' did not mean a personal affront calling for immediate, probably bloody, vengeance, but an unjust action in general, subject to legal sentence. In these matters Navarre and Aragon were closer to Castile than to Catalonia.[1]

The penetration of feudalism from France into Catalonia since the ninth century and the early influence of Roman law were behind the way the ordinary Catalan reacted in a crisis in the thirteenth century. They explain why his reactions to an injury would take a legal channel whereas the Castilian's reaction would be personal. Contacts between Barcelona and French and Italian cities, their sharing a common life based on trade, produced an urban society, with a bourgeoisie and an organization of artisans into guilds, aspects of life almost entirely lacking in Castile. This urban society, in its turn, supported its local assembly or Corts, far more powerful in the assertion of their rights than the corresponding Cortes of Castile.[2]

LINGUISTIC DIVERSITY

Outside Catalonia, with its cultural tradition stemming from Provence, all lyric poetry in the peninsula until the late fourteenth century was written in Galician. But, in prose, Castilian came into its own in the thirteenth century. There are many references to 'our language of Castile' in the time of

[1] R. Serra Ruíz, *Honor, honra e injuria en el derecho medieval español* (Murcia, 1969), pp. 251, 257–63, 191 ff., etc. See F. A. Roca Traver, *El Justicia de Valencia, 1238–1321* (Valencia, 1970), pp. 221, 369.

[2] See below, Ch. II, pp. 72–5; Part II, Ch. II, pp. 304–6.

Alfonso X (1252–84). Miss Procter believes that Alfonso 'aimed at making Castilian the official language of his realms.' She points out that it was employed in all internal administration. Latin was used for foreign diplomatic correspondence only. In Portugal Alfonso's grandson, King Dinis (1279–1325) was to imitate his grandfather and make Portuguese the official language of his monarchy.

The Crown of Aragon was plurilingual. Five languages attained cultural expression, Catalan, Aragonese, Provençal, Latin, and Hebrew. Arabic, by 1300, was of less importance in both Aragon and Castile than Hebrew.

Of the languages in use in the Crown of Aragon Catalan was certainly the most important. It was the most widespread, being spoken from Roussillon and Cerdagne to the southern border of the kingdom of Valencia at Alicante, and in the Balearic Islands. It had been widely diffused in Sicily and Sardinia by the Catalan armies. Catalan was spoken of as 'our language' by Alfons II in 1287. But Aragonese was also useful as a link with Castile and Navarre, while Provençal united Catalonia to southern France and was the language used by Catalan poets until the fifteenth century. There seems no evidence for a conscious attempt by the kings of Aragon to 'catalanize' non-Catalan territories under their rule. It was not until the fourteenth century that Catalan definitely began to supersede Latin as the language of administration.[1]

ECCLESIASTICAL DIVERSITY

The dynastic character of the crusades launched in the peninsula appeared in 1237 when the papal indulgence granted to all the faithful of the ecclesiastical province of Tarragona for a crusade against Valencia expressly excluded the dioceses of Pamplona and Calahorra. These dioceses were spiritually subject to the Catalan see of Tarragona but they were under the kings of Navarre or Castile and so could not be drawn into a Catalan crusade. The peninsular kingdoms were anxious to control their local churches. They sought to preclude any intervention by 'foreign' clerics in their realms. In 1317–18

[1] E. S. Procter, *Alfonso X of Castile* (Oxford, 1951), p. 4; eadem, in *Oxford Essays in Medieval History presented to H. E. Slater* (Oxford, 1934), p. 106; M. Batllori, *VII CHCA* i. 330 f.; *contra* Soldevila, *Història de Catalunya*, 2nd edn., p. 457.

Jaume II of Aragon largely succeeded in changing ancient ecclesiastical boundaries to bring this aim about.[1]

INTERNAL WARS

Much of the energy of rulers of the peninsula was spent on useless internecine struggles, such as the wars between Portugal and Castile over the failures to fulfil marriage promises.

A Portuguese chronicler describes one of these wars, in which Castilians enslaved and sold hundreds of Portuguese peasants while, in revenge, the Portuguese army spared no one they found in the country round Salamanca. Churches provided no shelter to those who took refuge there. They were robbed and killed as in any other place. These conflicts had no effect on the frontier between the two countries, which has hardly varied since 1267, nor were they as destructive as the wars of the late fourteenth century between Castile, Aragon, and Portugal, but they assisted the Muslims of Granada and demonstrated that if any consciousness of unity existed in the peninsula it had very little effect on the way its rulers behaved.

Professor Maravall has insisted that the plurality of the peninsula 'cannot be understood without the superior presence (*instancia*) of Spain'. While he admits the diversity of the later Middle Ages he sees the Iberian unity, the 'idea of the whole', as overriding. On the other hand Sr. Blanco-González holds that because spiritual unity 'crystallized prematurely' in three separate units (Portugal, Castile, the Crown of Aragon—Granada and Navarre being largely suppressed by Castile) 'not even in the modern period was a definite unity achieved. The municipalities . . . and Cortes maintained the individual character of each unit'.[2]

The evidence outlined here seems to show that one should incline to the view of Sr. Blanco-González. In the thirteenth century, as in earlier times, diversity, not unity, is the pre-

[1] P. Guichard, *AEM* 5 (1968), 729; J. Goñi Gaztambide, *Principe de Viana*, 23 (1962), 110–12; Vincke, *Documenta*, pp. 41, 46, 255. For the struggle between Toledo and Tarragona over Valencia see R. I. Burns, *The Crusader Kingdom of Valencia*, i (Cambridge, Mass., 1967), 253–81.

[2] J. A. Maravall, *El concepto de España en la edad media*, 2nd edn. (Madrid, 1954), p. 41 (and see pp. 341–99); B. Blanco-González, *Del cortesano al discreto*, i (Madrid, 1962), 374. C. da Silva Tarouca, *Crónicas dos sete primeiros reis de Portugal*, ii (Lisbon, 1952), 36–9.

dominant note of the peninsula. This diversity went deep, it was expressed in many different ways. Not only politics but art, literature, language, institutions separated rather than united Castile and Catalonia. It was hardly likely that a royal marriage in 1469 between the heirs of Castile and Aragon could unite peoples which had possessed for centuries 'their own character, their own language, and their mission to achieve'.[1]

[1] F. Soldevila, *Historia de España*, 2nd edn., i (Barcelona, 1959), 229.

II
Economy and Society

THE END OF THE 'RECONQUEST'

DURING the thirteenth century the Christian kingdoms of Aragon, Castile, and Portugal asserted not only predominance but control over the Islamic south of the Iberian peninsula. By 1300 the Crown of Aragon had taken over Valencia, part of Murcia, and the Balearic Islands; Castile Andalusia, Portugal the Algarve. It seemed unlikely that Granada could survive for long as an independent Islamic state. But these political conquests did not mean the end of Islam in the peninsula. In 1300 Iberia was, perhaps more than ever before, a land of three religions. Islamic culture was transmitted to the Christian rulers by a vastly larger number of newly acquired subject Muslims, the 'Mudejars', and by the Jewish communities dispersed throughout the peninsula. Islamic institutions and scientific skills, ranging from systems of irrigation to Arabic medicine, were used and transformed by the constant interaction, the *convivencia* of Jews, Muslims, and Christians in a world now won politically for Latin Christendom but where, below the surface, East and West continued to dispute for dominance.

The political change was sudden. In 1200 the Almohad empire, with its capital at Marrakesh in Morocco, extended from Tripoli to the Tagus and the Ebro. Its architectural achievements surpassed anything in the Islamic East; its philosophical thinkers dwarfed competitors both in Islam and in contemporary Christendom. The Christian rulers of Iberia seemed petty in comparison.

The enormous scale of the Almohad empire proved a disadvantage. Buildings such as the Giralda in Seville or philosophy as subtle as Averroes' touched few minds. The primitive Almohad doctrine had lost its hold even on the victor of Alarcos (in 1195), the caliph al-Mansūr. It was also significant that this great victory won back no important cities in Spain for Islam.

The Christian kings could not unite against Islam but they could resist and the Almohads did not keep up the pressure.

The defeat of the Almohad caliph al-Nāsir in 1212 at Las Navas de Tolosa by the kings of Castile, Aragon, and Navarre was not decisive in itself but the Almohads failed to recover from the blow. The same year the walls of Fez were restored; the heart of the empire was felt to be in danger. In 1213 the eventual supplanters of the Almohads, the Banū Marīn began to move against them. In the 1220s the great structure began visibly to dissolve. The dissolution came first in Spain, where the Almohads had long been regarded as Berber oppressors. As Ibn Khaldūn puts it: 'In the provinces of al-Andalus the "lords" [members of the reigning dynasty] sought to reign, each over his lands; at Marrakesh [the Almohads'] authority grew weaker. They had come to ask help from the king of Castile against each other and to give him Islamic fortresses in exchange.'[1] Dynastic quarrels led to the revolt of the Arabic aristocracy of Spain. The Christian rulers of the north profited from the ensuing anarchy. Even before the virtual end of the Almohad power in North Africa, with the death of al-Sa'īd in 1248, the Christian 'reconquest' of al-Andalus was almost accomplished with the capture of Seville.[2]

The first half of the thirteenth century was an age of expansion for western Christendom but the most important and lasting gains were made in the Iberian peninsula. The establishment of a Latin empire in Constantinople in 1204 and of Latin principalities in Greece were trivial and evanescent in comparison. From 1212 to 1248, with some small later conquests, Catalonia–Aragon, Castile, and Portugal together increased their territory by almost half again. Catalonia–Aragon grew from 85,000 to 112,000 square kilometres with the acquisition of the kingdom of Valencia (extended to Alicante in 1304) and of the Balearic Islands. León–Castile, through Fernando III's conquests in Andalusia, grew from 235,000 square kilometres

[1] Ibn Khaldūn, *Kitāb al-ᶜIbar*, transl. M. Gaudefroy-Demombynes, *Journal asiatique*, 9 série, 12 (1898), 311; cf. idem, *Histoire des berbères*, transl. Slane, ii (Algiers, 1854), 319–25.

[2] Roger le Tourneau, *The Almohad Movement in North Africa in the Twelfth and Thirteenth Centuries* (Princeton, N.J., 1969); A. Huici Miranda, *Historia política del imperio almohade*, 2 vols. (Tetuán, 1956–9). R. Arié, *L'Espagne musulmane au temps des nasrides* (Paris, 1973), pp. 49–60.

to 355,000 and Portugal, in less than twenty years (1220–38), from 55,000 to 90,000. In comparison the emirate of Granada, the only Islamic state left in the peninsula, was reduced to less than 30,000 square kilometres.[1]

The expansion of the Crown of Aragon was more important than the figures might suggest. Catalonia–Aragon now controlled the greater part of the Mediterranean coast of the peninsula and the Balearics. These acquisitions launched the rulers of Catalonia–Aragon on a route which took them, by the 1320s, to Sicily and Sardinia. Catalonia had found its maritime vocation. To contemporary Egyptian chroniclers the kings of Aragon appeared as 'kings of Barcelona'; to a Frankish chronicler in fourteenth-century Greece, 'kings of Catalonia'.[2] At the same time, in Valencia and the Balearics, Catalonia–Aragon incorporated a much greater proportion of the existing Muslim population than Castile in Andalusia for, by 1270, most of the Muslims had emigrated from Andalusia after a series of revolts. These two advantages enjoyed by the Crown of Aragon could not, however, outweigh the vastly greater territorial expansion of León–Castile, which, by 1300, occupied an area almost four times larger than Portugal and over three times greater than that of Aragon.

The small kingdom of Navarre was the one Christian state of the peninsula which did not profit from the break-up of Almohad rule in al-Andalus. Navarre remained bottled up in the Pyrenees, sealed off by Castile and Aragon from expansion southwards. From 1234 it was controlled by a French dynasty and tended to move in the orbit of French rather than of peninsular politics.

The fall of Seville in 1248 to Fernando III of Castile convinced both Muslims and Christians that the end of al-Andalus had come. The end was lamented by a Muslim poet of Ronda, for whom it meant that Muslims were 'strangers now in Spain'; it was celebrated by the future Alfonso X (then heir to the throne of Castile) and by the *Primera Crónica General*, which was begun at his court. For the *Crónica* the conquest displayed God's

[1] S. Sobrequés Vidal, in *Historia de España y América*, ed. J. Vicens Vives, ii (Barcelona, 1961), 8–12; M. A. Ladero Quesada, *Granada* (Madrid, 1969), p. 32.

[2] A. Masía de Ros, *La Corona de Aragón y los estados del Norte de Africa* (Barcelona, 1951), p. 102; A. Rubió y Lluch, in *Memorias de la Real Academia de Buenas Letras de Barcelona*, 4 (1887), 39 f.

special favour and the great loyalty of Castile's vassals. In fact there took part in the campaign not only forces from Asturias, Vizcaya, Guipúzcoa, Galicia, León, Old and New Castile, but also from Aragon, Catalonia, and Navarre. Contingents from Castilian cities and the Military Orders played a vital role. The siege had lasted seventeen months.[1]

Fernando III was planning conquests in North Africa. He already saw al-Andalus as conquered. The *Primera Crónica* imagines his dying speech to his heir: 'I leave you lord of all the land this side of the sea, which Moors took from King Rodrigo of Spain—all is in your power, conquered or tributary.'[2]

If one puts aside Portugal and especially Catalonia–Aragon—whose chroniclers presented their Jaume I as equal in fame to his contemporary Fernando, this dying speech of the conqueror of Seville may be regarded as accurate. Fernando III, aided by Muslim internal dissensions and lack of help from North Africa, had 'taken from the enemies of the faith of Christ the lordship [over Spain]'. For a Galician poet he was 'the king who conquered the land of Moors from sea to sea'.[3]

How did any part of al-Andalus escape being swallowed up by the triumphant Christians? In 1250 Castilian opinion believed complete victory must come soon.[4] Alfonso X's later *Cántigas* are less confident. His nephew, Don Juan Manuel, believed 'the House of Castile is disinherited and without great honour from neighbouring kings' because of the failure to complete the conquest of Granada.[5]

THE SURVIVAL OF GRANADA

The military aid Granada received from Tunis, and later from Morocco, contributed less to its survival than did the lack of

[1] *Primera Crónica General*, ed. R. Menéndez Pidal, cc. 1128–31, ii (Madrid, 1955), 768, 771; A. Ballesteros, *Sevilla en el siglo XIII* (Madrid, 1913), pp. 13–6; J. González, *Hispania*, 6 (1946), 515–631.

[2] *Primera Crónica General*, cc. 1131 f., pp. 771 f.

[3] ibid., c. 1131 (p. 771). Compare the Aragonese *Crónica de San Juan de la Peña*, ed. A. Ubieto Arteta (Textos Medievales IV) (Valencia, 1961), p. 143. See also the description of Fernando III taking Córdoba in 1236 by Rodrigo Ximénez de Rada, *Opera* (Madrid, 1793, facsimile Valencia, 1968); *De rebus Hispaniae*, ix, cc. 16 f. (pp. 205–7), and González, *Repartimiento de Sevilla*, i. 219 f.

[4] *Poema de Fernán González*, ed. A. Zamora Vicente (Clásicos Castelanos, cxxviii) (Madrid, 1946), p. 130 (v. 438).

[5] *Cántigas*, ccclx, cccci (ed. Mettmann, iii. 272 f., 349 f.); Juan Manuel, *Libro de los estados*, ii, c. 45 (*BAE* li. 363).

Christian unity. Treaties concluded in the twelfth century and reaffirmed later barred both Portugal and Aragon from any further territorial acquisitions east of the Algarve or south of Valencia, respectively. Granada was reserved for Castile. There was no reason for haste on the part of Castile—or for interest on the part of the other kingdoms of the peninsula. In 1309 Jaume II of Aragon, writing to the king of Portugal, might declare: 'It was our great shame that the king of Granada, having so little power, should stand so long, with great dishonour to Jesus Christ and to us and harm to all Spain.' But Jaume II's offer to join Castile against Granada the year this letter was written—in return for a promise of one-sixth of the kingdom to be attacked— was greeted with jealous rage on the part of the Castilian Cortes.[1]

What followed in 1309—the disastrous siege of Almería by Jaume, at the time that Fernando IV of Castile was besieging Algeciras—was seen by historians in the past as a striking example of a 'crusading' mentality, the *reconquista* transcending the divisions of Spanish kingdoms. The tragi-comedy of 1309 illustrates something less impressive. Castile and Aragon entered the war as 'auxiliaries of Morocco' against Granada.[2] A few years later the attack on Granada in 1319 by the Castilian Infantes Pedro and Juan was an unsuccessful intervention in the internal struggles of that kingdom. The conflict over the Straits of Gibraltar, over Tarifa and Algeciras, which went through several acts between 1292 and 1350, was of greater importance but it was essentially a defensive war against the growing power of Morocco, one in which Granada was at times on the Christian side.[3]

Perhaps Granada survived because it ceased to be dangerous. Islam in Spain could no longer provoke fear (though Morocco in the 1340s might do so), and fear, in the later Middle Ages, was needed to galvanize even the bungling crusades against the Turks. The Naṣrids of Granada entered skilfully into the interplay of the Spanish kingdoms. In the 1270s Muḥammad II of Granada allied with Castile against Morocco in order to avoid

[1] A. Giménez Solér, *El sitio de Almería en 1309* (Barcelona, 1904), pp. 36 f., 38 f.

[2] ibid., p. 57; cf. A. Ballesteros y Beretta, *Historia de España*², iii. 1 (Barcelona, 1948), 263 f.

[3] See below, Part II, Ch. II, and Part III, Ch. I.

being swallowed up by the victorious Banū Marīn. In the 1290s Muḥammad offered to mediate between the kings of Aragon and Castile. He again preferred to be one of the 'club' of Spanish kings rather than to depend for his survival on the Berbers of Morocco. Hence he joined with Castile in attacking Tarifa, which was held by his Moroccan co-religionists.[1]

After the disasters of 1309 Christian opinion outside the peninsula was summed up by the French pope Clement V: 'I fear they will say that the king of Aragon and the kings of Spain are neighbours of the Moors of Spain and want to use *other* hands to pluck the viper out of its hole.' The pope himself held that the vested interests of the Castilian nobility, who would sell God and all Christendom for money, explained the failure to conquer Granada.[2] In 1317 Clement's successor, John XXII, before he would allow the Spanish clergy to be taxed to finance a 'crusade' against Granada, demanded a previous promise to reduce all Muslim prisoners to slavery if they refused baptism, and to convert all mosques to churches, and not to make any peace or truce without papal consent.[3] Almost two centuries were to pass before Spanish rulers could contemplate imposing conditions so far removed from the traditions of the peninsula.

With the 'Reconquest' halted and—as it proved—at a virtual standstill until the Catholic Monarchs, Castile was to take refuge from boredom in civil strife, in wars with the other Christian kingdoms of the peninsula, or in attempts to intervene on the wider European stage. Catalonia–Aragon was to pursue possibilities of expansion in the Mediterranean, since southern France was barred to her by the Capetians, while the 'Reconquest' of Granada was monopolized by Castile.

REPOPULATION

The 'real Reconquest', as Vicens Vives called it, the colonization and settlement of the south and south-eastern sections of the peninsula, was painfully slow in comparison to the military campaigns.

[1] Ibn Khaldūn, *Histoire des berbères*, transl. Slane, iv. 97; Giménez Soler, *El sitio de Almería en 1309*, pp. 17 f.

[2] ibid., pp. 67, n. 1; 68, n. 1.

[3] Idem, *La Corona de Aragón y Granada* (Barcelona, 1908), p. 206.

CASTILE: ANDALUSIA

Until after the great revolt of the Muslims of Andalusia in the 1260s and their consequent expulsion *en masse* from large areas of the countryside, Christians settled almost entirely in the fortified cities. The devastation wrought in the countryside by the raids which accompanied and made possible the conquest from the 1220s to 1248 was severe. In 1253 a commission at Coria found that only 10,000 of the olive trees around the town were standing; 20,000 had been burnt.[1]

The first conquests of Fernando III in eastern Andalusia and the Islamic kingdom of Jaén (1225–46) were largely bestowed on the Military Orders of Calatrava and Santiago and on the archbishopric of Toledo, since the Orders and the archbishop had provided most of the troops used by Fernando. In Córdoba, taken in 1236, and Seville (in 1248) royal municipalities were created, but Muslims continued, as was the case elsewhere, to occupy the countryside until a revolt in 1264, instigated by Granada. After this rebellion the Orders of Calatrava, Santiago, and Alcántara again obtained vast grants of land with the responsibility of protecting the frontier against the kingdom of Granada. Écija (taken in 1263) and Carmona constituted royal municipalities, as did Arcos, Niebla (conquered in 1262), Cádiz (before 1260), and the most important, Jerez. Over half the land of Andalusia, however, was granted to, or acquired by, the Castilian nobility, the Orders, and the Church. Lower Extremadura, with the towns of Mérida and Trujillo, became almost entirely the possession of the Orders, the Temple, Alcántara, and Santiago, each of which received about 300,000 hectares (almost 700,000 acres) of land. The Orders failed to attract many Christian settlers: they preferred to carry on sheep-, horse-, and cattle-raising with the help of small numbers of subject Muslims. This general preference for the more dependent Muslims as against Christian vassals and workers appears in documents of the Order of Santiago of the 1270s ranging from lands around Uclés and Ocaña, to the east of Toledo, south to Murcia.[2]

[1] J. González, *Repartimiento*, 392.

[2] D. W. Lomax, *La Orden de Santiago (1170–1275)* (Madrid, 1965), pp. 271–4, 112–15, 127 f.; F. Fernández y González, *Estado social y política de los Mudéjares de Castilla* (Madrid, 1866), pp. 321 f.; C. J. Bishko, in *The New World looks at its history*, ed. A. R. Lewis and T. F. McGann (Austin, Texas, 1963), pp. 53 ff.

The general result of royal policy was that, by 1300, Extremadura and large areas of Andalusia were very sparsely populated and that the area actually settled by Christian colonists from the north was far smaller, proportionately, than was the case in the Crown of Aragon. However, a large number of settlers continued, for centuries, to move slowly south from the Meseta, while other areas, such as the northern part of the province of Madrid, were gradually settled by colonists, in this case coming from Segovia.

There exists a detailed description of the way in which the city and lands of Écija were divided in 1264 among the new settlers. The city was divided on the lines of a great cross which was traced by the royal commission, looking down from the minaret of the principal mosque. The division was intended to represent Christ on the Cross between his Mother and the beloved disciple, with the faithful at his feet. Christ crucified was to redeem the newly Christian Écija.

> We divided the town [we read] into four sections in memory of the Cross: the first, the greater, the Holy and Venerable Cross; on the right that of Santa Maria; on the left that of St John; and, in front of all three, St. Barbara, as a semblance of the people before the Cross, asking for mercy and praising the name of Jesus Christ.

The country immediately round the city was also divided into four parts, each of which was presumably assigned to the settlers of one of the four sections of the city itself. The more remote countryside had been abandoned by the Muslims. No farms were in use, even their names were forgotten. The countryside was divided up into small properties to support the settlers, who lived in small villages or hamlets of four to twenty houses. Many of these settlers seem soon to have tired of Andalusia. They sold their lands—often to the Order of Calatrava—and returned to their homes in northern Spain.[1]

Other newly created municipalities had difficulty in finding settlers. Cádiz was at first granted an extensive area dependent on the city, but this was soon reduced by royal gifts and powerful neighbours. The settlers of Cádiz came mainly from the Basque ports of the north though they also included Frenchmen,

[1] E. Tormo, *BRAH* 118 (1946), 176; González, op. cit., i. 58–63.

Portuguese, and Catalans. They probably did not number much more than 500 families—Jerez in 1260 comprised less than 2,000 houses (probably less than 10,000 people). The new inhabitants of these towns were apportioned houses, land outside the city walls, and farms in the rural area under the city's jurisdiction, according to their rank in society. A noble received more than a non-noble mounted man-at-arms (a *caballero villano*), and the latter twice the portion of a foot-soldier. The members of the royal court, leading nobles and ecclesiastics, and the local Church, thus newly endowed, all received portions of the city and its dependent countryside.[1]

SEVILLE

The repopulation of Seville can be studied in detail, on the basis of the original *Repartimiento*, a register of the lands and houses allocated to settlers by a royal commission. The first commission of *partidores* was active from 1249 to 1253 and lesser bodies completed the task from 1255 to 1257. (This was not an exceptionally lengthy process—in Córdoba the work took from 1236 to 1241, in Murcia and Orihuela far longer.) Yet in 1263 Alfonso X discovered that 'Seville was [already] becoming depopulated'. He ordered the redistribution of houses abandoned by the original settlers. In Seville, more than elsewhere, since the court was often there, many properties had been given to nobles, royal officials, and members of the royal family. Two hundred heads of noble families were settled in Seville, as compared to forty in Jérez and thirty in Carmona. By 1254 there was little property left in the king's hands.

It is thought that the settlers of Seville numbered over 20,000. There were few Muslims, an important colony of Jews, many of whom probably arrived with Fernando III in 1248, Italians, especially Genoese, some French, and more Catalans but the great majority of settlers came from Old Castile, especially Burgos, Palencia, and Valladolid.

The municipality (*concejo*) of Seville governed an area which was larger than the modern province, although the city's juris-

[1] J. González in *La reconquista española y la repoblación del país* (Saragossa, 1951), pp. 197–206; Sobrequés, op. cit., pp. 12–21; H. Sancho de Sopranis, *Hispania*, 15 (1955), 483–539, esp. 515 ff.

diction was restricted by Alfonso X's grants to the Military Orders. The actual settlement of new colonists was concentrated round Seville itself.[1]

MURCIA

In 1243 the Muslim king of Murcia became a vassal of Castile. He kept much of his independence, however, and, apart from military garrisons, few Castilians settled in the kingdom of Murcia. In 1257 Alfonso X attempted to increase the number of Christian settlers; pressure was put on the Muslim king and local chiefs to give up their lands. This pressure probably helped to bring about the revolt of 1264, which followed that of the Muslims of Andalusia.[2]

By 1266 the revolt of Murcia had been put down by Jaume I of Aragon, who then returned the kingdom to his son-in-law Alfonso X. The settlement of the country by Christians now began on a large scale. From Jaume I's *Book of Deeds* it appears that he only intended that a limited number of knights should be settled in Murcia to prevent a further rising. Alfonso X, however, followed the same policy as in Andalusia, the intensive settlement of towns, ruled by municipal councils (*concejos*), under the Crown, and large grants in rural areas to the Military Orders. Accordingly, the city of Murcia was placed under a (mainly bourgeois) council. The Muslims were removed to a fortified suburb. The land round the city which could be irrigated was divided into two halves, one of which was reserved for Muslims. Gradually this zone was penetrated by Christians as discontented Muslims emigrated to Granada.[3]

The surviving *Repartimiento* of Murcia is incomplete. About 45 per cent of the settlers recorded came from the territories of Jaume I of Aragon; most of them were probably soldiers in his invading army of 1266, who chose to remain behind. Over 1,000 Catalan settlers appear in the *Repartimiento* and about 100 Aragonese, compared with some 500 Castilians (18 per cent of

[1] González, *Repartimiento*.

[2] *Documentos de Alfonso X el Sabio*, ed. J. Torres Fontes (Murcia, 1963), pp. 7–14; *Documentos del siglo XIII*, ed. idem (Murcia, 1969), pp. 17 f.

[3] J. Torres Fontes, *La conquista de Murcia en 1266 por Jaime I de Aragón* (Murcia, 1967); idem, *VII CHCA* ii. 329–40; idem, in *Murgetana*, 17 (1961), 57–89; *Documentos de Alfonso X*, pp. 83 ff.

the whole) and under 500 Muslim names (16 per cent). The origin of 17 per cent of the settlers is not clear. A large number of Catalan names also appear in the *Repartimiento* of Orihuela, which was carried out in several stages from 1265 to 1314.[1]

The strong Catalan element in the settlement of Murcia is also shown by the very high proportion (perhaps 50 per cent) of Catalan words in the local dialect today. In about 1335 we are told that Catalan was spoken throughout the kingdom of Murcia. Jaume II of Aragon's conquest of the kingdom from Castile in 1296 (he held it until 1304 and retained Orihuela and Alicante after that) no doubt brought more Catalan settlers there.[2]

In the late thirteenth century the Christian population declined in numbers. The lesser nobles and citizens lived as rentiers, maintaining horses and arms. Their lands were worked by Mudejars. What Christian artisans there were suffered from the competition of Mudejar craftsmen. The Military Orders, as usual, did not attract or encourage many Christian settlers on their lands. The loss of population by the emigration of many Mudejars to Granada in the thirteenth century was not made up until the reign of the Catholic Kings. In spite of this emigration the southern part of the kingdom of Murcia, along the border with Granada, remained for centuries a mainly Islamic country.[3]

THE CROWN OF ARAGON

In the thirteenth century the Crown of Aragon conquered the Balearic Islands and the Muslim kingdom of Valencia. The ways in which colonization proceeded were very different in these two regions.

Majorca was divided in 1232 into two halves. The king, Jaume I of Aragon, received half the houses, shops, ovens, and

[1] M. Gual Camarena, *VII CHCA* ii. 303–10, based on *Repartimiento de Murcia*, ed. J. Torres Fontes (Madrid, 1960); J. Mª. Font Rius, in *HV* i. 417–30 (on Orihuela).

[2] Ramon Muntaner, *Crónica*, c. 17; F. Soldevila, *Els grans reis del segle XIII*, p. 42.

[3] J. Torres Fontes, *La repoblación murciana en el siglo XIII* (Murcia, 1963), cited by M. Gual in *EEMCA* 8 (1967), 783 f.; J. Mª. Font Rius, in *La reconquista*, pp. 107–26.

baths of the City of Majorca (today Palma) and half (150,000 hectares) of the land in the rest of the island. The *Repartiment* we possess describes the distribution of the royal half (houses, etc. in the city, and farms, mills, etc. in the island) to a very large number of mainly small proprietors. Eighty-three per cent of the beneficiaries received less than 150 hectares (about 370 acres), 50 per cent less than 70 hectares (170 acres). The men of Barcelona received 455 farms, totalling 11,500 hectares (about 28,500 acres), and 256 houses and shops in the city. The men of Marseille received almost as much land and 297 houses in the city. The men of Tarragona and Lérida also received large grants of land and houses, as did the Order of the Temple.[1]

The main problem with regard to the colonization of Majorca concerns the fate of the large Muslim population. Most of the Muslims surrendered unconditionally. It is generally supposed that they either became slaves or were allowed to emigrate to North Africa. This may be questioned, however. It is true that the royal *Repartiment* does not record any Muslim proprietors. But this document (originally drawn up in Arabic) concerns only half the island. We have practically no record of how the other half was distributed by the nobles to whom it was given. It seems reasonable to suggest that, as happened elsewhere (for instance, in Valencia and Ibiza), the nobles kept on the Muslim inhabitants to work their lands, probably with the semi-free status of the *exaricos* of Aragon, owning goods and being able to transmit them to their children but not allowed to leave the estate to which they were attached. One may also note the appearance of native and foreign free Muslims in Majorca in thirteenth-century documents, both working the land and as artisans (painters, blacksmiths, bakers, etc.) in the towns. They provided a regular source of taxes. They did not, however, play a part comparable to that of the free Muslims (Mudejars) of Valencia. It seems probable that many Muslims in

[1] *CDIACA* xi. 7–141. There is a useful résumé by S. Sobrequés, loc. cit., pp. 22–6, but the numbers given need to be checked (e.g. for Marseille). The best account of the *Repartiment* is in J. Mª. Quadrado, *Historia de la conquista de Mallorca* (Palma, 1850). pp. 432–535. The articles by J. Busquets Mulet, *BSAL* 30 (1947–52), 708–58, and in *HM* i. 243–95, add interesting details from a hitherto unused manuscript, partly written in Arabic. See the statistical calculations of J. Bisson, *BSAL* 33 (1968–), 51–8.

Majorca became free after a number of years and received baptism. They would then have been assimilated with comparative ease into the Christian population.[1]

Ibiza (in 1235) and Minorca (in 1287) were taken over and resettled by Catalans in much the same way as Majorca. In Ibiza the Muslims mainly continued to work the land as slaves. Most of the Muslims of Minorca were either expelled or sold as slaves, in general outside the island, but in both islands some free Muslims appear in the sources.[2]

VALENCIA

The Balearics, in their Christian population, institutions, and government, were 'a prolongation of Catalonia'.[3] Valencia, in contrast, conquered from 1232 to 1245, remained for centuries mainly Muslim in population and its Christian settlers were of Aragonese as well as Catalan origin.

The repopulation of the northern region of the kingdom of Valencia was hardly attempted. Large areas were granted to the Military Orders; these grants produced the same results as in Andalusia. Along the border with Aragon the land was mainly held by Aragonese nobles who did not displace the Muslim inhabitants. In 1270, at the end of Jaume I's reign, the king remarked that there were only some 30,000 Christians in the whole kingdom. The large grants in the city of Valencia and other towns to Catalans—the men of Barcelona, Tortosa, Lérida, Tarragona—to settlers from Aragon (particularly Teruel, Saragossa, Daroca, Tarazona), and to citizens of Montpellier, recorded in the *Repartiment*, were apparently not successful in drawing a large population to Valencia and keeping it there. In 1300, despite successive rebellions and expulsions of Muslims, and the occasional foundation of a

[1] Verlinden, i. 262 f., 276, n. 122. For grants within the City by one of the leading nobles cf. E. de K. Aguiló, *BSAL* 14 (1912–13), 209–24, 241–56, 273–85; 15 (1914–15), 53–62. See L. Lliteras, *Artà en el siglo XIII* (Mallorca, 1967), pp. 59 f., 135–7, 166 f., 175. The views expressed in the text are reinforced by the independent conclusions of Elena Lourie, *Speculum*, 45 (1970), 624–49, who produces the first evidence for free Muslim artisans in Majorca. Non-native free Muslims in the 14th cent. are discussed by N. Gais, *RHCM* 9 (1970), 19–30. See also Dufourcq, p. 35, Villanueva, xxi. 131 (a document of 1248).

[2] See below, Part II, Ch. I, p. 260, n. 3; Lourie, pp. 631 ff.

[3] J. E. Martínez Ferrando, *VII CHCA* i. 168.

new town such as Villarreal, Christians still constituted a minority.[1]

Internal colonization and resettlement continued in the thirteenth century in Catalonia itself. Jaume I and Pere II granted new royal charters or founded new towns both in central Catalonia and along the Pyrenees (Figueras 1267, Palamós 1277). Jaume II founded several towns in the deserted region round Balaguer. The Catalan nobility were forced to issue more liberal terms to their dependants to prevent mass emigration to newly conquered Majorca and Valencia. There are cases of attempted colonization by the Military Orders and by the Cistercian monastery of Poblet.[2] Other regions of Spain need to be studied to see if the emigration to the south was accompanied by general resettlement elsewhere.

The large conquests made by Portugal south of the Tagus river were generally distributed, on the same pattern as was followed in Extremadura, to monasteries, Military Orders, and leading nobles.[3]

THE POPULATION OF THE PENINSULA

We do not have even partly reliable figures for the general population of Majorca before 1329, of Navarre before 1350, of Catalonia before 1365, of Aragon before 1404, of Castile–León before 1482, or of Valencia before the sixteenth century. It is clear, however, that the great territorial growth of the Christian monarchies of the peninsula in the thirteenth century did not mean a great growth of population for either Castile or Portugal. Andalusia had been densely populated by Muslims but, except in Murcia, they had largely emigrated by 1270. Many went to North Africa but it is reasonable to suppose that the population of Granada, the last Islamic kingdom left in the peninsula, was doubled as a result.

[1] J. Mª. Font Rius, in *La reconquista*, pp. 94–107; S. Sobrequés, pp. 28–42. The basic source is the *Repartiment* (of 1237–52), *CDIACA* xi. 145–656. Ch. de la Véronne, *Bulletin hispanique*, 51 (1949), 423–6, calculates that by 1244 3,191 Christians had been given grants in the city of Valencia and there were 3,378 Mudejar and 103 Jewish proprietors in a suburb; only thirty-four Muslims remained in the city proper. See also L. Torres Balbas, *Al-Andalus*, 16 (1951), 167 f. On Villarreal (1274) see J. Ma. Doñate Sebastía, *VIII CHCA* ii. 1, 149–63.

[2] J. Mª. Font Rius, *Cartas de población y franquicia de Cataluña*, i (2 parts) (Madrid–Barcelona, 1969).

[3] V. Rau, *Estudos de história económica* (Lisbon, 1961), p. 19.

The Crown of Aragon, in contrast, probably retained the majority of the Muslim population of Valencia, and, in my view, a considerable proportion of the Muslims of Majorca. This brought with it certain disadvantages. The Mudejars proved very hard to assimilate and might revolt if Muslim invaders appeared from Granada or North Africa.

Despite the inclusion of many more Muslims in the new territories of the Crown of Aragon than in Andalusia there can be no doubt that the population of Castile–León was far greater than that of the Crown of Aragon. Reckoning back from an estimated 7,000,000 or 8,000,000 in 1482, it is conjectured that the population of Castile–León in 1225 was about 4,000,000 (another estimate is 3,000,000) and that the conquests perhaps added 300,000 more. By a similar process one can arrive at a population of 100,000 for Aragon and of about 130,000 for Valencia in the late thirteenth century. To this one may add a conjecture of 500,000—550,000 for Catalonia and perhaps 40,000 for Majorca—almost certainly less than 1,000,000 for the whole Crown of Aragon. In Navarre there seems evidence for a small and virtually stationary population, which was perhaps less than 100,000. We cannot even conjecture the population of Granada in the thirteenth century. In the fifteenth century Portugal seems to have contained about 1,000,000 inhabitants. In the thirteenth century the number was probably less than this.[1]

THE JEWISH POPULATION

Scholars are not agreed as to the numbers of the Jewish population in the peninsula in the thirteenth century. The most careful estimate for Castile–León, that of Professor Yitzhak Baer, is 3,600 families. This is based on the tax-rolls for the 1290s. The largest (and richest) community, that of Toledo, apparently numbered only about 350 families, that of Seville about 200 and Burgos 120–50. It is impossible to estimate the

[1] S. Sobrequés, pp. 46–51. For a discussion of the figure for 1482, which seems far too high, see below, Vol. II, Part III. For Portugal see A. H. de Oliveira Marques, in *Revista da Faculdade de Letras de Lisboa*, 3rd ser., 2 (1958), 47–88 (repr. in his *Ensaios de história medieval portuguesa* (Lisbon, 1965), pp. 71–123); V. Rau, in *Do tempo e da história*, i (Lisbon, 1965), pp. 7–46. J. A. G. de Cortázar, *La época medieval* (Madrid, 1973), p. 206, has slightly different figures, which he offers with more assurance than others could command.

number of children and servants per household or the numbers of Jews too poor to pay taxes. It seems unlikely, however, that the Jews of Toledo can have numbered many more than 2,000. There were perhaps ten other cities in Castile–León with fifty to a hundred families (probably less than 1,000 persons), and a large number of smaller groups. It is difficult to arrive at a probable figure of much over 20,000 Jews in Castile–León.[1] I cannot see any basis for supposing a large Jewish population in Castile–León in 1300, reaching perhaps 200,000 (about 5 per cent of an estimated total of 4,000,000).[2]

The number of Jews in Navarre, settled notably in Tudela and Pamplona, in the thirteenth century was small, perhaps 300–400 families in all. In Portugal, also, the Jewish community was as yet of slight importance.[3] In the Crown of Aragon Jews may have formed a higher proportion of the population than in Castile. It is, however, impossible to agree with the suggestion that there were 25,000 Jews in Catalonia, 20,000 in Aragon, 10,000 in Valencia, and perhaps 5,000 in Majorca. These figures seem far too high and should probably be reduced by at least half. The Jews in Barcelona seem not to have numbered much more than 200 families (perhaps 1,200 to 1,500 persons out of a probable city population of some 30,000); there were probably fewer than 2,000 in the city of Valencia and fewer than 2,000 in the whole of Majorca.[4]

A prudent conclusion would seem to be that the numbers of the Jewish population were very much smaller than recent estimates have suggested. They probably did not number more than 2 or 3 per cent of the population of the Crown of Aragon and formed a smaller proportion still of that of Castile–León. Their importance was due not to their numbers but to their

[1] Baer, *History* i. 190–3, 418–20, based largely on Baer, *Die Juden* ii. 81–8. See also F. Cantera, *Sefarad*, 1 (1941), 95–7.

[2] For the numbers expelled in 1492 see below, Vol. II, Part III, Ch. III. Sobrequés, pp. 54 f.; J. Vicens Vives, *Manual de historia económica de España*, 4th edn. (Barcelona, 1965), pp. 224 f.

[3] Baer, *History* i. 193, 420; M. Kayserling, *Geschichte der Juden in Portugal* (Leipzig, 1867), is the only reliable work on the subject. Far more remains to be done.

[4] Sobrequés, pp. 56 f.; Baer, *History* i. 193–5; ii. 46. It is not clear how Sobrequés arrives at his figures, which are repeated in Vicens Vives, op. cit., p. 163. There were 2,580 Jews in Majorca after the Black Death; 2,000 seems a possible figure for 1300. Cf. A. Santamaría Arández, *VIII CHCA* ii. 1, pp. 103–30. For Perpignan see R. W. Emery, *The Jews of Perpignan* (New York, 1959), pp. 11 f. (about 100 families in 1290).

wealth and industry and especially to the fact that they possessed in their Hebrew-Arabic learning a culture and a tradition superior to that of the Christians among whom they lived.

THE MUDEJAR POPULATION

Far less work has been done so far on the Mudejars than on the Jews of the peninsula. In Castile, apart from Murcia, they were far less numerous than in the Crown of Aragon. Mudejar quarters (*morerías*) are found, however, in many cities from León and Burgos southwards. Large farms round Seville were worked mainly by Muslims, though they were often slaves. There were free Muslims in Seville itself. I have already referred to the use of Muslims by the Military Orders.[1]

In the Crown of Aragon estimates for the proportion of Mudejars to the total population have gone as high as 50 per cent.[2] This very high figure is less improbable than some others given for the Jewish population, but it is reached by the same process of arguing back from figures of later centuries, in this case from those calculated for the Moriscos expelled in the seventeenth century.[3] Only in the kingdom of Valencia (and its extension southward to Alicante) did the Mudejars constitute a large majority of the population; in Majorca they may have formed 50 per cent. They were very numerous in Aragon proper. They were also found in Catalonia, in the lower Ebro valley. In contrast, there is little trace of Mudejars in Navarre. They were of greater importance in Portugal, where they worked as skilled agricultural labourers; they seem to have been assimilated more easily there than elsewhere into the life of the people.[4]

THE ECONOMIES OF THE PENINSULA

The thirteenth century was a prosperous age in the economy of western Europe. In this prosperity the Iberian peninsula seems to have shared. In Castile this century saw the creation

[1] J. González, *Repartimiento de Sevilla*, i. 444; see above, p. 22 n. 2, and below, Ch. V, p. 180, n. 2.

[2] Sobrequés, p. 61.

[3] See J. Reglá, *Estudios sobre los moriscos* (Valencia, 1964), and especially H. Lapeyre, *Géographie de l'Espagne morisque* (Paris, 1959), who calculates the Moriscos of the Crown of Aragon as numbering about 200,000 in 1609–11.

[4] Sobrequés, pp. 61 ff.; J. Lúcio de Azevedo, in *História de Portugal*, ed. D. Peres, ii (Lisbon, 1929), 443 f.

of the Mesta, in the Crown of Aragon the rise of the Consulate of the Sea. These two institutions will be discussed in later chapters. They are mentioned here because they represent two of the main directions the economies of the two kingdoms were to take. Castile was to become increasingly geared to the production and export of wool, Catalonia, Valencia, and Majorca to Mediterranean trade. There follow some general notes on the agriculture, manufactures, exports, and imports of the different kingdoms of the peninsula.

AGRICULTURE

The vast majority of the population of the peninsula was occupied, for many centuries after 1200, with agriculture. Most medieval trade, apart from luxury articles such as spices, was concerned with foodstuffs. Cereals, rice, fish (perhaps more than meat), wine, fruits, and olive oil were the most important items of exchange. The mining of iron and salt was of importance. Timber was essential for naval construction and for all building. The increasingly pastoral economy of Castile produced wool first and foremost but also sheepskins and leather; these things rivalled foodstuffs in importance. Among manufactured goods cloth was the principal object of large-scale trade.

Medieval technical improvements in land cultivation were introduced and used far more extensively in northern than in Mediterranean Europe. A great deal of the land of the Iberian peninsula was uncultivated. Muslim techniques of irrigation were in use not only in Islamic Granada but in the fertile lands round Valencia, Murcia, and other cities of the eastern coastal regions, and in Majorca. Water mills were in extensive use in the plain of Vich in Catalonia. They enabled water to be raised to terraces far above the natural water level. In contrast, very little land was irrigated in Castile, except in the Rioja, and, in Andalusia, the extent of irrigated land may have declined after the Christian conquest. In Portugal almost half the soil was uncultivated as late as 1868; in Spain in 1965–9 33.7 per cent of the soil produced virtually nothing.[1]

[1] A. H. de Oliveira Marques, *Introducão a História da agricultura em Portugal*, 2nd edn. (Lisbon, 1968), pp. 61 f.; J.-P. Cuvillier, *MCV* 4 (1968), 73–103. For Aragon see J. Mª. Lacarra, in *Aragón, cuatro ensayos*, i (Saragossa, 1960), 248 f. For irrigation techniques see below, Ch. V, p. 188. A. Cabo, in *Historia de España Alfaguara*, i (Madrid, 1973), p. 131.

CEREALS

Despite technical backwardness, Castile and Aragon proper were usually not only self-sufficient in cereals but able to export them to Portugal and Catalonia. Cereals from Aragon and northern Catalonia were exported down the Ebro river through the port of Tortosa, which 'regulated the price of wheat in a great part of the western Mediterranean'.[1] But cereals also had to be imported to the peninsula, in particular from North Africa. Sicily and Sardinia were constant sources of supply for the Crown of Aragon. The export of cereals from Portugal was allowed in good years but often forbidden by the Portuguese monarchy.[2]

In the peninsula rice was produced mainly in Valencia; Valencian rice reached Castile and Genoa in the fourteenth century. Pegolotti's trade manual compares the 'rice of Spain' to that of Naples and Syria. In the fifteenth century Valencian and Portuguese rice was listed by the customs officers of Bruges among dutiable goods often imported.[3]

FISH

In a world where Lenten and other seasons of abstinence occupied much of the year fish was as important as meat. The Portuguese court consumed large quantities of dried fish, eels, and whale. In the epic battle of Doña Cuaresma against Don Carnal, chronicled by the Archpriest of Hita in the fourteenth century, the eels of Valencia, the trout of the Alberche, the dogfish of Bayonne, the sardines, crabs, and oysters of Biscay, the lobster of Santander, the herring and sea bream of Bermeo, the lamprey of Seville, the salmon of Castro Urdiales contest with, and finally defeat, the domestic animals, chickens, rabbits, capons, ducks, geese, goats, and suckling pigs; the wild game which covered Spain, the pheasants and partridges, the deer, stags, wild boars; and the great flocks of sheep which crossed the Meseta every year.[4] The Archpriest's lists of warriors on

[1] Vicens Vives, op. cit., p. 180.

[2] Oliveira Marques, op. cit., pp. 153–7, 168.

[3] M. Gual Camarena, *Vocabulario del comercio medieval* (Tarragona, 1968), pp. 217 f.; J. Finot, *Étude historique sur les relations commerciales entre la Flandre et l'Espagne au moyen âge* (Paris, 1899), pp. 304–6.

[4] A. H. de Oliveira Marques, *Daily Life*, p. 22; Arcipreste de Hita, *Libro de Buen Amor*, vv. 1067–1127, ed. M. Criado de Val and E. W. Naylor (Madrid, 1965), pp. 312–32.

each side in this battle are perhaps more useful historically than Homer's catalogues of champions. Many of the Archpriest's fish came from Cantabria. We know from other sources that already in the fourteenth century—perhaps earlier—Basque seamen were transporting fish from the Atlantic to eastern Spain, often to return laden with salt from Ibiza. 'Arenchs', dried herrings perhaps from the Baltic, appear in seven custom tariffs of the Crown of Aragon by 1365.

WINE

Perhaps the best definition known of the bourgeois is one of 1252 which describes him as the man who drinks wine. The history of the wine trade has been studied less for the peninsula than for France. It seems that Castile, Portugal, and Valencia exported wine in the thirteenth century, Castile on a particularly large scale. The customs tariffs of the Crown of Aragon record wine from Marseille, Tarascon, Agde, Narbonne, Roussillon, Collioure, and Barcelona, as well as 'Greek wine', highly prized by successive kings of Aragon, Jaume II, Pere III, and Martí. Wine was often drunk mixed with water; it was also too frequently adulterated with lime, salt, and plaster.[1]

VEGETABLES

The Archpriest of Hita tells us that during Lent, while undergoing penance, Don Carnal was obliged to live, on Sunday on chickpeas with olive oil, on Monday on locust beans, on Tuesday on asparagus and bread, on Wednesday on a little spinach, on Thursday on salted lentils, on Friday on bread and water, and on Saturday on beans.[2] This vegetable diet was probably common to many of the poor throughout the year.

FRUIT

The customs tariffs of the Crown of Aragon often list almonds (from Valencia, Málaga, and Portugal), and figs (presumably dried) from Valencia, Alicante, Catalonia, Majorca, Murcia, and Málaga. Figs were exported to Italy. Olive oil was produced in Catalonia, Valencia, and Majorca and shipped from Seville by Catalan merchants. Catalans sold oil to Sicily and

[1] Gual Camarena, pp. 212, 355, 450–4.
[2] Arcipreste, vv. 1163–9 (pp. 348–50).

Tunis. Genoese merchants exported large quantities of oil from Andalusia to Egypt. Portugal exported oil to northern Europe. Oranges were produced in Valencia but not on a great scale. In 1305 Jaume II of Aragon attempted to introduce sugar-cane from Sicily to Valencia but it did not become important there until the fifteenth century. Sugar was produced on a greater scale in the kingdom of Granada. Honey was exported both from Castile and the Crown of Aragon. Well-known cheeses came from the Balearics, Sardinia, Sicily, and Peñafiel near Valladolid. Goat and sheep cheeses were as well known as they are today.[1]

SALT

In the medieval economy salt was perhaps as important as wheat and wine. Neither fish nor meat could be preserved without salt; without it men would have gone very hungry in the winter. Salt was also essential for migrant flocks of sheep and one of the Mesta's most prized privileges was exemption from paying the salt tax. This tax, paid by all consumers, formed one of the more important sources of revenue of the monarchies of the peninsula.

The Crown of Aragon's main salt mines were in Aragon (in the province of Teruel), in Catalonia (Cardona), and in Ibiza in the Balearics. From the 1320s the Crown also controlled the salt mines of Sardinia. Castile possessed sources of supply in the provinces of Guadalajara and Cuenca. It seems that the export of Portuguese salt began in the last quarter of the thirteenth century. From about 1450 the salt of Setúbal became the main export of Portugal.[2]

SHEEP-RAISING: WOOL

It has been suggested that the economy of Andalusia changed with the expulsion of the majority of the Muslim rural popula-

[1] Gual Camarena, pp. 345, 203 f., 316 f., 371 ff., 441 f., 359 f., 320; Martínez Ferrando, *Jaime II*, ii. 20; *Homenaje a D. Francisco Codera* (Saragossa, 1904), p. 470 (a text of 1337 on Granada); A. H. de Oliveira Marques, *Ensaios de historia medieval portuguesa* (Lisbon, 1965), p. 45.

[2] M. Gual Camarena, 'Para un mapa de la sal hispana en la Edad Media', *HV* i. 483–97; V. Rau, 'Problèmes de l'histoire du sel au Portugal', *Association pour l'histoire de la civilisation* (Toulouse, 1956–7), pp. 16–23; eadem, *Estudos de história*, i (Lisbon, 1968), 175–202.

tion in 1264 and that an intensive type of agriculture based on irrigation was replaced at this time by olive-growing and sheep-raising. However, the Muslim geographer al-Idrīsī, writing in the twelfth century, already describes the landscape around Seville as covered with olives and figs as far as Niebla. It is possible that the amount of land given over to wheat declined somewhat after 1264 and that more vines were planted, but the only real change appears to be the appearance of large flocks of sheep in documents dating from 1266 onwards.[1] In the Extremadura and in Portugal, in the Algarve, the same type of cattle economy was carried on by the same type of large proprietors as was probably practised under the Muslims. In these adjoining regions the Military Orders, so richly endowed at the Reconquest, now reigned supreme.

The Christian conquest of Andalusia undoubtedly led to a great increase in sheep-raising in Castile–León. The migration of sheep from winter to summer pasturage and back again is attested at a far earlier time but now these migrations could be extended over almost the whole length of the Iberian peninsula.[2] The official royal recognition of 'the Mesta of the Shepherds' by Alfonso X in 1273 is a sign of the importance sheep and cattle-raising had attained by this time. In the next two centuries they were to go from strength to strength in Castile.[3]

From 1303 onwards the ports of Cantabria, particularly San Sebastián, Santander, and Bilbao, were engaged in the regular export of Spanish wool to England. The second half of the fourteenth century was to see a great increase in the export of wool from Castile, especially to Flanders and Italy, but the ground for later expansion was laid before 1350.[4]

The rapid growth of sheep-farming in Castile may have been assisted by cross-breeding between North African and Spanish sheep which produced the merino breed. The name probably came from the Banū Marīn of Morocco. 'Merino

[1] Vicens Vives, *Manual*, p. 150; cf. Al-Idrīsī, transl. A. Blázquez, *Boletín de la Real Sociedad geográfica*, 43 (1901), 15 f.; Al Himyarī, *Kitāb ar-Rawd al-Mi ᶜtar*, transl. Mª. P. Maestro González (Textos Medievales X) (Valencia, 1963), p. 50, follows al-Idrīsī; González, *Repartimiento de Sevilla*, i. 446.

[2] See below, Part II, Ch. II, pp. 288 f.

[3] J. Klein, *The Mesta* (Cambridge, Mass., 1920).

[4] Klein, *The Mesta*, pp. 34 f.

wool' is first mentioned as being shipped from Tunis to Pisa in 1307 but we do not know that this shipment consisted of the 'white, kinky staple' which later became Castile's major export.

Although on a lesser scale than in Castile wool was also produced in Aragon, which exported it to France, around Valencia, in Catalonia, and in Majorca. Valencia exported wool to Italy in the fourteenth century. It also exported sheepskins.[1]

INDUSTRY: TEXTILE

One hundred and fifty places in the peninsula where weaving took place have been noted but only about thirty were of any importance. The most considerable textile industry of the peninsula was situated in Catalonia. In the thirteenth century its main centre was at Lérida. By the 1300s other centres had developed, from Perpignan to Barcelona. Textiles were also made in many places in Castile. Segovia, Zamora, Avila, and Soria were exporting cloth to Portugal in 1268. All four cities were situated on main routes taken by the sheep flocks and so had ready sources of wool available.

Cloth was exported from Catalonia and Valencia to Sicily, North Africa, and the eastern Mediterranean. Most Catalan cloth was of relatively inferior quality; accordingly it was cheap. Silk was produced at Valencia and Játiva and exported to Italy. This silk, like that of Almería, and of Jaén, in Castile, was produced by Mudejar workmen.[2]

The richer classes of the peninsula preferred to buy cloth from abroad. Most of this cloth came from France and Flanders, though cotton was imported from the East (it was also produced in Granada and Valencia). A legal compilation drawn up at Tortosa in Catalonia in the 1270s mentions cloth from Arras, Châlons, Saint-Omer, Provins, Ypres, Ghent, Douai, Valenciennes, Cambrai, Narbonne, and perhaps from Rouen. These

[1] R. S. Lopez, 'El origen de la oveja merina', *EHMod* iv (1954), 3–11. Vicens, p. 231, appears to date the appearance of the merino sheep in Spain earlier than Lopez would do. See also Gual Camarena, *Vocabulario*, p. 342. For the Crown of Aragon see idem, *EHMed* ii (1970), 71–84.

[2] M. Gual Camarena, 'Para un mapa de la industria textil hispana en la Edad Media', *AEM* 4 (1967), 109–68; idem, 'El comercio de telas en el siglo XIII hispano', *AHES* 1 (1968), 88, n. 14, 92, n. 30; Vicens, p. 238.

cloths may have come through Perpignan, where some of them are documented in the 1260s. Lists of the customs duties to be paid in four Cantabrian ports in the thirteenth century mention twenty-seven centres from which cloth was being imported. All of these centres, except for a general mention of England, were in France or Flanders. Sixteen different types of cloth appear in these lists. The accounts of Sancho IV show that the value of the cloth actually imported in 1293–4 was very considerable, almost 900,000 maravedis. The prices for which foreign cloth were sold were correspondingly high—in 1268 a length of cloth from Montpellier cost as much as a cow and its calf in Castile. In contrast, the imports of cloth to the Crown of Aragon recorded in 1303–4 amounted only to about a thirtieth of the imports into Castile ten years before. The difference here was probably due to the fact that Catalan textiles were of a relatively higher level than those produced in Castile and so were better able to compete with foreign imports. French and Flemish cloth also reached Portugal, mainly through Oporto, but some foreign cloth may have travelled to Portugal through Castile.[1]

The textile industry was inseparable from the art of dyeing. Many dyes were produced in the peninsula. Saffron, used to dye cloth and leather as well as in cosmetics, medicine, painting, and as a condiment, was produced on a large scale in Catalonia, Aragon, and Valencia, for export as well as for domestic uses. 'Gleda', a substance used to clean cloth, often appears in customs tariffs. It was produced in Valencia. Antimony, used to colour textiles as well as for ceramics and cosmetics, was produced near Tarragona and exported on a large scale from Barcelona. Alum, used in dyeing cloth as well as on leather and skins, in painting, etc., was imported from Syria and North Africa. It was also produced in Castile.[2]

Leatherwork continued to be produced in Andalusia though possibly on a less high level of quality than before the Christian

[1] Gual Camarena, *Vocabulario*, pp. 284 f. (and *passim*); idem, 'El comercio de telas en el siglo XIII hispano', pp. 85–106, especially pp. 104 f.; *Libre de les costums de Tortosa*, ed. B. Oliver (Madrid, 1881), p. 413; R. W. Emery, in *Essays in Medieval Life and Thought presented in honor of A. P. Evans* (New York, 1955), pp. 153–65; M. Gaibrois de Ballesteros, *Historia del reinado de Sancho IV de Castilla*, i (Madrid, 1922), pp. iii-xxii; Ch. Verlinden, *Revue du nord*, 22 (1936), 5–20; Sobrequés, p. 306. The amounts recorded for Aragon are 26,723 sueldos of Barcelona and 2,057 of Jaca.

[2] Gual, *Vocabulario*, pp. 412 f., 271 f., 195, 200 ff.

conquest. It was being exported by merchants from Lérida to the fairs of Champagne in 1259. In 1316 hangings of gilded or painted leather were being made in Barcelona and Valencia.[1]

MINING

Iron was mined in the Catalan Pyrenees but on a larger scale in Castile, especially in Biscay. In 1293 very large quantities of iron were exported from the Cantabrian ports, probably to Flanders. Iron was also exported to England in the fourteenth century. It seems likely that, before the boom in the export of wool, iron was Castile's principal export.

Castile produced and exported lead and copper from Andalusia; lead was also mined in Aragon. Silver was mined in Ibiza, in Sardinia (under Catalan control from the 1320s), and elsewhere; it was sometimes exported to Castile. Quicksilver was exported by Castile; in the thirteenth century its production was mainly controlled by the Order of Calatrava.

Steel was used by the armourers of Toledo and the jewellers of Barcelona. Toledo also competed with Andalusia in its ceramics, although the pottery of Islamic Málaga was still unrivalled in the thirteenth century. The Mudejars of Murcia produced glass and carpets as they had done before the Christian conquest. The work of Muslim craftsmen enjoyed greater prestige than anything produced by Christians.[2]

TRADE-ROUTES

It was very much easier to transport goods by water than by land. However, the use of rivers for transport was imperfectly developed in the Iberian peninsula. It was very limited in Portugal. The Guadalquivir and Guadiana rivers were navigable as far as Córdoba and Mérida, respectively. In 1310 Fernando IV of Castile granted the ships plying on the Guadalquivir protection against the interference of local officials. The kings of Aragon made considerable efforts to improve navigation on the Ebro down which cereals were brought from Aragon to Catalonia and for export abroad. In 1310 Jaume II, travel-

[1] ibid., pp. 281 f., 288 f., 335.

[2] ibid., pp. 313–16, 395, 285 f., 212–15; M. del C. Carlé, *CHE* 21–2 (1954), 165–208, presents much evidence for industries in Castile but admits they were not on a large scale ('de gran producción').

ling down the Ebro from Saragossa to Lérida, observed that there was 'great danger for ships' and ordered the Confraternity of Our Lady of the Merchants of Saragossa, which had been placed in charge of the river in 1264, to make good the damage.[1]

In large parts of Castile and León there was no alternative to land transport. This probably proceeded in much the same way as it continued to do in 1730 when the Royal Association of Teamsters (Cabaña Real de Carreteros)—officially recognized in 1497—brought a suit against the Mesta in which it described how the ox-drawn carts of its members transported goods from Toledo to Seville, then from Seville, bringing salt, to Coria and Plasencia, grain to Segovia, wool from there to Vitoria, and iron from Vitoria to the Cantabrian ports. Along the rudimentary roads of Spain the carts of these teamsters could hardly cover more than 25 miles a day and less than this in the thirteenth century. It was they, however, with carts or with mules and horses, who supplied the many fairs of Castile with goods, especially the fairs held at Medina del Campo, which brought merchants from Flanders, Ireland, and Italy to Castile.[2]

In the thirteenth century Portuguese trade was already focused towards northern Europe. Portugal's products—mainly raw materials and foodstuffs—were so similar to those of Mediterranean countries that it had little worth sending east except dried fish. Portugal imported cereals, cloth, and minerals from Castile, silks, arms, and spices from eastern Spain, Italy, and the eastern Mediterranean.[3]

In contrast to Portugal, the Crown of Aragon traded mainly with the Mediterranean. Its essential interests lay in the western part of that sea and its bulk trade was carried on with Sicily, Italy, Sardinia, southern France, and North Africa. A few ships every year risked the longer voyage to Alexandria in search of spices, indigo, and ivory, or, less often, traded with Cyprus and Constantinople. Catalan and Majorcan galleys also sailed to Seville and the Atlantic coast of Morocco. Occasionally they attempted the longer journey to England and Flanders but

[1] Benavides, ii. 746–9; *CDIACA* vi. 422–6.

[2] Klein, *The Mesta*, pp. 22 f.; M. del C. Carlé, loc. cit., 152–65; C. Espejo and J. Paz, *Las antiguas ferias de Medina del Campo* (Valladolid, 1908–12).

[3] A. H. de Oliveira Marques, *Ensaios*, pp. 43–5.

only the Genoese and Venetians could maintain that voyage as a regular affair.[1]

In 1300 Catalonia–Aragon was the only one of the Christian kingdoms of the peninsula to possess a navy of its own. The navies of Castile and Portugal were often commanded by Genoese mercenaries and consisted of Genoese galleys, hired when necessary.

In naval construction, particularly that of galleys, Barcelona was outstanding in the peninsula, but galleys were also built at Málaga, Almería, and Almuñécar in the kingdom of Granada, and the struggle for control of the Straits of Gibraltar was not yet decided in favour of Castile. Customs tariffs often list hemp —used for sails—tar, and pitch, both produced at Valencia.[2]

In the Mediterranean, a ship could pay for its construction by five or six months' profitable trade. A galley, though expensive, could do so too if it was hired for four months.

PIRACY

But the risks of piracy were also very considerable in a world where Catalans attacked Majorcans from Sardinia, Majorcans Catalans from Sicily, and both Catalans and Majorcans vessels sent to Egypt to ransom Christian prisoners there. In the early fourteenth century Muslim pirates from Granada and North Africa were growing in daring and raiding the coasts of the Balearics, Valencia, and Catalonia.[3]

Treaties between Catalonia–Aragon or Majorca and an Islamic state such as Tunisia prohibited piracy against the other nation. That these prohibitions were seen to be ineffective is shown by the stipulation inserted in several treaties by which no piratical actions shall affect the general peace, if reasonable satisfaction is given.

The treaties were frequently violated by Christians. Tunisia claimed that the treaty of 1301 with Catalonia–Aragon was broken on nineteen occasions in 1303–5 by Catalans, five times by the admiral of a royal squadron—this included three disembarkations on the Tunisian coast and attacks on populated places, with the object of acquiring slaves. There were similar,

[1] For details see Part II, Ch. I, below. cf. Gual, *Vocabulario*, pp. 428 f. (spices).
[2] ibid., pp. 251 f., 199, 386 f.
[3] Dufourcq, pp. 536–43, 574 f.

if perhaps less frequent, breaches of treaties by North African admirals and by Genoese in the service of Granada.

Many merchants, Christians and Muslims alike, would become pirates when it suited them. In August 1341 a Catalan ship, 'charged with merchandise of Christians and Moors, was taken by two armed ships from Algiers laden with wood'.

Cities such as Barcelona often armed galleys to take reprisals against the fellow subjects of some Muslim or Christian pirate. Individual nobles, merchants, and adventurers also armed galleys or rented them—as did Barcelona—from the king of Aragon, with the same purpose in view.

No treaties normally protected those wrecked on foreign shores from having their possessions seized and often from being themselves enslaved. These misadventures not only befell Christians wrecked in North Africa or in the kingdom of Granada (or Muslims wrecked on Christian coasts) but also Castilians wrecked in Catalonia or the Balearics.[1]

On the Atlantic side of the Straits of Gibraltar there were far fewer pirates. In Seville and, more so, in the Cantabrian north, Castile was gradually developing into a maritime power. In Seville goods came in and the produce of Andalusia flowed out, honey, wax, oil, wine, nuts, figs, raisins, almonds, chestnuts, cheese, cereals, rice, leather, cloth, iron, and lead, all enumerated in a tariff of 1302. A very high proportion of these goods was transported, however, by foreign ships. The situation in Cantabria was different.[2]

In the north the foundation of the *Hermandad de la Marisma* in 1296 united the ports of Santander, Laredo, Castro Urdiales, San Vicente de la Barquera, Bermeo, Guetaria, San Sebastián, and Fuenterrabía. The Cantabrian ports united in this 'Brotherhood' wished to act together to preserve a profitable state of neutrality between France and England, to resist paying taxes to Burgos, and to monopolize the export of iron. The foundation of Bilbao in 1300 is another sign pointing to the future of Basque seamen.

From the 1220s the Basques are attested as trading with

[1] J. Mª. Ramos y Loscertales, *El cautiverio en la Corona de Aragón* (Saragossa, 1915), pp. 2–100; A. Giménez Soler, *BRABL* 6 (1909–10), 198 f., 295.

[2] R. Carande, *AHDE* 2 (1925), 302 ff.; C. López Martínez, *Archivo hispalense*, 9 (1948), 205–23. See below, Part II, Ch. II, pp. 290 f.

Bruges and as helping to transport wine from Bordeaux to England. In 1297 Edward I of England granted privileges favouring Spanish and Portuguese merchants; he did so at the request of the count of Flanders. The trade in iron and, later, in wool in exchange for fine cloth and luxury goods was to give the Cantabrian ports international importance.

In its maritime development Castile in 1300 was still behind Catalonia, though not far behind. In finance it was far behind. Its finances were still entirely in the hands of Jews or of Italian bankers.[1] This had ceased to be the case in Catalonia in the 1280s. There was to be no change here in Castile for a century. In industry Castile was also behind Catalonia, and this also was to remain unchanged. Through its vastly greater size and its far greater population Castile was almost bound in the end to surpass Catalonia but its lack of a middle class and its one-sided reliance—ever greater as time passed—on sheep-farming and the wool-trade were ill omens for future empire.

SOCIETY: VISIONS OF SOCIETY

Alfonso X of Castile's *Cántigas* (1252–84) and the works of his Majorcan contemporary Ramon Lull present us with the most detailed portraits we possess of thirteenth-century society in the peninsula.

The miniaturists of the *Cántigas* journeyed with Alfonso's travelling court from Galicia through Castile to Seville and Murcia. They painted almost 3,000 scenes. Their work adds to our understanding of Alfonso's poems. Together, poems and illustrations provide a faithful, though stylized, picture of the society of Castile–León in the second half of the thirteenth century, a picture to which the illustrations of Alfonso's work on chess, the *Tratado de ajedrez*, add significant touches. The whole of life is here, 'from birth to death, from the font to the coffin'. Monks and nuns are seen singing in choir but also fleeing from their abbeys to their lovers. Pilgrims often pass across the scene or prostrate themselves before the Virgin, but we also have a cleric in bed with his concubine and thieves

[1] Vicens Vives, *Manual*, pp. 242–4, 248 ff.; Carande, pp. 287–96; Finot, op. cit., pp. 18–29, 47; Benavides, ii. 118; J. Maréchal, *Revue du nord*, 35 (1953), 7, 11 f.; on banking see Carlé, loc. cit., 295–8; E. Benito Ruano, *La Banca toscana y la Orden de Santiago durante el siglo XIII* (Valladolid, 1961).

praying to the Virgin when about to rob. There are kings, emperors, and nobles, at court or at the head of their armies, but also black and white slaves and the scum of the Castilian earth at dice in taverns. There are banquets, battles, wrecks at sea, pharmacies, and money-changers' booths, buildings going up and being pulled down, Muslims, Jews, soldiers, monks, friars, minstrels, painters, peasants ploughing, shepherds, artisans. Horses provide the main transport for people but carts and litters are also used. On the road merchants travelling to fairs may pass lesser gentry—*infanzones*—hawking. If a cleric or Jew strays from the road he is liable to be seized by robbers and thrown down a well.

The physical background is lightly but authentically brought in, from the great barns of Galicia to the Mediterranean palm trees of Elche. French Gothic models appear in church architecture but also Mudejar influence, both in the painting of animals—where the artists may have drawn on Islamic bestiaries—and in the horse-shoe arches which are anachronistically made to adorn the Roman aqueduct at Segovia.[1]

Ramon Lull's view of the society of the Crown of Aragon is equally interesting although unfortunately it was not illustrated, as were Alfonso's *Cántigas*, by miniaturists working under his direction. Lull had lived for thirty years in the world before his conversion to a religious life. As a knight and later as seneschal of the Infant Jaume, second surviving son of Jaume I of Aragon, the destined heir to the kingdom of Majorca, Lull must have come to know Catalonia, Aragon, Valencia, and probably also the court of Castile. After his conversion (about 1263) he travelled even more widely. Lull's criticism of society is, however, based on his early years as a courtier and is mainly expressed in his *Book of Contemplation*, completed about 1274, and in *Blanquerna*, written one or two decades later, where, as Menéndez Pelayo remarked, 'the whole thirteenth century is displayed before our eyes'. Lull's view of society is unsparing.

It is a hierarchical view. At the top of the hierarchy are the clergy, 'honoured [by God] in the world above all men', because they maintain the faith and interpret the Bible. The

[1] J. Guerrero Lovillo, *Las Cantigas*, Madrid, 1949. See also the reviews by L. Torres Balbas, *Al Andalus*, 15 (1950), 193–5; F. J. Sánchez Canton, *Arbor*, 14 (1949), 474–8. For Segovia see Guerrero, lám. 119 on *Cántiga* 107.

pope 'holds [God's] place on earth'. Under him are the secular clergy and religious orders.

Below the lowest cleric come, descending in order, kings and barons, knights, pilgrims, judges, lawyers, doctors, merchants, seamen, minstrels, shepherds, painters, farm labourers, and, lastly, artisans. The positions given to pilgrims and minstrels in this hierarchy appear to be peculiar to Lull and display his high estimate of minstrels, who can play for God, though they often prefer to please men. The only classes Lull praises in the *Book of Contemplation* are the clergy—whom he was to censure in *Blanquerna* and later works—and the farm workers.

Kings appoint 'vile men', of low birth, to act for them. These officials devour their people as wolves do sheep. Instead of preserving peace kings 'keep the whole world in war and travail'. Kings adorn their fingers with gold and jewelled rings but their hands are filthy with the blood of poor men to whom they refuse justice. Kings hunt wild beasts and birds but not the evildoers who destroy their kingdoms.

Knights use the arms given them against wrongdoers to attack the innocent, rob men, and rape women. Once armed and on his war horse the knight thinks he is a lion and disdains the mercy he may soon need for himself. Lull points out the failure and folly of the crusades to the East and the fundamental mistrust between kings and knights, both of whom try to use the other for their own ends.

Pilgrims pursue a devout calling but many of them do so riding on palfreys and mules, carrying fine linen with them, barrels of wine, money, and spices. Many go seeking Christ in Compostela or Rome or Jerusalem with the devil slung round their neck. When they reach their goal they are often defrauded by greedy innkeepers and custodians of the shrine and return worse than when they set out.

Judges and lawyers, instead of defending the injured party, make truth appear falsehood. 'By false judges and lawyers and witnesses almost the whole world is betrayed.' Judges and lawyers are loved and honoured by princes, barons, and rich men, but hated by the poor and powerless. Doctors also grow rich by the tricks they play on their patients. Merchants accumulate riches and vices together. Minstrels are clothed in royal clothing, banquet with princes, and are loaded with silver and gold while the poor shiver in rags outside the palace doors.

Lull has heard of no king who rules as he should do, of few knights who discharge their duty, of few judges not corrupted by gold, of few minstrels who will not lie for money. In his *Doctrina pueril* (*c.* 1282) Lull, like Alfonso X in the *Partidas*, puts artisans together with labourers as supporting society with their skills but he points out that almost all craftsmen want to be burgesses though 'there is no office in the world as unstable as that of a burgess . . . since he spends and does not earn. . . . No men have such a short life as burgesses . . . since they eat too much and do not work. . . . This office is punished more severely by God than any other'.[1]

HIERARCHIES: THE THREE 'ESTATES'

The *Partidas* contain the classical medieval division of men into three estates, those who pray, those who fight, and those who work. The king should protect all three estates. In each men can attain excellence in different ways, whether as a theologian or jurist, as a soldier, or as a merchant or artisan. Writing some sixty years later Alfonso's nephew, Don Juan Manuel, repeats this static picture of the world, with the clergy above the warriors and the latter above workmen. The social body, with its diversity, is the work of God. In it each member has an organic task which he must perform within the estate God has given him, whether it is that of the clergy, the warriors, or the workmen. 'The first thing a man can do is to know his estate and to maintain it as he should; and the greatest error a man can make is *not* to know or keep his estate.'

However, Juan Manuel is exceptionally sensitive to the changes proceeding in this hierarchical world. His account of knighthood is largely based on Lull's *Book of the Order of Chivalry* but, unlike Lull, he not only recognizes that contemporary rulers are making use of non-noble officials but sees this as legitimate. Juan Manuel is also aware that the old estate of workmen now covers many different classes of men, ranging from merchants to labourers.

[1] Ramon Lull, *Libre de contemplació*, cc. 110–22 (*Obres essencials*, ii (Barcelona, 1960), 334–69). There is some veiled censure of the clergy in c. 119 (on 'shepherds'). Idem, *Doctrina pueril*, c. 79 (*Obres de R. Lull*, i (Palma, 1906), 146–8). *Partidas*, ii. x. 3. See Menéndez Pelayo, *Orígenes* i. 132.

It seems unlikely that the lower levels of society saw it in the same light as Alfonso X, Lull, and Juan Manuel. Instead of seeing it as an organic unity they may have conceived of it as a hostile system, devised to keep them down. This is speculation, however, since we have no vocal artisans or labourers in this period unless we are to accept Lull's picture of the mob in *Blanquerna*, howling for food in front of rich men's houses.[1] The following discussion will be concerned with Christian lay society, from king to peasant. Secular clergy and Religious Orders will be discussed in Chapter IV, Jews and Mudejars in Chapter V.

DIFFERENTIATION: DRESS

Never has it been as true as it was in these centuries that 'the dress *is* the man'. The *Partidas* remark that 'clothes make men *known* as noble or vile'. To dress above your estate required special permission. The Cortes of Castile–León established minute dress regulations for all stations in society from falconers to great nobles. In 1340 Afonso IV of Portugal restricted the use of hose to the nobility and rich bourgeoisie, forbidding peasants to expose their legs in this way. In 1393 Joan I of Aragon allowed two *bourgeoises*, inhabitants of Puigcerdá, to transgress the local town ordinance and to wear 'clothes of gold or silver or of wool of any colour you prefer', or furs or silk, adorned with pearls, gold, or silver. Similar permission to dress as aristocrats had often been granted in the thirteenth century to Jewish courtiers at the court of Aragon.

The illustrations to Alfonso X's *Cántigas* show how men and women dressed. Cloaks were reserved for the nobility, scarlet cloaks for the king, according to the Cortes of 1258. A shorter cape was used by the lower classes. The use of fur trimmings was restricted by law to the nobility. The *Partidas* dictate the appearance of knights. They were always to wear their swords—

[1] *Partidas*, II. x. 3. xxi (transl. into Catalan in *Tractats de Cavallería*, (*ENC* A57), ed. P. Bohigas (Barcelona, 1947), p. 111); Juan Manuel, *Libro del caballero y del escudero*, cc. 17, 38; *Libro de los estados*, i. 92 f. (*BAE* li. 236, 246, 337 f.); cf. Lull, *Libre qui és de l'Orde de Cavallería*, ii (*Obres essencials*, i. 530 f.); J. A. Maravall, *Estudios de historia del pensamiento español, Edad Media*, i (Madrid, 1967), 453–72, a review of L. de Stéfano, *La sociedad estamental de la baja edad media española a la luz de la literatura de la época* (Universidad Central de Venezuela, 1966). For Blanquerna see below, pp. 150 f.

the sign of their order—and cloaks, even at meals, with a knot over their right shoulder, in token of the obedience they owed their lords. Their clothes were to be of gay colours, not sombre, red, crocus-coloured, or green.[1]

WINE

Other hierarchical means of differentiation appear in legal codes. The codes establish sharply differing penalties for many crimes, depending on the rank of those convicted. The *Fuero general de Navarra* prescribes that peasants working for lords should be given 'well-tempered wine, with only the *colour* of wine but not gone bad or entirely sour'. The wife of a lesser noble, an *infanzón*, fared only slightly better, receiving 'half must and half water and wine'. In 1331 the *Book of the Cook of the Cathedral of Tarragona* prescribed that the canons of the cathedral should receive 'as much wine as they want, pure, without water', whereas the lowlier chaplains had their wine 'conveniently tempered with water'.[2]

HORSES

Castilian legislation from Alfonso X onwards was greatly preoccupied with the need to maintain and increase the number of horses in the kingdom. This obligation extended to all classes, but especially to knights. The *Partidas* declared that knights were to ride only horses (not mules). Maltreatment or neglect of their horses was a sufficient reason for them to lose their rank. The price of a horse was normally as high as that of several slaves. In Catalonia the price of a horse would have consumed several months of the salary paid to Christian knights in service with North African princes. In a crisis a horse could cost as much as a sixth of a war galley.[3]

The legal codes of the time establish sharply differing penalties for many crimes, depending on the rank of those convicted.

[1] *Partidas*, II. v. 5. xxi. 17 f.; Oliveira Marques, *Daily Life*, p. 56; *CDIACA* vi. 451 f., cf. 474; *Cortes de León*, i. 55 ff.; Ballesteros, *Alfonso X*, p. 71; Guerrero Lovillo, op. cit., pp. 47–111.

[2] *Fuero general de Navarra*, ed. P. Ilarregui and S. Lapuerta (Pamplona, 1869), pp. 51, 86; *Libre del coc de la seu de Tarragona*, ed. J. Serra i Vilaró (Barcelona, 1935), fols. 42v-43v.

[3] *Partidas*, II. xxi. 17, 25; C.-E. Dufourcq, *MÂ* 71 (1965), 477 f., 505.

THE KING AND HIS COURT

The ideal king is described by Don Juan Manuel in traditional terms. He should be God's image and representative on earth. His people, if they obey him, should live with him 'as sons with their father'. Tyrants are God's punishment for disobedience.

In another passage Don Juan comes closer to the conditions of the day. A king must be sure of his lodging, of the food he is served, of his guards by day and night. He should always exceed other kings in gifts and should reward his vassals. He should stand out visually, either by being more finely dressed than his courtiers or else by deliberately dressing simply so as to set a good example. His bed, his eating and drinking vessels, the hangings of his chamber (all transported from place to place on his travels) should be very fine but should not preoccupy him excessively.

An earlier Castilian didactic work also stresses the need for the king to be generous to his nobles and to attach them to him by being open, companionable, and visible to his people. 'The king should be the companion of his followers . . . drinking and joking with them, showing he is joyful and pleased with them . . . Every lord should *show himself* to the people.'

One way in which attention could be focused on a king in the midst of his court appear in the *Ordinances* of Pere III of Catalonia–Aragon (of 1344 but derived from earlier sources). Elaborate directions prescribe how a royal dinner is to be illuminated. The king's table and especially the place where he sits are to be surrounded by candelabra. The knights at other tables have only one light for four persons and the non-noble tables two small candles for four. No wall or ceiling lights are indicated. Anyone entering a large Gothic vaulted room such as the Tinell of Barcelona would at once have had his eyes drawn to the royal table and to the king. The accounts of Sancho IV of Castile in the 1290s mention 'the great candles which burn before the king and queen the whole month'; these candles cost as much as the wages of six armed knights but they were evidently felt to be worth the expense.[1]

[1] Juan Manuel, *Libro de los castigos*, 4; *Libro de los estados*, i. 62 (*BAE* li. 268, 313 f.); *Libro de los XII Sabios*, ed. M. de Manuel Rodríguez, *Memorias para la vida del S. Rey D. Fernando III* (Madrid, 1800), 11 f., pp. 194 f.; *CDIACA* v. 182 (= Jaume III of Majorca, Leges Palatinae, MS. Brussels 9169, fol. 55v); Gaibrois de Ballesteros, *Sancho IV*, i. 38, n. 1, 46.

Seven occupations of the court and of nobles in general were singled out by Pedro Alfonso in the twelfth century. Riding, swimming, shooting with the bow, hunting, hawking, playing chess, and composing verses were designed to form the knight as the seven liberal arts formed the scholar. In the thirteenth century Aristotle and his commentators had largely replaced the seven arts in the universities but, for the knight, little had changed except that swimming was replaced by dancing. The correspondence of King Jaume II of Aragon (1291–1327) shows him exercising with the crossbow, acquiring and training falcons and hounds from Majorca, France, and England, hunting wild boar and stags on the slopes of the Pyrenees, partridges and quail in Aragon, and wild ducks in the Albufera of Valencia. Jaume naturally displayed great interest in finding the best mounts. He was also interested in raising wild animals in zoos. The royal family looked down from the terraces and galleries of the palace outside Valencia or the Aljaferia in Saragossa on the sport caged lions provided when they were let loose on horses and other animals.

When he could not exercise himself out of doors Jaume II often played chess or composed verses. On a special occasion, such as the reception of an embassy, it was necessary to bring out hangings to decorate the house or palace where the king was. In his palace in Barcelona Jaume was troubled by the noise and dust from the building going on in the cathedral across the street. He suffered from a neighbouring blacksmith, whom the king paid not to work while he was ill, and from men selling straw in the palace courtyards.

Jaume's main palaces, at Barcelona, Valencia, and Saragossa, generally needed urgent repairs when the king and queen were expected, as did the less usual royal residences in the kingdom of Valencia: Murcia, Elche, Gandia, Alcira, Játiva; in Aragon at Daroca, Teruel, Tarazona, Huesca, Castellar, Ejea; in Catalonia at Lérida, Poblet, Santes Creus, Montserrat, and many other places.

All medieval kings were normally on the move. Only by continually visiting their different domains could they fulfil their role as supreme judge, prevent rebellion, and avoid crushing any one locality by the expense of maintaining their court over a long period. The kings of Castile travelled even more widely than those of Aragon, from Zamora, León, and Burgos in the north to Toledo, Seville, and Córdoba.

Because of the constant travelling of kings and nobles more attention was paid to dress and to easily portable luxuries than to buildings which only provided shelter for a month at most. Jewels, gold, splendid clothes, all symbolized the dominion their owner and wearer had achieved by the sword. Hence the attention devoted by chronicles and poets to descriptions of the arms, jewels, and armour of their heroes. In Jaume's court French and Flemish taste prevailed in dress, Muslim or Mudejar in the hangings, leather screens, silver mirrors, or ivory combs and chess-sets from Murcia.[1]

The court of Jaume II was simply a more elaborate version of the existence of lesser princes and great lords. A study of the court of Jaume's father, Pere II, when he was still heir to the throne, shows us how such men lived.

The basis of the diet at Pere's court (as at that of his contemporary, Sancho IV of Castile) consisted of meat, especially mutton, but also veal and goat-meat. Fish was less often eaten away from the coast and apart from days of abstinence. Vegetables were sparsely used. White sugar and rice appeared at feasts. Great use was made of spices and aromatic herbs. The usual number of persons eating at Pere's court was about 150. At one great banquet 420 persons were present. They ate thirty-one sheep, nine fish, a large quantity of veal, sixteen goats, pork, salt meat, sixty-eight chickens, and eighty hens. On most days, however, 'moderation and abundance' were the main notes of the prince's court. Half a kilo of meat (usually mutton) was the average amount dealt out each day to each of Pere's followers, though the prince and his leading servants received veal and other supplementary fare. Bread was a staple food.

Like all kings and great nobles Pere never travelled without his huntsmen and falconers. The trumpeters in his suite may have been a distinction of royalty. Many of his followers must have gone on foot. The 150 to 170 horses and mules mentioned

[1] Petrus Alfonsus, *Disciplina clericalis*, ed. A. Hilka and W. Söderhjelus (Helsinki, 1911), p. 10; Martínez Ferrando, *Jaime II*, i. 304–6, 32–5, 64, 72–5, 78 f.; ii. 89, 139 f., 144 f.; J. Mª. Madurell, *AST* 12 (1936), 494–9; B. Blanco-González, *Del cortesano al discreto*, i (Madrid, 1962), 165 f., 366–8.

in the accounts had to transport everything the mobile court needed, down to its travelling kitchen and the prince's bed. Many animals were hired for a short distance. Pere seems to have had only four horses of his own. On a very exceptional occasion, when he met the king of France at Toulouse in 1281, Pere (now himself king) was preceded by 400 pack mules. In his usual train there would be Catalan and Aragonese nobles and knights, his chaplain and notary, and his minstrels. The accounts often record gifts to friars but they probably did not form part of the permanent suite. Runners, on foot, connected Pere to his father Jaume I and to his relations, or went to Valencia for falcons or to Lérida for cloth for his clothes. In one year (1262), which is not fully documented, Pere, as heir, was present in the south of his realms, at Valencia, Játiva, and Gandia, then at Collioure, near the Pyrenees, at Perpignan, then at Gerona, Vich, and Barcelona, then back to Perpignan and Montpellier.

After his marriage to Costanza of Sicily Pere's accounts reveal greater variety in diet—doves become a favourite dish—and more mention of baths, mirrors, and musical instruments. The personnel of the court also becomes more varied and now includes some Muslim painters and four black waiting women in attendance on Costanza.

The accounts also show that there was a sharp difference of prices between Barcelona, for instance, and Huesca. A sheep at Huesca cost half as much as at Barcelona. This provides a good reason why Pere and his wife spent such long periods at the remote Aragonese mountain city of Huesca.[1]

When Pere II became king of Aragon he issued the first existing *Ordinances* we possess on the royal household. They regulate the rights of all household officials, from the majordomo down to porters, mule drivers, and huntsmen. These *Ordinances* are the ancestors of the elaborate codes drawn up by Jaume III of Majorca and Pere III of Aragon in the 1330s and 1340s.

Although we do not possess a similar code for the court of Castile in this period the accounts of Sancho IV preserved from the 1290s show that the same type of court life existed in Castile as in Aragon. Sancho's court normally consisted of at

[1] F. Soldevila, *Pere el Gran*, i. *L'Infant*, 1, pp. 50–79; 2, pp. 156–75; 3, pp. 428–51, 454–6, 481. Desclot, c. 76 (Coll, iii. 52 f.) records the visit to Toulouse.

least 250 persons, including forty muleteers, forty knights and squires, a bodyguard of thirty archers, the eighteen clerics of the royal travelling chapel, Master Martin the organist, royal scribes, Jewish and Christian doctors, sixty-five huntsmen and—on one journey—as many as thirty-six falconers, pages, cooks, minstrels, buffoons, Moorish drummers and trumpeters. There was also a favourite dwarf who received almost as large a present at his wedding as a knight received in a year's pay.

The court of Aragon under Pere II and his son Jaume II had an international quality probably absent from that of Castile after the death of Alfonso X in 1284. Jaume II, for instance, entertained English musicians in 1315, a foretaste of the presence of composers from Tours, Germany, and the papal chapel at Avignon at the Aragonese court in the later fourteenth century.

Minstrels already played a considerable role at the court of Pere II. They were defended by the Catalan troubadour Cerverí de Girona, who recalls Pindar as among the minstrels of the past—he himself, as a troubadour, considered himself to be far above minstrels and on a level with a king. We know that minstrels were sometimes used for political missions. Pere II, as heir to the throne, entertained Moorish and Lombard *jongleurs* as well as Lombard falconers and Italian merchants. Unlike the court of Castile there were no female minstrels or dancers at the court and hence no need for a king pimp (*rey arlot*). But Jaume II's court welcomed minstrels from Portugal, Castile, Navarre, France, Venice, Sicily, and Majorca as well as Jewish and Muslim musicians.[1]

THE HIGHER NOBILITY

The higher nobles of Castile and Aragon were known as 'ricos hombres'—a term derived from the Gothic 'reiks' ('powerful') which first appears in the *Cantar del Cid*, those of Catalonia, Valencia, and Majorca as 'nobles, richs hòmens, magnates, barones'. In Catalan territories the term 'noble' was only

[1] *CDIACA* vi. 5–14 (cf. Soldevila, *Vida de Pere el Gran*, p. 275); Gaibrois, op. cit., i. 37–47; H. Anglès, *VII CHCA* iii. 283 f., 288 f.; Cerverí de Girona, *Obras completas*, ed. M. de Riquer (Barcelona, 1947), pp. 233 f.; H. Wieruszowski, *Archivio storico italiano*, 96 (1938), 160; J. Miret, *Butlleti del Centre excursionista de Catalunya*, 18 (1908), 204; L. Batlle Prats, in *Estudios dedicados a Menéndez Pidal*, v. 165–73.

applied to the higher nobility—lesser nobles were known as knights, 'donzells' or 'gentils homes'. In Castile and Aragon 'caballeros, infanzones, hijosdalgos' were all considered noble, though in Aragon, unlike Castile, the higher and lower nobility constituted separate branches of the Cortes.

The higher nobility was very small in numbers—perhaps a thousand families by 1500 in Castile, the Crown of Aragon, and Navarre together. It was very important, however, since its members owned over a tenth of the land of the peninsula and held a very high proportion of the leading posts in Church and State. It was far from being a closed caste. Royal favour could raise a man from bourgeois or petty noble to become the head of a leading family. Kings such as Jaume I of Aragon or Alfonso XI of Castile could and did do even more for their illegitimate sons.

In the Crown of Aragon the higher nobility reached its zenith of power and influence in the late thirteenth century. Its decline was rapid in the fourteenth century, catastrophic in the fifteenth. In Castile, on the other hand, the power of the greater nobles enormously increased during these centuries. This difference between the two Crowns was partly due to the different way in which the territories conquered in the thirteenth century were distributed—the Castilian nobility's gains in Andalusia were far greater than any made by Catalan or Aragonese nobles in Majorca or Valencia—but also to the fact that in Castile the Crown either did not possess, in the cities, the strong ally against the nobility which existed in Catalonia, or else did not know how to use its allies.

The ideal noble appears in a thirteenth-century Catalan text as 'a very fine man, agreeable, young and wonderfully valiant, shining in arms and large in gifts'. Alfonso X's *Cántigas* also portray him: 'he was frank and daring and of good manners and never would have peace with Moors'.[1]

Don Juan Manuel describes in detail the life a great noble should live—a miniature reflection of royalty. It is a life lived mainly in the noble's own castles and in the country, travelling from one castle to another, not in towns. The noble has not yet become urbanized or a courtier. In the morning he should rise as

[1] Sobrequés, op. cit., pp. 107–24; Desclot, *Crònica*, c. 89 (ed. Coll, iii. 93); *Cántigas* lxiii (ed. Mettmann, i. 778).

early as possible and at once commend himself to God's protection and hear Hours (probably of the Virgin) recited and Mass. If he has to travel he can hunt on the way to practise horsemanship. At the inn he should eat with his followers (not apart) and after the meal listen, if he feels so inclined, to his minstrels singing and playing before him songs of chivalry and reciting *chansons de geste*. After the siesta he should hear more Hours and then convoke his counsellors and dispatch urgent affairs, not putting them off or entrusting essential questions to others.

As he goes on his way, riding or hunting, he should take petitions handed in to him and have them dealt with by his counsel. He should sit down to dine even if he is not himself hungry. On fast days he should at least have wine served to his suite. Before going to bed he should again commend himself to God and examine how he has passed the day. If he wakes during the night he should think of what he can do to save his soul and increase his honour and estate and should instruct whichever servant sleeps in the room to remind him next day of his decisions. 'If he cannot sleep he should have some good histories read to him from which he may take good examples.' He should practise a detached attitude towards his actions and try to judge them as if they were done by someone else.[1]

EDUCATION OF THE NOBILITY

Don Juan Manuel also drew up a scheme of education for the children of kings and great nobles. They were to have wet-nurses of good blood, and, later, male tutors to teach them moderation in eating and drinking and especially in the use of wine. From the age of five they should gradually be taught to read and learn to speak and understand Latin. Their interest should be aroused in 'chronicles of good deeds and great conquests and deeds of arms and chivalry, of how lords won to great estate through goodness and valour and of the evil fame those who did ill left behind them'.

From the time the child can walk he should be taught to ride and later to hunt, to ride across any type of country, and to bear arms. On Sundays, after Mass, he should spend the day in exercise on foot or horseback. The days of the week should

[1] Juan Manuel, *Libro de los estados*, i. 59 (*BAE* li. 310 ff.). At the end of the chapter we are told that the advice applies equally to emperors, kings, and great lords.

be spent, alternately, on study and riding. The child should be accustomed to eat at different hours. His bed should sometimes be hard and badly made and he should be trained to sleep through noise.

It seems that this was the way Don Juan himself had been brought up by his mother. What other evidence we possess suggests that the chronicles and chivalric legends Don Juan mentions played a considerable role in the education of the nobility. The *Partidas* prescribe that knights should have 'stories of great deeds of arms' read aloud to them while they are eating. When no books are available 'good old knights' should recount such stories. Minstrels should recount *chansons de geste* before knights at meals or when they cannot sleep. The Catalan chroniclers, for their part, compare their heroes to Roland, Oliver, Tristan, Lancelot, Galahad, and Percival. Juan Manuel speaks of a falcon called Lancelot and the slightly later *Poema de Alfonso XI* alludes to 'the harp of Don Tristan' and refers to Merlin. Examples from history blended with those of legend. The palace of Guimarães in Portugal contained tapestries displaying the stories of Hercules, Theseus, Troy, Alexander, Hannibal, and Julius Caesar. Mural paintings preserved in the castle of Alcañiz, in Aragon, represent chivalric legends and probably also the conquests of Jaume I of Aragon. They may have been inspired by lost *chansons de geste*, as were parts of the *Book of Deeds* of Jaume. In 1961 wall paintings were discovered in the Palacio Aguilar in Barcelona, probably inspired by a similar poem, representing the conquest of Majorca in 1229.

Another wall painting has appeared in the Palacio del Marqués de Llió, in Barcelona, showing King Frederic of Sicily (the younger brother of Jaume II of Aragon) striking down an Angevin prince. Other thirteenth-century paintings in the Tinell, in the royal palace at Barcelona, represent the Catalan army of the age. It is notable that only infantry is represented. Ramon Lull describes a knight having a picture of his son painted on the wall of his chamber so as to remember his son while he was absent 'in feats of arms in a strange land'.

The Arthurian literature celebrates love as well as chivalry. The *Cancioneiros* of the period preserves over a thousand poems written between about 1250 and 1325 by the cultivated nobles of Castile and Portugal. They are in Galician, the language used in both kingdoms for lyrical poetry at this time. There is only one important theme for the great majority of those poems that are not satirical—love. Love here is not the conjugal union of the earlier *Cantar de Mio Cid*, nor is it the erudite gallantry of the fifteenth century. It is fuller of feeling and passion than much troubadour verse. The Church, marriage, conjugal rights, and children are notable by their absence.[1]

THE NOBILITY: IDEALS

Despite his insistence on Christian observance and his undoubtedly sincere faith, there is a strong streak of worldliness in Don Juan Manuel. For him the ideal is to attend to God and the world at the same time. Shame is the most important quality a man can possess since it makes him die for the sake of honour and abstain from evil actions. In the *Partidas*, too, 'shame' is an essential condition of a knight. One is reminded of Newman's diagnosis of shame as the governing motive behind the code of behaviour of English gentlemen in the nineteenth century. If he is governed by shame, Don Juan holds, 'a man may die but not his name'. Juan Manuel holds that 'in things a man can remedy he should seek the means to do so, without waiting for God or chance to set it right . . . Since man has understanding and reason he should do all he can'.

WAR WITH THE MOORS

'The best way' for a noble 'to save his soul, according to his estate and dignity', Don Juan makes Patronio advise Count Lucanor, is 'to die fighting the Moors. If you do this or even if you wish death in this way you will be a martyr, and even those who wish to say evil of you will not be able to do so, since all men see that you leave nothing undone of what you should do for chivalry . . . He who considers himself a knight should not

[1] Ibid. i. 67 (pp. 316 f.); *Partidas*, II. xxi. 20; Muntaner, cc. 51, 134; Desclot, c. 159 (ed. Coll, v. 87); Juan Manuel, *Libro de la caza*, 8, ed. J. Mª. Castro y Calvo (Barcelona, 1947), p. 56; *Poema de Alfonso XI*, vv. 409, 1832 (*BAE* lvii. 489, 532); Oliveira Marques, *Daily Life*, p. 133; Riquer, i. 374 and Plate; Lull, *Libre de meravelles*, viii. 53 (*Obres essencials*, i. 401); Blanco-González, op. cit., pp. 200–13. Good reproductions of the Tinell paintings in *Història dels Catalans*, ed. Soldevila, iii (Barcelona, 1969), 1349–78.

shut himself up in a monastery', but serve God in war. The whole of this passage reminds one strongly of Archbishop Turpin's exhortation to the Franks at Roncesvalles in the *Song of Roland*. In another story Patronio tells his master that in fighting Moors 'you will do many good things. First of all, you will serve God, and, for the rest, you will gain honour and live in your office [of knight], and not live idly, which does not *look well* for any great lord'.[1]

REALITIES: CIVIL WAR

The reality of fourteenth-century Castile naturally differed from its ideals. Don Juan Manuel's own life shows that he spent far less time in wars with the Moors of Granada than in fighting his own king. Maitland's phrase, coined for medieval English barons, applies perfectly to nobles like Don Juan. 'They were ready to fight for their king, unless they happened to fight against him.' Heroism against 'the Moors' existed. Some modern historians have questioned the story of Alfonso Pérez de Guzman's defence of Tarifa in 1294 when he refused to surrender the town to save his son's life. However, a document of 1297 declares that Guzman 'himself threw a knife to the Moors with which they should kill his son, so that they might be sure that he would not give up the town . . . and the Moors, beholding this, slew the son with his father's knife'.

The hero of this superhuman act of devotion to his king and defiance of 'the Moors' had made his reputation as a commander of Castilian mercenaries serving Morocco. In this earlier part of his life he was more typical of the great nobles of Castile than in the glorious tragedy of Tarifa.

Don Juan Manuel described the situation that actually existed between king and nobles when he advised his son

> not to believe that [even] meeting the king in the country, with many followers, can [a noble] be safe from death, if the king wishes to kill him. He should be on his guard night and day wherever he stays and not put himself in the power of any town or man he does not completely trust, for most men do much to gain favour with kings . . . He should seek to have great power of fortresses and

[1] Juan Manuel, *Libro de Patronio*, 16, 18, 3, 33 (*BAE*, li. 384, 386, 374, 404); *Partidas*, II. xxi. 2.

vassals and relations and friends to defend himself . . . He should always be prepared . . . as in time of war [with the king, though] he should never begin it, except for something which would be great dishonour to him if he did not act upon it.

One such *causa belli*, given as an instance, is an attack by the king on a great noble which seems unjust to his equals in rank.[1]

Private war between nobles was generally assumed to be normal. Alfonso X's *Partidas* regulate how friendship should be renounced, truces granted, and reconciliation achieved. Civil wars tended to drag on since it was very hard even for a king to capture a strong castle. Juan Manuel makes Patronio tell count Lucanor: 'No fortress can be taken except by scaling or mining its walls, but if the walls are high the ladders cannot serve. A mine takes a great time to make, and so fortresses are taken because the besieged lack supplies or become needlessly afraid.'

On this basis Juan Manuel traces a plan by which a great noble can make war successfully on a king. He advocates the sort of guerrilla warfare he practised in fact. The noble needs a number of fortresses adequately supplied with arms and food and must not be caught in any one of them. He should fight only when he has a chance of a decisive victory but he can harry the rear of the force besieging his castle or make them raise the siege by attacking their fortresses. He should aim for a truce in the summer so as to get in his crops, and fight in the winter. He must divide his enemies by intrigue, keep absolute secrecy over his own plans, and wring every advantage he can from night marches, terrain, and weather conditions.[2]

Juan Manuel's advocacy of the right of nobles to resist their king was naturally not shared by kings themselves or by a Christian thinker such as Ramon Lull. Jaume I of Aragon, in his advice to his son-in-law Alfonso X of Castile, told him to prefer the Church and cities to knights, because of the disruptive nature of knights. For Lull, himself a knight by birth, knights are 'the Devil's ministers'. 'Who is there in the world', he asks, 'who does as much harm as knights?'

Despite their dislike of the nobles' private wars it was

[1] Benavides, ii. 145; see M. Gaibrois, *BRAH* 76, pp. 146 f.; Juan Manuel, *Libro de los castigos*, cc. 4, 7 (*BAE* li. 269 f.).

[2] *Partidas*, VII. XI–XII; Juan Manuel, *Libro de Patronio*, 12 (*BAE* li. 381); *Libro de los estados*, i. 70 (ibid., pp. 319 f.).

impossible for the kings of the time to prevent these wars occurring outside certain seasons of the Christian year such as Lent, when they had long been condemned by the Church, or a grave crisis concerning the whole kingdom. In 1314 Jaume II of Aragon wrote to a Catalan noble, noting that his subject was at war with another noble family and merely asking him not to harm the hospital the king was building on the Coll of Balaguer, since Jaume planned to use it when he passed that way.

In 1293 Don Gonzalo Ruiz de Zúñiga, who had served Don Juan Núñez de Lara and other warlords of contemporary Castile, made his will. The list of debts he admitted owing gives us a picture of the wars of the time.

When Don Juan was raiding towards Burgos I had from this raid 120 sheep and they were worth, on the average, 3 maravedis each, and an ox perhaps worth 40, and 40 pigs which I ate . . . worth 8 maravedis, not more . . . and I had 1,000 maravedis from the town [*concejo*] of Trepeana. And when I was a vassal of Don Diego [López de Haro] I had a load of barley from Castiel de Peones, and when I was a vassal of Don Jaime I took three loads of wheat in Quintanilla de Sant García. In Ebriones [I took] a mule worth as much as 120 maravedis, and when they took prisoner Don Simón [Roiz de los Cameros] I had four loads of wheat from a man of Ventosa, near Navarrete, and when I went to Albarracín to Don Juan I took a mule. . . . I sold it for 100 sueldos. I took another mule from Fuente Burueba worth 100 maravedis . . . I owe the town of Eglesia Saleña 120 mrs. and 200 [for] a Moorish woman of Toledo and 200 for a Moor. In all the war of Albarracín all my gains might amount to 2,000 mrs. of Castile and Aragon. When Don Juan broke with the king of Castile and went over to the king of Aragon I got 2,200 mrs. for two horses . . . apart from 400 sheep which Don Juan gave me and up to 150 loads of wheat and rye which he took from labourers . . . A house I burnt in Salas might be worth up to 40 mrs.

Don Gonzalo had evidently been a successful condottiere. Now repentant, he instructed his executors to pay for these debts with the 'bread, money, arms, and jewels' he left behind him. Against some of the debts the word 'paid' is written in the original document.

The general attitude of the nobility to war was expressed by Juan Manuel through the fictional Count Lucanor: 'I was born, grew up, and have always lived in the midst of wars, now with Christians and now with Moors, and at times with kings, my lords, and with my neighbours.' In another story Patronio defines the situation very clearly when he tells Lucanor that the count's friends and enemies desire neither real war (for which they lack the means) nor real peace, but a state of confusion, 'in which they can rob and attack your lands and force you to give them what you have'.[1]

HUNTING

It is hardly surprising that Count Lucanor should have wished to escape a state of affairs in which he was always at war or exposed to it and to have remarked: 'I would like to rest from now on, hunting and living free of troubles and worries', a wish many contemporary nobles must have shared. We have already seen hunting to be the main diversion of the kings of the time and an essential part of the noble's education. The Cortes of Castile-León prohibit the export of falcons unless with special royal permission. Juan Manuel himself wrote a book on falconry which ended with a discussion of the places where he had hunted, from León and Burgos to Seville and Murcia. The *Partidas* sum up admirably the attractions hunting possessed for the ruling class:

> Hunting contributes greatly to diminish serious thoughts and passions . . . and it confers health, [causing] a man to eat and sleep well, which is the principal thing in life. The pleasure which is derived from it is, moreover, a great source of joy, obtaining possession of birds and wild beasts and causing them to obey and serve man, by bringing others into his hands . . . Hunting is an art and imparts knowledge of war and conquest, with which kings should be thoroughly familiar.

A moralist like Lull tended to view hunting with less favour. There were kings 'so given up to hunting that they were very displeased if men mentioned anything else to them'. The *Primera Crónica General* describes other amusements of the nobility, jousting and bull-fighting on horseback, a specialized

[1] Jaume I, *Libre dels feyts*, c. 498; Lull, *Libre de contemplació*, c. 112 (*Obres essencials*, ii. 340); Martínez Ferrando, *Jaime II*, ii. 101; Gaibrois, *Sancho IV*, iii. p. cccxlix; Juan Manuel, *Libro de Patronio*, 3, 15 (*BAE* li. 372, 384).

form of the struggle with wild beasts which occupied so much of the noble's time.[1]

LESSER NOBLES: CASTILE

Below the few counts and the many *ricoshombres* of Castile, with their vassals and banners, who were almost on the same level as the king, came the far more numerous *hidalgos* (*hijosdalgo*). There was no rigid division; the distinction between *ricoshombres* and *hidalgos* was due to wealth. In Portugal 'whoever possessed an inhabited country estate, a yoke of oxen, forty sheep, a donkey, and two beds moved from the social class of peasant to that of knight'. *Caballeros* could be created by the Crown. In theory *hidalgos* could not but in fact their position could alter, depending on their fortunes, and the Cortes complained that many men were ennobled illegally. *Caballeros* have been defined as 'soldiers on active service', *hidalgos* as 'a passive class', with military obligations normally limited to their local area, though subject to service further afield if called on by the king. These two (often overlapping) classes were the 'living forces' of Castile up to the virtual end of the reconquest of Andalusia in 1250. Their military service made them necessary to society. Their privileges, which were not very numerous, sprang from the function they fulfilled. They were, like the clergy, free from taxes which were intended to finance the expeditions to which they contributed their personal service while the clergy contributed their prayers. A lesser noble had wide rights to choose a male heir so as to continue his lineage. Heavier fines were levied for damage done to nobles' houses and animals than to the property of non-nobles. For most serious crimes they were judged by the king or a major noble, as his deputy, not by the local judge. On the other hand they were punished with especial severity for treason (their sons could not become knights), heresy (by loss of their fiefs), and blasphemy.

Restrictions on all nobles—*hidalgos* and *caballeros*—also sprang from their function in society. They could not practise any profession or trade of which the object was making money.

[1] Juan Manuel, ibid. 16 (p. 384); Ballesteros, *Alfonso X*, p. 72; *Cortes de León*, i. 62, 72; Juan Manuel, *Libro de la caza*, 12, ed. cit., pp. 85–109; *Partidas*, II. v. 20 (transl. S. P. Scott, p. 296); Lull, *Libre de meravelles*, viii. 99 (*Obres essencials*, i. 473 f.); *Primera Crónica General*, c. 712, ed. Menéndez Pidal, ii. 415.

This situation had begun to break down by 1300. The economic position of the lesser nobility began to collapse as their military function decayed. The *Partidas* show that they had always had to have a minimal income to maintain their rank, though the *caballero* needed less than the *hidalgo*. As they were increasingly replaced as soldiers by infantry, as administrators and judges by royal officials, they ceased to be the directing force of Castile. Profits from war—booty in arms, clothes, horses, plate—now virtually ceased except for the fortunate brigand on a large scale such as Don Gonzalo. The landed property available decreased rather than increased since most of Andalusia was divided into great estates. Profits from the increasing sheep-farming and especially from the Mesta also went, in the main, to the rich. In 1289 the 'caballeros y escuderos' of Cuenca felt it necessary to form a league of mutual defence against the townspeople and peasants.

The decay of the lesser nobles appears in the vulgarization of the term 'hidalgo', which was used much less carefully in the fourteenth century. A new hierarchy of dukes, marquises, and *privados*, the king's special counsellors, forerunners of the *cortesano*, arose between the king and the *caballero* or *hidalgo*. The Archpriest of Hita's belief that money alone can make a labourer a *hidalgo* was not far removed from the concern for money of the *hidalgos* themselves, who, in 1309, refused to fight against Granada unless they were paid before the campaign, or to cease to wage private war when Fernando IV sought to mobilize them against Islam. In the 1270s the Castilian treasury was already trying to collect fines from the many *caballeros* who did not equip themselves for the king's service as they were obliged to do, or took the king's money and remained at home, or appeared on parade with borrowed horses and arms.[1]

Don Juan Manuel makes Count Lucanor say: 'At times I found myself in such need for money that I would not have objected to death.' Lucanor here represents the whole nobility. From princes like Don Juan down nobles were continually demanding and extorting grants (*mercedes*) from the king, either

[1] Oliveira Marques, *Daily Life*, p. 123; Blanco-González, op. cit., pp. 61 f., 107–12, 114–18, 129–36, 19–22, 29–31; Gaibrois, iii, pp. cxlviii f.; *Libro de Buen Amor*, v. 491, ed. M. Criado de Val and E. W. Naylor, p. 138; *Crónica de Fernando IV*, 16 (*BAE* lxvi. 162); *MHE* i. 314 ff.

in land or money. Lesser nobles had merely fewer opportunities for profit. Their decline is reflected in the satirical *Cántigas d'escarnho*, and in the *Debate de Elena y María*, of about 1280. Here the sister who loves a cleric describes the hard life of the *hidalgo*: 'When he goes to the palace we know how they treat him. His bread is measured out, his wine is tasteless . . . He smiles more than he eats . . . He is always hungry and cold.' If he ever makes money he loses it gambling and has to wager his horse and arms (an action which could cause him to lose his rank).

If he goes on an expedition
He does not do so willingly.
If he goes out to fight
It is not of *his* volition.

In 1348 Alfonso XI extended the privileges of immunity which had long protected the houses, arms, and horses of *hidalgos* from seizure for debt to the horses and arms of the plebeian horsemen (*caballeros villanos*) of his cities, who had now reached a position differing very little from that of *hidalgos*. Some years before this Don Juan Manuel had recognized the existence and usefulness of non-noble officials. This recognition was even clearer in Catalonia than in Castile.[1]

THE CROWN OF ARAGON

The legal codes of Aragon and Valencia reveal a large and generally poor class of lesser nobles which resembles that of Castile. The codes attempted to stabilize the situation, fixing the size of dowries according to class distinctions and only allowing marriages between nobles and non-nobles in return for financial compensation. In 1333 the Catalan Corts, in a similar attempt to perpetuate noble lineages, fixed the proportion of a noble inheritance due to the male heir as three-quarters. In fact, however, marriages between daughters of merchants and nobles occurred not infrequently. In 1280 a daughter of a cloth merchant of Lérida married Ot de Moncada, a member of a leading noble house. The Pauli family of Vich rose by

[1] *Libro de Patronio*, 10 (*BAE* li. 378); *Cántigas d'escarnho*, ed. M. Rodrigues Lapa, e.g. nos. 274, 351; R. Menéndez Pidal, *RFE* 1 (1914), 57, 59 f., 63; Blanco-González, p. 53; see p. 47 above.

loaning money to the nobles of the region, by handling clerical finances, and by disguised usury. The father, Ferran Pauli, whose accounts run from 1280 to his death in 1312, sold cloth, leather, and arms locally. His son Jaume's commercial interests went as far as Sicily. He also bought land. In 1330–1, by exploiting his position as the creditor of a noble family, he became 'Venerable citizen of Vich, draper, and Lord of Sentfores'. Like other (born) nobles of the age he lived in his country house, waited on by Greek slaves. Jaume's son, the third generation Pauli, married a daughter of the lord of Taradell and one of his daughters married Pauli's debtor, the lord of Sant Feliu. In three generations the Paulis had entered the local nobility.

By lending money to the Crown and acquiring its rights other Catalan merchants could rise higher than the Paulis. They could become administrators of Crown revenues. 'Textile merchants and horse traders often rose to become state officials and in some instances even admirals of the fleet.' The highest posts were usually for sale and, after the 1280s, when Jewish competition was removed, opportunities for advancement multiplied for the bourgeois of Catalonia.

Ramon Lull, in his *Book of Wonders*, describes the prosperous Catalan merchant of his day in the process of becoming a noble.

> A merchant had 1,000 besants and desired to have 1,000 more, and . . . so he gained 100,000 besants but he could not be satiated. At this the merchant was much amazed and thought that his desires could not be fulfilled in money and believed that it could be in castles, towns, and estates, which he wanted to have and had.[1]

THE CITIES OF THE PENINSULA: ISLAMIC AND CHRISTIAN CITIES

In the thirteenth and fourteenth centuries the peninsula contained two different types of city, those of the south, which long preserved their Islamic character, and those of the north, founded by Christians during their resistance to Islam. Neither

[1] J.-P. Cuvillier, *MCV* 5 (1969), 168–80; idem, in *Miscel·lània històrica catalana* (Poblet, 1970), p. 246; J. Lladonosa, *Arnau de Solsona, un mercader lleidatà a Tunis (1218–1297)* (Barcelona, 1967), p. 13; Baer, *History* i. 145, citing L. Klüpfel, *Verwaltungsgeschichte des Königreichs Aragon* (Berlin, 1915), pp. 4 f.; Lull, *Libre de meravelles*, i. 2 (*Obres* i. 322). See also A. García, *Ausa*, 4 (1961–3), 321–9; 64–5 (1970), 165–85.

type of city bore any real relation to the Roman cities which had existed in the peninsula until the coming of the Muslims.

The Islamic type of city, such as Seville or Toledo, was differentiated from the northern city by the houses it contained and by its street-plan. While Christians emphasized the façade of their houses, since they wished to impress the passer-by, the Muslim built for himself. His house had scarcely any opening on the street other than wooden balconies, closed by screens, from which the women of the house could watch the street without being seen. Although these closed-in balconies gradually disappeared the majority of Christian *bourgeoises*, especially in Andalusia, continued to live very much as their Muslim predecessors had done, essentially within their houses, looking out on the world through screens which continued to be built until at least the eighteenth century.

Parts of cities such as Toledo and Écija still preserve the typical Islamic street-plan—or lack of plan—which one finds in modern Morocco. Streets twist and turn, they are often crossed by arches and end in a cul-de-sac. The reason why many Spanish cathedrals are so closely surrounded by houses is that the cathedral stands on the site of the main mosque and open spaces were not thought necessary even around the mosque. Richard Burton's description of Al-Madina and Mecca in 1853 shows how the holiest places of Islam were hemmed in by buildings in the same way as Toledo Cathedral.

Fifteenth-century visitors to the newly conquered Granada and Málaga were amazed at the narrowness and gloom of the streets of these cities. No street in sixteenth-century Toledo was wider than 2·25 metres. Up to the nineteenth century the cities of southern Spain preserved much of their Islamic character.

The main differences between Seville or Toledo and Burgos or Barcelona in 1300 or 1500 were due to the fact that in Islamic Andalusia the houses had been built first, the streets second, whereas in the north the reverse was the case. The northern cities were also far less densely populated than the cities of al-Andalus. In Salamanca—the most populous city in the kingdom of León—it took centuries for the population to fill the space within the thirteenth-century walls. The large open spaces were needed for the flocks of sheep which supported the clergy and warriors who owned them. Towns in Aragon such as Daroca or Teruel were mainly inhabited by peasants who could not remain long at a siege because they had to go home and get in the crops. Avila and Salamanca were inhabited by sheep-owners.

The origin of the Christian cities of the north was most often military. They had been created to defend mountain passes or passages over rivers. Sometimes, as in Navarre, along the pilgrim route to Compostela, or in Valencia, in the lands conquered by Jaume I, new towns were laid out in regular patterns such as squares. But even if streets curved they generally went in a clear direction. The streets were narrow but without the numerous blind alleys of the Islamic south and there were open spaces around the churches or serving as markets.[1]

Muslim poets recounted the beauties of the cities which had fallen to the Christian conquerors in the thirteenth century. They celebrated the palaces of Seville, the rivulets of water flowing through the orange and lemon groves of their patios. They celebrated Valencia, 'surrounded by rivers and gardens. One only hears the murmuring of water spreading out in every direction and the singing of countless birds'. For a native Muslim author 'the brilliance of the light of Valencia exceeds that of the other cities of al-Andalus'. This was the same southern city that captivated the Franciscan Eiximenis when he arrived from his native mountains of Gerona, so that he hymns Valencia's Mediterranean air and the extraordinary fertility of its soil in the prologue to his *Regiment de la cosa pública*. Writing in 1383, Eiximenis was as well aware as any later author of the differences between the two types of city in the peninsula. He wished to reform the 'almost Moorish' city he lived in and replan it along classical lines. In fact this proved impossible; in 1762 Valencia was still a maze of 428 'streets' and some 130 narrow squares, yet more was done in Valencia than elsewhere. In Murcia no new Christian churches were built before the fourteenth century and no stone bridge over the river until almost 1400. In the far richer Seville the Gothic cathedral was not begun until 1401.

[1] L. Torres Balbas, *Al-Andalus*, 12 (1947), 415–27; idem, in *Resumen histórico del urbanismo en España* (Madrid, 1954), pp. 9–87.

THE CITY: A STATE WITHIN A STATE

The differences between the architectural character of the two types of cities in the peninsula remained as acute as the climatic differences between Seville and Avila. But the effort was made to transplant the whole structure of society, which had been created in the north, to the conquered south. Town councils were created in Seville, Córdoba, and Murcia, and guilds, with separate streets assigned to armourers, saddlers, shoemakers, carpenters, leather-workers, and so on. Cloth was produced in Seville and leather in Murcia as they had been before the Christians arrived on the scene but the way in which these goods were made was now governed by new authorities, by guilds.[1]

The Christian conquests of the thirteenth century extended the type of city that had gradually evolved in western Europe throughout the peninsula. Out of markets and fortresses there had slowly developed the idea of a city as a state within a state, possessing, in widely varying degrees, juridical and economic autonomy. There were great differences here between the Spanish kingdoms and Italy and Flanders, where cities enjoyed a political independence never possessed by any city in the peninsula. When a king of Castile was in urgent need of money he might be prepared to recognize that Seville had entire control over its own revenues. His successors revoked this concession. Barcelona won a stronger position as against the ruler of Catalonia–Aragon than Seville ever possessed. Even so, the cities of Castile could act, especially during royal minorities, as a decisive political force, a force usually on the side of royal order as against anarchy fomented by the nobility. The town councils (*concejos*) of Seville, Córdoba, and some other cities in Andalusia ruled enormous dependent areas, far larger than those controlled by the *concejos* of Toledo, Avila, and other northern cities. These areas were controlled by castles. The main expenses of Castilian cities were military. The maintenance of the city's walls and castles and the occasional military expedition constituted the principal items in the budget.

[1] González, *Repartimiento de Sevilla*, i. 498; Abulfeda of Damascus, *Boletín de la Real Sociedad geográfica de Madrid*, 48 (1906), 99 f.; for Eiximenis see below, Vol. ii, Part I, Ch. II; *Documentos de Alfonso X el Sabio*, ed. J. Torres Fontes (Murcia, 1963), pp. 44 f., 76 f.

The military character of the medieval city in general and its separation, as a definite unit, from the countryside was accentuated by the way in which, to quote Huizinga, 'it stood forth as a compact whole', surrounded by its walls. Its gates were closed and guarded at night. All the city's male inhabitants, except for the very young and very old, were liable for watch service, though the clergy, the Jews, and, in Seville, seamen, were only called upon if the city was actually attacked.

In the *Partidas* Alfonso X remarks: 'The king should honour his land and especially in encircling his cities and towns and castles with good walls and towers.' Poets praise a city if it is defended not only by walls but by water. They describe their ideal city as on guard, with its sentries sounding trumpets or horns, 'as is the custom of those who watch'. When the garrison sallies out against a besieging force they are watched by their womenfolk.

In the thirteenth century these walled cities developed suburbs where life was pleasanter than in the narrow streets of the old city, where 'it is the hour of terce (about 9 a.m.) when they receive the light and heat of the sun'. But the suburbs might be torn down in an emergency such as the French invasion of Catalonia in 1285 when the walls of Catalan cities were being feverishly repaired and cleared of surrounding houses.[1]

THE CITY'S INHABITANTS: THE BOURGEOISIE

In the late thirteenth century the term 'burgués' ('bourgeois', 'burgess') was used in the Crown of Aragon (Catalonia, Aragon, Valencia, Majorca), Navarre, and Galicia, but not in Castile. Alfonso X's *Partidas* speak of citizens as 'the roots and treasure's of kingdoms' and of merchants as those 'who bring from other parts to their seignories the things that are needed there', but burgesses are not mentioned. They are defined, however, by the leading Aragonese lawyer, Vidal de Canellas, a contemporary of Alfonso, as inhabitants of cities who live from some industry or office but without manual labour. Vidal includes as 'burgesses' cloth merchants, money-changers, lawyers, and doctors.

[1] R. Carande, 'Sevilla', *AHDE* 2 (1925), 251, 256, 392–401, 315 f.; *Partidas*, II. xi. 2; Rubió, *Vida*, pp. 17–30. For the position of Barcelona and the invasion of 1285 see below, pp. 258, 280.

Professor Valdeavellano has noted Vidal's recognition of a 'primitive industrial and mercantile bourgeoisie', which also included the legal and medical professions.

Outside the Crown of Aragon the phenomenon of the bourgeoisie was mainly restricted to the towns along the pilgrimage route from Navarre to Galicia where French immigration had affected society. Of these towns Burgos was the most important. Toledo also contained a French colony. The other towns of the Meseta were, as has been said, military and agricultural in character. Trade and industry in Castile, outside the Basque ports, was mainly carried on by Muslims and Jews, in Seville by foreigners, particularly the Genoese. In a town such as Avila the non-noble and non-clerical Christian citizens lived by sheep-farming. Their ambition was to become assimilated into the lesser nobility by becoming 'plebeian knights' (*caballeros villanos*), exempt from taxes in return for military service as cavalry. Their world was totally distinct from the 'urban patriciate' which was developing in Catalonia and the areas conquered by Catalans—Valencia and Majorca—along essentially the same lines as in Florence, Venice, or Bruges. Catalonia was at least a century, perhaps two centuries, ahead of Castile as far as the development of the bourgeoisie was concerned.

THE URBAN PATRICIATE

In contrast with Castile, nobles played virtually no part in the city life of the Crown of Aragon. In order to become a citizen of Barcelona a knight had to begin by renouncing his military privileges. In return he entered the class of 'honoured citizens', 'men of honour', which was also recruited from successful merchants and artisans, doctors, royal officials, and converted Jews. A citizen of Barcelona, Valencia, or Majorca, enjoyed the same rights as a noble, including that of entry into the Military Orders. This type of urban aristocracy or patriciate hardly existed in Castile, where sheep-farming *caballeros* dominated most of the towns. Catalans appear to have been free of the veneration for 'knights' found in Castile. In Catalonia a second son would become a knight while the eldest son and heir would continue to be a 'citizen', leading, probably, a richer, more cultivated life than his younger brother.

The 'honoured citizens' of Barcelona or Valencia, the cream

of contemporary bourgeoisie in the peninsula, were few in number, less than a hundred in Barcelona. They were rentiers. They did not themselves act as merchants or industrialists but their money financed workshops, built ships, was invested in land or in the public debt of their own or other cities. Their sons were prominent in the universities, in law, medicine, and theology. Some of them divided with the higher clergy the confidential posts of the Crown of Aragon while others led their cities in jealous maintenance of their independence, or, simply, of the interests of their own class.

CATALONIA AND CASTILE

In the Iberian peninsula in 1306 only a Catalan could have written: 'To work wool and cloth is the cause of great *honesty* in men and women, of *whatever* estate, and to those noble ladies and others who make clothes for themselves or their households, and it is of great profit and much more economical than if they purchased the clothes.'

One may compare this bourgeois glorification of work with the Archpriest of Hita's description of Lot as the prototype bourgeois—a man so governed by gluttony that he committed incest with his daughters. In the early fifteenth century Gutierre Díez de Games, in his account of the deeds of Pero Niño, sees the bourgeois as merely one of the 'common offices' opposed to that of knights.

For those who pursue common occupations eat their bread in idleness, wear exquisite clothes, eat well-dressed food, enjoy soft, perfumed beds. They sleep safe and arise without fear; they dwell in fine houses with their wives and children and servants; they grow double chins and pot-bellies and have a great opinion of themselves. What reward or honours do they deserve? None.[1]

The precocious urban prosperity of Catalonia brought with it social instability. The widening gap between rich and poor produced, in 1285, an attempted social revolution in Barcelona,

[1] *Partidas*, II. x. 3; Vidal de Canyellas, *In excelsis Dei thesauris*, vii. 29, ed. G. Tilander, *Vidal Mayor*, ii (Lund, 1956), 460; L. García de Valdeavellano, *Sobre los burgos y los burgueses de la España medieval* (Madrid, 1960), pp. 150 n. 339, 156–9; Sobrequés, op. cit., pp. 150–63; Finke, *Acta* iii. 160; *Libro de Buen Amor*, v. 296, ed. M. Criado de Val and E. W. Naylor, p. 77; Díez de Games, *El Victorial*, c. 8, ed. J. de Mata Carriazo (Madrid, 1940), p. 42.

and efforts to form communes in other seignorial and royal towns. This movement has no known parallel in contemporary Castile though it has many in Italy and Flanders. It was firmly put down by royal and local authorities.

In Castile the late thirteenth and early fourteenth century saw control of the towns pass to groups of *caballeros villanos* who secured exclusive rights of access to municipal office. The general assembly of qualified 'neighbours' lost power to these groups. The Castilian assembly formally lost the right to elect local officials in about 1340 but the effective change came earlier.

This shift of power did not occur without conflict, recorded for several towns (Toro, Zamora, and Córdoba) from the 1280s to the early fourteenth century. These cases of conflict were probably not unique. It seems mistaken to see this as a class struggle comparable to that of Barcelona. It was merely a matter of which privileged group was to prevail. At times both opposing groups consisted of *caballeros*. The only conflict in Castile into which an element of social rebellion entered was when, during the anarchical minority of Alfonso XI, the peasants and workmen of some towns turned against the nobles oppressing them. This movement resembles the 'Jacquerie' of France during the Hundred Years War. We know very little about it and it appears to have been short-lived.[1]

THE LESSER BOURGEOISIE: MERCHANTS

In the cities of Catalonia, Valencia, and Majorca there existed a second urban aristocracy, below the 'honoured citizens' but of great importance since all long-distance, especially maritime, trade was in its hands. This type of capitalist appears in Catalonia in the late twelfth century. Merchants played a considerable role in Seville, Burgos, and the Basque ports but they were still grouped with rag-dealers and butchers by the Cortes of Castile of 1351. In Catalonia many merchants were also bankers

[1] J. M. Font Rius, *Annales du Midi*, 69 (1957), 304–6; M. del C. Carlé, *Del concejo medieval castellano-leonés* (Buenos Aires, 1968), pp. 78 f., 90, 126–9, 145–8, 151–60. See the *Crónica de Alfonso XI*, c. 37 (*BAE* lxvi. 197). The case of Ubeda (ibid., c. 109, p. 244) might also be cited as exceptional. Carlé exaggerates the social significance of most of the cases she cites. The use of the term 'patriciate' for Castilian cities is misleading. It is preferable to reserve this term for its usual connotation, a bourgeoisie ruling over a city of the Italian or Flemish type.

while in Castile banking remained mainly in Jewish or Genoese hands during the fourteenth century.

Below the merchants was the 'lower-middle class' of notaries and smaller traders, painters, sculptors, etc., which was to become more important politically in the fifteenth century. Below these men came the mass of the city population, recruited constantly from the peasants fleeing from the labour of the fields. It was possible to rise from an artisan to the middle class in Catalonia by municipal decree, in Castile and Aragon simply by income—a higher income brought with it higher taxes and military duties. One could also officially descend the ladder and be reclassified as a workman. Reclassification reduced one's obligations as well as one's privileges.

The artisan-shopkeeper, making and selling his own wares, assisted by his family, some apprentices, and perhaps a slave, was the basis on which the city rested. As he was mainly self-employed he felt no hatred for alien 'capitalists' but he wanted a share in governing his city. But in 1338–9 the elected assembly, the *Consell de Cent*, of Barcelona only included twelve workmen—a far smaller proportion than the eighty-nine workmen in the *Consell* of 210 of 1257, and, as proportional representation, absurd since the *Consell* of 1338 contained sixty-three representatives of the hundred or so families of the 'honoured citizens'. Nor could workmen hold municipal office in Barcelona before 1455.[1]

GUILDS

Guilds of workmen began, as in other countries of western Europe, as religious confraternities grouping the practitioners of the same craft together for religious functions and mutual assistance. In Seville by 1250 the tailors owned a hospital where the members of their confraternity could receive free treatment. By 1500 there were almost fifty such guild hospitals in the city. The guild also supported members who were out of work and gave pensions to their widows and dowries to their daughters.

In the Crown of Aragon the guilds, with their elected officials, were the means by which the workmen organized their drive for political power in cities such as Barcelona. The guilds also acted, in both Catalonia–Aragon and Castile, to exclude com-

[1] Sobrequés, pp. 184–208; A. Altisent, *BRABL* 32 (1967–8), 45–65.

petition and enforce 'union rules'. In Castile the guilds were much less powerful than in Catalonia. Whenever they attempted to develop beyond the stage of a religious, charitable association they were prohibited by the Crown of Castile. In 1250, for instance, Fernando III ordered the dissolution of *confradias* in Segovia because they withdrew their members from royal authority and that of their town council and attempted to fix prices differing from those established by the *concejo*. Alfonso X's *Partidas* echo this opposition to monopolistic guilds. Together, the Crown and the *concejos* of *caballeros*, acting through the Cortes, were strong enough to prevent guilds developing in Castile as closed corporations until the late fifteenth century. Just as most of Castile lacked a true bourgeoisie so it lacked the powerful semi-political guild organizations found in Catalonia, as in Italy and Flanders. Laws against the guilds were enacted in Valencia and Aragon (not in Catalonia) but they were soon repealed. In 1337 Pere III granted each city the authority to regulate the local guilds. From then on they multiplied.[1]

TOWN LIFE

City life, for virtually all the population except members of religious orders, was lived much more in the open than it is today. The ordinary house possessed few attractions. Work was normally done—shoes were mended, or armour repaired—in the street, in front of the shop—in Catalonia probably under porticoes, which provided shelter in the winter. Alfonso's *Partidas* refer to barbers shaving their clients on the open street or in a plaza. They may be jostled by a passer-by and the man being shaved or bled may be injured. They should work in 'retired places'.

The northern cities had *plazas* (squares) and even the smallest *plaza* surprised men emerging from tortuous, narrow, and evil-smelling streets. Town ordinances recognize that the '*plaza* is the most noble and suitable place in the whole city, for all men, natives, and foreigners'. Ramon Lull remarks: 'Every day we see the streets and *plazas* full of merchants who exchange silver for gold and things of little price for precious objects.' The *plazas*

[1] Sobrequés, pp. 214–16, 296–300; Carlé, pp. 221 f.; *Partidas*, V. VIII. 2; A. Rumeu de Armas, *Historia de la previsión social en España* (Madrid, 1944), Chs. V-VIII.

are the places where minstrels perform. In the *Libro de Apolonio*, when Tarsiana goes out to play her viol in the *plaza*, the people flock to hear her. There is not room for them all in the *plaza*. They fill the windows and galleries of the houses around. Other spectacles in the *plaza* included the exceptional tournament, the fair, and the more common market, frequented, as always, by conjurers, cheats, and pickpockets. The *Partidas* tell us that men produce serpents 'and suddenly throw them down before people in markets and fairs, frightening men and women so that they abandon their merchandise and robbers steal their property . . . Others pretend to fight and draw knives against one another', with the same end in view.[1]

The Archpriest of Hita's description of the reception of 'Don Amor' shows a town of New Castile in the fourteenth century celebrating a festival. Don Amor is received with drums and guitars, lauds, flutes, viols, trumpets, dulcimers, and harps. He is received by Jews and Muslims, by the parochial processions, by Benedictines, Cistercians, Cluniacs, the Military Orders of Santiago, Calatrava, and Alcántara, by friars in their habits, Dominicans, Franciscans, Augustinians, Trinitarians, Carmelites, Mercedarians, Friars of St. Anthony, and by every Order of nuns. All vie with each other to receive Don Amor and his suite. The monks—who often entertained royalty when inns were lacking—promise him superb refectories and dormitories.

Less joyous sights than the reception of Dom Amor, or of a king or great prince, were seen every day in a great city. Ramon Lull describes many of the street scenes common to a Catalan city, such as Barcelona, Majorca, or Perpignan. A brawl could break out suddenly. Two young men, sons of leading burgesses, angered by a pretentious-looking stranger, might set upon him and tear off his fine tunic, his red breeches, and his painted shoes. Knives would be out and men killed in a moment. The beautiful lady passing by on a palfrey was led by a cleric who had been sent to bring her to his bishop. Another passage of Lull's *Book of Wonders* almost films the street life he knew.

Through a noble city there went a poor man. He saw many men bearing falcons, who had come from one end of the world and were taking them to the Tartars to gain money. Then he saw a bishop

[1] Rubió, *Vida*, pp. 31–8; *Partidas*, VII. xv. 27; xvi. 10; R. Lull, *Libre de contemplació*, 116 (*Obres essencials*, ii. 350); *Libre de Apolonio*, vv. 426 f. (*BAE* lvii. 297).

going with a great following to Rome to ask that he might be confirmed [in his see] by the pope. Then that poor man passed through the *plaza* where he saw many workshops full of fine cloth and in the silversmiths many silver-gilt cups and many more vanities. Then in the streets poor men, naked, weak, famished, who asked and demanded alms for the love of God, and there was none who had pity on them but rather refused them and abused them.

These extreme contrasts were looked out on by religious recluses, walled up in small cells beside the street, living on alms given by passers-by, gazing 'through a window all day long as people went up and down', enjoying or abusing a liberty the recluse had renounced for ever for the love of God.

The streets of cities were infested by bogus beggars who, if they persisted in begging, were whipped through the town, paying their tormentor's salary. Recaptured slaves were led along, or, exceptionally, there were executions in which the criminal was deprived of one member after another, as he was driven round the city. The justice of the day could be brutal. Jacques Licras, doctor of laws and procurator of the queen of Navarre, had exploited his office to obtain bribes. He had imprisoned, tormented, and killed innocent men. At last, in 1346, he was tried, convicted, and dragged through the streets of Pamplona, with a bugler going before him. His tongue was cut out at the foot of the scaffold and he was hanged at noon. His documents were transported on three mules from the castle of Olite to Pamplona.

The men who witnessed such justice no doubt applauded it but they did not care to associate with its instruments. The municipal regulations of Valencia and Majorca forbade the public executioner to touch the food in the market. He had to point to it with a stick and wearing gloves. Nor could he drink in a tavern except out of a glass he had brought with him.[1]

CATALAN TOWN ORDINANCES

By 1300 it was customary to promulgate ordinances in Catalonia even for small towns. These ordinances provide a clear picture

[1] *Libro de Buen Amor*, vv. 1225–55, ed. cit., pp. 377–92; F. Sevillano Colom, *Valencia urbana medieval* (Valencia, 1957), pp. 50, 346; F. A. Roca Traver, *El Justicia de Valencia, 1238–1321* (Valencia, 1970), pp. 377–83, 473; Rubió, *Vida*, p. 64; Lull, *Libre de meravelles*, viii, Proemi; i. 7; viii. 65, 105 (*Obres essencials*, i. 391, 331, 418, 483); J. Goñi Gaztambide, *Principe de Viana*, 23 (1962), 79 f.

of town life, regulating property, the use of streets, squares, and aqueducts.

ARMS

Many prohibitions concern carrying arms through cities. In 1290 it was forbidden to carry a lance, crossbow, or shield through Barcelona. Even a noble was only permitted to carry a short dagger, except when entering or leaving the city or moving from one inn to another. Fines for transgressions were very high. If the fine could not be paid the man responsible had to choose whether to lose a foot or a hand. Tortosa in 1341 was more lenient. You could carry arms there by day but not by night unless you were also carrying a light.

Normally it was forbidden to move around at all at night, whether armed or unarmed. There is no evidence for street lighting before the fourteenth century. Fiancés were forbidden to take minstrels to serenade their betrothed at night. If you went through Barcelona at night playing a musical instrument you risked losing it. Many streets had chains across them at night so as to limit street fights between rival gangs.

GAMBLING AND BLASPHEMY

Dicing was prohibited, in one small town, on Sundays and Feast days until after Mass. Even then it was limited to the main square. In larger cities penalties concerned the blasphemy which often arose from gambling. It cost 5 *sueldos* to swear by the head, womb, or 'other parts' of God or the Virgin Mary. Other blasphemies were more expensive. If the fine could not be paid the culprit spent twenty days on bread and water. In Barcelona he was beaten, put in the stocks, and heavily fined. If he could not pay he spent three days half naked in the stocks after being driven round the city. In 1335 Bagà, in the Pyrenees, ordered that the tongues of those 'swearing horribly by God and the Madonna' should be torn out. But even here, by 1400, fines had replaced corporal punishment.

HYGIENE

What seem to us more practical regulations concern hygiene. The first municipal orders as to cleaning Barcelona that are known date from 1301; from the 1350s the streets were cleaned every Saturday. Some wells for drinking water had been sunk in 1263. By 1313 the town council was bringing water in by conduits from Montjuich. In 1366 a covered sewer existed along the length of the Rambla to the sea. Fines were levied for throwing filth or dead animals into the streets. The household refuse might be dumped out of the window on the passer-by. Valencia appears to have been behind Barcelona in hygiene. In 1396 even excommunication could not prevent the Valencians from filling the approaches to their cathedral with filth and dead cats. In 1397 a certain Juan of Saragossa, known as 'mala ropa', proposed to the *concejo* of Valencia that he should act as a one-man street-cleaning agency; his proposal was not accepted until 1401.

Ordinances issued in Tortosa show that even a large Catalan city, with considerable maritime trade down the Ebro, was still largely agricultural in the 1340s. Within the walls of Tortosa there were many vineyards, fig orchards, and gardens. Barcelona in 1301 also had large spaces taken up by vines and ploughed land. In 1385 the streets of a smaller town, Fullola (near Tortosa) were infested with pigs and goats wandering about with no guardians and drinking from the communal springs in which the local women washed their clothes, though all this was contrary to local law.

Improvements were gradual—most rapidly felt in Barcelona. By the 1300s a stone bridge there had replaced the wooden crossing over the Llobregat. Only the very poor continued to live in adobe buildings; most men now lived in stone houses. Windows and doors were growing in size. Windows were divided by slender columns with sculptured capitals. The houses of the rich were now set off by a Gothic cloister or a gallery. Country houses arose for the 'honoured citizens', the oligarchs of Barcelona; they were provided with defensive towers. Many town houses were now ornamented on the outside with sculpture or paintings. The traveller, however, who had to rely on inns was less fortunate. Most inns had an unsavoury reputation, doubling as brothels and gaming houses. Many murders were committed within their walls.[1]

[1] *Libre de les costums generals de Tortosa* (*circa 1272*), ed. B. Oliver (Madrid, 1881); F. Carreras y Candi, *BRABL* 11 (1923–4), 292–334, 365–431; 12 (1925–6), 37–62, 121–53, 189–208, 286–95, 368–80, 419–23, 520–33; idem, *Geografia general de*

THE MUSTAÇAF

By 1300 the cities of Majorca and Valencia, which were largely self-governing, possessed similar institutions to those of Barcelona. The *Books* of the Mustaçaf of Majorca and Valencia provide much information as to life in these cities. The Mustaçaf controlled the local market and a great deal of the life of the city. The office also existed in Barcelona from 1339. The Castilian equivalent was the Almotacén.

The Mustaçaf was primarily concerned with the market of the city. He controlled the weights and measures used and inspected the food offered for sale, especially cereals, meats, and fish, but also fuel (charcoal, wood), candles, tiles, bricks, raw materials, and industrial products, cloth, leather, ironwork. Every day the Mustaçaf fixed the maximum prices, a very delicate task, especially in time of scarcity when the city would sell wheat at almost half the price it had paid for it in an attempt to stabilize the market. Every effort was made to prevent speculation in foodstuffs. The guilds of the various crafts, such as textile workers, were also supervised by the Mustaçaf, to make sure that guild regulations approved by the Crown or the city were enforced.

The Mustaçaf and his assistants (*veedores*), chosen from the local merchants, dealt with butchers who disguised one meat as another or sold meat gone bad, and with fruit sellers who crushed figs or sold them when they were not in prime condition. Shoemakers and leather-workers were chosen to verify the quality of leather of the finished product; builders and carpenters inspected the materials being used for new buildings or for paving streets. Inspectors also examined all medicines and drugs offered for sale. They were responsible for destroying any dangerous or spoilt medicines.

From controlling the market the Mustaçaf came (as he had done in Islamic Spain) to control the hygiene of the city. He was much concerned with cleaning the streets and also with preventing the erection of buildings which lent forward, covering most of the street. This was partly to prevent fraudulence,

---

Catalunya: la ciutat de Barcelona (Barcelona, n.d.), pp. 340–44, 360–400; Rubió, *Vida*, pp. 50 ff., 57–62. On gambling and blasphemy see also J. Serra i Vilaro, *AST* 12 (1936), 415–23. For hygiene in Valencia cf. Sevillano, op. cit., pp. 47 f.

since if a shop was overshadowed it became too dark to judge the quality of the goods offered for sale; there were many cloth merchants who sold 'Ypres for Bruges and Rouen for Malines, violet for red'.

The Mustaçaf had to protect the public interest, to prevent, for instance, damage to the city walls or buildings going up in public squares and streets, to regulate the height of houses which might cut off a neighbour's light or enable one family to spy into another's private life.

The Mustaçaf regulated transport. Carts were not normally allowed within the walls because of the narrowness of the streets and the damage the weight of the carts would cause the pavement and the covers of the sewers. The Mustaçaf's duties included preventing manual labour on Sundays and Christian festivals, seeing that men and women did not visit the public baths together, enforcing the statutory limitations on expenditure at weddings and baptisms (only twenty married couples could be invited), and attempting to regulate gambling and punish blasphemy. Almost any case could be brought before him. For instance, in 1400 Joan Guerau complained to the Mustaçaf of Majorca that he was often kept awake by two Tartar neighbours—presumably freed slaves—who, even on Saturdays and vigils of Saints' days, treated their friends to banquets of four or five sheep, which they had killed illegally, singing while they ate into the small hours.

The temptations offered the Mustaçaf of the Crown of Aragon were much the same as those described by Ibn al-Khaṭīb in a letter to a friend appointed Almotacén of Málaga in the fourteenth-century emirate of Granada. Ibn al-Khaṭīb sees his friend on horseback in the market, surrounded by booth-keepers trying to bribe him:

> Do not let yourself be won over by pastries and forget the fish in the basket. Confronted with [a present of] flour display the asceticism of an apostle and renounce the 'loans' that men press on you. Leave sweets on one side as if you were indifferent to them and disdain roasted meats . . . Throw yourself on the wedding feast like a lion and keep the young libertines of the market in terror.

The office of the Mustaçaf was one of the ways in which the cities of the Crown of Aragon sought to control the lives of their citizens. The seaports exercised particularly close vigilance over their merchants. The merchants of Majorca, for instance, who left the island in January or February, had to pledge all their goods and find sureties for their return in March or April. The city authorities were concerned lest the citizens of Majorca hire out their services elsewhere. They must be ready every spring to serve their city. Its collective interests overrode those of any individual citizen. The *Fueros* of Castile illustrate this principle just as clearly. They deal with a simpler economy than that of the Crown of Aragon. They are mainly concerned with sheep- and cattle-raising but they also attempt to regulate every other feature of economic life, shops, fairs, and markets. In these centuries the individual was everywhere bound by the duties he owed to the communities and associations to which he belonged, the kingdom, city, trade association, the real family or artificial brotherhood he had entered.[1]

WOMEN

The role of women in medieval society has hardly been investigated. One can note some changes in the thirteenth century. The very influential *Fuero de Cuenca* (1177–89), on which many later Fueros were based, provided detailed protection for women in a way that does not appear in earlier legislation. We are now in a more urban society where women play a greater, or at least more visible, role in the street, the market, going to and returning from church, than was possible in a rural setting. Hence they were now exposed to greater risks. Fines were now levied for calling a woman an evil name, for seizing her by the hair, stealing her clothes while she was in the public baths, throwing her to the ground, etc., and also for fixing horns to a neighbour's house. (The prostitute shared with the Muslim slave the disadvantage of being unprotected from affront.)

A rudimentary equality between men and women now appears in questions of inheritance, in the joint power both parents share over their children, in the independent situation of a widow, and in the arrangement by which goods were held

[1] For the Islamic origins of this office see below, Ch. V, pp. 186 f., and Ibn al-Khaṭīb, transl. by F. de la Granja, *Al-Andalus*, 26 (1961), 474 f. The sources used here are Sevillano Colom, op. cit.; A. Pons, *Libre del Mostassaf de Mallorca* (Mallorca, 1949); Dufourcq, pp. 32 ff.; M. del C. Carlé, op. cit., pp. 207–25.

in common between husband and wife—at their marriage the husband normally gave his wife half his present and future goods.

In the population of the time women clearly predominated over men. Hence many women were forced to work with their hands, not only in the fields but in cities, where they were even found in the building trade.[1]

THE COUNTRYSIDE: PEASANTS

Although, by 1300, the cities of the peninsula were greatly increasing in size and importance, their inhabitants formed a small minority of the population. Most men lived outside towns and most were peasants. Unfortunately we know far less about them than we do about the town dwellers.

Two main types of Christian peasant population can be broadly distinguished (Mudéjares will be discussed in a later chapter), the farmer and the labourer. Farmers predominated in the north, except in Galicia, and among the Christian population (a minority compared with the Mudéjares) in Valencia and Majorca. Labourers formed the mass of the rural population in the centre and south of the Meseta and in Andalusia, regions where the extent of land available and the lack of irrigation made a régime of small properties impossible, except for the lands belonging to municipalities in Castile–León, which were normally distributed among small farmers. The farmer could be a free man who farmed Crown lands in return for a rent. He could also be subject to varying obligations to a lay or ecclesiastical lord. The labourer, without ties to a specific piece of land, could hardly not be free juridically but he was not free economically.

The richer labourer owned a team of oxen or mules with which he would contract to work for a year, being paid partly or wholly in kind. In the irrigated lands round the cities of Andalusia a skilled gardener could earn a good annual wage in money. The shepherd or cattle-herd was also generally paid by the year and paid well. He also had free access to a substantial diet of meat, milk, and cheese. Most labourers, however, lacking

[1] R. Serra Ruiz, *Honor, honra e injuria en el derecho medieval español* (Murcia, 1969), pp. 65–7, 249; E. de Hinojosa, *Obras*, ii (Madrid, 1955), 361–79.

oxen or special skills, were hired by the month or the day, which lasted as long as there was light; the pay decreased with the hours worked. The position of these labourers was precarious, especially as they had to pay taxes to the king or lord to whom they were subject. They would take any work they could get and were as much builders (in the winter) as, in the summer, they were harvesters. They took part in sporadic attacks on ecclesiastical lords or on Jews but their attachment to the land was too slight for them to engage in a specifically agrarian movement such as we find in Catalonia.

The farmers who populated northern Spain, from Asturias to Catalonia, lived mainly in isolated farms, unlike the villages or small towns inhabited by the labourers of Castile and Andalusia. Most farmers did not own their land but owed service to a lay or ecclesiastical lord. In Valencia and in Majorca—for about a century after the Christian conquest of 1229—free farmers subject only to the Crown predominated.

In Castile the situation of the small farmer seems to have deteriorated markedly from the thirteenth century onwards. Many royal estates passed to lay lords, with very serious consequences to the farmer, and lay lords' demands increased everywhere.

The non-free farmers of northern Spain owed a number of tributes and personal services to their lords, most of which had been converted into money payments by 1200. In the thirteenth century the movement of settlers southwards at first improved the position of the farmers who remained, but eventually the proprietors reacted by forcible methods in an attempt to keep what labour they could. The *remensa*, a fine the farmer had to pay to leave his farm, received legal sanction in Catalonia from 1283. Similar measures were taken in Castile, though there the Crown resisted rather longer the pressure brought to bear by the lay nobles. In 1293 we have a local peasant revolt in Catalonia. It is surprising that similar revolts are not attested for Aragon. There the *Fueros* of 1247 authorized a secular (not an ecclesiastical) lord to kill, by hunger, thirst, or cold, a peasant who had slain one of his fellows. Fourteenth-century Aragonese jurists maintained that any lord could do this. Roman law on slaves was applied to peasants. In 1332 the Justicia of Aragon recognized 'that the lord can maltreat his vassal whenever there is "just cause".' It is not clear who, other than the lord himself, was to determine justice in the matter.[1]

THE LIFE OF THE COUNTRYSIDE

The thirteenth-century *Libro de Alixandre* preserves the traditional scheme by which the labours of the soil were distributed among the months of the year. January was given up to roasting chickens and taking sausages down from where they hung, February to warming one's hands at the fire, March to planting, pruning, and digging vines. In April armies assembled for the year's campaign; as the days grew longer the peasant trained his vines. In May the country took on varied colours. In June harvests ripened and trees were charged with cherries, in July the harvest was gathered in, in August the threshing floors were busy. September was taken up by the vintage and by gathering walnuts and figs. In October the fields had to be sown again while the new wine was tried as it fermented. In November the pigs were brought in for the great pig-killing which closed the year as the clouds lay heavy over the Meseta. The days, the Archpriest of Hita tells us, grew short, while wheat had to be sown and the hills cleared of dead wood. Old women were telling stories by the fire.

The Archpriest gives us the Castilian winter: snow on the heights of the Guadarrama north of Madrid, oak fires in the huts of the shepherdesses beside which the traveller trapped by the weather or by his hostess might warm himself before eating a vast meal of rabbits, roasted partridges, great pieces of bread and suckling pig, a quart of good wine, cow's butter, smoked cheese, milk, berries, and trout. If he was less fortunate he might receive stale, dirty, black bread, bad wine, sour and thin, salted meat, and goat cheese.

The Cortes of Aragon and Catalonia, assembled at Lérida in 1214, proclaimed a constitution protecting a different sort of peasantry who enjoyed a settled existence on their farms with their domestic animals and farm instruments, their bee-hives and dovecots, mills and olive trees, until a sudden raid by a neighbouring noble on the lands of their own lord brought

[1] Sobrequés, pp. 223–30, 234–50, 253 f.; *Vidal Mayor*, ii, ed. G. Tilander (Lund, 1956), 510; J. Mª. Lacarra, op. cit. (p. 33, n. 1), pp. 226 f. For Portugal see Oliveira Marques, *Daily Life*, pp. 182–9.

disaster upon them. Ramon Lull wrote of the same type of peasant farmer, as he had known him in Majorca, and of his trials.

> The greatest and most useful skill in the world is that of the labourer, for all men live off labourers . . . the most injured and despised men in the world. All men and birds and beasts harm them, for kings and knights rob them and make them fight in war . . . and destroy their crops and vines and burn their houses.

A recent study has shed light on the development of Catalan peasant life in the plain of Vich during the thirteenth and fourteenth centuries. Here much land belonged to the local clergy, especially the cathedral chapter of Vich. The chapter proved much more successful than the local nobility in adapting to a money economy. The clergy substituted money rents for rents in kind from 1250 whereas the nobility only began to do this over sixty years later. The Church offered the rich peasants in the irrigated lands round Vich short contracts (for four years) in return for half the value of their harvests. Peasants farming unirrigated areas paid less. The clergy rented out large farms to the rich burgesses of the town. They were liberal in allowing the construction of mills, fed by dams or canals, which were used for textile production as well as for grinding wheat. Reservoirs were built and made available to farms growing vegetables and fruit trees. The general picture is one of a peasant society whose members were not badly off and could become free. The clerical landlords of Vich, unlike the local nobles, were not attacked in the peasant revolt of 1293. It may be, however, that this was an exceptionally fortunate region.[1]

SLAVES

Up to the virtual end of the 'Reconquest' of Islamic Andalusia the main source of supply of slaves for all the Christian kingdoms was war. Slaves were normally Muslims, captured during military campaigns. When the Christian conquests came to an end in the 1260s the supply of slaves fell off sharply in Castile and Portugal. It was maintained in the Crown of

[1] *Libro de Alixandre*, ed. R. S. Willis, Jr. (Princeton–Paris, 1934), pp. 440–3 (or *BAE* lvii. 220 f.); *Libro de Buen Amor*, vv. 968 f., 1030 f., 1272 f., ed. Criado de Val and Naylor, pp. 279 f., 300, 399; *Cortés de Cataluña*, i. 1. 91; R. Lull, *Libre de contemplació*, 121 (*Obres essencials*, ii. 365); J.-P. Cuvillier, *MCV*, 4 (1968), 73–103.

Aragon by the slave trade which began there relatively early. Muslim slaves appear in a list of custom dues for Barcelona of 1222.

THE CROWN OF ARAGON

By the 1240s Catalan merchants were buying slaves in North Africa and selling them in Italy as well as at home. Barcelona was rivalled as a slave market by Majorca. White slaves appear in documents from the 1250s, mulattos and blacks from the 1270s. A few Muslims who were settled in the Crown of Aragon sold themselves into slavery or were enslaved as a punishment for conversion from Islam to Judaism.

The number of slaves in Catalonia was high. Most slaves were found in towns and not in the country. Their owners were often far from rich and included artisans, though about 1300 the price of slaves rose. In Tortosa slaves sold wheat, cloth, wine, and oil, acted as money-changers, and ran inns. According to a Castilian jurist whose work was translated into Catalan in the thirteenth century, a slave could sue his master if he was not fed or was cruelly treated. Slaves could become free. They could make money and keep their earnings and so buy their liberty. Sometimes they could get a loan for the sum they needed to be free. In 1284 one slave lent his master money, thus getting permission to work wherever he liked. He was soon mortgaging his cape to a Jew, lending wheat to one villager and money to another. Muslim slaves—most slaves were still Muslims in the early fourteenth century—could be freed by the local Mudejar community, which they would then join. Slaves could also become Christians. The effect of baptism on their status depended on their master's religion. In Tortosa in the 1270s a slave who belonged to a Christian remained a slave after his baptism but he could be sold only to other Christians, not to Jews. If the Christian master had a child by his own slave, the child was born free, but the woman, unless already baptized, remained a slave. If a Christian had a child by a Muslim belonging to another person neither slave nor child were freed. Slaves could marry but they and their children did not thereby become free. It was far easier for the Muslim slave of a Jew to become free after baptism, on payment of a small sum to his master.

Although a slave in Tortosa could be kept in prison, in chains, the type of urban slavery revealed by the local law code and, in much more detail, by contemporary documents, does not seem to have been unbearable. In the Balearic Islands many more slaves worked on the land than in Catalonia. In 1335 it was stated that in Ibiza 'all the agricultural work is done by slaves'. The proportion of slaves to free peasants was probably far smaller in Majorca at this time but the number of slaves increased there as the fourteenth century advanced.[1]

CASTILE

Slaves appear in the documents of late thirteenth-century Castile, though they appear to have been far less numerous there than in Catalonia or Majorca. Families of Muslim slaves helped to work the farms round Seville and lived in the city. In 1272 one proprietor gave his wife 'Axa with his son and Mariem and Mahomat my Moorish weaver and the other five Moors I have in Mures and eight pairs of oxen'. In 1266 a Mozarabic Christian couple in Toledo owned ten Moorish slaves, nine of whom had been baptized. These slaves, and others in Toledo, were apparently from Murcia, which was in revolt that year. In 1287 some slaves in Toledo were working outside their master's house. Enfranchisement after a stipulated time was common.

Alfonso X's *Partidas* follow Roman law in holding that slaves can testify in cases of treason, in the event of the murder of their master or mistress, or in other exceptional cases. But they must be tortured first, 'because slaves are desperate men, on account of the condition in which they are, and every person should suspect that they will easily lie and conceal the truth when some force is not employed against them'. Alfonso also prescribes very severe punishment for those who conceal fugitive slaves; if they cannot pay the fine due they 'shall be publicly whipped'. The *Partidas* were not in force as law until 1348 but they considerably influenced legal procedure before that date.

[1] Verlinden, i. 258–319. For Tortosa see *Libre de les costums de Tortosa*, ed. B. Oliver (Madrid, 1881), especially II. xvii, vi (p. 99), VI. i–iv (pp. 268 f., 276); for Majorca see below, Vol. II, Part I, Ch. I, for Ibiza, I. Macabich, *BSAL* 17 (1918–19), 254 f.

PORTUGAL

The situation in Portugal appears to have been much the same as in Castile, except that the Portuguese began to bring in Muslims captured at sea or in raids on the North African coast before this was done by Castilians.

GRANADA

There were large numbers of Christian slaves, captured in war or in frontier or sea raids, in Islamic Granada and in North Africa. They seem to have been treated more harshly than Muslim slaves were by Christians. Christian slaves were made to work as servants, in domestic industries, and, especially, on the land. They replaced donkeys tied to the wheels (*norias*) which brought up water used for irrigation. They were under constant pressure to become Muslims. Many, no doubt, did so. Many of those who escaped attributed their good fortune to the intervention of San Domingo of Silos on their behalf. To San Domingo are attributed the murders of Muslims committed by the escaping Christians.[1]

[1] Verlinden, pp. 562–5, 600 f., 547 f., 238 f.; González, *Repartimiento de Sevilla*, i. 444; on Granada see J. Mª. de Cossío, *Al-Andalus*, 7 (1942), 49–112; *Partidas*, III. XVI. 13; VII. XIV. 23–9.

III

The International Church, International Law, Royal and Local Institutions

THE Iberian Church, in its internal workings, will be the subject of Chapter IV. Here I wish to discuss the relations between the Church, as an international body, and the monarchies of the peninsula, and try to see how these monarchies were affected by changes in the international law and political concepts of the thirteenth century.

THE PAPACY

By 1100 the reformed Gregorian papacy had asserted its control over the peninsula. Spanish bishops had had to acknowledge its jurisdiction: Spanish kings had become its vassals. The ancient Mozarabic liturgy had gradually given way to the Roman Office and Mass, Visigothic script to the international Carlovingian minuscule, which was to be replaced, in its turn, by the equally international 'Gothic' script. Foreign, particularly French, monks had founded or acquired monasteries throughout the peninsula. To the wave of Cluniac influence in the eleventh there succeeded the Cistercians in the twelfth and the Orders of friars in the thirteenth century.

For the papacy the thirteenth century began with the great Innocent III. It ended, disastrously, with the humiliation of Boniface VIII at Anagni and the removal to Avignon. Although the struggles with the Hohenstaufen emperors, their Italian allies, and later with France, took up most of their attention, the popes continually attempted to intervene in the Iberian peninsula, not always with success.

The papacy's most notable intervention was in 1245–8 when Sancho II of Portugal was replaced, with papal approval and encouragement, by his brother, Afonso III. Once he was king Afonso proved less satisfactory than the papacy had hoped. The papacy also intervened to assure the succession of Fernando III, first in Castile and later in León, while it defended Navarre against annexation by Castile. The popes repeatedly authorized the taxation of the Spanish clergy to support the conquest of Andalusia and later projects of conquest in Morocco. By the end of the thirteenth century ecclesiastical administration had been restored. Through the whole of the peninsula apart from the Islamic kingdom of Granada dioceses had been set up again. They were grouped in five ecclesiastical provinces, Toledo, Compostela, Braga, Seville, and Tarragona. Saragossa was to be added in 1318.[1]

Jaume I of Aragon records the advice he gave his son-in-law, Alfonso X of Castile, to keep the love of the Church and the people and to prefer these estates to the nobility. But (as will appear in Chapter IV) the Church in Castile was far weaker, *vis-à-vis* the Crown, than in Aragon. Alfonso seems to have paid little attention to Jaume's advice. He had little need to do so.

Jaume and Alfonso's heirs were even less amenable to papal influence than their fathers had been. In the 1280s serious conflicts arose between both Aragon and Castile and the papacy. Pere II of Catalonia–Aragon was invited to Sicily by the Sicilians, in rebellion against Charles of Anjou. The papacy considered Naples and Sicily a papal fief and had conferred them on Charles. When Pere refused to withdraw from Sicily he was excommunicated and deposed by the French pope Martin IV. Pope Martin also excommunicated the Infante Sancho who had raised a successful rebellion against his father Alfonso X and was acting as Pere's ally. The whole peninsula, except for Portugal and Seville—held by Alfonso—was placed under interdict, an interdict scarcely observed even by the Orders of friars. Martin IV then 'conferred' Catalonia–Aragon on Charles of Valois, the younger son of Philippe III of France. The attempt, through a French 'crusade' against Catalonia, to make this papal donation a reality failed miserably in 1285. Pere II had refused to allow the publication of the papal sentence in his dominions and continued to make church appointments, although appearing to observe the correct forms. In October 1284

[1] L. Gonzaga de Azevedo, *História de Portugal*, vi (Lisbon, 1944), 101–16; D. Mansilla Reoyo, *Iglesia castellano-leonesa y curia romana en los tiempos del Rey San Fernando* (Madrid, 1945), pp. 17, 26, 50–64; J. Goñi Gaztambide, *Historia de la Bula de la Cruzada en España* (Vitoria, 1958), pp. 139–86. For one diocese see R. I. Burns, *The Crusader Kingdom of Valencia*, 2 vols. (Cambridge, Mass., 1967).

he wrote to the pope who had excommunicated him, asking him to appoint the abbot of a vacant abbey. The same day, however, he appointed his brother Ferran, telling him: 'We concede to you the abbey in full legality, as the appointment belongs to Us and Our predecessors.'

In 1290 Pere's eldest son and successor, Alfons II, remarked that the Church had sent armies against Aragon for five years, 'changing the preaching of the Cross, which used to be preached for the aid of the Holy Land . . . into the conquest of Our Kingdom'. The papacy wished to subject a land, which the Lord of Hosts won for Christendom, to France. A few years later Jaume II of Aragon and Sancho of Castile were turning for weapons to the anti-papal propaganda of the Emperor Frederick II. The papacy was wise to annul its donation in 1295.[1]

CHURCH AND MONARCHY

Less far-reaching events than the depositions of kings often brought the monarchies of the peninsula into collision with the Church. Jaume I of Aragon did not become immune from censure because of his crusading against Muslims. He was repeatedly reproved by the papacy for attacking churches and for leading an immoral life. The papacy failed to persuade him to expel all Muslims from his realms. It also failed to persuade Sancho IV of Castile to give up his wife on the ground that they were too closely related. It was obvious to Sancho that the papacy was ruled by political considerations in this matter and he appealed to God to judge his cause.[2]

TAXATION OF THE CLERGY

There were a number of general grounds of conflict between Church and monarchy. By 1300 European monarchies considered that they were entitled to tax their clergy to help to pay

[1] Jaume I, *Libre dels feyts*, c. 498; A. Ballesteros, *Alfonso X*, pp. 1034–7; A. Marcos Pous, *Cuadernos de la Escuela española de historia y arqueología en Roma*, 8 (1956), 41 f.; Carini, *Archivi*, pp. 34 f., 195–200; Finke, *Acta* iii. 3, 9 f.; Rubió, *Documents* ii. 3 f.; Vincke, *Documenta*, pp. 26–33; see A. Fábrega Grau, in *Miscellanea Historiae Pontificiae*, 18 (1954), 161–80, and below, Part II, Ch. I, pp. 254 ff.

[2] J. Mª. Pou y Martí, *Miscell. Hist. Pont.*, *loc. cit.*, pp. 145–55; T. Ripoll, *Bullarium ordinis FF. Praedicatorum*, i (Rome, 1729), 478 f. (a bull of 1266); *Crónica de Sancho IV*, c. 2 (*BAE* lxvi. 73). See *Crónica de Fernando IV*, c. 13 (ibid., p. 139).

for anything that could remotely be construed as a crusade, but for this they needed papal permission. Alfons III of Catalonia–Aragon was particularly indignant when he was actually planning a crusade against Granada and was only given a tenth of clerical revenues for two years, whereas the king of France received this for six years.

When the kingdom was invaded its ruler assumed the right to tax the local church. In 1285 Pere II of Aragon compelled the Catalan clergy to assist him to defend Catalonia against a French 'crusade', which was accompanied by a papal legate. He had already taken a large sum from a papal collector to use against a Muslim rising. In 1294 Sancho IV of Castile told his officials to force his bishops and abbots to contribute the sums he needed to fight the Muslims besieging Tarifa. If they did not contribute voluntarily their goods were to be seized and sold.

CHURCH APPOINTMENTS

There was constant friction over church appointments. The formal royal right of presentation to church office (the later *Patronato Real*) began with Fernando III of Castile in 1236 and Jaume I of Aragon in 1238 but it was, as yet, very limited in the extent of the offices affected. In contrast, the papacy's direct interventions in appointments, both to bishoprics and to lesser benefices, greatly increased in number in the thirteenth century, though papal appointments often favoured royal candidates. More and more benefices were given to the same person who, increasingly often, did not reside in any of them since he was attached either to the papal or to a royal court.[1]

The kings of Aragon objected to the appointment of foreigners to benefices. In 1335 Alfons III claimed that Catalans and Aragonese did not receive benefices abroad while Italians and Frenchmen obtained church office in the Crown of Aragon. The kings of Aragon continually interfered in elections to bishoprics and abbeys though their repeated attempts to secure the appointment of a cardinal from their dominions proved unsuccessful. At times the king could act on the pope through his relations. A nephew of Clement V writes to Jaume II: 'I

[1] See below, Part II, Ch. I, p. 256; Ch. II, pp. 295 f.; Mansilla, op. cit., pp. 89 f., 166–253; P. Linehan, *The Spanish Church and the Papacy in the thirteenth century* (Cambridge, 1971), pp. 215 f.

have made our Lord the Pope dispose of the priory of Crosilla as Your Highness wished.'[1]

CONFLICTS OVER JURISDICTION

When the monarchies had been weak the Church had taken over many areas of life. Church courts tried all cases involving the most nominal cleric. They also claimed jurisdiction over all Christians in cases concerning tithes due to the Church, heresy, usury, and any question that involved an oath. This was a very wide field of jurisdiction. In addition, many bishoprics and abbeys in the northern part of the peninsula possessed temporal lordships. Jaume II of Aragon remarked in 1320 that if the Church's claims to judge 'by reason of sin' were all admitted, 'all secular jurisdiction would be done away'.

The monarchies protected the friars, whom it used and trusted, and also monasteries and the Military Orders, which were under ecclesiastical jurisdiction, from attack by the bishops or by nobles, who made war on the Orders as they did on each other. But at the same time there was a tendency to try to recover from the hands of the Church duties and powers it had assumed in the past. Hospitals, for instance, were being taken over by the local city or by the Crown. Sees founded in the thirteenth century, such as Majorca or Valencia, were endowed from tithes paid by the inhabitants of the diocese and did not receive the feudal rights of older dioceses. The Crown of Aragon began to buy up the feudal rights of the bishops of Vich and Tortosa. Jaume I tried to prohibit the coining of money by the bishop of Vich. In 1315 Jaume II acquired the episcopal right to mint through an exchange.

ATTACKS ON THE CHURCH'S TERRITORIAL LORDSHIPS

Temporal (feudal) rule by the Church was now resented in many places, particularly in Galicia. A bishop of Lugo was condemned to death by the city in the fourteenth century; he escaped with banishment. The inhabitants of Santiago de Compostela repeatedly attempted to become free of the rule of

[1] Finke, *Acta* iii, pp. xli, xliv-vii; R. Oliver Bertrand, *EEMCA* 4 (1951), 156–76; Vincke, *Documenta*, pp. 71 f., etc. For royal patronage in the Crown of Aragon see Vincke, *SFG* i, 10 (1955), 55–95; for papal provisions there, idem, *Römische Quartalschrift*, 48 (1953), 195–210. See also C. Bauer, *SFG* i, 11 (1955), 43–97.

their archbishop. They almost succeeded in doing so in 1347. In 1291 Orense was divided into the followers of the bishop and of the town council. The episcopal party, rising in arms, killed the royal judge and burnt down his house.

The case of Navarre has been studied in detail. In 1200 Pamplona, the one see in this small kingdom, possessed a large temporal sovereignty and played a decisive role in Navarre. The king could hardly enter Pamplona, his capital, without the bishop's leave. The local rulers worked to weaken the Church. The men of Pamplona preferred royal rule to ecclesiastical. Complaints were made that the bishop did not keep crime in the city under control.

In 1319 the bishop and cathedral chapter of Pamplona gave up their temporal rule. This concession eliminated a cause of perpetual quarrels between Church and monarchy. In return for a larger income the Church of Pamplona abandoned rights it could no longer enforce. It is notable that John XXII, one of the shrewdest and most determined popes of the century, confirmed the agreement.

The Church's concession did not end the monarchy's demands. The influence of French regalian ideas in Navarre may explain an edict of 1340 annulling gifts made to the local churches in recent years, though the right of the Church to acquire land—which would thus become free of tax—was also being limited in the Crown of Aragon and Portugal at this time.

In 1343 the French prince who was king of Navarre demanded military service from the bishop of Pamplona, who was to produce 100 armed horse and 300 foot, although he had given up his fiefs. This and other matters in dispute led to the Crown's seizure of the bishop's lands and palace. It took six years before they were recovered.[1]

In Castile the situation was much the same. A document of 1275 records the complaints of the church hierarchy. The clergy were forced to appear before lay judges while the sentences of church courts were not respected. In Seville in 1276

[1] J. Segura, *Revista de ciencias históricas*, 5 (1887), 212 f.; J. Vincke, *VII CHCA* i. 267–85; idem, *Documenta*, p. 251; F. Mateu y Llopis, *Numario hispánico*, 3 (1954), 187–91; M. Pérez-Villamil, *BRAH* 68 (1916), 361–90; M. Gaibrois de Ballesteros, *Sancho IV*, ii. 110 f.; J. Goñi Gaztambide, *Principe de Viana*, 18 (1957), 41–237; idem, ibid. 23 (1962), 5–194, 309–400; A. López Ferreiro, *Historia de la Iglesia de Santiago de Compostela*, vi (Santiago, 1903), 129–34.

the royal authorities were taking over the Church's revenues. In 1277 the archbishop of Seville complained that the Sevillanos paid no attention to his sentences of excommunication. Alfonso X was repeatedly obliged to intervene to protect the Church's rights. At other times Alfonso could act decisively against clerics whom he saw as usurping royal jurisdiction.

The situation continued unchanged under Sancho IV (1284–95) and Fernando IV (1295–1312). Fernando evidently tried to protect the clergy from being illegally taxed by the local authorities. He also defended the episcopal jurisdiction of the bishops of Lugo and Palencia. In May 1311 he issued a formal promise to respect ecclesiastical privileges. But two months later a number of the leading bishops of Galicia, Asturias, and Castile felt it necessary to form a 'Brotherhood' (*Hermandad*), to defend themselves against a general 'lack of justice'. We know that in 1301 a great noble had seized the possessions of the bishop of Coria and refused to return them without special concessions.

In 1302 the church council of Peñafiel agreed on measures to be adopted if the king attacked ecclesiastical liberties, in justice or taxation. If he did so, any place he visited would be put under interdict. The Castilian Church expected to be attacked. It was on the defensive.[1]

MILITARY ORDERS

By 1300 many men in western Europe considered that the Military Orders, founded for the crusades in the East, no longer fulfilled their functions. In Castile the main Orders were native foundations, Santiago, Calatrava, and Alcántara. These Orders were enormously rich but they still carried on some of the border fighting with Granada. In the Crown of Aragon and Navarre the principal Orders were the Temple and Hospital. In Navarre these Orders had become large landowners. In Aragon and Catalonia this may have been the case, though in Valencia the Orders continued to play an important military role in defence of the frontier with Castile and in raids against Granada. After the suppression of the Temple in 1312 its lands were given by the papacy to the Hospital. Jaume II of Aragon refused to agree to this principle being applied to his kingdoms.

[1] Ballesteros, *Alfonso X*, pp. 736–8, 740, 787 f., 840; *MHE* i, 265 f.; Gaibrois, iii, p. xiii; Benavides, ii. 16, 238 ff., 261 f., 283, 513 f., 800–5, 816.

His attempt to secure the Temple's lands for his Crown failed. In 1317, as a compromise, the Order of Montesa was created to defend the kingdom of Valencia. It received the property belonging to both the Temple and Hospital in Valencia and was placed directly under the Crown. (In Portugal the same aim was achieved by the transference of the Temple's goods there to the new native Order of Christ.) In Catalonia and Aragon the Hospital received the Temple's lands. It now owned 'almost all southern Catalonia' and large parts of Aragon. It possessed many castles and very wide jurisdiction. It was also exempt from most taxes.

Jaume II and his successors sought to reduce this privileged position, enjoyed by a body which was responsible not to the Crown but to the Master of the Order, with his headquarters in Rhodes, and to the papacy. By 1350 the monarchy had largely succeeded in acquiring control of the Hospital in the Crown of Aragon. The Hospital served the Crown in its wars, not only with the Muslims but with Christians, and gave large sums to the Crown. The support it gave Pere III in his struggle with the nobility in the 1340s was essential to his success. The papacy was unable to prevent this increase of royal power at the expense of one of the main international Orders which was theoretically subject only to itself. In 1372 the Crown of Aragon's control over the Military Orders was further strengthened when the Castilian Orders of Santiago and Calatrava gave up their lands in Aragon to the Hospital in return for lands claimed by the Hospital in Castile–León.

Although less research has been done on the Hospital in the other peninsular kingdoms the same subordination to the Crown seems to have obtained there. In 1298 the Portuguese members of the Order informed the Master that they had been forced to accompany their king in his war with Castile.[1]

CLERICAL PRIVILEGES: THEIR ABUSE

Royal officials complained of the clergy's abuse of their privileges. For one infringement of canon law all the inhabitants of a district or town could be put under interdict. The existence of

[1] A. Luttrell, 'The Aragonese Crown and the Knights Hospitallers of Rhodes, 1291–1350', *English Historical Review*, 76 (1961), 1–19. See also Vincke, *Documenta*, pp. 493 f.; Burns, i. 173–96; Benavides, ii. 170 f.

many nominal clerics was also a constant cause of trouble. These men lived as laymen but, when accused of a crime, claimed to have been tonsured and so to be subject only to the Church, which tended to impose far lighter sentences on them than they would have received from a lay court. These pseudo-clerics included butchers, carpenters, cobblers, minstrels. A banker went bankrupt in Valencia. He immediately claimed clerical protection against paying his debts. A doctor was denounced in Játiva for using magical arts. Terrified, he tonsured himself. Was he a genuine cleric?

In 1318 the Provincial Council of Tarragona issued a constitution attempting to deal with these 'clergy', but four years later Jaume II of Aragon claimed that matters were no better. He threatened to issue an edict himself. The question dragged on unresolved. Many questions were bound to do this in a society in which a large number of the more influential and educated, as well as wealthy members, were subject to the pope as spiritual sovereign, and at the same time to a local lay ruler. In the fourteenth century church law and administration were often in conflict with the law, government, and resources of the emerging monarchies of western Europe. The Crown could win practical control on occasion, as in the case of the Military Orders, but such triumphs were as yet fragile and insecure. Professor David Knowles, in a discussion of this question as it affected England, stated the situation very clearly:

It was not a matter of State versus Church as in the Roman Empire or the modern world. It was, rather, that two authorities, both acknowledged, at least so far as words went, by the whole population, claimed control of the activities of that population. In an ideal world a division and separation of jurisdiction might have been conceivable. In the world as it was—and is—the overlapping of rights and the extravagant claims of both sides ensured perpetual controversies.[1]

UNIVERSITIES

The thirteenth century saw the official 'foundation' of the leading universities of western Europe, Paris, Bologna, and

[1] Finke, *Acta* ii. 848, 852, 854 f., 858; iii, pp. lvii, 95 f.; David Knowles, *Thomas Becket* (London, 1970), p. 155; cf. Vincke, *Documenta*, pp. 146, 177 f.; T. del Campillo, *Documentos históricos de Daroca y su comunidad* (Saragossa, 1915), pp. 439 f. (1325); O. Engels, *VIII CHCA* ii. 253–62.

Oxford. There had been important schools at all these places long before they received papal or imperial charters. The Iberian universities, on the other hand, were deliberate creations of the different kingdoms of the peninsula. Between 1208 and 1214 Alfonso VIII of Castile granted royal privileges to the cathedral school of Palencia. About 1218 Alfonso IX of León gave a similar grant to the schools of Salamanca. Because of the royal patronage Salamanca received it far outdistanced Palencia, which, by about 1250, had ceased to be of any importance. A papal grant to Valladolid in 1262 did not enable it to compete with Salamanca, which had been well endowed from church revenues. In 1300 Jaume II of Aragon founded the first university in his Crown at Lérida—the attempt to create a university at Valencia in 1245 is not known to have produced any definite results.

Salamanca and Lérida were essentially schools of law, Roman and canon. The teaching of the liberal arts, grammar, rhetoric, and logic, and of medicine, was subordinate to that of law. There were no schools of theology at either place. For this subject Spaniards still had to travel abroad, especially to Paris. In Portugal the University of Lisbon was founded in 1288–9; it was transferred in 1308 to Coimbra. It was as deliberate a creation of the local monarchy as Salamanca in Castile or Lérida in Catalonia–Aragon, and was as completely focused on legal studies. None of these universities had a faculty to compare in numbers with Paris. Salamanca in 1254 had twelve professors with assured salaries, Lérida seven in 1300; Coimbra, in 1323, had six only.[1]

LAW: LOCAL AND ROMAN

Roman and canon law were rediscovered and reorganized in the twelfth century at Bologna. As systems they were incomparably superior to traditional customary law which varied

[1] H. Rashdall, *The Universities of Europe in the Middle Ages*, ed. F. M. Powicke and A. B. Emden, ii (Oxford, 1936), 63–114; C. M. Ajo G. y Saínz de Zúñiga, *Historia de las universidades hispánicas*, i (Madrid, 1957), 195–201; V. Beltrán de Heredia, *Ciencia tomista*, 81 (1954), 69–116 (origins of Salamanca); idem, *Cartulario de la Universidad de Salamanca (1218–1600)*, i (Salamanca, 1970), 37–124, 604–6; Burns, i. 101–6. See also Part II, Ch. I below, p. 284. For Portugal A. Moreira de Sá, *Revista da Faculdade de Letras* [of Lisbon], 3rd ser., 8 (1964), 5–38; idem (ed.), *Chartularium Universitatis Portugalensis (1288–1537)*, i (Lisbon, 1966), 85.

throughout western Europe. Roman law, as codified by the Emperor Justinian in the sixth century, dealt with powers and offices, marriage and property, obligations and punishments. It provided a model for a centralized state, with a prince and a hierarchy of functionaries, a theory of law and an organization of justice. Almost all Roman law could be, and was, taken over and applied by canon lawyers to the Church. It could also be used by the servants of the rising monarchies of the West.[1] Men trained in the revived legal systems could act as the administrators Castile–León and Catalonia–Aragon needed if they were to maintain any central government against the continual attempts of the nobility to disrupt these rudimentary states as they expanded southwards and took over Muslim populations. Hence the enthusiasm of Alfonso X of Castile for legal studies and his view of a 'Studium' or university as incomplete without 'Masters of Decretals and of Laws', i.e. of canon and Roman lawyers. Alfonso's *Siete Partidas* hold that 'the science of laws is the source of justice and the world profits from it more than from the other sciences . . . We hold it good that the Masters [of Laws] should have in Our dominions the honours that the ancient law commands'.[2]

In the twelfth and thirteenth centuries Roman and canon law, in the form of their practitioners, invaded the Iberian peninsula, as they did the rest of the Christian West. Italian 'Masters' of law are found in Castile from 1184. Fernando III and Alfonso X of Castile were surrounded by *sabidores de derecho*.[3] Their permanent Council included jurists trained in Bologna, later perhaps in Salamanca. Jacobo de las Leyes was one such lawyer. He was the author of an introduction to law written for his pupil Alfonso and also of the third *Partida*. Jaume I of Aragon was much influenced by his confessor, the great Dominican Ramon de Penyafort, by Vidal de Canellas, bishop of Huesca, and by Pere Albert, canon of Barcelona, all of whom had been trained as lawyers in Italy.

In the *Partidas* Alfonso X spoke as the Roman emperor he hoped to be (he had been elected 'King of the Romans' in

[1] G. Le Bras, *Institutions ecclésiastiques de la chrétienté médiévale*, i (Paris, 1959), 33.

[2] Alfonso X, *Partidas*, II. xxxi. 1 and 8.

[3] J. F. O'Callaghan, *American Historical Review*, 74 (1969), 1509, n. 26; *MHE* i. 197 (a document of 1262).

1256), but as an emperor of Muslims as well as Christians—the work is dated by the Hegira as well as by the Christian era. The *Partidas* are a summary of Roman and canon law. Alfonso's nephew, Don Juan Manuel, rightly said that Alfonso 'put into romance all ecclesiastical and secular laws'.[1]

The *Partidas* may not have been intended by Alfonso to be immediately applied as actual law but, as an authoritative Castilian version of the law studied in the universities, they naturally exercised great influence on lawyers. Alfonso's other legal compilations sought to impose common norms based on Roman law, interpreted by new royal judges, on his subjects. The *Espéculo*, apparently a first draft of the *Partidas*, was drawn on for a sentence issued by Alfonso in 1261. Under Alfonso and his successor, Sancho IV, there was a strong reaction in favour of local law. Many men agreed with the representatives of the city of Santiago de Compostela, who complained in 1253 that the Church there had learned clerics who, 'by their subtleties and by Roman laws . . . cause the *concejo* to lose its rights'.[2]

The kings of Aragon had the same view of law as Alfonso X. In 1247 Jaume I, the still-youthful conqueror of the Balearics and Valencia, claimed, as a new Justinian, to promulgate laws after victories in arms. His *Fueros de Aragón* introduced principles from canon law by which illegitimate sons had a right to share in an inheritance, and replaced the Germanic trial by ordeal by witnesses and written testimony. The systematization of law Jaume I aimed at met with the same bitter resistance in Aragon that greeted Alfonso X in Castile. But Jaume's successors gave even greater weight than he had done to Roman as well as canon law. Jaume II, in 1301, decreed that judges should pursue homicide as a crime against society irrespective of any arrangements arrived at between the murderer and his victim's relations. The Germanic idea of composition for blood guilt was being replaced by the Roman concept of public good.

[1] Juan Manuel, cited below, p. 218, n. 1. For the *Partidas* see R. Gibert, *Historia general del derecho español* (Granada, 1968), pp. 41–5; also E. N. van Kleffens, *Hispanic Law until the end of the Middle Ages* (Edinburgh, 1968), pp. 155–211; for canon law in *Partida* I see J. Giménez y M. de Carvajal, *Anthologica annua*, 2 (1954), 239–348; 3 (1955), 201–338.

[2] E. Procter, 'The Towns of León and Castile as Suitors before the King's Court', *English Historical Review*, 74 (1959), 16; J. L. Bermejo Cabrero, *Hispania*, 30 (1970), 169–77.

Only Navarre, among the monarchies of the peninsula, maintained in its *Fuero general* (1266–1304) Germanic practices such as the judicial duel and ordeals. Even there Roman law influenced legal practice in the royal court.[1]

ROMAN LAW AND POLITICAL CONCEPTS

Roman law was bound to influence politics and political ethics very considerably. It contained a number of commanding principles, the notion of equity, that of the natural equality of all men, and of the sovereignty of the people, while also proclaiming the principle of royal absolutism; once the 'people' had conferred their mandate it could not be revoked. The ideas of 'public utility', of the supremacy of the 'patria' had re-entered a world long oblivious of the State and structured by feudal bonds of vassalage which united only individual men.[2]

Both Alfonso X in Castile and Pere Albert in Catalonia used Roman law to interpret a world for which feudal law had ceased to provide an adequate frame of reference. By interpreting the world they knew, including the existing feudal law, by Roman legal concepts, they greatly changed it both for their contemporaries and for later generations. Feudal forms and institutions did not disappear overnight; they survived until the eighteenth century. But they had become essentially irrelevant since society was now focused on 'the prince of the land', the 'sovereign lord', 'superior' because he represented the overriding claim of 'public utility', almost 'reason of State'.

In Catalonia, more clearly than in Castile, society was becoming a unity centred on a dynasty. The Catalan chronicles of the thirteenth century express this sense of unity around the House of Barcelona. Pere Albert sees only one superior court of appeal for all feudal cases 'throughout Catalonia'. Only the prince, the count of Barcelona, has a '*general* right of jurisdiction'

War against Islam is only to be waged by a 'superior lord', who can command 'his vassals and other men *naturally* his'.[3]

[1] Gibert, pp. 70–2, 79–82; F. A. Roca Traver, *El Justicia de Valencia, 1238–1321* (Valencia, 1970), p. 230. See below, Part II, Ch. I, pp. 276 ff. For Navarre see J. Mª. Lacarra, *AHDE* 11 (1934), 457–67.

[2] See Gaines Post, *Studies in Medieval Legal Thought, Public Law and the State, 1100–1322* (Princeton, N.J., 1964); E. H. Kantorowicz, *Selected Studies* (Locust Valley, N.Y., 1965), pp. 157–61, 308–22.

[3] J. A. Maravall, *Estudios de historia del pensamiento español, Edad Media*, i (Madrid, 1967), pp. 89–140, 143–56.

In other words the 'natural' lord is above the feudal superior. In the *Book of Deeds* of Jaume I a knight says to the king: 'Though he is my lord, you are my natural lord.' Even in Castile, in the perpetual rebel Don Juan Manuel, one finds a recognition of the king as '*natural* lord'. The 'natural' relationship of all men of the 'land' (*tierra*) to the king appears. Juan Manuel recognizes that there is a duty 'to defend law and the land to which men are born'. Pere Albert also holds that 'men are bound to fight for the land and to obey the king'.[1]

The existence of such a thing as the will of the people was gradually being recognized. In 1304 Jaume II of Aragon acknowledged that the claim of Alfonso de la Cerda to Castile was hopeless—despite his superior rights as the legitimate dynastic heir to Alfonso X—'seeing, above all, that the cities and other peoples of the kingdoms of Castile were obstinate and firm in their decision not to receive Don Alfonso as Lord'. By 1240 the Navarrese had already affirmed that they, as free men, were the source of law, and that their king owed his power to election by his people. In 1328 Navarre declared that Jeanne d'Evreux should be its ruler, in preference to Philippe VI of France.[2]

INSTITUTIONS: ROMAN LAW AND THE CORTES

Roman law influenced the growth of royal institutions. The Chancery, the Council, and the royal central court were being slowly organized in the Iberian monarchies by men trained in the revived laws.[3] Roman legal influence appears even more strikingly in the development of the Cortes, the parliamentary assemblies of the peninsula which were gradually emerging from sessions of the full royal court held on exceptional occasions.

Alfonso X, recognizing the dependence of the monarchy on the person of the king, holds that all the subjects of a king who is a child should be concerned for the kingdom, 'for the

[1] Jaume I, *Libre dels feyts*, c. 133 (see Part II, Ch. I); Juan Manuel, *Libro de los estados*, i. 86, 92 (*BAE* li. 332 f., 337); Pere Albert, *Commemoracions*, ed. J. Rovira i Ermengol (*ENC* A43–4) (Barcelona, 1933), p. 187. See *Partidas*, IV. xxv. 5.

[2] Salavert, *Cerdeña* ii. 141 f. J. Mª. Lacarra, *El Juramento de los Reyes de Navarra (1234–1329)* (Madrid, 1972).

[4] See below, Part II, Ch. I, pp. 282 f., and Ch. II, pp. 297 ff. For Navarre see F. J. Zabalo, *El registro de comptos del reino de Navarra de 1280* (Pamplona, 1972).

matter of the king *touches all men* and all have a part in it'. The maxim of Roman and canon law, 'quod omnes tangit', was to be one basis for seeking the participation of all 'estates', including the representatives of towns, in the Cortes.[1]

The informal representation of towns in Cortes is attested in León from 1188, in Castile from 1217 at least, in Aragon from 1164, and in Catalonia from 1214. In Castile–León from 1255, at the latest, and in Catalonia and Aragon from at least 1283, the representatives sent to Cortes had to possess the 'full power' (*plena potestas*), that Roman and canon law demanded, as procurators, corporate representatives of their cities. This stipulation was clearly to the advantage of the ruler, who wanted the cities represented to be bound by the decisions of their agents. He needed the towns' support and subsidies against his nobles. As time passed the Cortes of León–Castile and of Catalonia, Aragon, and Valencia were to be concerned with a wide range of other subjects, judicial questions, the regulation of the coinage, weights, measures, prices, trade, usury, Muslims, and Jews.[2]

FEUDALISM IN THE PENINSULA

The waves of Roman legal influence that entered the peninsula in the twelfth and thirteenth centuries met with strong resistance from entrenched local customs and especially from feudal institutions. These had long existed in Catalonia. In the other Christian states, from Portugal to Aragon, feudalism had been greatly reinforced by increased contact with France since the late eleventh century. Terms such as vassal, hommage, and fief were now used throughout the peninsula although they appeared less often in popular than in learned works, such as the *Partidas*.

It was probably largely under the influence of French practice that the government of districts, the command of a castle, or the right to receive a local tax, was conceded as a *prestimonio* in Castile–León or as an 'honour' in Navarre and Aragon. In

[1] Alfonso X, *Espéculo*, II. xvi. v, cited by Maravall, op. cit., p. 162; G. Post, op. cit., pp. 163–238.

[2] G. Post, pp. 70–9; Procter, loc. cit., pp. 1–22; J. F. O'Callaghan, 'The Beginnings of the Cortes of León-Castile', *American Historical Review*, 74 (1969), 1503–37. For Catalonia–Aragon, see below, Part II, Ch. I, pp. 278 ff. and, for Portugal, C. Sánchez-Albornoz, *La Curia Regia Portuguesa, siglos XII y XIII* (Madrid, 1920).

Castile–León concessions of offices, lands, or castles by kings or by secular or ecclesiastical magnates to nobles—who might or might not be called their vassals—were not inheritable and could generally be revoked. They were held by the 'custom of Spain', to distinguish them from Catalan feudal usage. In Catalonia, as in France, it was far more difficult to reclaim a 'fief', once it was granted. In Navarre and in Aragon, from 1283, it was very difficult to take an 'honour' from the *rico hombre* to whom it belonged and who had usually inherited it. Catalonia had been organized on feudal principles from the time of its conquest by the Franks in the ninth century. Long before 1200 the full feudal hierarchy existed there, with lesser nobles (*cavallers*) below barons (*richs hòmens*). The hierarchy culminated in the count of Barcelona, who normally reserved for himself jurisdiction over the more important civil and criminal cases.

The virtual end of the 'Reconquest' in the thirteenth century brought with it great changes both in Catalonia and Castile–León. In Catalonia the development of trade and industry promoted the growth of a bourgeoisie which generally sided with the ruler against the nobility; in Castile–León, on the other hand, there was an increase in the number of men termed 'vassals' both of the king and the magnates while the temporary nature of the grants they received was largely forgotten. Far more land was granted, either for past services or for military service in the future, to favoured nobles as their unrestricted property, which they could leave to their descendants. Many nobles were now rewarded in money rather than land but, even so, the growth of large estates which could not be reclaimed from their noble owners is one of the main features of the next two centuries.

The power of the *terratenientes* of Castile–León was strengthened by the grant of many 'immunities', mainly of jurisdiction over estates and their peasant population. This type of grant, because of French influence, had become much more frequent in the west of the peninsula from the twelfth century onwards. The lord of an 'immune' or exempt estate controlled the justice, taxes, and administration within the estate, issued all local laws and had a right to the military service of his dependants. He was bound to the king only by vassalage, a bond which had proved fragile in Carolingian France. In Castile and León the king could intervene if the possessor of an immunity did not 'do justice' to his men. Royal officials could pursue those guilty of grave crimes into 'immune' areas. The Crown normally maintained the right to judge cases on appeal, to found markets and fairs in seignorial domains, and to call up men for military service. Nevertheless, a very large proportion of Castile–León consisted, in the fourteenth century, of areas under nobles, Military Orders, episcopal sees, or abbeys, which were, in general, exempt from royal inspection or control.[1]

[1] L. García de Valdeavellano, 'Las instituciones feudales en España', in F. L. Ganshof, *El feudalismo* (Barcelona, 1963), pp. 245–305, with the many bibliographical references there given. See the review by S. de Moxó, *Hispania*, 24 (1964), 123–33.

IV

The Christian Church in the Peninsula

THE traditional view of the late-medieval Church, both secular and monastic, in the Iberian peninsula, is that it was rich, privileged, and powerful. Recent research suggests that this picture is almost the reverse of the truth. When the 'Reconquest' virtually came to an end in Castile–León in 1248 the Church there was far from rich. For over thirty years it had been steadily milked to finance the Crown's campaigning in Andalusia. Even more serious, a third of its future income from the ecclesiastical tithes paid by the general population had been granted in 1247 by the papacy to the Crown. This grant was never to be recovered. Nor was the Church, as a whole, rewarded for its financial sacrifices by large grants of property in the conquered south. The new archdiocese of Seville was well endowed but the bishoprics of León and Old Castile were conspicuously ill treated. In the second half of the thirteenth century, the Military Order of Santiago and numbers of bishops and cathedral churches fell into the hands of Italian banking houses. The bankers were supported in their claims by the ecclesiastical penalties imposed by the papacy on indigent clerical debtors. In 1283–4 the primate of Spain, Archbishop Gonzalo of Toledo, holder of one of the richest sees in Castile, was forced to spend over a year near Avignon until he had paid some of his debts to the Chiarenti Company of Pistoia.

In the Crown of Aragon the situation was less desperate. Although the Church, particularly in Aragon itself, was not very rich, the bishops of the province (of Tarragona) could and did act in concert to a far greater extent than their colleagues in Castile–León. They were able to defend their corporate interests and to exercise some control over grants made to the Crown.[1]

[1] P. Linehan, *The Spanish Church*, pp. 101–51; for the traditional view see Sobrequés, in *Historia de España*, ed. Vicens, ii. 75, 163–7; see also E. Benito Ruano, *La Banca toscana y la Orden de Santiago durante el siglo XIII* (Valladolid, 1961); J. Mª. Lacarra, in *Aragón, cuatro ensayos*, i (Saragossa, 1960), 238.

It is far easier to estimate the Church's wealth in material goods than it is to assess its spirituality. There is little reason to suppose, however, that the Iberian Church possessed either unity within itself or unity of purpose with the papacy. The levels both of sexual morality and of education within the clergy seem to have been remarkably low and the clergy's relations with the laity correspondingly poor. The older Religious Orders, both male and female, though still an impressive feature of the social scene, did not flourish. In all these matters Castile was far worse off than the Crown of Aragon. Only the friars' rise seemed, as everywhere in western Europe, to redeem the general decline. Yet, before the thirteenth century was over, the friars' light, too, was greatly dimmed.

THE SECULAR CLERGY: BISHOPS

The secular clergy was deeply divided among itself. It was as hard for the higher clergy not to be identified with the nobility from which it was recruited, as it was for the lower clergy not to be merged with the peasantry from which its members came. A sharp differentiation existed between the two classes of clergy. In 1252 Jaume I of Aragon declared that the clergy of Valencia should pay a tax on the property they owned in and around the city, but clerics of noble birth were only to pay this tax for the property they held from the Crown. The bishop of Saragossa who journeyed to Barcelona in 1262 with his suite borne by at least seventy horses and mules could hardly avoid being the great noble he appeared to the world. Ramon Lull's novel *Blanquerna*, written in the 1280s or 1290s, tells us that the cathedral clergy considered themselves dishonoured if their bishop did not travel with a large retinue and have gold and silver cups on his table and a great company of guests entertained by minstrels, singing and dancing, speaking words which contradicted the grace said at table. The higher clergy also believed that their bishop should have 'many beasts in his stable, many clothes in his wardrobes, much money in his chests'. In another novel, the *Book of Wonders*, Lull refers to a bishop who 'had a nephew, whom he loved more than God, for when he died he left his nephew 1,000 silver marks and only 1,000 sous to the poor of Christ'.

Alvaro Peláez, bishop of Silves in Portugal, writing in the

1320s, declared that his Castilian colleagues were 'rarely found in their churches but spend almost their whole lives in princely courts, the Roman Curia, and their family's houses'. They normally 'heard' the Divine Office 'lying in bed, moving around, or judging cases'. There is a great deal of evidence to support this harsh view of the leaders of the Castilian Church. A recent historian declares that 'the royal court exercised a fatal fascination over the entire peninsular Church'.

THE PAPACY AND THE BISHOPS

The papacy found Spanish bishops far from easy to bring to heel. Spaniards were, not unnaturally, disinclined to finance papal crusades to the East when they were already burdened with the support of continual royal campaigns against Muslims in Spain itself. Emissaries from the Curia were at times set upon and wounded, or almost drowned, by the local clergy. Less dramatically but even more effectively, papal provisions and requests for money could be simply ignored. In 1313–14 the expenses of papal collectors touring Castile–León actually exceeded their receipts. (The situation seems to have been better for the papacy in Aragon and Navarre; the only published collectors' accounts for these kingdoms, for 1279–80, show substantial receipts.) It was as difficult for the papacy to persuade the bishops of Castile to gather in council and apply its reforming decrees as it was to raise money from them for papal projects. Papal legates came and went. Occasionally they issued decrees intended to secure a properly educated and continent clergy but their legislation was often not applied. Provincial and diocesan councils met fairly frequently in the Crown of Aragon, very seldom in Castile. In 1279 the Castilian bishops informed the pope that 'the bishops and churches are not free to meet and discuss their grievances or to refer them to the Apostolic See'. They were under royal control and their sporadic attempts to assert 'ecclesiastical liberty' were short-lived. Alvaro Peláez stated the position in symbolic terms. For him a bishop was far above a king in dignity but he had to admit that 'the vile prelates of Spain kiss the hands of kings. I confess that I, rather by fear than humility, was forced to kiss the right hand of the king of Portugal, although I do not hold fiefs from him'.

In the Crown of Aragon the Church was less dependent on the monarchy than it was in Castile. Catalan and Aragonese bishops were able to meet regularly in council. The difference between the conciliar activity here and the sloth of Castile was also partly due to the presence in Catalonia (and absence in Castile) of a group of reforming bishops recruited from the Dominican Order in the 1240s and under the influence of the leading canonist and former Master General of the Dominicans, St. Ramon of Penyafort. Although even in Catalonia too much depended on the personality of the archbishop of the province, and not all archbishops of Tarragona were interested in reform, the general tide was set towards reform in the Crown of Aragon whereas it was set against it in Castile.

Don Juan Manuel tells us that the duties of the clergy included participation in war against Muslims. The figure of an archbishop of Toledo at Las Navas de Tolosa in 1212 or of his successor at the battle of the Salado in 1340, leading the Christian hosts against the infidel, might seem glorious to a Christendom whose greatest patron saint, an apostle of Christ, was normally represented killing Moors, but this warlike mentality sometimes brought undesirable accompaniments with it. They appear, for instance, when a diocesan council of Santiago itself was obliged to decree that 'if the clergy of the diocese use armed resistance against the bishop, archdeacon, or archpriest they are excommunicated'.[1]

Even one of the best bishops of the time, Arnault de Barbazan, a French bishop of Pamplona, could use violent methods. Irritated with a canon of his cathedral, Barbazan summoned him to appear at his palace. When his brothers appeared to represent the canon, the bishop's armed men rushed out and tried to kill them. It took eight months before a superior ecclesiastical judge ordered the bishop to raise his excommunication of the canon for refusing (wisely) to appear before him.

[1] Huici, *Colección*, i. 553 ff.; Soldevila, *Pere el Gran*, i. 1, p. 56; Lull, *Blanquerna*, 58, 68 (*Obres essencials*, i. 194, 211); *Libre de meravelles*, viii. 79 (p. 442); Alvarus Pelagius, *De planctu ecclesiae*, ii. 20, 18 (Venice, 1560), fols. 55, 52; Linehan, pp. 6 f., 11–4, 37 f., 78 f., 147, 174, 183 f., 188–240, 247–9 (the quotation in the text from p. 239); *Rationes decimarum Hispaniae*, ed. J. Rius Serra, ii (Barcelona, 1947), 301–7; R. I. Burns, *The Crusader Kingdom of Valencia*, i (Cambridge, Mass., 1967), 22–8; for the revenues of the diocese of Valencia, ibid., pp. 131–72; Juan Manuel, *Libro de los estados*, ii. 3 (*BAE* li. 344); A. López Ferreiro, *Historia de la Santa A. M. Iglesia de Santiago de Compostela*, v (Santiago, 1902), 80 (appendices).

In 1321 the suggestion was made to Jaume II that he should found many new bishoprics in Aragon proper, thus dividing up the revenues enjoyed by only a few sees. If any rebellion occurred in Aragon the few bishops there joined the rebel forces or else they took sides in the feuds of the nobility. 'The bishops of our land,' the king was told, 'have become as warlike as those of Germany, not against lesser men but even against your sons.'[1]

SEXUAL MORALITY

Clandestine marriages were frequently denounced by church councils. Great numbers of illegitimate children appear – cited as 'Bort', 'Burdus', 'Spurius'—in the documents of the thirteenth and fourteenth centuries in the records of all social classes. The clergy were no exception. They simply had the misfortune that their sins were more fully recorded than those of their lay contemporaries, since they flagrantly contradicted the celibate rule they were required to observe.[2]

In 1251 Pope Innocent IV revoked earlier sentences issued by a papal legate which excommunicated all priests, deacons, subdeacons, and beneficiaries who publicly kept women, and the women themselves. The sentences were suspended because they affected too many people. They were changed to a fine for beneficed clergy and half the amount for the non-beneficed and for the women involved. This system of fines seems also to have proved ineffective. In 1359 the bishop of Tortosa decreed that no one in Holy Orders should make his son his heir or leave him a legacy. Other councils had tried another tactic. They ordered that any cleric's concubine should be buried in the pit used for dead mules.

In 1318 Pope John XXII wrote to the bishops of the province of Toledo complaining that they caused great scandal to the faithful, publicly breaking the vow of celibacy and dividing the Church's goods among their offspring instead of using them for pious purposes. A council held in 1321–2 in Castile by John's legate declared that no cleric, secular or religious, should officiate at the baptism, betrothal, or marriage of their child or

[1] J. Goñi Gaztambide, *Principe de Viana*, 23 (1962), 90 f.; Finke, *Acta* ii. 855 f.

[2] Tejada y Ramiro, iii. 574; Segura, *Aplech*, pp. 238 ff.

grandchild, or endow them with the Church's property. The council established a graduated system of fines by which the beneficed cleric who refused to abandon his 'concubine' would eventually lose all his revenues, and the non-beneficed could not receive a benefice. The clerics with 'infidel' (Jewish or Muslim) mistresses were to be imprisoned for two years by their bishop. Those laity or communities who had 'compelled' clerics to take mistresses were to be excommunicated. The Provincial Council of Toledo in 1323 forbade the wife or child of the celebrant to assist him at Mass. That this legislation was ineffectual appears from the constant repetition of the same complaints.[1]

Literary evidence highlights the picture provided by contemporary laws. The *Debate de Elena y María*, written about 1280, is a realistic satire in the form of a debate between two sisters, both *hijas de algo*, one of whom loves a poor knight, a *hidalgo*, the other a cleric. In contrast to the *hidalgo*, the cleric 'eats and drinks and lies in fine beds'. He has fur capes, mules, horses, and vassals, wheat, wine and money, 'he lives as a noble'. Kings and counts, nobles and great ladies are happy to kiss his hand. Clearly the fact that he has a mistress is far from spoiling this picture. Any lack of worldly honour she may suffer is compensated for by her lover's riches.

The Archpriest of Hita gives us an unsurpassed portrait of Castilian life in the fourteenth century. It would be hard to know how far the picture of the clergy he shows us going through their clerical duties as pure routine with their minds fixed only on women was true to fact if one only had his book as evidence but there is much to corroborate it. In 1295 thirteen of the twenty-four clerics attached to the Church of Artajona in Navarre were publicly living with women. In the whole diocese of Pamplona there were 450 clergy with mistresses. They were found throughout the diocese, in villages and towns, except for Pamplona itself.

If the secular authorities had resolutely supported the conciliar prescriptions clerical concubinage might have been put down. In fact—as in the case of Jews and Mudejars—the civil

[1] Linehan, pp. 51 f.; Villanueva, v. 356; J. Goñi Gaztambide, *Hispania Sacra*, 8 (1955), 409–13; Tejada y Ramiro, iii. 325 f., 396, 482–6, 514; vi. 49; Burns, i. 112 ff.

authorities' theory differed greatly from their practice. Alfonso X's *Partidas* decree that a cleric marrying or living with a woman should lose his benefice, and his wife, if a vassal of the Church, should be enslaved. But in *practice* Alfonso granted the clergy of the diocese of Salamanca the right to leave their property to their descendants. An illustration to Alfonso's *Cántigas* represents a cleric in bed with his concubine, as a normal fact of life.

The Cortes of Castile were equally ineffective in their attempts to deal with the problem. In 1351 they complained that clerics' mistresses, 'barraganas de clérigos', formed a caste on their own. They were ordered to wear distinctive head-dress but in 1380 the Cortes complained that they had not done so. Earlier in the fourteenth century Alvaro Peláez had denounced the clergy of the peninsula for entering into public contracts with women, especially of noble blood, and endowing them with the Church's goods. The bishop also remarked that the clergy often seduced their female penitents. He believed that there were almost as many children of the clergy in Spain as of the laity.[1]

There existed a large clerical 'fringe', denounced repeatedly by church councils and royal decrees, carrying arms, drinking in taverns, going hunting with their falcon or sparrow-hawk. In 1316 the bishop of Gerona denounced the clergy in his diocese who kept taverns and gambling hells, cultivated fields, acted as shopkeepers, usurers, or artisans or as municipal police. If they continued to do any of these things they would lose their clerical privileges.

One reason for this behaviour was that most clergy—not only those in minor orders—habitually dressed as laymen, despite decrees to the contrary, and often wore beards instead of tonsures. In 1267 a council at León ordered the local clergy not to wear red or green clothes or large, enveloping capes. In 1274 another council, in the Crown of Aragon, forbade the

[1] *Debate de Elena y Maria*, ed. R. Menéndez Pidal, *RFE* I (1914), 52–96; see O. H. Green, *Spain and the Western Tradition*, i (Madison, 1963), 53–60; J. Mª. Jimeno Jurio, *Documentos medievales artajoneses (1070–1312)* (Pamplona, 1968), pp. 281, 293; Goñi, *Principe de Viana*, 18 (1957), 189; Alfonso X, *Cántigas*, no. 151 (ii. 139 f.); J. Guerrero Lovillo, *Las Cántigas* (Madrid, 1949), lám. 165; *Partidas* I. VI. 41; *MHE* i. 193; *Cortes de León*, ii. 14 f., 304; Alvarus Pelagius, op. cit., ii. 27, fols. 64v, 67.

clergy to wear elaborately adorned tunics, with gold or silver buttons, striped garments, or long hoods.[1]

LACK OF CLERICAL EDUCATION

Many of the more striking defects of the secular clergy were due to their lack of training. No theological faculties of importance existed at any Iberian university until the end of the fourteenth century. The court of Alfonso X of Castile encouraged scientific and legal studies, but not theology. Alfonso's *Primera Partida* draws its theology direct from the Catalan Dominican Ramon of Penyafort. Theology was systematically studied and taught only in the convents of friars, especially Dominican and Franciscan. In the Crown of Aragon, from the mid-fourteenth century, the friars were appointed to teach theology in most cathedral churches to the members of the chapter. Cathedral chapters, in Castile and Aragon, were repeatedly ordered to send some of their younger members abroad to study theology or canon law. Councils held at Valladolid and Lérida, in 1228–9 prescribed that all beneficed clergy, except for the old, should be forced to learn to speak Latin, 'for many want the tonsure to have the freedom [i.e. the privileges] of the clergy and do not want to learn'. In Castile, from 1322 onwards, the attempt was made to establish several grammar schools in each diocese and in the more important monasteries, and schools of logic in the larger cities where the secular clergy could study. It is not clear how effective this attempt proved but it seems likely that many of the rustic clergy were well represented by the ignorant hermit of Lull's *Libre de Sancta Maria* (about 1290) who confessed he was unable to pray to the Virgin except for material goods, for his donkey, his chickens, and for the cure of his dog, which had been bitten by a wolf.

In *Blanquerna* Lull displays the bitter resistance of cathedral canons at the thought of devoting a third of their revenues to the study of theology and canon law. In the novel the reform is (as always) carried through, but how often was it carried out in fact?[2]

[1] Villaneuva, xiii. 340–2; Tejada y Ramiro, iii. 389; F. D. Swift, *James I*, p. 241, n. 1.

[2] See Ch. III, p. 101, n. 1, above; P. Sanahuja, *Historia de la seráfica provincia*

In a visitation of the diocese of Pamplona in 1318 only one beneficed cleric is listed with a Master's degree. Cathedral canons might be expected to be better educated but at an election of new canons of Pamplona cathedral the same year only two of the twenty-three electors were Doctors and three did not know how to write. In 1330 Bishop Arnault de Barbazan of Pamplona stated that he would refuse ordination to those not familiar with Latin grammar. This was an extreme measure by a reforming bishop. It evidently failed. In 1354 Bishop Arnault was obliged to publish a compendium of theology in romance for clergy ignorant of Latin. This summary exposition of doctrine was so badly needed that it was still in use in the sixteenth century. By about 1350 the papacy had accepted a lower standard of education for beneficed clergy in Spain than it would have tolerated elsewhere. Other cathedral chapters, notably in Catalonia, included a higher proportion of educated men than Pamplona. However, the library of Gonzalo Palomeque, canon of Toledo, who died in 1273, with its range of translations of Aristotle, Avicenna, and Averroes, was very exceptional for the age. That of the famous lay doctor, Arnau de Vilanova (d. 1311), with its Greek and Hebrew Biblical manuscripts and its Arabic scientific works, was probably unique. These libraries were, of course, largely irrelevant to any theological or pastoral concern.[1]

THE HIGHER CLERGY: CATHEDRAL CHAPTERS

The behaviour of the higher clergy was not edifying. Señor Goñi Gaztambide's studies of the diocese of Pamplona reveal successive archdeacons who were principally occupied in causing trouble to their bishop, the municipal authorities, and the cathedral chapter. One archdeacon refused either to provide the existing canons with a minimum wage to live on or wood for their kitchen fire, or to pay for prayers for deceased members of the chapter. Punishments, including excommunica-

[1] Goñi, *Principe de Viana*, 18 (1957), 189 f.; ibid. 23 (1962), 84, 88 f.; J. Vincke, *SFG* i. 9 (1954), 144–63; R. Beer, *Handschriftenschätze Spaniens* (Vienna, 1894), no. 127; Carreras Artau, i. 79–83; Linehan, pp. 236 f.

de Cataluña (Barcelona, 1956), pp. 170–4, 185–93; V. Beltrán de Heredia, *Estudis franciscans*, 34 (1924), 38–58; idem, *Escorial*, 3 (1941), 289–98; idem, *RET* 6 (1946), 313–57; Tejada y Ramiro, iii. 325, 332; vi. 66; R. Lull, *Libre de Sancta Maria*, Pròleg (*Obres essencials*, i. 1158); *Blanquerna*, 68 (ibid. 211 f.).

tion and suspension of revenues, seem to have had little effect on him. One is reminded of the archdeacon in Lull's *Blanquerna*, a steadfast opponent of any reform. He is depicted feasting on meat and partridges and travelling out to dine at one of his castles with barrels of wine and hens 'already killed, so that they might be tenderer, and white bread, sauces and sweetmeats. The archdeacon was very fat and a great trencherman'. The Master of the Schools in Lull's novel was nearly as rich. By 'cornering' corn he was able to buy a castle for his nephew. A historical parallel to this exists in the canon of Valencia who died in 1256, leaving 'my castle at Espioca', 'my armour', 'all my vineyards', 'my wine cellar', and many buildings.

The members of the Pamplona chapter, when 'visited' by the bishop in 1265, had a casual attitude towards the disciplined communal life they were supposed to lead, as Regular Canons of St. Augustine. Not all the canons ate in the refectory or slept in the common dormitory. In the refectory the noise was so great during meals that it was hardly possible to hear the Biblical or patristic text being read aloud. Many canons went outside the refectory on fast days to eat meat. A similar confusion obtained in the choir offices. Some canons, instead of joining in the chant or listening to the reading, carried on conversations in loud voices, others moved around within and outside the choir during the service. The bishop ordered that this behaviour should be severely punished. The prior was also to see that all canons went to confession three times a year. Similar evidence exists for Catalan cathedrals (Vich, Gerona) and for Castile–León. In many cathedrals only a small minority of the canons bothered to take priest's orders. They wished to be able to return to lay life if opportunity beckoned.[1]

THE CLERGY AND THE SACRAMENTS

The clergy often neglected the sacraments. In 1317 a Council of Tarragona stated that canons and other beneficed clergy, who were not in priest's orders, should receive communion at least twice a year (the laity were required to receive it once a year). Rectors of churches and other priests were to celebrate

[1] Goñi, 18 (1957), 193 f.; 23 (1962), 53 f., 88, 90–4; on the visitation of 1265 see 18 (1957), 115 f.; *Blanquerna*, 68–70, 72 (*Obres essencials*, i. 211–13, 217); Linehan, pp. 44–8; Burns, i. 35 f.; ii. 388 (n. 122).

Mass at least three times a year. These minimal requirements were not complied with. In 1329 another Council of Tarragona stated: 'many parish priests do not celebrate Mass in their churches or anywhere else.' They were suspended from office if they did not celebrate Mass within three months of ordination.[1]

THE CLERGY AND THE LAITY

Many benefices had been obtained in dubious ways. 'Conspicuous' simony—the purchase of bishoprics or abbeys—had been made more difficult by the reforms of the eleventh and twelfth centuries. An apparently simoniacal election to the see of Palencia in 1296 was immediately investigated by Rome. However, the use of money to obtain lesser benefices was denounced in a diocesan synod of Pamplona in the early fourteenth century. At the other end of the Iberian peninsula a synod held at Santiago in 1322 tells us that some fathers gave the same name to two or more of their sons so that if one son, who was beneficed, died or married, the next son could step in with no institution or examinaton by the bishop. Another Council of Santiago in 1324 reveals that benefices could be obtained without even the first tonsure, the most superficial token of the clerical state. The Portuguese bishop of Silves, Alvaro Peláez, writing about this time, took his usual gloomy view of the situation. He remarked:

> I scarcely believe that, especially in Spain, there is *one* bishop out of a hundred who is not simoniacal in conferring orders and benefices. ... In one ordination a bishop [in Spain] will get, either by express or tacit simony ... 450 florins and often more ... nor do [bishops] absolve anyone except for money.[2]

Only in the Basque provinces, Guipúzcoa, Alava, and Vizcaya, did the old unabashed lay control of the Church which had been normal in western Europe before Pope Gregory VII continue. Here, in 1390, laymen still received the tithes and gave a mere pittance to the clergy they appointed to churches.

[1] Tejada y Ramiro, iii. 475, 541.

[2] Benavides, ii. 104 f., Goñi, *Principe de Viana*, 23 (1962), 28; López Ferreiro, vi (Santiago, 1903), appendices, pp. 32, 41; Alvarus Pelagius, ii. 20, fol. 54. A general prohibition of laymen holding churches under royal patronage (1288) in M. Gaibrois de Ballesteros, *Historia del reinado de Sancho IV de Castilla*, iii, pp. cxxv ff.

When the bishop of Pamplona tried to appoint parish priests and recover tithes for the Church he caused a mass protest by the *caballeros e hijosdalgo* of these provinces and matters remained unchanged. In other areas of the peninsula, however, lay patrons continued to choose their parish clergy. The Council of Valladolid in 1322 denounced the appointment of children to church office by laymen some of whose rights of patronage were non-existent. The newly appointed cleric was forced to curry favour with the local laity and neighbouring clergy by entertaining them to splendid banquets and by gifts of money.

The Council of Tarragona in 1292 presented a remarkable picture of the sufferings of the clergy at the hands of the laity. Many laymen regarded it as their right to eat with their parish priest once a week. At Christmas, Easter, and Pentecost some laymen, immediately after receiving communion, insisted on the Church regaling them with barrels of wine, on which they got hopelessly drunk and began violent quarrels, which often led to bloodshed.

When the crops were harvested certain laymen insisted on transporting the clerical tithe of the harvest to the Church's barns, making the clergy pay them two or three times the normal cost.[1]

Evasion or direct refusal to pay tithes was very common. In 1255 Alfonso X of Castile issued a general decree: 'Since we find that many tricks are played, no one from now on shall dare to collect or measure the wheat he has threshed until he has first rung the bell three times and summoned the collectors of tithes . . . No one is to threaten the collectors or pursue or injure them.' We find the same resistance in the 1330s both in Castile and among the nobles of the ecclesiastical province of Tarragona. The attempt by the Council of Salamanca in 1335 to 'extend' the text of Christ's condemnation of the wicked in the Gospel from an infernal to an earthly malediction, 'Because you did not pay me tenths and first fruits . . . you are condemned to suffer hunger and misery . . . You have lost the fertility of your fields', evidently had as little effect as it deserved.

Many violations of church property are recorded. The Church was often seen simply as the economic rival of a neighbouring town. A bridge built by a convent might be broken

[1] Goñi, ibid. 341 f.; Tejada y Ramiro, pp. 491 f., 496 f., 416. See Burns, i. 70 ff.

down by a city whose control of passage over a river it threatened. Nor was the sacred character of churches respected. Churches were used as markets or turned into fortresses. It was not uncommon for blood to be shed in a cathedral or its cloister.[1]

Making every allowance for clerical bias, this evidence shows very clearly that, despite the triumphs of the Church from the eleventh to the thirteenth centuries, the same evils, often vanquished, continued to return. Not only clerical incontinence but simony and lay control of the Church were still rampant, at least below the highest levels. Pope Boniface VIII's famous manifesto, 'Clericis laicos', was issued in 1296, only four years after the Council of Tarragona, from whose decreees I have quoted. Boniface was engaged in combat with the monarchies of France and England, the fathers of Tarragona with the petty nobles and farmers of Catalonia, but the council could have made its own Boniface's opening words, 'That laymen have been very hostile to the clergy . . . is proved by the experience of the present age'. In 1302 the Council of Peñafiel echoed Boniface's words.

The clergy were largely responsible for the lack of respect they received from the laity. The Basque nobles who defended their out-of-date privileges against the bishop of Pamplona in 1390 found a ready audience when they claimed that the bishops wanted to swallow up everything and would do better if, instead of intriguing in royal courts, they saw to the discipline of the lower clergy, many of whom 'do not know how to consecrate the Body of God'. Many bishops had given several churches to one favourite, who might hold four parishes, distant from each other, one of which could have supported him. The canons of Pamplona received parish churches; there was no possibility of their preaching to their parishioners. A recent historian has noted in the clergy of thirteenth-century Valencia 'a worldly preoccupation with every petty right or claim' which may have angered laymen even more than absenteeism or concubinage.

The reaction to any sin committed by a layman often took the stereotyped form of excommunication and a large fine. The normal level of Christian instruction among the laity was

[1] *MHE* i. 70–5, 131 f.; see Gaibrois, iii, pp. cliii f. (1289); Tejada y Ramiro, pp. 554–7, 569, 493–5. The text 'extended' by the council is Matthew 25:45.

extraordinarily low. In 1273 the clergy of Valencia admitted that 'there are many in our city and diocese who do not know the Lord's Prayer . . . or else do not know it well; and there are very few who know the Creed'. The Council of Valladolid of 1322 told parish priests to display in church in Latin and romance the Articles of Faith, the Ten Commandments, a list of the sacraments of the Church, and of the types of vices and virtues. These lists were to be read out to parishioners on the greater feasts and on Sundays in Lent. This attempt at elementary instruction in doctrine was repeated by diocesan synods. It was accompanied, in 1330, in Pamplona—where the bishop was the same Barbazan who later published a compendium of doctrine for his clergy—by the following regulations regarding 'public sinners', usurers, adulterers, the incestuous. They were first to be admonished in general sermons by their parish priest. Next he was to reason with them privately. He was then to single out the sinner for admonition from the pulpit. Only after these methods had been tried and failed was such a man to be excommunicated. I cannot say if these sensible regulations were peculiar to Pamplona or were found in other dioceses, or how faithfully they were applied. They demand a better trained and more carefully selected parish clergy than other evidence suggests existed.

Alvaro Peláez laments the way peasants heard Mass: 'They stand outside the church . . . They do not go in except to see the Lord's Body [at the Elevation of the Host] and many look on from outside. There, like brute beasts, they talk of their animals and of other vulgar things.'

Alvaro Peláez saw peasants as only concerned with gain. Even rich peasants, he remarks with amazed contempt,

> work with their own hands and do not cease to do so in old age, twisting their bodies and corrupting their souls . . . All day long they plough and dig the earth so that they are wholly *earthy*. They suck up earth, they eat it, they talk of earth, in their land they have placed all their hope . . . They are commonly inhumane to pilgrims and the poor.

Perhaps the clergy were in part responsible for the 'earthiness' of their rural congregations. Bishop Alvaro makes it clear that old peasants, who insist on working, should by no means be let off observing fast days on account of age. Other evidence shows that the Christianity taught the peasantry was highly legalistic.

The peasant or artisan who was confessed by a priest using the thirteenth-century manual *Los Diez Mandamientos* would be asked if he had sworn by God or the Virgin Mary and if he had broken Sunday observance by ploughing, working his mill, or going to market. The priest would concentrate especially on the sins of the flesh. Not only incest, adultery, and fornication but sexual relations between married persons on feast or fast days or in the open country, in vineyards and fields, were sanctioned by penances, adjusted by bargaining between priest and penitent, but as heavy as the sinner would bear, 'fasts and disciplines and pilgrimages'. (Most penances, even the pilgrimage to Jerusalem, could customarily be discharged either by almsgiving or by the recitation of many psalms.)

There existed other and better manuals for the clergy than *Los Diez Mandamientos*, among others the *Summa Septem Sacramentorum* of Pere d' Albalat, archbishop of Tarragona (1238–51), which told the confessor to judge penitents as individuals, considering each one's merits and character before imposing a penance out of a textbook. Pere's manual was used from Barcelona to Valencia; it was still in use in the late-fourteenth century. It required, however, a knowledge of Latin which many parish clergy did not possess.

The main feature of religion, as presented either at a royal court or in a rural parish, was the celebration of Mass. This loomed far larger, for most Christians, than the reception of the sacraments—laymen were only obliged to receive Communion and to make their confession once a year but they had to attend Mass every Sunday and on many other feast days. Alvaro Peláez remarks that

so many Masses are said every day to please men or to conceal crimes that the Lord's Holy Body has become vile for both people and clergy . . . Our church is full to overflowing with altars, Masses, and Sacrifices, but the sacrificing priests are also full of murders, sacrilege, uncleanness, simony . . . The Lord God does not regard a great multitude of Sacrifices, gilded vessels, and singers like tragedians, who use drugs to make their throats supple and smooth.

Bishop Alvaro, as on other occasions, may have been somewhat carried away by his own style.

In his study of the thirteenth-century Church in Valencia Professor Burns sums up the positive achievements of the parish system, set up in the newly created diocese within thirty years of the conquest. Even the most ill-trained and unimpressive clerics of the day could convey much to the people.

[The system] was admirably suited to do the one essential: it could carry [everywhere] the sacraments, the liturgy, and the whole range of para-liturgical ceremonies and customs. Each separate church . . . was thus able to create its own atmosphere, an added dimension of symbolism by which the ordinary was clothed with sacramental signifieance. The liturgy, pageantry, and customs transported to the frontier a religious world of sight and sound, the daily public office and sung Mass, the procession and the ceremony, the votive lamp and the wayside shrine. It was an Old Testament world of tithes and theocratic overtones. It was a world which somewhat neglected preaching (though this was now changing) but which fed upon the chanted service and occasional confession, the blessing of crops, the solemnities of the current marriage, baptism, or funeral, and the recurrent feast days in the cycle of ecclesiastical seasons. These set the mood and temper of the people.[1]

THE RELIGIOUS ORDERS: MONKS

The impetus that had created hundreds of monasteries in the Iberian peninsula had largely spent its force by the thirteenth century. From now onwards, here as elsewhere in western Europe, monasticism lived mainly on the spiritual and economic legacy of the past. The monasteries were now on the defensive. The thirteenth and fourteenth centuries saw fewer than twenty new monasteries founded in the peninsula, four of which were Cistercian creations in the lands conquered by Catalonia–Aragon: Majorca, and Valencia. In Castile Silos founded the only Benedictine monastery established in the whole of Andalusia, San Benito, near Seville; in 1301 San Isidoro was erected near the same city by the Cistercians.

Donations to existing monasteries also diminished sharply. Monasteries possessing temporal jurisdiction came under the same attack from town councils and from the Iberian monarch-

[1] Goñi, 23 (1962), 341, 132, 29, 84; Tejada, pp. 408, 481; Villanueva, xvii. 242 f. (Lérida, 1325); Benavides, ii. 287; Alvarus Pelagius, ii. 43; 5, fols. 84^{r-v}, 14^{v}; A. Morel-Fatio, *Romania*, 16 (1887), 379–82; Linehan, pp. 71–7, 98; idem, *Hispania Sacra*, 22 (1969), 11 f.; Burns, i. 114 f., 124, 87; the quotation from pp. 54 f.

ies that assailed the bishops of the time; they were even less successful in defending themselves. Royal law was penetrating the fiefs belonging to monasteries, *abadengos*. Many towns now refused to pay the customary tribute to their abbatial lords. But the monarchy continued to exact feudal service from the impoverished monasteries, which vainly struggled in the meetings of the Cortes of Castile with the representatives of the towns.[1]

MONKS AND BISHOPS

The monasteries had also to contend with their bishops. Many monasteries possessed jurisdiction over parish churches. In Castile San Millán, for instance, had complete control over many parishes and was subject to the papacy only. This exemption from local episcopal control had, in general, served the cause of church, and especially of monastic, reform up to the twelfth century. After that time bishops, whose rights had now been more clearly defined by canon law, were often more interested in reform than were most abbots. The following centuries saw conflicts between almost every main exempt monastery and the local bishop. These conflicts led to lengthy and expensive litigation which often reached Rome. The results of the struggle differed widely in different areas. Silos in Castile and Ripoll in Catalonia came out on the whole victorious in 1236 and 1260 against the bishops of Burgos and Vich respectively. The bishops of Pamplona eventually succeeded in asserting their jurisdiction over Montearagón and its many dependent parishes. On the other hand Pamplona was not successful with the Cistercian monastery of La Oliva. The Cistercian abbeys were linked far more closely together under Cîteaux than were Benedictine monasteries. They were thus better able to resist episcopal intrusion. In 1305 the founder of a new convent of nuns placed the convent clearly under

[1] For the temporal jurisdiction of certain sees, see above, Ch. III, p. 95, n. 1; J. Pérez y R. Escalona, *Historia del Real Monasterio de Sahagún* (Madrid, 1782), pp. 643–7, 664; J. Pujol y Alonso, *El Abadengo de Sahagún* (Madrid, 1915), pp. 118 ff., 135 f., 208–11, and other references cited by J. Pérez de Urbel, *Los monjes españoles en la edad media*, ii (Madrid, 1934), 526–32; see J. A. García de Cortázar y Ruiz de Aguirre, *El dominio del monasterio de San Millán de la Cogolla (siglos X a XIII)* (Salamanca, 1969), pp. 333 ff.; for Cistercian foundations see M. Cocheril, *Études sur le monachisme en Espagne et au Portugal* (Paris–Lisbon, 1966), pp. 372–6.

episcopal jurisdiction, thus seeking to avoid conflicts which plagued older foundations.[1]

MONKS AND THE NOBILITY

The worst enemies the monasteries possessed were the local nobility. Even under a strong king such as Sancho IV, Castilian monasteries found it hard to collect rents—and they were increasingly rentiers—from their tenants. The nobility came into their own in Castile during the minorities of Fernando IV and Alfonso XI. In 1295 a deputation of bishops and abbots complained to the child King Fernando and his mother that when any church became vacant it was seized and all its goods and revenue taken and pressure put on the cathedral chapter or the monks of the abbey in question to bring about the election of the candidate the local nobles wanted. Similar complaints had been raised in 1283, during Sancho's revolt against Alfonso X, and they appear again in 1315 when Alfonso XI was a child. In 1284 the monks of Lorenzana in Galicia complained to Sancho that

> Ruy González de Bollano with his father and brothers and his whole company seized the abbot, broke open the treasury, and took thence all the letters of the monastery and the privileges it had from . . . popes and emperors, kings, infantes, bishops, counts, *ricos hombres*, *hijosdalgo*, countesses, ladies, and many others.

To a corporation struggling for existence in a world of incessant litigation, this violent intrusion could well have been a deathblow.

MONKS AND PEASANTS

Lull, in *Blanquerna*, describes monks' lands being invaded by the local peasantry. A document of 1347 shows this invasion occurring in Castile. Clerical and lay representatives of the town of Madriz appeared before the abbot and monks of San Millán, assembled in chapter, and confessed, kneeling, that they had taken over and ploughed lands reserved by the abbey;

[1] A. Pladevall i Font, in *I Col. loqui d'història del Monaquisme Català*, i (Santes Creus, 1967), 263–95; M. Férotin, *Recueil des chartes de l'abbaye de Silos* (Paris, 1897), pp. 142 f., 148–50, 152 f., 185, 205, 345–97, 353–56, etc.; Goñi, *Principe de Viana*, 23 (1962), 102–10, 121 f., 158 ff., 327–9; Pérez de Urbel, pp. 532–6.

had killed cattle and sheep belonging to the monastery which were being pastured on its lands, and had refused to perform labour services they owed to the monastery.

In return for this confession and a large fine they obtained favourable terms from the abbey. This case was far from unusual. In 1290 another document reveals villagers 'coming by night with arms to move boundary stones and steal the cattle' of the convent of Fresnillo in Castile. Other villagers harvested the convent's wheat and carried it off.

In order to obtain protection many monasteries had, in the past 'commended' themselves to the Crown. In the reign of Fernando IV (1295–1312), despite royal prohibitions, monasteries turned instead to a local noble whose aid seemed likely to be more efficacious than that of the enfeebled monarchy. The monks hoped that in return for a sum of money their fief would be properly administered and their revenues assured. In many cases their hopes were deceived.[1]

The main monasteries of Castile and Navarre, which possessed, in theory, jurisdiction over sixty or more lesser monasteries and towns, Nájera, Leyre, Oña, Sahagún, Silos, San Millán, were in serious financial trouble by 1300. In 1338 Silos had to alienate many properties in return for money to carry on lawsuits with secular clergy and the Franciscans. But if Silos had not had to alienate property it would still have been in debt. The richest monastery of all, Oña, could only maintain monks in four of the eighty dependent priories it had once had.

CISTERCIAN HOUSES

The Cistercian monasteries of Castile were no more able to defend themselves than the Benedictine houses. The miserable state of the Cistercian monasteries of Galicia emerges in a memorial addressed to Fernando IV in 1309. The memorial states that the Cistercians were exploited by royal officials, who levied far larger taxes than were due and—together with the

[1] García de Cortázar, pp. 345 f.; Benavides, ii. 33–5; *MHE* ii, 94–7; see L. Fernández Martín, *Hispania Sacra*, 25 (1972), 30–4; Gaibrois, *Sancho IV*, iii, pp. iii f., clxxxvii f.; *Cortes de León*, i. 296; *Cartulario de San Millán de la Cogolla*, ed. L. Serrano (Madrid, 1930), pp. xcix f; cf. Férotin, *Recueil*, pp. 358 f. (1326); Lull, *Blanquerna*, 63 (*Obres* i. 203); J. L. Santos Diez, *La encomienda de monasterios en la Corona de Castilla* (Rome–Madrid, 1961), pp. 26, 41.

local towns—forced the monasteries to plead cases before them, instead of before clerical judges. Local nobles made the monks contribute to their expenses when they went to court and forced the monastery's vassals to abandon monastic lands and accompany them on expeditions against other nobles. The Galician squirearchy invaded the monastic enclosure, gave banquets there and brought in their women.[1]

CATALONIA: POBLET

Conditions were somewhat less serious in Catalonia. The continued prosperity of the great Cistercian monastery of Poblet was not due only to the royal protection it received or to the great extent of its lands—with some 55,000 acres, 20,000 of them administered directly, it was probably the largest landed proprietor in Catalonia—but to the fact that these lands continued to be farmed by lay brothers (*conversi*) and were not in the hands of lay tenants who only provided a nominal rent. Poblet also had over eighty (in 1316, ninety-two) choir monks (clerics) in the fourteenth century; it maintained a school of polyphonic music of the first order. At the other side of the peninsula another great Cistercian monastery, Alcobaça in Portugal, maintained its standing. None of the great monasteries of Castile had more than the fifty-two monks of Oña at this time. Arlanza had fallen in a century from 180 to twenty.[2]

HANGERS-ON: SILOS

While the number of actual monks had fallen the usual Benedictine monastery was inhabited by a swarm of lay servants who did the work done by lay brothers in Cistercian houses. In Silos in 1338 there were three men working under the cellarer, a man bringing wood for the oven and the kitchens, two cooks, two other men baking bread, two porters, two women recluses (walled up in cells with an opening on the church or cloister), two shepherds, several gardeners, the monastery tailor, the servant of the infirmary, the man in charge of the refectory,

[1] Pérez de Urbel, pp. 541–4; Benavides, ii. 645–8; Férotin, pp. 386 f.

[2] J. Finestres y de Monsalvó, *Historia del Real Monasterio de Poblet*, iii (Barcelona, 1948, 1st edn. Cervera, 1796), 'Disertaciones' iv-v. 117–52; L. McCrank, *Analecta Cisterciensia*, 29 (1973), 57–78; Pérez de Urbel, pp. 544–6; H. Anglés, *La musica de las Cántigas de Santa María del Rey Alfonso el Sabio*, iii. 1 (Barcelona, 1958), 90.

the doctor or surgeon, a woman who washed the clothes of the monastery, two chaplains to say Mass in the village, the pig-man, eight *racioneros* (laymen who had handed over their possessions to the monastery and lived there at its expense), four 'poor' men who lived at the abbey, three men working in the vineyards, and a forester. There was also the abbot's separate establishment, his chamberlain, doorkeeper, private cook, muleteer, thirteen other men who saw to the abbot's animals and went on his messages, the abbot's judge, to whom he delegated local cases in his feudal jurisdiction, his representative at Burgos, several tax-collectors in the abbey's service, and four young boys who were being brought up as a service to God. This makes a total of some seventy hangers-on at Silos, as against thirty choir monks. One should add the guests and pilgrims always passing through a great monastery, and the neighbouring poor, on whom much of its revenues were spent. And nobles still chose to be buried at Silos, near the high altar, 'seeing the miracles and benefits which Christ bestows by the prayers of the glorious confessor Lord Saint Domingo de Silos'.[1]

Some monasteries had attached to them a kind of Third Order or confraternity, whose members gave alms and had a place in the prayers of the monks. One such confraternity, established in Navarre in 1241 around a convent of Benedictine nuns, constituted a mutual-aid society, whose members were bound to avenge any injury done to one of their number. It included clergy, a local squire, and the women in charge of the convent's hens and oven. Less suitable monastic hangers-on no doubt resembled the knight Narpan of Lull's *Blanquerna*, who lived in the monastery exactly as he would have done in the world, eating meat, wearing soft linen, sleeping on a soft bed, waited on by his squire, providing a thoroughly bad example deeply envied by the regular inhabitants of the monastery.

From the thirteenth century onward the monastery's revenues were often divided between the monks and the abbot. The aim of this division was to prevent the abbot taking all the revenues for himself and allowing his monks to starve. As

[1] Férotin, *Recueil*, pp. 349 f., 264 ff. (1279); later demands for burial at Silos, pp. 293 ff., 296 f., 341 f.; idem, *Histoire de l'abbaye de Silos* (Paris, 1897), pp. 124 f.

one can see at Silos in 1338 the abbot now had his separate staff and lived largely apart from the monks. He was often mainly concerned with the affairs of court and Church.[1]

It is very difficult to estimate the internal spiritual life of medieval monasticism at any period. What we have, on the one side, are accounts or documents referring to the exceptionally gifted or saintly monk and, on the other, the denunciations of church councils, episcopal visitors, and contemporary satirists. Certain differences appear between different regions and between Benedictines and Cistercians.

ATTEMPTS AT MONASTIC REFORM

The Fourth Council of the Lateran in 1215 sought to remedy the isolation existing between Benedictine monasteries. The council prescribed the celebration of regular regional chapter meetings between the abbots of these monasteries, a system imitated from the Cistercian statutes. The chapters were to appoint visitors who would see that the Rule of St. Benedict, with its supplementary legislation, was observed. In 1336 Pope Benedict XII divided Benedictine monasteries into thirty-two regions, four of which—Compostela–Seville, Braga, Toledo, and Tarragona—Saragossa—corresponded to the Iberian peninsula.

The legislation of 1215 was immediately applied in Aragon and Catalonia, which came under Tarragona. Here chapters and visitations continued throughout the thirteenth and fourteenth centuries. In Castile there is very little evidence that the legislation was applied at all consistently. This difference may help to explain the lower level of monastic observance which appears in Castile, for instance, in the acts of the Council of Valladolid of 1322, which state that the *Rules* of St. Augustine—applying to regular canons—and of St. Benedict were 'wholly unobserved'. Even papal delegates were sometimes forbidden entrance to the greater monasteries of Castile such as Sahagún, while the accounts of visitations from 1312 to 1314 of smaller Catalan monasteries contain few irregularities and none of importance. In Navarre, on the other hand, it proved impossible to reform the Benedictines of Leyre. Cistercian monks were

[1] Férotin, *Recueil*, pp. 234 ff.; Lull, *Blanquerna*, 52 (*Obres* i. 185–8); Pérez de Urbel, pp. 552–60.

brought in to replace them, but the Benedictines refused to give way and repeatedly invaded the monastery by force. The struggle continued from at least 1235 to 1306. In 1296, because of the inconsistent policy of successive bishops of Pamplona, the unreformed Benedictines secured the monastery's treasures.[1]

A number of causes for the low state of many Benedictine monasteries have already appeared. They were continually subject to harassment by royal officials, by local towns, nominally their vassals, local nobles, and their diocesan bishop. They had to support large numbers of lay hangers-on. Their abbots' interests were increasingly focused outside the monastery and, in Castile, there was no efficient external agency to exercise a minimum of control over monastic observance.

The life of the ordinary monk lacked the spiritual stimulus which might have counteracted these negative factors. His days were spent in attendance at two sung Masses every day and at increasingly lengthy choir offices, modelled on the system derived from Cluny in former centuries. The endless recitation of psalms, lessons, and litanies was only interrupted by a siesta and by increasingly lavish meals, where meat, contrary to the Benedictine Rule, figured at least three times a week. The life of the greater monasteries has been well defined as one 'neither of scandalous relaxation nor of great enthusiasm . . . The monks are men who have an assured income and believe they earn it by ceaseless psalm-singing. A long recitation deserves a good meal. It is a tepid and colourless atmosphere'.

The Cistercian monasteries maintained a somewhat higher level of observance. Their abbots met in regular chapter meetings and they were subject to visitation by the abbots of the French monasteries which had founded the first houses in the peninsula or by their delegates, although these meetings and visitations became less frequent in the late thirteenth century. The lowest level of monastic discipline was to be found in the Benedictine monasteries subject to the abbey of Cluny, despite the regular visitations carried out by some of their priors. At times these visitors were refused admission, on other occasions bandits were paid to kidnap them. If they did reach their goal it was often to find the monastery had been taken over by local

[1] Pérez de Urbel, pp. 569–75; Tejada, p. 490; Pladevall i Font, pp. 290–5; Goñi, *Principe de Viana*, 18 (1957), 88–92, 116–9, 151–3, 196–9.

nobles. The General Chapter of Cluny of 1296 declared: 'almost all the Order has in Spain is alienated.' Attempts at reform proved hopeless. Many of the priors were French; many of them set examples of evil living which were naturally imitated by their monks.[1]

LACK OF MONASTIC EDUCATION

The decline of Latin monasticism from the thirteenth century onward is shown by the general failure of monasteries to assimilate the new studies pursued in the universities and by the friars. The General Chapter of Cîteaux in 1287 and Pope Benedict XII in 1336 saw the necessity of sending chosen monks to study in the universities if the tradition of learning was not to die in the monasteries, but not every abbot appears to have complied with these general recommendations.

The monastery described in Lull's *Blanquerna* was probably a Cistercian house. Its abbot, though a good man, was better at entertaining the neighbouring knights to a banquet than at preaching, 'since he neither knew Latin nor how to expound the Scriptures'. The monastery had no place for study though it had sent two monks to study law at Montpellier, 'so as to assist the monks in their temporal affairs', their lawsuits. While Lull, through his hero Blanquerna, favoured studies in the monastery he evidently had doubts as to the advisability of sending monks away to universities where they might be corrupted. The average monk felt, however, that the monastery's prestige was increased by 'great clerks'. The cellarer, a particularly well-drawn worldly monk, tried to persuade a leading preacher to abandon another monastery and join his so that the neighbouring people should come to hear him. The cellarer was mainly concerned, however, to increase the monastery's lands and was prepared to raise the money by making the monks eat less meat, despite the fact that the monastery was already in debt to pay for its last purchase.

The Cistercian monasteries of Alcobaça, in Portugal, and of Poblet, in Catalonia, which stood out, among the general

[1] Pérez de Urbel, pp. 575–88 (the quotation from pp. 577 f.); J. M. Canivez, *Statuta Capitulorum Generalium Ordinis Cisterciensis ab anno 1116 ad annum 1786*, 8 vols. (Louvain, 1933–41), e.g. iii. 49, 83 (1267–70); Cocheril, op. cit., pp. 397–415; U. Robert, 'État des monastères espagnols de l'ordre de Cluny aux XIIIe–XVe siècles', *BRAH* 20 (1892), 321–431, especially pp. 356, 365, 369 f.

decline, in their numbers and prosperity, also led the movement to the universities, as far as the Iberian peninsula was concerned. The Cistercian Order possessed houses of study in Paris (1244), Montpellier (1260), and Oxford (1280), among other universities. Both Alcobaça and Poblet sent monks to study theology at Paris and Toulouse though in far smaller numbers than the Orders of friars. Alcobaça also established a house of study in Lisbon in 1294, attached to the university just founded there. When this university was transferred to Coimbra in 1308 the monks followed it. Poblet established a similar house attached to the University of Lérida in 1420. Another Cistercian house of studies founded at Estella in Navarre in 1260 was later transferred to Salamanca.[1]

In France and England the Benedictines, although less active than the Cistercians, founded similar houses at Paris and Oxford in the thirteenth century. It is difficult to find parallels to these efforts among the Benedictines of the peninsula. The plan to establish the study of theology and canon law in 1348 at a university level inside the monastery of Sahagún was more limited in character and its precise results before 1400 are uncertain.

MONASTIC LIBRARIES

There exists no satisfactory general study of the libraries of medieval Spain. Books continued to be copied by monastic scribes but far more were now acquired by monasteries by gift or purchase, especially by students sent to the universities. Cistercian libraries, especially Poblet and Santes Creus, in Catalonia, and Alcobaça, in Portugal, again led in the acquisition of books. In 1520 Alcobaça possessed somewhat less than 500 manuscripts. This is not a large number, compared with the 1,200 volumes of Cîteaux and 1,700 of Clairvaux or the 2,000 or more of the great Benedictine abbeys of England, but it is probably a larger number than even such celebrated Benedictine abbeys as Ripoll in Catalonia or Silos in Castile, cultural centres of great importance in earlier centuries, could boast.

[1] Lull, *Blanquerna*, 53, 56–8 (*Obres* i. 188, 191 f., 193, 194 f.); M. Cocheril, 'Les Cisterciens portugais et les études', *Los monjes y los estudios* (Poblet, 1963), pp. 235–48; Rubió, *Documents*, ii, pp. lxxix-xcix; Finestres, *Historia de Poblet*, iii. 229.

Ripoll, however, continued to acquire books in large numbers throughout the Middle Ages.[1]

MONASTIC WRITINGS

The works written by the monks of the thirteenth and fourteenth centuries in western Europe are of far less interest than those of the twelfth century. Dom Hoste has remarked that three-quarters of the works by Benedictines consist of monastic chronicles, usually very limited in their scope, the remainder being lives of local saints or ascetic treatises, in general anthologies of earlier authors. The Cistercians launch out more into the world of contemporary thought and provide a number of scholastic authors, though their contribution is slight in comparison with that of the friars or of the secular clergy.

These remarks are applicable to the monks of the peninsula. They produced a number of chronicles in Latin, of which the most interesting is the intensely patriotic *Acts of the Counts of Barcelona*, continued by a monk of Ripoll or possibly by a cleric attached to the monastery up to 1299.[2] In Castile his contemporary, a prior of Silos, Pero Marín, wrote, in romance, an account of the miracles by which his monastery's patron saint had delivered captives from the Moors. In the first half of the thirteenth century the most notable Castilian poet, Gonzalo de Berceo, a secular priest, spent his life attached to the monastery of San Millán and his religious poems celebrate the saints of monastic Castile.

NUNS

The history of the convents of women in the Middle Ages has received far less attention than that of the male Orders. In general the convents were fewer and poorer than the monasteries. The very rich Cistercian convent of Las Huelgas outside Burgos served as a burial place for many members of the royal family of Castile. Its blend of Gothic and Muslim architecture

[1] J. Pérez y R. Escalona, op. cit., p. 171; see my article, 'Una biblioteca cisterciense medieval: La Real (Mallorca)', *AST* 32 (1959), 89–191; Cocheril, p. 240, n. 19; Beer, *Handschriftenschätze Spaniens*, especially nos. 391, 455; Férotin, *Histoire de Silos*, pp. 259–86; Carreras Artau, i. 72 f.

[2] A. Hoste, 'Les Études chez les moines des XIIIe et XIVe siècles', *Los monjes y los estudios*, pp. 249–60; *Gesta comitum Barcinonensium*, ed. L. Barrau Dihigo and J. Massó Torrents (Croniques Catalanes ii) (Barcelona, 1925), p. liii.

will be touched on later. In church music Las Huelgas led the field, introducing new melodies from Paris into Castile and adding new compositions of its own. Las Huelgas was unique. In 1257 it had a hundred noble *dueñas de velo* (choir nuns), forty *niñas hijasdalgo* being brought up in the convent, and forty lay sisters to serve the nuns. There was also a community of priests to assist the nuns in the execution of the liturgy, which was performed with two choirs, nuns and clerics. In Aragon Sigena harboured two daughters of King Jaume II. Although perhaps the nearest equivalent one could find in the peninsula, it was far behind Las Huelgas in its resources. But of the interior spiritual history even of Las Huelgas we are ignorant.[1]

In 1285 Doña Pascuala de Talavera, after a year as a novice, made her profession as a Poor Clare, a follower of St. Francis, in the convent at Seville. The notarial act drawn up on the occasion declared that the new nun was 'in good health, in full possession of her memory, acting under no pressure. Of her own free will she wished to enter God's service, for her soul's salvation'. Kneeling, she promised obedience, to keep the Rule of the Order, to keep chastity, to renounce the goods of this world. Clothed in the habit of the Order she was raised to her feet and saluted with the kiss of peace.[2]

This is an official statement of the ideal way in which a woman would become a nun. Many nuns, like the protagonist of a fourteenth-century Catalan poem might have said: 'I was made a nun to my harm . . . may God punish those who brought me to this evil!' This poem was almost certainly written by a professional poet but evidence exists to show that it did not greatly misrepresent the facts. The Archpriest of Hita knew the world he depicted. He enumerates at length the presents sent to nuns by their gallants—sweetmeats, spices, and strong red wine from Toro. Even the name, Trotaconventos, which the Archpriest gives the procuress in his book, reveals the nature of the case. According to Trotaconventos, nuns are 'beautiful painted images, ladies who are generous and free by nature'.

[1] See below, Ch. V, p. 199; H. Anglés, *El Còdex musical de Las Huelgas*, 3 vols. (Barcelona, 1931); A. Rodríguez López, *El Real Monasterio de las Huelgas de Burgos . . .*, 2 vols. (Burgos, 1907) (see i. 457); A. Ubieto Arteta, *El Real Monasterio de Sigena (1188–1300)* (Valencia, 1966).

[2] A. Ballesteros, *Sevilla en el siglo XIII* (Madrid, 1913), p. 146.

The picture evokes the beauty competition between nuns of Seville and Toledo described by a slightly later poet.[1]

If one turns from literary to documentary evidence one finds many wills by which daughters of a lesser noble are left small sums and directed to use them as an entrance fee (a dowry) to a convent. Other documents display girls being received in convents when they are under age, in return for a dowry. It is hardly surprising that church councils denounce the abduction of nuns from convents which they had probably entered without any vocation. Alfonso X's *Cántigas* gloss this development when they display a pregnant abbess saved by the Virgin Mary's miraculously removing the child.[2]

Lull's novel *Blanquerna* provides an excellent picture of a late-thirteenth-century convent, based on real convents in Majorca or Montpellier. It is a credible picture of a community of generally devout women, alive to the difference the entry of a rich novice would make to their life, terrified by threats from the novice's relations to destroy the convent unless they refuse to receive her, but who can be swayed by being reminded of the example of Christ and the martyrs.

Normally the nuns of *Blanquerna* resemble the religious depicted by the Archpriest of Hita.

> Joyfully goes the nun from choir to the parlour,
> Joyfully the monk from terce to the refectory,
> The nun wants to hear news from the outside world
> The monk greedily anticipates his meal.

Lull's nuns cannot resist gossip of weddings brought to their parlour by the ladies they know. Nor can they resist inspecting closely the dress and make-up of the ladies who come to the convent or the waft of the musk and amber they are drenched in. The sermons of Lull's abbess, Natana, are directed against temptations which affect her nuns. Many nuns, while physically present in the convent, are in the world by their desires. They want to eat fish with special sauces as a substitute for the meat

[1] Riquer, i. 516; Arcipreste de Hita, *Libro de Buen Amor*, vv. 1333–9, 1341, ed. M. Criado de Val and E. W. Naylor (Madrid, 1965), pp. 425–9; *Cancionero de Baena*, ed. Azáceta, no. 98 (i. 200).

[2] J. Segura, *Revista de ciencias históricas*, 5 (1887), 322 f.; Benavides, ii. 100 f.; López Ferreiro, op. cit., vi. (1903), appendices, pp. 24–41; *Cántigas*, no. 7 (ed. W. Mettmann, i. 24 f.).

they are proud of having renounced. They have only one meal on fast days but one as large as two normal meals. 'Many religious houses are poor and in debt through too great superfluity of food.' One nun confesses she entered the convent because she was too poor to live as she wished in the world. Another nun wanted the honour of being abbess. Another is imprisoned in a special cell, alone and in darkness, lying on vine-branches, 'who had greatly erred and sinned against her honour and her Order'. Another nun is so ignorant that she did not know the basic Articles of the Faith. Natana found it necessary to have one of the nuns act as a spy on the others and to have spies in the city to watch the nuns when they went out of the convent.[1]

THE FRIARS

Far more than the earlier monastic Orders the friars acted as direct servants of the papacy. They were well trained in canon law and theology. Through their sermons, incomparably superior to those of the parish clergy, and their direct contact with the people, they continually strove to do away with Islamic or Jewish customs, and, in particular, to restrict the power and influence of the richer Jews. Wherever they were allowed to do so they entered synagogues and mosques to address captive audiences of Jews or Muslims. The role of the friars in newly conquered regions such as Valencia was indispensable and their popularity there, in the thirteenth century, is undeniable. Here, as elsewhere, they directed the lay confraternity guilds which were being organized among the city's artisans.

The papal Inquisition had been introduced from southern France into the Crown of Aragon in the reign of Jaume I (1213–76). It was soon entirely controlled by the Dominican Order. Its activities against heretics will be referred to later. There was no Inquisition in Castile until the time of Fernando and Isabel and none in Portugal. What heretics there were in these countries were dealt with by the ordinary episcopal courts.[2]

[1] Lull, *Blanquerna*, 20–41 (*Obres*, i. 150–70). See M. M. Riu, *AEM* 7 (1970–1), 595 f. Arcipreste de Hita, *Libro de Buen Amor*, v. 1399, ed. cit., p. 458.

[2] Burns, i. 198–213; J. Vincke, *Zur Vorgeschichte der spanische Inquisition: Die Inquisition in Aragon, Katalonien, Mallorca und Valencia während des 13. und 14. Jahrhunderts* (Bonn, 1941).

The Franciscans possessed great influence with the ruling dynasty of Catalonia–Aragon. From 1286 to 1491 they acted as confessors to the ruling king, and often as royal ambassadors. Like the Dominicans they held many sees. Convents of Franciscans and Poor Clares were founded by members of the dynasty. In 1292 Jaume II told the Minister General of the Franciscans that he had always chosen St. Francis as his patron, after the Virgin Mary. His mother Costanza was to die as a Poor Clare. Jaume defended the Franciscans against encroachments on their rights by the secular clergy. The friars had the right, he insisted, to hear the laity's confessions, to preach, and to inter the laymen who preferred to be buried in their cemeteries.[1]

In Castile the Dominicans appear to have enjoyed greater favour with royalty. Queen María of Molina, widow of Sancho IV and guardian of two later kings, was one of the most devout women of her day. She chose to be buried in the Dominican habit. Don Juan Manuel's life was less edifying than Queen María's but his writings reveal deep concern with religion. His rigid orthodoxy also owes much to the Dominicans.[2]

The new Orders of friars, Dominicans, Franciscans, Carmelites, Augustinians and the rest, had, however, considerable difficulty in establishing themselves in the peninsula. In 1245 the Franciscans of Pamplona tried to found a convent in the middle of the city without episcopal—though with papal—permission. The prior of the cathedral of Pamplona, the archdeacon, and other canons took every opportunity, including funerals, to denounce the Franciscans as excommunicate. In their sermons the cathedral clergy forbade the laity to assist at Franciscan sermons or to make their confessions to Franciscans, under pain of deprivation of the Eucharist and of church burial. The Franciscans were described as heretics, falsifiers of papal bulls, worse than Jews and Muslims. The cathedral clergy even invaded the Franciscan convent, breaking down its doors. They severely wounded two friars and imprisoned others for three days on bread and water. Violent resistance to the friars by local vested interests existed in many other places. In Galicia in 1289, the bishop of Orense himself invaded the Franciscan church, seized the corpse of a lady just buried there, and had it

[1] P. Sanahuja, op. cit., pp. 194–203, 106–12; Finke, *Acta* iii. 16–9.

[2] Benavides, i. 680 ff.; Ch. VI, below, p. 223.

moved to the cathedral cemetery. But in the end the friars, through papal and royal support, proved victorious over cathedral chapters and monasteries and established themselves almost everywhere.[1]

One reason for the friars' success was their gift for attracting far more talented men than now entered either the secular clergy or the monasteries. Unlike these other orders of men the friars were in touch with new and alive elements in thirteenth- and early-fourteenth-century thought. They understood the need for a new type of apostolate, based on cities, with a strong emphasis on teaching. The Dominicans insisted that no convent could be founded that did not include a Doctor of Theology. The post of prior of a convent was less important than that of the conventual Reader in Theology. It is estimated that by the late-thirteenth century the Dominicans included at least 1,500 teaching members, half of whom taught theology, spread among conventual, cathedral, and monastic schools and the universities. The Dominicans were imitated, on a lesser scale, by the other Orders of friars.

Lull, with his instinct for the truth of a situation, describes friars coming to a monastery and teasing the monks with Biblical problems which they cannot solve. The friars' libraries presented a contrast to the outdated erudition of Benedictines and Cistercians and the haphazard accumulation of cathedral chapters. In the second half of the thirteenth century the Dominican convent at Barcelona received the latest works of Albert the Great and Thomas Aquinas as soon as they were written. It seems probable that other Dominican and Franciscan convents were almost as well off, although, by the 1320s, some friars were becoming more interested in the outward appearance of their books, with their silver and silk bindings, than in their contents.[2]

Students from Barcelona followed the courses given by

[1] Goñi, *Principe de Viana*, 18 (1957), 126 f.; Gaibrois, *Sancho IV*, ii. 55, 111 f. See the case of Silos (1300–1), Férotin, *Recueil*, pp. 309, 312–19, and that of Burgos in P. A. Linehan, in *El Cardenal Albornoz y el Colegio de España*, ii (Bologna, 1972), 270.

[2] P. Amargier, in *Les Universités du Languedoc au XIIIe siècle* (Toulouse, 1970), pp. 119–44; Lull, *Blanquerna*, 57 (*Obres* i. 193); Carreras Artau, i. 16 f., 76 f.; Alvarus Pelagius, op. cit., ii. 76 (fol. 207). See also Alvarus's criticism of Franciscans' vanity in dress (fol. 206).

Albert the Great and Aquinas in Paris or Cologne. A series of Catalan Dominicans themselves taught at Paris. In the fourteenth century they reacted to Arnau de Vilanova's attacks on Aquinas by securing the condemnation of Arnau's theological works immediately after his death. A Catalan friar even translated part of the *Summa theologica* into Armenian to assist his mission to that country.

The Franciscan writers of fourteenth-century Spain were—like the Dominicans—mainly Catalans. Their great master was Duns Scotus. His teaching reached Barcelona by 1321, within fifteen years of his death. Although the Catalan friars were not strikingly original they were in touch with European thought to a far greater extent than appears to have been the case in Castile.

But by 1300 even the friars had lost much of their prestige. They were still needed by the papacy and the monarchies and by an ignorant clergy, but, apart from the occasional scandal, the quality even of the Dominican or Franciscan bishop had cheapened. These friar bishops were no longer apostles of reform but lawyers, doctors, and, increasingly often, promoted civil servants. The glory had largely departed from the friars.[1]

POPULAR RELIGION

In about the year 1250 Arias Nunes, a cleric of Santiago, wrote a poem in which he described his search for truth. Since truth had abandoned the world he hoped to find it in monasteries, but Benedictines told him it had left their houses many years ago. Even among Cistercians, 'where truth used to dwell', it had vanished, nor had the pilgrims to Santiago met truth on the road. Another satiric poet of the time, Martin Moxa, sees anti-Christ's rule established. War is everywhere. Justice is everywhere despised. Churches and hospitals are robbed by *hidalgos* and women raped with impunity. Workmen are not to be found in towns for there is no man to defend them. Vines are uncultivated, rents unpaid, Christ no longer wishes to behold the world. Every day it goes from bad to worse.[2]

[1] Carreras Artau, i. 147–98; ii. 444–75; Linehan, pp. 224–9, 313–6; F. E. de Tejada, *Historia del pensamiento político catalán*, i (Seville, 1963), 181–202.

[2] *Cántigas d'escarnho*, 69, 275–278, ed. M. Rodrigues Lapa (Coimbra, 1965), pp. 115 f., 412–19.

The *Cántigas d'escarnho* of the late thirteenth century surprise us by the intensity with which they blaspheme the Christian creed. In a poem attributed to Alfonso X of Castile a prostitute considers that her suffering—in not completing the act of sexual intercourse because it is Good Friday—is greater martyrdom than Christ's crucifixion. A poet tells an abbess that she can instruct him in every detail of the art of love. Gil Pérez Conde complains to God that He has taken his lady from him for the same reason that He formerly destroyed Sodom and Gomorrha, because of His detestation of earthly love. Another poet sees God as a poor liege lord to His vassals, whom He does not protect and love as the meanest earthly lord does his dependants, seeing to their earthly happiness.[1]

Most men, however, could not entirely forget that this life was not the only one. A conscientious man would not die without making arrangements to repay any sums he might owe as an administrator of a great estate. In Seville pious legacies appear in virtually all wills, legacies to Religious Orders or cathedral chapters; to pay for candles to be burnt for the testator; for scholarships for pupils in the cathedral school, on condition they should assist at the burials of the poor or recite psalms for the crusade; for Masses of the Virgin or the dead.[2]

This is an age when all the trappings of religion, like those of ordinary life, paintings, reliquaries, banners borne in procession, processional crosses, become more sumptuous. The first sumptuary laws of the peninsula—directed against excessive personal expenditure on dress and appearance—were issued by Jaume I of Aragon in 1234. But no regulations could prevent expenditure on religion. What Huizinga called the 'hunger for colour and brilliance' of the later Middle Ages was legitimate here, since it might move men to devotion. One of Alfonso X's *Cántigas* tells us how 'a sinful woman who entered a church, as often happens, seeing the monks' sacred vestments, and God sculptured in stone with His Mother, was forced down on her knees and began to reproach herself.'[3]

[1] ibid. 14, 37, 162, 394 (pp. 23 f., 69 f., 253 f., 580).
[2] Segura, *Aplech*, pp. 231–7; Ballesteros, *Sevilla en el siglo XIII*, pp. 146 f.
[3] *Cántigas*, no. 38, ed. W. Mettmann, i. 112.

DEVOTION TO THE VIRGIN

Men continued, Alfonso X remarks, to 'commend their beasts to St. Anthony [of Egypt], their flocks to St. Pastor, and their throats to St. Blas', but no other saint received the devotion given to the Virgin Mary. The *Cántigas*, an enormous collection of earlier legends and contemporary anecdote, expound the view that every sin could be forgiven in a devotee of Mary. A monk drowned while on his nightly journey from his monastery to his concubine, a cleric 'who was a gambler and thief', another priest who was so ignorant that the only Mass he could chant was that of the Virgin, are all saved by her intervention. A noble robs his lay and monastic neighbours. Because he thought before dying of founding a monastery in honour of the Virgin he is restored to life to carry out his promise. He dies a monk.

The world is a battlefield between the Virgin and the Devil. The Virgin has her fortresses. Alfonso's poems range over the Marian shrines of his age, from Chartres in France, through Montserrat in Catalonia and many lesser-known Iberian shrines to Marian wonder-working images in Murcia and Puerto de Santa María, near Cádiz. Demons—fully as real to most men's minds as the saints—attack pilgrims, tricking them into committing suicide out of despair. They lure a judge from his dinner-table into the street and hurl him down to Hell. Clerics invoke demons to get the girls they want. But the Virgin is always there, to intervene and defeat the demons, protect pilgrims, save the 'honour' of her devotees, free captives of the Moors, or act, like St. Anthony of Padua in later piety, as general retriever of lost property. In return she exacts precise payment in wax candles and cloths for her altar or image, and, like a jealous woman, refuses to allow a man who has pledged his faith to her to marry an earthly bride.

RELICS

As María Rosa Lida observed, the men of this age moved easily between sacred and profane. The faith of 'the bandit who always wears a scapulary' is that described in these miracles. 'The devout thief, the cleric with a concubine, the pregnant abbess, the incestuous mother who kills her infant child, [all] insupportable for modern piety, are treated with sympathy by medieval authors.'[1]

Faith in miraculous images is linked to faith in relics. It was necessary to believe absolutely in the power of relics of the Virgin, such as her shoes or her milk. Other relics of saints attracted devotion. The discovery of the bodies of the Eighteen Martyrs of Saragossa—whose martyrdom was recorded by Prudentius in the fourth century—in 1319 caused a great stir. Jaume II of Aragon made great efforts to obtain the Chalice used at the Last Supper and the body of the early martyr St. Barbara from Egypt. A contemporary document describes the arrival of Jaume II at the monastery of San Cugat near Barcelona in May 1299. The king came with a train of knights and citizens. He found a woman 'out of her mind, lying half-dead before the altar of St. Michael, gravely tormented by an unclean spirit named Pilot'. The abbot and monks in vain applied relics of the True Cross, of apostles and martyrs, to the woman. They finally elicited from her the name of a hitherto unknown St. Albus, supposed to be buried near where she lay in the church. This identification was confirmed by application of relics to other demoniacs present. King Jaume left for a neighbouring castle but sent three knights back to ask for relics of the mysterious St. Albus. After due prayer the floor of a chapel was taken up and a tomb found. Jaume hastened back and duly received the relics he wanted after they had demonstrated their efficacy by being hung round the neck of the possessed woman and so curing her.

The most powerful of all relics was the consecrated Host. Hence it was stolen, on occasion, in the hope that it would bestow magical force on its possessor. But, according to the *Cántigas*, the stolen Host bled and revealed its true nature.[2]

[1] Alfonso X, *General estoria*, i. xxi. 18 (ed. Solalinde, p. 607); *Cántigas*, nos. 11, 24, 32, 45, 26, 119, 125, 83, 42–4, etc. (i. 34–6, 68 f., 95 f., 130–3, 76–9; ii. 54–6, 67–71; i. 240–2, 121–7); M. R. Lida, *NRFH* 13 (1959), 47. There are many more parallels, or versions of the same stories, in Berceo's earlier *Milagros de Nuestra Señora* (see p. 132 above). See A. Valbuena Prat, *Historia de la literatura española*, 6th edn., i (Barcelona, 1960), 125–35; E. S. Procter, *Alfonso X of Castile* (Oxford, 1951), pp. 24–46.

[2] *Cántigas*, nos. 35, 61 (i. 102, 174 f.); Martínez Ferrando, *Jaime II de Aragón*, ii. 235 f.; Finke, *Acta* ii. 756, 910–12; *Cántigas*, no. 104 (ii. 8–10). For Jaume II and other relics (in Armenia) see K. J. Basmadjian, *Revue de l'orient latin*, 11 (1905–8), 1–6.

MAGIC

The belief in the reality of magic, of the evil eye, of astrology and alchemy, was shared by Muslims and Christians. Among Christians leading 'scientists' of the thirteenth century, such as Robert Grosseteste, considered knowledge of astrology essential to successful agriculture, medicine, and alchemical experiments. The Archpriest of Hita's remark 'I believe the astrologers [interpret] the truth of nature', though God could change nature and chance, represented the common view.

Alfonso X, in the *Partidas*, distinguished between divination by 'the art of astronomy', which was legitimate since it was based on Ptolemy, and predictions made by augurers and witches, which were linked with necromancy and deserved the death penalty. He then added:

> But those who carry out enchantments with a *good* intention, such as removing demons from men's bodies, or freeing those who are husband and wife who are under a spell so that they cannot fulfil their conjugal duties, or dissolve a cloud which might bring down hail or mist, so that it should not destroy the fruits of the earth, or kill locusts or insects which are harming grain or vines, or [labour] for some other profitable end, should not be punished but rather rewarded.

The *Lapidario* written under Alfonso's direction contains 'information and actual recipes for the practice of magic and alchemy'. Medical science of the time prescribed that blood-letting should only take place when the moon and stars were found in specified conjunctions. The great doctor Petrus Hispanus (born in Lisbon) advised wearing, as a general preventive against disease, a bag containing the eyes of a magpie, a crab, or a wolf slung round one's neck.

The importance of astrology to Ramon Lull appears in his medical treatises as well as in the role elemental theory played in his Art. Don Juan Manuel considers that the use of 'virtues' of precious stones to obtain knowledge of the future is perfectly possible (though wrong) while the attempt to bring pressure on God by having Masses celebrated and magical prayers said is clearly very wrong. A thirteenth-century manual for confessors speaks of 'those who make encantations or charms through women or throw lots for lost objects or seek out augurers or go to diviners'. In *Blanquerna* Lull describes a knight seeking omens from the flight of birds, though Lull's hero considers this to be a waste of time.[1]

The documents of the time corroborate the literary evidence. In 1325 a Muslim dyer in Tarazona complained that a certain Don Bueno and his wife had bewitched him so that he could not work at his craft. A local lawyer was instructed to investigate the matter.

Jaume II of Aragon had studied magical books when he was a young man. In 1302 he ordered that they should be sent to him at Jaca, secretly and urgently. Jaume II's grandson, Pere III, was to devote inordinate attention to astrology. Like alchemy, it was a reputable science. The practitioners of these sciences were not dependent on kings alone. A document of 1298 reveals an English alchemist in debt to someone who was probably an innkeeper in Tarragona: 'I John the Englishman, scribe, owe you P. Zavit 30 sol. for food and drink, which I promise to pay when the secret of making gold permits me.'

Magical swords enjoyed great prestige. In 1270 Jaume I of Aragon annulled a judicial duel because one of the two challengers had used the 'sword of Vilardell', which was said to have slain a dragon. It was stated that the sword 'had such virtue that no one bearing it can succomb or be overcome'. This sword was bought by Alfons II of Catalonia–Aragon in 1285 for a very large sum.[2]

Many church councils condemn witchcraft and forbid the faithful to consult magicians. A contemporary Penitential lists among popular beliefs those in witches, vampires, and the evil eye. In Navarre in 1329 the civil power seized on some women accused of witchcraft and burnt them alive. This seems to have been a rare intrusion into the domain of the Church.[3]

[1] *Libro de Buen Amor*, v. 140 (ed. cit., p. 46); *Partidas*, VII. xxiii. 3; J. H. Nunemaker, *Speculum*, 7 (1932), 558; Oliveira Marques, *Daily Life*, pp. 145, 150; my *Ramon Lull*, pp. 13 f.; Juan Manuel, *Libro del caballero et del escudero*, 45 (*BAE* li. 252 f.); *Libro de Patronio*, 45 (ibid. 415 f.); A. Morel-Fatio, *Romania*, 16 (1887), 379; Lull, *Blanquerna*, 47 (*Obres* i. 177). For Islam see E. Lévi-Provençal, *Al-Andalus*, 6 (1941), 395; Ibn Khaldūn, *Muqaddimah*, transl. F. Rosenthal, i. pp. lxxii f.

[2] Finke, *Acta* ii. 867 f., 920; p. 351 below; Segura, *Aplech*, p. 276; F. Carreras y Candi, *Revue hispanique*, 15 (1906), 652–67; Guerrero Lovillo, op. cit., pp. 137 f.

[3] Oliveira Marques, pp. 226 f.; Goñi, *Principe de Viana*, 23 (1962), 72; cf. e.g. the Council of Salamanca of 1335 (Tejada y Ramiro, iii. 576).

Magic played a large role in popular religion. Other components of the Christian world-picture should now be noted.

MILITANT CHRISTIANITY

Religion in the Latin West had a strongly militant note. This is well illustrated by one of the *Miraculos romanzados* of Pero Marín, prior of Silos. These stories celebrate the wonders performed by Santo Domingo, the monastery's patron. Alfonso X of Castile kneels throughout Vespers and Matins before the body of Santo Domingo, praying for aid against his enemies. The Saint appears to Alfonso in his sleep. When Alfonso asks how he should live with neighbouring kings he is answered in a quotation from Psalm 2, 'Thou shalt break them with a rod of iron; thou shalt dash them in pieces like a potter's vessel'. Alfonso carries out the Saint's advice, triumphs, and, in gratitude, gives the monastery all the royal revenue from the town of Silos. The deed of gift of 1256 still exists. The story was no doubt woven round it but it is quite possible that Marín has used some statement made by the king. A mind familiar with the Psalter and intent on approaching conflict would naturally phrase what seemed a divine vision in the language of that book.

Jaume I's *Book of Deeds*, in its description of the conquest of Majorca, includes a sermon promising Paradise to those who die fighting the Muslims. St. George, patron of Catalonia, is seen entering the breach in the city walls at the head of Jaume's troops. One seems to be reading a chronicle of the First Crusade.

Even Lull, a great propagandist for missions rather than crusades, shared the common feeling. In *Blanquerna* a knight resolves to serve the Virgin Mary in arms—since he cannot do so by writing—by doing battle for her in Muslim lands. His death is seen as martyrdom. Lull's hero, Blanquerna, when pope, recommends this behaviour to the Military Orders in general.[1]

PILGRIMAGE

Pilgrimage played an even larger part than holy war or crusade in the religion of late-medieval Europe. There were many

[1] Férotin, *Recueil*, pp. 226 ff.; Jaume I, *Libre dels feyts*, cc. 62, 84; Lull, *Blanquerna*, 64, 80 (*Obres* i. 205 f., 231). On the cult of St. George in Aragon see A. Canellas López in *J. Zurita, cuadernos de historia*, 19–20 (1966–7), 7–23; see Burns, op. cit. i. 12–15.

shrines in the Iberian peninsula but far the most important was Santiago de Compostela. A thirteenth-century diocesan synod of Santiago declared: 'Whoever comes on pilgrimage to the church of St. James is forgiven a third part of all his sins and if, coming, staying or returning, he shall die *all* are forgiven him.' So many pilgrims arrived, by night and day, that violent collisions between them were not infrequent, the more so that it was a point of national honour for Germans, French, and Italians to seize the place nearest the tomb of St. James in the night vigils. Violent deaths of pilgrims within the cathedral were so common that in 1207 Pope Innocent III agreed that church offices need not be suspended on these occasions. The church could be purified by a rapid sprinkling with holy water mixed with wine and ashes. In 1328 a later pope made it simply holy water, to save time.

At the morning Mass and in the afternoon a cleric in his surplice took his place on top of the enormous chest for offerings to the shrine and proclaimed the official indulgence in garbled French, Italian, or Spanish, depending on which group was approaching, for instance, in so-called French, 'Zee [ici?] larcha de lobra mon señor Samanin; zee lobra de lagresa [la Grace?]'. The scale of the pilgrimage in the thirteenth century appears from the fact that over a hundred shops selling shells—the official token of the Santiago pilgrim—and other souvenirs existed in the city itself.[1]

Compared with the pilgrims to Santiago the Spaniards who ventured to Jerusalem were few in number. A Catalan pilgrimage took place in 1323, led by Dominicans. This was part of Jaume II of Aragon's attempt to get control of the Holy Places. The account of the pilgrimage, following a tradition going back to the fourth century, identified minutely the place where every event in the New Testament—and some in the Old Testament—had taken place, for instance, 'In front of this church there is a fine palm tree to which St. Peter fastened his boats when he was fishing. At the foot of the tree there is a stone where St. Peter sold the fish.'[2]

[1] López Ferreiro, op. cit. v. 49, 94, 98, appendices, pp. 64–7, 74; vi. 296. For English pilgrims see D. W. Lomax, *Principe de Viana*, 31 (1970), 159–69. For the shrine of S. Ildefonso at Zamora see J. Gil de Zamora, *BRAH* 6 (1885), 60–71.

[2] J. Pijoan, *AIEC* 1 (1907), 370–84, especially p. 383; see Finke, *Acta* ii. 756.

SOURCES OF LAY PIETY: THE BIBLE

The lay piety of the age was fed by a number of different sources. In Castile, unlike the rest of western Europe, many translations of different books of the Bible were based on the Hebrew text, not on the Latin Vulgate. Castilian translations were made by and for Jews. There is evidence for an almost complete translation of the Bible by the reign of Alfonso X. Alfonso's *General estoria* also included the text of the Bible, together with much else. The earlier poems of Berceo show the poet's complete familiarity with Biblical texts used in the Liturgy, and especially with the Gospels of Matthew and John. By 1300 many liturgical and devotional phrases coming ultimately from the Bible had entered Castilian.

Less is known of Catalan translations of the Bible than of Castilian. There seems no evidence for translations from Hebrew into Catalan. On the other hand, as in secular literature, there is a strong link between France and Catalonia. The Bible was translated from the Latin of the Vulgate into Catalan. Between 1282 and 1313 it was also largely translated from a French version into over 11,000 Catalan verses. The translation was incomplete. In the Old Testament the Prophets were omitted in favour of the Books of Kings and Maccabees. The choice was possibly due to the preference of the lady, a countess of Ampurias, to whom the translation was dedicated—in the dedication she was correctly told she would find 'many battles' in the work before her. A brief compendium of the Bible was translated from Provençal into Catalan.[1]

RELIGIOUS DRAMA

Catalonia adopted the Roman-Gallican rite and abandoned the Mozarabic in the ninth century, over two hundred years before the rest of Christian Spain took this step. This difference in time largely explains why Catalonia developed a far richer liturgical drama than the rest of the peninsula. In contrast to Castile 'Catalonia was a part of that general territory which saw the tradition of the liturgical play begin'. Catalan abbeys such as Ripoll were in close touch with French monasteries. The

[1] M. Morreale, 'Vernacular Scriptures in Spain', *The Cambridge History of the Bible*, ii (Cambridge, 1969), 465–71, bibliography, pp. 533–5; Riquer, ii. 117–21; D. Catalán, *Hispanic Review*, 33 (1965), 310–18.

same Latin plays were staged at Easter and Christmas in the cathedrals and monasteries of Catalonia, Valencia, and Majorca that could be seen in France or Germany. Vernacular religious plays, with elaborate stage machinery, were also presented, at least in Valencia, at Christmas, Pentecost, and the Assumption. The dramatic monologue spoken at Christmas by a child impersonating the Sibyl, surviving today in Majorca, appears to be a native Catalan development.

Little Latin liturgical drama existed in Castile (or in Portugal). The Castilian twelfth-century vernacular play the *Auto de los Reyes Magos*, was modelled on a play or poems in French. The *Auto* describes the visit of the three kings, Caspar, Melchior, Baltasar, to Herod with 'the same ingenuous piety that appears in contemporary sculpture'. There existed in Castile two cycles of vernacular plays, now lost, one devoted to the Nativity, the other to the Resurrection.

VERNACULAR RELIGIOUS LITERATURE

The devout vernacular literature of the age included a number of narrative poems, mostly modelled on French or Provençal sources. The *Libre dels Tres Reys d'Orient* narrated the legends of Christ's infancy. The *Vida de Santa María Egipciaca* described the dramatic change wrought by grace in a prostitute who becomes a saint in the desert. Gonzalo de Berceo's poems (written 1220–50) are no more 'original' than these works but they are more remarkable. They present lives of saints or miracles of the Virgin, or explain ceremonies of the Mass or the signs which will announce the Last Judgement in language which could be understood by the least-educated laity. Berceo's San Millán or Santo Domingo of Silos are shepherds before they are saints, shepherds Berceo has seen in his native Rioja.[1]

LAY PIETY

From the twelfth century onwards piety turned more and more to loving, emotional contemplation of the Passion of Christ. This tendency appears as clearly in literature as it does in Gothic

[1] H. Anglès, *La musica a Catalunya fins al segle XIII* (Barcelona, 1935), esp. pp. 24–34, 267–311; R. B. Donovan, *The Liturgical Drama in Medieval Spain* (Toronto, 1958), esp. pp. 29, 67–73, 143, 165–7; *Auto*, ed. R. Menéndez Pidal, *RABM* 3ª. época, 4 (1900), 455–62; *Libre dels Tres Reis*, ed. M. Alvar (Madrid, 1965); this and other texts mentioned are in *BAE* lvii; Valbuena Prat, op. cit., i. 65–7, 75–93.

sculpture. Ramon Lull's *Book of Contemplation* returns throughout to the suffering of Christ on the Cross.

If women paint their mouths red, Your mouth, Lord, was dyed with gall and soot and vinegar: and if women dye their hair blond and black, Your hair was dyed with red blood. If women paint their side and breasts with silk and lace and gold and silver, Your side and breast were painted on the Cross by the wound which split Your heart in half.

Don Juan Manuel's detailed meditation on the Passion also brings out the sufferings of every part of Christ's body, his eyes, his hair, his cheeks, his neck, his side, arms, shoulders, legs, hands, feet . . .

Many nobles of the time, while reciting their prayers, mechanically interspersed clauses of the 'Our Father' with shouted orders to their servants. Juan Manuel felt it necessary to insist that it is better to say one 'Our Father', thinking over what one is saying, rather than mumble many prayers unthinkingly.

Many nobles fasted only when they were not hungry and gave alms only when they did not feel the loss. Lull tells us that it was commonly held that alms were a substitute for fasting in Lent. Other evidence for the uninspired character of much popular religion has already been presented.[1]

The *Castigos e documentos* attributed to Sancho IV of Castile contain much practical advice to the king or lay noble. He should above all hear Mass devoutly, give alms, and suppress the desires of the flesh. He should also treat prelates politely. It is seldom that this rather low level of piety is transcended, though we are told that the whole Christian religion is founded on justice, patience, and mercy.

The main sources of the *Castigos* are the canonical and apocryphal scriptures and the compilations due to Alfonso X, especially the *Primera Crónica* and the *Partidas*. It seems clear that the book is mainly due to some member of Sancho's clerical entourage. It contains a number of miracles of the Virgin and stories of demons.[2]

[1] Lull, *Libre de contemplació*, 120, 15 (*Obres* ii. 362); Juan Manuel, *Libro de los estados*, i. 57, 60 (*BAE* li. 309,312); Lull, *Blanquerna*, 72 (*Obres* i. 217); see pp. 119 ff. above.

[2] See the edn. by A. Rey (Bloomington, Indiana, 1952), cc. 4, 6, 7, 10, 17, 30; see p. 140 above, and Valbuena Prat, pp. 135 ff.

PRACTICAL GOOD WORKS: RANSOMING CAPTIVES

Among the more striking signs of the actual influence of the Christian religion in the thirteenth century is the success of the Trinitarian and Mercedarian friars, whose task was the ransoming of Christian captives from Muslim Spain and especially from North Africa. These Orders founded convents all over the peninsula. When the alms they could collect failed, they were prepared to risk papal censure by trading with Muslims to raise the money they needed. They acted as regular intermediaries between Christian slaves and their families just as did the Muslim *alfaquequer* who visited Christian countries to free Muslim slaves. A document of 1410 shows us the Mercedarians at work. It presents an arrangement which must often have been made before this time. A group of Christians had been ransomed in North Africa by the Mercedarians and now swore to accompany the friars in their propaganda tours for a year to raise funds. They would wear the clothes they had worn as slaves, not wash their hair without the friars' permission, not swear, gamble, or frequent brothels, they would recite stated prayers, and hand over the alms they were given to the Order. If they broke their oath they conceded they could be imprisoned, chained, and even tortured. Another document of 1412 shows us another group of twenty-eight Christians from all over the Crown of Aragon following the friars in the same way.[1]

HOSPITALS

The endowment and upkeep of hospitals was an increasingly common form of lay piety. In 1218 a female recluse who came from an aristocratic family retired to the hospital attached to the monastery of Silos and gave herself up to the service of the poor there. In the 1220s a hospital for the poor was founded at the Cistercian monastery of Santes Creus in Catalonia by a noble, Ramon Alamany. Between 1260 and 1278 two women, a layman and a canon, endowed beds in the hospitals of other Cistercian monasteries in Catalonia, Poblet and Escarp. The endowment was assured from the revenue of vineyards, a house, and an oven.

[1] Verlinden, i. 537–43, 606–14; E. Pascual, *BSAL* 6 (1895–6), 123–6; see Burns, op. cit., i. 247–52.

Hospitals were also founded in towns. Alfonso X remarks in a *Cántiga* that a good man built a hospital where he 'gave [the sick] bread and wine and meat and fish and beds to lie in in winter and summer'. In 1285 the bishop of Pamplona reorganized the cathedral hospital, which was to have fifty beds. Leper hospitals existed at Pamplona and along the pilgrimage route to Santiago. In 1288 Sancho IV issued a privilege protecting a hospital founded by the dean of Burgos cathedral just outside the town. Such protection was necessary. In 1315 the prelates of Castile complained that hospitals 'made for the poor and sick' were used by knights who 'threw the poor out to die in the streets'.

Lull's *Blanquerna* has an elaborate description of the hospital founded by Blanquerna's parents, Evast and Aloma. After Blanquerna, 'captured by God', has withdrawn to the life of a hermit, his parents decide to sell all their possessions and endow a hospital. In it every poor patient had 'a very fine bed, with the food he needed', and was waited on by many servants, among whom Evast and Aloma themselves took their place.

The foundation of a hospital is only part of the 'lay apostolate' exercised by Evast and Aloma. Their adoption of complete poverty for the sake of Christ, their extreme humility, and the love that continues to unite them affects the modern reader as it does the gluttonous bishop, lustful nobles, avaricious banker, overproud cloth merchant, envious, rich, and vainglorious friar of the novel. All these are types, however well drawn. Evast and Aloma (particularly the latter) are real people and their approach to others as 'brothers and friends' expresses a vital spirit in Lull which comes from St. Francis.[1]

Much more information as to contemporary religion can be drawn from *Blanquerna*, for instance the imbalance of preachers between the well-supplied towns and the deserted countryside, or the type of burgesses who live outwardly in great splendour but have secret rooms in their house where they dine meagrely,

[1] Férotin, *Recueil*, pp. 139 f.; E. Fort i Cogul, in *Miscel·lània històrica catalana* (Poblet, 1970), pp. 181–213; A. Altisent, *Studia monastica*, 12 (1970), 107–13; Alfonso X, *Cántigas*, no. 67 (ed. Mettmann, i. 198); Vázquez de Parga, *et al.*, *Las peregrinaciones a Santiago*, iii (Madrid, 1949), 70 f., 73 f.; Gaibrois, *Sancho IV*, p. cxviii; *Cortés de León*, i. 295; Lull, *Blanquerna*, 5, 10–18 (*Obres* i. 134, 143–8). For Valencia see Burns, i. 237–46, 285–94; see also J. M. Miquel Parellada, *Los hospitales de Tarragona* (Tarragona, 1959).

sleep on an uncomfortable bed, wear hair shirts, and pray for hours before a crucifix.[1]

It is more difficult to say to what degree Lull's programme for 'social action' corresponded to reality. Blanquerna, when bishop, supports his canons when they lead demonstrations against over-rich clergy. One canon leads a crowd of the poor going through the streets to the houses of rich men crying, 'Hunger, hunger!'. Another canon pleads cases for the poor in the courts. He is ready to lead a crowd to the royal palace to dramatize injustice. Another canon leads a mob of gamblers and harlots to tear down the shutters with which drapers darken their shops so as to conceal the poor quality of the cloth they are selling. Lull has captured a fact of contemporary life, the wide gap between the rich (including many of the clergy) and the poor, and the violent resentment the poor felt at this. This resentment appeared in the attempted popular revolt of Barcelona in 1285. I do not know of any evidence that the higher clergy, anywhere, took the popular side in this struggle. Other features of Blanquerna's programme are closer to reality.

His attack on mourning garments as ostentatious, and as involving misuse of money which should be given to the poor, finds some echo in contemporary sumptuary laws. Bishop Blanquerna's use of a third of his income to make peace, to end blood feuds in his city, probably only goes somewhat beyond contemporary evidence.

If the religion of the age is to be evaluated fairly, its ideals must be included in the balance as well as its failings. The ideals expressed in *Blanquerna* must be taken into account as well as the denunciations of evils by church councils. Lull's criticisms of processions imploring rain as self-interested must be recalled as well as the materialistic superstition of many of Alfonso X's *Cántigas*.

Some contemporary changes in private institutions show Christian ideas translated into action. In 1337 Valencia saw the creation of the office of 'father of orphans' and the abolition of that of 'king of the harlots' (king pimp). In 1343 a 'procurator of the miserable' was appointed in Valencia to defend the rights of prisoners too poor to pay a lawyer. This institution corresponds very closely to an idea advanced in *Blanquerna* (c. 73). Is

[1] *Blanquerna*, 66, 69 (pp. 207, 213).

it possible that the Lullists of Valencia, who were active in the 1330s, were behind this application of Lullian ideas to a concrete situation?

One may wonder, however, if the remark of the royal treasurer of Castile that sanctity was only possible to members of the nobility did not reflect contemporary reality. Perhaps the widespread influence of Christianity can be seen mainly in such central features of medieval life as the horror attached to perjury—oaths were seen as the one cement binding society together—but there are other indications that Christian ideas were slowly penetrating the popular mind. The criminal records of Valencia include the account of a murder. The dying victim was surrounded by his neighbours who implored him to forgive his murderer so that Christ would forgive him his own sins.[1]

HERETICS

Heretical Christians bulked very small in the Iberian kingdoms compared to Jews and Muslims. The *Partidas* prescribe the death penalty against obstinate heretics who insult God or the Virgin Mary but the prescription was seldom invoked. Fernando III had ordered some heretics to be hanged or burnt alive. Others were merely branded on the face with a hot iron and lost their possessions.[2]

It is not clear if these heretics were Albigensian (Cathar) missionaries, who had penetrated to Castile and León. One Alfonso X's *Cántigas* depicts unspecified heretics who cut out the tongue of a cleric because he sang the praise of the Virgin Mary. Another *Cántiga* describes the trick by which an undoubtedly Albigensian heretic had a pilgrim to Santiago hanged as a thief.[3] Catharism, in its passion for poverty and hatred of corruption—whether or not this was combined with Manichaean beliefs—was the most formidable rival of the Catholic Church in the twelfth and thirteenth centuries. It loomed larger in Catalonia than in Castile. Catalonia shared the same language and culture as Provence and Languedoc. The cause of the

[1] ibid. 72 f., 75 f. (pp. 217, 218, 220–3). For the revolt of Barcelona see below, Part II, Ch. I, p. 281, n. 1. For Valencia see J. Lalinde Abadía, *VIII CHCA*, i (1967), 46. See F. Fita, *BRAH* 9 (1886), 118 (cited Linehan, p. 187); F. A. Roca Traver, *El Justicia de Valencia, 1238–1321* (Valencia, 1970), p. 325.

[2] *Partidas*, VII. xxvi. 2; Mansilla, op. cit. (p. 91, n. 1), pp. 148–50.

[3] *Cántigas*, nos. 156, 175 (ii. 149 f., 187–90).

Cathars had become inextricably confused with that of the resistance of the rulers of southern France to the Capetian monarchy of the north. Jaume I's father, Pere I, although orthodox himself, had died in 1213 at the head of a partly Cathar army.

The recent studies of Joan Ventura have shown that a large number of the feudal lords of Roussillon and Cerdagne and of the diocese of Urgel in the Pyrenees—all part of the Crown of Aragon—were Cathars. A number of other nobles from Languedoc who were Cathars or suspected of heresy took refuge in Catalonia under Jaume I. Some of them received as a penance the obligation to go on crusade and discharged this by taking part in Jaume's conquest of Majorca and Valencia. It has yet to be proved that 'Cathar gold' contributed to any significant extent to these conquests. No doubt some Cathar merchants, as well as nobles, emigrated to Catalonia, but more Cathars took their capital to north Italy. The Cathars seem only to have been strong in the north of Catalonia and across the Pyrenees. Their presence there may explain the foundation of convents of friars in Pyrenean towns such as Puigcerdá. Heresy called forth vigorous opponents. But, by 1300, the Cathars had virtually ceased to exist, even in these areas. The Dominican Inquisition had triumphed here as in southern France.[1]

The early fourteenth century shows Jaume II of Aragon occasionally worried by isolated cases of heresy. In 1307, for instance. Jaume was informed that a certain Joan Despuig of Tortosa, aged seventy, held fatalist views, disbelieved in the Resurrection of the dead, was never known to attend Mass, receive the Sacraments, or give alms, and was wont to read from a mysterious—perhaps magical—book. Jaume merely told the bishop of Tortosa to 'take counsel' on the matter, but it is of some interest that Despuig's opinions were seen as liable to spread. (A Council of Tarragona in 1292 had denounced disbelief in the Resurrection as the foundation of many heresies.) In general Jaume was concerned to keep the Inquisitors within bounds—he insisted on being kept informed of any process for

[1] J. Ventura Subirats, *BRABL* 28 (1959–60), 75–168 (see esp. p. 117); idem, *VII CHCA* iii. 123–34. The author places far greater emphasis on Catharism in Catalonia than I would do. For convents in Puigcerdá, etc., see M. M. Riu, cited above (p. 135, n. 1).

heresy, especially any directed against Jews. This did not mean that Jaume was not deeply concerned with the morality of his subjects. His letters testify to his disgust at hearing that in Valencia men and women used the public baths together and that some notaries of Valencia spent their days at dice and their nights in revelry. A girl from Játiva was summoned to appear before the king to present a charge of rape. Jaume's successor, Alfons III, was equally concerned for his subjects' salvation. He often issued invitations to his subjects to join in prayer so as to avert public calamities, and exhorted them to fulfil the precepts of the Church. In 1317 'a new type of life, not approved by the Church', was being introduced into Catalonia by 'Beguines', men and women, who had 'books of theology in romance', Provençal or Catalan. These Beguines were connected with the Third Order of St. Francis, whose members were ordered not to live together or to have theological books in romance or to preach, teach, or repeat anything concerning the Faith, except in church.[1]

[1] Finke, *Acta* ii. 846 f., 851, 853, 856 f., 860; Tejada y Ramiro, iii. 414, 474 f.; Martínez Ferrando, *Jaime II*, i. 298; ii. 300, 32, 173; E. Bagué, in *Els descendents de Pere el Gran*, p. 172.

V
A Land of Three Religions

In the thirteenth and early fourteenth centuries the Iberian peninsula continued to act as it had done since at least the tenth century as a mediator between Islam and the Christian West. At the courts of Castile and Aragon, in the island of Majorca, in the castles of Don Juan Manuel and the taverns frequented by the Archpriest of Hita, Jewish scholars and financiers, Mudejar minstrels and artists met architects from the Île de France, friars trained in theology at Paris, canonists and Roman lawyers from Bologna, merchants from Genoa, troubadours and political exiles from Provence and Sicily.

The art and literature of the age reveal with particular clarity the fusion of Islamic, Hebraic, and Christian. This fusion also appears in social customs and popular beliefs and superstitions. It was naturally repugnant to Frenchmen and Italians, who could not understand how it could have developed, and to faithful servants of the international Church.

THE PENINSULA AND ISLAM: RELATIONS WITH ISLAMIC COUNTRIES

Relations between Castile, Aragon, or Portugal, and Islamic countries were somewhat more difficult but no less important than those with France or Italy. Since one Islamic country, Granada, formed part of the peninsula, relations with its rulers were as important, to Castile in particular, as close connections with France were to the Crown of Aragon, with its possessions north of the Pyrenees.

Embassies were also exchanged with Egypt and with the emirates of North Africa, Tunisia, Tlemcen, and Morocco. Muslim emissaries were treated with understanding. In 1293 the envoys of Tlemcen to Castile received a double allowance for food, 'the day of their Easter', that is for the end of Ramadan, the 'Lent' of Islam. Official relations between Castile and Egypt were comparatively slight, except perhaps in the reign of

Alfonso X; there is little evidence even for Granada's relations with Egypt before 1350. In contrast, the Crown of Aragon, as it grew into a political and economic power in the Mediterranean, was in fairly continuous diplomatic touch with Egypt. Egypt and Aragon concluded two important treaties in the 1290s.[1]

The Crown of Aragon maintained constant diplomatic relations with Tunisia and Tlemcen. Both countries, at different times, became tributaries of Aragon. Castile and Portugal were more concerned with Morocco. The Banū Marīn of Morocco continually intervened in the peninsula, and frequently occupied such key positions as Tarifa, Algeciras, and Ronda. In 1288 Sancho IV of Castile sent troops to assist Morocco. In doing so Sancho complied with a treaty in exactly the same way as his successors complied with their obligations when they sent war-galleys to assist France.[2]

Granada was woven into the fabric of Castilian politics. From 1246 onwards its ruler had been legally a vassal of Castile, with heavy monetary and military obligations, and the duty to attend meetings of the Castilian Cortes. Jaume I of Aragon accepted this situation and treated the rulers of Granada as vassals of Castile. Jaume's successors pursued a different policy, treating Granada as an independent country. Alfons II allied with Granada against Castile, Jaume II with Castile and Granada against Morocco. In later years one of Jaume II's main aims was the partition of Castile. He was prepared to ally with Granada or with Morocco and agree to their conquests from Castile if that furthered his main goal.[3]

The Christian rulers of the peninsula were well informed as to the affairs of their Muslim neighbours. Jaume I of Aragon's conquests were made easier by the information he received from Catalan merchants trading with Majorca and from one of his nobles who had spent two years in exile in Valencia and who

[1] M. Gaibrois de Ballesteros, *Historia del reinado de Sancho IV de Castilla*, i (Madrid, 1922), p. cxxi. P. Martínez Montávez, in *Al-Andalus*, 27 (1962), 343–76, and in *Hispania*, 23 (1963), 505–23, argues for, but does not prove, intense relations between Castile and Egypt from the 1250s, though Alfonso X sent four or five embassies to the East. R. Arié, *MCV* 1 (1965), 87–107, can produce no evidence of diplomatic relations between Granada and Egypt before the 1340s. For the Crown of Aragon see Part II, Ch. I below, p. 268.

[2] See below, Part II, Ch. I, pp. 247 f., Ch. II, p. 327, n. 1.

[3] A. Giménez Soler, *La Corona de Aragón y Granada* (Barcelona, 1908), e.g. pp. 76 ff.

knew both the attractions of that kingdom and where it was vulnerable to attack. The details of the assassination of Abu Yaᶜqūb of Morocco at Tlemcen on 13 May 1307 were known by 5 June in Castile. Granada was even better known. Treaties with Castile normally contained a clause allowing merchants of each country free access to the other. The history of Granada was especially interesting to Castilians. The *Crónica de Alfonso XI* contains a résumé of the reigns of its first five kings, which were regarded as part of the history of Castile. The fuller (unpublished) version of this *Crónica* contains over fifty chapters devoted to the history of the Banū Marīn of Morocco. Aragon, also, had its sources of information on Granada. An envoy of Jaume II to Pope Clement V in 1309 could provide an estimate of the forces of Granada and Morocco.[1]

Granada, in return, was well informed about the situation in Castile and Aragon. Ibn Khaldūn, who was at one time employed by the court of Granada, has left us a brief history of Christian Spain which is superior to any contemporary Christian account of an Islamic state. Leading Castilian nobles, when they rebelled, often turned for shelter to Granada. The Alhambra knew when the resources of Alfonso X were overstrained by his bid for the Holy Roman Empire, the right moment (in 1275) to call in the Banū Marīn from Morocco. Infantes of Castile fought against their king, under the banner of Granada, while princes of Granada fought for Castile. Not only Castilian émigré magnates temporarily out of favour at home, but Catalan merchants appear in the service of Granada in the fourteenth century. This situation appeared normal to contemporaries. Even an official chronicler might blame disloyalty to one's own king but not alliance with those of another faith. On the frontier, in particular, 'peace and war were not affairs of State [still less of religion] but a private matter for each man, determined as his interests indicated'. In 1329 the king of Castile, when preparing to join with Aragon against Granada, had to promise Aragon 'that he would not allow his bishops, the Military Orders, nobles, knights, or

[1] Jaume I, *Libre dels feyts*, cc. 47, 58, 128; A. Canellas López, *BRAH* 145 (1959), 256–8, 279 f.; Giménez Soler, pp. 167–70; *Crónica de Alfonso XI*, c. 55 (*BAE* lxvi. 206 f.); D. Catalán Menéndez Pidal, *NRFH* 7 (1953), 570 f.; Finke, *Acta* ii. 765 f.

town councils to make peace or truce with Granada on their own.'[1]

The general Catalan attitude towards Islamic states was one of recognition and tolerance. The chronicler and royal official Bernat Desclot characterizes the crusade of St. Louis of France against Egypt by remarking that the princes of France 'had gone to a land of strange people to destroy them and to take their land'. Another Catalan, Ramon Lull, imagines the sultan of Egypt sending a mission to the pope to remark how strange it was that the pope and Christian princes used force to conquer the Holy Land—thus imitating Muḥammad—rather than preaching and martyrdom, the arms by which Christ and the Apostles converted the world. This scepticism towards the value of crusades helps to explain the refusal of Jaume I to join in a crusade against Tunis and the readiness of later kings of Aragon not only to ally with Granada and Morocco against Castile but to promise to aid the sultan of Egypt against any crusade directed against him. On the other hand the Muslims of Granada soon developed a 'siege mentality'. The permanent inclination of the doctors of the law and the populace to Holy War could only with difficulty be restrained by the wiser emirs.[2]

Official diplomatic envoys were the exception rather than the rule. The main contacts between Christian and Islamic countries were provided by the mercenaries, merchants, missionaries, and slaves who shuttled between Castile and Catalonia–Aragon and Granada, North Africa, and the East.

These travellers ranged downwards in the social hierarchy from the Infante Enrique of Castile, a brother of Alfonso X, and various illegitimate sons of Sancho IV of Castile and of Jaume II of Aragon, through Castilian or Catalan nobles, such as Guzmán el Bueno or Guillem Ramon de Moncada, to friars, adventurers, mercenary commanders, and pirates.

The papacy prohibited the export of war materials—principally arms and timber, etc. for naval construction—to Muslims.

[1] Ibn Khaldūn, in R. Dozy, *Recherches sur l'histoire* . . ., 3rd edn., i (Paris, 1881), 89–116; Ibn Abi Zar', *Rawd al-Qirtas*, transl. A. Huici Miranda, ii (Textos Medievales XIII) (Valencia, 1964), 591, 617; Giménez Soler, pp. 257, 261, 290 f.; J. de Mata de Carriazo, *Al-Andalus*, 13 (1948), 92; Zurita, *Anales* vii. 7.

[2] B. Desclot, *Crònica*, c. 63, ed. Coll, ii. 182; R. Lull, *Blanquerna*, c. 80 (*Obres essencials*, i (Barcelona, 1957), 229; transl. E. A. Peers, p. 323); see p. 262 below; H. Terrasse, in *Mélanges offerts à M. Bataillon* (Bordeaux, 1962), pp. 253–60.

Similar prohibitions existed in Islam. The merchants of neither side respected them. Even the sale of a ship to Muslims could be compounded for by a relatively small fine. The export of cereals to Islam was prohibited, but treaties included freedom from duties on grain.

There was always the risk of piracy, Christian and Muslim. However, from 1250, the kings of Aragon forbade and attempted to punish piratical attacks by their subjects on Muslims who were protected either by treaties between Aragon and their rulers or by individual safe-conducts.[1]

There were Christian mercenaries, merchants, and slaves in North Africa and Muslim mercenaries, merchants, and slaves in Castile and Aragon. In the twelfth century Christian mercenaries had fought for the Almoravids against the Almohads in Morocco. In the thirteenth century the declining Almohads depended largely on Castilian and Portuguese mercenaries. When the Almohads fell Castilian and, at times, Catalan mercenary captains recruited bands to serve the new masters of Morocco, the Banū Marīn. There were Catalan militias in Tunis and Tlemcen from the 1250s onwards for at least two centuries. The commanders of these mercenary forces were highly honoured and very well paid. They received much more than the officers of state of Christian kingdoms. Ibn Khaldūn acknowledges that the North African rulers were right to use Christian mercenaries since they lent solidity to Maghribí armies.[2]

Most of the North African mercenaries serving in Spain came from the Zanāta tribe in Morocco. They served principally in Granada, where they provided the cream of the army. They also served Castile and Aragon; they gave the term designating a light horseman to the languages of the peninsula; 'jinete' in Castilian, 'genet' in Catalan, 'ginete' in Portuguese. Some Banū Marīn princes also served Aragon in the

[1] Dufourcq, pp. 84 ff., 90 f., 521. An excellent example of *modus vivendi* in 1313, ed. E. K. Aguilo, *BSAL* 15 (1914–15), 227–32.

[2] Dufourcq, pp. 21, 24 f., and *passim*; Ibn Idārī, *Al-Bayān al-Mughrib*, transl. A. Huici Miranda, *Colección de crónicas árabes*, iii (Tetuán, 1954), 31 f., 90; J. Alemany, in *Homenaje a D. Francisco Codera* (Saragossa, 1904), pp. 133–69; A. Giménez Soler, in *Revue hispanique*, 12 (1905), 299–347; 16 (1907), 56–69; idem, *El sitio de Almeria en 1309* (Barcelona, 1904), pp. 80 ff.; Dufourcq, *MÂ* 71 (1965), 508 f.; Ibn Khaldūn, *The Muqaddimah*, transl. F. Rosenthal, ii (Princeton, N.J., 1967), 80 f.

1290s and 1300s. Other mercenaries were recruited from Tlemcen.[1]

Far more numerous than the mercenaries were the thousands of Muslim slaves—in the Crown of Aragon and Majorca alone—and the thousands of Christian slaves in North Africa. Raids by land from Aragon on Islamic Spain ceased with Jaume I while the border warfare between Castile and Granada continued. Corsairs, chartered by everyone with the money, from the archbishop of Tarragona down, preyed on the North African coast. In 1317 King Dinis of Portugal agreed to give his newly established Genoese admiral a fifth of the value of the slaves taken by his ships on the Atlantic coast of Morocco.

Muslim slave-traders also had their sources of supply in their own corsairs, and in Christian traders, such as the Genoese who sold Catalans in Almería. There were many Christian slaves in the kingdom of Granada and in North Africa. They were usually kept imprisoned and in chains—this was normally only done in the Christian countries of the peninsula to slaves accused of a crime. In 1320 the emir of Tlemcen informed Jaume II of Aragon:

> With regard to your demand for liberty for all the slaves of our lands, it is impossible to carry this out, as it would also be if we were to ask you to free the Muslim captives in your land, for you must know that in our [realm] all work is done by slaves, most of whom are artisans . . . To free them all would mean the depopulation of the land and the end of the working of the different services.[2]

The Christian mercenaries had, at times, great political influence in the Islamic states of North Africa. They exercised it almost entirely for their own profit. One can trace little systematic attempt to use the mercenaries to undermine Islamic rule politically in North Africa. The mercenaries had no effect on Islamic religion. The influence of the slave population was slight. North Africa was also penetrated by Christian merchants who reached not only the coastal cities but the interior of the Atlas mountains. A (probably far smaller) number of

[1] Giménez Soler, *Revue hispanique*, 12 (1905), 348–72; Part II, Ch. I, below, p. 242, n. 3; H. Lüdtke, *ER* 8 (1961), 117–19.

[2] J. Vincke, *SFG* i. 25 (1970), 43; Verlinden, i. 258 ff., 547–50, 238 f.; Dufourcq, pp. 75, 81; M. A. Alarcón y Santón and R. García de Linares, *Los documentos árabes diplomáticos* (Madrid, 1940), p. 185.

Muslim merchants also visited the peninsula, particularly the Crown of Aragon. It does not seem that these merchants penetrated much deeper than the mercenaries into the lives of the people among whom they lived.

Some exceptional Christians tried to go further. Groups of Dominican friars studied Arabic and Islam and spent years in Tunis. The Catalan missionary and mystic Ramon Lull travelled repeatedly to Tunisia to try to engage the Doctors of the Law in a dialogue, to demonstrate to them, by means of his Art, the superiority of Christianity over Islam. Lull was outstanding among Christian apologists in his real knowledge of Islam but he had no more effect than the Dominicans on the fortress of Islamic faith. It seems true to say that 'Christians were simply *tolerated* in North Africa, in as much as they were useful to the trade and politics' of the local rulers. On their side the kings of Aragon, while at times stung by Muslim pirates into planning a crusade at sea, remained essentially on the defensive. The result of a century of mutual relations could be summed up, by Christians, as a favourable balance of trade.[1]

THE PENINSULA: A LAND OF THREE RELIGIONS

External relations with Islamic countries, even with Granada, were less important to most medieval Castilians or Catalans than the presence of Islam among them as an intimately known reality.

The Christians of the peninsula were linked to western Europe by their religion, and, increasingly, by their laws and political concepts. They were bound to Islam by the weight of the past, the Islamic culture which had dominated the Iberian world for four hundred years; by the daily presence among them of Muslims and of Jews trained in Arabic culture; by the physical setting in which they lived, the Islamic cities which covered the peninsula from Toledo and Saragossa southwards, which, for centuries, the conquerors hardly attempted to change.

The Primera Crónica General sees the past history of 'the Spains' as dealing 'as much with Moors as with Christians and even with Jews, if necessary'. When it was important to make clear

[1] Dufourcq, pp. 512–24, 580 f. See A. López, *Obispos en el Africa septentrional desde el siglo XIII* (Tangier, 1941).

that a statute applied to all men the text would read: '*all* can come to buy and sell, Christians and Moors and Jews.' When the author of the fourteenth century *Poema de Alfonso XI* tried to imagine a foreign ruler he could only do so in terms of the pluralistic society he himself knew. The titles of the 'emperor of Babylon' include 'lord of the three laws', Islam, Judaism, and Christianity. The contemporary *Crónica de Alfonso XI*, especially in its later unabbreviated version, presents the Muslims of Granada and Africa with great sympathy and as holding exactly the same chivalric ideals as Christian knights.[1]

In the poems of the age Jews and Muslims always figure in the scene, whether imaginary or real. *La danza de la muerte* includes in its long procession, which begins with the heads of the two hierarchies of contemporary Christendom, the pope and the emperor, and ends with labourers, friars, and hermits, the 'bearded Rabbi who always studied the Talmud' and the Muslim *Alfaqui*, clinging to his wife to the end. The *Poema de Alfonso XI*, describes the coronation of Alfonso in 1332 at Burgos:

> The jongleurs were strumming
> Their instruments through Las Huelgas,
> Touching their beguiling lutes,
> Plucking their viols,
> The Rabbi with his psaltery,
> The mountain guitar,
> The Moorish flute . . .[2]

THE PROBLEM OF SECURITY

The fact that no picture of the world, whether visionary or naturalistic, could be complete, for Spaniards of this age, without the presence of Jews and Muslims, did not mean that this presence was always welcome. After the expulsion of the 1260s Muslims ceased to be, by their numbers, an internal danger to Castile. In Valencia the case was different. There free Muslims (Mudejars) continued to form a majority of the population. This was bound to cause friction. In the 1270s the king of

[1] *Primera Crónica*, c. 972, ed. Menéndez Pidal, ii. 653; *MHE* i. 23 (privilege of 1254); *Poema de Alfonso XI*, v. 917 (*BAE* lvii. 505); D. Catalán Menéndez Pidal, *NRFH* 7 (1953), 570–82.

[2] *BAE* lvii. 385, 489 (vv. 406–8).

Aragon had to restrain attacks by Christians on Muslims, and then put down a formidable Mudejar rebellion. In 1323 the bailiff of Valencia was informed that once the royal expedition had sailed to Sardinia a concerted Mudejar rising would take place in conjunction with an invasion by the kings of Granada and of Tlemcen in North Africa. Similar conspiracies were expected in 1332 and 1340. As late as 1455 the Christians of Valencia were seized with panic at the rumour that the city was about to be attacked by the neighbouring Mudejar peasantry.[1]

This problem of internal security was not sufficiently pressing. however, for the kings of Aragon to carry out the mass expulsion of Muslims from Valencia which was repeatedly counselled by the papacy. The emigration of individuals or of small groups of Mudejars was usually permitted but no general emigration was allowed.[2] This was not only because the Mudejar labour force was essential to the economy of Valencia. There was also the hope that the Mudejars and the Jews would be peacefully assimilated into Christian society.

AN AGE OF OPTIMISM: CONVERSION BY REASON

The thirteenth century, for Latin Christianity, was an age of optimism with regard to the possible conversion of Islam and Jewry. It was also an age when the desire to learn from a superior civilization—and the idea that Islam possessed this superiority—still influenced leading minds. Hence a general atmosphere of tolerance. Out of this grew, in Castile, the study of Arabic science at the court of Alfonso X and, in Catalonia–Aragon, the foundation by the Dominicans and by Ramon Lull of colleges for oriental languages to train missionaries to work in the peninsula and in North Africa. The difference between interest in science and in conversion was largely due to the greater scale of the internal problem in Aragon and its contacts, far closer than Castile's, with North Africa.

The most careful and elaborate discussion of the relations of Islam and Judaism to Christianity is found in Ramon Lull. His

[1] F. Soldevila, *Pere el Gran*, i. 3 (Barcelona, 1956), 403–23, 474–6; R. I. Burns, in *American Historical Review*, 66 (1961), 378–400; A. Giménez Soler, *La Corona de Aragón y Granada*, pp. 226, n. 2, 253; J. A. Robson, *English Historical Review*, 74 (1959), 390; M. Gual Camarena, *IV CHCA* i. 479.

[2] See Part II, Ch. I, below, p. 252; Giménez Soler, p. 321 (1392).

Book of the Gentile, one of his first works, originally written in Arabic in Majorca about 1272, contains reasoned expositions of the rival faiths in the form of a dialogue between 'three wise men' who represent the faiths, and a curious and intelligent 'Gentile' or pagan. The book has no conclusion. We are not told which faith the Gentile ends by embracing.

The young Lull of the 1270s had seen the failure of the crusades—in 1270 Louis IX of France (St. Louis) had died during a futile 'crusade' against Tunis. At this time Lull believed passionately in the use of reason rather than force to convert non-Christians. He also held that he had received, through divine revelation, an Art by whose irrefutable arguments all men could be converted.

The college to train Franciscan missionaries to Islam, which Lull persuaded Jaume II of Majorca to found in 1276, probably did not outlive the century. Lull's immediate influence in the Crown of Aragon was less pronounced than in the University of Paris. However, Lull's ideas influenced a leading Castilian writer of the early fourteenth century, Don Juan Manuel (1282–1348).[1]

Don Juan Manuel is as emphatic as Lull in denouncing any attempts to force men to become Christians. 'No man of another law [i.e. religion] should be tricked or compelled by force to believe [in Christ] for forced services do not please God.' Later he writes: 'There will be war between Christians and Moors until Christians recover the lands Moors took from them; there would be no war because of the law or sect [Moors] hold to, for Christ never commanded that anyone should be slain or forced to receive his law.' Juan Manuel did not see all those who 'died in the war with Moors as martyrs or saints'. Their sanctity depended on their intention in going to war. For Juan Manuel, as for the *Crónica de Alfonso XI*, God was above both Christians and Muslims and rewarded men not according to their creed but according to their deserts. These views were shared by Don Juan's uncle, Alfonso X of Castile, who described God in his *Cántigas* as 'He who can pardon Christian, Jew, and Moor, as long as they have their *intention* fixed on Him'. A synagogue is a 'house where God is praised'. Alfonso's *Partidas* clearly prohibit conversion by force.

[1] *Libre del gentil e los tres savis*, in Lull, *Obres essencials*, i (Barcelona, 1957).

Alfonso extended the same protection to Jewish orthodoxy as he did to Christian dogma. His *Fuero Real* (*c.* 1255) declared: 'We forbid any Jew reading books on his Law, which undermine it; nor is he to keep them secretly. If any such books are found they are to be burnt at the door of the synagogue.'

It seems likely that this measure was inspired by Alfonso's Jewish courtiers, but its enforcement by a Christian king would have been inconceivable outside the peninsula.[1]

Don Juan Manuel's confidence in the possibility of converting Jews and Muslims 'by science and reason' went even further than Lull's had gone. Don Juan stated that 'the *foundation* of our law and salvation is attained by reason'.[2]

This remark, unqualified by reference to the necessity of faith for the comprehension of Christian doctrine, would have seemed suspect to the many friars who laboured to convert Jews and Mudejars and who probably made a far greater impact than the more tolerant lay writers, such as Lull, Alfonso X, or Don Juan Manuel. The Dominicans of the Crown of Aragon were particularly active in these missions. Under the inspiration of their former Master General, Ramon de Penyafort, the Dominicans founded a school of Arabic studies at Tunis before 1250, which came to an end by 1259, and a school of Hebrew and Arabic at Murcia in 1266 (the Hebrew school was transferred to Barcelona in 1281). Schools existed at Valencia and Játiva until 1313. The Dominicans preached regularly (as did the Franciscans and Ramon Lull) in synagogues and mosques and engaged in public disputations, such as the famous debate of 1263 in Barcelona between the Dominican friar and convert from Judaism, Pau Cristià, and Moses ben Nahman (Nahmanides), a leading Rabbi of Gerona. The Catalan Dominicans also included one famous literary controversialist, Ramon Martí. His *Pugio fidei* (*Dagger of Faith*) followed a cruder approach than that of Lull, that of inventing forgeries which he attributed to the Talmud and used to support his arguments against the Jews' refusal to accept the Christian Messiah. Martí influenced the famous

[1] *Libre de los estados*, i. 19, 30, 76 (*BAE* li. 289, 294, 323); Catalán, loc. cit.; Alfonso X, *Cántigas* (cited from the Florence MS. by A. Castro, *La realidad histórica de España*, 2nd edn. (Mexico, 1962), p. 40); *Partidas*, VII. xxiv. 4; xxv. 2; *Fuero Real*, cited A. Castro, ibid. (1954), 491 f.; idem, in *Estudios filológicos*, 5 (1969), 24, n. 19. But see also below, p. 210.

[2] Juan Manuel, *Libro de los estados*, ii. 3, 6 (*BAE* li. 344 f., 347). See c. 32 (p. 355).

doctor and religious fanatic, Arnau de Vilanova, but his reliance on 'authorities' was explicitly rejected by Lull.[1]

Efforts at evangelization were made possible by royal support. Royal permission to friars to preach to Jews and Muslims was given by Jaume I of Aragon. Similar permissions were issued by later rulers. In general there was no obligation to assist at Christian sermons outside the Jewish or Muslim quarters or to engage in argument with the preacher. Jaume I took part in the Jewish–Christian disputation at Barcelona in 1263 and addressed the local synagogue on this occasion. This, in itself, was an extraordinary action. Even more extraordinary was Jaume's allowing the leading Jewish spokesman to answer him freely. In 1279 Pere II ordered that a Dominican trained in Arabic should be allowed to preach to Muslims in Valencia. A fair number of converts from Islam were made in Valencia; their conversion had been favoured by the Crown from 1242 onwards. Mockery of converts was severely punished.

There was a considerable incentive to conversion for Muslims who were slaves of Jews, as they became free upon baptism on payment of a small sum to their former owner. There was, however, opposition to the baptism of Muslims, whether free or slaves, by the nobility both of Majorca and Valencia. This opposition, together with the cohesion of the Mudejar and Jewish communities, made conversion by reason a slow process. The royal authorities were also quite as concerned to avoid scandal and riot as to further conversion of Muslims or Jews. In 1330 Eximén Pérez, a convert from Judaism, appeared in Valencia with a royal privilege entitling him to preach to the Jews. The Bayle General of Valencia accordingly arranged for him to address the Jews in the episcopal palace—with the doors closed to prevent a Christian mob entering—and also in the Jewish synagogue. However, the Bayle refused to make the Jews come to the cathedral of Valencia to hear Pérez preach because of the danger to them which would ensue.[2]

[1] J. Mª. Coll, *AST* 17 (1944), 115–38; 18 (1945), 59–89; 19 (1946), 217–40; C. Roth, *Harvard Theological Review*, 43 (1950), 117–44; Baer, *History* i. 152–5, 185, and n. 54 on p. 411. For Lull and Martí see my *Ramon Lull*, pp. 21 f. A. Díez Macho, *Sefarad*, 9 (1949), 165–96, attempts to clear Martí of the charge of forgery. See Bernardo Oliver, *El tratado 'Contra caecitatem Iudaeorum'*, ed. F. Cantera Burgos (Madrid, 1965) (*c.* 1317).

[2] Baer, *History* i. 153; F. Janer, *Condición social de los moriscos de España* (Madrid,

Alfonso X of Castile wished to further the conversion of Jews and Muslims, although he was far less active in the matter than were contemporary kings of Aragon. The *Partidas* state that the convert can keep his wife even if he is related to her within degrees normally prohibited by the Church.[1]

CHURCH LAW AND IBERIAN PRACTICE

Throughout the Iberian peninsula a gulf existed between the decrees of the Church as to the treatment proper to non-Christians and the legislation on the subject by the local Christian rulers. The Third and Fourth Lateran Councils (1180 and 1215) decreed that Jews and Muslims should be clearly distinguished from Christians. They should dress differently, live separately, pay taxes to the Church, and not hold any public office. None of these decrees was strictly enforced in Spain. In 1219 a leading churchman, Rodrigo Jiménez de Rada, archbishop of Toledo and primate of Spain, who had himself been present at the council of 1215, had its decrees suspended as regarded the Jews of Castile since they provided the greater part of the royal revenue. He made an agreement with the Jews of his own diocese in which he promised to defend and assist them as far as he could. The Fourth Council's decrees were also suspended in Aragon at the request of Jaume I.[2]

DRESS

The Cortes of Valladolid of 1258 stated that Mudejars in Christian towns should wear beards and their hair cut in a wheel round their head. Neither they nor Jews were to be allowed to wear brightly coloured clothes or white or gilded shoes, dress considered proper to nobles. In Catalonia and Aragon it was not until 1301 that the Cortes issued similar orders for the local Mudejars. The Jews of Catalonia and of

[1] Alfonso X, *Partidas*, IV. VI. 6. For a discussion of the Koran in Murcia see F. de la Granja, *Al-Andalus*, 31 (1966), 47–72.

[2] L. Torres Balbas, *Algunos aspectos del mudejarismo urbano medieval* (Madrid, 1954), p. 69; Baer, *Die Juden* ii. 24 f.; D. Mansilla Reoyo, *Iglesia castellano-leonesa*, p. 143.

1857), p. 14; R. I. Burns, *Speculum*, 35 (1960), 337–56; L. Piles, *Sefarad*, 8 (1948), 91–6.

Valencia (from 1283) were required to wear a round cape and a red-and-yellow badge, the colours of the Crown, to signify royal protection. Many Jews connected with the court received exemptions. No similar regulations existed for Castile until 1405, though they were demanded by the Cortes in 1313. The miniatures of the *Cántigas* and *Libro de ajedrez* prepared for Alfonso X suggest that—at least in the thirteenth century—the dress regulations of the Cortes were not enforced on the Mudejars of Castile. They continued to wear richly coloured and silken garments and jewels, including heavy golden bracelets. One may also note that in 1292 Sancho IV ordered coloured *aljubas* to be presented to two Muslims at his court. (The miniatures of the *Cántigas* do show Jews, however, wearing capes and pointed caps as the *Partidas* indicate they should do.) The arabicized Christians (Mozarabs) who formed an important community in Toledo continued—to judge by their surviving documents—to dress very much as did the Mudejars. Their women wore veils when they left the house.[1]

Rather than the clear distinction in dress between infidels and Christians demanded by the papacy, there was a tendency to imitate the appearance of the rival community. In the late-thirteenth century Ibn Saᶜīd tells us that 'the sultans and warriors [of Granada] imitate the dress of the Christians their neighbours, their weapons are the same and their cloaks, even their banners and the saddles of their horses, even their way of fighting with shield and long lances'. A century later Ibn Khaldūn remarks that the Spanish Muslims 'assimilate themselves to the [Christians] in their dress, their emblems, and most of their customs and conditions . . . The observer will conclude that this is a sign of domination [by others]'. Christian influence appears in the dress of the doctors of the law represented in the Sala del Tribunal of the Alhambra. Jewish courtiers at the Christian courts of the peninsula also aped Christian knights, to the scandal of the devout of both religions.

Meanwhile Christian nobles were adopting the ample, flowing robes and turbans of Muslim aristocrats. Ramon Lull

[1] *Cortes de León*, i. 59, 227; ii. 553; *Cortes de Cataluña*, i. 190; F. Fernández y González, *Estado social y política de los mudejares de Castilla* (Madrid, 1866), p. 369; *Partidas*, VII. xxiv. 11; R. Arié, *MCV* 2 (1966), 59–66; Gaibrois de Ballesteros, *Sancho IV*, i, p. lxxix; J. Guerrero Lovillo, *Las Cántigas*, p. 188, lám. 29.

praised Muslim dress as far more comfortable, sensible, and hygienic than Christian. The inventory of the possessions of a bishop of Cuenca, drawn up in 1273, lists cushions and carpets from Murcia, Tlemcen, and Toledo, cloaks from Murcia, writing desks and chess sets of ebony and ivory made by Muslim craftsmen. Christian liturgical vestments of this century bear Arabic inscriptions. The tombs of Las Huelgas and fragments found elsewhere reveal that members of the royal family of Castile were buried as they had lived, when at their ease, in silks and muslins from North African or Mudejar workshops, occasionally in 'Tartar' silks from China or Central Asia. The bodies of Queen Berenguela, the mother of Fernando III (d. 1246) and of her sister, Queen Leonor of Aragon (d. 1244) reposed on cushions covered with Islamic invocations. The cloak in which the great Fernando himself was buried in the cathedral of his conquered Seville was woven of silk and gold-thread by Mudejar workmen.[1]

'CONVIVENCIA'

The Cortes of Jerez of 1268, following the teaching of the Church, prohibited Christians living together with Muslims or Jews. In theory the two subject communities should have been confined to separate quarters, *Morerías* or *Juderías* in each town, and only allowed to own shops outside these areas. In fact this separation was never entirely realized until the expulsion of Jews and Moriscos from the peninsula. Attempts to prevent Christians and Jews and Muslims from engaging in business together repeatedly failed.

Royalty set the example in disregarding the decrees of Cortes and church councils. In 1292 Sancho IV of Castile spent the feast of Christmas in Córdoba as the guest of a rich Jewish financier. The *Chronicle* of Sancho's reign shows us one of his greatest nobles, Don Juan Núñez de Lara, playing at dice at night in the Dominican convent outside Toledo. His companion was a Jew. These casual glimpses of real life show us

[1] E. García Gómez, *Cinco poetas musulmanes*, 2nd edn. (Madrid, 1959), p. 176; Ibn Khaldūn, *Muqaddimah*, ii. 22 (i. 300); R. Arié, *Arabica*, 12 (1965); 252, Ramon Lull, *Libre de meravelles*, viii, 50 (*Obres essencials*, i. 399); M. Gómez-Moreno, *El Panteón Real de las Huelgas de Burgos* (Madrid, 1946); J. L. Nevinson, *The Connoisseur*, 146 (1960), 10–15; C. Bernis, *Archivo español de arte*, 29 (1956), 95–115; L. Torres Balbas, in *Ars Hispaniae*, iv. 384.

more of the age than many decrees. The example of kings and nobles was generally followed.[1]

The church councils of Valladolid and Toledo in 1322–3 complained that Jews and Muslims often assisted at Mass, that Muslim minstrels were hired to play in church during night vigils of the greater Christian festivals, and that Christians were present at Jewish and Muslim marriages and funerals. Christian women especially used to bring their Jewish and Muslim women friends to Mass. Another council, in 1335, tells us that Jews and Muslims often rented houses conveniently near churches. These practices were condemned, but over a century later little had changed. An ecclesiastical visitation in 1436 of Brihuega in the archdiocese of Toledo revealed that 'Jews and Moors publicly have Christian servants, men and women, in their houses and eat and drink with them continually, and Jewish and Moorish doctors and carpenters enter convents without Christians accompanying them and act as lawyers of convents against Christians.'[2]

The Jews of León never lived cut off from contacts with Christians. 'Their participation in the common life of the city has hardly left a trace of resentment' in the surviving records. The cathedral chapter of León employed Jews as their doctors, surgeons, and painters. Jews intervened as witnesses in contracts between Christians and Christians in contracts between Jews. The attempts by the church councils and by the Cortes (for instance at Valladolid in 1293) to prevent commercial relations between Jews and Christians seem to have had no effect. The Jewish community of León was relatively small, but many contracts between Jews and Christians survive. In the smaller towns of Castile and León, such as Aguilar de Campóo or Bembibre, the Jews lived in the middle of the town, in Aguilar beside the pilgrimage way to Santiago. In Calahorra, near Navarre, in 1320, the clergy, citizens, *hidalgos*, and Jews co-operated as equals in the construction of new mills to use water from the Ebro.[3] In León in 1305 the Jewish community

[1] *Cortes de León*, i. 77; see below, p. 184, and Part II, Ch. I, p. 239; Gaibrois, *Sancho IV*, ii. 189; *Crónica de Sancho IV*, c. 7 (*BAE* lxvi. 84).

[2] Tejada y Ramiro, iii. 499, 516, 575; Torres Balbas, *Algunos aspectos*, p. 78. See the anti-Jewish decrees of the Council of Zamora (1312–13) in F. Fita y Colomé, *Actas inéditas de siete concilios españoles* (Madrid, 1882), pp. 138–46.

[3] J. Rodríguez Fernández, *La Judería de la Ciudad de León* (León, 1969), pp. 146–9;

reached a fairly satisfactory compromise with the town council over justice. The Jews could elect their own judge to judge cases between members of the different faiths. They could change him if he could be proved to have acted unjustly. If the king sent a special judge to León the Jews would contribute to his salary. Cases between Jews were, as was normal elsewhere, decided entirely by the local Jewish authorities.[1]

The canon law insisted that no Jew or Muslim should hold any office over Christians. In the thirteenth century this legislation was hardly observed at all. Jews acted as royal administrators both in Castile and Aragon. The protests of the papacy and of general and local church councils reveal their ineffectiveness by the frequency with which they return to the same points.[2]

The Church could not even prevent public display of the Islamic religion. In 1311–12 the Council of Vienne prohibited the public invocation of Muḥammad in Christian countries. This prohibition was echoed by local church councils and inserted by Jaume II of Aragon in the laws of Valencia.

But in 1357 his successor was allowing the invocations (in return for money) and when a Christian noble needed Mudejar settlers, as at Chelva, in Valencia, in 1370, he had to permit public prayer from minarets. Mosques are attested in Majorca as late as 1327. In 1331 Jaume III of Majorca rejected an attempt by the papacy to prevent the Jews of the island from building a synagogue to replace one confiscated some years before.[3]

ROYAL ATTITUDES TO JEWS AND MUDEJARS

The general attitude of the rulers of the peninsula was expressed by Alfonso X in the *Partidas*. Mudejars and Jews should 'observe their law and not attack ours'. If they met the Host being carried through the streets they should kneel as Christians would do. 'If they are not willing to do so they should leave the street.' Punishment for failure to obey this statute, even for

[1] Rodríguez Fernández, pp. 119 f., 204–7. For a similar settlement in Murcia in 1294 see J. Torres Fontes, *Murgetana*, 18 (1962), 12–20.

[2] Torres Balbas, pp. 69 f.

[3] Fernández y González, pp. 376 f.; John Boswell's dissertation, cited in the Bibliography for this chapter; F. A. Roca Traver, *EEMCA* 5 (1952), 141; E. K. Aguiló, *BSAL* 4 (1891–2), 72; J. Goñi Gaztambide, *Sefarad*, 22 (1962), 103–6.

Cortes de León, i. 128; F. Cantera, *Sinagogas españolas*, pp. 176–9; idem, *Sefarad*, 16 (1956), 79 f. (see 15 (1955), 357).

repeated offences, should not be unreasonably severe, 'that the Jews and the Moors may not be able to say that they are wrongfully subjected to injury in Our Dominions'. The blood-price of any Muslim must be paid by the town of the crime to the local Muslim community, in the case of a Jew, to the Crown.

The attempts of Christians to avoid paying their debts to Jewish creditors, under the plea of usury, were generally rejected by the ruler who needed Jewish financial support. Jaume I of Aragon repeatedly enforced the payment of debts to Jews, together with the interest due, which could be compounded as the years passed. In 1275 Jaume ordered his representatives in Perpignan to fine heavily any Christian layman who cited a Jew before a church court. If a cleric did so he was to be boycotted. No one was to assist him in any way. These measures did not entirely prevent appeals to the church courts but must have made them far more difficult. The same situation obtained in Castile. In 1307, when the cathedral chapter of Toledo, following canon law, tried to force the local Jews to return the interest they claimed, Fernando IV prohibited the use of papal letters by Christian debtors and told the chapter that they would have to repay double any sum they extorted from the Jews.[1]

In the Crown of Aragon—where alone in the peninsula the Inquisition operated at this period—it was not concerned with Muslims and very little with Jews. When, in 1323, an Inquisitor began to meddle with the Jews of Lérida Jaume II told him: 'This is to destroy Our Laws under the veil of the crime of heresy.' Jaume tried to protect other Jewish communities against the local Inquisitors; in this he was generally successful.[2]

CULTURAL INTERPENETRATION

When the synagogue of Córdoba was reconstructed in 1315 a number of remarkable inscriptions were placed there which still survive. Drawing on Psalms 122 and 57 these inscriptions tell

[1] Fernández, pp. 127 f.; *Partidas*, VII. xxiv. 2; I. iv. 63 (119); *Leyes de estilo*, CIII, in *Opúsculos legales del Rey D. Alfonso*, ii (Madrid, 1836), pp. 280 f.; R. W. Emery, *The Jews of Perpignan in the thirteenth century* (New York, 1959), pp. 81, 84, 88–93; Fita, op. cit., pp. 203–8; for Alfonso XI see F. Cantera, *Sefarad*, I (1941), 107–9, 132–7. For Navarre in 1277–81, F. Arroyo, *Ligarzas* 2 (Valencia, 1970), 87–108.

[2] Finke, *Acta* ii, pp. liii f., 859 f., 862, 870; Baer, *History* ii. 7–17.

the congregation to pray for the peace of Jerusalem. 'May [her] lovers enjoy prosperity! May peace reign within [her] walls, prosperity in [her] palaces!' 'Take pity on me, O God, take pity on me, for in Thou my soul takes refuge and I fly to the shadow of Thy wings until the devastation passes by.' Another inscription commemorates the restoration of the synagogue; 'Sanctuary in miniature and dwelling of the law, completed by Isaac Mohab, son of the lord Ephraim Waddawa . . . Return, O God, and hasten to rebuild Jerusalem!'

These inscriptions tell us much of the mind of Spanish Jewry. The Jewish communities lived always under the menace of 'devastation', in an alien land. They existed in provisional 'sanctuaries', for all synagogues were provisional compared to the Temple of Jerusalem which all Jews longed to see rebuilt. A contemporary poem by a Jewish poet of Castile, Yosef ben Abraham ibn Chicatella, celebrates Jerusalem as 'door of heaven, archetype of the law, the throne and chariot of God'.[1]

However, in 1315 no one could foresee the wholesale pogroms of 1391, still less the expulsion of 1492, while the Talmud taught that the Dispersion was part of God's providential design. Professor Yitzhak Baer believes that in the thirteenth century the position of the Jews in the peninsula, despite periodic outbursts of hostility, was superior to that they enjoyed in the rest of Christian Europe. Christian and Jewish societies were interwoven throughout the peninsula. Synagogues are known to have existed in 118 places; in twenty-three towns there were more than one synagogue. In Toledo in 1391 there were at least seven synagogues and five centres of study and prayer. 'There is no city in the world which surpasses Toledo in the interest of its Hebrew inscriptions.'[2]

In 1342 Alfonso XI asked the papacy to permit the use of a new synagogue in Seville on the grounds that 'the Jews are very necessary, since they contribute to the needs of the city and sometimes go out with the Christians against Muslims and do not fear to expose themselves to death.'[3]

[1] Cantera, *Sinagogas*, pp. 7–32; J. Mª. Millás, *La poesía sagrada hebraicoespañola* (Madrid–Barcelona, 1948), pp. 147 f., 333 f.

[2] Baer, *History* i. 181, 247; F. Cantera and J. Mª. Millás Vallicrosa, *Las inscripciones*, p. 36.

[3] Baer, *Die Juden* ii. 163.

Spanish synagogues followed no set prototype. A synagogue near Soria looked like a Romanesque church. The surviving synagogues of Toledo and Córdoba are Mudejar in style. Like the King's daughters of the Psalms the riches of these synagogues were within. Their external appearance must not provoke hostility. In 1250 there were protests in Córdoba because of the unusual height of a new synagogue. Internally the synagogues were as bright with votive lamps as contemporary churches with votive candles. 'It must have been easy for the *converso* from Judaism to vary his gift.' It was also easy to convert a synagogue into a church, eliminating or painting over the Hebrew inscriptions and covering the niche of the *hekhal* with a Christian retable, in much the same way, as, throughout the peninsula from the thirteenth century onwards, mosques had become churches by the placing of an altar in front of the *mihrab*.

The decoration of the synagogue of the Transito at Toledo recalls the Sala de Comares in the Alhambra. The chant of the synagogues was influenced by Arabic culture. The Spanish Jews chanted Arabic melodies as well as Hebrew chants in Arabic metres.[1]

The centuries of Islamic cultural dominance of the peninsula influenced the Jewish communities of Spain in many ways, notably in the development of Arabic literature and scholarship among the Jews. From the thirteenth century onwards the Jews drew, in turn, on the Christian culture which now dominated the world in which they lived. Jewish communal institutions in Navarre and in the Crown of Aragon developed on the model of municipal administration. In Barcelona Jewish communal affairs were handled by thirty elected members, a clear imitation of the *Consell de Cent*. The statutes the Barcelona Community adopted in 1327 were written in Catalan, with an admixture of Hebrew. The oligarchical type of self-government they prescribe—adopted by other communities—was modelled on that of the city of Barcelona. 'Democratic' tendencies triumphed simultaneously, though briefly, in Barcelona in 1386 in both the city government and the Jewish *aljama*.

[1] J. A. Gaya Nuño, in *Collected Studies in Honour of Américo Castro's Eightieth Year*, ed. M. P. Hornik (Oxford, 1965), pp. 122–4; Cantera, *Sinagogas*, pp. 4 f.; H. Anglès, *VII CHCA* iii. 288.

Jewish judicial institutions were also influenced by Islamic and, later, by Christian models. The Muslim authorities had granted Jewish communities very wide criminal jurisdiction, which included the power to impose the death sentence on their members. This jurisdiction—not enjoyed by Jews in other parts of western Europe—continued to be exercised in the Christian kingdoms of the peninsula, though with much greater freedom in the more Islamicized Castile than in the Crown of Aragon. The way Jewish criminal justice was carried out in Castile and Aragon, by means of secret trials, was influenced by the methods of Roman law adopted by the papal Inquisition in the thirteenth century. Leading Jewish rabbis such as Solomon ibn Adret of Barcelona (*c.* 1233–1310) were familiar with Roman law.

In the fourteenth century Jewish scholars took to Catalan and Castilian to instruct contemporary kings, Jaume II of Aragon or Pedro I of Castile, in ethical lore as, in earlier centuries, they had taken to Arabic to charm and edify the caliphs of Córdoba or the rulers of the eleventh-century *Taifa* kingdoms. They exploited and were exploited by the dominant culture, whether it was Islamic or Christian. Professor Baer has pointed out that a cultivated Jewish courtier such as Todros ben Judah Halevi (1247–*c.* 1306), brought up in the tradition of Arabic scholarship, could turn as easily for his models to Galician or Provençal lyric poets as to Hebrew poems written in Muslim Spain. Todros describes the worldly Jew as despising Talmudic study and as saying: 'Hebrew we need not know; Castilian is our tongue, or Arabic.' Although such men were few in number compared with the crowd of pious Jewish artisans, they 'set the social tone for the Jewish aristocracy' in Castile and Aragon. Catalan Jews wrote wedding songs in Catalan (the language they normally spoke), though in Hebrew characters.[1]

JEWS IN SOCIETY: FINANCIERS

The most well-known and the richest Jews were tax-collectors, an office leading Jews had often held in Islamic Spain. In Aragon Jaume I's and Pere II's most trusted administrators

[1] Baer, *History* i. 219–42, 282 f.; ii. 21 ff., 42 f. For Magister Judah of Barcelona see below, p. 285. J. Riera i Sans, *Cants de Noces dels Jueus Catalans* (Barcelona, 1974).

were Jews. Only internal pressure during Pere's war with France forced him to dismiss them. In Castile there was no break, for there did not exist in Castile the Christian bourgeoisie of Catalonia who could replace Jews as administrators. During Alfonso XI's reign the office of Almojarife was abolished. The chief tax-collector, usually a Jew, was to be replaced by a Christian Treasurer. In fact Pedro I's chief Treasurer was the Jew Samuel Halevi. These high financiers amassed great riches. Their careers often ended abruptly and disastrously, but the rulers of Castile could only replace them by another Jew. In Portugal, also, Jews were at the head of royal finances from the fourteenth century onwards. On a lower level Jews acted as financial administrators for towns in Castile and for many ecclesiastical corporations.[1]

DOCTORS

Jewish doctors were of great importance. Alfonso X and Sancho IV of Castile trusted them. Don Juan Manuel recommended the descendants of Don Isaac ibn Wakar to his son as the best doctors he could find. In his will of 1339 he made another Jewish doctor one of the executors even of his bequests to Christian religious foundations and named him as his closest friend.

In Catalonia Arnau de Vilanova, possibly actuated to some extent by professional jealousy, complained that, although Christians who used Jews as doctors were told by friars that they were excommunicated, normally all religious communities—nuns as well as monks—preferred Jewish to Christian doctors. The court of Aragon employed Arnau himself as its principal doctor but both Arnau's patron, Jaume II, and—much more so—his grandson Pere III employed many Jewish doctors. (Both kings also employed Jewish scholars as translators and scientists.) There is much evidence—the cases of Brihuega and León have already been cited—that ordinary Christians preferred the risk of excommunication to bad medical treatment. This must have been the attitude of the municipal governments

[1] For Aragon see Part II, Ch. I below, p. 239; for Castile Part II, Ch. II, p. 296. J. Lúcio de Azevedo, in *História de Portugal*, ed. D. Peres, ii (Lisbon, 1929), 444.

of Barcelona and Saragossa, both of which employed Jews as their official physicians.[1]

At a lower level Jews played a considerable role throughout the peninsula as merchants and artisans, often in partnership with Christians. In Avila in 1306 they, like Christians, were scribes, carpenters, shoemakers, saddlemakers. In León the Jewish community was mainly engaged in transactions in land and houses. There is no apparent difference between most of their activities and those of their Christian fellow citizens, though some Jews lent money to individuals and to convents. The Jewish role in the economy of a small Catalan town emerged in 1304 at Valls, near Tarragona, when the town authorities admitted that the vines—the main riches of the town—had been planted because of loans provided by the local Jews. In 1286–7 the Jews of Puigcerdá in the Pyrenees were lending money to virtually every surrounding village. In the 1270s and 1280s the Jewish community of Perpignan existed mainly by money-lending. Loans were made to many villages around the city. They were generally made at the end of the harvest season and so were probably not 'distress loans'. The cloth-dealers of Perpignan, who were a prosperous group, relied largely on loans from Jews to finance their operations on credit. The case of Perpignan shows how Jewish money-lending could play an essential role in a prosperous and expanding economy, where money was dear and credit was hard to find. The Perpignan Jews were atypical, however. Their almost exclusive reliance on money-lending may have been due to the fact that their community was relatively new. It hardly existed before 1200. Most Jewish communities, both in Castile and Catalonia–Aragon, had existed for centuries and had far deeper roots. It is probably true to say that 'the majority of the Jews earned their livelihood by petty trade, handicrafts and the sale of produce from their fields and vineyards' rather than by lending money at interest. For the many poorer Jews there existed pious foundations such as the hospital founded in Barcelona in the thirteenth century, possibly on the model of contemporary Christian hos-

[1] Juan Manuel, *Libro de los castigos*, 2 (*BAE* li. 267); A. Giménez Soler, *Don Juan Manuel*, pp. 634, 702 f., 707 f.; Baer, *Die Juden* ii. 139 f.; *History* i. 182 f.; Arnau de Vilanova, *Interpretatio de visionibus*, in M. Menéndez y Pelayo, *Historia de los heterodoxos españoles*, vii (Madrid, 1948), 235; J. Rubió y Balaguer, *EUC* 3 (1909), 489–97. See below, p. 330.

pitals. At this period the Jews of Barcelona owned farms all round the city, alternating with Christian properties. Many Jewish farms were worked by Christians.[1]

MUDEJARS IN SOCIETY

The position of the free Muslims, or Mudejars, was in many ways different to that of the Jewish communities in Spain, though, like the Jews, the Mudejars possessed considerable rights of self-government. The Jews had leaders whose families had enjoyed wealth and learning for centuries. They had leading financiers and doctors who had the entrée to every royal court and most bishops' palaces as they had had to the courts of Islamic Spain. In contrast the Mudejars had few leaders. The Arabic aristocracy of al-Andalus and the leading scholars, the doctors of the law, generally refused to live under Christian rule. They emigrated to Granada or North Africa. A number of craftsmen from al-Andalus even reached Egypt and many more Andalusí lawyers moved there. The small number of Muslim scholars patronized by Alfonso X or by the kings of Aragon could not fill the gaps left by this emigration of the natural leaders of a people. The few Arabic inscriptions that survive, erected by Mudejars in Toledo or Avila, show that epigraphic formulas were still correctly transmitted, but these inscriptions are poverty itself compared to those either of earlier Islamic Spain or of contemporary Jewish communities. In Valencia Mudejar lords remained prominent until the failure of the revolt of the 1270s; after this they fade away.[2]

One can find occasional figures such as Juan Martínez Omar, probably a baptized Mudejar, who played an important part in guiding Alfonso XI's military manoeuvres against the kings of

[1] M. del C. Carlé, *CHE* 21–2 (1954), 171; Rodríguez Fernández, op. cit., pp. 131, 135 f.; F. Carreras y Candi, *BRABL* 12 (1925–6), 199; Baer, *History* i. 361, 197–211; for Puigcerdá see M. Delcor, *Sefarad*, 26 (1966), 17–46; for Huesca, R. del Arco, ibid. 7 (1947), 280; for Calahorra, F. Cantera, ibid. 6 (1946), 37–61; for Barcelona, A. Cardoner, ibid. 22 (1962), 373–5; J. Mª. Millás, ibid. 27 (1967), 64–9; for Morella (Valencia), M. Grau Monserrat, ibid. 24 (1964), 294–8; for Perpignan, R. W. Emery, op. cit., esp. pp. 26–66, 101 f.; for Navarre, Arroyo, *Ligarzas* 2, 87–108.

[2] Ibn Khaldūn, *Muqaddimah*, iv. 17; v. 29 (ii. 290, 386), etc.; G. Marçais, in *Mélanges d'histoire et d'archéologie de l'occident musulman*, i (Algiers, 1957), 147; E. Lévi-Provençal, *Inscriptions arabes d'Espagne* (Leyden–Paris, 1931), pp. 80 f. R. I. Burns, *Islam under the Crusaders, Colonial survival in the thirteenth-century Kingdom of Valencia* (Princeton, 1973).

Morocco and Granada in the 1340s. Jaume II of Aragon possessed similar Muslim agents in Valencia, who controlled spies working in Granada, and in 1323 we hear of *infanzones* (lesser nobles) among the Muslims of Daroca in Aragon, but this is as high in the social hierarchy as one can go by this time among the Mudejars.[1]

There were many Mudejar communities. In Castile–León fifty-five urban communities have been listed for the thirteenth century; this list is far from exhaustive. Many Mudejars also lived outside towns. These communities were far less rich than the Jewish *aljamas* of Castile—in 1293–4 the Mudejars of Seville paid only 5,500 maravedis compared to 115,333 paid by the local Jews—but they should not be underestimated. The Mudejars of Murcia were particularly important. They needed and received protection from the Castilian Crown. In 1305 Fernando IV recognized 'the many and great services they perform'. In the hope of attracting more Mudejars from Granada or Aragon he guaranteed the Murcian Muslims liberty to travel and to name their own officials. Cases brought against them would be judged only by Muslim judges. This privilege was confirmed by later rulers, down to the Catholic Monarchs.[2]

There was a very much larger Mudejar population in the Crown of Aragon. The Mudejars of Aragon proper and Valencia were called on for military service against the French in 1285 and against rebellious nobles in 1347. Until 1366 they normally served together with Christian troops from the same town. In Castile in 1241 the bishops of Cuenca and Sigüenza were not unnaturally angered by being set upon suddenly by the Commander of Uclés, of the Order of Santiago, and a troop of Moorish archers employed by the Order. Mudejars appeared in more decorative roles on royal occasions. When the Infant Pere, heir to Aragon, entered Toledo on a state visit in 1269 he did so preceded by a hundred Moorish trumpeters and minstrels, no doubt hired locally for the occasion. Moorish minstrels

[1] *Crónica de Alfonso XI*, c. 268 (*BAE* lxvi. 342 f.); M. Gaspar y Remiro, *Revista del Centro de Estudios históricos de Granada y su reino*, 13 (1923), 180; T. del Campillo, *Documentos históricos de Daroca y su comunidad* (Saragossa, 1915), p. 434. For an exceptional case see the Bibliography, p. 419.

[2] Fernández y González, p. 134; Gaibrois, iii, p. cccxcvi; Baer, *Die Juden*, ii. 81–92; J. Torres Fontes, *AHDE* 32 (1962), 138 f.; see above, Ch. II, p. 26, n. 3.

appear at Pere's court and at that of Sancho IV of Castile.[1] The part played by the Mudejars in the society of the peninsula can be seen by glancing successively at Seville, Burgos, and Avila in Castile and then at Aragon and Valencia.

SEVILLE

In Seville, despite the change from an almost entirely Islamic city to one mainly inhabited by Christians, the same industries continued; soap, pottery, and cloth were produced as before the conquest of 1248 and were exported to the same markets in Egypt and North Africa, and also, for the first time, to northern Spain and England. Mudejar doctors, some rentiers, builders, tile-makers, and smiths appear in the records of Christian Seville. Muslim builders were working in the cathedral (still a transformed mosque) in 1306. Mudejars probably assisted Christians to learn the cultivation of olives and mulberries, perhaps of cotton and sugar-cane. In the fourteenth century Mudejar peasants recolonized abandoned areas of the country-side. The archbishop of Seville used them in 1345 to settle Cantillana.[2]

BURGOS

Mudejar communities existed against what might appear a far less propitious background than Andalusia or even than the formerly Islamic Toledo. In Burgos in Old Castile, a Mudejar community is documented from the early-twelfth century onwards; it appears to have increased in numbers as time went on. The Mudejars of Burgos included doctors, surgeons, and rent-collectors for the cathedral chapter. Mudejars took part in all the building that went on during the fourteenth and fifteenth centuries in Burgos. Almost all the carpenters of Burgos were Mudejars. Mudejars worked in the gardens belonging to the chapter and to the many monasteries in Burgos. The shoe-makers' guild, in 1259, was controlled by two Christians, a Muslim, and a foreigner. Mudejar builders and gardeners

[1] D. W. Lomax, *Hispania*, 19 (1959), 364; Soldevila, *Pere el Gran*, i. 2, p. 255; i. 1, p. 72; Gaibrois, i. 37, 40. See John Boswell's dissertation, cited above, p. 171, n. 3.

[2] Carande, *AHDE* 2 (1925), 272 f.; González, *Repartimiento de Sevilla*, i. 508–20, 546; see Ch. II, p. 43, n. 2 above; Ballesteros, *Sevilla en el s. XIII*, p. 105.

employed or worked side by side with Christian women—this practice was only prohibited in 1484. Mudejar women entered Christian houses as midwives and *curanderas*, the semi-witch healers still popular today in rural Spain, or to sell cosmetics and trinkets.

The great Cistercian convent of Las Huelgas, which possessed feudal jurisdiction over hundreds of villages and the area immediately outside Burgos where the convent was situated, employed Mudejar officials to look after its property. They were authorized by a royal decree of 1304 to live tax-free, inside the monastery. Las Huelgas also employed Jewish doctors, placed under its jurisdiction by Alfonso X in 1270. It is hardly surprising that Las Huelgas contains, as we shall see, some of the most interesting examples of Muslim art in Christian Spain.[1]

AVILA

It is even more surprising to find a flourishing Mudejar community in Avila, with its harsh climate and poor soil. 'Only military necessity would seem to justify the creation [in Avila] of an important urban centre.' The life of medieval Avila was centred on sheep- and cattle-raising and on war. Jews and Mudejars filled roles in Avila which the local Christians were not interested in undertaking. Jewish and Mudejar communities are recorded from the twelfth century. The Mudejars rented so many lands, vineyards, and mills from Christians, while refusing to pay a tithe to the church on the produce of these lands, that ecclesiastical revenue shrank alarmingly. The Mudejars of Avila also constituted, as late as 1255, an important part of the troops the town could send out in the king's service. In the fourteenth century there existed three separate Muslim *aljamas* (communities) in Avila, each, presumably, with a separate mosque. A register drawn up in 1306 of the property belonging to the cathedral shows that its tenants included almost as many Jews and Mudejars as Christians.[2]

[1] Torres Balbas, op. cit., pp. 25–34, and bibliography there cited; idem, in *Al-Andalus*, 19 (1954), 197–202; see below, p. 199.

[2] Torres Balbas, pp. 34–46; *Crónica de la población de Avila*, ed. A. Hernández Segura (Textos Medievales XX) (Valencia, 1960), p. 47; Mª. del Pilar Laguzzi, *CHE* 12 (1949), 145–80 (the remarks on the proportion of Christians to the rest of the population on p. 149 are misleading).

ARAGON

The distribution of Mudejar populations in the Crown of Aragon has already been noted.[1] The Mudejars of Aragon proper were mainly settled along the rivers, in the fertile lands they had held before the Christian conquest. They lived on there with little variation from the twelfth century to the expulsion of 1610. In one region, the lower valley of the Jalón, the same authorities controlled irrigation rights after the conquest of 1120 as before. Up to 1247 the baptism of Jews and Muslims was prohibited in Aragon. This prohibition was removed by Jaume I, but many villages remained entirely Mudejar. Mudejars governed small towns in the area and sometimes represented the Christian inhabitants as well as themselves in dealing with other towns ruled by Christian town councils. Most Mudejars were tenant farmers, "between serfs and free-renters". They were not notably worse off, as regarded their individual obligations, than free Christian peasants, but a special corporate tax was levied on all Muslim communities. Other taxes could at times rise to a third of the harvest. The Mudejar *aljamas* were ruled by a *qadi*, or judge, appointed, or at least approved of, by the Crown or the feudal lord responsible. He was assisted by elected *adelantati* or *Jurados* (like the Jewish communities, the Mudejars imitated the development of Christian municipal institutions). The local mosques, like the local churches, owned their own property. There seems little evidence for separate *barrios* for Mudejars or for Christian intolerance. The decrees ordering Mudejars to dress differently from Christians were probably not well observed in these rural communities. On essential questions, such as that of irrigation, collaboration between Muslim and Christian communities was essential. In any legal dealing between Christians and Muslims two witnesses of each religion were necessary to prove the case. Although many measures of the Cortes of Aragon sought to protect the Mudejars both of royal and non-royal *aljamas*, numbers of Mudejars emigrated from the mainly urban royal *aljamas* to those under seignorial jurisdiction because of the lighter taxes they were subject to from feudal lords.

[1] See above, Ch. II, footnotes on p. 32.

Mudejars were also to be found in the cities of Aragon. In the episcopal city of Huesca they were important as artisans and, despite measures favouring Christians, continued to maintain a superior position as workers in ceramics in the fifteenth century.[1]

VALENCIA

The Christian conquest of the kingdom of Valencia by Jaume I in 1232–45, like that of Aragon a century before, was mainly effected by pacts between the conquerors and the Muslim population. The pacts stated that the Mudejars would preserve their religious customs and their property—that is that they would continue to work the same land as tenant-farmers for a different (now a Christian) lord. The *aljamas* of Valencia were ruled by Muslim authorities, in much the same way as in Aragon. They were governed by Islamic law, supplemented by the local *fueros* which Mudejars were capable of manipulating against Christians in lawsuits. The local *aljama* possessed a mosque, religious school, and cemetery. If a Mudejar became a Christian he lost his immovable goods which could not pass to a Christian. If a Christian became a Muslim or reverted to Islam he could hardly escape punishment, however.

Mudejars were free to travel. They could leave the kingdom, taking their family, slaves, animals, and movable goods and sell their houses before they left. They could go to North Africa and as pilgrims to Mecca, and return, and often did so, travelling as merchants. Muslims from abroad could enter and leave the kingdom provided they had a safe conduct. (In Aragon free Mudejars were even better off in this respect since they had to be paid for the goods they left behind.) They were free to work on the land or inside their shops, not outside in the street as they would generally do, on all but four of the greatest Christian religious festivals. Apart from agriculture, the production of pottery was the most important occupation of the Mudejars of Valencia. They also produced silk in large quantities and worked in silver. Shops in the *Morería* of Valencia were valuable and were rented by Christians to Mudejar workmen for large

[1] F. Macho y Ortega, in *Memorias de la Facultad de Filosofía y Letras*, i (Saragossa, 1923), 147 f., 155–9, 192; Mª. L. Ledesma Rubió, in *Miscelánea José Ma. Lacarra, estudios de historia medieval* (Saragossa, 1968), pp. 63–79; F. Balaguer and A. Durán Gudiol, *VI CHCA*, pp. 221–39, at 222. Burns, *Islam*, pp. 102–4.

sums. The Mudejars played a considerable part in the textile industry of Valencia, Játiva, and Seville in the thirteenth century; the paper factories continued at Játiva.

Three of the *cartas pueblas* (documents governing the settlement of a new area), granted by the Crown and by individual lords in the kingdom of Valencia, permitted Christians to live in a local *Morería*. More generally this *convivencia* was prohibited. But in fact Muslims and Christians often lived even in the same house, though in 1382 the public authorities of Vallbona considered this 'the occasion of many evils and of danger of death and of violation of the Catholic Faith'. In 1409 Christians were still living in the *Morería* of Valencia.

The rights of the Mudejars were much restricted in the fourteenth and fifteenth centuries. Emigration became more difficult. There was more interference with local *aljamas* than in Aragon or Catalonia. The local *qadi* lost much of his judicial powers to Christian officials, who often interfered even in cases between Muslims. Forced-labour services gradually appeared and were to become very heavy. Taxes increased. Taxes on fruit amounted, in the thirteenth century, to a sixth, at most, of the crop. In the fourteenth century they rose to a third or a fifth (in the case of non-irrigated land). Special tributes multiplied, on vines, figs, flocks; personal services increased, either in work on the land or in weaving cloth or silk. In the fifteenth century many Mudejars moved from seignorial to royal *aljamas*, the reverse of the tendency in Aragon. They were assisted to do so by the Bayle General of Valencia, under whose jurisdiction all Mudejars in the kingdom came.[1]

To grasp the cultural interpenetration of Jewish, Muslim, and Christian societies in the peninsula it is necessary to examine many types of evidence, linguistic, institutional, artistic, literary, and religious.

LINGUISTIC EVIDENCE

The Arabic element in Castilian is the most important after Latin. Over 4,000 words in Castilian derive from Arabic.

[1] M. Gual Camarena, *Saitabi*, 7 (1949), 165–99; idem, in *AEM* 4 (1967), 110 f.; F. A. Roca Traver, *EEMCA* 5 (1952), 115–208; L. Piles, in *Estudios de historia social de España*, 1 (1949), 227–74; Macho y Ortega, p. 194; *CDIHE* xviii. 146 f. See now the basic work of Burns, *Islam under the Crusaders*, and Boswell's dissertation.

Arabic terms have penetrated particularly into the vocabulary employed for war, agriculture, industry, finance, household furniture and furnishing, institutions and science. Professor Rafael Lapesa remarks that the great number of Arabisms Castilian and Portuguese contain still distinguishes these languages from the other romance tongues. Arabic influence is also notable in Catalan, though to a lesser extent.

Many military terms and words for institutions, coins, measures, and agriculture entered Castilian before 1200 but far more are attested after that date. Arabisms common to different peninsular languages which first appear in the thirteenth century include the words for rice, barley, and tax-collector, and terms for cosmetics, water-conduits, the parapet of a fortress, a war-machine, a well, a trumpet, a shepherd, for cushions, caravans, poisons, and musical instruments.[1] The Castilian ploughman adjures his horse to plough by *Harre!* the Portuguese by *Arre!*, the Catalan or Majorcan by *Arri!* In every case the root is the Arabic *Harra!* Many other Arabisms only entered one or two languages, for instance, *azeite*, the word found in Castilian and Portuguese for oil (Catalan has *oli* from the Latin *oleum*). Apart from the numerous Arabisms in popular use many 'cultisms' appear in the thirteenth century. They are found particularly in the compilations produced by the court of Alfonso X, such as the *Libro de ajedrez*, *Lapidario*, and *Primera Crónica General*, works in which Mudejar scholars and Jews familiar with Arabic collaborated.

A recent study of the influence of Arabic on medieval Castilian prose works concludes that Arabic models were more important as models in the thirteenth century than the documents of the royal Chancery. The Castilian translators from the Arabic who worked for Alfonso rejected the dominant French linguistic influence and turned deliberately to Arabic for the modes of expression they needed.

The process by which Arabic terms entered Castilian has been thoroughly examined only up to 1300. The current of Arabicization was probably even stronger in the fourteenth century. About a hundred Arabisms appear for the first time in the Archpriest of Hita's *Libro de Buen Amor* (about 1350). A new

[1] The words cited are *arroz, alcacer, almojarife, alcohol* (for make-up), *alcaduz, adarve, algarrada, algibe, añafil, rabadán, márfaga, recua, rejalgar*, and *albogón*.

tendency, visible in 1300, is a greater proportion of non-military terms. Large numbers of names of animals and plants and of musical instruments appear in the thirteenth century. Together these classes of words constitute 21 per cent of the new Arabisms as compared to only 6·2 per cent for military terms. The 'Reconquest' was virtually over and Castilians could begin to profit extensively from Arabic science and arts of enjoyment.

It is particularly interesting to note expressions of Latin origin which changed their meaning under the influence of similar Arabic terms, for instance, *infante* (from *infans*) ceased to mean any child and came to mean (under the influence of the Arabic *walad*) the son of a king or a noble. *Hidalgo* (from *hijo dalgo*) derives from the Arabic concept of calling a man 'the son of something', for instance a rich man is described as 'son of riches'. Alfonso X defines *hidalgo* as 'son of good things'. Religious invocations and blessings in Castilian, such as 'May God guard' or 'maintain' a king or lord, accompanying his name, are Christianizations of Arabic formulas. Other words, already attested in Castilian as derived from Latin, were simply replaced by Arabisms or became synonymous, for instance *alcalde* (mayor) and *mezquino* (miserable) replaced the Latin-derived equivalent. In the thirteenth century Alfonso X already noted this process at work.[1]

INSTITUTIONS

Recent studies have helped to clarify the difficult question of institutional continuity after the Christian conquests of the thirteenth century. Some claims made by Arabists in the past—such as the supposed derivation of the Justicia of Aragon from an Islamic official—are no longer seriously entertained. On the other hand it is now generally agreed that the Mustaçaf of Catalonia, Valencia, and Majorca, an official fulfilling the same functions as the Almotacén of Castile, derives not only his name but the nature of his office from the Islamic *muḥtasib*.

[1] R. Lapesa, *Historia de la lengua española*, 7th edn. (Madrid, 1968), pp. 97–110; Eero K. Neuvonen, *Los arabismos del español en el siglo XIII* (Studia Orientalia x. 1) (Helsinki, 1941), esp. pp. 138–310; A. Galmés de Fuentes, *BRAE* 35–6 (1956), esp. 36, pp. 300, 305 f.; Alfonso X, *Partidas*, II. xxi. 2.

THE MUNICIPAL ECONOMY

The *muḥtasib* was in charge of the Islamic institution of the *ḥisba*. He supervised the local market, policed the roads leading to it, suppressed fraudulent combinations by guilds of workmen, and even came to control local building. The Mustaçaf first appears in a Christian town in Valencia in 1238, the very year of the conquest. He is documented in Majorca from 1309 but the office probably existed here too from the conquest (1229–30). In 1339 Pere III created the office of Mustaçaf in Barcelona at the wish of the town council. In Valencia the Crown had a say in the appointment, but the Mustaçaf carried out the orders of the city. In Majorca and Barcelona he was a royal official, chosen and controlled by the Crown. His jurisdiction included every class in the city and all religions, except that in Majorca the Jewish community was exempt, at least from 1344.

The Mustaçaf administered justice summarily, with no recourse to written documents and no right of appeal—the same procedure used in the Water Court of Valencia, to which I shall return. The office was held in alternate years in Valencia and from 1392 in Majorca, by a knight or a citizen. Other Catalan cities adopted the institution. It continued virtually unchanged until 1718.[1]

IRRIGATION

When the Christians conquered the great cities of Islamic Spain they naturally took over the municipal economy—they had nothing comparable of their own to substitute for it. Where they could do so they also took over the system of irrigation which had been brought to a high degree of development by the Muslims. The effect on an invading Christian army of an intensively irrigated Muslim *huerta* is vividly described by Jaume I of Aragon in his *Book of Deeds*. Writing of the *huerta* round Játiva he says: 'We saw the most beautiful *huerta* which we had ever seen of town or castle, with more than two hundred farms in it . . . and we had great joy in our heart.' The imitation of the

[1] Ibn Khaldūn, *Muqaddimah*, iii. 29, transl. F. Rosenthal, i. 462 f.; F. Sevillano Colom, *AHDE* 23 (1953), 525–38; idem, *Valencia urbana medieval a través del oficio de Mustaçaf* (Valencia, 1957); A. Pons, *Libre del Mostassaf de Mallorca* (Mallorca, 1949). See above, Ch. II, p. 80.

existing system was deliberate, in both Crowns, Castile and Aragon. In 1254 Alfonso X of Castile ordered the *concejo* of Seville 'to make the water come as it used to do in the time of the Moors'. The existing aqueducts were used to supply the city and the whole sewer system had been organized before the conquest.

In Seville the Christian conquerors had the disadvantage of not being able to consult the Muslim officials who had been in charge of the irrigation system since the Muslim population of the city had been expelled wholesale. In Valencia Jaume I was more fortunate; he immediately directed inquiry to be made of the local Muslim officials so as to learn how the local system worked. Alfonso was to do the same in eastern Spain, at Alicante and Orihuela, where the Muslim population remained.[1]

The information obtained made it possible to specify in the *Repartiments* of property, drawn up immediately after the conquest, which lands had a right to be irrigated and which did not have this right. In Valencia not only orange trees but grain, vineyards, and even locust-bean trees were irrigated when this was possible.

During the thirteenth and fourteenth centuries all the Christians did was 'maintain and repair' the existing irrigation system. Large-scale projects to improve it were planned but not executed. However, the system was considerably extended; many irrigated areas were enlarged.

Professor Thomas Glick has shown how the same techniques of irrigation (the diversion dam, the *noria*, or Persian wheel, and the *qanat*, or horizontal well) existed in the Near East, were brought to Spain by the Arabs, and were taken over by the Christian conquerors of the Islamic south, who later transmitted these techniques to the New World. The cultivation of oranges travelled by the same route.

The system by which water was controlled in Christian Valencia seems to derive almost entirely from earlier Muslim customs. Professor Glick remarks: 'When *all* the synonyms describing a simple phenomenon [in irrigation] are Arabisms,

[1] Jaume I, *Libre dels feyts*, c. 318; González, *Repartimiento de Sevilla*, i. 476, 480 ff.; Roque Chabás, *Distribución de las aguas en 1244 y donaciones del término de Gandia por Don Jaime I* (Valencia, 1898), quoted by Glick (see the next note), pp. 233 f. For Alfonso X in Alicante and Orihuela see Glick, pp. 371 f.

there is a strong presumption that the concept or technique was unknown or undeveloped outside of the Islamic orbit or, at any rate, was very intimately associated with the Islamic style of irrigating.' It seems reasonable to posit a Muslim municipal official before the conquest who controlled water rights in Valencia, as the *muḥtasib* controlled the market. Just as the *muḥtasib* became the Mustaçaf so the 'master of water' developed into the *cequier* of Valencia or the *çabacequier* of other towns.[1]

PUBLIC BATHS

Closely associated with public control of water is the institution of public baths. These were found in many cities in western Europe in the Middle Ages but their exceptional importance in the peninsula and the similarity of construction of baths in Islamic and Christian Spain is proof of the influence of Islam, a religion in which great emphasis is laid on personal cleanliness and in whose cities public baths are as inevitable as mosques and schools.

The objections raised by some ecclesiastics in Spain to the use of baths were not successful during the Middle Ages. Given the general use of baths they proved very profitable institutions and were often reserved as Crown property, or granted to cathedrals, churches, religious communities, or to private individuals. As far north as Gerona stone baths were built in the late-thirteenth century on the Muslim model. The nuns of the Aragonese convent of Sigena possessed baths.

Some cities contained separate baths for Jews, Muslims, and Christians. In others there was a communal bath. The *Fuero de Cuenca* (1189–90)—adopted by other cities—regulated the use of these communal baths. Christian men could bathe on Tuesday, Thursday, and Saturday, women on Monday and Wednesday, Jews on Friday and Sunday. The *Libre de les costums generals* of Tortosa of about 1272 merely remarks of the town baths 'all the citizens and inhabitants, Saracens, Jews, like Christians, should use them'. In Tarazona in Aragon the cathedral chapter rented out the public, communal baths to a local Mudejar.

[1] Thomas F. Glick, *Irrigation and Society in Medieval Valencia* (Cambridge, Mass., 1970). The quotations in the text are from pp. 94 and 223 (the italics are mine). See also R. I. Burns, *Speculum*, 44 (1969), 560–7.

Baths were constructed in royal palaces on Muslim models. Those built in 1328 in the Alcazar of Córdoba for Alfonso XI have recently been discovered with their three rooms, cold, intermediate, and hot. Alfonso also had baths built at Tordesillas in Castile, on the Duero, by Mudejar craftsmen. At the other end of the social hierarchy agricultural labourers, after spending the day threshing, entered the nearest steam baths available—and public baths were available, even in villages.

During the fifteenth century attacks on the practice of bathing gathered strength. Public baths were seen as occasion for immorality. In Valencia they were the scene of feasting, dancing, and drinking at night, according to a contemporary poet. Alfonso XI's bath at Córdoba was given up by Fernando and Isabel. This decline of concern for cleanliness is characteristic of the sixteenth century in all western Europe but in Granada the suppression of public baths was an essential part of the attempt to extirpate Islamic practices among the conquered Moriscos.[1] In other parts of the peninsula the change may have stemmed in part from a general aversion to all things Arabic, seen now as barbarous and non-Castilian. It will be necessary to return to this sixteenth-century revolt against the past of Spain.

ART

The art of the Iberian peninsula displays perhaps more clearly than anything else the extraordinary interpenetration of western European and Islamic influences which characterized Portugal, Castile, and the Crown of Aragon from the thirteenth to the fifteenth century.

GOTHIC ART

Gothic art began to enter the peninsula in the twelfth century along much the same routes as those traversed by Romanesque art before this time. Gothic architectural forms spread slowly along the pilgrimage road from the Pyrenees to the shrine of St. James at Compostela. They also travelled—rather later—through Languedoc to Catalonia. Gothic sculpture had reached

[1] Torres Balbas, pp. 46–68; on Tortosa, *Libre de les costums generals*, I. I. xv, ed. B. Oliver (Madrid, 1881), p. 16; on Tarazona, J. Mª. Sanz Artibucilla, *Al-Andalus*, 9 (1944), 218–26; on Tordesillas, Torres Balbas, ibid. 24 (1959), 409–25; on Valencia, see Jaume Roig, *Llibre de les dones o Spill* (*ENC* A. 21) (Barcelona, 1928), p. 58, and R. I. Burns, *Speculum*, 46 (1971), 453–8.

Castile by 1230. The French style of Gothic painting took far longer to displace Romanesque models.

ARCHITECTURE: CASTILE–LEON

The fully developed Gothic cathedral did not evolve in Spain from native precedent and experiment, as was the case in France. It was exported whole on to the soil of Castile by two outstanding bishops who had probably studied at Paris and certainly knew at first hand the new art of the Île de France, Rodrigo Jiménez de Rada, archbishop of Toledo (1209–47) and Mauricio, bishop of Burgos (1213–38). These two men were evidently determined to provide the 'royal cities' of New and Old Castile with cathedrals to rival Notre-Dame de Paris, the capital of Castile's main rival in western Europe. Notre-Dame was almost finished when Toledo and Burgos were begun, in 1226 and 1222 respectively. A contemporary, Bishop Lucas of Tuy, recognized the novelty of Gothic in Spain when he hailed the 'marvellous work' of Toledo and the 'strong and beautiful church of Burgos' as among the greatest achievements of the age of the 'Reconquest' of the Islamic south. Rodrigo Jiménez de Rada demolished the main mosque of Toledo, which had served as a cathedral since the Christian conquest in 1085. Bishop Mauricio pulled down an existing Romanesque fabric. It seems probable that in both Toledo and Burgos the original architect of the new work was French. If he was not French he was certainly a man who knew contemporary French Gothic very well. Street remarks that Toledo cathedral is 'thoroughly French in its ground plan and equally French in all its details . . . and it is not until we reach the triforium of the choir that any other influence is visible . . . The whole work is a grand protest against [the] Mahomedan architecture [of the rest of Toledo]'. Of the original work at Burgos Street says 'there is little, if anything, to show that we are not in France, and looking at some of its best and purest thirteenth-century Gothic'. Although neither cathedral was completed until 1300 or later, and changes were introduced, particularly in Toledo, into the original plan, recent scholarship has endorsed Street's insistence on the French inspiration behind these buildings. Not only the architecture but the music of the liturgy for which these churches were created was French; the music performed in

Toledo in the thirteenth century came from Notre-Dame in Paris.[1]

The cathedral of León (about 1255–1302) represents a later stage in Gothic art than Toledo or Burgos. The surface covered with stained glass is much larger, the unity of style more apparent, and Spanish features even less noticeable. The plan is a copy, reduced about a third in scale, of the cathedral of Reims but with some improvements, probably due to the influence of other French churches such as Beauvais.

León is an extreme example of French influence. It seems 'a building transplanted to the south of the Pyrenees'. The exotic character of this and of the other great cathedrals of Castile–León appears in the fact that they had very little influence on smaller churches. This was partly because of the great cost of building in stone and partly, no doubt, because a building like León—as Street says, 'a mere lantern', where light is allowed to pour in—is unsuited to Spain.

In contrast to the cathedrals of Toledo and León, which had little influence on their surrounding regions, Burgos cathedral and the contemporary Gothic conventual church of Las Huelgas, situated just outside the city, influenced churches as far as Seville and Aragon and a number of parish churches and abbeys in Castile, where good stone was available and funds abounded. It seems true to say, however, that the later development of French Gothic architecture in Castile is disappointing and adds little to what had already been achieved at Toledo and León.

CATALONIA

Navarre, also, under a French dynasty from 1234 to 1425, did little to add to the models it received, though it could copy them with skill and ingenuity. It is only in Catalonia and the territories colonized by Catalans that one finds a new school of Gothic architecture, something Castile does not achieve before

[1] Marqués de Lozoya, *Historia del arte hispánico*, ii (Barcelona, 1934), Ch. 3; G. E. Street, *Some Account of Gothic Architecture in Spain* (London, 1865), pp. 235 f., 15; see B. Bevan, *History of Spanish Architecture* (London and New York, 1939), pp. 79–82; L. Torres Balbas, *Arquitectura gótica* (*Ars Hispaniae* VII) (Madrid, 1952), pp. 59–77. See also E. Lambert, *L'Art gothique en Espagne aux XIIe et XIIIe siècles* (Paris, 1931); H. Anglés, *La música de las Cántigas* iii. 1 (Barcelona, 1958), 90.

the fifteenth and sixteenth centuries with the cathedrals of Seville and Segovia and the new cathedral of Salamanca.[1]

Catalan Gothic begins with the churches built by the new Orders of friars in the thirteenth century. The Dominicans were established in Barcelona in 1219, the Franciscans by 1229. The Dominican church was begun in 1243, that of the Franciscans was built in the second half of the century.

These churches and many later copies consisted of a broad single nave, with rectangular side chapels between its internal buttresses and a presbytery at the east end. The models used by the builders are in dispute but their aim is clear. It was to get as many people as possible into a large hall where they could see, hear, and be dominated by a preacher. The 'hall-churches' of the friars followed a totally different plan from that of the northern French cathedral which had been transplanted to Toledo, Burgos, and León. These cathedrals with their three naves, transept, and chapels radiating off the apse, offered no chance of an uninterrupted view. They were not churches for sermons but churches for prayer, particularly for the regulated chant of the choir office by the clergy. In the friars' churches space was unified, the choir office was minimized, decoration and mystery disappeared, and the preacher, in long, vibrant, and intensely personal sermons, peppered with striking anecdotes, sought to confront his hearers with the new vision of Christ and the way to follow Him, in simplicity and poverty, which Francis and Dominic had discovered. Gothic architecture, in its most simplified form, suited the friars because it enabled them to cover a large unified space, which was lit by plain glass—stained glass was prohibited by the new Orders in their churches—except in the presbytery.

The great Catalan Cistercian churches of Poblet and Santes Creus, built or begun in the twelfth century, and the cathedrals of Tarragona (1171–1308) and Lérida (1203–78) had contained Gothic features. It was the friars who first introduced Gothic architecture, in an unadulterated form, into Catalonia. The strength, simplicity, and relatively slight cost of their single-nave churches proved enormously attractive to Catalans. They were imitated in the royal chapel of Santa Águeda in Barcelona

[1] Torres Balbas, pp. 84–94, 108 f., 174; Street, pp. 105–21, esp. 111; Bevan, pp. 82–6.

(1302–11), in most of the parish churches of that city, and in the conventual church (a royal foundation) of Pedralbes just outside Barcelona, begun in 1326. Single-nave churches of the same type are found all over Catalonia, in Majorca, and in Valencia.

The other Gothic form introduced into Catalonia came later. This was the church of three naves. This may have been derived in part from the cathedrals of southern France, which begin the necessary adaptation of the northern-French cathedral to the climate and customs of the south, an adaptation not attempted in León. The windows grow smaller and the triforium is closed. But Catalan architects carry the adaptation very much farther; their greatest achievements, the cathedrals of Barcelona, Majorca (Palma), and Gerona, display a native school developing its own forms, distinct from those one finds elsewhere. This development tends to produce vast 'hall-churches', in which beauty emerges from the perfect control of mass and volume.

Barcelona cathedral was begun in 1298 but was largely the work of Jaume Fabre of Majorca, the architect of the great (destroyed) church of Santo Domingo in that island's capital, who took charge of Barcelona cathedral in 1317. By 1338 Fabre had finished the chevet and the crossing. The work continued according to a uniform plan and the cathedral, completed by 1420, is a unity, only diminished by the pseudo-Gothic nineteenth-century façade.

Although Barcelona cathedral has three naves the central nave is far wider than the side aisles, and the transepts are hardly noticeable. One can see here the influence of the single-nave church of the friars. This influence is still clearer in the collegiate church of Manresa, begun in 1328, whose nave, 'a vast hall sixty feet wide, is flanked by narrow aisles', with virtually no transepts. Santa Maria del Mar in Barcelona (well advanced by 1340) is 'a simplification of, yet an advance upon, the plan of the cathedral'. There are no transepts and the columns are simple and unadorned. They raise the main nave to the same height as that of the cathedral.

The cathedral of the City of Majorca (today Palma) carries even further the soaring tendency of Catalan churches on the mainland. The central vault of its nave is 140 feet high, higher than all French cathedrals except Beauvais. It is 190 feet across.

The extraordinary sense of unlimited space in the cathedral and the daring of its construction are only surpassed, if at all, by the nave of the cathedral of Gerona, which may have been inspired by the Majorcan example.

In both Majorca and Gerona the original intention was to continue the three naves of the chevet—built in both cases by 1350—throughout the church. In Majorca three naves were built (from 1368 onwards) but at a far greater height than that contemplated in the original plan. In Gerona a conference of architects, held in 1416, was divided between three naves and one. The members of the cathedral chapter adopted the minority opinion in favour of one nave. This was to be a broader single nave (73 feet), than that of any contemporary cathedral. They made their choice, the document states, not only because one nave would cost less but because they held the result would be 'more solemn and noble' and the interior would be lighter. In the naves of Palma and Gerona cathedrals engineering becomes great art. These cathedrals are as original as Chartres was in its day, the culmination of two centuries of continuous experiment in the mastery of space.

The achievements of Catalan architecture were not limited to religious buildings. They also produced a series of secular buildings in the Gothic style which are unparalleled in Castile. However, as these all date from the second half of the fourteenth or from the fifteenth century, it seems better to discuss them at a later point in this book.[1]

SCULPTURE

French sculptors reached Castile at the same time as French architects, drawn by the same ecclesiastical patrons. Two French sculptors were at work by about 1230 on the south-transept door of the cathedral of Burgos. A more natural and realistic style gradually evolves. It can be seen in the statue of Queen

[1] J. Puig i Cadafalch, in *Miscel.lània Prat de la Riba*, i (Barcelona, 1921), pp. 65–87; Torres Balbas, pp. 120–30, 150, 173–217, 269–75; Bevan, pp. 87–96 (the quotations in the text are from pp. 92 f.); Street, pp. 291–329; Lozoya, Chs. 4, 5; P. Lavedan, *L'Architecture gothique religieuse en Catalogne, Valence et Baléares* (Paris, 1935); M. Durliat, *L'Art dans le royaume de Majorque* (Toulouse, 1962), pp. 150–67; see also R. A. Cram, *The Cathedral of Palma de Mallorca, an architectural study* (Cambridge, Mass., 1932). The consultation of architects at Gerona in Villanueva, xii. 324–38, and transl. in Street, pp. 501–13. For secular Catalan Gothic see below, vol. ii, Part I, Ch. IV.

Violante in the cloister at Burgos, which is alive and personal, and in the tomb of the founder of the cathedral, Bishop Mauricio, in the choir. Realism becomes theatrical exaggeration in the Descent from the Cross at Las Huelgas, near Burgos. In general Gothic sculpture in Castile is less lyrical and idealized than its French models. Its Virgins are rounder, fuller, closer to the people who prayed before them. The Annunciation in the old cathedral at Salamanca is worth citing, for the extreme dignity and serenity with which spiritual values are presented to the worshipper.

Sculpture in Toledo cathedral displays, as at Burgos, the influence of Reims, but at Toledo Italian masters seem also to have been at work on the doors. In more outlying regions of Castile, such as Asturias and Galicia, the Romanesque tradition long persisted and what Gothic sculpture one finds seems to have been imported, on occasion from England. In Andalusia and Extremadura little, if any, monumental sculpture worthy of note seems to have been executed but many fine images were made, usually in wood. Navarre, on the other hand, was faithful to France in sculpture as in architecture.

Catalan artists took longer to evolve a native school in Gothic sculpture than they did in architecture. In the thirteenth and the early fourteenth centuries Italian is as important as French influence in the work done at the cathedral of Tarragona, at Gerona, and on the royal tombs at Santes Creus. Italian sculptors seem to have been imported to execute the tomb of Santa Eulalia in the crypt at Barcelona (about 1330) and that of the Archbishop Infant Joan of Aragon at Tarragona (1337). The evolution of a distinct native style is linked with the court of Pere III of Catalonia–Aragon (1336–87). It was to issue in the free, imaginative work of fifteenth-century Catalan sculptors.[1]

PAINTING

What the late Chandler Rathfon Post called the 'Franco-Gothic' style of painting has been rebaptized as 'estilo gótico lineal' by the Catalan scholar Dr José Gudiol Ricart. The latter defines this style as two-dimensional and with a monochrome back-

[1] A. Durán Sanpere and J. Ainaud de Lasarte, *Escultura gótica* (*Ars Hispaniae* VIII) (Madrid, 1956); Lozoya, Ch. 6. See Vol. ii, Part I. Ch. IV.

ground, recalling scenes from stained glass which often served as models. Evolving out of late-Romanesque painting this style dominated the peninsula during most of the fourteenth century. Mural paintings continued to be executed as well as retables. From about 1330 the 'Franco-Gothic' style was challenged, especially in Catalonia and Majorca, by painters who had probably studied in Italy and had certainly absorbed much of the emotional interest in detail of Giotto and Duccio. From about 1340 the retable appears to triumph over the mural painting. The evolution of retable-painting is connected, like that of Gothic sculpture in Catalonia, with the court of Pere III.[1]

MUDEJAR ART

In Catalonia a native school of Gothic art found acceptance at every level, from the cathedral to the parish church. In Castile Gothic art, and especially architecture, hardly penetrated below the level of the great cathedrals and abbeys. Mudejar art was much more economic than Gothic. Instead of stone it used the cheaper and more readily available brick, plaster, wood, and lime. It naturally remained the predominant art form in Andalusia. In cities such as Seville or Córdoba mosques became and often continued for centuries to serve as churches. The markets, public baths, and ovens built by Muslims continued to be used by Christians. The street plan hardly changed. These cities reached the nineteenth century with many traces of their Islamic past. Up to 1500 the changes were relatively slight. All this contributed to maintain continuity in building. New buildings were generally erected in the same materials as of old, in adobe, plaster, brick, rather than stone. They were adorned with Mudejar woodwork, superior to anything Gothic artists achieved in wood, and defended by fortifications which followed Islamic traditions.

The first churches built in Andalusia after the Christian conquest, such as Santa Ana de Triana at Seville, represented an attempt to be true to Gothic forms. But other churches there and at Córdoba grew further and further away from Gothic as their builders were captured by the Mudejar atmosphere of the

[1] C. R. Post, *A History of Spanish Painting*, ii (Cambridge, Mass., 1930); J. Gudiol Ricart, *Pintura gótica* (*Ars Hispaniae* IX) (Madrid, 1955).

south. Gothic vaulting only appears at the chevet. The nave and aisles are covered with wooden Mudejar ceilings. Above square chapels rise cupolas decorated with interlace. Seville still has a most impressive series of these Mudejar churches, Santa Catalina, La Encarnación, San Pablo (La Magdalena), El Salvador. Against this background the enormous late-Gothic cathedral seems a complete exotic. In Córdoba San Pablo is outstanding. It has an extraordinary chapel with tiles and plaster-work with horseshoe arches, which seems a direct echo of Granada.[1]

In and around Toledo and León and in Aragon Muslim architecture through its derivatives—Mozarabic and Mudejar —was, as in the south, too firmly rooted not to remain the predominant style. The Gothic cathedrals of Toledo and León had virtually no influence on later buildings. It is notable that the parish church of San Román, with its Mudejar decoration, was consecrated in 1221 by the builder of Toledo cathedral, the great Archbishop Rodrigo Jiménez de Rada. Muslim influence is visible even in the cathedral itself, French as its inspiration is, in the triforium over the choir, as well as in later details from the splendid tomb of Don Fernán Gudiel (d. 1278) and in the sixteenth-century door of the Sala Capitular.

Through the patronage of kings and nobles Mudejar architecture and decoration reached other regions such as Old Castile and Navarre which had never had a large Muslim or Mozarabic population. Mudejar influence was impressed on all the forms that entered the peninsula from outside, Romanesque, Gothic, Plateresque, Italian Renaissance. On all of them—except, perhaps in Catalonia—it stamped variations which are only found in the peninsula and in Spanish conquests overseas. If Spain ever had a style that can be called national, Mudejar deserves that name. For many centuries it was 'the most genuine expression, the traditional language' of the people. The influence of Mudejar art in Portugal was far slighter than in Spain and only appeared very late, under Manuel I (1495–1521). In Castile Mudejar art interested all classes from kings to the rag-dealer who built the chapel of the Concepción Francisca in Toledo in 1422. Mudejar art could be and was executed not

[1] L. Torres Balbas, *Algunos aspectos del mudejarismo urbano*, pp. 21–3; E. Lambert, *Études médiévales*, iii (Toulouse, 1956), 163–6.

only by Mudejares but by native Christian workmen and even by foreigners working in Spain. It was as much appreciated and used by Jews as by Christians. In Toledo about 1200 the same Mudejar artists were at work in mosques, synagogues, and churches. In later centuries opportunities to build mosques hardly existed but synagogues and churches prove that the preference for Mudejar art continued.[1]

The *Primera Crónica General* records the impression made in 1248 on the conquerors of Seville by the minaret of the principal mosque, the Giralda as we call it. The great mosque at Seville, built from 1172 to 1182, which existed until 1400, was as large as that of Córdoba. Its decoration and that of the Patio de Yeso which survives in the Alcazar of Seville helped to inspire later work in the Alhambra. The influence of these Almohad works can also be seen in the Chapel de las Claustrillas in the royal foundation of Las Huelgas, outside Burgos. The chapel was built by Muslim artists, probably from Seville, before 1225. Its sober decoration, which stemmed from the puritanical drive for simplicity of the Almohad movement, was perfectly suited to a Cistercian convent. The fact, as Torres Balbas says, 'demonstrates the intimate communion, the symbiosis between the two medieval Spains'. It is particularly striking that the king who was responsible for this chapel, chose Muslim, not Christian, workmen to build it at a time when Castile was engaged in a desperate struggle with the Almohad empire. Throughout the thirteenth century Muslim art continued to be used at Las Huelgas, in union with the best French Gothic.[2]

The same style of decoration in plaster appears in the second half of the thirteenth century in Las Huelgas and in the synagogue of Santa Maria la Blanca in Toledo. The style adopted in these two places follows the essentially abstract lines of Islamic art which 'converts decoration into geometry', but, like Arabic poetry, Islamic decoration can produce infinite variations within the same canon. In the fourteenth century Mudejar decorative style becomes more varied as it is influenced at the

[1] L. Torres Balbas, *Arte almohade, arte nazarí, arte mudejar* (*Ars Hispaniae* IV) (Madrid, 1949), p. 246; Lambert, op. cit., pp. 119–30, 253 ff.

[2] Torres Balbas, pp. 39–43; *Primera Crónica General*, c. 1128, ed. R. Menéndez Pidal, ii. 768.

same time by the models evolved in the Alhambra and by the more naturalistic repertoire of Gothic sculptors.[1]

Mudejar art influenced church builders in different ways in Castile, León, Andalusia, and Aragon. The most striking example of continuous development can be seen in and around Toledo, where large Mudejar and Mozarabic communities existed which continued to be in touch with Andalusia, and especially with the still independent Islamic Granada. In Toledo stone was expensive and difficult to work. Until the late fifteenth century the cathedral was the only church in Toledo built in stone. The Mudejar workmen of Toledo, and also of Castile and León, adapted Romanesque architecture to brick, changing it as they did so. The changes are more evident in Toledo where the towers of the churches clearly descend from minarets and where horseshoe and lobed arches and blind arcades often replace the rounded Romanesque forms.[2] In Old Castile and León Mudejar workmen were employed not only on many parish churches but in completing the great Cluniac monastery of Sahagún and on later Cistercian abbeys.

Toledan Mudejar influence was felt as far west as Talavera and as far north as Guadalajara. The first churches of Madrid were modest Mudejar buildings. Don Juan Manuel, a great admirer of Arabic literature and of Hebrew medicine, also chose Mudejar (probably Toledan) workmen to build a Dominican church in Peñafiel near Valladolid, which was begun in 1324. Here a Mudejar exterior is wedded to interior Gothic vaulting.

The monastic church of Guadalupe in the mountains south of Toledo was built from 1389 to 1412, at the order of Juan I of Castile. It was built by the architect in charge of Toledo cathedral, in Gothic style but with Mudejar decoration. Its cloister contains some of the finest Mudejar work in brick and tiles.

As we have seen, almost all the parish churches of Seville and Córdoba, all the monasteries built in Andalusia from the fourteenth to the sixteenth centuries, and many of those erected in

[1] See below, Vol. ii, Part I, Ch. IV. On the synagogues of Toledo see Lambert, pp. 131–43.

[2] M. Gómez-Moreno, *Arte mudéjar toledano* (Madrid, 1916). For Talavera, M. Terrasse, *MCV* 6 (1970), 79–112.

Castile and Aragon contain elements taken from Mudejar art. Sepulchral chapels built by kings and nobles displayed cupolas with rich decoration in plaster or painting, rising on a system of vaults which is found in the great mosque of Córdoba. The Capilla Real was built in 1258–60 by Alfonso X in the middle of that mosque in clear imitation of its tenth-century vaulting. It has been called 'a Christian chapel which could not be more completely Muslim'.[1] Other similar chapels were erected by Alfonso XI in his palace in Tordesillas in Old Castile, and in Toledo, Seville, and Olmedo. They are prototypes of the splendid chapels and domes of the late fifteenth and sixteenth centuries which adorn the cathedrals of Burgos and Murcia and San Juan de los Reyes in Toledo.

Mudejar style does not seem to have been introduced into Aragon much before 1300 but, once introduced, it flourished there. Aragon contains numbers of churches built on Catalan Gothic models, with wide single naves covered with ogival vaulting, or with three naves and no transepts but in brick instead of stone. The interior decoration in plaster or wood, the impressive exteriors, with green and white tiles inset in brick, the extraordinary variety of the bell-towers beside the churches, with their terracotta columns, varying from purple to deep blue, all reveal Mudejar work. This impression is confirmed by the published documents and surviving inscriptions which show that the majority of the builders of these churches were Muslims. One of these builders, at Maluenda, even placed the invocation of Allah and his prophet Muḥammad (in Arabic script) after a Gospel text in Gothic lettering. The combination still attests the church's origin.[2]

SECULAR ARCHITECTURE

Mudejar influence appears even more clearly in secular than in religious architecture. Just as the Christian conquerors of Seville attempted to import there the Gothic type of church they had only recently received from France, so Alfonso X and his brother Don Fadrique built palaces in Seville in the Gothic

[1] V. Escribano Ucelay, in *I Congreso de Estudios Árabes e Islámicos* (Córdoba, 1962), *Actas* (Madrid, 1964), p. 398.

[2] J. Galiay Sarañana, *Arte mudéjar aragonés* (Saragossa, 1950); Bevan, *History of Spanish Architecture*, pp. 107–10, esp. 108; G. M. Bonas Gualis, *Al-Andalus*, 22 (1967), 399–414.

style.[1] This attempt to import a style proved an even more complete failure in secular than it was in ecclesiastical architecture. There were, in the thirteenth century, no Christian models that could challenge the mastery of the art of palace-building attained by Muslims. The simple effectiveness of a Gothic castle hall, its only adornment tapestries on a festival occasion, could hardly compete with marble floors, walls covered with brilliantly coloured tiles and gold, blue-and-red designs in stucco, elaborately worked and gilded ceilings, cushions and carpets of great beauty, an architecture suited to a climate where life could be lived round patios and gardens, where dazzling heat was filtered by marble lattices and silk hangings, and the air cooled by the continual sound of fountains. It is hardly surprising that within far less than a century the kings of Castile had ceased to build Gothic castles, that Alfonso X's palace at Seville was swallowed up in Pedro I's Mudejar Alcazar, and that not only in Andalusia but throughout northern Spain, as far as the Pyrenees, there arose imitations of Seville and Granada, where the king, leading prelates and nobles 'enjoy poetry, learn to play chess, listen to Indian tales of Kalila and Dimna, and receive foreign envoys to the sound of Moorish flutes . . . The way of looking at the world has changed.'[2]

Only fragments of many of these Mudejar palaces have survived, such as the façade of the palace built about 1300 outside Valladolid, by Doña María de Molina, the widow of Sancho IV, or the ruins of the palaces of the archbishop of Toledo at Brihuega or in Toledo itself. The convent of Santa Clara at Tordesillas on the Duero contains the palace built by Alfonso XI in the 1340s, with its Arabic inscription over the door, its patio and baths. These palaces prepare for Pedro I's buildings at Seville. Mudejar craftsmen took part in the majority of public works, bridges, town halls, hospitals, baths, in the docks built by Alfonso X at Seville in 1252, and in the fortification of towns and castles so necessary in the unquiet Castile of the next two centuries. Only in Catalonia does one find, in the peninsula,

[1] Lambert, pp. 166–71.

[2] M. Gaibrois de Ballesteros, cited by L. Torres Balbas, *Arte almohade*, p. 312 (slightly paraphrased). See the *Libro de Alixandre*, vv. 1956–9 (*BAE* lvii. 207; ed. Willis, p. 369).

palaces and public works which derive from a pure Gothic tradition, with little or no Mudejar influence.[1]

There is overwhelming evidence of the appreciation of Muslim and Mudejar work in the 'minor' arts by the Christian ruling classes—notably in the textiles preserved at Las Huelgas, but also in episcopal inventories, in surviving liturgical vestments, and in silks used to wrap relics of saints. Leather hangings from Granada and Andalusia were highly prized. In ceramics, too, first Málaga, in the kingdom of Granada, and later the Mudejar workmen of Manises, near Valencia, were supreme. In 1303 plates and jugs of 'Malyk' appear in the lists of goods brought in through the English customs at Sandwich. The first mention of Manises ware is in 1317. By 1400 Manises was exporting to Italy, France, and England. Manises ware was acquired by the royal house of Portugal and the great merchants of Florence.

The Muslims of Granada, under Christian influence, painted the walls of their houses and palaces with human representations. A few of these paintings survive in the Alhambra, some probably executed by Christian artists, some by Muslims.[2] Alfonso X, in the thirteenth century, and the Archpriest of Hita in the fourteenth, record the mural decorations of Christian churches and houses in Toledo. Mudejar painters decorated the church of San Román in Toledo where Arabic inscriptions accompany Christian scenes. Formal decoration inspired by Arabic script accompanies wall paintings representing the conquest of Majorca, recently found in Barcelona. Many citizens were enlivened by the polychromy of their church towers. The outer walls of buildings glowed with coloured ceramics and paintings. Muslim influence also appears in retables by Christian painters, particularly in ornamental borders with animals, which derive from Islamic textiles or ivory caskets.[3] Wherever fine work was needed, one can find Mudejars providing it. As carpenters they made not only doors and ceilings but choir stalls in Majorca, Pamplona, Huesca, reliquaries, frames for retables, organs. In Segovia Christians and Mudejars belonged to the

[1] For Catalan Gothic secular buildings see below, Vol. ii, Part I, Ch. IV; for Mudejar work from Pedro I to Juan II, ibid.

[2] See C. R. Post, *A History of Spanish Painting*, ii. 160–71; Torres Balbas, *Arte almohade*, pp. 191, 377.

[3] Torres Balbas, *Al-Andalus*, 7 (1942), 409–17; Post, i. 64 f.

same guild of ironworkers. The sword attributed to Roland, and perhaps actually used by Fernando III, now in the Royal Armoury in Madrid, was probably made by Mudejars. Only in sculpture do they seem to have taken no part.[1]

The *convivencia* of members of the three religions brought about borrowing by Christians in the spheres of language, institutions, and art. What is perhaps the most difficult question to answer with regard to the relations that existed between Christians and Muslims in the Iberian peninsula has been posed as follows: 'Could [these] physical and spiritual contacts achieve a transference of *ideas*?'[2] The same question could be asked with regard to relations between Christians and Jews. A later examination of some key figures of the age, Ramon Lull, Alfonso X of Castile, Don Juan Manuel, and the Archpriest of Hita, may help to answer this question. There follow some general remarks on the literary and religious evidence.

LITERATURE: FRENCH INFLUENCE

In the thirteenth century French influence in the peninsula appears as clearly in literature as it does in the increase of feudal institutions and in trappings of chivalry such as heraldry. Many men, like the 'student' (*escolar*) of the poem, *Razón feita de amor*, had lived 'in Germany, France, and in Lombardy to learn courtesy'.[3] No doubt it was the example of France and especially of Provence and Languedoc that made not only Alfons I of Catalonia–Aragon (1162–96) (who was also marquess of Provence) and his grandson, Jaume I (1213–76), but Fernando III of Castile (1218–52) and his son Alfonso X (1252–84) become troubadours themselves or at least protect troubadours at their courts. These rulers were imitated in a later generation by King Dinis of Portugal (1279–1325), and, on a smaller scale, by the leading nobles of the Spanish kingdoms.

The Catalan poets of the twelfth and thirteenth centuries are troubadours; they 'belong to Provençal literature not only by their language and style but also by their personal and cultural

[1] The section on Mudejar art is principally based on Torres Balbas, *Arte almohade*. See also Lozoya, Ch. 3.

[2] Dufourcq, p. 3.

[4] For feudalism see above, Ch. III, pp. 104 f.; *Razón de amor*, ed. R. Menéndez Pidal, *Revue hispanique*, 13 (1905), 608. See M. Rodrigues Lapa, *Liçoes de literatura portuguesa*, 6th edn., pp. 118–24.

relations with troubadours beyond the Pyrenees'. Ramon Lull, while creating Catalan prose as a literary instrument distinct from any other language, continued to write verse which is almost Provençal. At the end of the fourteenth century the verse of another leading Catalan author, Bernat Metge, was still full of Provençal terms.

Northern-French novels and romances were also known in Catalonia. About 1170 a Catalan troubadour expected his minstrel (*joglar*) to be familiar with Arthurian themes. In the thirteenth century these themes had penetrated aristocratic circles in Castile. Alfonso X's poems show a knowledge of Arthurian legends, as do the poems of his grandson King Dinis of Portugal. Arthurian romances influenced the great Catalan chroniclers, who saw their heroes as men of the Round Table or of the *Song of Roland*, come to life again. The *Roman de Renart* was cited by Catalan troubadours and by Ramon Lull. At the beginning of the fourteenth century the castle of Alcañiz in Aragon was decorated with frescoes inspired by the *Romans*.[1]

In Castile Alfonso X, like Ramon Lull, considered himself to be a troubadour and wrote both profane and sacred poetry. Like Lull, Alfonso did not write his poems in the same language that he employed—and largely created—for prose, in Castilian, but, in this case, in Galician, but the influence of Provençal lyric models is as strong in Alfonso as it is in Lull. At least nineteen troubadours dedicated poems to Alfonso or were connected with his court. Other Castilian poets, such as the author of *Fernán González*, are as conscious of the *chansons de geste* and of the northern-French heroic models as any Catalan writer.

A count of Castile is seen as one in a long line of heroes, from Alexander and David down through Roland and Oliver, all of whom will be remembered 'for what they *did*'. The mystique of action and exaltation of glorious deeds found in the *chansons* and in the northern-French novels inspired by Geoffrey of Monmouth entered both Castile and Catalonia. The *Libre de saviesa* attributed to Jaume I of Aragon begins: 'Man should live in this world for two things, to enjoy God's glory and to gain

[1] Riquer, i. 22, 13 f., 59, 307, 313–6; Part II, Ch. I, below, p. 236. M. R. Lida de Malkiel, in *Arthurian Literature in the Middle Ages*, ed. R. S. Loomis (Oxford, 1959), pp. 406–18.

fame in this earthly life.' The two ends seem equivalent in value.[1]

EASTERN INFLUENCE

France and Provence played a preponderant part in influencing the style and content of Castilian and Catalan lyric poetry and also in promoting a more 'secularized' approach to this world, fame, and glory, although Arabic legends combine with Latin and French sources in the *Libro de Alixandre*. In the creation both of Castilian and Catalan prose and particularly in philosophy and science, French influences were of slight importance compared to Arabic and Hebrew models. The influence of Roman and canon law on the legal compilations produced in the vernacular in Castile under Alfonso X and in Aragon under Jaume I has already been discussed.[2]

The list of translations made from Arabic or Hebrew into Castilian in the thirteenth century is a long one. Castile in this century refused to imitate the lyric poem and short story of Islam but it adopted its moral wisdom. A number of didactic political-moral catechisms were composed under Fernando III. These works and also novelistic collections such as *Kalila and Dimna*—translated in 1251— are indisputably derived from Arabic originals. It was through these translations that Castilian prose began to develop. The didactic works were drawn on by Alfonso X's *Partidas*. Eastern influence is still apparent behind the *Libro de los castigos e documentos* attributed to Sancho IV of Castile, and in the far more impressive works of Don Juan Manuel, who adopts the Eastern short story as his model.[3]

The use of Castilian instead of Latin is the most striking feature of the translations brought about by Alfonso X, as

[1] M. R. Lida de Malkiel, *La idea de la fama en la edad media castellana* (Mexico–Buenos Aires), 1952), esp. pp. 159, 197–206; cf. R. W. Hanning, *The Vision of History in Early Britain, from Gildas to Geoffrey of Monmouth* (New York–London, 1966), esp. Ch. 5, pp. 121–72.

[2] E. García Gómez, *Un texto árabe occidental de la leyenda de Alejandro* (Madrid, 1929), esp. pp. lxxi-viii. See above, Ch. III.

[3] For a bibliography of the didactic works see Carreras Artau, i. 27 f.; A. Millares Carlo, *Literatura española hasta fines del s. XV* (Mexico, 1950), pp. 113–22, 125–8. See A. Castro, *La realidad* (1954), pp. 358 f.; also Menéndez y Pelayo, *Orígenes* i, Chs. 2–3 and, below, Ch. VI. A new edn. of *El libro de Calila e Digna*, ed. J. E. Keller and R. W. Linker (Madrid, 1967), has an improved text; see J. E. Keller, *Alfonso X, El Sabio* (New York, 1967), pp. 51–63. For Alfonso X's translations see below, Part II, Ch. II.

against earlier translations made in Spain in the twelfth century. This preference for Castilian is certainly largely due to a desire to secure the greatest possible diffusion for the works translated. It may also be due in part to the use of Jews—and some Muslims—rather than clerics. As Muslim and Jewish scholars became more familiar with Castilian they began to write in it. We possess the curious *Poema de Yuçuf*, written in Castilian in Arabic characters, evidently by a Mudejar, and the later poem of Rabbi Sem Tob, addressed to Pedro I.[1]

Alfonso X's patronage of translators was only continued on a very reduced scale by his successors. Greater interest in scientific culture was now displayed by the court of Aragon. Ramon Lull (1232–1316), whose first book was a translation of a work on logic from Arabic, was not principally interested in the natural sciences but he encouraged very strongly the study of Arabic and Hebrew thought. The court doctor, Arnau de Vilanova (d. 1311) enjoyed greater influence than Lull with Jaume II (1291–1327). It was probably because of Arnau's interest in Arabic medicine and astronomy that Jaume II ordered the translation of medical works from Arabic into Latin. Arnau's own first works had included six such translations. He also made considerable use of Arabic ideas in his own medical works, and of works on the occult sciences in his polemical writings. Although Arnau, like Lull, urged the rulers of his time to arrange debates on religions between Christians and Muslims, his knowledge of Islamic thought was slight in comparison to Lull's. Arnau had learnt Hebrew from the Dominican Ramon Martí. He endeavoured to imitate Martí by writing against Judaism. What is curious is that, despite his claim of originality, the methods he pursued in Biblical exegesis were derived from the prophetic Cabalism of his contemporary Abraham Abulafia, who came close to professing a belief in the Trinity. There is a parallel here to Lull's possible use of Cabalism and certain use of Islamic theology. It is hardly surprising that both Arnau and Lull were considered to be heretical by thinkers formed in schools outside the peninsula. Arnau was denounced in 1312 for his 'Judaizing' exegesis by Henry of Harclay, chancellor of the University of Oxford. Lull was

[1] *Poema de Yuçuf*, *BAE* lvii. 413–23; Sem Tob, ibid. 331–72. See R. Lapesa, op. cit., p. 166.

considered a heretic by the fashionable theologian Augustinus Triumphus.[1]

Jaume II received a *Book of Proverbs* from Ramon Lull. He was also presented with a *Book of the words and savings of wise men* by Judah Bonsenyor, a compilation of Catalan maxims drawn from Latin as well as Arabic and Hebrew sources.[2]

RELIGIOUS EVIDENCE: VISIONARIES

In 1300 the whole Iberian peninsula was as full of visionaries as Muslim Spain had been a century earlier. Indeed Ibn Arabī's description of the holy men of al-Andalus, 'full of prodigies and wonders', endowed with the supernatural gift of 'discernment of spirits', capable of prodigies of asceticism, surrounded by groups of disciples, living on dry figs or beans, passing their nights in vigils, their days in reading the Qurān, possessing the 'gift of tears', bringing down rain by their prayers, caring for the poor and cursing the rich, sometimes living as hermits, sometimes teaching, venerated by merchants, damned by the worldly doctors of the law, very strongly recalls the Spiritual Franciscans and other visionaries who flourished, especially in Catalonia, and whose leading allies were Arnau de Vilanova and Ramon Lull. The fearless attitude of these Muslim ascetics, when faced with the rulers of their day, and their constant mobility recall Lull's fictional hero Blanquerna and much of his own life.

Other spiritual descendants of Ibn Arabī's ascetics existed in Lull's time besides the Spiritual Franciscans. The Jewish mystics who appear in the Cabalist writings originating in Castile in the 1280s behave in very much the same way as the Franciscans. They are popular preachers of morality, begging their bread as the early friars had done. Like the Franciscans the Cabalists are engaged in a perpetual struggle with devils, while they also love, like Lull's heroes, to sit beside fountains under trees and contemplate the beauty of nature. The reference to King David as God's minstrel reminds one of the minstrels

[1] J. M[a]. Millás Vallicrosa, *VII CHCA* iii. 315 f.; J. Carreras Artau, in *HM* i. 309–21; idem, *Sefarad*, 7 (1947), 49–61; see my *Ramon Lull*, pp. 55 f. G. Scholem, in *Essays presented to Leo Baeck* (London, 1954), pp. 171 f., questions a direct relationship between Abulafia and Arnau.

[2] See Part II, Ch. I, below, p. 285, n. 2. The *Libre de saviesa*, attributed to Jaume I, cited above (p. 205) is a very similar work to Bonsenyor's.

who appear as God's spokesmen in Lull's novels. The Cabalists' opposition to the worldliness of the leaders of Jewish communities in Spain also parallels the Franciscan attack on much in the contemporary Church. The Cabalists and Lull shared a common aversion to 'Averroist' views, which appeared to undermine traditional religious faith. In the 1300s, while Lull was asking the king of France to ban Averroist writings in Paris, orthodox Catalan Jews were attempting to enact similar prohibitions in their communities. Jewish mystics, like the Spiritual Franciscans, see poverty not as a trial but as 'a religious end in itself'. One must agree with Professor Baer in seeing Christian influence 'colouring the Jewish outlook in spite of the stubborn opposition of the rabbis and religious teachers'.[1]

ARRESTED FUSION

The *convivencia* which existed between Christians, Muslims, and Jews in the Iberian peninsula was not assured of permanence. Despite the optimism of men like Ramon Lull and the Dominicans of Aragon assimilation remained incomplete and fusion was arrested. The Iberian *modus vivendi* was constantly under fire from the papacy and from the more fanatical elements of the Spanish clergy.[2] The toleration displayed by the Spanish Muslim thinker Ibn Arabī (d. 1240) was highly exceptional and was only imperfectly reciprocated even by Lull, who believed that if Jews and Muslims left Christian lands to escape proselytism this would not greatly matter. He objected as violently as any contemporary noble to a Christian king employing Jewish officials or honouring rich Jews who lent him money. Lull's objections were not based on vested interests but on religion, because Jews 'wish ill to Christ and to all his followers', but they were the more significant for that reason.[3] Evidence of the mutual hostility between the different religious

[1] M. Asín, *Vidas de santones andaluces* (Madrid, 1933), pp. 52–186; *Sufis of Andalusia*, transl. R. W. J. Austin and M. Lings (Berkeley, 1971); Baer, *History* i. 261–305; see my *Ramon Lull*, Ch. II. J. Mª. Pou y Martí, *Visionarios beguinos y fraticelos catalanes* (*siglos XIII–XV*) (Vich, 1930); M. D. Lambert, *Franciscan Poverty* (London, 1961).

[2] T. F. Glick and O. Pi-Sunyer, 'Acculturation as an Explanatory Concept in Spanish History', *Comparative Studies in Society and History*, 2. 2 (1969), 153 f.

[3] For Ibn Arabī see A. Castro, *La realidad histórica de España*, new edn. (Mexico 1962), p. 430; for Lull my *Ramon Lull*, p. 24, and Lull, *Blanquerna*, iv, c. 80, 6 (*Obres essencials*, i. 230 f.); *Libre de meravelles*, viii. 86, 92 (pp. 452, 462).

communities exists in the thirteenth century in the midst of the *convivencia* already described.

MUTUAL HOSTILITY

The attitude of Alfonso X was far from consistent. Some of his more tolerant remarks have already been quoted and in practice he made considerable use of Jewish scholars and financiers. But the *Partidas* also contain a general statement, explaining why Jews are allowed to live among Christians, 'so that they may live forever in captivity that men may remember that they come from the lineage of those who crucified our Lord Jesus Christ'.[1]

The general attitude of Jaume I of Aragon to Muslims was also far more hostile than his protection of the Muslims of conquered Majorca and Valencia would suggest. When a large Muslim revolt broke out in Valencia in the 1240s, his *Book of Deeds* records:

> It pleases me much, for on account of the treaties made with the Saracens I did not drive them out of this country. Since they have done something now by which I should [be justified] in driving them out, I am delighted that where the name of Muḥammad has long been invoked men will call on the name of Our Lord Jesus Christ.

Even those Muslims who had not rebelled should, Jaume considered, be expelled. Many Muslims were in fact expelled after this revolt, despite the resistance of those barons whose lands were worked by Muslims, though other Muslims were granted lands in later decades.

In the 1270s the authorities of the Catalan port of Tortosa promulgated a new law code which contained the usual regulations enforcing distinction in dress on the local Jews and Muslims. They also stated that when attending Court they were to sit 'at the feet of Christians'. The fallen and conquered state of non-Christians must be made visible and humiliating.[2]

As we have seen, the peaceful conversion of Jews and Muslims was strongly favoured, especially by the kings of Aragon. But the missionary campaigns conducted by Dominicans and

[1] Alfonso X, *Partidas*, VII. xxiv. 1; for other views of Alfonso and for his Jewish financiers see above, p. 165, n. 1; p. 172, n. 1; p. 176, n. 1.

[2] Jaume I, *Libre dels feyts*, cc. 361, 365–7. See below, Part II, Ch. I, p. 252; *Libre de les costums generals de Tortosa*, I. ix, ed. B. Oliver, pp. 56 f. See R. I. Burns, 'Immigrants from Islam', *American Historical Review*, 80 (1975).

Franciscans from the 1240s onwards, with sermons delivered in mosques and synagogues to captive audiences of Muslims and Jews and occasional public disputations, could produce fanatical demonstrations on the part of Christians. In 1263, 1268, and 1279 the Jewish communities obtained royal privileges limiting attendance at these sermons to the Jewish quarter. The number of Christians allowed to accompany the preacher was restricted to ten. These privileges were paid for, a Jewish document records, by 'large expenditures by the communities in the interests of public welfare and *safety*'. Riots against Jews or Muslims could break out very easily, fomented by clerical fanatics. On one occasion Jaume I had to draw his sword to disperse a mob of clerics about to attack the Jews of Barcelona. In 1278 Jaume's son Pere II, had to rebuke the clergy of Gerona for celebrating Easter by bombarding the *Judería* in Gerona with stones from the cathedral steeple, severely damaging Jewish gardens and vineyards and the Jewish cemetery. The monarchy succeeded with some difficulty in preventing serious anti-Jewish riots in the thirteenth century. It was not so successful in protecting the Muslims of Valencia.

In 1236, before Valencia fell, Jaume I secured a papal letter ordering the clergy to protect conquered Muslims from violence. In 1238 the bishops of Catalonia and Aragon issued an excommunication against those who maltreated Mudejars. Christian converts from Islam were no safer than Muslims. In 1275–6 very serious anti-Mudejar riots broke out throughout the kingdom of Valencia. The rioters were mainly townsmen. Many Mudejars were enslaved and sold. These riots may have been due to the same causes that had brought about the anti-Jewish movement of the 1260s, that is, to a misplaced confidence in the possibility of the rapid conversion of the non-Christian masses to Christianity—a confidence which had probably spread from Ramon Lull and the Dominican preachers to many of the less intelligent laity.[1]

In the *Partidas* Alfonso X legislated to protect Jews and Muslims from injury but he also prohibited communal living or the sharing of meals or of public baths. These laws were not applied at this time but they indicate the theoretical acceptance by Alfonso of church legislation. Similarly, in 1228, Jaume I

[1] Baer, *History* i. 156, 159–67; R. I. Burns, in *American Historical Review*, 66 (1961).

decreed that Jews should not hold public office and limited the interest they could collect on loans to 20 per cent. The first law was never applied by Jaume. Jaume varied his policy as to usury, sometimes assisting Jews to collect their debts and sometimes enforcing laws restricting interest.[1]

All Christian rulers were decided on two points. Any Jew or Muslim who converted a Christian to his religion and any Jew or Muslim who seduced a Christian woman (intermarriage was prohibited) should receive the death penalty, normally by being burnt alive. Alfonso explains the reason for this. Christian women are 'spiritually spouses of Christ'. The death penalty extended to all Christian women, even to a prostitute who twice had intercourse with a Muslim. These laws existed in Catalonia and Valencia as well as in Castile. In 1321 a Christian woman was accused in Valencia of having travelled through North Africa 'and not denied your person to any Moor or Jew who wanted to have it'. These 'crimes' were often remitted with a fine. According to the *Furs* (the local law code) of Valencia, if a Christian man had sexual relations with a Jewess they were both to be burnt; a Christian seducing a Mudejar woman got off more lightly; they were both to be beaten naked through the city. The general Christian feeling on this point is unmistakable. In 1371 a Mudejar in Valencia was fined merely for saying he had slept with a Christian woman.[2]

Another indication of growing hostility towards non-Christians is in the legends that first appear in the Iberian peninsula in the thirteenth century. An early thirteenth-century *Disputa* in Castilian between a Christian and a Jew, packs an alarming quantity of hatred and ignorance into a few lines. The author believes for instance, that the Rabbi who performed the rite of circumcision drank the blood of the child. He also misinterprets, probably wilfully, the Jews' invocation of God to try to make them into polytheists.

In 1250 the story of a Christian boy ritually murdered by Jews in an imitation of the Crucifixion appears at Saragossa. The legend that such murders took place on Good Friday

[1] *Partidas* VII. xxiv. 8; Huici, *Colección*, i. 126 f.; Baer, *History* i. 147 ff.

[2] *Partidas*, VII. xxiv. 2 and 9; xxv. 4 and 10; *Libre de . . . Tortosa*, IX. ii. vii (p. 368); *Furs de Valencia*, IX. 2, cited by M. Gual, *Saitabi*, 7 (1949), 193, n. 100; L. Piles, in *Estudios de historia social de España*, 1 (1949), 270. F. A. Roca Traver, *El Justicia de Valencia, 1238–1321* (Valencia, 1970), pp. 377 f.

originated in northern Europe and only spread slowly southward. It is referred to, but only as a possibly true story, in the *Partidas*. A contemporary Castilian author, Berceo, in his *Milagros de Nuestra Señora*, tells a story of some Jews at Toledo who re-enacted the Crucifixion on a wax figure. Discovered by the intervention of the Virgin Mary they were put to death.[1]

The *Cántigas* of Alfonso X, which, like Berceo's poem, celebrate the miracles wrought by the Virgin, repeat Berceo's story. They contain other examples of anti-Judaism. A Jew who insults the Virgin's image is struck dead. Christians take a synagogue from the local Jews. When the law should make them give it back a miracle enables them to keep it. On two occasions the discovery of Jewish wickedness ends satisfactorily in a pogrom. Jews naturally try to cheat Christians whenever they can. They, can, however, be converted by a miracle. A Jew is converted by a vision of the Virgin and by being shown all Jews burning in Hell.

The picture of Muslims in the *Cántigas* is less insistently hostile than that of the Jews. Alfonso includes a story of a Christian commander of a castle on the frontier with Granada who is betrayed by the Muslim commander of a neighbouring fortress who had long pretended to be his close friend. This story probably represents accurately the friendly relations that often existed on the frontier and may simply be meant as a warning to Christians placed in such a position to be cautious. Muslims can certainly be converted to Christianity. In one of the *Cántigas* 'a good man' reasons with his Moorish slave to try to convert him. By the help of the Virgin he is successful. The Muslim defeats the demon who has entered him and becomes a Christian. The *Cántigas* remain above the level of the slightly later *Castigos e documentos* attributed to Sancho IV, where we read 'the Moor is simply a dog and the Mooress a bitch'. This passage also contains the legend that because he lived for seven years with a Jewess in Toledo Alfonso VIII of Castile lost the battle of Alarcos and his sons died.[2]

[1] A. Castro, *RFE* i (1914), 173–80; Baer, *History* i. 149; *Partidas*, VII. xxiv. 2; Gonzalo de Berceo, in *BAE* lvii. 116.

[2] *Cántigas*, ed. W. Mettmann, i (Coimbra, 1959), nos. 34 (pp. 100 f.); 27 (pp. 80 ff.); 4 (p. 23); 12 (pp. 37 f.); 25 (pp. 70–5); 85 (pp. 246–8); 185 (ii. 1961, 211–14); 192 (pp. 229 ff.); see R. I. Burns, *American Historical Review*, 76 (1971), 1429–31. Sancho IV, *Castigos e documentos*, c. 21, ed. A. Rey (Bloomington, Indiana).

Both the tendency towards assimilation, found in the worldly Jewish courtier class, and Christian intolerance, expressed in literary works and popular riots, helped to provoke a mystic reaction in Spanish Judaism. This reaction is behind the Cabala, whose central canon, the *Zohar*, was produced in Castile during the reigns of Alfonso X and Sancho IV (1280–6). For the Cabalists, 'to compromise with the outlook of the non-Jewish world or with rational philosophy, even to accept service in the princely courts, and—worst of all—to enter into intimacy with Gentile women, is to surrender to Satan.'

The same apocalyptic tendencies one finds in the contemporary speculations of the Spiritual Franciscans appear in the Cabala. For both Jewish and Christian mystics the end of the world seemed imminent. In the light of this belief the *convivencia* of the peninsula, the attempt to profit from the thought and culture of another religious community, seemed blasphemous folly.[1]

[1] Baer, *History* i. 243–50, 269 f., 433 f.

VI

Some Figures of the Age: Ramon Lull, Alfonso X, Don Juan Manuel, the Archpriest of Hita

RAMON LULL AND ALFONSO X OF CASTILE

THE writings of Ramon Lull, King Alfonso X of Castile, Don Juan Manuel, and the Archpriest of Hita are among the most precious sources we possess for the century from 1250 to 1350. They have been put to constant use in the previous chapters. Here I shall attempt to capture some essential features of these four writers in the hope that thereby the main lines of their age may become clearer.

A comparison between Ramon Lull and King Alfonso X of Castile serves to bring out some characteristics of these two personalities and, through them, of their age. The contrasts between their different positions in society were vast. Alfonso X (1221–84) was one of the most powerful kings of the thirteenth century. He aspired to the Holy Roman Empire and attempted to revive Castilian imperial claims over the peninsula. His policies ended in disaster but his great wealth financed the encyclopedic labours of his school of translators. Lull (1232–1316), on the other hand, was born in Majorca, the son of a knight of moderate means. As a young man he had a successful career at the court of Alfonso's father-in-law and rival, Jaume I of Aragon, but all his real achievements came after his conversion to a religious life and renunciation of his possessions.

The lives of Lull and Alfonso were lived against very different backgrounds. Alfonso X's life, apart from one journey in 1275 to meet Pope Gregory X at Beaucaire, was spent in Castile or on its borders. His travels, though constant, were slight in comparison with those of Lull. Lull's journeying covered the whole of the Mediterranean. He followed the routes traced by the merchants of Barcelona and Majorca. He is found in the ports of the East where they obtained trading privileges,

Famagusta in Cyprus, Laiazzo in Lesser Armenia, Rhodes. He followed his compatriots to Tunis and Bougie where the kings of Aragon and Majorca were represented by consuls and Catalan militias. Lull appears in the Italian and southern-French maritime cities which were rivals of the Catalans, Genoa, Pisa, Venice, Marseille. At the end of his life Lull spent two years in Sicily, the island whose sensational conquest by Pere II of Aragon in 1282 had changed the bases of power in the Mediterranean. Lull also knew Naples, ruled by the Angevin rivals of the Catalans of Sicily. He was familiar with the papal court, whether it dwelt at Rome or Anagni under Boniface VIII or at Avignon under Clement V. He knew the universities of Montpellier and Paris and he spent years soliciting aid not only from the court of Aragon but from Philippe IV of France.[1]

The contrasts between the lives of Lull and Alfonso make the similarity between their achievements and aims all the more striking.

With Alfonso X's compilations Castilian prose came of age. For the first time it now expressed historical, legal, scientific concepts. Lull, similarly, was the first to make Catalan express theological, philosophical, and scientific ideas. 'By a completely personal effort Lull changed Catalan prose, as it were overnight, into an instrument which could express perfectly any kind of feeling or argument.' He did this by fusing popular and learned language in one. It has been shown that 72 per cent of the words he used were employed by earlier Catalan writers, 18 per cent are Latinisms and only 7 per cent were words coined by Lull. But no one before Lull had used Catalan as he did, to discuss theology, science, and philosophy, both in the form of technical treatises and in the first philosophical novels of western Europe. *Blanquerna* and the *Book of Wonders* (*Felix*). Some of Arnau de Vilanova's medical works and polemical tracts were also written in Catalan, but Latin was the language he principally employed. Arnau began to write later than Lull and his Catalan works are slight in comparison with Ramon's.

Alfonso X's contribution to the development of Castilian was less personal than Lull's contribution to that of Catalan, but it

[1] A. Ballesteros-Beretta, *Alfonso X el Sabio* (Barcelona, 1963); my *Ramon Lull and Lullism*, Chs. 1 and 2, or the classic works of S. Galmés, *El dinamisme de Ramon Lull* (Palma, 1935), and M. Batllori, *Introducción a Ramón Lull* (Madrid, 1960).

should not be underestimated. Not only epic and narrative poems but also a number of prose works already existed in Castilian but Alfonso 'had to mould a new language' in order to incorporate Arabic literature and classical and patristic Latin into Castilian. Alfonso himself revised an earlier translation of the *Libro de la ochava esfera* in 1276. The translations produced by the scholars working for Alfonso are not absolutely uniform in their language but the speech of Toledo seems to have been used as a general model. Works like the *Partidas* employed a fuller and more varied phraseology than had existed before in Castilian. The *Partidas* are an extraordinary achievement in systematic exposition. The only works produced in romance by any author of the peninsula in this century which can be compared to them are Lull's *Art*, in its various versions, and his *Tree of Science*.

Ramon Lull created Catalan as a language of high culture, which could handle concepts previously only discussed in the peninsula in Latin, Arabic, or Hebrew. Alfonso X, through the *Partidas* and the historical works he patronized, did the same for Castilian. He 'definitely created Castilian prose'.[1]

What impelled Lull and Alfonso to act as they did?

The apologetic aim behind Lull's works is indisputable. He was born and brought up in Majorca. When he was converted from a worldly to a religious life in about 1263 Majorca was still a largely Islamic country. The Dominicans and Franciscans whom Lull knew were already preoccupied with the conversion of the Muslim and Jewish communities which played so large a role in the Crown of Aragon. It was almost inevitable that Lull should be caught up in the same apostolate. In action and in writing it was to consume his life. But, in order that Christians should convert the world, they must live Christian lives. Hence Lull's constant advocacy of reform within the Christian world. Menéndez Pelayo remarked that Lull was the most practical of reformers. 'Not one of the social, educational or ecclesiastical reforms proposed [in *Blanquerna*] was not based on some Catalan institution, none of which he sought to destroy but rather to revive by the infusion of a Christian, active and civilizing spirit.'

[1] Riquer, i. 14, 342–4; J. Rubió, in *HGLH* i. 690; A. G. Solalinde (ed.) Alfonso X, *General estoria*, i (Madrid, 1930), p. xix; R. Lapesa, *Historia de la lengua española*, 7th edn. (Madrid, 1968), pp. 165–78.

Alfonso X's aims are less clear than those of Lull. There is no doubt that the wish that knowledge should be more widely diffused lay behind his translations. In the prologue to the *Lapidario* he remarks that 'he ordered it to be translated from Arabic into Castilian so that men might understand it better and make greater use of it.' Alfonso X's nephew, Don Juan Manuel, saw more than this in the translations produced under Alfonso's patronage.

He desired so greatly that those of his kingdoms should be learned that he had all the sciences translated into this language of Castile, as much theology as logic, and all the seven liberal with all the mechanical arts. He also had translated the whole sect of the Moors, so that there might appear in this way the errors Muḥammad their false prophet taught them, in which they are today. He also had translated the whole Jewish law and even their Talmud, and another very secret science the Jews have, which they call Cabala. And he did this so that there might clearly appear through [the Jewish] law that it was all a figure of the law we Christians have. And that as much they as the Moors are in great error and in a state to lose their souls. He also translated all the ecclesiastical and secular laws, so that no man could say how much good this noble king did, especially in increasing and stimulating learning.

Juan Manuel may have emphasized the apologetic element behind Alfonso's translations because of his own interest in converting Muslims and Jews, but Alfonso did include most of the Old Testament in his *General estoria* and he also sponsored a translation of the account of Muḥammad's ascent into heaven. He sought—though less energetically than contemporary kings of Aragon—to further the conversion of Muslims and Jews by rational discussion. A clear 'moralist intention' lies behind Alfonso's works. He sought, Solalinde observes, 'to determine the right conduct for human beings by discovering what man had achieved in the past, to discern the influence on him of divine powers and of the stars, and to state his duties as a citizen.' This is the main reason for his historical, astronomical, astrological, and legislative works.[1]

[1] Menéndez Pelayo, *Orígenes* i. 130; Alfonso X, *Lapidario*, facs. reproduction (Madrid, 1879), fol. 1^{v}; Juan Manuel, *Libro de la caza*, ed. J. M^{a}. Castro y Calvó (Barcelona, 1947), pp. 11 f.; see E. S. Procter, *Alfonso X of Castile* (Oxford, 1951), pp. 4–6; Solalinde, p. ix; Ch. V, above, p. 167.

What made possible Alfonso's and Lull's achievements?

In the case of Lull the answer, again, is clearer than in that of Alfonso. When Lull turned to a religious life he was over thirty years old. His only accomplishments were those of a courtier who could write love poems in Provençal. The contemporary *Life*—inspired by Lull's memories as an old man—tells us that, after his decision to devote himself to Christ's service, he spent nine years studying Arabic while 'he learnt a little Latin grammar'. The *Life* is confirmed by other sources. Lull's first works were written in Arabic before he translated them into Catalan. There is no evidence that he ever wrote a book in Latin, though most of his works (over two hundred) were soon translated by others into that language. Lull's knowledge of contemporary scholastic thought was rudimentary compared to the thorough grounding he possessed in Islamic logic, philosophy, and religion. Lull's emphasis on the role of reason in proving the truths of the Christian faith, so great that it led him to be accused of rationalism and heresy, is clearly influenced by the Islamic theologians' emphasis on proof and demonstration in the sphere of theology.

Alfonso X's *Partidas* incorporated, as Juan Manuel saw, much Roman and canon law. His other compilations, however, were more deeply influenced by Islamic science and by didactic moral works than by Latin writings. Even the *Partidas* use literal translations from Arabic moralists while the *Primera Crónica General*, under the influence of its Arabic sources, takes on the use of anecdote, the detail and intimacy of Arabic historians, in contrast to the dry brevity of earlier Hispano-Latin texts. Even when recounting Biblical history Alfonso uses Arabic sources to flesh out Exodus. His criterion is stated in the *General estoria:*

> The Arabs have their Bible translated from the Hebrew, as have we . . . and although they err in their faith . . . they said many good and true things on the Bible . . . and were very wise men *and still are today*: and in what they said well we believe that it is not unreasonable to compare, where need be, our sayings with theirs.

Alfonso's aims differed from Lull's in that Alfonso was not primarily interested in converting Muslims, but both Alfonso and Lull created schools for Arabic, Alfonso in Murcia and possibly in Seville, Lull in Majorca.

Alfonso and Lull were bound to the Latin West not only by their religion but by many other links. They shared the same poetic tradition. They both considered themselves troubadours. Lull began by writing love poems and ended by becoming the troubadour of the Virgin Mary, 'Lady of Love', for whom he wrote poems to be sung by all men. Alfonso appears to have alternated secular and Marian poems throughout his life. He intended his *Cántigas* to be sung on the feasts of the Virgin in the church where he was buried. The music of the *Cántigas* includes many popular melodies, rondels, and *virolais* from Provence. But these links with the West are less striking than the influence of the Islamic world. Both Lull and Alfonso are essentially focused towards Islamic thought—Lull towards its mysticism and philosophical theology, Alfonso towards its science, history, and didactic morality. Even Alfonso's *Book of Chess* 'begins with an Oriental fable'. The players appear in Oriental dress and are entertained by Mudejar musicians. Both Lull, in Majorca, and Alfonso, in Toledo or Seville, were living on the geographical and spiritual frontier between Christianity and Islam, where both religions met in what was still relative tolerance. Lull's thought has rightly been described as a 'frontier philosophy'. Some of the central doctrines of his Art and their development within his system were due to his living contact with Jewish Rabbis and Muslim Doctors of the Law. In a less dramatic way the same is true of Alfonso's efforts to civilize and educate his people. They are inconceivable without the Islamic example and the help of Muslim, and, especially, of Jewish scholars. If Lull is in many ways closer to a wandering mystical preacher of Islam than he is to a scholastic thinker at Paris or Oxford, Alfonso is closer to a caliph such as al-Hakam II in tenth-century Córdoba or to his own contemporary the great al-Mustancir of Tunis, with his literary and philosophical salon, than he is to a crusader such as St. Louis or Edward I of England.

The most important of Alfonso's translators or editors were Italians or Jews—out of some twelve names only three were certainly Castilian—and it seems probable that the Jews and Italians may not only have been behind Alfonso's compilations but also have inspired the imperial dreams in which his reign foundered. It was two Jewish astronomers who proposed to date a new era from Alfonso's reign, a chronology which would have cast that of the Incarnation into oblivion. The five Jews whose names are known translated twenty-three works, as against eight produced by non-Jews.

The fact that the works of Alfonso and of Lull grew out of a situation only fully intelligible within the Iberian peninsula explains the limited success of their writings in western Christendom. Alfonso's Castilian compilations did not travel beyond the Pyrenees. Some Latin translations made from Castilian were more widely known. The most curious case is that of *The Ladder of Muḥammad* (*al-Miʿrāŷ*), translated from Castilian into French and Latin by an Italian notary at Alfonso's court. This translation of an account of Muḥammad's journey to the other world was perhaps due to Alfonso's desire to demonstrate the falsity of Islam. It is entirely possible that Dante knew the story and drew from it some of the ideas of the *Divine Comedy*. Many of Lull's works were widely diffused. Unlike most of Alfonso's they were translated into Latin and, in a few cases, into French or Italian. Even so, Lull's *Art* met with suspicion and incomprehension from the ordinary scholastic thinker. Lullists have almost always been men somewhat apart from the main currents of European thought.[1]

DON JUAN MANUEL: HIS CHARACTER

Menéndez Pelayo called Don Juan Manuel (1282–1348) 'perhaps the most *human* man of his time'. It is truer of him even than of Ramon Lull that all his works were autobiographical. In the *Libro de Patronio* he is at once the wise steward Patronio and the great noble Patronio serves. He is present in Prince Joás in the *Libro de los estados*. Like Lull, he continually refers to himself and to his writings. The *Libro de las armas* conveys his idea of the greatness of his family. His works on chivalry and

[1] See my *Ramon Lull*, Chs. 1 and 7; A. Castro, *La realidad histórica de España* (Mexico, 1954), pp. 323 n. 43, 358, 456, 463; J. B. Trend, 'Alfonso el Sabio and the Game of Chess', *Revue hispanique*, 81. 1 (1933), 393–403; R. Menéndez Pidal, *Estudios literarios* (Madrid, 1920), p. 242; Procter, op. cit., pp. 113–39; G. Menéndez Pidal, *NRFH* 5 (1951), 363–80; H. Anglés, *La música de las Cántigas de Santa María del Rey Alfonso el Sabio*, 3 vols. (Barcelona, 1943–64); G. Levi della Vida, *Al-Andalus*, 14 (1949), 377–407; E. Cerulli, ibid. 21 (1956), 229–53; idem, *Il Libro della Scala e la questione delle fonti arabo-spagnole della Divina Commedia* (Vatican City, 1949); Alfonso X, *General estoria*, i., ed. Solalinde, 85 f.

hunting describe his social life. His theological and didactic works give his personal vision of society and his beliefs.

In the *Libro de las armas* Don Juan recounts how his father, the Infante Manuel, had been defrauded by his brother, Alfonso X, of the kingdom of Murcia. But Manuel had inherited the great sword (the *espada lobera*) of the conqueror, his father Fernando III. Don Juan describes the conversation he had as a boy of twelve with the dying Sancho IV. This conversation made an extraordinary impression on him. From then on he believed that the line of Fernando III's descendants to which he himself belonged was blessed, the line of Alfonso X and Sancho accursed. All this goes far to explain Don Juan's actions during the minority of Alfonso XI (1312–25). Alfonso XI's later behaviour towards him, promising to marry his daughter, then imprisoning her and preventing her for years from marrying the king of Portugal, provided further justification for Don Juan's allying with Granada against his king. In the *Libro de los estados* Don Juan remarks that he embarked on war with the king of Castile, who was aided by Aragon and Portugal. He refused to make peace, in this struggle against great odds because he had suffered wrong and dishonour, until he received 'the most honourable peace with the king that ever man got in Spain'.

In the *Libro de los castigos* (*Libro infinido*), written after Don Juan's peace with Alfonso XI, he told his son and heir the position he had won for him.

> Now, praised be God, there is no one in Spain of higher rank than you except the king. And since kings are more honoured than other men for the estate God gave them, you should always do them honour in your speech . . . But as for *works* you should treat with them as with your neighbours . . . You can maintain some 1,000 horse without the king's help and go from Navarre to Granada, sleeping each night in a walled town or in castles I command . . . Your estate . . . is nearer to that of kings than to that of *ricos hombres*.

Don Juan was not the Machiavellian schemer he has sometimes been portrayed. If he was 'obsessed with the question of honour' he was typical in this of the Castilian nobility as a whole. The continual attacks on him in the *Crónica de Fernando IV* and the *Crónica de Alfonso XI* can largely be discounted as royal propaganda. In Portuguese sources he appears as a generally honourable man and as virtually an equal of the kings of Castile and Portugal. The fact that the people of Murcia continually strove to be free of his authority shows, however, that in real life he did not entirely correspond to the ideal noble of his writings. His exaltation of war against the Muslims of Spain did not prevent him spending more time fighting the king of Castile than the emir of Granada. From the point of view of the monarchy and of the *concejos*, whose representatives spoke through the Castilian Cortes, Don Juan was an overproud vassal who had virtually achieved independence. The existence of such men was a major obstacle to royal power and to the unity of Castile, but if they were responsible for much of the confusion of the age they also gave it much of its colour and movement.[1]

Juan Manuel, in a younger generation, continued the work both of Alfonso X and of Ramon Lull. As Menéndez Pelayo remarked, 'his teaching is addressed to all states and situations of life. . . In this sense he is a popular educator'.

INFLUENCES

In this desire to teach Juan Manuel was largely inspired by the example of his uncle, Alfonso X. I have cited Don Juan's summary of Alfonso's works, where the stress is laid on the king's wish to instruct his people and to convert Muslims and Jews. María Rosa Lida has pointed to the influence on Don Juan of the Dominican Order. Don Juan founded a Dominican convent at Peñafiel where he intended to be buried and where the final copy of his works was to be preserved. One of his close friends was the Dominican Ramon Masquefa. It is very possible that Juan Manuel's writings were influenced by the Dominican attempt to reach the people.

Two other main influences behind the educational slant in Don Juan's writings are equally clear, that of Ramon Lull and that of Islamic literature.

Juan Manuel had read Lull's *Book of the Order of Chivalry* as well as his philosophical novels, *Blanquerna* and *The Book of Wonders*. Don Juan's *Libro del caballero y del escudero* is clearly

[1] Carreras Artau, ii. 499–522, esp. 506–8; Juan Manuel, *Libro de las armas*; *Libro de los estados*, i. 70; *Libro de los castigos*, 5–6 (*BAE* li. 260–4, 319, 269, or ed. Castro y Calvó and Riquer, pp. 108 f.); C. da Silva Tarouca, *Crónicas dos sete primeiros reis de Portugal*, ii (Lisbon, 1952), e.g. p. 172. See also, below, Part II, Ch. II. Castro, *La realidad*, pp. 369–72 (on Sancho IV and Don Juan).

inspired by Lull's treatise on chivalry. In both works what is stressed is the religious end to which chivalry should be directed. Don Juan's *Libro de los estados* follows *Blanquerna* in presenting a vision of the society of the time. This vision is presented within an apologetic for Christianity against Islam and Judaism which draws on Lull, perhaps especially on the *Book of the Gentile*. Given his indebtedness to Lull, it is just as possible that Don Juan took from Lull his use of 'examples' to reinforce his arguments (these 'examples' constitute his *Libro de Patronio* or *Conde Lucanor*) as that he drew here on the practice of Dominican preachers. Don Juan's use of Castilian rather than Latin was probably mainly due to the example of Alfonso X, though Lull may also have influenced him here. Don Juan probably read Lull in Catalan. That he knew Catalan is shown by his correspondence with his father-in-law, Jaume II of Aragon. He borrowed books from Jaume. These may have included works of Lull who had worked for Jaume and dedicated books to him.

Menéndez Pelayo pointed out that Don Juan was 'brought up in the Eastern wisdom, which indoctrinated the princes and magnates of Castile', and that, for this reason, his moral teaching was philosophical in inspiration rather than chivalric. The *Libro de los estados* draws on the legend of Buddha; the precise way this legend reached Don Juan is not clear. The argument of the book coincides with that of the *Kitāb al-Khazar* of the Spanish Jew Judah Halevi. It has been shown that Don Juan's teaching is close to *The Lamp of Princes* of al-Tartushi. There is no doubt that, like Lull, Don Juan knew not only popular Arabic (spoken on his estates in Murcia) but literary Arabic. Although he knew Latin well he conceals his knowledge, probably because he did not wish to write as a cleric. It was perfectly acceptable for a noble to cite Arabic phrases, to describe Arabic musical instruments, or recount stories of Islamic courts. Don Juan treats Muslim princes, whether in Spain or the East, as knights who are on the same level as Christian knights. Their discipline and military talents are admired. Even when Don Juan is defending the doctrine of the bodily Assumption of the Virgin into heaven he brings in an Arabic refrain. Like Lull, again, Don Juan could converse with Muslim Doctors of the Law on difficult points of theology as well as with the Jewish physicians he so greatly esteemed, one of whom may have provided the model for the wise steward Patronio of his masterpiece. I have already shown that Dom Juan fully shared or even surpassed Lull's spirit of tolerance for Islam and his confidence in the use of reason in theological argument.[1]

THE ARCHPRIEST OF HITA

Very little was known until recently as to the external life of the Archpriest of Hita. The discovery of new documents has shown than Juan Ruiz (or Rodríguez) de Cisneros was the illegitimate son of a noble, that he was born in Muslim Spain in 1295–6 and died in 1353, having held a series of high church benefices in Toledo, Burgos, etc. The first edition of his *Libro de Buen Amor* or *Libro de cantares* was finished in 1330 and revised in 1343 when the Archpriest speaks of himself as an old man and in prison. (There is a gap of ten years, 1343 to 1353, in the documents so far discovered.)

Ramón Menéndez Pidal remarked that the Archpriest is extraordinary in that he is a very personal and at the same time a completely popular author. Don Ramón pointed out that the Archpriest was a minstrel, who left his book to minstrels (*juglares*) of all kinds, from serenading students to blind beggars, Christians, Jews, and Muslims, and urged them to add to it. The 'revised edition' of 1343 differs from the first form of the book by adding to the poems which could be sung, to the repertoire immediately available to the minstrel. There is evidence that the *Cantares* in the *Libro* were sung and that they were popular. This is hardly surprising if one considers not only the very personal style of the Archpriest but his extraordinary range.

The *Libro* has rightly been called the 'human comedy' of the fourteenth century. It contains unscrupulous judges, intriguing

[1] Menéndez Pelayo, op. cit., pp. 138–52; M. R. Lida de Malkiel, *La idea de la fama en la edad media castellana* (Mexico, 1952), pp. 207–20; eadem, *Romance Philology*, 4 (1950–1), 155–94; J. Mª. Castro y Calvó, *El arte de gobernar en las obras de Don Juan Manuel* (Barcelona, 1945), pp. 99–107. The more important passages cited in the text are *Libro de Patronio*, cc. 28, 50; *Libro de los estados*, i. 76; ii. 3; *Tractado en que se prueba por razón que Sancta María esta en el cuerpo e alma en paraíso* (*BAE* li. 400, 420 ff., 323 f., 345, 440). For Don Juan's views on the war with Granada see Ch. II above, p. 58; for his Jewish doctors and his 'rationalism' see Ch. V above, pp. 165, 176. See now *Libro de los estados*, ed. R. B. Tate and I. Macpherson (Oxford, 1974).

lawyers, nuns, ladies, Muslims and Jews, wild countrywomen, knights who rush to be paid but tarry on the way to the frontier. Menéndez y Pelayo's general view of the book is excellent:

> [The Archpriest] put the whole of himself into his book and all he knew of the world and life . . . As a historical source it is worth so much that, if it was lacking, we should not know a whole side of our Middle Ages, as it would be impossible to understand Imperial Rome without the novel of Petronius . . . The chronicles tell us how our fathers fought; *Fueros* and the records of the Cortes how they legislated; only the Archpriest tells us how they lived in their house and at the market, what were the dishes served at their tables, what instruments they played, how they dressed and adorned themselves, how they made love in the city and in the mountains.

The *Libro de Buen Amor* is a series of episodes. The two main characters are the Archpriest himself and Trotaconventos, a skilful old bawd whom the author employs as an intermediary in his attacks on the virtue of widows, singing girls, and nuns. When Trotaconventos dies the Archpriest laments her death in a long poem. As Américo Castro remarks, 'her death and the pain with which he laments it made Trotacontentos a living person'. The Archpriest himself is also a very real person. He has caught his own appearance in a speech he makes Trotaconventos address to Doña Garoza. This description, as Rafael Lapesa observes, 'corresponds perfectly to the vigorous, sensual person' who appears in the whole *Libro*.

> He has a strong, hairy body, large limbs and head, broad shoulders, and a thick neck. His hair is dark and his ears large. His eyebrows are apart and black as coal. He walks erect as a peacock; his gait is composed. His nose is long. This detracts from him. His voice is ponderous, his mouth regular, with thick, sensuous lips, red as coral. His eyes are small. His complexion is rather dark, his chest juts out, his arms and wrists are strong, his legs shapely, his feet small. He is gay, brave, and young. He can play musical instruments and knows the whole minstrel's art. He is a gay lady's man. By my slippers, you won't find such a man in every country fair!

Critics disagree—perhaps they will always do so—as to the Archpriest's intentions in writing his book. This disagreement is partly due to the skill with which he alternates moralizing with amorality. No one today sees him simply as the 'severe moralist and exemplary cleric' of Amador de los Ríos, but it is virtually impossible to separate autobiography and fantasy in the Archpriest's adventures. He is a brilliant satirist. One may agree with Menéndez Pelayo that he had no conscious intention of undermining the Church he served but, unconsciously, he represents the crisis of faith of fourteenth-century Castile as Don Juan Manuel symbolizes the crisis of political authority when great nobles became rivals of their king. Much evidence exists to corroborate the Archpriest's picture of the decadent and worldly clergy and Religious Orders of Castile.[1]

Leo Spitzer and, following him, María Rosa Lida de Malkiel, have argued that the *Libro de Buen Amor* had an essentially didactic purpose. María Rosa Lida held that the Archpriest imitated the *maqāmāt*, an Arabic form of literature cultivated in Hebrew by the Jews of Catalonia and southern France. The *maqāmāt* is a flexible type of fictional autobiography, with many insertions in verse and prose.

The real contrasts in the *Libro de buen amor* are not between soul and body. As Américo Castro remarks: 'For the author life is a *whole*, composed of bodily, sensible, subjective joy *and* of transcendent morality.' (I italicize.)

Professor Lapesa has observed that the treatment of death in *Libro* reveals that, for the Archpriest, the usual medieval Christian equivalence of spirit (= good) and flesh (= evil) does not obtain. The system of values is not based on an opposition between 'flesh' and 'spirit' but between 'death' and 'life'. There is no pagan goliardic rebellion against asceticism but an almost indissoluble mixture of religion and sensuality. So, for instance, immediately after recounting some unedifying adventures with mountain shepherdesses the Archpriest enters the hermitage of Santa María del Vado and prostrates himself before 'the light shining in the world, the brilliance of heaven', and addresses the Virgin: 'I offer my soul and body before Your Majesty with songs and great humility'. Even clearer instances of the Archpriest's view of life are his descriptions of the day of the clerical

[1] E. Sáez and J. Trenchs, in *Actas del I Congreso internacional sobre el Arcipreste de Hita* (Barcelona, 1973), pp. 365–68. R. Menéndez Pidal, *Poesía juglaresca y juglares* (Madrid, 1924), pp. 266, 271; Menéndez Pelayo, *Antología* i. 258–314; Castro, *La realidad*, pp. 378–442, esp. p. 441; R. Lapesa, in *Diccionario de literatura española* (Madrid, 1949), p. 37; *Libro de Buen Amor*, vv. 1513 f., 1520–75, 1485–9, ed. Criado de Val and Naylor, pp. 508 f., 512–34, 494–6. For religion in Castile see Ch. IV above.

lover, singing psalms and making love alternately, the confessions of Don Carnal, the account of the reception of Don Amor at the end of Lent by the Religious Orders and clergy, or the verses in which the death of Trotaconventos is celebrated as a 'martyrdom' for love which will deserve God's grace.

Professor Castro has shown that the way the Archpriest enjoys the whole of life, without drawing sharp lines between worldly and other worldly, flesh and spirit, is typically Muslim while it is extraordinary for a Christian. The Archpriest's knowledge of popular Arabic speech and customs are abundantly clear; he could quote Arabic phrases knowing his audience would understand them. The question goes deeper than a specific literary source. The fact that the Archpriest spent the first ten years of his life in the emirate of Granada no doubt influenced his whole life. The recent discovery of a cache of Arabic manuscripts at Ocaña reveals the strong Arabic tradition of the region where he lived.

Menéndez Pelayo remarked that the *Libro* is 'a *composite* monument in which capricious details, belonging to different architectures, surprise and delight the eyes by the very variety and violence of their contrasts.'

This description applies very well to many Mudejar churches being built in the Archpriest's archdiocese of Toledo during his lifetime, churches in which Romanesque or Gothic architectural forms are combined with Mudejar plasterwork and carpentry. Castro brilliantly defines the Archpriest's art as

> consisting in giving a Christian meaning to the literary forms of some Islamic ascetics. It parallels the Mudejar buildings so frequent in his time. Love can benefit both the senses *and* the spirit, and so his book diverts *and* indoctrinates, interweaving Islam and Christianity ... Not only did Juan Ruiz take fables and stories from Arabic, or moral anecdotes such as the censure of drunkeness, but the *central motif* of the book is Islamic, that is, erotic experience directed *both* into sensual impulse and ascetic control. Narration followed by moral gloss, the tireless repetitions of analogous themes, the double and reversible meaning of everything said, all this is found in *The Ring of the Dove* and in other Arabic ascetic and mystical treatises. (I italicize.)

The Archpriest had probably studied at Toledo, where, as nowhere else in Spain, Islamic traditions met Christian sources.

He drew on all the sources he could find, French 'fabliaux'; the Latin satirical verses of Walter Map; the twelfth-century comedy, *Pamphilus*; perhaps the *De Amore* of Andrew the Chaplain (*c.* 1180); he used tags from the Bible, the church liturgy, canon and civil law, Ovid's *Art of Love*, Aristotle, but the ties which united him to his contemporaries in France or Italy are less significant than his links to the Islamic world. As María Rosa Lida remarked, it is very misleading to call the Arch priest 'a man of the age of Boccaccio'. He was alive at the same time as Boccaccio but his poetry does not spring out of the humanism of Boccaccio's Florence but out of the Arabic–Jewish–Christian tradition of his country. This tradition saw no inconsistency in teaching men while amusing them, in 'rejoicing bodies while assisting souls', the Archpriest's aim according to his opening prayer to the Trinity. This tradition lies behind the novels of Ramon Lull, the *Cántigas* of Alfonso X, the writings of Juan Manuel—especially the stories of the *Libro de Patronio*—and the Archpriest's celebration of life as a whole. For the Archpriest life is not divided, in the usual Christian fashion, into antagonistic realms of impure flesh and pure spirit. He accepts, unembarrassed, the richness of life and the *Libro de Buen Amor* conveys it to us as he knew it.

Lull, Alfonso X, Juan Manuel, and the Archpriest, all, in different ways, paid tribute to the Islamic world on which they drew. The episode of the Mudejar girl who rejects the Archpriest's advances with four brief Arabic phrases contrasts with the loquacity of the nun, Doña Garoza, who engages in an elaborate flirtation. The story of the girl has rightly been characterized, by María Rosa Lida, as

> a voluntary embellishment of the Muslim world, with the same meaning—although expressed on a humble social plane and accentuating only moral superiority—with which Don Juan Manuel dazzles his readers [in the *Libro de Patronio*] with visions of the elaborate courtesy of Hispano-Arabic kings. Both [tributes] are, in fact, the most perfect literary expression of the Arabic impact on Castilian life in the middle of the fourteenth century and the first step in the long process of its nostalgic idealization.

In the thirteenth century Ramon Lull had already recognized his debt to Islamic thought and mysticism. The form of his most famous mystical work, *The Book of the Lover and the Beloved*, was taken from an Islamic model.

> Blanquerna remembered how once, when he was pope, a Sarracen had told him that the Sarracens had religious men and among the most esteemed there are *sufis*, and they have words of love and short examples [on which they meditate] which arouse great devotion; and they are words which need exposition and by this the understanding is aroused and the will . . . When Blanquerna had considered thus, he set out to write the book in the manner set out above.[1]

The work of Lull in the Crown of Aragon, of Alfonso X, Juan Manuel, and the Archpriest of Hita in Castile, grew out of the Islamic background and would be unintelligible without it, though these writers produced works very different from those achieved by Muslims. In view of the recognition of this fact by the authors concerned, it is surprising that it should still be necessary to argue the case, that there should be Spanish scholars so anxious to appear fully 'European' that they deny the unique richness of their own spiritual ancestry, in which alone in Europe—apart from the brief experience of Sicily in the twelfth and thirteenth centuries—the Islamic and Latin Christian perspectives meet and combine.

[1] M. R. Lida de Malkiel, *NRFH* 13 (1959), 17–82; A. N. Zahareas, *The Art of Juan Ruiz, Archpriest of Hita* (Madrid, 1965); see the review by S. Gilman, *Romanische Forschungen*, 78 (1966), 607–10; Castro, pp. 387, 388, 423; R. Lapesa, in *Estudios dedicados a J. H. Herriott* (University of Wisconsin, 1966), pp. 127–44; J. Oliver Asín, *BRAE* 30 (1950), 389–421; idem, *Al-Andalus*, 21 (1956), 212–14; F. Rico, *AEM*, 4 (1967), 301–25; F. Márquez Villanueva, *Revista de occidente*, ser. 2. ix. 27 (1965), 269–91; *Libro de Buen Amor*, vv. 1045, 375–86, 1128–30, 1225–58, 1569 f., 13, 1509–12 (pp. 304 f., 101–5, 332 f., 377–93, 532 f., 8, 506–8); Lull, *Blanquerna*, c. 99 (*Obres essencials*, i. 260); on Mudejar art see Ch. V, above; on Arabic influence see now J. Martínez Ruiz, in *Actas del I Congreso*, pp. 187–201, and J. Albarracín Navarro, ibid., pp. 488–94.

PART II

CASTILE and CATALONIA–ARAGON
1225–1330

MAP II THE WESTERN MEDITERRANEAN
c. 1300
0 50 10 200 300 400 miles
0 50 100 200 300 400 500 600 km
Guienne
FRANCE
Rhône
Avignon
Provence
Marseilles
Montpellier
Narbonne
Milan
Venice
Genoa
Pisa
Papal States
Rome
Anagni
Naples
Naples
Corsica
Sassari
Alghero
Sardinia
Arborea
Cagliari
Minorca
Palma
Majorca
Burgos
NAVARRE
Cerdagne
Roussillon
Ebro
ARAGON
Barcelona
Valencia
Oporto
Duero
CASTILE
PORTUGAL
Tagus
Lisbon
Guadiana
Guadalquivir
Córdoba
Seville
Murcia
Granada
GRANADA
Almería
Málaga
Cádiz
Gibraltar
Ceuta
Arcila
Salé
Marruecos
Tlemcen
Bougie
Collo
Constantine
Tunis
Tunis
Djerba
Messina
Reggio
Palermo
Trapani
Sicily
Malta

I

The Crown of Aragon, 1229–1327: a Mediterranean Empire?

THE CATALAN CHRONICLES

THE three Catalan chronicles of King Jaume I, Desclot, and Muntaner are among the most impressive of the Middle Ages. Between them they span the period from the defeat and death of Jaume's father, Pere I, at Muret in 1213, and Jaume's accession to the throne of Aragon as a child of five, to the coronation of Alfons III in 1327. This is the age of the expansion of the federation of Catalonia–Aragon (principally of Catalonia) into the Mediterranean, of the conquest of the Balearic Isles and Valencia, Sicily, and Sardinia. Since so much of our picture of this decisive century is necessarily formed and coloured by the three chronicles—documentary sources can correct, often greatly expand but hardly change in essentials the picture they present—it seems worth while to begin by considering the nature of these three works.[1]

The *Libre dels feyts* or *Book of the Deeds* of Jaume I is now considered 'fundamentally the personal work' of the king and as the first in date of the chronicles. It is particularly detailed and valuable for the years 1228–40 and 1265–74. The last chapters and perhaps the prologue were added by a clerical author, probably not long after Jaume's death in 1276.[2]

Bernat Desclot, an official and perhaps an ecclesiastic in the royal court, may have originally intended his work to be a genealogy of the Counts of Barcelona but almost the whole of his chronicle is devoted to Jaume I's son and successor, Pere II the Great (Pedro III of Aragon). Desclot evidently wrote between

[1] Editions and translations of these chronicles are listed in the Bibliography to this chapter.

[2] Riquer, i. 398–408. F. Soldevila, *Els grans reis del segle XIII* (Barcelona, 1955), pp. 77 f.; idem, *Al marge de la Crònica de Jaume I* (Barcelona, 1967); L. Nicolau d'Olwer, *EUC*, 11 (1926), 79–88.

1283 and 1288, very soon after most of the events he describes. His work ends in 1285, with Pere's death.[1]

Ramon Muntaner was born in 1265 at Peralada in northern Catalonia and died in 1336 in Ibiza. His extremely eventful life took him from service in the royal court under Pere II to the Balearic Isles and Sicily, and, in 1302–9, to Constantinople, Asia Minor, and Greece, with the Catalan Company. From 1309 to 1315 he was governor of the Moorish island of Djerba off Tunisia for Frederic of Sicily. His last decades were spent in Valencia and the Balearics. His *Chronicle* covers the period from 1205 to 1327 and was written between 1325 and 1336.[2]

The three chronicles all see history as centred on the Royal House. They are either concerned with the person of a particular king, or, as in the case of Muntaner, with the dynasty, the House of Barcelona, as a whole. Jaume I's *Book* says—or leaves out—what Jaume wanted said—or left out. The tone is set almost from the beginning, when the king is taken, as a new-born child, to the churches of Montpellier and omens predict his future greatness. Desclot glorifies Pere II as 'the second Alexander in chivalry and conquest'. Desclot's aim is to write 'the great deeds and conquests of the kings of Aragon of the high lineage of the Count of Barcelona'. Muntaner, in his turn, celebrated Jaume I's birth, comparing it to that of Christ. Muntaner sought to hold up a 'mirror for princes' to future kings of Aragon, for whom he even foresaw universal dominion. He meant his book to be read aloud to future rulers. We know that all three chronicles were in fact possessed, and, in some cases, studied, by later members of the royal dynasty, as well as by many other Catalans. They influenced deeply the development of Catalan historiography and helped to inspire the greatest Catalan novels of the fourteenth and fifteenth centuries, *Curial e Güelfa* and *Tirant lo blanc*.[3]

These chronicles are successive chapters of royal history, of the history of the same dynasty. It is doubtful if one can describe

[1] M. Coll i Alentorn, in his edition of Desclot, i. 116–74; J. Rubió, *ER* 5 (1955–6), 211–25; Riquer, i. 429–34.

[2] M. de Barcelona, *Estudis franciscans*, 48 (1936), 218–33, and in *SFG* i, 6 (1937), 310–26; Riquer, i. 449–56.

[3] Jaume I, *Libre dels feyts*, 5; Desclot, *Pròleg*; Muntaner, 4, 72, 292; J. Massó Torrents, *Revue hispanique*, 15 (1906), 503–43; Coll, i. 174–88.

Jaume I, Desclot, or Muntaner as setting out to provide propaganda for the House of Barcelona. But it would be mistaken to see any of the chronicles as the spontaneous personal expression of the individual chronicler's feelings. The form the books took was largely inspired by the *chansons de geste* their authors used. These *chansons* were poems in Provençal by troubadours attached to the court, recited in public years before the chronicles were written. When it proved necessary to raise levies and taxes for a new enterprise or when the morale of a hard-pressed force had to be sustained through long months of siege warfare a troubadour might well be asked to describe the glories of recent Catalan achievements. It has been shown that the account in Jaume I's *Book* of the conquests of Majorca and Valencia is largely a prose version of a series of *chansons*. Throughout Desclot we can see traces of the poet speaking to his audience—'in this book you will find and *hear*'. In a non-noble, probably ecclesiastical official such as Desclot, with a bureaucrat's love for documents of every sort (juridical acts, royal accounts, correspondence, war communiqués), the presentation of history as a series of chivalric scenes is very striking. It must spring from the chivalric poems on which Desclot drew. Much of the 'fantasy' of Muntaner also comes from the books he had read, troubadours and novels of chivalry. He, also, speaks of the 'lords who will *hear* this book'.[1]

The poetic origin of the chronicles explains much of their popular style and the epic tone which gives the narrative unity and force. The closeness of the poems the chroniclers used to the events they described, their concern for telling and vivid detail, also gives us the feeling that we can see the men they portray. Of Jaume I and Pere II 'we not only know what they did and why but also how they felt, how they loved and hated'. The chronicles 'have left us the physiognomy which the [kings] wished men to remember them by in later centuries'. Often, it seems, there is an attempt to reproduce, as precisely as possible, the actual words used.[2]

The epic tone and extraordinary detail of the Catalan chronicles bring with them some disadvantages. Desclot's

[1] Coll, i. 50–4, 89 f., 99–103; Desclot, 47; Soldevila, *Els grans reis*, p. 93, n. 299; J. Rubió, loc. cit.; Riquer, i. 373–94, 457–66.

[2] Riquer, i. 394.

portrait of Jaume I is so closely modelled on a legendary account of Charlemagne as to lose its value as history.[1] At times, in the *Book of Deeds*, one wonders if one is reading an account of Jaume I of Aragon or the *Chanson de Roland.* It was not a question of direct literary imitation of the epics but of the assimilation of their spirit and style. For Jaume I his sword Tisó had become the sword of the—to him—entirely 'historical' hero, Roland. In the same way Pere II's very impolitic acceptance of a challenge to a duel shows that his mentality was that of the chivalric novels of the day.[2] Desclot and Muntaner, also, see their heroes as on the same level with Roland, Tristan, Lancelot, and the other knights of the Round Table. The tendency to embroider and 'improve' on history in Muntaner, and his frequent inaccuracies, are less important than his 'mentality and emotionalism which make us understand and feel the force which drove the Catalans of his age, the reason for their expansive drive and their victorious enthusiasm'.[3]

In the chronicle of Jaume I the scene is already large: the different territories of the Crown of Aragon, from Montpellier to Murcia, come into view. In Desclot Castile and France are included, and, with Pere II's expedition to North Africa and Sicily, Catalonia enters the central Mediterranean. In Muntaner the canvas becomes even broader. Among the western-European histories of his age his is the richest in its scope, in the knowledge it displays of the lands and islands of the Mediterranean, not only of Spain but of Italy, North Africa, and the Greek East. Muntaner takes us to the rising cities of the Catalan world, Valencia, Murcia, Majorca, to the battlefields, from the Pyrenees to Gallipoli, where Catalans defeated their enemies. He shows us the men who guided the Catalan victories, not only Pere II and his son Frederic of Sicily but the Italians Ruggiero di Loria and Ruggiero di Flor. Unlike Desclot, Muntaner, as he shows by his constant personal interventions in the narrative, wanted to be known for himself and he is known. In his book he gives us himself, and, with himself, much of the contemporary opinion of Catalonia, of the 'nobles and knights and

[1] Desclot, 8 (ed. Coll, ii. 64 f.; cf. i. 48).

[2] *Libre dels feyts*, 174; Riquer, i. 434–6; see p. 254, n. 1 below.

[3] Soldevila, *Vida de Pere el Gran i d'Alfons el Liberal* (Barcelona, 1963), p. 198.

citizens and merchants, captains of ships and sailors and almogàvers and soldiers' to whom Muntaner appeals to act as one in defence of the integrity of the territories of the Crown of Aragon, and who stood in fact behind its rise.[1] Desclot also, while vastly more discreet than Muntaner in presenting his own views, was writing under the stimulus of the conquest of Sicily by Pere II and of the heroic defence of Catalonia against the French invasion of 1285. He identifies intensely—as does the contemporary monastic author of the Latin *Acts of the Counts of Barcelona*—with Catalonia and its dynasty against its French and papal opponents. Desclot enables one to penetrate below the level of the leading classes of the day. He gives us the feelings of the ordinary Catalan during the crucial hours of the French invasion: the people of Perpignan, torn between allegiance to Pere II and to his brother, their immediate lord, Jaume II of Majorca; the rage of the people of Barcelona when a small Catalan squadron fails to destroy, at once, a French fleet ten times greater in numbers.[2]

These Catalan chronicles, then, are prime sources of enormous value and not only for political history. Their dynastic bias can usually be detected, their mistakes corrected, their deliberate silences explained with the help of foreign chronicles and contemporary documents. The chronicles do not provide us with economic explanations. They see the events they describe as the divinely ordained victorious progress of the Crown of Aragon. They give us, however, something perhaps more valuable than economic theories, the ideas and the mentality without which one could not begin to explain a century of astonishing achievements.

Modern historians naturally seek to supply the economic explanations lacking in the contemporary chronicles. The theories advanced in recent years to account for the rise of Catalonia–Aragon and for the Catalan expansion into the Mediterranean suffer from the imbalance between the relatively rich political evidence and far poorer economic sources. They

[1] Muntaner, 15; see A. Rubió y Lluch, *Paquimeres i Muntaner* (Barcelona, 1927), p. 9; Soldevila, *Pere el Gran*, i. 1 (Barcelona, 1950), pp. xi-xiii.

[2] Desclot, 134 f., 157; cf. Coll, i. 7 f.; *Gesta comitum Barcinonensium*, e.g. XXVIII. 47 f., ed. L. Barrau Dihigo and J. Massó Torrents (Barcelona, 1925), pp. 89 f.

also often attempt to make out Catalan policy as far more consistent than it was.[1]

The rulers of Catalonia–Aragon were subject to a number of severe internal limitations on their policy. They may be summed up as the nature of the Catalan-Aragonese federation, the relatively undeveloped nature of the economy, and the poverty of the Crown, with its, consequently, very limited military and naval resources. These internal restrictions were often combined with the pressure of external enemies, the most important of which were France—often allied with the papacy—Castile, and the Italian maritime republics.

Aragon and Catalonia attained union as late as 1137. The so-called confederation was only united in the person of its ruler, who was both king of Aragon and count of Barcelona, and who also became, in the thirteenth century, king of Majorca, of Valencia, for some years of Sicily, and, later, of Sardinia. The personal union of these countries could be dissolved by the ruler's will. It was nearly so dissolved by Jaume I.

AN UNDEVELOPED ECONOMY

During the thirteenth century the economies of the lands of the Crown of Aragon developed slowly. Aragonese economy was almost entirely agricultural and it was only in 1316 that Orihuela and Alicante, in the kingdom of Valencia, were authorized to export cereals, to buy wool in order to make cloth. Even in Catalonia the prices of manufactured goods were disproportionately higher than those of agricultural products.[2] The most important Catalan industry, the manufacture of cloth, only became of international importance from the 1280s onwards because of the political and economic conflict with France. In about 1306 the prohibition of the export of crude cloth from France could still cause a major crisis in Catalonia. Counter-measures proposed included a general prohibition of exports to France and of the import of finished cloth from

[1] This is particularly clear in the case of Jaume II. V. Salavert, *Cerdeña y la expansión mediterránea de la Corona de Aragón, 1297–1314*, i (Madrid, 1956), 160–79, expends much ingenuity arguing to the contrary.

[2] J.-P. Cuvillier, in *MCV* 6 (1970), 123; Soldevila, *Pere el Gran*, i. 3 (1956), 482.

France, as well as the encouragement of sheep-raising in the Crown of Aragon. It was hoped that over 100,000 people could be induced to move from France to Catalonia.[1] It seems that many textile workers did move to Barcelona—the first regulations for their guild there date from 1308—and that it was this foreign labour force that really launched the Catalan industry.[2] Cloth became the main Catalan export of the fourteenth century. Other Catalan products will be discussed later but it seems clear that in the thirteenth century Catalonia was well behind France in industrial development, let alone Italy or Flanders.

THE ROLE OF THE JEWS

Dependence on Jewish expertise in finance and administration provides further proof of the relatively backward place of the Crown of Aragon in the thirteenth century. Jews had played a crucial role in developing the cities conquered from the Muslims in the twelfth century, Lérida, Tortosa, Huesca. They continued to act as diplomats and administrators for Jaume I during the conquest of Majorca, Valencia, and Játiva. In Valencia Jewish officials acquired 'vast estates'. Privileges were granted to Jewish communities for trade in grain, oil, and cattle. In 1228 Jaume I issued a law forbidding Jews holding office over Christians. This law was never observed during Jaume's reign. Jaume's reliance on Jewish officials was very considerable. He repaid their loans and their services as bailiffs of the main cities of Aragon, Catalonia, and Valencia by privileges and estates and by protecting the Jews of his realms. In return Jewish aid made it possible for Jaume to undertake his campaign against the Muslims of Murcia in 1265 and his journey to the church council of Lyon in 1274.[3]

Jewish officials were of even greater importance and value to Pere II, not only in affairs requiring a knowledge of Arabic, but in royal administration. Like his father, Pere sought to attract Jews from North Africa. Jews served both as envoys to Muslim

[1] Finke, *Acta* iii. 155–62; J. Reglá, *El comercio entre Francia y la Corona de Aragón en los siglos XIII y XIV* (Saragossa, 1950).

[2] E. Asensio Salvado, in *VII CHCA* ii. 407–16; M. Riu Riu, ibid. 547–59. See also Capmany, ii. 23 f., 109 f., 174 f.

[3] Baer, *Die Juden* i. 16 f., 23–7, 97 f.; Baer, *History* i. 91, 139–47; J. Millás i Vallicrosa, *Documents hebraics de jueus catalans* (Barcelona, 1927); Huici, *Colección* i. 127; F. de A. de Bofarull y Sans, *I CHCA* ii. 819–943 (168 documents).

rulers and as administrators in the largely Muslim kingdom of Valencia. Joseph Ravaya acted as general royal treasurer and carried out technical improvements in the central administration. Apart from Pere and his heir he was the only person active in the government of Aragon, Catalonia, and Valencia. All local administrators were subject to him. During the rebellion of the Catalan nobles in 1280 the Ravayas largely took over the royal administration.[1] It was only as a result of the weakness of the Crown during the war with France that anti-Jewish feeling forced Pere to dismiss some of his Jewish officials. Christian lay middle-class officials who already held local office became much more prominent. In this respect Catalonia was ahead of Aragon—where Jews continued to serve unofficially as financial advisers under Alfons II (1285–91)—and the Crown of Aragon in general was ahead of Castile, but the development of the Christian bourgeois class was still rudimentary. It was only under Jaume II (1291–1327) that Jewish officials were replaced even as envoys to Islamic North Africa by Christians.[2]

THE CROWN'S FINANCIAL RESOURCES

In finance the Jewish contribution continued to be of great importance. In 1294 it is estimated that the Jewish communities contributed 22 per cent of all direct taxes in Aragon. In Catalonia the proportion contributed by Jews was probably higher, since the Catalan communities were richer. In 1323 the Catalan Jewish communities contributed as much as all the Catalan cities to the expedition to Sardinia. The Jewish contribution (500,000 ss.) constituted 35 per cent of the sum raised in Catalonia.[3]

The general financial resources of the Crown of Aragon, as compared to those of the French or Castilian monarchies, were very limited. In 1268 the French Pope Clement IV remarked contemptuously that all the church tithes of Jaume's realms only amounted to 10,000 lb. and it was not worth sending a legate to receive such a small sum towards a crusade. Compared to the King of France, Pere II of Aragon seemed to his

[1] Baer, *History* i. 163–71, 411 ff.; D. Romano, in *HM* ii. 243–92.
[2] Baer, *History* i. 171–7, ii. 1–6.
[3] Baer, *History* i. 179, 415 (n. 77); *Die Juden* i. 112 f., 120; A. Arribas Palau, *a conquista de Cerdeña por Jaime II de Aragón* (Barcelona, 1952), pp. 183–4.

servant Desclot 'one of the poor kings of the world, in lands and possessions'.[1] Jaume II was apparently richer than his predecessors. His officials made every effort to exploit his rights but his revenues reflected very imperfectly such features of the Catalan economy as the rise of the textile industry. There were signs of strain. One of Jaume's ministers advised him to devalue the coinage.

In 1281 Pere II informed an Italian prince that 'neither We nor Our predecessors ever made or had treasure'. Jaume I had also had to admit that he possessed 'no treasure'. This lack of 'treasure' (of a large monetary reserve), as well as of considerable steady revenues, probably explains much of the hesitation and caution of Jaume I and Jaume II.[2] The Castilian monarchy's total revenues cannot be stated with precision but they seem to have been four or five times larger than its rival's. The revenues of the French Crown in the early fourteenth century also far exceeded those of Catalonia–Aragon.[3] The limited financial resources of the Crown of Aragon were its Achilles' heel. It was because of royal poverty that the Catalan Corts were enabled to challenge the monarchy in the late fourteenth century.

MILITARY FORCES

The relative poverty of the rulers of Catalonia–Aragon is reflected in the limited military and naval forces at their disposal. The figures given for medieval armies by contemporary chroniclers are notoriously unreliable but, in a few cases, such as the expedition of Jaume I to Majorca in 1229, of Pere II to Sicily in 1282, and of the Infant Alfons, as heir to the throne, to Sardinia in 1323, the chronicles' figures can be checked with those in contemporary documents. The largest force of armed horse mentioned on any occasion is the 1,300 knights and squires of 1229.

This was a small force and the feudal contingents which provided most of the cavalry could only be maintained, after a

[1] E. Martène and U. Durand, *Thesaurus novus anecdotorum*, ii (Paris, 1717), col. 564. Desclot, 136.

[2] Pere II in *MHE* ii. 17; Jaume I, *Libre dels feyts*, 180.

[3] M. Gaibrois de Ballesteros, *Historia del reinado de Sancho IV de Castilla* (Madrid, 1922–8), i, pp. i-cxlviii, iii, pp. ccclx-lxxiii; F. Lot and R. Fawtier, *Histoire des institutions françaises du moyen âge*, ii (Paris, 1958), 183–238.

short time, by large payments in money. The numbers of heavy-armed horse Castile or France could muster were far larger, 4,000 to 6,000 men-at-arms.[1] In Majorca and Valencia the kings of Aragon could defeat Muslim troops because Muslim cavalry could not stand against even a small number of heavily armed knights, provided they kept together. But it was their *almogàvers* that rendered Catalan armies formidable to the French.

Almogàvers wore no armour and their only weapons were two javelins, a lance and dagger. They excelled in their use of javelins, which they could hurl with enough force to pierce through the best armour of the age, and in extreme rapidity and agility of movement. The inability of French chivalry to do more than charge in a massed phalanx made it relatively easy for light infantry, with projectiles, such as the *almogàvers,* and the ability to manœuvre on rough ground to defeat them. The *almogàvers* dealt as effectively with French cavalry in South Italy, Catalonia, and Greece as the English archers did in the following century at Crécy and Poitiers.[2] Aragon also made much use of Muslim light horse, or *zenetes*. They were hired in large numbers from Granada and others were sought from Morocco (the best Muslim light cavalry in Granada was North African in origin).[3]

NAVAL FORCES

A study of the naval forces of the Crown of Aragon reveals the same relatively small numbers and, consequently, the same need and ability to create new types of tactic and recruitment that one finds in its armies. The number of Catalan galleys—and it was galleys that counted in Mediterranean warfare—seems never to have been large, only in 1323 rising above twenty-two to fifty-three. These are not impressive figures, compared with the large fleets of fifty to eighty galleys that Genoa, Venice, or Pisa could put to sea. In the 1280s Charles of Anjou's Provençal, Neapolitan, and other galleys consistently outnumbered Pere's fleets. It is clear that Pere could not have

[1] F. Lot, *L'Art militaire et les armées au moyen âge en Europe et dans le proche orient* ii (Paris, 1946), 298–303, 240 (for the French army invading Catalonia in 1285), For Castilian forces in 1356–66 see R. d'Abadal, in *HE* XIV, pp. clxvii-clxxiii.

[2] F. Soldevila, *Els almogàvers* (Barcelona, 1952).

[3] F. D. Gazulla, in *BRAH* 90 (1927), 174–96; Finke, *Acta* iii. 122–4.

taken Sicily from Charles if the Sicilians had not already rebelled against him, or if Charles's navy had been united and had wanted to fight.[1]

EXTERNAL LIMITATIONS

Not only were the rulers of Catalonia–Aragon handicapped by the lack of unity between these two countries—each country possessing different and often incompatible aims—and by the relatively undeveloped state of the Catalan economy, which led to very limited financial, military, and naval resources. They were also confronted by much richer and more powerful enemies.

The defeat and death of Jaume I's father, Pere I, at Muret in 1213 by Simon de Montfort, was a very severe blow to the Crown of Aragon, which had, until then, been the major power in southern France. Throughout the first half of the thirteenth century the French monarchy advanced steadily south towards the Pyrenees. Jaume I was not willing to fight to prevent this advance and his attempts to prevent it by diplomacy failed.

In 1258 Jaume signed the Treaty of Corbeil with Louis IX. Jaume retained Montpellier, which he had inherited from his mother, some small neighbouring lordships, and the counties of Roussillon and Cerdagne, which had been in the hands of the House of Barcelona since 1182. He renounced all his other claims in southern France, in return for the French renunciation of claims of overlordship over Catalonia which dated back to Charlemagne.[2] By this treaty Jaume accepted the fact that the expansion of his monarchy in southern France was no longer possible. Almost immediately he seems to have begun to prepare other possibilities in Italy. Here he again came into opposition to France, represented, as in Provence, by Charles of Anjou, Louis IX's younger brother. In 1262 the marriage between Jaume's heir, Pere, and Costanza, daughter and heiress of Manfred, ruler of Naples and Sicily, was concluded at Montpellier, but Jaume was obliged to promise Louis IX that he would not aid Manfred against the papacy.[3] In 1262 Charles of Anjou had not yet accepted the papal offer of Manfred's kingdom

[1] F. Giunta, *Aragonesi e catalani nel Mediterraneo*, ii (Palermo, 1959), 54 f.; Arribas Palau, *Conquista de Cerdeña*, pp. 143 ff.

[2] O. Engels, in *SFG* i. 19 (1962), 114–46.

[3] D. Girona, *I CHCA* i. 232–99.

or set out to conquer it. But Jaume's promise prevented his opposing that conquest. He and Pere were forced to stand by in 1266 when Manfred was defeated and killed by Charles at Benevento. Pere's succession to Naples and Sicily now appeared impossible.[1]

During Jaume's long reign, whenever the two countries came into conflict, France checkmated Aragon, whether in Navarre, southern France, or Italy. French success was largely due to the support France received from the papacy, then at the height of its prestige. Jaume had seen the way the papacy put down its enemies. He was unwilling to fight a king supported by the Church. Pere II, when he became king, was prepared to vindicate his wife's rights to Sicily by force. He was successful, but his successors were unable to maintain all he had achieved.

Throughout the thirteenth century and the first half of the fourteenth, until France became involved in the Hundred Years War with England, French pressure on the Crown of Aragon was constant and conflict between the two monarchies was always possible. While France pushed the Crown of Aragon back to the Pyrenees and sought to prevent her expansion to Italy, Castile barred expansion by land towards the south of Spain.

As well as France and Castile, Catalonia–Aragon had to face the inevitable rivalry and opposition of the Italian maritime republics. It was very fortunate for Pere II that his rival Charles of Anjou was not a close ally of Genoa or Pisa, so that the Catalan fleet did not have to deal with more than Provençal and South Italian sailors in the 1280s. The internal and external limitations on the possibilities open to the Crown of Aragon were numerous and severe. How did it develop, politically and economically, from 1229 to 1327? This century is divided almost exactly in half by the death of Jaume I in 1276, which in many ways marks a dividing line. Jaume's policies and those of his successors differed in many ways.

JAUME I: THE BEGINNINGS OF MARITIME EXPANSION: THE FIRST CONQUESTS

During the thirteenth century the Crown of Aragon (for all practical purposes one may substitute here Catalonia) became

[1] S. Runciman, *The Sicilian Vespers* (Cambridge, 1958), pp. 65–70.

a Mediterranean power. It did so by the conquest of ports of great importance in the Balearic Isles and the Muslim kingdom of Valencia.

CONQUEST OF THE BALEARICS

The conquest of Majorca was popular with the barons and bishops of Catalonia and was urged on by the merchants of Barcelona, whose ships were being intercepted by Majorcan Muslims as they traded with Bougie (in modern Algeria) and with Ceuta in Morocco.[1]

The interest of Barcelona and its rulers in the Balearics was not new. Majorca's geographical position in the western Mediterranean inevitably gave it importance. The Muslim sea kingdom stretching from Denia to the Balearics in the eleventh century revealed how this geographical position could be used. In the late twelfth century the successful war carried on for years from the sea by the Banū Ghāniya of Majorca in North Africa repeated the demonstration.[2]

In 1114 Count Ramon Berenguer III of Barcelona, in alliance with Pisa, captured Majorca and Ibiza. This conquest was intended to be permanent. Although the islands were recovered by the Muslims in 1115 Ramon Berenguer's exploit gave Barcelona a title over the Balearics and placed the Catalans in touch with Italian maritime republics and Sicily. At this time Genoa dominated the western Mediterranean. In 1143 Genoa obtained control of the port of Montpellier, in 1166 of that of Narbonne. Barcelona did not become a Genoese colony, however. The count of Barcelona was able to force Genoa to recognize his sovereignty from Nice to the Ebro river by imposing a tax on Genoese ships sailing along this coast. Throughout the twelfth century the counts of Barcelona (who became, in 1137, also rulers of Aragon) continued to plan the conquest of Majorca but Genoa and Pisa preferred the privileged commercial position they soon secured from the island's Muslim rulers to the establishment there of their Catalan rivals. When Jaume I demanded restitution for the seizure of Catalan ships in the 1220s the Muslim emir was encouraged by the

[1] Desclot, 14; Capmany, i. 278.

[2] A. Campaner y Fuertes, *Bosquejo histórico de la dominación islamita en las Islas Baleares* (Palma, 1888); A. Bel, *Les Benou Ghanya* (Paris, 1903).

Genoese, Pisan, and Provençal merchants in Majorca to refuse the demand.[1]

Barcelona's rise as a port came long after that of Genoa and Pisa but it had the advantage, denied to these republics, of being united with a large inland territory which could produce materials for export. In the eleventh century one can see the rise at Barcelona of 'men of affairs' (*negotiatores*), who became rich through accumulating lands, especially vines, and water-mills. Slave-trading and tributes in gold from Muslim rulers were only some of the lesser sources of Barcelona's wealth. In the 1160s Benjamin of Tudela records the presence of merchants from the eastern Mediterranean, as well as Italians, in the 'small and beautiful' city of Barcelona. Catalan merchants are also recorded in the crusading Palestinian port of Tyre in 1187 but they were not important enough to act independently of the merchants of Marseille, Montpellier, and St. Gilles. In 1222 an agreement made by Jaume I defines the dues levied on spices imported from Egypt and Syria and on other articles, including cloth, livestock, oil, honey, iron, fish, lead, paper, and sulphur. In 1227 Jaume forbade foreign ships taking on cargoes for Egypt, Syria, or Ceuta if there was a ship of Barcelona willing to undertake the voyage.[2] These documents show that Barcelona was growing in importance as a port before the conquest of the Balearics (1229–35) but the new conquest marked an important stage in the progress of Catalan trade.

The conquest of Valencia (1232–45) took far longer than that of the Balearics and subsequent Muslim revolts occurred throughout Jaume's reign. The advance along the Mediterranean coast as far south as Denia eventually added weight to the maritime tendencies of Catalonia, but it seems that, under Jaume, what shipping Valencia possessed was mainly engaged

[1] P. Piferrer and J. Mª. Quadrado, *Islas Baleares* (Barcelona, 1888), pp. 31–43; Desclot, 14; L. Nicolau d'Olwer, in *Revista de Catalunya*, 13 (1930), 97–112; R. Lopez, *Storia delle colonie genovese nel Mediterraneo* (Bologna, 1938). Genoa had a representative in Majorca in 1191; see *Annales Januenses*, 1174–96 (Fonti per la storia d'Italia, xii (1901), 38). See now J. E. Ruiz Doménec, in *I Congresso storico Liguria-Catalogna* (Bordighera, 1974).

[2] J. E. Ruiz Doménec, in *Miscellanea Barcinonensia*, 11 (1972), 55–88; Baer, *Die Juden* i. 7 f. J. Mª. Lacarra, *HV* i (1965), 255–77; Benjamin of Tudela, *Itinerary*, ed. M. N. Adler (London, 1907), p. 2; L. Méry and F. Guindon, *Histoire analytique et chronologique des actes et des délibérations de Marseille*, i (Marseille, 1841), 190–2; Capmany, ii. 6–13.

in piracy. The development of Valencian trade and industry seems to have been slower than was the case in Majorca. From the time of its conquest by Jaume I the role of Majorca is intertwined with that of Barcelona in the development of Catalan trade. This involvement did not preclude economic rivalry, which attained new heights with the creation of a separate kingdom of Majorca in 1276, on the death of Jaume I.

SPHERES OF INFLUENCE: NORTH AFRICA: TUNISIA

The conquest of the Balearics advanced Catalans half-way to North Africa. The Balearics are almost 125 miles from Catalonia and only about 150 from Algeria. Barcelona had been trading with North Africa long before 1229, but this trade was now far easier.[1] An obstacle—a hostile Majorca—had been removed and a staging-point secured.

Our earliest document recording a Catalan consulate in Tunis dates from about 1253 and the earliest evidence for one in Bougie (now in Algeria), the other main port of the Tunisian kingdom, from 1259. By 1257, at the latest, there was a Catalan militia in Tunis. The earliest surviving formal treaty between Tunis and Aragon was concluded in 1271.[2]

Jaume I drew considerable sums from Tunis, not only through regular payments from the caliph for permission for his subjects to enlist in the militia there but principally by selling to private merchants the right to act as consul in Tunis or Bougie and so to receive dues paid by all Catalan merchants trading with these ports. Jaume maintained Crown control over the North African consulates in 1266 when he allowed the city of Barcelona to appoint Catalan consuls elsewhere.[3]

TLEMCEN: MOROCCO

Relations with the kingdom of Tlemcen, in central Algeria, with Oran as its main port, developed more slowly, but a Catalan militia was created in the 1250s at Tlemcen, paralleling that at Tunis. In 1271–2, if not before, Jaume received a tribute in exchange for Tlemcen's right to recruit this militia and to trade with Jaume's subjects. This tribute consisted largely in

[1] Dufourcq, pp. 26, 31.
[2] ibid., pp. 93–131.
[3] Dufourcq, *AEM* 3 (1966), 469–79.

returning part of the custom dues paid by Catalan merchants to the ruler of Catalonia. This system was to be followed elsewhere. Jaume I's relations with Morocco were less active than those maintained by Castile.[1]

Catalan exports to North Africa during this period consisted of cloth, mainly manufactured at this time at Lérida, oil and wine (both sent from Majorca, as well as Catalonia), and salt from Ibiza. Some spices from the eastern Mediterranean were resold to North Africa. In return the Crown of Aragon imported gold, black slaves, paper, sheepskins, leather, wool, and wax.[2]

ITALY: THE EASTERN MEDITERRANEAN

The Crown of Aragon did not maintain the same constant political contacts with Italy or the eastern Mediterranean as it did with Tunis and Tlemcen. The beginnings of Catalan trade with the East were due to private merchants of Barcelona who followed the Genoese, the Marseillais, and the men of Montpellier to the spice markets. It does not seem that the Catalan presence in the East was of great importance until the second half of the thirteenth century. Nor can one trace more than a few references to Catalan merchants in the Low Countries and at the fairs of Champagne at this period. Trade with southern Spain, especially with Seville, was of greater importance but still, it would seem, marginal in comparison with relations with North Africa.

THE END OF JAUME I'S REIGN

The death of Jaume I marks the end of an age in the history of the Crown of Aragon, the virtual end, for Catalonia–Aragon, of the *reconquista* in Spain and the beginning of new and daring Italian enterprises which Jaume may have foreseen but had himself avoided. Outside the Iberian peninsula the main line of Catalan expansion had reached through the Balearics to North Africa. It had been a commercial expansion but with political overtones—the question of tribute had already been raised and tribute had been received by Jaume from Tlemcen.

[1] Dufourcq, pp. 133–68.

[2] Dufourcq, *MÂ* 71 (1965), 479 f., 488 ff.; J. Lladonosa, *Arnau de Solsona, un mercader lleidatà a Tunis* (Barcelona, 1967), pp. 14 f.

Jaume's *Book of Deeds* reveals what the king thought he had achieved. The *Book*'s omissions are also very significant. It is entirely silent on Jaume's repeated failures in southern France. The *Book* presents God's champion against Muslims. It describes Jaume's miraculous rise from miserable beginnings. 'When I entered Monzón,' he writes of himself when he had just become king at the age of six, 'I had not food for one day, the land being wasted and mortgaged.'[1] He was formed in Monzón by the Templars who sheltered him. It was probably they, official warriors of the Faith, who gave him his crusading zeal and they —together with gratitude to Pope Innocent III for his protection when he was friendless—who gave Jaume his lifetime loyalty to the papacy, which he was never willing to oppose. Jaume left Monzón at the age of nine, before his literary education had begun. He could probably understand simple Latin when it was read to him, but his culture was essentially that of the troubadours, a cult of chivalry and love.

Jaume's early struggles, at times hand to hand, with rebellious nobles forged in him a remarkable strength of will. His complete confidence that God would not abandon one employed on His service won him Majorca and Valencia, when his barons would gladly have withdrawn, given the chance. At the same time his success in Valencia, and also in Murcia in 1266, was largely due to the liberal terms he was prepared to grant to Muslims who surrendered and to their faith in his word. Muslims would accept his verbal promise as sufficient, and, knowing that they would do this, he could remain alone outside a castle with two hundred Muslims, though 'I took care that none of them could seize the reins of my horse'. It is characteristic of Jaume that after 1266, when there were no more Muslims he could conquer left in Spain, he should have turned to a (fruitless) crusade in the East.[2]

'Many books were made on [Jaume's] life and his conquests and his excellence in chivalry and his feats and prowess'. Many contemporaries saw Jaume as he wished to be seen. Desclot, for instance, wrote: 'All his heart and will were to war with Muslims.'[3] The troubadour Cerverí de Girona saw the other

[1] Jaume I, *Libre dels feyts*, 11.
[2] ibid. 184. See 306.
[3] Muntaner, 7. Desclot, 12.

side of Jaume, the chivalric and amorous knight of Arthurian legend, who held that

a just and courteous man is never without ladies and anyone who has value in the Court has it by right of love . . . Wherever the sky was clearer and more luminous he believed his lady was there, her brilliance increasing the brilliance of heaven . . . Before [his confessor] fray Ramon [de Penyafort] the king adduced authors, kings and emperors, who are and have been, to prove that man's valour comes through woman . . . Solomon and Vergil, Homer and Porphyry, David and Plato, Lot and Samson, Lancelot and Tristan, Perceval and Yvain, Roland and Oliver, Bernard of Montleidier and Charles, who conquered Spain . . .[1]

ERRORS OF JAUME'S REIGN

Brilliant, attractive, chivalric, and successful in war against the Muslims, Jaume left a troubled heritage to his eldest surviving son, Pere. Despite Jaume's repeated victories over rebellious nobles his willingness to pardon rebels meant they would soon rebel again. The town council of Lérida told him: 'You always end by forgiving [your vassals] so that they are emboldened to do you mischief.' The Cortes of Ejea in 1265 revealed that the nobles of Aragon considered Jaume 'as little more than their feudal superior, with . . . a limited right of leading them to battle'.[2] Jaume's concessions to the Aragonese nobles were to hamper his successors. In Catalonia magnates such as the viscount of Cardona considered that they ruled their fiefs by the same 'grace of God' as their king his kingdom. Many peasants accepted Cardona's protection (in return for a tribute), since royal protection was not effective. Cardona held that he could not normally be prevented by the king from waging private war or from employing siege-engines, considered a privilege of royalty. He was at war with Jaume in 1252–3, again in 1259–62, and in 1274. In 1280 Cardona led a raiding party to the gates of Barcelona. He was never seriously punished by Jaume.[3] In 1273 Pere, as heir to the throne, accused his illegitimate half-

[1] Cerverí de Girona, *Obras completas*, ed. M. de Riquer (Barcelona, 1947), pp. 330 f.

[2] *Libre dels feyts*, 458; F. D. Swift, *The Life and Times of James the First the Conqueror* (Oxford, 1894), p. 150.

[3] F. Carreras y Candi, *BRABL* 6 (1911–12), 361–74, 502–40; J. Coroleu, *Revista de ciencias históricas*, 5 (1887), 374–8.

brother Fernando Sánchez, a great favourite of his father, and 'the greater part of the Aragonese barons' of preparing treason. For a time Jaume turned against his heir but was eventually reconciled to him. During Jaume's last years Pere was the dominant influence. He was able to crush Fernando Sánchez in June 1275 and to overcome the leading Catalan magnate, the count of Ampurias, the following year. These successes made possible Pere's peaceful succession in 1276.[1]

Jaume's indulgent policy towards rebellious nobles harmed his successor less than his policy of dividing his kingdoms. The final division, of 1262, left the Balearics, the counties of Roussillon and Cerdagne, and Montpellier, to Jaume, Jaume I's second son, who became king of Majorca at his father's death in 1276.[2]

PERE II: HIS AIMS

Pere II (1240–85) resembled his father in a number of ways. Active and vigorous as a child, taking at once to the use of arms, he was also trained in courtly culture and could exchange verses with any troubadour. The title he used most often, from the age of fourteen onwards, was 'Heir of Catalonia', the one region always left to him in Jaume's successive partitions. In 1257, at the age of seventeen, he received the office of Procurator of Catalonia, which gave him delegated royal powers there. For the next twenty years, while his father lived, he was mainly engaged in fighting against the rebellious Catalan nobles. He gained wider fame in the expeditions against the Muslims of Murcia of 1265–6. In 1269 he visited the kingdom of Castile and in 1275–6 he was at Paris. From 1273 he virtually ruled with his father.

Pere was to attain, if possible, greater fame than Jaume I. For Muntaner his work was that of God himself. Pere was 'the best knight in the world and the wisest and the most gracious to all men ever born'. The author of the *Acts of the Counts* sees him as the perfect knight. When he was told of the death of his great enemy, Charles of Anjou, 'no sign of joy appeared in him . . . but he said that one of the best knights in the world was dead'.

[1] *Libre dels feyts*, 514, 550; Soldevila, *Pere el Gran*, i. 3, pp. 326 ff., 348; Desclot, 69–72.

[2] Soldevila, i. 1, p. 115; Huici, iii. 164–7.

The author sees Pere, however, as surpassing his father: 'for a good father the best of sons.'[1]

Pere was more determined to vindicate his rights both within the kingdom and outside it than his father had been. In doing this he was ready to use law but also force, if this proved necessary. A troubadour blames him for trapping and drowning a noble rebel, treating him as if he were a peasant. Desclot remarks that Pere 'would not curry favour with knights or barons as [Jaume] had done'. Pere's decidedly authoritarian rule was only checked when internal difficulties, combined with external dangers, forced him to make concessions to his subjects in 1283.[2]

As heir to the throne Pere had been the leader of the anti-French cause in Provence, in Marseille in 1263, and Toulouse in 1271. The troubadours of Provence turned to him when they despaired of his father. 'From his early years,' the *Acts* say, 'he hated the French.' His marriage to Costanza, the heiress of Naples and Sicily, made him the natural champion of her cause when her father, Manfred, was slain by Charles of Anjou in 1266.[3]

INTERNAL SUCCESSES

Pere proceeded by degrees. He could not move against Charles of Anjou in Italy until internal rebellion was over. Jaume I died on 27 July 1276 in the middle of a major revolt of the Muslims of Valencia. It took Pere fourteen months to force them to submit. He did not follow Jaume's dying instructions and order a mass expulsion of Muslims from Valencia. Pere expelled some leading rebels but punished severely any attack on the Muslims communities after their surrender and welcomed Muslims fleeing from other lands. The new king was less immediately clement, on the other hand, than Jaume might have been to the Catalan nobles. He had refused to issue a general confirmation of their privileges, some of which he considered harmful. A rebellion followed. In 1280 he captured its leaders. They were imprisoned for a year and had all their possessions confiscated.

[1] *Gesta comitum* XXVIII. 1, 6, 30, pp. 62, 64, 75; Soldevila, i. 1, p. 33; Huici, ii. 92; Muntaner, 145.

[2] Desclot, 68; Soldevila, i. 3, pp. 307–13; Cerverí de Girona, *Obras*, p. 88. See below, p. 255, and n. 2.

[3] *Gesta comitum* XXVIII. 42, p. 85; Soldevila, i. 2, pp. 188, 193 f., 195 ff., 202 ff.; i. 3, p. 454.

With one exception they were then released and restored their fiefs. Henceforth the viscount of Cardona and the rest were to be Pere's loyal collaborators.[1] Neither Valencia nor Catalonia was to move against him again. No active danger of revolt appeared as yet in Aragon. In January 1279 Pere had forced his younger brother, Jaume II of Majorca, to become his vassal. Jaume's resentment of his loss of complete sovereignty was so bitter, however, that he was to seize the first opportunity of turning against Pere.[2]

INTERNATIONAL POLICY

Pere's international strategy as king was a continuation of the policy he had pursued since 1266 as heir to the throne. Pere sought to use the Infantes de la Cerda as hostages, in order to neutralize his two most powerful neighbours, France and Castile. He was not successful with France but he did achieve an alliance with Castile in 1281, which lasted until after Pere's Sicilian expedition.[3] Pere was also in touch with Pope Nicholas III, who he hoped might at least remain neutral when Pere attacked Charles. Nicholas's death in August 1280 and the election of another French pope (Martin IV), brought about by Charles's influence, came too late for Pere to postpone his plans.[5]

Pere's North African policy was a far more ambitious continuation of that of Jaume I. He was principally interested in Tunisia because of its nearness to Sicily. The expedition of 1282 was officially prepared against Tunis, but, although Pere's 'official' historian, Desclot, does not admit this, there can be no doubt that the expedition was ultimately directed against Charles of Anjou's kingdom of Naples and Sicily.[5]

Summoned by the Sicilian rebels against Charles of Anjou, Pere was able, within a month, to occupy the whole of Sicily. By January 1283 the *almogàvers* were carrying out successful

[1] *Libre dels feyts*, 564; Desclot, 73, 75; Soldevila, i. 3, p. 417, n. 86; ii. 1, esp. pp. 55–60, 82 f., 107–11; Zurita, *Anales* iv. 5, 9; F. Carreras y Candi, *Miscelanea histórica catalana*, ii (Barcelona, 1906), 33–56.

[2] A. Lecoy de la Marche, *Les Relations politiques de la France avec le royaume de Majorque*, i (Paris, 1892), 446–9; Zurita, iv. 7.

[3] A. Ballesteros Beretta, *Alfonso X el Sabio* (Barcelona, 1963), pp. 937–41.

[4] H. Wieruszowski, *BRAH* 107 (1935), 547–602; Carini, *Archivi*, ii. 17 f., 40–3, 46.

[5] Dufourcq, pp. 238–49; Desclot, 88; cf. Carini, *Archivi* ii. 45.

raids across the Straits of Messina. The Angevin troops began to withdraw. In February Pere had crossed to Reggio in Calabria. Pere did not advance more rapidly in Italy, partly, perhaps, because of lack of money but mainly because he had consented to try the justice of his claims to Sicily in a personal duel with Charles of Anjou at Bordeaux, in neutral Gascony, then under English rule. No more rebellions occurred in southern Italy after Pere's departure. He was trapped by his chivalric nature into accepting the challenge.[1]

The duel at Bordeaux was set for 1 June 1283. Pere was obliged to leave Sicily in May. He sent for his Queen Costanza and his younger sons and left them there in his place but they could not in fact replace him. The war was carried on successfully at sea by Ruggiero di Loria (appointed Admiral on 20 April 1283), but there were no more advances by land, since, as Desclot tells us, 'the greater part of the good men-at-arms had returned to Catalonia with the king'. Meanwhile Pope Martin IV forbade Edward I of England to supervise the duel and, despite the safe-conducts which had been promised, the hundred knights who were to joust with Pere against Charles and his hundred were prevented from reaching Bordeaux. Pere himself arrived there in disguise on 1 June, accompanied by only three knights. They travelled as attendants of a horsedealer 'who knew all the ways, the forests, and mountains from Castile to Gascony'. Pere discovered that Charles of Anjou was already in Bordeaux, accompanied by King Philippe III of France and a large body of French knights. Edward I's seneschal in Bordeaux warned him that he could not safeguard him. He had a notary attest his presence there and returned with honour across the Pyrenees. This exploit aroused enormous interest in contemporary knights, from England to Frankish Greece, but the main result was that Charles had gained time and Pere had lost the best chance he or his successors were to have of conquering the whole of Charles's kingdom.[2]

On 21 March 1283 Martin IV had formally deposed Pere II as a rebel against the papacy, the overlord of Sicily. He urged Philippe III of France to invade Pere's realms as those of a

[1] Desclot, 98 f.; Muntaner, 74, 72; Carini, *De rebus*, pp. 110 f., 225 f., 296 f., 510.

[2] Desclot, 104 f., 110; Muntaner, 85–91; Carini, *De rebus*, pp. 617 f., 706 f.; F. Soldevila, *EUC* 9 (1915), 123–72.

deposed enemy of the Church. Philippe's younger son, Charles of Valois, was named King of Aragon by the pope. Jaume II of Majorca now had an excuse to ally himself with France against his brother and overlord.[1]

INTERNAL TROUBLES: ARAGON

Pere's position was greatly weakened by internal dissension. The Aragonese nobles resented the Sicilian expedition, on which they had not been previously consulted. In October 1283 Pere was obliged to confirm the General Privilege of the newly established *Unión* of Aragon. The nobles of the *Unión*, soon joined by most of the towns of Aragon, were not content with this. On 20 October they issued 'Ordinances', by which they swore 'not to hold [Pere] for king or to obey him', and to depose him, with the help of his heir, if he did not respect the laws of Aragon. By March 1284 the *Unión*'s pretensions were increasing. They were sending envoys to the king of Navarre (the eldest son and heir of the king of France), with whom Pere was at war. They were threatening to seek foreign help against the king. Pere would have been lost without the support of Valencia, and especially of Catalonia. In 1283–4 he held his first Corts at Valencia and Barcelona. He was obliged to make considerable grants to nobility, clergy, and bourgeois to secure their support, but he obtained this.[2]

THE FRENCH INVASION

Fortunately for Pere the French threat took a long time to develop. But Pere was increasingly isolated. As Muntaner saw it, he was 'deserted by all his friends on earth'.[3] Pere's poetical appeal to Catalonia's former vassals in southern France fell on deaf ears. Bernat d'Auriac of Béziers had predicted a French victory. Pere would be hanged from a common gibbet as a public robber, since he had stolen Charles of Anjou's kingdom. In fact contingents from southern France provided the core of the invading army.[4] It was clear that there would be little

[1] Zurita, *Anales* iv. 26, 36 f.; Lecoy de la Marche, i. 185–93, 453 f.

[2] Zurita, iv. 38; L. González Antón, in *Miscelánea J. M. Lacarra, estudios de historia medieval* (Saragossa, 1968), pp. 51–62. See below, p. 278, n. 2.

[3] Muntaner, 120.

[4] A. Jeanroy, in *Homenaje a Menéndez Pidal*, iii (Madrid, 1925), 77–88; F. Lot, *L'Art militaire*, i. 243, n. 5; Riquer, i. 166–9.

help from Aragon against the French. Nor was all Catalonia loyal.

Pere acted with his usual energy. In January 1285 he summoned Valencia, Catalonia, and Aragon to arm against the French, 'who seek unjustly to take from us our kingdoms, annulling our royal title'. Any attempt by the clergy to publish the papal bulls excommunicating and deposing Pere would meet with a death sentence. If the clergy of Cervera did not immediately assist in levying men for the royal army the local officials were 'to burn and destroy their lands'.[1]

Leaving Huesca in Aragon, Pere reached Barcelona. He was only just in time. An attempt to form a popular government in Barcelona, directed against the richer bourgeoisie, the Church, and the Jews, was led by a certain Berenguer Oller. It was rumoured that he planned to surrender the city to France, and would act on Easter Day (25 March 1285). Entering the city at dawn on 24 March, Pere surprised and seized Oller. On Easter Day he and seven of his companions were hanged and 600 of his followers fled to escape arrest. Pere was sure of his capital. He could hold his Easter feast in his palace.[2]

Losing no time, Pere advanced by forced marches across the Pyrenees and entered Perpignan, again at dawn, probably on 14 April. His plan was to surprise his brother, Jaume II of Majorca, whom he suspected, rightly, of a secret alliance with France, and so take control of his castles in Roussillon and Cerdagne. This would have forced the French to waste the greater part of 1285 campaigning north of the Pyrenees. Jaume, however, escaped from the castle of Perpignan through a sewer. A local rising forced Pere to withdraw to the Pyrenees.[3] On 22 April he summoned the men of Barcelona to come at once, 'since there is clear danger in delay'. The same day he excused himself to his feudal vassals for not paying them the usual stipend for military service: 'God knows it is impossible.' In spite of the large sums he had raised from the Jews and the clergy he was very short of money. At first the towns and nobles of Aragon had merely been ordered to defend the Aragonese

[1] Carini, *Archivi*, pp. 7, 87 f., 177.

[2] Desclot, 133. See p. 281, n. 1 below.

[3] Desclot, 134 f.; *Gesta comitum*, XXVIII. 31, pp. 76 f.; Soldevila, *Els grans reis del segle XIII*, p. 125 and n. 131 (p. 161).

frontier against the French in Navarre. In May Pere summoned the Aragonese forces to the Catalan Pyrenees.[1] All these preparations came late, for the French were almost upon him.

The numbers of the French army were vastly swollen by contemporaries, especially by the victorious Catalans. The real figures were probably nearer 4,000 horse and 8,000 foot than the over 135,000 given by Desclot, but 4,000 horse was far more than Pere could muster. But the French expedition was officially a crusade, launched by the papacy, against a refractory and deposed ruler, and the French army was accordingly accompanied by hordes of peasants, men, women, and children who hoped to gain the spiritual blessings that accompanied crusades, without travelling to the East. They apparently believed that they could gain the papal indulgence by throwing a stone in the direction of Pere's forces, while crying out: 'I throw this stone against Pere of Aragon.' These mobs of 'crusaders' slowed down the French advance while they consumed the provisions the army needed.[2]

The French attempted to cross the Pyrenees by the Col de Panissars on 7 May 1285. Pere had reached the pass the evening before with only thirty-eight knights and seventy followers. By lighting hundreds of fires over the mountainside he convinced the French that he was there with his whole army. Soon the Catalan town militias began to appear and the pass was effectively blocked. The French were stopped for a month. They could only plunder and burn Roussillon and commit atrocities which Pere's propaganda hastened to diffuse and French propaganda to justify, as committed 'against the enemies of the Christian Faith'.[3]

The French crossed the Pyrenees, probably by the difficult passage of Massana, on 8 June. Panic set in in the north of Catalonia, aided by treason. Sancho IV of Castile not only did not send the aid he had promised Pere but made overtures to France. It proved necessary to divert troops to the Castilian

[1] Carini, *Archivi*, pp. 74 f., 123, 76 f., 80 ff., 85. For the contribution of Valencia see R. Arroyo Ilera, *EEMCA* 8 (1967), 429–34.

[2] Desclot, 131, 137; *Gesta comitum* XXVIII. 41, p. 84. See Lot, i. 239 f.

[3] Desclot, 138–41; Carini, p. 82; Guillaume de Nangis, in *Recueil des historiens des Gaules et de la France*, xx. 530.

frontier. By late July practically no troops had arrived in Catalonia from Aragon.[1]

All Pere could do was slow the French down. Gerona was garrisoned and surrounded by an evacuated belt of territory between it and Barcelona. Pere himself returned to Barcelona. While 'hunting, eating, and drinking', he was ordering the fortification of Barcelona and of the cities of western Catalonia. Full emergency powers were given to the Jew Muça de Portella to handle the revenues of Aragon. Corrado Lancia was given the same powers for Valencia. The clergy were forced to contribute large sums.[2]

The French played into Pere's hands. As in later invasions they wasted their strength before Gerona, instead of pressing on to Barcelona which would probably have fallen. The enormous French fleet spread fire and devastation along the Catalan coast. There were few temptations for Catalans to go over to the papal nominee as king of Aragon, Charles of Valois. The French army was wasted by disease. Its communications and supplies depended on maintaining control of the sea. The French were thus vulnerable to attacks by corsairs, who came from Valencia, Alicante, and Ibiza, as well as Catalonia. On 28 July ten or eleven galleys from Barcelona defeated a larger French fleet. On the night of 3 September the fleet of Ruggiero di Loria, just arrived from Sicily, fell on the remaining French galleys and virtually destroyed them. Without supplies all the French could do was withdraw. The retreat through torrential rain and mud was disastrous. As the beaten army passed through the Col de Panissars on 3–4 October the *almogàvers* descended on them from one side and Loria's sailors from the other. Only the dead or dying Philippe III, 'flying and dishonouring the lilies', as Dante saw him, his sons, the papal legate, and a knot of nobles clustered round the Oriflamme were spared, by the mercy of Pere II. A French historian sums up the invasion as 'one of the most unjust, most useless, and most disastrous expeditions the Capetians undertook'.[3]

[1] Desclot, 146; L. Klüpfel, *Die äusserige Politik Alfonsos III. von Aragon* (Leipzig, 1911–12), p. 166; Carini, pp. 102, 88.

[2] Desclot, 148–53, 157. Carini, pp. 92–8, 125 f.; Baer, *History* i. 414 (n. 69).

[3] *Gesta comitum* XXVIII. 44, 47, pp. 87, 89; Desclot, 154–9, 166 f.; Muntaner, 130, 138 f.; Carini, pp. 60–2; Guillaume de Nangis, pp. 536 f.; Ch.-V. Langlois, *Le Règne de Philippe III le Hardi* (Paris, 1887), p. 165.

The French had achieved nothing. They had to surrender Gerona after holding it for only a month. 'One of the poor kings' of western Europe had not only taken Sicily from the great Charles of Anjou but held it against him and the papacy. Despite the treasonable indifference of Aragon and the uncertain loyalties of much of Catalonia he had completely vanquished the leading monarchy in Europe.[1] The southern summer, Pere's sailors, and his own tenacity had overcome greatly superior numbers and resources.

Pere did not intend to rest on his laurels. An expedition to Majorca was under preparation to seize the island as punishment for his brother Jaume's treason. Pere set out from Barcelona, only to fall ill and die, aged only forty-six, during the night of 10 November. Before he died he may have made his peace with the Church, giving up Sicily—which he had already formally transferred to his younger son, Jaume; he also made sure that his heir Alfons would carry on the expedition against Majorca. It is possible that he may also have determined to punish Sancho of Castile and to set up Sancho's nephew, Alfonso de la Cerda, as a rival king.[2]

THE SUCCESSORS OF PERE II: ALFONS II AND JAUME II

Ten years passed after Pere's victory before the Crown of Aragon attained peace with France and the papacy. Pere's gains proved too great for his successors to maintain. The Peace of Anagni of 1295 provided a compromise which left important issues unsettled.

Pere's death-bed renunciation of Sicily was not divulged. Pere was succeeded in the Crown of Aragon by his eldest son, Alfons II, and in Sicily by his second son, Jaume. He had arranged this division in 1283 but intended that his sons should collaborate very closely. Alfons was only twenty in 1285 and Jaume eighteen, but they had been trained for years to act as their father's deputies and they were surrounded by remarkably talented advisers. Loria, in particular, acted as liaison between

[1] Carini, pp. 60–2. See Desclot, 136.

[2] Desclot, 168; Muntaner, 142, 156. See Carini, pp. 119, 177 f. S. Sobrequés, in *Els descendents de Pere el Gran* (Barcelona, 1954), pp. 20, 47, n. 58, questions the authenticity of Pere's renunciation. *Contra*, Soldevila, *Història de Catalunya* (Barcelona, 1963), p. 374 and n. 171.

them and immediately obtained sworn guarantees of mutual aid, in return for Jaume's homage to Alfons.[1]

Alfons began his reign happily. The expedition to Majorca was successful. The City of Majorca surrendered within ten days of Pere's death although resistance in the island continued for some time, possibly for years.[2] Ibiza also surrendered immediately. The only other military success of Alfons's reign followed on from this. The Muslims of Minorca had remained semi-independent vassals of Aragon after Jaume I's conquest of Majorca. It is uncertain whether Alfons hoped to impress the hostile papacy by a minor 'crusade' against infidels or merely wished to round off his control of the Balearics. Before he landed in Minorca in January 1287 he had decided to enslave a large part of the Muslim population. The richer Muslims were allowed to ransom themselves and sail to Tunis. The rest filled the slave-markets of Majorca, Valencia, Barcelona, and Sicily. White and black slaves were distributed as presents to the king's relations, their ladies in waiting, the Dominican convent of Majorca, and the abbey of Montserrat. The land was distributed to Catalan settlers and a few religious foundations. The whole enterprise was 'une magnifique affaire' for the Crown.[3]

The complete conquest of the Balearics strengthened Alfons's strategic position in the western Mediterranean and gave him another bargaining counter he could use in peace negotiations. He already had the hostages acquired by Pere II, the Infantes de la Cerda, and the heir of Charles of Anjou, now Charles II of Naples since his father's death in January 1285, who had been captured by Loria in 1284. Negotiations could not long be delayed. The Aragonese *Unión* caused Alfons II even more trouble than it had caused his father. It now included all the towns of Aragon. It demanded control over foreign policy as

[1] G. La Mantia, *Codice diplomatico dei re aragonese di Sicilia*, i (Palermo, 1917), 269–71; idem, in *AIEC* 2 (1908), 346–63; Carini, pp. 208, 210 f. For Alfons II cf. F. Carreras y Candi, *BRABL* 10 (1921–2), 61–83; Sobrequés, pp. 11–54; Soldevila, *Vida de Pere el Gran*, pp. 283–349.

[2] Zurita, *Anales* iv. 74; Lecoy de la Marche, i. 454 f.; M. Bonet, *BSAL* 7 (1897–8), 37–41, 57–9, 80 f.; M. Ferrer y Flórez, ibid. 30 (1947–52), 274–88; B. Guasp, *AST* 18 (1945), 91–102; cf. La Mantia, ii (1956), 45 f. (an attempted rising in 1291).

[3] C. Parpal y Marqués, *La conquista de Menorca en 1287 por Alfonso III de Aragón* (Barcelona, 1901); Muntaner, 172; Verlinden, i. 253–8.

well as over the royal household, lands and revenues. It claimed that Alfons should not act without the consent of a permanent delegation of Aragonese nobles, knights and cities. At one point it even claimed to control Alfons' policy in Catalonia. The *Unión* sent envoys to Alfons's enemies, the papacy, France, Castile, and Granada. While Alfons was in Minorca the Aragonese invaded Valencia to force the Valencians to accept the *Fuero de Aragón*. Having tried force against the *Unión* and failed, Alfons was obliged to confirm their Privileges on 28 December 1287. He had to swear not to proceed against any members of the *Unión* without the consent of the Justicia of Aragon and of the Aragonese Cortes. If he did so the *Unión* could refuse to obey him and could choose another king. This last clause, as a royal concession, is probably unique. The king was forced to hand over a number of hostages and twelve castles, as pledges of his sincerity. In return he received some military aid against France but in 1288 a group of leading Aragonese nobles was still negotiating with Charles of Valois and offering to recognize him as king.[1]

In Sicily Jaume, also, had to contend with a disloyal faction. 'Only the naval power of the Catalan–Sicilian coalition, the daring of its rulers, and the genius of Loria had been able to create a momentary superiority which could not long be maintained' against the greatly superior forces of France and Naples and the moral force of the papacy, which deprived the people of Catalonia–Aragon and Sicily of the Christian sacraments for over ten years.[2]

By February 1286 Alfons was engaged in peace negotiations in which his captive, Charles II of Naples, took a large part. Both Charles II and Philippe IV of France were peacefully disposed, but no agreement was possible without the papacy, and the papacy wished to persuade Aragon to make a separate peace and abandon the Sicilians to the Angevins of Naples. Alfons remained loyal to his brother as long as he could. His fleets devastated the coasts of Provence and the bay of Naples. Jaume held his own in Calabria and Alfons in the Pyrenees. One peace conference succeeded the last. The situation became more

[1] Zurita, iv. 83, 93, 97; Soldevila, *Història*, pp. 381 ff.; Sobrequés, pp. 31 f.; R. E. Giesey, *If Not, Not* (Princeton, 1968), pp. 89 f.

[2] Sobrequés, p. 29.

serious when Castile allied with France in 1288. Alfons's proclamation of Alfonso de la Cerda as king of Castile had little effect. In an attempt to escape from his diplomatic isolation Alfons concluded an alliance with Egypt in 1290 but he was eventually forced to make peace with the papacy, very much on its terms, in February 1291 at the Treaty of Brignoles or Tarascon. He promised to go to Rome to ask pardon for his father's actions and then to go on crusade to the East. He engaged to recall his subjects from Sicily but did not promise to intervene there himself, against his brother Jaume. The question of the Balearics was left unsettled. Alfons's successor was to get no better terms four years later, at Anagni.[1]

Alfons's sudden death in June 1291 left Aragon to his brother Jaume and again threw the whole situation into confusion. Jaume refused to accept the wills of his father and brother, which had declared the separation of Aragon and Sicily. He left his brother Frederic in Sicily only as viceroy, not as king, and immediately took control of the Crown of Aragon.[2]

JAUME II: HIS CHARACTER

Jaume II was to reign as king of Aragon for thirty-six years (1291–1327). Unlike his grandfather and father, Jaume I and Pere II, he was not the main subject of any chronicle, but he is known to us through his enormous diplomatic correspondence. His family life has also been studied in detail.[3] He was to attain a remarkable position, respected, if not liked, by all the rulers of western Europe. Jaume succeeded in making peace with the papacy without ceasing to advance in the Italian world, although his path of advance was changed. The acquisition of Sardinia in the 1320s sealed the policy he had pursued since the 1290s. These successes were attained at a high price. Against Castile and against his brother Frederic Jaume's policy was unscrupulous but he was soon reconciled with Frederic and—on less advantageous terms—with Castile.

[1] Carini, p. 211; Salavert, *Cerdeña*, i. 63, 78; Soldevila, in *Studi medievali in onore di A. de Stefano* (Palermo, 1956), pp. 519–27.

[2] *MHE* iii. 426–47. See Soldevila, *SFG* i. 21 (1963), 149–54.

[3] Finke, *Acta*; Martínez Ferrando, *Jaime II de Aragón, su vida familiar.*

JAUME II AND HIS BROTHER FREDERIC OF SICILY

The contrast is extreme between Jaume, the crowned bureaucrat, in many ways resembling the later Philip II of Spain, and his younger brother Frederic. Jaume was prudent and prolix, sending, according to one contemporary, 'more solemn envoys to the papal court in one year than the kings of France and England in ten'.[1] Cautious in everything, often rigid and tyrannical with his family, minutely officious in religion, justice, and administration, Jaume always sought for a peaceful solution to every problem. Frederic, on the other hand, rushed headlong into every crisis. His ideal of a united Christendom led him to ally, to the rage of successive popes, with German emperors whose position in Italy was so insecure as to be little use to him. He protected the extreme Spiritual wing of the Franciscan Order against the papacy. He believed in the visionary ravings of Arnau de Vilanova; when Jaume II tried to show him the harm Arnau had done to both of them at the papal court he refused to listen. Unlike Jaume, Frederic never realized or allowed for the strength of the papacy. Frederic had all the impulsive daring of Pere II, Jaume all the prudence of Jaume I, with whom he was compared by a contemporary.[2] Perhaps only Frederic could have held Sicily against the papacy, France, the Angevins of Naples, and his own brother. Certainly only Jaume could have schemed and manœuvred for twenty-five years to gain Sardinia.

From 1291 to 1293 Jaume fought to keep Sicily united to the Crown of Aragon. He won over Aragon from its usual opposition and made peace with Castile. Sancho IV secured a favourable settlement at Monteagudo in November 1291. Jaume abandoned the Infantes de la Cerda. Sancho's hands were freed against Morocco, Jaume's against France. This was only a pause in the conflict with Castile. Sancho used Catalan help against Tarifa while assuring France that he was 'not so mad that I would wish to lose the king of France and the Church of Rome for Aragon'. By 1293 Jaume had seen through Sancho.

[1] Martínez Ferrando, *Jaime II*, ii. 333.

[2] Finke, *Acta* i. 340, 440; ii. 668 f., 673 f., 834; 'Nachträge', in *SFG* i. 4 (1933), 463 f.; J. Carreras Artau, *Relaciones de Arnau de Vilanova con los reyes de la Casa de Aragón* (Barcelona, 1955); Bernat de Canals, cited by J. Rubió, in *Homenaje a J. Vincke*, i (Madrid, 1962–3), 235; see Rubió, *EUC* 12 (1927), 280.

He turned first to a marriage alliance with France and then to one with Blanche, daughter of Charles II of Naples.[1] On 24 December 1294 a new pope was proclaimed as Boniface VIII. He was to lend his authority and iron will to break Jaume's ties to Sicily and forge instead an Aragonese–Neapolitan alliance.

THE TREATY OF ANAGNI

The essential clauses of the 'Treaty' of Anagni were drawn up on 20 June 1295. Apart from the marriage between Jaume II and Blanche they included the abandonment of Sicily to the papacy (and hence to the Angevins), the renunciation by France of the papal donation of the Crown of Aragon to Charles of Valois, and the lifting of papal censures on that Crown and its subjects. The papacy was to decide the question of the Balearics. They were returned to Jaume II of Majorca in 1298; he was to hold his kingdom (as before the war) as a vassal of Aragon.[2]

The treaty enabled Jaume to profit from the death of Sancho IV in April 1295, which left Castile under Fernando IV, a child of nine, whose legitimacy was disputed. Jaume again supported Alfonso de la Cerda in an attempt to partition Castile. In 1296 Jaume himself occupied most of the kingdom of Murcia.[3]

From 1297 to 1299 Jaume was mainly occupied with Italy. On 4 April 1297 he received from Boniface VIII in Rome the solemn investiture of the title to the kingdoms of Sardinia and Corsica. He had been largely induced to renounce Sicily by the possibility of this investiture.[4] Jaume was obliged to become a vasal of the pope for his new kingdom and to promise the papacy armed assistance in Italy and an annual tribute. He was also to assist in taking Sicily from his younger brother Frederic, who had been crowned king in Palermo in January 1296. Jaume's expedition to Sicily in 1298 was inconclusive. On 4 July 1299 he and Loria won a sea battle against Frederic, but Jaume almost immediately returned to Catalonia. Jaume returned to Catalonia not only—probably not mainly—to save his brother

[1] Gaibrois de Ballesteros, *Sancho IV*, iii, p. ccci; ii. 240–8; *MHE* iii. 452–8, 460–8; Zurita, iv. 124; Finke, *Acta* iii. 19 f., 21–3; H. E. Rohde, *Der Kampf um Sizilien in den Jahren 1291–1302* (Berlin, 1913), pp. 28 f.

[2] V. Salavert, *EEMCA* 5 (1952), 209–360. Lecoy de la Marche, i. 351–60.

[3] Muntaner, 188.

[4] Soldevila, *Història*, p. 396, n. 71; Jaume was interested in Sardinia in 1290–1 (Finke, 'Nachträge', p. 436).

Frederic from collapse but to forestall internal revolt and external danger from Castile and Granada, and also because he could not pay his troops over the winter.

Jaume's withdrawal and the Sicilian resistance resulted in the Peace of Caltabelotta of 1302. Frederic kept Sicily and gave up Calabria. Until 1310 Jaume was mainly occupied with the Iberian Peninsula. In 1304, by the treaty of Agreda with Castile, he secured a large part of the kingdom of Murcia. In 1309, in alliance with Fernando IV of Castile, Jaume invaded Granada and unsuccessfully besieged Almería. Only after recovering from this reverse could he devote his whole energies to the acquisition of Sardinia.[1]

THE CONQUEST OF SARDINIA

It took twenty-six years to make the title to Sardinia good. (No serious attempt was made on Corsica until the fifteenth century.) Jaume could not acquire control of Sardinia without the help, or at least the neutrality, of either Pisa or Genoa. He also needed the assistance of the main local noble families and especially of the Judges of Arborea.

Jaume pursued his goal with extraordinary persistence, anxious to achieve it by peaceful means. It eventually became clear that he could hope for no direct aid from the divided forces of Italy and that the papacy refused to assist him to implement its grant of 1297. He had to act with only his own resources, those of Majorca (as vassal to Aragon), and assistance from the Judge of Arborea, who contributed large sums.[2]

A relatively small Catalan–Aragonese expeditionary force vanquished the Pisans and conquered the island in about a year (June 1323–July 1324). The conquest was rapid because of the general detestation of the Pisans felt by most of the Sards and because of the decisive support received from the Judge of Arborea and the other leading local dynasties.[3]

But within a year the Doria and Malaspina and the town of

[1] Giménez Soler, *Aragón y Granada*, pp. 59 f.; Soldevila, pp. 408–10; Muntaner, 247; Martínez Ferrando, in *Els descendents*, pp. 106–10; Giménez Soler, *El sitio de Almeria en 1309* (Barcelona, 1904).

[2] Salavert, *passim*; Finke, *Acta* ii. 581–9, 574, 619 f., 631; C. Manca, *Fonti e orientamenti per la storia economica della Sardegna aragonese* (Padua, 1967), p. 34; Arribas Palau, *Conquista de Cerdeña*, pp. 137, 183–90, 376–9, 385 f.

[3] Muntaner, 271–9; *Crònica de Pere III*, i, ed. A. Pagès (Toulouse, 1942), 20–47.

Sassari were in revolt. Peace was re-established with the help of Arborea. The main cause of this revolt and of countless later revolts in Sardinia against the Crown of Aragon was stated by the Judge of Arborea in 1325: 'The Sards believed they would have one king and now have as many kings as there are villages around Cagliari.'[1] This was not what the Sards—and especially the local noble dynasties—had bargained for. The struggle between the family of Arborea and the Crown of Aragon was inevitable as soon as a clash occurred between two strong personalities. This situation arose in the 1340s under Pere III of Aragon.

Economic aspects of the expansion of the countries of the Crown of Aragon, during the reigns of Pere II, Alfons II, and Jaume II, must be briefly studied before one attempts to discuss the possible general causes for that expansion, from 1229 to 1327.

ECONOMIC EXPANSION (1282–1327): SICILY

The conquest of Sicily in 1282 by Pere II gave Catalan merchants a favoured position in Sicilian ports. The main Catalan export to Sicily and southern Italy was cloth. The victory of Pere and his successors over the Angevins meant that the growing Catalan textile industry competed with Tuscany as the supplier of cloth for Sicily. The Catalans also secured control of Sicilian grain and wool. 'Sicily became the granary of Catalonia.'[2]

SARDINIA

As a result of the War of the Sicilian Vespers Catalan merchants had been installed in a privileged position in the central Mediterranean. In the 1320s Jaume II acquired Sardinia. Sardinia, like Sicily, produced substantial exports of grain, which were needed by Catalonia. It produced salt, which was exported up the Rhône valley and to Naples. The salt mines of Sardinia were immediately taken over by the Crown. Silver was produced in the mines of Iglesias, another Crown monopoly from the 1320s.

[1] Arribas, pp. 430 f.

[2] C. Trasselli, *I privilegi di Messina e di Trapani (1160–1355)* (Palermo, 1949), pp. 41–3, 54 f.; Capmany, i. 285–88, ii. 86 ff.

But the attempt to impose feudal as well as mercantile control over the island proved fatal.[1]

SICILY AND SARDINIA

The main difference between Sicily and Sardinia appears in the fact that no member of the ruling House of Barcelona ever visited Sardinia except on a punitive expedition. Sardinia, for the Crown of Aragon, was never more than a colony, and the Sards were treated, from the beginning, as the conquered by their conquerors. Sicily became a completely independent kingdom. Its rulers recognized that the king of Aragon was the head of the dynasty to which they belonged but they pursued their own policy.[2]

SPHERES OF INFLUENCE: NORTH AFRICA: TUNISIA

The conquest of Sicily placed Catalans less than 100 miles from Tunisia, that of Sardinia only 125 miles from eastern Algeria. The Crown of Aragon continued to concentrate its attention, as under Jaume I, on Tunisia. After 1295 it seems that Tunisia profited from the enmities between Naples, Sicily, and Aragon to avoid paying any tribute at all. There was no attempt to penetrate politically into North Africa west of Tunis. Relations with Tlemcen continued to be close, however, Catalan naval superiority was acknowledged in North Africa and could be exploited.[3]

Although the Crown of Aragon could use its galleys to levy tribute from North Africa it did not deepen its hold in the first quarter of the fourteenth century. Like Tlemcen, Tunisia now took a more independent line. It was possible to play off the Italian republics, Majorca and Sicily, against Aragon. The direct profits derived by the monarchy itself from consulates in North Africa and from the Catalan militias there were less than they had been in the thirteenth century.[4]

The trade balance continued to be favourable to the Crown of Aragon and to Majorca. The main articles of trade acquired

[1] Salavert, i. 132; A. Boscolo, *VI CHCA*, pp. 73–84. M. M. Costa, ibid., pp. 601–11; C. Manca, *Aspetti dell 'espansione economica catalano-aragonese nel mediterraneo occidentale* (Milan, 1966), pp. 22–9.

[2] La Mantia, i. 460; Trasselli, pp. 44 f.; Giunta, op. cit., ii. 161 ff.

[3] Dufourcq, pp. 238–310.

[4] ibid., pp. 450–510, 556–64.

in North Africa were much the same as in 1250. The value of trade with Tunisia was probably greater than that of trade with Tlemcen. In a good year, it has been estimated, the value of exports from Catalonia and Majorca to North Africa was 400,000–500,000 dinars, a very considerable increase from the reign of Jaume I.[1]

THE EASTERN MEDITERRANEAN

Diplomatic relations between Egypt and the Crown of Aragon only became important after the Sicilian Vespers. Confronted with France and the papacy the Crown of Aragon needed allies, even if they were infidels. After Jaume II made peace with the papacy at Anagni in 1295 his relations with Egypt were to be less close. However, he and his son, Alfons III, exchanged more than ten embassies with the sultans. Jaume sought to establish a protectorate over Eastern Christians and the Holy Places of Palestine. His embassies achieved some results because Egypt was dependent on trade with the West, which seems to have been carried on by relatively few rich merchants in Barcelona and to have proved principally profitable to them and the Crown.[2]

Although Jaume II underwent moments of enthusiasm in which he seemed about to intervene in the East, through Cyprus or in alliance with the Mongols—those implausible allies against Islam who fascinated Latin Christendom in the thirteenth century—the king's Eastern policy was one of non-involvement. He steadily refused to be drawn into papal crusades in the East. Jaume's general policy is illustrated by his dealings with the Catalan Company.

THE CATALAN COMPANY

Muntaner, one of its leaders, gave great space to the Company in his *Crónica*. He treated it as part of the history of the Crown of Aragon. This, together with the unique character of the Company's adventures and the brilliance with which Muntaner recounted them, has misled later historians into seeing the Company's career as more important than it was, and as an

[1] ibid., pp. 543–56.

[2] A. S. Atiya, *Egypt and Aragon* (Leipzig, 1938); A. Masía de Ros, *La Corona de Aragón y los estados del norte de Africa* (Barcelona, 1951).

integral part of the reign of Jaume II, though it had no direct connection with him. Until 1312, when it came under the nominal authority of Frederic of Sicily, the Company retained complete independence. It had no juridical link with the Crown of Aragon until 1379. After the recognition of the authority of Frederic III the Company continued to exist as a largely independent entity, ruling Athens and Thebes until the 1380s. Its links with Catalonia and its role in promoting Catalan and Sicilian trade with the East seem to have been slight.[1]

This survey of the political and economic expansion of the Crown of Aragon from 1229 to 1327 may conclude with a discussion of the general causes which may have helped to bring this expansion about.

All Catalonia was behind the conquest of Majorca in 1229, the nobility and the Church as much as the cities. The Sicilian expedition of 1282 was directed by Pere II; only he decided that it would go first to Tunisia and then to Sicily. The Sardinian expedition was also long in preparation and its direction was due to Jaume II. He was doubtless aware of the island's economic resources but certainly as interested in its strategic possibilities.

In the thirteenth and fourteenth centuries the Crown of Aragon's conquests in the Mediterranean were confined to islands, the Balearics (conquered in 1229, reconquered from its independent dynasty in 1285–98, and, finally, in 1343), Sicily, with the adjacent islands of the central Mediterranean (1282–6), and Sardinia (1323–6). Corsica, also, was claimed. All these islands lay in the western or central Mediterranean. Did the Crown of Aragon attempt or plan conquests farther afield?

It has been stated that Pere II envisaged the conquest of Tunisia in 1282 and might have planned to create a New Catalonia there. There seems to be no proof of this. Pere did not even aim at direct rule over the islands of the central Mediterranean.

It has also been argued that the Crown of Aragon was focused essentially on the eastern Mediterranean, both because of the draw of the crusade and because of the markets of Alexandria and Constantinople. It is impossible to agree that 'the Mediterranean enterprise was a religious ideal' of the

[1] Muntaner, 193–244.

monarchy, as a whole. Nor does it seem demonstrable that the Crown of Aragon 'established itself on the spice route' to Egypt, or that the spice trade provided 'the fundamental structure of the great trade of Barcelona and the basis of the Mediterranean Imperialism of its kings'.[1]

ESSENTIAL AREAS

If one looks at the Mediterranean policy of the rulers of Catalonia–Aragon it is clear that it was not consistent. It suffered a major change in 1295. Before this date Jaume II was concerned to keep Sicily, after this date to gain Sardinia. But, in either case, he was concerned essentially with the western Mediterranean, from Tunis to Spain.[2] He had no need and evinced no real desire to intervene politically outside this area. But he did need to control the western Mediterranean in order to protect trade with North Africa and Sicily, and, to a lesser extent, with the East.

WHO DIRECTED THE EXPANSION?

How was the policy of the Crown of Aragon formed? Who directed it? The intimate association of the rulers of Barcelona with their capital city and its leading class was grasped by contemporaries. It appears in all the great Catalan Chronicles. This close association with their subjects made it natural for the kings of Aragon to further their interests. The Crown itself engaged in trade. The municipal government of Barcelona kept in close touch with political developments. In 1302, for instance, it sought to use the good relations obtaining between Jaume II and Morocco to buy up wheat and barley, not only for Barcelona itself but for the whole Crown of Aragon, no doubt hoping to make a large profit. Bribes were offered to the royal officials concerned. But Barcelona did not in fact control Jaume II's policy. No royal embassy was sent to Morocco to further the wishes of Barcelona.[3] The Catalan–Aragonese federation should not be equated with Barcelona or described as a state-city. Catalonia–Aragon was more than Barcelona and its policy was formed by its count-kings not by the city bourgeoisie.

[1] J. Vicens Vives, *VI CHCA*, pp. 105 f. See Manca, *Aspetti*, pp. 8–13.
[2] I agree with Giunta, ii. 7 f.; see also Manca, p. 13.
[3] Dufourcq, pp. 358–60.

Dynastic right and religious feeling were perhaps more important to its rulers than economic interests.

A CATALAN 'EMPIRE'?

Can one speak of a Catalan 'empire' or of Catalan 'imperialism' in the thirteenth and fourteenth centuries? It seems unwise to use the nineteenth-century term 'imperialism' to describe a very different age. The idea of a Catalan 'empire' seems even more misleading. Such an empire could only have taken real form if the Crown of Aragon had really controlled the kingdoms ruled by junior branches of the House of Barcelona, Majorca, and Sicily. In fact, in 1327, after a century of struggle, the Crown of Aragon only controlled directly one island in the Mediterranean, Sardinia, and its hold there was soon to be revealed as feeble. The Crown, by itself, was too weak financially and too limited in its military and naval resources to be able to defeat, except in exceptional circumstances, France or Castile by land or Genoa or Venice by sea. This fact was to become clear in the reign of Pere III (1336–87).[1] The basis for any real Catalan 'empire' must be considered fragile when no major challenge could be overcome except by luck.

If one cannot affirm the existence of Catalan imperialism or of a Catalan empire one cannot deny great advances in Catalan trade. These advances accompanied and were assisted by limited and mainly temporary territorial acquisitions, though territorial expansion was not principally dictated by economic motives. Catalan trade, especially with North Africa, Italy, and the eastern Mediterranean, increased very greatly in the thirteenth century. Catalan competition in North Africa helped to turn Genoa and Marseille towards the East. However, these Mediterranean advances probably meant losses, or a failure to advance, in other directions, especially in Seville, Málaga, and the whole south of Spain, and along the Atlantic trade-routes.[2]

ADVANCES IN COMMERCIAL METHODS: BANKING

Considerable advances in commercial methods are visible at Barcelona in the thirteenth and early fourteenth centuries. In

[1] See below, Part III, Chs. II and III.

[2] This is noted by M. Del Treppo, in *Nuove questioni di storia medioevale* (Milan, 1964), p. 264.

the thirteenth century the terminology of early capitalism was no less precise than in Italy or Provence and commercial partnerships were no more limited in their scope. Catalans may have been somewhat less willing than Italians to risk lending money to develop trade but we know of groups of capitalists entrusting goods to a merchant in return for a share, half or three-quarters of the profits he might make. It is perhaps less important that before 1300 there is no evidence of banks in Barcelona, only of money-changers. The great Tuscan bankers of the age were possibly not interested in establishing agencies in Barcelona. In 1268 they were forbidden to do so by Jaume I; this exclusion continued, because of the Tuscan support of the Angevins of Naples during the war over Sicily.[1] Rich Jews and Christians and the Order of the Temple provided loans when the Crown needed them. In 1300–1 the Catalan Corts established the first general regulations on banking in Barcelona. Money-changers were required to provide considerable sureties if they took deposits. In 1302–4 the published royal accounts mention seven of these money-changers, two each in Lérida, Valencia, and Barcelona, and one in Tortosa. Other private bankers from Barcelona appear in the city records from 1302 onwards.[2]

In 1231 the citizens of Barcelona were relieved of all customs dues when trading with the Balearics; in 1232 they were given this freedom in all the realms of the Crown of Aragon. The ships of Marseille, and no doubt also of Genoa, were still important in linking Barcelona to the new conquests of Valencia and Majorca but in 1243 Jaume I stated that the city 'grows every day because of the frequent arrival of ships'. It had become necessary to define the area around the port within which no buildings could be allowed.[3]

THE CONSULATE OF THE SEA

In 1258 Jaume I granted permission to the 'good men' of Barcelona to elect each year one of their number to conduct the

[1] A.-E. Sayous, *EUC* 16 (1931), 155–98; A. Altisent, *BRABL* 32 (1967–8), 45–65; Capmany, ii. 38; A. García Sanz (*et al.*), *Comandas comerciales barcelonesas* (Barcelona, 1973), pp. 63–73.

[2] A. P. Usher, *The Early History of Deposit Banking in Mediterranean Europe*, i (Cambridge, Mass., 1943), 239 f., 256 f.; E. González Hurtebise, *Libros de tesorería de la casa real de Aragón*, i (Barcelona, 1911). For Valencia, A. García Sanz, *BSCC* 33 (1957), 201–5.

[3] Capmany, ii. 14–16, 19 f.

defence and improvement of its port. They could also establish the necessary Ordinances. Jurisdiction over the port was separated from that of the ordinary royal officials. The same year regulations for the port of Barcelona were duly drawn up and approved by the king. They ordained that every ship should carry a scribe, who would keep its log. They also regulated closely how cargoes should be stowed on board and the arms that must be carried for self-defence.[1]

A document of 1257 records the beginnings, in Barcelona, of the institution of the 'Consulate of the Sea' (*Consolat del Mar*). The regulations of 1258 are at the origin of a long process of codification of maritime law which was to produce the *Libre del Consolat del Mar*. The Consulate, as a guild court designed to expedite maritime cases, is first found in Pisa and Genoa about 1200. It was adopted from there in southern France and the Crown of Aragon. When Pere III established the Consulate of Valencia in 1283–4 he referred to the Barcelona Consulate as an already existing model for the new institution. In both places two consuls were elected each year by the local seamen, with jurisdiction over seamen and merchants and the right to decide maritime cases. Appeals from the consuls' decisions were heard by a special judge, who was also elected by the seamen of the port in question.[2] Similar Consulates were introduced in Majorca in 1326, and in Tortosa, Gerona, and Perpignan in the second half of the fourteenth century. They were also introduced, probably on the Catalan model, into Sicily, at Messina and Trapani. Eventually the consuls decided almost every commercial case disputed at law. They came to be elected primarily from guilds of merchants instead of seamen. In Barcelona, by 1436, they were chosen by members of the *Consell de Cent*. One consul had to be an 'honoured citizen', the other, and the judge, merchants.[3]

CATALAN CONSULATES ABROAD

In 1266 the municipal Council of Barcelona was given power by

[1] *CDIACA* viii. 119 f.; Capmany, ii. 25–30.

[2] R. S. Smith, *The Spanish Guild Merchant* (Durham, N.C., 1940). A. García Sanz, *BSCC* 35 (1959), 180–9; see Capmany, ii. 44.

[3] García Sanz, *VIII CHCA* ii. 1, p. 268, n. 18; Trasselli, *I privilegi*, p. 108; L. Genuardi, *Il libro dei capitoli della corte del Consolato di mare di Messina* (Palermo, 1924); C. Carrère, *Barcelone, centre économique à l'époque des difficultés, 1380–1462* (Paris, 1967), i. 38–47.

Jaume I to name consuls in Syria and Egypt. In 1268 this privilege was made general, although Jaume I kept the lucrative consulates of North Africa in his own hands. During the following reigns the city of Barcelona sought to protect the interests of its merchants, either directly or through its ruler. It acquired privileges in southern France, Valencia, Seville, Sicily, Sardinia, Naples, Tunis, Tlemcen, Morocco, Constantinople, Cyprus, and Egypt.[1]

SHIPS AND THEIR OWNERS

The new names of ships which appear in Catalan documents suggest progress in developing shipping which could compete with Barcelona's Italian rivals, perhaps particularly in the Atlantic trade. The name 'coca' appears in the records by 1310 but its relation to the *coca* of the Bay of Biscay or to the Hanseatic *kogge* is not clear. We also have 'uxer', a large galley used for transport and by a Majorcan explorer of the West coast of Africa in 1346. (In 1278 a merchant from Barcelona had reached Safi on the Atlantic coast of Morocco, thirteen years before a recorded Genoese voyage there.) The tonnage of Catalan ships had reached several hundred tons, a figure comparable to other Mediterranean fleets. Direct sailings all round the year to North Africa were now common, thanks largely to the use of the compass by Catalans and Majorcans, which had become current by 1300.

In general a ship was owned by a group of co-proprietors who could be far from rich as individuals. The crew often owned part of the cargo. By 1300 more stable 'firms' were developing, some of them with agents resident in North Africa. In 1307 five 'firms' in Barcelona each had an agent in Arzila, on the Atlantic Moroccan coast.[2]

JEWS AND MUSLIMS

Jews played a limited role in developing both internal and external Catalan trade. In 1302-4 we find Jews from Catalonia in Alexandria but they only formed a small proportion of the

[1] Capmany, ii. 35 f., 39-180.

[2] Dufourcq, pp. 40-62. See *Die Bremser Hanse-Kogge, ein Schlüssel zur Schiffahrtsgeschichte* (Bremen, 1969).

merchants engaged in the Alexandrian trade. They were more important in maintaining trade with North Africa, where leading Jews were employed as diplomatic agents. The Jewish community in Majorca had particularly close ties with Morocco and Tlemcen. Jewish merchants from Majorca appear at Murcia in 1273–4 and off Tunis in 1289.[1]

In the Crown of Aragon and Majorca it was possible for Muslims, as well as Jews, to form partnerships with Christians. At times they received royal protection despite a state of war between Aragon and their own country. In 1294 Jaume II of Aragon declared that 'it is no slight loss to Our Court if Muslim and Jewish merchants, who were and are *accustomed* to sail, under Our surety, from Barbary to Majorca, should cease to do so . . . Our Court would lose over 20,000 ss. a year' in the fees paid by Muslims for such sureties.[2] Restored in 1298 to its independent dynasty, Majorca continued to be a centre for Jewish and Muslim trade.

'LIBRE DEL CONSOLAT DEL MAR'

The *Libre del Consolat del Mar* is evidence of the great advances in Catalan trade in the thirteenth century. The probable date of the first redaction of the *Costums*, which form the nucleus of this work, goes back at least to 1231. Its place of origin is certainly Barcelona. The *Costums* was a private, anonymous, eminently practical work, produced by the expert merchants and seamen of Barcelona, the 'skilful men who go through the world' of the introductory paragraph. To the *Costums* were added fourteenth-century Ordinances from Valencia. The text we have of the *Libre* reveals many later additions, completed before 1385, the date of the earliest existing manuscript. The work represents 'the first attempt at a systematic regulation of maritime law'. The work stipulates maritime contracts and trade, the rights and obligations of merchants, seamen, and passengers, from the first construction of a ship onwards. Catalan maritime law, as it evolved in the thirteenth century,

[1] González Hurtebise, pp. 8, 98, 215; Masía de Ros, *La Corona de Aragón*, pp. 353–74; Baer, *History* i. 427 (n. 23); *Die Juden* i. 146 f.; Villanueva, xxii. 327 f. Dufourcq, pp. 142 f.

[2] A. Giménez Soler, *BRABL* 5 (1909–10), 191, n. 1, 297; E. de K. Aguiló, *BSAL* 4 (1891–2), 224 f.; F. Giunta, *Uomini e cose del medioevo mediterraneo* (Palermo, 1965), pp. 162 f.

in Barcelona, Valencia, and Tortosa, and is codified in the *Libre del Consolat*, made it possible for a man who never went to sea to invest in a ship, as he might invest in a piece of land, with the clear knowledge that his responsibility, in the event of disaster, was limited to what he owned of the ship. It is this principle that largely explains the success of Catalan law throughout the Mediterranean. The clarity and equity of the *Libre* are also notable, for instance its stipulation that the obligation to pay the ship's sailors comes before all other obligations. The *Libre* became 'the Bible of maritime law'.[1] There were many printed editions from the 1480s onwards and it was translated into Italian, Castilian, French, Dutch, and German.

INSTITUTIONAL DEVELOPMENT

The thirteenth century is the crucial period in the development of the main institutions of the Crown of Aragon. In the early thirteenth century the Cortes (Corts in Catalonia and Valencia), the royal chancery, the municipal institutions of Catalonia were in a more or less fluid state. By the death of Jaume II in 1327 they had achieved the form that was to continue, with only slight changes, until the sixteenth or, in many cases, the eighteenth century.

LEGAL COMPILATIONS

Although the Roman and canon laws did not formally become the law of any of the realms of the Crown of Aragon they deeply affected not only the plan but many details of the *Fueros de Aragón*, drawn up by Vidal de Canellas, and promulgated in 1247. Roman and canon law were also among the main sources of the *Costum* (later called *Fuero* or *Furs*) of Valencia, a collection of statutes granted by Jaume I from 1240 to 1271 to the 'royal towns' of Valencia, and later extended, despite Aragonese opposition, to most of the kingdom.[2]

[1] *Libro del Consulado del Mar*, ed. A. de Capmany, new edn. (Barcelona, 1965), p. 73; A. García Sanz, *BSCC* 36 (1960), 47–74. The last quotation from L. Perels, *Revista jurídica de Cataluña*, 23 (1917), 71.

[2] See Bibliography to Part I, Ch. II; S. Cebrían Ibor, *III CHCA* i. 605–65; H. García, *BSCC* 23 (1947), 428–50; 24 (1948), 5–14; A. García Sanz, ibid. 41 (1965), 1–26; idem, in *Ligarzas*, 1 (Valencia, 1968), 207–21; M. Gual, *EEMCA* 3 (1948), 262–89.

Catalonia and Majorca did not possess general legal codes to compare to those of Aragon and Valencia. The Catalan *Usatges* had reached their original form about 1150. They dealt with feudal relationships and with some norms of private law. In the twelfth century they were supplemented by *Cartas de población*, granted originally to Tortosa and Lérida and later applied to Majorca, and by Ordinances enforcing peace and forbidding (for set periods) private war. All these were issued by the counts of Barcelona. An expanded version of the *Usatges* was declared the fundamental law of Catalonia in 1243 and 1251 and was translated from Latin into Catalan. It still needed supplementing by the local codifications of the main Catalan towns, by compilations of feudal law, and by maritime law, which has already been discussed. These supplementary compilations, for instance the *Consuetudines* of Lérida (1228), the *Costums* of Tortosa (1272), or the *Commemoracions* of Pere Albert, which deal with feudal law, are deeply influenced by Roman and canon laws. In Majorca Roman law played a greater part than did the *Usatges* in the *Ordinances* issued by the local government, the Jurats, with royal approval.[1]

ARAGONESE RESISTANCE

The monarchy naturally favoured the increasing systematization of law, under the influence of the centralizing Roman and canon laws. This systematization met with a bitter reaction from the nobility of Aragon. In 1265, at the Cortes of Ejea, the Aragonese claimed that Jaume I had 'infringed the *Fueros* of Aragon in that [he] had with him a number of clerks learned in civil and canon laws, and gave judgement according to them'. Jaume's explanation, that 'neither I nor any layman could know all the law writings there are in the world . . . especially on account of my different states not being under one *Fuero* or one custom' had little effect. The Aragonese waited until the monarchy was in serious trouble. In 1283–5 they used Pere II's critical situation to wring considerable concessions from him.[2]

[1] J. Mª. Font Rius, *VII CHCA* i. 289–326; E. de Hinojosa, *Obras*, ii (Madrid, 1955), 389–404; L. París i Bou, in *Miscel. lània històrica catalana* (Poblet, 1970), pp. 155–9.

[2] Jaume I, *Libre dels feyts*, 395 f. See above, p. 255, n. 2.

THE CORTES

Pere II's war with France brought the Aragonese Cortes into prominence as an instrument of resistance to royal authority. It also produced a great rise in the importance of the Corts of Catalonia and Valencia. In Aragon and Catalonia, as in other countries, the Cortes had begun as an expanded meeting of the royal court. Its functions, not clearly defined, had been principally consultative and occasionally judicial. The ruler had normally legislated, though the Cortes might be asked to consent to a new law.

During the reign of Jaume I the Aragonese Cortes became separated from the Catalan Corts, though the two bodies could meet together at Lérida or Monzón, on the frontier between the two countries. Jaume I had a low opinion of parliamentary assemblies and only summoned them when he needed grants of money and support for some exceptional venture. Pere II was even less favourably disposed towards the Cortes and did not call them until he was forced to do so.[1]

In 1283, immediately after his defeat by the Aragonese, Pere summoned Corts, first at Valencia, then at Barcelona. On both occasions he made important concessions to secure the support of the nobles, clergy, and bourgeois. In Valencia these concessions affected the municipal organization of the city, the organization of banks, guilds, and of the Consolat del Mar, which was now established there. In Barcelona Pere restricted a tax on cattle to certain areas, abolished taxes on salt and all taxes on nobles and clergy, and granted an important statute affecting the municipal government of Barcelona. In both countries he promised to call the Corts regularly (in Catalonia every year, in Valencia every three years). He acknowledged that any new general statute or special tax needed the Corts' sanction.[2]

In 1283 the basis was laid for the considerable later intervention of the Cortes of Aragon, Valencia, and Catalonia in the life of the Crown of Aragon. By 1300 the composition of these

[1] E. S. Procter, *EUC* 22 (1936), 525–46; *Libre dels feyts*, 382; Soldevila, *Els grans reis*, pp. 134 f.

[2] *Cortes de Cataluña*, i. 140–53; Zurita, iv. 40; Procter, pp. 536, 544–6; A. García Sanz, *BSCC* 35 (1959), 181–4; Soldevila, pp. 136–45; J. M. Font Rius, *Orígenes del Regimen municipal de Cataluña* (Madrid, 1946), pp. 388 ff.

three bodies was virtually defined, as it was to remain. In Catalonia and Valencia there were three branches (or estates) in the Corts, which deliberated separately, the nobility, clergy, and the representatives of the towns which were under royal (not seignorial) authority. Representatives of some Catalan towns had taken part in various Corts from 1214 onwards. Their presence had not been considered essential and the number of towns represented varied widely. It only gradually became fixed at eighteen in Catalonia, thirteen in Valencia. Barcelona and Valencia each sent five deputies to their separate Corts, the other towns one or two each. It was established which nobles and prelates should be summoned.[1] In Aragon the Cortes were dominated throughout the thirteenth century by the first 'estate', the *ricos ombres*, representatives of the thirty-nine families of upper nobility. The second estate, the middle nobility and the representatives of five small towns, normally followed the lead of the first. The clergy did not appear as an estate until 1301; the fourth estate, the representatives of the larger towns, had appeared in 1283 (with twenty-one towns represented) but they enjoyed far less importance than in Catalonia or Valencia. But, whatever the social balance or imbalance of the three Cortes might be, the monarchy had henceforth to reckon with them as permanent institutions, called to consider 'the good state and reformation of the land', empowered to hear complaints against royal authority, and necessary collaborators, without whose agreement legislation was impossible.[2]

Compared with the events of 1283 the changes that took place in the organization of the Cortes during the reigns of Pere II's successors were slight. In 1300 Jaume II sold the right to impose a general tax, the *bovatge*, in Catalonia. He was now more dependent than ever on the Corts. In 1301 meetings of the Catalan Corts became triennial, and in 1307 those of the Aragonese Cortes biennial, rather than annual. In 1289 a delegation of the Corts appears, collecting the taxes they had voted (royal officials were not allowed to take part in this collection). In Catalonia and Valencia this delegation was to become the

[1] Soldevila, *Els primers temps de Jaume I*, pp. 79 f.; Cebrián Ibor, pp. 646–51.

[2] L. F. Arregui Lucea, *Argensola*, 4 (1953), 1–36; *Constitucions de Catalunya*, I. xiv. 1, cited by Soldevila, *Els grans reis*, p. 136.

Diputació del General. A similar *Diputación del Reyno* emerged in Aragon during the reign of Pere III.[1]

MUNICIPAL INSTITUTIONS

The reign of Jaume I saw the first clear appearance of typical Catalan municipal institutions, both in the main cities subject to the Crown and in the seignorial towns. As towns attained greater economic importance they became able to bargain with the Crown. One can see this happening in 1266 when Jaume I promised not to alter the value of the coinage in return for financial aid from Valencia.[2] A slow process of bargaining and experimentation is also visible in the development of town constitutions. This is particularly clear in the case of Barcelona. In 1226 Jaume I, 'given the loyalty of the people of Barcelona and considering the frequent complaints made to Us', ordered the election of representatives of the different classes of the city to collect taxes. This election of representatives to a limited and temporary office is found earlier in Catalan towns. In 1249 four *Paers* were named by Jaume for Barcelona; they could co-opt counsellors and, with them, elect their successors each year. Judicial and coercive powers over the inhabitants of Barcelona were still in the hands of the royal vicar (*veguer*).[3] In 1258 Jaume allowed the election of eight *prohoms*. They, with the vicar, were to choose 200 other counsellors; the latter chose the eight *prohoms* for the next year. The general assembly mentioned in 1249 has virtually been replaced by this group of 200, which included, in 1258, 114 merchants and artisans and a sprinkling of doctors of law and medicine. In 1260 the number of *prohoms* was reduced to six, in 1265 to four, and the counsellors to 100. The *Consell de Cent* of medieval Barcelona had appeared. In 1274 the number of *prohoms* was fixed at five. The royal vicar and bailiff could be present at the meetings by invitation only. Each year the next five *Consellers* were to be chosen by twelve electors, themselves chosen by the old *Consell de Cent*. The new five were to choose the new *Consell*. The statute of 1274 marks

[1] Martínez Ferrando, in *Els descendents de Pere*, pp. 139 f.; R. B. Merriman, *American Historical Review*, 16 (1911), 487–93; C. Salord Comella, *EEMCA* 6 (1956), 247 ff.

[2] Font Rius, p. 377; F. Mateu y Llopis, in *Studi in onore di A. Fanfani*, iii (Milan, 1962), 185–216; Huici, *Colección* ii. 303–6.

[3] Huici, i. 101; Font Rius, pp. 478–81; Capmany, ii. 20.

the triumph of municipal over royal officials in Barcelona, though the virtual disappearance of the general assembly and the system of elections also ensured the dominance of a small number of rich families. The system was only to be modified in detail. The popular revolt in Barcelona in 1285 was probably a reaction against the establishment of oligarchical government there. Similarly, Lérida received definite confirmation of its *Paers* in 1264, Valencia and Majorca of its *Jurats* in 1266 and 1273, respectively. In Valencia, as in Barcelona, the *Consell* was chosen by the *Jurats*.[1]

In 1283–4, the Corts of Barcelona passed a decree which recognized that a special urban regime existed in the royal cities and towns which differentiated them from the rest of the country. The municipal institution had received a general legislative sanction. During this session of the Corts Pere II also confirmed a series of economic privileges of Barcelona and established further limitations on the city's royal vicar and bailiff. In 1284 he granted privileges to Gerona and Montblanch.[2]

Under Jaume II the municipalities continued to rise, and privileges extended to other towns the type of government enjoyed by Barcelona. The jurisdiction of Barcelona was extended up to the neighbouring mountains which enclose the plains of the rivers Besòs and Llobregat. Variations on a proportional representation of social classes became general in Catalan towns, but the richer classes in fact ruled.

Town development in the Crown of Aragon did not have the same results as in Italy. The social character of Barcelona or Valencia might resemble contemporary Genoa or Venice, but juridically even Barcelona never became an independent city state or republic, free of royal control, able to determine its international policy. Even its internal affairs were constantly subject to royal intervention. It is a 'piece or organ of the administration of the state', though a vital piece, without which it is hard to imagine the Crown of Aragon in the fourteenth and

[1] Capmany, ii. 24 f., 34 f.; *CDIACA* viii. 137–9, 143–6; Huici, ii. 301, 307 f., 360; Font Rius, pp. 383–6; Soldevila, *Els grans reis*, pp. 60–7. On the revolt of 1285 see P. Wolff, *VII CHCA* ii. 587–92; idem, *AEM* 5 (1968), 207–22; C. Batlle, *EHMed* 2 (1970), 21–9.

[2] Font Rius, pp. 388–91; Soldevila, pp. 145–8.

fifteenth centuries. Through the Corts, in particular, and administrative agencies developed by the Corts, Barcelona and the other cities took a central part in the formation and execution of policy for the whole confederation.[1]

ROYAL INSTITUTIONS

During the reign of Jaume I the monarchy attempted to develop new administrative instruments with which to handle its growing territory and the new problems with which it was confronted. The office of *Procurador*, either as the king's representative in one of the separate kingdoms or as *Procurador general*, appears during Jaume's minority. The *Procurador general* became an office associated almost automatically with the heir to the throne.

In the central administration of all the Crown's territories the Chancellor appeared as perhaps the most important royal official. Registers of royal letters began to be kept. The Chancellor not only directed this royal correspondence but presided over the central court—this charge was handed over to the Vice-Chancellor in the fourteenth century—and the royal Council, membership of which was not yet closely defined but was largely left to the king to determine on an *ad hoc* basis. The Chancellor had to approve all appointments of judges and notaries for the whole Crown of Aragon. He was normally a bishop, or at least a cleric.[2]

The Chancellor's financial equivalent in the central administration, the Maestre Racional, probably appeared under Pere II and became more important than the Treasurer. Under these central officials (normally travelling with the constantly moving monarch) there multiplied local royal officials. Separate general bailiffs administered the royal patrimony in Catalonia, Aragon, and Valencia. The royal household had a chamberlain and separate majordomos for the three countries. In Catalonia the royal vicar had administrative, military, and judicial responsibility for his district, the bailiff financial (he was paid from the revenue of his bailiwick). In Aragon the *merino* acted as judge, the *zalmedina* as administrator. In Aragon there was also

[1] F. Carreras y Candi, *La ciutat de Barcelona* (Barcelona, n.d.), pp. 331–8; Font Rius, pp. 462–7.

[2] Swift, *Life and Times of James the First*, pp. 149–234; Soldevila, pp. 47–71; F. Sevillano Colom, in *Martínez Ferrando, archivero* (Barcelona, 1968), pp. 451–80.

the Justicia. Beginning as a local official he only attained importance after the crisis of 1283. In Catalonia the Corts acted instead of the Justicia as a mediating power between king and people.

The Justicia of Valencia is not to be confused with his more important namesake of Aragon. His functions were similar to those of the Catalan vicar and Aragonese *zalmedina*. His competence was restricted to the city of Valencia and he soon came to be appointed by the city authorities.[1]

Pere II tried to improve the efficiency of his administration. He issued the first known Ordinances of the royal household. They specify the duties of his servants from the majordomo down to the mule-drivers. Complaints raised by the Catalan Corts of 1283–4 against royal officials show that many of these men, like their counterparts in other western-European countries, were trying to evade baronial and ecclesiastical jurisdiction.[2]

Alfons II and Jaume II issued further regulations for the royal household. Under Jaume the office of Vice-Chancellor appears. Other offices, such as Protonotary, were probably created by Jaume II. Pere II and his sons also made attempts to control local officials through periodic inquiries, known as the 'Purga de Taula'. From 1311 this inquiry was to be triennial and was carried out by three judges, one lawyer, and one knight or citizen.[3]

In 1319 Jaume II issued a 'Privilege of Union', by which 'whoever may be king of Aragon shall also be king of Valencia and count of Barcelona'. This was to bar further attempts, like those of Jaume I, to divide the Crown of Aragon, and it was successful. When Pere III reconquered Majorca in 1343 he included that kingdom in Jaume II's Privilege.[4]

Jaume also attempted to unify his disparate realms by using a small group of privileged servants, *familiares*, men directly

[1] Soldevila, *Historia de España*, ii (Barcelona, 1962), 82 ff.; F. Udina, *RABM* 65 (1958), 50; J. Lalinde Abadía, *AEM* 4 (1967), 169–299; F. A. Roca Traver, *El Justicia de Valencia, 1238–1321* (Valencia, 1970).

[2] *CDIACA* vi. 5–14. Soldevila, *Els grans reis*, pp. 133 f., 141 f.

[3] F. Carreras y Candi, *BRABL* 5 (1909–10), 105–8; Martínez Ferrando, in *Els descendents*, pp. 135–9; Lalinde Abadía, *HV* i. 499–523.

[4] P. E. Schramm, *Historisches Jahrbuch*, 74 (1955), 99–123. See Part III, Ch. II below.

attached to the ruler. Non-noble *familiares* were permitted to bear arms and, if Jews, not to wear Jewish dress. Only a few members of the royal Council were *familiares*. The latter included the doctor and mystic Arnau de Vilanova, archdeacons who represented Jaume at the papal court, some officials and diplomats. The queen and the heir to the throne also had their own *familiares*. They were generally well rewarded and included a few foreigners, such as papal courtiers, and, for Alfons III apparently, one Muslim official at Granada.[1]

THE UNIVERSITY OF LÉRIDA

Jaume II's foundation of the first university to exist in the Crown of Aragon took place in 1300, at Lérida. The new university was to have the same freedom and privileges as were enjoyed by the University of Toulouse. The foundation was certainly part of Jaume's attempts to unify his realms. In 1302 Jaume decreed that no student should be allowed to leave the kingdom to study, since at Lérida he could now pursue not only the liberal arts but also civil and canon law and medicine. The university at Lérida had difficulty in overcoming the opposition of the city. Jaume was continually concerned with it until his death. Its statutes are among the most impressive of the age in their precision and clarity. In 1313 Jaume gave the appointment of doctors and the supervision of the university to the municipal authorities of Lérida, removing it from the bishop and cathedral chapter, but this did not end the conflicts of town and gown. These conflicts did not prevent the university from continuing to flourish throughout the Middle Ages.[2]

JAUME II'S CULTURAL INTERESTS

In 1315 Jaume II asked for a copy of Livy which one of his ambassadors had seen in Naples, 'in which good and pleasant matters', he had heard, 'are treated'. It is uncertain if one should credit Jaume with great discrimination here. A year before he had written for the second time to ask for a compilation of legends about the crusading East, 'a book of the Histories

[1] J. Vincke, *AEM* I (1964), 333–51.

[2] Rubió, *Documents* i. 14–27, 32 f., 82–8; ii, pp. lix–lxvi; Villanueva, xvi. 26–49, 196–246; Finke, *Acta* ii. 921. More references in Soldevila, *Història de Catalunya*, p. 437, n. 123.

of the Conquest of Antioch, in which there are stories of King Godefroi . . . and of the count who had seven children with seven silver collars', almost certainly the *Gran conquista de ultramar*, recently translated into Castilian from French.[1]

As a young man Jaume II may have been interested in writing and reading verses in Provençal. He was to give one of his sons a copy of the romance of *Lancelot* in French. But there is little evidence that he promoted any new works in Catalan, to compare with his elder brother Alfons II's patronage of a translation of the Bible from French. Jaume's patronage of Ramon Lull and Arnau de Vilanova was largely due to the use they could be to him at the papal court. Arnau was of greater interest still to Jaume as a doctor. 'The true passion of [Jaume's] whole life was medicine.' He was constantly demanding the latest medical works. He greatly appreciated Avicenna as a medical authority and assisted his numerous doctors to acquire Avicenna's works. The translations from Arabic he encouraged and assisted were almost all of medical works. Jaume's practical nature also appears in his care to see that the correct text of an *Usatge* was substituted for a corrupt version. In moral teaching he favoured compilations of short and pithy ethical maxims, whether by the Jewish doctor Judah Bonsenyor of Barcelona or by Ramon Lull.[2]

ROYAL ART

The reigns of Jaume I, Pere II, and Jaume II saw the rise of some of the most striking monuments of Catalan Gothic. It does not seem that the great Catalan cathedrals of this century owe much to royal patronage. This does appear in the royal tombs of Jaume I at Poblet and of Pere II and Jaume II at Santes Creus. Jaume II's directions to the artists of Pere's tomb show that masons were brought from Sicily to work on it. For the tomb of his first queen, Blanche, Jaume attempted to get porphyry from Attica. An English sculptor also worked on these tombs.[3]

[1] Rubió, i. 64; Martínez Ferrando, *Jaime II*, ii. 88, 111; *Castigos e documentos del rey Don Sancho*, ed. A. Rey (Bloomington, Ind., 1952), p. 20, n. 26.

[2] Rubió, i. 6 ff., 10, 41; ii. 4 f., 33, xxxi, 9, 13–15, 20; Riquer, i. 170–3; Martínez Ferrando, *Jaime II*, ii. 235; Baer, *History* ii. 6. On Bonsenyor see J. Cardoner Planas, *Sefarad*, 4 (1944), 287–93.

[3] Finke, *Acta* ii. 905–7; Rubió, ii. 6 f., 23 f.; Martínez Ferrando, ii. 41.

The House of Barcelona not only protected writers and artists (and here Jaume II's grandson, Pere III, and Pere's sons far surpassed him) but also included troubadours, historians, and orators. Pere II, Jaume II, and his brother Frederic of Sicily were poets, as were the last three kings of the Catalan dynasty. Jaume I, Pere III, and his son Martí were historians, Jaume II was the first notable orator of his dynasty. In his speech at Portfangós, addressed to his heir Alfons and to the expedition leaving for Sardinia in 1323, Jaume, who so often seems cold and calculating, attained eloquence. His evocation of 'the royal standard, of the Royal House of Aragon, which has never been conquered or overcome' was recorded by his grandson Pere III in his *Chronicle* and recalled by his great-grandson, Martí, in his speech of 1406 to the Corts of Perpignan.[1]

THE DYNASTY AND THE LANGUAGE

Jaume II's oratory at Portfangós, the royal tombs at Santes Creus, and the translation into Latin of his grandfather Jaume I's *Book of Deeds*, which he sponsored, were all designed to exalt the dynasty as the symbol and centre, the unifying force of the Crown of Aragon. In this Jaume II was in agreement with Jaume I, Desclot, and Muntaner. Jaume might not speak with the same joy as Muntaner of Catalan as a language, 'the finest Catalan in the world', but it was largely through Jaume that Catalan had become by 1300 one of the international languages of diplomacy as well as trade.[2] This success of Catalan as a language mirrors the political and economic achievements—all the more remarkable because of the handicaps which I have stressed—of the Crown of Aragon from 1229 to 1327.

[1] Rubió, ii, pp. x f.; Pere III, *Crònica*, i. 12, ed. Pagès, p. 22; *Parlaments a les corts catalanes*, ed. R. Albert and J. Gassiot (Barcelona, 1928), p. 71.

[2] Rubió, i. 6, 57 f., ii, p. lxxi; Muntaner, 18.

II

Castile and Granada: 1252–1325: The Crown and the Nobility

At the end of the thirteenth century the Franciscan Juan Gil de Zamora looked back with longing on the days when the enemies of all good Christians were clearly identifiable. 'O what blessed times were those, in which the cities and castles of the Saracens were laid waste by the sword of the faithful!' A modern historian sees things in much the same way. 'For the time being the king [Fernando III] was the central and predominant figure in the political life of [León and Castile].' He directed the 'Reconquest' and distributed its spoils.

What went wrong? Why was the heritage won by the sword of San Fernando dissipated by his successors? Why is it that the seventy odd years between the death of Fernando III in 1252 and the coming of age of Alfonso XI in 1325 form so checkered and confused a postscript to the vast expansion of Castile–León between 1212 and 1248, so striking a contrast to the great age of Catalan–Aragonese adventure in the Mediterranean? How is it that a contemporary can sum up Castile in the 1300s as follows: 'There are no other news from Castile except that the king and all the rest fight among themselves to destroy her . . . they do not know what justice is nor does it please them'?

For the history of Castile in the late thirteenth and early fourteenth centuries we do not possess contemporary chronicles or collections of royal documents to compare with those available for the Crown of Aragon. Nor has the Castilian history of this age received anything approaching the same attention as that of Catalonia. No reliable works of synthesis exist. This means that any discussion of Castile in this period must be difficult and its conclusions hesitant.[1]

[1] Juan Gil de Zamora, *Liber illustrium personarum*, ed. F. Fita, *BRAH* 5 (1884), 311; J. F. O'Callaghan, *American Historical Review*, 74 (1969), 1532; A. Giménez

Certain facts appear assured, however. The 'Reconquest' is virtually over. By 1300, in the economy of Castile, large estates and sheep-rearing are already of central importance. The country is rich but the Crown has great difficulty in transferring part of these riches into its treasury or in formulating any economic policies. Royal financial administration is heavily dependent on Jewish expertise. In the development of non-financial institutions the political principles, borrowed by Alfonso X from Roman law, are more impressive than the actual achievements of the Crown. The cities (*concejos*) are full of life. Their activity is displayed in *Hermandades* (Brotherhoods) —when the monarchy is weak—and in the increasingly frequent meetings of the Cortes. But the overwhelming fact of Castilian history in the age that follows the Reconquest is the dominance of the nobility. It is this that sharpens every internal political crisis, that negates the foreign policy of the monarchy in western Europe, that assures the survival of Granada.

CASTILIAN INTERNAL HISTORY: THE ECONOMY

With the Reconquest at an end the kings of Castile were faced with the colossal task of organizing, peopling, and policing the vast, newly acquired south. It has already been shown that they were obliged, for lack of settlers from the north to fill the gaps left by Muslim peasants expelled in the 1260s, to hand over very large areas to the Military Orders, to a few selected dioceses, and to leading nobles. This decision was to influence the history of Castile not only during the next two centuries but down to modern times.[1]

SHEEP

Castile was bound to be, for many centuries, an agrarian country. The particular importance there of sheep- and cattle-raising, however, not only as compared with industry but with agriculture, is linked with the form taken by the Reconquest in Andalusia and Extremadura.

In 1253 some of the main routes later to be followed by the

[1] See above, Part I, Ch. II, p. 22.

Soler, *Don Juan Manuel* (Saragossa, 1932), p. 67; see above, Ch. I, pp. 233–7, and the Bibliography below, to Chs. I and II.

flocks of the Mesta were already established. The three principal routes ran: from León south to Extremadura below Badajoz and Mérida; from Logroño on the border of Navarre, by way of Soria and Segovia, south to Talavera, Guadalupe, and Córdoba; and from Cuenca and the border with Aragon across La Mancha to the plains of Murcia. The main routes were defined as about 250 feet wide when marked off between cultivated areas. There were many lesser routes also. The sheep travelled south in October and returned northwards in April and May. The distances traversed ranged between 450 and 150 miles.[1]

In 1273 Alfonso X of Castile–Léon included 'all the shepherds of his realms' in one association, the 'Honourable Assembly [*concejo*] of the Mesta of the Shepherds'. The charter of 1273, which renewed and strengthened earlier (lost) royal grants, was designed to protect the stockmen from paying taxes to the towns on the routes they travelled. Taxes were paid, however, to the Crown and also to the Military Orders which owned the main southern pasture lands used by the flocks of sheep in the winter and who naturally opposed the unrestricted use of these lands by the northern flocks. Alfonso's aim was to secure a reliable tax on cattle and sheep; in return he granted the new organization control of sheep throughout his realms. The political and economic importance the Mesta acquired in later centuries was very considerable.[2] Its triumphs were not to be achieved without opposition from the towns, who resented the loss of their power to levy local taxes on sheep and cattle passing through their lands. The temporary success of the towns under Sancho IV and Fernando IV and their failure under Alfonso XI illustrates the political fortunes of the Castilian Crown. The towns' opposition to the Mesta was based on fiscal and judicial questions. The towns were not concerned to defend agriculture against sheep. Like the other powers of the day, the nobility, the Military Orders, they were themselves considerable sheep-owners. By 1300 the process by which the whole economy of Castile was to become

[1] J. Klein, *The Mesta, a Study in Spanish Economic History, 1273–1836* (Cambridge, Mass., 1920), pp. 18–20, 28 f., 171 f.

[2] ibid., pp. 176 ff.; the text of the Charter in *BRAH* 64 (1914), 205–17; C. J. Bishko, in *The New World Looks at its History*, ed. A. R. Lewis and T. F. McGann (Austin, Texas, 1963), pp. 61–4.

geared to sheep-raising and the export of wool was well under way.[1]

SHIPPING

Vigorous life was stirring in the ports of Castile both in the north and the south, but the development of Castilian overseas trade owed little to the assistance of the Crown.

BASQUE TRADE

In the north Basque trade with Flanders was growing steadily. In 1280 Spanish merchants in Bruges represented not only their own interests but those of the German cities trading there. Basque ships had taken a vital part in the capture of Seville in 1248. Even before this, in 1230, a ship of Bayonne was hired by an Aragonese noble for an expedition to Majorca. It is not, however, until the early fourteenth century that evidence accumulates for Basques in the Mediterranean.[2]

SEVILLE

The situation in Seville was different. The rulers of Castile seem to have been long unsuccessful in developing the strategic possibilities of Seville as a naval base against Muslim North Africa.

THE CASTILIAN NAVY

When Alfonso X came to the throne in 1252, he ordered the completion of the docks at Seville; they were to provide ample space to build and shelter royal galleys and large ships. In 1253 Alfonso was planning a fleet of eighteen galleys. Its commanders included Frenchmen, Catalans, and Italians. This dependence on foreigners is symptomatic of the whole early history of the Castilian navy and of the maritime development of Seville, where the Genoese colony played a far greater role than Italians did in Catalonia. Alfonso could project, and at times launch, fleets as large as those of contemporary Catalonia–Aragon, but they proved singularly ineffective. In 1256 Alfonso was planning an attack on Sicily. It never took place, but even to plan it

[1] Klein, pp. 302–12. See below, p. 346.

[2] See above, Part I, Ch. II, p. 44, n. 1; Jaume I, *Libre dels feyts*, 104; M. Durliat and J. Pons i Marquês, *VI CHCA*, pp. 353 f.; J. Mª. Ramos y Loscertales, *El cautiverio en la Corona de Aragón* (Saragossa, 1915), p. 93, n. 5.

Alfonso needed to be sure of the participation of Pisa and Marseille. After the disastrous failure of the Castilian attack on Salé in Morocco in 1260 a Genoese admiral was appointed and galleys ordered from Genoa, but nothing came of this. In 1279 Alfonso collected a large fleet commanded by a Castilian to blockade Algeciras. After this fleet had been utterly destroyed Alfonso appealed for galleys to Pere II of Catalonia–Aragon. Alfonso appears to have summoned to his aid another Genoese commander, the famous Benedetto Zaccaria, but Zaccaria did not enter Castilian service until the 1290s when his naval victory in the Straits of Gibraltar over the Moroccan fleet was largely responsible for Sancho IV's capture of Tarifa. Later Castilian victories over Morocco in the struggle for the Straits—the capture of Gibraltar in 1309 and of Algeciras in 1344—would have been impossible without the collaboration of foreign naval forces and commanders—of Catalan galleys and a Catalan admiral in 1309 and of Catalans and a Genoese admiral in 1344.[1]

ABSENCE OF CASTILIAN MARITIME POLICY

The absence of a native Castilian navy in the century following the capture of Seville may have been largely due to the failure of the Castilian Crown to enact any measure corresponding to Jaume I of Aragon's 'navigation act' of 1227, which forbade foreign ships taking on cargoes in Barcelona for Egypt, Syria, or Ceuta, if a native vessel was willing to make the voyage. The Castilian failure to seize a major opportunity to promote maritime growth seems to have been characteristic of the Castilian monarchy as compared to the rulers of Catalonia–Aragon, who were generally aware of the possibilities of overseas trade though their policy was not determined only by economic considerations.[2]

ECONOMIC LEGISLATION

The Castilian Crown was not uninterested in regulating economic matters. In his *Partidas* Alfonso recognized the value of

[1] F. Pérez-Embid, *El almirantazgo de Castilla hasta las capitulaciones de Santa Fe* (Seville, 1944); idem, *MÂ* 75 (1969), 268–89, 479–87; idem, *AEM* 6 (1969), 141–85; R. Lopez, *Genova marinara nel duecento* (Messina–Milan, 1933), pp. 166–176; idem, *CHE* 14 (1950), 5–16; *MHE* ii. 7; see below, Part III, Ch. I, p. 343.

[2] Capmany, ii. 6–13; see above, Ch. I, p. 246.

merchants to a country. He also issued general regulations protecting them. Alfonso and his successors sought to regulate wages and prices, whereas these questions were usually left untouched by the Crown of Aragon. In 1252 Alfonso attempted to fix prices and introduce a stronger currency. These attempts seem to have soon proved an expensive failure.

Most of Alfonso's legislation on economic affairs, such as the laws against usury and against excessive expenditure on dress, weddings, and banquets, was impelled by non-economic moral motives. Similar laws were issued by other monarchies. They were only irregularly enforced.[1] Like other rulers Alfonso sought to promote the celebration of fairs such as those held twice a year at Seville. Merchants attending these fairs were exempted from many customs dues. At the same time other regulations forbade the export of horses, cattle, pigs, silk, leather, bread, wine, precious metals, falcons, etc. Yet despite this mania for regulations, the balance of trade appears to have been unfavourable. No attempt seems to have been made to prevent the constant importation of large quantities of expensive foreign cloth or to encourage a native textile industry. The interests of the sheep-owners and wool exporters were allowed to prevail.[2]

ROYAL INSTITUTIONS: FINANCES

The Castilian Crown possessed many sources of revenue. Apart from the regular tax (*moneda*)—supposed to be paid every seven years by all non-nobles and clerics—the Crown had acquired vast lands in Andalusia. It could raise money through customs dues, in tribute from Granada, from the Church, the Jews, and, during a war, from the general population in lieu of military service.

The ordinary and special war taxes affected the majority of the population. A man with five maravedis or more in coin or goods had to pay a tenth of this sum. In 1286 Sancho IV conceded that a man's 'oxen and ploughing animals should not be

[1] S. Sobrequés, in *Historia de España y América*, ed. Vicens, ii. 305 f.; Alfonso X, *Partidas*, V. VII; A. Ballesteros Beretta, *Alfonso X el Sabio* (Barcelona, 1963), pp. 70 ff.; M. del C. Carlé, *CHE* 15 (1951), 132 ff.; I. García Ramila, *Hispania* 5 (1945), 179–235, 385–439, 605–50. V. Romero Muñoz, *Archivo hispalense*, 41 (1948), 21–6.

[2] Carlé, *CHE* 21–2 (1954), 152–65, 304 ff.

seized' to pay the tax, '*provided* there exist other goods to take' in their place.

Yet, in the second half of the thirteenth century, the royal treasury veered from one expedient to another. Fernando III debased the coinage. Alfonso X carried this process further. He began to exact the *alcabala* already raised by certain municipalities, a sales tax of 5 per cent on all transactions.[1]

Alfonso agreed to receive 50,000 fewer maravedis in tribute from Granada than his father had done. He was generous to the Military Orders, to his relations, and to the nobility. In 1276 Alfonso was in severe need of money. He was obliged to contract with five financiers, four of whom were Jews, for the collection of all taxes in arrears since 1261. In 1277 he secured the promise of an annual grant (*servicio*), in return for exemption from other taxes, but this proved insufficient.[2]

The heavy taxes raised by Alfonso made him very unpopular. In 1281, when his son Sancho was preparing to rebel against him, Sancho's supporters represented him as pointing out to his father 'how men were very poor and taxes great'. Jofre de Loaisa, the contemporary Archdeacon of Toledo, saw Sancho as rebelling because of the 'immense exactions' levied by Alfonso.

In the process of his successful rebellion Sancho distributed the royal revenues among his supporters. The *Crónica de Alfonso X*, written by a supporter of Sancho, tells us that the Infante gave away what was needed to maintain the Crown. Once king (1284–95), Sancho was soon in acute need of money. He turned, as Alfonso had done, to Jewish financiers for aid, and imposed, in 1294, a new tax, the *sisa*, a levy of 1 per cent on all transactions, from building houses to selling a few eggs. Loaisa, though he praises Sancho, remarks that 'he imposed more tributes on his subjects than his father ever did'.[3]

The *sisa* was so unpopular that the Crown was obliged to renounce it during the minority of Fernando IV (1295–1312), though it was soon to return. It does not appear to have been

[1] N. Tenorio y Cerero, *El concejo de Sevilla* (Seville, 1901), pp. 229 f.; *Cortes de León*, i. 98; S. de Moxó, *La Alcabala* (Madrid, 1963), pp. 13–23; Ballesteros, *Alfonso X*, pp. 60 f.

[2] Ballesteros, pp. 65 f., 77–84; *MHE* i. 308–24. J. F. O'Callaghan, *Traditio*, 27 (1971), 391 f., 397.

[3] Ballesteros, pp. 946 f.; Loaisa, *Crónica*, ed. A. Ubieto Arteta (Valencia, 1971), pp. 22, 33; *Crónica de Alfonso X*, 76 (*BAE* lxvi. 61).

very productive. Larger sums could be raised from other sources. The resources of Castile were very considerable even during Fernando's minority. The Cortes voted five *servicios* in 1300 and five more, despite a severe famine, in 1301. The queen mother, María of Molina, was able to raise 1,500,000 maravedis to support an expedition to Murcia of 4,000 knights and to send 10,000 silver marks to Rome to secure Fernando's legitimization by the pope.

In 1309 it was estimated by the Cortes that the ordinary revenues of the Crown were so far below the sums paid annually to 'the great men, the Infantes and the *caballeros*', and the amount needed for the support of the Court, that 4,500,000 maravedis had to be raised from other sources. This sum could have been raised—and assured for the future—by a vote of the Cortes, but the nobles preferred that the Crown should not be so strengthened. The Infante Juan instead proposed the revival of a series of claims for arrears of taxes, fines for usury and illegal exports, the same set of expedients for raising money to which Alfonso X and Sancho IV had had recourse through their Jewish financiers. The weak young King Fernando IV agreed to the second alternative.[1]

Some of the tax documents of Sancho's reign survive. They provide concrete, though incomplete, evidence which is lacking for the reigns of Alfonso X and Fernando IV.

In an ordinary year, such as 1291, when no large military expenses were necessary, the bishop of Astorga, who was in charge of the royal finances, could balance the budget with a revenue of 320,754 maravedis. In other years much more money was necessary. The royal household's expenses alone, when the king of Aragon had to be entertained twice in seven months (1292–3), could soar to over 300,000; this swallowed up all the general receipts.

Customs dues provided 120,000 mrs. in 1291. In 1293 dues levied in the Cantabrian ports on imports brought in about 150,000. In Seville customs in 1294 amounted to almost the same. Along the frontier with Portugal many posts brought in nothing, because they were in the hands of the Order of Alcántara or of nobles who would not tolerate royal customs

[1] On the *sisa* M. Gaibrois de Ballesteros, *Sancho IV de Castilla*, i, p. lxiii, iii pp. cdiv-vii. See *Crónica de Fernando IV*, 7 f., 16 (*BAE* lxvi, 117 ff., 160).

officers in their lands. The total for a year was only 30,577 mrs. The total amount for customs was about the same as the 275,000 mrs. paid in fees to the royal chancery for the same year.

It is more difficult to summarize special taxes. They could yield large sums. In 1293 the *fonsadera*, a special tax to support a military campaign (in this case the capture of Tarifa in the previous year) raised 212,272 mrs. from the dioceses of Burgos, Calahorra, and Palencia. This tax was paid even by widows and orphans, normally exempt from taxation. The *servicios* voted by Cortes in the kingdom of León in 1294 raised over 400,000. In Extremadura the *servicios* were rented out for 250,000 to a Christian tax-farmer. Many more revenues, amounting to over 1,500,000 mrs., were rented to a group of Jewish financiers. This group stated that it had outbid all its rivals in the sum they offered.

1294 was an expensive year. Over 3,000 mrs. were paid 'to hasten the tax-collectors'. Foot messengers were sent all over Castile 'to bring maravedis in great haste'. The money was sent south with armed escorts through the mountains between Toledo and Seville. The campaign in Andalusia cost 910,282 mrs. A third of this sum constituted the salary of Benedetto Zaccaria, the Genoese admiral of Castile, for eight months (282,805 mrs); provisions for the army cost a little more, the pay of the garrisons less. The revenue of Andalusia just covered the cost of the military campaign, but not of the Catalan galleys, which were paid for separately. An estimate for thirty galleys for the projected campaign of 1295 came to 1,440,000 for six months.[1]

The Castilian Crown had two special sources of income which merit attention—the Church and the Jews.

In 1294 the Castilian Church—which already contributed to the monarchy a constant stream of money in the shape of a third of the ecclesiastical tithes—was summoned to support the Holy War against Islam being waged in defence of Tarifa. The sums levied were very large. When the archbishop of Santiago refused to pay Sancho IV ordered his goods to be seized to the

[1] Gaibrois, iii, pp. ccxxxix-xli (1291); i, pp. i-cxlviii (1293–4). The totals are in most cases mine. The Jewish group paid 519,446 mrs. as a third of the revenues agreed upon (p. lxxi; see p. lix); iii, pp. cccxcv-cd (expenses for the campaign of 1294); eadem, *BRAH* 76 (1920), 125 f.; 77 (1920), 212–15.

value of 30,000 maravedis. The clergy of the archdiocese of Santiago had to pay 50,000, those of the dioceses of Burgos and Palencia 60,000 each, those of Toledo 100,000. Over 800,000 was raised from all the prelates of León–Castile. Monasteries were obliged to contribute also though some exemptions from taxes were admitted.

Jewish contributions were also large. In 1293–4 the Jews of Castile paid 900,000 maravedis which appears to be more than the Church contributed.[1]

JEWS IN CASTILIAN FINANCIAL ADMINISTRATION

The Jews contributed more than money to the Castilian Crown. They were indispensable as financiers to the monarchy. Alfonso X's *Partidas* prohibited Jews from holding public office. They did not in fact hold the highest posts in the administration, which were reserved for nobles and prelates, but they were found in the lower echelons. They were employed especially in diplomatic missions to Muslim states—where their knowledge of Arabic made them invaluable—and in taxation.

Alfonso X and his successors employed some Jews as royal secretaries. His Jewish doctors were among his most trusted advisers. A small group of Jews, mainly from Toledo, played a vital role. They did not form the majority of the tax-collectors but they organized what financial administration existed. Other Jews performed the same service for leading bishops, the Military Orders, and many Castilian towns.

Alfonso X employed Don Meir ibn Shoshan as his chief *Almojarife* (tax-collector) and also Don Solomon ibn Zadok and his son Don Isaac. A young Jewish poet looking back years later celebrates the prosperous days of Castilian Judaism in the 1270s. He describes Don Isaac's tour of inspection of the Castilian ports, 'in royal style'. A sudden reversal of fortune at court brought down Don Isaac. In 1281 Alfonso had all the Jews of his kingdoms arrested and made them ransom themselves for a sum equal to twice their annual tribute.

Under Sancho IV the Jews returned to royal favour. Don Abraham *el Barchilón* (of Toledo) became the main financier of the Crown. In 1288 and 1293 Sancho, who needed the

[1] Gaibrois, iii, pp. ccclx-lxxiii; ccclxxxi f; eadem, *BRAH* 76 (1920), 430–4; 77 (1920), 210. See Baer, *Die Juden* ii. 81–7 (1291).

Cortes' grant of money for his military campaigns, agreed that no Jew be employed as tax-collector. He did not carry out this legislation. During the minority of Fernando IV it seems to have been applied but in 1302 Fernando returned to Jewish administrators and defended the Jews against attempts by the Church to defraud them of interest on loans. The minority of Alfonso XI saw another clamour against Jewish officials but the Infantes who acted as regents continued to employ them.[1]

NON-FINANCIAL INSTITUTIONS

The non-financial royal institutions of Castile developed less rapidly than did corresponding institutions in the Crown of Aragon. The most important developments in Castilian institutions came in the middle and late fourteenth century, under Alfonso XI, Pedro I, and the first Trastámaras.[2] On the other hand the political concepts put forward by Alfonso X, especially his view of a king's place in society, are of great importance for later Castilian history. How far were Alfonso's views on royal government reflected in the actual justice and administration of Castile? What were the Castilian Cortes in the thirteenth century?

LEGISLATION AND ALFONSO X: POLITICAL CONCEPTS

Alfonso X's predecessors had respected the local customs of each city. This could lead to great confusion. In Toledo there were separate judges, one using the Visigothic *Fuero juzgo*, the other Castilian *Fueros*. In 1254 Alfonso had to intervene to prevent the second judge from interfering with the first. Alfonso is the first Castilian ruler to issue general legislation. His *Fuero Real* (*c.* 1255) was intended to be a supplementary law code for all León and Castile. It was granted to Burgos, Madrid, and many other cities. It regulated obligations, contracts, and legal procedure. It was used for the appeals to the court tribunal which it encouraged. The *Fuero Real* began slowly to replace local customs and Visigothic law. The *Leyes nuevas* and *Leyes del*

[1] Baer, *History* i. 112–37, 306–11; *Cortes de León*, i. 105, 110; for the Order of Santiago and the Jews see D. W. Lomax, *La Orden de Santiago (1170–1275)* (Madrid, 1965), pp. 271–4; Baer, *Die Juden* ii. 78–80.

[2] For Aragon see above, Ch. I, pp. 282 f.; for later institutional development in Castile, below, Part III, Ch. IV.

estilo, judicial decisions of the period, show how many questions were raised and decided by the *Fuero Real*.[1]

About 1260 Alfonso X issued his *Espéculo* (Mirror of Law). It was intended as general law for the king, his officials, and the judges of the Royal Court. The *Espéculo* was the first version of the *Siete Partidas* (or *Book of Laws*). *Partida I* was probably finished in 1265. The other *Partidas* appear to be later; they went through several stages and were only promulgated in a more or less definitive text in 1348, by Alfonso XI, as a supplement to royal decrees and local *Fueros*. The long delay before Alfonso's general legislation was adopted was due to the 'intense opposition' it provoked in the defenders of local customs. For a time the new law was not even applied in the Royal Court. Under Sancho IV 'the kingdom again became a collection of territories and cities'. But the royal jurists had not forgotten Alfonso's laws. As the monarchy regained strength it returned to the principles he had enunciated.

These principles appealed to jurists trained in the universities for the same reason that they disgusted traditionalists, because they were drawn from Roman law. The *Partidas* see the king and his kingdom as a corporate unity superior to feudal and local ties. The king possesses the 'full power' (*plena potestas*) of a Roman emperor. He can issue laws, do justice, strike money, declare war or peace, establish taxes, fairs, appoint governors, delimit provinces. He is God's Vicar. No other power in his kingdom can challenge his. Royal power is 'public power'. It is, therefore, inalienable and indivisible. The grant of a fief does not alienate jurisdiction over war and peace, money, justice. The king is concerned to do 'justice' to all the people of his lordship.[2]

ADMINISTRATION

Alfonso's principles were resoundingly clear. Their application met with enormous difficulties. Alfonso wished to apply one

[1] R. Gibert, *Historia general del derecho español*, i (Granada, 1968), 40 f., 45–8; *MHE* i, 38, 97; *Documentos del Archivo General de la Villa de Madrid*, ed. T. Domingo Palacio, i (Madrid, 1888), 85–91.

[2] A. García Gallo, *AHDE* 21–2 (1951–2), 345–528; Gibert, pp. 48–50; J. A. Maravall, *Estudios de historia del pensamiento español, edad media*, i (Madrid, 1967), pp. 89–140 (from *BRAH* 157 (1965)). See especially *Partidas*, II. i. 2, 4; x; see above, Part I, Ch. III, pp. 102 f. and accompanying notes. Also, E. S. Procter, *Alfonso X of Castile* (Oxford, 1951), pp. 47–77.

law throughout his kingdoms—this desire appears, for instance, in a decree of 1261: 'Since Our rule is one We wish all weights and measures of Our kingdoms should be the same'. But to most men of the time, what mattered was their own city or at most León or Castile, not the over-all unity (only achieved as recently as 1230) over which Alfonso reigned. Although less obvious than in the Crown of Aragon, substantial internal differences existed between León and Castile, each of which had its separate institutions. In 1274 the Cortes of Zamora, reacting against Alfonso's legislation, restricted the type of case which could come to the royal court. They also decreed that judges from León were to hear cases in the royal court from León, judges from Castile Castilian cases. These judges were to be 'laymen' (not clerics and presumably not professional Roman lawyers from Bologna). In 1279 Alfonso conceded that cases should not be brought before the royal court until they had been adjudicated by the judge of the local town.[1]

THE ROYAL COUNCIL

The king, Alfonso stated, was the 'head, life, and support' of his people. He was assisted by a Council whose membership was largely undefined at this period. During the minorities of Fernando IV and Alfonso XI the municipalities (*concejos*) named representatives to join the bishops and nobles who were royal counsellors. This mixed composition of the Council was confirmed in principle by later rulers, though they normally selected their own particular counsellors.

The Castilian Royal Council had to decide many questions of jurisdiction raised by recent conquests in Andalusia, such as the boundary lines between the *concejos* of Córdoba and Toledo. It also had to try to supervise the permanent administrative officers, the governors (*Adelantados* or *merinos*), of Castile, León, Galicia, Murcia, etc., the tax-collectors, with their (usually Jewish) head (the *Almojarife*), and the judges, with their *Justicia Mayor*, a definite post from Sancho IV's time. To dispatch the Council's orders there existed the Chancery, which was rapidly developing.

[1] Aly Aben Ragel, *El libro conplido de los iudizios de las estrellas*, ed. G. Hilty (Madrid, 1954), p. xxvi, n. 30; *Cortes de León*, i. 87–94 (see pp. 122 f.); *MHE* ii. 1 f.

CHANCERY

Castilian was increasingly used in royal letters, as against Latin. The titular Chancellors (or, at times, separate Chancellors for Castile, León, and Andalusia) were normally leading prelates but their duties were discharged by notaries, who were generally clerics on their way to high office. These notaries also intervened in the collection of taxes and in administration in general. Under Alfonso X registers of royal letters began to be kept—almost all of which are lost. It is possible that the *Canciller de la poridat* who appears as one of Sancho IV's main ministers, holding a privy seal, may have existed earlier. Over a hundred scribes appear in documents of Sancho's reign, though some worked in the royal household or served the judges of the royal court. The scribes also carried out many other duties which were only slightly less important than those entrusted to the notaries. Although a notary might be paid ten times as much, the scribe received a fee from the suppliant in question for each document he issued. There also existed an Arabic Scribal Office (*Escribanía del Arábigo*), of which the head was a Jew. This office was necessary to maintain correspondence between Castile, Granada, and Morocco.[1]

ADMINISTRATIVE PROBLEMS: THE AGENTS OF THE CROWN

The Royal Council and its officials were confronted by situations partially reflected in the *Partidas* and the complaints of the Cortes. Powerful men with armed retinues appeared before judges and terrified witnesses and advocates. 'Persons unite to commit violence with arms and kindle fire', and to seize property or land by force. Bishops and the *concejos* of towns behaved in the same way. Alfonso X was obliged to permit his nobles to retain armed men for self-defence. In 1293 the Cortes complained 'that when good men go to fairs and markets and sea-ports . . . they are robbed and captured on the road and even if they complain to the *merinos* they cannot have justice.' Sancho IV decreed that the local *merino* 'should be

[1] *Partidas*, II. x. 3; *MHE* i. 212 ff.; E. S. Procter, in *Oxford Essays in Medieval History presented to H. E. Salter* (Oxford, 1934), pp. 104–21; L. Sánchez Belda, *AHDE* 21–2 (1951–2), 171–223; Gaibrois, *Sancho IV*, i, p. cxlvii.

obliged to inform Us of the evildoers. If he does not do so he shall make good the loss.' At the same meeting the Cortes stated that bandits attacked shepherds passing by with their flocks.

The *Adelantado* and his subordinate *merinos*, the *Partidas* remark, 'should travel through the land to punish criminals, render justice, and to acquaint the king with the conditions of the country'. He should avoid burdening the land with a numerous retinue but should have an expert legal staff with him.[1]

Although there was no regular system of travelling judges, as in England, royal judges could be sent out on occasion to carry out inquiries. Their fees were paid by the local *concejo*. They were naturally unpopular. In 1286 and 1293 Sancho IV was asked to withdraw the royal judges he had sent to various cities. He agreed to do so provided he did not receive a request from a town for a judge. This proviso is also found in royal replies to later Cortes; it left the king a pretext to continue to intervene in local judicial affairs.

One of the means that the Castilian Crown used to exercise control over its vast realms was the *pesquisa*, a judicial investigation carried out by special agents. It could be a general inquiry extending over a whole region or might be confined to a particular case. By 1300 the *pesquisa* was ceasing to be used for civil cases, such as the investigation of royal fiscal rights or the resumption of royal land by the Church, and becoming more general in criminal cases. It was also used by *concejos* within their local jurisdiction.

During the reign of Sancho IV a new type of 'civil servant' emerges, a member of the lesser nobility who was not swayed by the grandiose ambitions of the leading noble houses. Two such men were Juan Mathe de Luna, Head Chamberlain (*Camarero Mayor*) and Fernán Pérez Maimón, holder of the privy seal. It is significant that Mathe was of Aragonese origin and Maimón probably a convert from Judaism. Both men came from outside the Castilian aristocracy, and, being dependent on the Crown, were prepared to devote their strength to its service. In the struggle with Morocco for Tarifa in 1294 they both held key posts. Mathe was in command of the frontier forces in

[1] *Partidas*, VII. x. 6 f., 9 f., 17; II. ix. 22; *Cortes de León*, i. 108 f., 123.

Andalusia, Maimón hastened the coming of the Catalan fleet which saved Tarifa.[1]

THE CROWN AND THE CITIES

Royal servants such as Mathe and Maimón were bound to come into conflict with the powerful cities of Castile. The support of the municipal governments, the *concejos*, was essential to the Crown. Their tributes enabled it to 'pay the *ricos omes* and knights and their vassals'. Yet the Crown was steadily encroaching on the *concejos*' rights. The appointment of almost all the municipal officials of Seville was reserved to the Crown from the time of Alfonso X. As membership of the town councils shrank in numbers they were easier to influence.

Conflicts arose over attempts to introduce royal jurisdiction. The Mesta is a case in point. In 1276 Alfonso X, instigated by the Mesta, placed three royal agents in charge of a campaign against unauthorized town taxes on sheep. The Mesta helped to collect the fines due for levying such taxes.

Reactions against royal power at the end of Alfonso's reign and during the later minorities of Fernando IV and Alfonso XI gave the towns an opportunity to assert their independence. Towns, bishops, and the Order of Calatrava received the privilege of levying taxes on sheep.

In 1282 Sancho, rebelling against his father Alfonso X, favoured a *Hermandad* (Brotherhood) of *concejos* which supported him. Once he was king Sancho decreed that this association should disappear but the precedent had been created. In 1295 and 1315, during minorities, the towns joined together against royal misgovernment.

On these occasions the Crown was forced to make concessions. In 1295 Seville secured the privilege that its officials should only be local inhabitants. In 1315 the general superiority of royal judges over those of the cities was annulled. These victories were transient. After he came of age in 1325 Alfonso XI was able to reassert royal control both in the general question of judicial authority over the *Hermandades* (which were

[1] *Cortes* i. 96, 120; M. Gaibrois de Ballesteros, *BRAH* 74 (1919), 420; 76 (1920), 59–62, 147 f.

suppressed), and in that of the Mesta. Grants of local sheep taxes to the towns came to an end.[1]

MALADMINISTRATION

For the ordinary inhabitant of Castile–León all officials were enemies. Among the *Responsa* of Rabbi Asher b. Yehiel of Toledo (d. 1328) there is one concerning 'an artisan, a dyer or saddler, [who] has an annual expense in the form of gifts to the judges and officials, to keep them from trumping up charges against him—the *usual* contribution that handicraftsmen are required to make out of their handiwork'.

Similar statements abound in the Christian sources. In 1286 Sancho IV had to promise the Cortes that his officials would not seize men's property without the order being passed by a royal judge. In 1293 the Cortes complained that whenever the king, the queen, or the Infantes reached a town royal officials 'broke into houses and took the bread and wine and fish and straw and wood [they needed]'. This complaint can be confirmed from the royal accounts, where it is stated that the royal household seized many things without payment. Sancho decreed that royal judges, at the end of their term of office were to hold an *audiencia* for thirty days, during which complaints could be brought against them before two men of the town. The Franciscan Juan Gil de Zamora addressing the future Sancho IV, remarked that the only law princes and prelates obey is that of extortion. 'Spain is tortured with unpredictable oppression.' She suffers from 'Pseudo-kings, pseudo-governors, pseudo-bishops'. This rhetoric is less impressive than the casual way in which the poet Gonzalo de Berceo describes Heaven as a place 'where no thief *or merino* can enter'.

The difficulties that beset the royal administration are well illustrated by the case of Don Alvaro Páez, bishop of Mondoñedo in Galicia. Don Alvaro had rented from Sancho IV the right to collect the local taxes. When he was three days late in paying a third of the sum due, Sancho, writing from Valladolid

[1] *Crónica de Fernando IV*, 5 (*BAE* lxvi. 115); M. del C. Carlé, *Del concejo medieval castellano-leonés* (Buenos Aires, 1968), pp. 234–42; Klein, op. cit., pp. 100–3, 180–3; *MHE* i. 308–24; J. Pujol y Alonso, *Las Hermandades de Castilla y León* (Madrid, 1913), pp. 23–40; L. Suárez Fernandez, *CHE* 16 (1952), 5 ff., 28 f.; Tenorio, op. cit., pp. 235 f.

on 18 August 1291, threatened him with the seizure and sale of his own goods and those of his see to make up the amount. The bishop did not pay at once. On 4 October, from Toro, the king complained to the local royal *Alcalde* that he had not yet carried out the royal threat to seize the bishop's goods, despite Sancho's promise to protect him against ecclesiastical censure. The *Alcalde* was galvanized into action by the threat of being brought before the king. But, while the *Alcalde* was seizing the bishop's goods, the bishop succeeded, on 1 November, in catching up, in Medina del Campo, with the travelling Court. He was able to prove that the reason why he had defaulted on his payment was that he had been forced to pay a large sum to the royal governor of Galicia, who was in rebellion against the king. Sancho was obliged to order his *Alcalde* to restore the bishop's goods. The *Alcalde* would have to make good out of his own pocket double the loss sustained by the bishop.[1]

THE CORTES OF CASTILE–LÉON

The way in which Roman law influenced the development of the Cortes in the various peninsular kingdoms has already been touched on. The Cortes emerged from meetings of the royal court because the monarchies, in their efforts to unify their countries against local, noble, or ecclesiastical resistance, needed the support, moral and financial, of all their subjects. The basis of the Cortes was seen in subjects' duty to give counsel and aid to the king in his court, when he summoned them. The king promised not to act without taking counsel, but he was not bound to follow the counsel he received. The Cortes should be seen as an administrative organ of the royal government. They could not function without the king. They scarcely ever, in Castile–León, worked against him. In Castile one cannot speak of clearly separate branches or estates of the Cortes such as existed in the Crown of Aragon. The nobles and prelates of Castile–León were not summoned as representatives of their estates but as holders of government office—nobles as governors of provinces, bishops as royal servants. The king was not obliged

[1] Baer, *History* i. 201; *Cortes de León*, i. 97, 110; Gaibrois, *Sancho IV*, i, pp. cxviff.; iii, documents 365, 376, 379; ii. 113 f. (the Mondoñedo case); Juan Gil de Zamora, *De preconiis Hispanie* (1278), ed. M. Castro y Castro (Madrid, 1955), pp. 341 f.; Berceo, *Milagros de Nuestra Señora*, XXI. v. 581 (*BAE* lvii. 121).

to call them, although there was a protest in 1295 when a number of bishops and nobles were excluded—at the desire of the representatives of the *concejos*. It was these representatives who really constituted the Cortes in Castile–León.

The *concejos*' representatives were there because the *concejos* (unlike the nobles and clergy) were taxable as a group. As the Castilian monarchy's expenses increased it summoned the *concejos* increasingly often. Their representatives were present at meetings of Cortes on at least ten occasions during the reign of Alfonso X (1252–84), four times under Sancho IV (1284–95), and fifteen times under Fernando IV (1295–1312). On most of these occasions we do not know how many *concejos* were represented. In 1315 the number was 101. This number was to shrink as the fourteenth century progressed.

The Cortes of León and Castile met separately during the minorities of Fernando IV and Alfonso XI and sometimes on later occasions because of the Crown's desire to divide its opposition. Normally the Cortes of the two kingdoms were called together.

The first collective petition of the *concejos* dates from 1293. In the next century most legislation in Cortes took the form of such a petition. If it was granted it became law.

The period from 1295 to 1324, the minority of Fernando IV, of his weak rule, and of Alfonso XI's minority, was one of the high periods of the Castilian Cortes. Petitions were normally answered soon and satisfactorily. In 1307 and 1315 it was recognized that the Crown could not levy extraordinary taxes without the Cortes. In 1295 the towns' representatives demanded an accounting of the sums voted in the previous reign, in 1315 an estimate of the total royal revenues. In 1317 they had the Jewish treasurer dismissed. In 1297 and again in 1313 they elected twelve citizens to accompany the young king and take part in the Royal Council.

These successes were transient. The Cortes failed to exploit the weakness of the Crown. They did not establish any permanent control over it. Very significant differences existed between Castile–León and the Crown of Aragon.

In Castile–León, unlike Aragon, the homage of the Cortes to the king or the heir to the throne always preceded the king or prince's oath to observe the laws. The taxes (*servicios*) demanded by the Crown were usually granted before the *concejos*' petitions were answered. Often petitions were rejected or evaded. The king could legislate outside Cortes. The *concejos*' right to petition (on virtually any subject) never became control over legislation such as existed in Catalonia–Aragon.

There was no prescription as to when or how often the Cortes should meet. In 1313 a meeting was decreed for every two years; this decree was not observed after Alfonso XI's minority. In Catalonia, in contrast, the Cortes met, by statute, every year, in Aragon every two years.

The Castilian Cortes failed to establish any financial machinery such as existed in the Crown of Aragon to collect and administer the sums it had voted to the Crown. This and other failures of the Cortes of Castile may perhaps be due to the virtual absence from its meetings of the nobility and clergy which play so large a role in the Catalan Corts.[1]

THE CROWN AND THE NOBILITY

The nobility overshadowed the Castilian scene. Leading nobles did not need to appear at meetings of Cortes. They could get what they wanted in other ways. Constant military campaigns and conquests had brought the Castilian nobility rich rewards from the Crown in towns, lands, and lordships. As Castile expanded many more administrative posts were created. At the highest level these posts were reserved for nobles.

The nobility sought to achieve full jurisdiction over their new estates. They were often successful. Their power expanded not only in the newly conquered south but in Old Castile, where, by 1350, many formerly free villages had passed under seignorial jurisdiction. As early as 1293 the Cortes complained that nobles were gaining control of the districts round the towns. The towns could no longer mobilize the men of their districts for a military campaign. Given the weakness of the towns in Castile the Crown was driven to rule by using one league of nobles against another.

Alfonso X greatly assisted the rise of the noble houses. Years

[1] See, above, Pt. I, Ch. III, pp. 103 f.; for the Crown of Aragon, above, Ch. I, pp. 278 ff. E. S. Procter, *English Historical Review*, 74 (1959), 18–22; W. Piskorski, *Las Cortes de Castilla, 1188–1520* (Barcelona, 1930); H. Grassotti, *CHE* 41–2 (1965), 340–5.

later he was forced to admit the excessive favour he had shown when young to Don Nuño González de Lara. Don Nuño received vast gifts in Seville and Jerez and all the royal revenues of Old Castile. Alfonso departed from custom in granting Don Nuño's sons lordships in their father's lifetime. Alfonso was also the first king to grant lands in New Castile to members of the royal family. He thus laid the foundation for the alliances his brothers and sons formed with leading magnates, alliances which were to undermine royal rule.[1]

Alfonso X's nephew, Don Juan Manuel, one of the greatest magnates of his day, named Haro and Lara as the leading noble houses of Castile. Slightly below them came Castro and Cameros. These were the main houses, which, in alliance or at variance with minor branches of the royal family, disputed power. Haro had its stronghold in virtually independent Viscaya; Lara in Albarracín, between Castile and Aragon. A contemporary chronicle tells us that Diego López de Haro arrived at the royal court 'with as an escort 700 horse and 5,000 foot'. In contrast the Crown often found it hard to muster troops. When Sancho IV needed to get an army under way early in the year he had to spend the previous winter 'campaigning' to persuade the *concejos*, by personal contact and promises, to send their forces when they were summoned. A less vigorous king such as Fernando IV found it easier to raise an army by handing over his revenues in Andalusia to four nobles, two of whom were each to provide 1,000 knights.

Can one ascribe any general aims to the nobility? In their rebellion against Alfonso X in the 1270s they complained that royal officials interfered with their seignorial rights and that the Crown was settling new towns in León and Galicia and was favouring cities against them. They claimed to be defending themselves and their *fueros* and acting 'for the good of the land'. Alfonso commented on this claim in a letter to his heir: 'They act as they do so as to keep kings under pressure and take what is their own from them. They look for ways in which they can disinherit and dishonour them . . . they want always to have a foot [in Granada], as well as one here.' During the revolt at the end of Alfonso's reign, led by the Infante Sancho, the rebels, who

[1] S. de Moxó, *Hispania*, 30 (1970), 30–49; *Cortes de León*, i, p. 112; Ballesteros, *Alfonso X*, pp. 106 f.; *Crónica de Alfonso X*, 30 (*BAE* lxvi. 25 f.).

included bishops and towns as well as nobles, again claimed to be defending their *Fueros* and customs. There was a genuine dislike for Alfonso's centralizing Roman legal principles behind this revolt. But when the nobles rebelled without the towns, as they did during the reign of Fernando IV, their motives seem less complex. A Catalan observer, writing in 1300, summed them up in one phrase 'All love land'. Without an unmeasured greed for land and the power it conferred it would be difficult to explain the ceaseless manœuvres and betrayals of the Castilian nobility. They could shift their loyalties with extraordinary agility from Castile to Navarre, France or Aragon, or to alliance with Granada. This agility appeared to contemporary nobles highly praiseworthy. It also made it very difficult to pin rebels down. The nobles of the day had written their own rules of war in which there was a strong element of make-believe. Don Juan Manuel tells us that any great noble should act to defend his equals against any attack by the king which seems to him unjust. If a noble joined the king in besieging one of his rivals he did so principally so as to extort concessions from the Crown and he was careful to see that none of his equals should be seriously hurt or his castles taken.[1]

The three kings who reigned in Castile between 1252 and 1312 differed widely in their character.

ALFONSO X AND THE NOBILITY (1252–1284)

Alfonso X, when he came to the throne in 1252, was in a stronger position than his son Sancho or his grandson Fernando when they began to reign. Alfonso inherited a vast patrimony and the prestige of his father Fernando III's conquests. He had been well educated and was highly gifted intellectually. His modern biographer sees him as 'inclined to clemency, munificent to the point of prodigality, and excessively tolerant'. He was to enjoy few peaceful years. By 1269, though only aged forty-eight, he was a man of highly nervous temperament who complained of his nobles' misdeeds. From 1270 his health

[1] Juan Manuel, *Libro de los castigos*, 6 f. (*BAE* li. 269 f.); Jofre de Loaisa, *Crónica*, ed. Ubieto, p. 48; Gaibrois, *Sancho IV*, ii. 359 f., 64; Giménez Soler, *Juan Manuel*, pp. 363 f.; *Crónica de Alfonso X*, 23, 52 (*BAE* lxvi. 20, 39); *Crónica de Fernando IV*, 15 (ibid. 158 f.); Procter, *Alfonso X*, pp. 59 f.; Giménez Soler, *La Corona de Aragón Granada*, p. 58 n. 1. See, above, Pt. I, Ch. II, p. 60, notes 1–2.

deteriorated sharply.[1] The struggle between Alfonso X and his nobles constituted a drama in three acts, in each of which the struggle was more severe than in the last. Alfonso's reign began well but within two years, in 1254, he was faced with a revolt by his brother, the Infante Enrique. Enrique and the House of Haro, jealous of the favour shown to the House of Lara, entered into alliance with Alfonso's father-in-law, Jaume I of Aragon. Alfonso was forced to send Queen Violante to beg for mercy from Jaume. Enrique and his brother Fadrique were banished from Castile (1255–56).

The relative peace that followed lasted eight years. Alfonso used the time to make minor conquests in Andalusia (Niebla and Cádiz), and an unsuccessful expedition to Morocco. He also, in 1256, became involved in the hopeless contest for the Holy Roman Empire. In 1264 a large-scale Muslim rebellion broke out in Andalusia, assisted by Granada. Alfonso, with the help of Aragon, was able to suppress the revolt by 1267. But Granada was already intriguing with Alfonso's favourite, Don Nuño González de Lara, who allied with the House of Haro against his benefactor. In 1271 rebellion broke out, led by another of Alfonso's brothers, Don Felipe. Virtually all the leading nobles of Castile and León were in alliance against the king. They were intriguing with Portugal, Navarre, Granada, and Morocco. It was impossible to placate the rebels, who included a number of bishops. It was also impossible to defeat them. Even the towns were not prepared to fight for the king. After the leading rebels had taken refuge in Granada, Alfonso, impelled by his desire to intervene in Italy, gave way to their demands in 1273. They received large sums from the tribute of Granada. Don Nuño was appointed governor of Andalusia (*Adelantado de la Frontera*). Alfonso's attempt to create a uniform law-code for his realms was one casualty of the contest.[2]

THE INHERITANCE OF ALFONSO X

In 1275, while Alfonso was on his way to see the pope at Beaucaire, the first wave of raids from Morocco struck Andalusia. Castilian forces were repeatedly defeated and Don Nuño

[1] A. Ballesteros, *Sevilla en el siglo XIII* (Seville, 1913), p. 67 (based on Juan Gil, p. 319); idem, *Alfonso X*, pp. 484–508; Jaume I, *Libre dels feyts*, 494–9.
[2] Ballesteros, *Alfonso X*, pp. 111, 119, 517–34, 556–673.

killed. Alfonso's heir, Fernando de la Cerda, died while preparing another army. He left two sons by his French wife Blanche. The eldest, Alfonso, was five. Fernando entrusted his son's cause to the son of Don Nuño, Don Juan Núñez de Lara. The House of Haro inevitably turned to Fernando's younger brother Sancho. Don Lope Díaz de Haro could not allow Lara to dominate a future king. He persuaded Sancho to style himself at once 'eldest son and heir'. Sancho's leadership in the military crisis won him a large following. A royal minority was unacceptable during a war. French attempts to defend the cause of Alfonso de la Cerda proved ineffectual.

In 1278 the Cortes recognized Sancho as heir. Fernando's widow, Blanche, and her sons took refuge in Aragon. Control of the Cerda princes gave Pere II of Catalonia–Aragon a weapon against Castile.

SANCHO'S REBELLION

Sancho was in a strong position. Covered with renewed glory by a campaign against Granada, he was able to reject Alfonso X's attempt to please France by giving Alfonso de la Cerda a subordinate kingdom in Jaén.

Royal princes, nobles, bishops, Masters of Military Orders stampeded to join the rebellious prince, who soon had Portugal and Granada on his side. Adroit propaganda won over the cities. During the last two years of his life (1282–4) Alfonso kept the loyalty of only Seville and Murcia. He had been formally deposed by an assembly in Valladolid in April 1282.

In November in the Alcázar of Seville, Alfonso solemnly cursed and disinherited Sancho. In his will he denounces 'the traitors to God and Us and Spain' who had betrayed him. Having found no aid in Christian rulers he had been forced to turn to Morocco and pledge his crown in return for a subsidy. The Merinid army appeared before Córdoba and raided as far as Toledo.

In 1283–4 Castile seemed to be dissolving in anarchy. Sancho's brothers and Don Lope Díaz de Haro were attempting to establish separate kingdoms in León, Extremadura, and Castile. Sancho tried to come to terms with his father but Alfonso was inflexible. He declared Alfonso de la Cerda his heir. If the Cerda princes died without sons Castile–León was to go to the king of France. In a second will the king left his sons Juan and Jaime kingdoms in Andalusia under vassalage to his Cerda grandson. It was fortunate for Castile that Alfonso died on 4 April 1284.[1]

SANCHO IV AND THE NOBILITY (1284–1295)

Sancho IV came to the throne under very unfavourable circumstances. He seems to have been of far more limited intelligence than his father and of a very violent nature. Until 1288 he was under the influence of his favourites. After this time he was somewhat more prudent but he was still very dependent on his nobles.

Sancho was not seriously threatened by France or Aragon, which were taken up in mutual conflict. At the beginning of the reign a desperate struggle with the Merinids was prevented by their concerns in Africa. The most serious threat to Sancho was Don Lope Díaz de Haro, who had been his main supporter against the Cerdas. In 1287 Sancho made Don Lope Count of Haro and *Mayordomo Mayor*. He received control of the Chancery and of all the castles of Castile. His brother, Don Diego, became *Alferez* (royal standard-bearer) and *Adelantado*, first of Castile, then of Andalusia. The Díazs wished to make these offices hereditary in their family. Don Lope married his daughter to Sancho's intriguing brother, the Infante Don Juan, and his brother to Sancho's sister. He planned to marry Sancho himself to one of his family, once he had had the king's doubtful marriage to María of Molina set aside. One contemporary remarks that Don Lope controlled León through Don Juan, Castile himself, Andalusia through his brother, another chronicler that he 'disposed of the royal household'. Through Jewish financiers Don Lope controlled royal finances. The people saw him as having bewitched the king. When Sancho at last realized the danger he was in he ordered Don Lope's arrest. Don Lope was killed at Alfaro on 8 June 1288 when he attacked the king. The Lordship of Vizcaya was bestowed on one of Sancho's sons.

[1] Ballesteros, pp. 763–9, 781–806, 818–27, 852 f., 872, 985–1008, etc. A more detailed account of Sancho's rebellion by Ballesteros, *BRAH* 119 (1946), 145–94. Alfonso's wills in *MHE* ii. 110–34, or, better edited, G. Daumet, *Bibliothèque de l'École des Chartes*, 67 (1906), 71–99.

The *Chronicle* of Loaisa sees Sancho as 'great in judgement . . . He executed many magnates . . . and he was feared by all the neighbouring kings'. In fact the reign was as much beset by internal feuds as those of Alfonso X or Fernando IV. Feuds between rival families tormented Badajoz, a struggle between the Order of the Temple and the city Plasencia. There was trouble in Toledo and Avila. The perennial conflicts in Galicia between *concejos*, bishops, and nobles continued. As soon as one over-powerful favourite was dealt with another arose and could not be disposed of by the same method. Don Juan Núñez de Lara refused to enter Valladolid while Sancho was there. He then fled to Aragon and defeated a Castilian force. But he had to be called back because Sancho could not afford to have Lara and Haro united against him. In 1293 Don Juan Núñez persuaded the Infante Don Juan that between them, and with the help of Portugal, they would rule Castile and León, 'for once they were one the king had no one else who could stop them.' The successful defence of Tarifa in 1294 was largely due to Don Juan Núñez's death earlier that year.[1]

THE MINORITY AND REIGN OF FERNANDO IV (1295–1312)

Sancho himself died, aged thirty-six, in 1295. He was buried in Toledo Cathedral on 26 April. His widow María of Molina refused to ride a mule in the procession and went on foot, 'tearing her hair and scratching her face and making great lament'.

Queen María had reason to lament the death of her husband. Her marriage was not recognized by the papacy until 1301. Until then her sons were officially illegitimate—a point exploited by the Cerda claimants and by other members of the royal family, by France, Aragon, and Portugal. Within Castile the Queen was faced with the same nobles Sancho had scarcely controlled and with the dislike of the towns for royal government. At the Cortes of Valladolid, in August 1295, King Fernando, a child of nine, was obliged to promise to dismiss all the officials of the Royal Household. By this time Alfonso X's brother, the Infante Enrique, an aged but formidable intriguer

[1] Gaibrois, *Sancho IV*, especially i. 88–204; ii. 7–18, 22 f., 29, 59–82, 108 f., 175; *Crónica de Sancho IV*, 3, 10 (*BAE* lxvi. 75, 88); Jofre de Loaisa, *Crónica*, ed. Ubieto, pp. 26, 33.

who had just returned to Castile after decades in exile, had persuaded the Cortes to name him joint tutor with Queen María. He was no doubt pleased to be rid of the clerics and Jews who had served Sancho well. Once regent 'he gave himself up more to hunting and frequent banquets than to anything else'.

These royal concessions did not satisfy the towns. They were easily stirred up by rumours of new heavy taxes. At Valladolid, Salamanca, and Segovia, the queen and the child-king found the city walls manned against them when they arrived. The plot to exclude the king from his cities while Castile was invaded by his enemies almost succeeded.

If the towns were uncertain allies the nobles were totally undependable, 'worse as allies than as enemies'. The new heads of the House of Lara promised to defend the child-king against Don Diego López de Haro. But having obtained a large sum of money from the queen they joined Don Diego 'and promised to make the queen give him Vizcaya which Sancho IV had bestowed on his younger son, and if she would not give it to him at once, they would take as king whoever Don Diego wished.' The queen had to give way. Don Diego received Vizcaya, his House and that of Lara received vast gifts of money, and Sancho's brother, the Infante Juan, the lands he had lost by a former rebellion. The Infante at once prepared a pact by which he was to receive León, Galicia, and Seville, Alfonso de la Cerda the rest, except for Murcia, which was to go to Aragon.

In 1296 Jaume II of Aragon, as the Cerda's ally, occupied most of the kingdom of Murcia. Alfonso de la Cerda crossed Castile with an Aragonese army and was crowned king at Sahagún in León. He could probably have captured Fernando and the Queen Mother at Valladolid. Instead the unsuccessful siege of Mayorga led to the retreat of the Aragonese. Fernando's betrothal to a Portuguese princess, and the cession of several frontier towns to Portugal appeared to remove another enemy. But the rebellion continued until 1300. The Infante Enrique was worse than useless as a regent. His proposal to surrender Sancho IV's one important conquest, Tarifa, to Granada was only prevented by the governor, Alfonso Pérez de Guzmán's refusal to give it up.

In these hazardous years the queen appears as almost alone

in sustaining her son's cause against his relatives and the great nobles. It is she who argues with one town delegation after another at the Cortes, who spends eight days in Segovia urging the need for the Crown to receive its usual tributes from the local Jewish and Muslim communities; who, when ill, travels in a litter born by mules to Burgos to obtain a loan from the merchants there. The queen struggles with the nobles to get them to push home a siege when all they want to do is 'eat and be quiet'. She makes the concessions that cannot be avoided to gain time. She is the only person a great noble such as Don Juan Núñez de Lara fears.

Queen María was assisted by the divisions between her enemies and by luck. Her task was vastly hampered by the weakness of the child for whom she had striven.

In 1301 Jaume II of Aragon believed, no doubt correctly, that 'it was a very easy thing to win over some of the principal *ricos hombres* of Castile with money... If, by the help of the king of France, the pope would assist Alfonso [de la Cerda], he would achieve his aims.' Fortunately for Castile France was taken up with the Flemish revolt. The queen was able to obtain letters from the papacy declaring Fernando IV legitimate.

In 1301 Fernando was sixteen years old. Contemporary chroniclers describe how easily he was turned against his mother by the men who had tried and were still trying to dethrone him. 'He was almost continually occupied in children's games rather than in trying to recover his land ... Indeed he alienated many other parts of his kingdom and gave them to barons, soldiers, and even to kings.' A modern historian sees Fernando as 'a mediocre monarch, guided by bad counsellors. He was fortunate that his mother lived ... Without her the kingdom would have perished, either by internal troubles or foreign enemies'.

Queen María was not all powerful. She could not prevent the permanent cession of much of the kingdom of Murcia to Aragon in 1304. Her authority was undermined by the rival bands of nobles, competing to see which of them could get Aragon on its side. At least the settlement brought with it a renunciation by the Cerdas of their claims to the throne. The queen tried to keep a balance in the kingdom. This was a difficult task when Fernando openly appeared as a 'partisan', now of one party, now of the other. The quarrels of the great nobles postponed for several years a campaign against Granada. In 1309 they rendered the siege of Algeciras futile. Fernando IV died aged twenty-six in 1312 leaving a child a year old as his heir.[1]

MINORITY OF ALFONSO XI (1312–1325)

The situation in 1312 was less serious than at the death of Sancho IV in 1295. Jaume II of Aragon recognized that the Cerdas were without substantial support in Castile. He was now mainly interested in Sardinia. Granada was engaged in civil war. It proved possible to arrive at a compromise on the government of Castile–León. From 1314 to 1319 it was shared by Queen María, her younger son the Infante Pedro, and Sancho IV's brother, the Infante Juan.

The death of the two Infantes in 1319 before Granada brought about a crisis. Queen María was old and ill. She died in 1321. There was no one with sufficient prestige to assume control. Don Juan, the son of the Infante Don Juan, allied with the *concejos* of Castile, Don Juan Manuel and the Infante Don Felipe, the feeblest of Sancho IV's sons, with those of Toledo and Extremadura. 'The land was divided in two.'

The chaotic conditions of the minority and reign of Fernando returned from 1319 to 1325. From 1301 onwards the Cortes had complained again and again of the illegal fortresses from which the evildoers terrorized the countryside. The Infante Pedro, when regent, had acted decisively to destroy these fortresses. But after his death they were again built not only by nobles but by Military Orders and prelates. In 1322 the Cortes complained that 'some *ricos omes*, *infanzones*, knights, squires . . . defy and threaten royal *concejos* . . . Diego López and Alfonso Fernández . . . entered by night the royal town of Vea, threw out those who lived there, took all they had, made a fortress there and hold it.' In 1315 the knights and towns of Castile-León had joined in a *Hermandad* to protect themselves from oppression by the earlier regents. This *Hermandad* was powerless to refuse

[1] Gaibrois, ii. 378 f., 394; *Cortes de León*, i. 131 f.; *Crónica de Fernando IV*, 1–4 (*BAE* lxvi. 93–112) and *passim*; Zurita, *Anales*, v. 50; Loaisa, pp. 33–49; A. Ballesteros, *Historia de España*, 2nd edn., iii. 1 (Barcelona, 1948), 85; A. Canellas López, *BRAH* 145 (1959), 233–55, 266–78.

recognition to the three new rulers, who, the archbishop of Toledo observed in 1322, 'are rather destroyers [of the land] than its protectors'.

War was carried on mainly by devastating the countryside. The *Chronicle* of Loaisa describes the conditions of 1300, which now returned. The roads of Castile were covered with grass and invaded by bands of peasants and labourers turned brigands. The regents could only agree to keep out their rivals. They were ready to give up royal rights to get control of a city. Under such rule the Crown's authority all but disappeared. Castile was fortunate that she possessed no serious external enemies.[1]

CASTILIAN EXTERNAL HISTORY: WESTERN EUROPE

The internal distractions of Castile made it very difficult for the monarchy to pursue any consistent external policies, either in or outside the Iberian peninsula. Fernando III had found it possible to direct the energies of Castile away from factional division into the struggle with Islam. Alfonso XI was to achieve the same object. In the period between 1252 and 1325 attempts to pursue the 'Reconquest' or to carry the war with Islam to North Africa were spasmodic, their results unimpressive. One of the reasons for this was the entanglement of the Castilian Crown in the politics of western Europe.

ALFONSO X AND THE HOLY ROMAN EMPIRE

Alfonso X was drawn into his hopeless quest for the crown of the Holy Roman Empire by way of his claim, through his mother, Beatrice of Hohenstaufen, to the duchy of Swabia. In 1255 Pope Alexander IV encouraged Alfonso to hope that he might succeed in this minor ambition. If the papacy wished to use Alfonso against the surviving members of the Hohenstaufen dynasty, it was unsuccessful. Alfonso was fatally drawn on to greater things.

In 1256 an embassy from the Ghibelline anti-papal republic of Pisa persuaded Alfonso to accept the Holy Roman Empire. In return for the promise of a crown Pisa had no right to offer, the republic acquired Alfonso's pledge to send Castilian troops

[1] Giménez Soler, *Don Juan Manuel*, pp. 451–55, 60, 491, 515; *Crónica de Alfonso XI*, 17, 23 f. (*BAE* lxvi. 186, 189 f.); *Cortes de León*, i. 147, 171, 188, 217, 361, 363, 367, 247–72; Finke, *Acta* iii. 404; Loaisa, pp. 37 f.

to defend it against its numerous enemies, who thus became Alfonso's.

Within a month of the Pisan embassy Alfonso had sent an ambassador to Germany to press his claims. In 1257 there followed the 'double election', in which three of the seven German electors chose Richard of Cornwall, brother of Henry III of England, as King of the Romans, while four chose Alfonso. This dubious triumph had been secured by enormous bribes. It proved illusory. Richard could visit Germany. Alfonso despite many promises, never succeeded in doing so. Nor did he achieve anything in Italy. He was soon abandoned by Pisa. Alfonso's alliance with the Ghibellines of North Italy turned the papacy against him.

At the Cortes of 1259, if not in 1258, Alfonso raised taxes to pursue 'the matter of the empire'. The sums raised were spent on his shadow Imperial Chancery and on large payments to peripheral magnates of the Empire such as the duke of Burgundy and count of Flanders. Embassies to the papacy merely procured neutrality. In 1270–1 a vacancy in the papacy appeared to give Alfonso an opening in Italy. More money was poured out to promote his claims. Even after the death of Richard of Cornwall and the election and papal recognition of Rudolf of Habsburg Alfonso was sending troops to North Italy. In 1275 he insisted on travelling to France to see Pope Gregory X. Morocco and Granada used his absence to invade Andalusia. Alfonso was forced to renounce his imperial claim in return for a grant of ecclesiastical revenues in Spain.

Alfonso's pursuit of the Holy Roman Empire won him nothing. The taxes he had raised to this end provided a good handle for his noble critics. In order to continue his imperial quest he had had to give in to their demands in 1273. Yet he returned to the title of King of the Romans when he again sent troops to North Italy in 1281 just before the last crisis of his reign.

Behind Alfonso's fascination for the Empire, which lasted almost thirty years, there was more than an interest in Italian politics or in Swabia. The *Primera Crónica General*'s interest in Julius Caesar, whom it sees as slain by 'traitors' (*ricos omes*), and the beginning of the Roman Empire, reveals something of Alfonso's mind. His legal compilations were inspired by Roman law. These interests blended with older claims by Castilian kings to 'empire' over Spain, claims which Alfonso tried to revive in 1259, only to be sharply rebuked by Jaume I of Aragon for doing so.[1]

CASTILE, ENGLAND, AND FRANCE: GASCONY (1253–1254)

Alfonso X's attempt to secure the Holy Roman Empire had little effect on Italy or Germany though it had a serious effect on the Castilian Crown. Before this imperial quest Alfonso made an attempt to assert older Castilian claims to Gascony, which was held by England. Alfonso was asked to intervene by rebellious Gascon nobles. Henry III of England apparently feared that Alfonso, 'with a great army of Christians and Saracens', was about to invade not only Gascony but England itself. Such was the reputation Castile enjoyed after Fernando III's victories. Alfonso renounced his claims in return for royal marriages and English promises, never fulfilled, to assist him over Navarre.

NAVARRE

Navarre would have been a good exchange for Gascony. Alfonso attempted to intervene at the death of the French king of Navarre, Thibaut I, in 1253, but was forced to withdraw by Aragon. Thibaut II became Alfonso's vassal but no land was gained by Castile. In 1274 the question of Navarre again arose, when the last king of the House of Champagne died, leaving only a daughter. Castile and Aragon both intervened in the country. The Queen Mother of Navarre chose to marry her daughter to the heir of France, the future Philippe IV. Navarre was directly united to France until 1328; after this time it was ruled by a minor branch of the French royal family.

France had acquired a foothold south of the Pyrenees from which it could menace or at any rate influence both Castile and Aragon. In 1276 France prepared to invade Castile to defend the rights of the Cerdas to the Castilian throne. This invasion was an even greater fiasco than the French attack on Catalonia in 1285. Alfonso X's appeal to France at the end of his life produced no response. However, France was sufficiently formidable

[1] Ballesteros, *Alfonso X*, pp. 135, 153–60, 177–89, 213–35, 240–3, 454–9, 536–44, 674–77, 683–97, 711–32, 769–74; R. Lopez, *Genova marinara*, pp. 78–85; Loaisa, pp. 16 f.; *Primera Crónica General*, ed. Menéndez Pidal, cc. 113, 118–20 (i, pp. 89–97); *MHE* i. 151. See also P. E. Schramm, in *Festschrift für E. E. Stengel* (Weimar, 1952), pp. 393–401.

to make Sancho IV prefer the French to the Aragonese alliance. In return Philippe IV of France was largely responsible in 1301 for the papal recognition of Fernando IV as legitimate. The Franco-Castilian alliance was confirmed in 1305.

Although Castile was not deeply embroiled in European politics before 1350—the imperial ambitions of Alfonso proving a flash in the pan—the geographical situation of Gascony, between Castile and France but held by England, was important for the future. Gascony was beginning to drag Castile into the international arena. In 1294 France required Sancho IV to send forces by land and sea against England. In return France promised aid against Portugal. We seem already in the Hundred Years War. Castile is becoming a firm ally of France. French influence with the papacy is as important to Castile in 1301 as it is throughout the fourteenth century, when the papacy was at Avignon. The geographical and demographic preponderance of Castile in the Iberian peninsula had already brought about an alliance of Portugal, Aragon, and Granada against her. This alliance was devised by Jaume II of Aragon in the 1290s. In the 1370s it was to be used by Pere III against Enrique II of Castile.[1]

CASTILIAN EXTERNAL HISTORY: THE PENINSULA: PORTUGAL

The frontiers between Castile–León and the other Christian kingdoms of the peninsula, Aragon, Navarre, and Portugal, scarcely changed after the thirteenth century. In 1304–5 the kingdom of Murcia was divided between Castile and Aragon on lines which were to prove permanent although they were the cause of much later conflict. Alfonso X ceded the Algarve to Portugal as a dowry accompanying the marriage of his illegitimate daughter to Afonso III. The frontier between Castile and Portugal was finally established in 1297.[2]

GRANADA

The frontier between Castile and Muslim Granada remained virtually stationary from 1246 until Alfonso XI's personal

[1] Ballesteros, pp. 92–9, 146, 697–706; see above, Ch. I, p. 258, n. 3. G. Daumet, *Mémoire sur les relations de la France et de la Castille de 1225 à 1320* (Paris, 1913); Gaibrois, *Sancho IV*, ii. 299–304.

[2] Ballesteros, pp. 74–7, 346 ff., 376 ff., 420–51.

reign (1325–50). Why was it that Granada survived? How did its survival affect Castile?

THE ECONOMY OF GRANADA

An Egyptian scholar, writing in the 1340s, gives us one of the best contemporary descriptions of Granada that we possess. He speaks of 'aqueducts flowing through Granada in all directions. The town has many gardens, very rich in fruits. Surrounded by mountains, it is protected against strong winds . . . on the two mountains within the city there are magnificent houses, with the most delicious views of the Vega, which is crossed by streams and covered with crops'. The Vega surrounding Granada impressed all visitors. Its richness seemed due to nature though in fact it was due to the skilful use of irrigation techniques. The intense exploitation of limited areas, not only round Granada but all over the small emirate, was already noted by Ibn Khaldūn in the fourteenth century. This was necessary to support the relatively dense population, swollen by Muslim refugees from other parts of Spain. The production of cereals was not enough for internal consumption. Cereals had to be imported. They were paid for by specialized crops, sugar-cane, figs, and almonds, and by industrial products, especially silk. The port of Málaga was one of the most important in the western Mediterranean. Through Málaga and Almería the emirate was in touch with Italy, the eastern Mediterranean, and North Africa.[1]

ITS INTERNAL WEAKNESSES: THE POLITICAL SITUATION

As long as specialized agriculture and overseas trade were not interrupted by prolonged periods of war Granada could survive. But it was difficult to assure the tranquillity it needed. From the beginning, in 1246, Granada was a vassal of Castile. This vassalage was a condition of survival but it also meant that a basic contradiction was built into the fabric of the State. For a Muslim ruler to be the vassal of a Christian king revolted every principle of Islamic law. And the vassalage of Granada was not only

[1] Ibn Faḍl Allah al-Umarī, transl. A. Zeki, *Homenaje a D. Francisco Codera* (Saragossa, 1904), pp. 465–72; M. A. Ladero Quesada, *Granada* (Madrid, 1969), pp. 18, 21 f., 36–41; Ibn Khaldūn, *The Muqaddimah*, transl. F. Rosenthal, ii (Princeton N.J., 1967), 278. R. Arié, *l'Espagne musulmane au temps des naṣrtides* (Paris, 1973), pp. 344–63.

humiliating but onerous. It involved the emir's attendance at the Castilian court and sending military contingents to fight against fellow Muslims as well as Christians. Granada also had to contribute large sums as annual tribute to Castile, the *parias*. In 1246 this tribute was fixed at half the revenues of the emirate. It never fell below a quarter or a fifth of these revenues. In order to raise *parias* and cover other expenses, the emirs taxed their subjects far more heavily than Islamic law allowed.

A 'SIEGE MENTALITY'

The situation of constant tension in which Granada existed had a pronounced psychological effect. It produced a 'siege mentality'. From the beginning Granada was 'a kingdom of refugees and so of intransigents'. In Granada there was little of the *convivencia* between men of different religions that one finds (together with intolerance) in Christian Spain. There were no organized Christian communities, though Christian renegades could rise, as individuals, to the highest posts. Jews were not numerous. They were of importance in overseas trade but do not seem to have attained the place as administrators and court scholars that they had had in former Muslim Spain and now enjoyed in the Christian kingdoms.

The intellectual life of Granada, sealed off from contact with Christian Spain, had also largely lost touch with Islamic traditions of scholarship. Ibn Khaldūn, who knew Granada, had a very low opinion of the standard of education there. His contemporary Ibn al-Khaṭīb's glowing praise of the intellectual attainments of several emirs is unconvincing. He wrote as a panegyrist. The Muslim scholars of Granada who could do so left the country to seek their fortunes in Baghdad, Damascus, Alexandria, or Timbuktu. In their place Ibn Baṭūṭa, who visited Granada in 1350, records the presence of fakirs from as far as Samarkand and India. These peripatetic holy men added, one suspects, more heat than light to the atmosphere of the city they inhabited.

RELIGIOUS FANATICISM

The odds against Granada in any direct encounter with Castile were so unfavourable that no intelligent statesman would have considered the possibility. But the politics of Granada, as of most other countries, were not determined only by the intelligent but very often by fanatics.

Spanish Islam had always been noted for its religious orthodoxy, often passing into bigotry. Ibn al-Khaṭīb, in his eulogy of the charming, modest, middle-class inhabitants of Granada, tells us that their 'beliefs are orthodox. Subversive opinions and heresies are unknown among them.' This orthodox population could be influenced by the Doctors of the Law, for whom the vassalage by which Granada lived was a dangerous error. The lawyers' views were preached to the crowds by numerous fakirs. Holy War was also popular with the Berber mercenary troops and volunteers from North Africa, who were always an important element in the country. As time went on the emirs found it more and more difficult to keep the Holy War Party in check. Most of the wars with Castile were caused by Granada. The epitaph of a North African sūfī Ḥasan ibn Ṣāliḥ gives us a picture of the type of man admired in Granada.

He came to this land desirous of waging the Holy War, of meeting virtuous men, and of visiting fortunate kings. . . . United in him there were the knowledge of the Religious Law and the sūfī method. He trained the novices and led them by the good road. He waged the Holy War in the Name of God and for love of God spent all he possessed. Polite assemblies benefited from his virtue and he defended garrisons and frontiers. He was one of the wonders of the age and the lights of the believers.

INTERNAL DIVISIONS

The power of these fanatics endangered the existence of Granada as a separate state. The emirate was troubled by other internal divisions also. It was plagued by the plague of all Muslim states, the power of the tribe, the lineage (*aṣabiyya*), as against the prince. Each lineage dominated a particular area or areas. Even in the large cities there were no officials named by the emir himself. Although Granada was freer from the feuds of the lineages in its first century of existence as an emirate than it was to be later, it had come into being as an alliance between the Naṣrid emirs and the Banū Ashīqlūla lineage. Their wars divided and nearly destroyed the State under Muḥammad I and II (1265–85).[1]

HOW GRANADA SURVIVED

Given the many internal weaknesses of Granada it is surprising that it survived for two centuries. Its survival was principally due to divisions within Castile but it also possessed military strengths of its own and powerful allies.

INTERNAL STRENGTHS: MILITARY

Ibn al-Khaṭīb tells us that the military forces of Granada were divided into the native inhabitants and the Berbers. The natives, or 'Andalusians', were commanded by a royal prince. Under the first emirs they were armed 'like their Christian neighbours and rivals'. By about 1350 they adopted normal Arab light arms. The Berber troops were commanded by a relative of the Merinid ruler of Morocco. They were armed with javelins and bows.

The Berbers were formidable adversaries. They were greatly appreciated by the Crown of Aragon, which employed them extensively. In Castile their tactics were imitated by native light cavalry. Don Juan Manuel, as *Adelantado* of Murcia, knew the frontier of Granada very well. He praises the raiding tactics of the 'Moors', who travel at great speed, without infantry, and with hardly any food and light arms.

Two hundred Moorish horse will cover more country and do more harm than 600 Christian . . . They are such good men-at-arms and know and wage war so well that, but for their false religion and because they are not armed or mounted so that they can endure hand-to-hand combat, they would be *unsurpassed* as warriors.

Don Juan's careful advice on the best tactics to adopt against the 'Moors', especially when invading their territory, shows that

[1] Ladero, pp. 50–5, 67; H. Terrasse, in *Mélanges offerts a M. Bataillon* (Bordeaux, 1962), pp. 253–60; Ibn Khaldūn, iii. 302 (see also ii. 430, iii. 117); Ibn al-Khaṭīb, *Ihata*, transl. Casiri, *Bibliotheca Arabico-Hispana Escurialiensis*, ii. 280 f.; transl. I. S. Allouche, *Mélanges d'histoire et d'archeologie de l'occident musulman*, ii (Algiers, 1957), 7–12; R. Arié, *MCV* I (1965), 103; Ibn Baṭūṭa, *Voyages*, transl. C. Defrémery and B. R. Sanguinetti, iv (Paris, 1879), 373; I. S. Allouche, *Hespéris*, 25 (1938), 1–11; E. Garcia Gómez, *Al-Andalus* 7 (1942), 293–6.

he considered war with Granada to be a very difficult undertaking.

GRANADA'S DEFENSIVE SYSTEM

The defensive system of Granada was organized by 1320. Along the vulnerable north and west frontiers it consisted of a line of great castles generally about ten kilometres apart. These castles often imitated the latest Christian techniques in fortification. They were sometimes linked by watch-towers. This defensive chain could not prevent Christian raids but it could send warning of their coming and hamper the raiders' communications with their base. Every town and village in the emirate was protected by some defensive work. This system of fortifications made the process of conquest so slow that, until the Catholic Kings, no ruler of Castile could pursue it except in a piecemeal fashion.

At the heart of the emirate was the Alhambra of Granada, a fortress city with its own population and life. Ibn al-Khaṭīb hails its 'white battlements, high towers, untakable fortress, palaces dominating the countryside.'[1]

GRANADA'S ALLIES: MOROCCO, ARAGON

Granada had allies it could deploy against its over-powerful liege-lord, Castile. By the 1260s the Merinids had emerged as rulers of Morocco. They could be invoked to assist their co-religionists in Spain. Their help needed, however, to be used with caution. They were apt to be as dangerous to the emirs of Granada as earlier African dynasties had proved to former princes of al-Andalus.

There was also Aragon, which was excluded by Castile from profiting from the conquest of Granada. From 1295 to 1303, and again in the fourteenth century, Aragon and Granada were in alliance. In order to survive the emirs of Granada were obliged to play off Morocco and Aragon against Castile. They profited from the internal divisions of Castile itself and from the fact that the Castilian Crown was far more concerned with other enemies than it was with Granada.

[1] Ibn al-Khaṭīb, transl. Allouche; Juan Manuel, *Libro de los estados*, i. 75–9 (*BAE* li. 322–6); H. Terrasse, *Les Fortresses de l'Espagne musulmane* (Madrid, 1954), pp. 25–35; see above, Part I, Ch. II, pp. 19–21; Arié, pp. 230–65.

ALFONSO X, GRANADA, AND MOROCCO

To Fernando III, in his last years, and to Alfonso X, at the beginning of his reign, the problem of Granada appeared to be settled. The emir of Granada was a vassal of Castile, and a constant source of gold. Granada, as Alfonso was to observe later, was inconsiderable in comparison with Castile. Once Alfonso had subdued the lower valley of the Guadalquivir he wished to extend his father's conquests to North Africa.

The construction of the dockyards of Seville was hurried on. In 1252 and 1255 the papacy issued letters exhorting the bishops of Spain to assist the crusade in Africa. In 1259, when the Cortes of Toledo were called to raise money for Alfonso's quest for the Holy Roman Empire, Muḥammad I of Granada himself proposed that the king should turn to the 'much greater and better empire than this' available in North Africa.

Although Alfonso's ambitions in Italy and Germany occupied much of his attention he made some small gains in Andalusia and launched one expedition to Salé in Morocco in 1260. A fleet of thirty-seven ships and a large expeditionary force took the port of Salé and held it for ten days but the return voyage, laden with booty and thousands of captives, was disastrous. The one attempt Alfonso made to carry out his African crusade was to have serious consequences. Abū Yūsuf, emir of the Banū Marīn, the conqueror of the Almohads, was not a ruler to tolerate a raid of this kind. A contemporary Arabic chronicler, Ibn Abi Zar', describes Abū Yūsuf as a conventional holy ruler of Islam; conventional piety included dedication to the Holy War against the infidel. Abū Yūsuf, as the founder of a new dynasty in Morocco, was in particular need of the prestige conferred by crusade. He achieved this prestige in Spain. The chronicler remarks: 'He was the first king of the Banū Marīn who defended Islam, destroyed the crosses, and laid waste the land of the Christians, subduing its kings and its *alcázares*.' Ibn Idārī describes Abū Yūsuf rebuilding the walls of Salé with his own hands. 'He did not cease to devote himself, from now on, to the Holy War.'[1] The first Berber volunteers, 3,000 horse, appeared

[1] Ballesteros, *Alfonso X*, pp. 68, 135 f.; *Crónica de Alfonso X*, 52 (*BAE* lxvi. 40); Ch-E. Dufourcq, *RHCM* 1 (1966), 27–51; T. Minguella y Arnedo, *Historia de la diócesis de Sigüenza y de sus obispos*, i (Madrid, 1910), p. 599; A. Huici Miranda,

in Granada a year after the attack on Salé. They were to assist Muḥammad I's onslaught on Castile in 1264. Muḥammad had seen Alfonso swallow one after another the tributary Muslim towns of Andalusia. Cádiz had been occupied before 1260, Niebla in 1262. Alfonso was demanding Tarifa and Gibraltar as bases for expeditions to North Africa. In 1264 the storm broke. All over Andalusia the subject Muslims (Mudejars) rose. Almost all the towns and castles along the frontier fell. Murcia revolted against its tributary status. Alfonso and his family were almost captured in Seville. As it was he escaped. The town militias and the nobles of Castile were called on for aid. Within a year the rising in Andalusia was subdued. In 1265 Alfonso invaded Granada. By allying with the rebellious Banū Ashqīlūla of Málaga and Guadix he forced Muḥammad to sue for peace and to abandon Murcia, which was conquered by Jaume I of Aragon.

Muḥammad was not conquered. He revenged himself by forming alliances with the Castilian magnates. When he died in 1273 his successor Muḥammad II adopted the policy of open alliance with Abū Yūsuf of Morocco. In 1273 Alfonso ridiculed the danger from Morocco. In 1275 he was to learn how mistaken he had been. While he was engaged in fruitless negotiation at Beaucaire over the Holy Roman Empire, Muḥammad II invited a large Merinid force to enter Spain. This invasion took Castile completely by surprise. Two Christian detachments led by Don Nuño González de Lara, *Adelantado de la Frontera*, and by the archbishop of Toledo, were destroyed. As the iron-clad Christian knights advanced Abū Yūsuf exhorted his Muslims to enter 'the great theatre of martyrdom' and conquer the 'polytheists'. The report of an eye-witness in Don Nuño's force describes how the *Adelantado* was urged in vain to wait for reinforcements, and his order to unfurl his banner. After the battle the Muezzins' call to prayer rang out from the top of mountains of heads of the dead Christians. It was a sight which had not been seen for many decades in Spain.

Abū Yūsuf's victorious troops appeared before the walls of Seville and carried off a huge booty in cattle and horses. Six months after his coming he retired to North Africa. His com-

Hespéris, 39 (1952), 41–74; Ibn Abi Zar', *Rawd al-Qirṭās*, ed. Huici, ii (Valencia, 1964), 565 ff.; Ibn Idārī, *Al-Bayan al-Mugrib*, ii, ed. Huici (Tetuán, 1953), 271.

munications were threatened by Christian ships in the Straits of Gibraltar.

This pattern of rapid raid and retreat was repeated in 1277 and 1282–5. The prestige of Islam was re-established in Spain. Castilian knights in gilded armour fled before the light-armed Africans. Andalusia and Extremadura were terrorized, though no important Christian city or castle was taken. Granada, which saw the Banū Marīn taking over its cities one after another, tried to find a way to escape.

Castile, Granada, and Morocco passed through a kaleidoscope of alliances. At one time Castile was allied with Granada, at another with Morocco, at another Morocco supported Alfonso X against his rebellious son Sancho, who was supported by Granada. Alfonso's will of 1282 expresses his gratitude to Abū Yūsuf, who 'seeing me destitute, although we were of different laws [religions] . . . did not regard that . . . We trusted in him so that we remained in his power for four months'. Whatever Abū Yūsuf's motives in assisting Alfonso in 1282–3, on that occasion, as before, he gained vast booty and weakened Castile.

SANCHO IV

At Alfonso's death Sancho IV found himself confronted with another Merinid raid. According to Ibn Khaldūn Sancho was forced to submit. He presented himself at Abū Yūsuf's camp, 'in the midst of the standards of Islam, surrounded by a large army and the brilliance of a strong and powerful nation.' The *Crónica de Sancho IV* sees Sancho as only prevented by his over-powerful magnates from winning a decisive victory. The truth appears to be that both Sancho and Abū Yūsuf wanted peace, though Sancho wanted it more.[1]

Abū Yūsuf's son and successor, Abū Ya^{c}qūb (1286–1307), for some years enjoyed peaceful relations with Castile. Sancho sent 300 men-at-arms to assist the emir in 1288. Granada, however, was not content with the situation. The Banū Marīn still occupied Tarifa and Algeciras and so controlled the Straits

[1] Ballesteros, pp. 313–20, 362–407, 740–65, 829–35, 866–9, 885–917; *Crónica de Alfonso X*, 52 (p. 39); Ibn Abi Zar', pp. 592–606; Pero Marin, *Miraculos*, *Al-Andalus*, 7 (1942), 58 f.; Alfonso X, in *Cantigas d'escarnho*, 21, ed. M. Rodrigues Lapa (Coimbra, 1965), pp. 37 ff.; *MHE* ii, 117 f.; Ibn Khaldūn, *Histoire des berbères*, transl. Slane, iv (Algiers, 1856), p. 118; *Crónica de Sancho IV*, 2 (*BAE* lxvi. 71 f.).

of Gibraltar. In 1291 Sancho IV partitioned future conquests in North Africa with Jaume II of Aragon. Morocco was reserved for Castile. Sancho may have promised Granada Tarifa. Certainly Granada assisted Sancho to capture the city in 1292. Jaume, Genoa, and Granada provided the fleet Castile needed, Jaume contributing eleven galleys, Genoa twelve, Granada twenty.

Morocco, now assisted by Muḥammad II of Granada, angry because he considered himself deluded by Sancho, only just failed to retake Tarifa in 1294. Catalan galleys again proved indispensable to Castile. Encouraged by this success, Sancho IV's counsellors proposed to him a plan by which he could take Algeciras as well: 'As soon as God has given it to you you are protected from all the enemies across the sea and may do what you will with those on *this* side.' In other words Granada would be in Sancho's power.

Sancho approved the plan but he died within a few months. Abū Yaᶜqūb turned away from Spain towards Tlemcen. He returned to Granada the custody of Ronda and Algeciras.

FERNANDO IV

During the minority of Fernando IV (1295–1301) Granada and Aragon joined together to collect what spoils they could from Castile. Aragon gained the kingdom of Murcia, Granada defeated several Castilian armies and conquered frontier places which it hoped to trade for Tarifa. In 1303 the new ruler of Granada, Muḥammad III, changed sides and allied with Castile. This change was enough to alter the balance of power in the peninsula and to force Aragon to give up part of Murcia to Castile in 1304.

Muḥammad III's own ambitious North African policy brought about an alliance of Morocco with Castile and Aragon. Aragon was promised a sixth of Granada. Jaume II's ambassador informed the pope that the time had come to extirpate 'the only corner of Europe inhabited by Saracens'. He did not disclose that Morocco was a party to the crusade for which he was demanding papal funds.

In 1309 Fernando IV of Castile besieged Algeciras, Jaume II Almería. This reliance on sieges, given the difficulty of taking walled towns, was probably mistaken. The victories of the past had been won by so devastating the land that its inhabitants were forced either to submit or emigrate. The sieges of 1309 were disastrous. Once Morocco had regained Ceuta from Granada she at once abandoned her Christian allies. Moroccan aid and the rivalries of Castilian magnates forced Fernando to withdraw from Algeciras. The Catalan fleet captured Gibraltar for Castile. Gibraltar was less important as a harbour than Algeciras but its capture was the main success of the campaign. By treaty with Granada (1310) Castile regained the towns lost during Fernando's minority. Jaume II's losses before Almería were very severe. The Crown of Aragon never again attacked Granada.

Fernando IV was planning a new campaign against Algeciras when he died in 1312. During the first years of Alfonso XI's minority Fernando's younger brother, the Infante Pedro, endeavoured to continue the war. His death and that of the Infante Juan during a raid on the Vega of Granada in 1319 led to a complete halt in hostilities which lasted ten years. From 1312 to 1329 Morocco was engaged in Africa and absent from Spain.

The results attained by three kings of Castile from 1252 to 1312 in the struggle against Islam were slight. Control over Murcia and the lower valley of the Guadalquivir were assured, Tarifa and Gibraltar were won, but the only attempt at a general crusade, in which Aragon shared, proved a dismal failure, and the struggle for the Straits of Gibraltar was not concluded. In the 1340s the body of the Infante Pedro was still suspended in a coffin over the door of the Alhambra, a trophy and a sign that Islam in Spain was not yet a thing of the past.[1]

THE CASTILIAN COURT AND LEARNING

The traditional picture of Alfonso X as a political failure must be held to be largely true. If his failure in politics extended to his two immediate successors his patronage of learning was not continued by them. Miss Procter has remarked that what

[1] Gaibrois, *Sancho IV*, i. 179 f.; ii. 123, 387; iii. ccl-lvi; Ibn Abi Zar', pp. 696 f.; Giménez Soler, *La Corona de Aragón y Granada* (Barcelona, 1908); idem, *El sitio de Almeria en 1309* (Barcelona, 1904); Dufourcq, pp. 376–405, 454–9; Finke, *Acta*, iii. 219; I. S. Allouche, *Hespéris*, 16 (1933), 122–38; Ibn Faḍl, op. cit., p. 469. For repercussions of 1319 see two North African texts in E. Fagnan, *Extraits inédits relatifs au Maghreb* (Algiers, 1924), pp. 259 f., 262 ff.

differentiates Alfonso's literary court from those of other rulers is that 'the major works produced under Alfonso's patronage are not individual compositions . . . but great works of *co-operative* scholarship . . . due to the initiative of the king and produced under his *personal* direction'. (My italics.) The great manuscripts of the *Cántigas*, the *Primera Crónica General*, the *General estoria*, were the work of *équipes* of scholars and artists. The manuscripts of the *Cántigas* at the Escorial, unique in their variety of content and perfection of execution, were the result of the collaboration of Provençal and Galician troubadours and minstrels with Muslim as well as Christian musicians and with scribes and miniaturists of the highest quality. The historical, legislative, and astronomical works were produced by corresponding groups of scholars. We do not know the names of the compilers of the historical and legislative works. The prologues of the astronomical works show that they were produced by the collaboration of Jews, Italians, and (a few) Castilians.[1]

ASTRONOMY-ASTROLOGY

That Alfonso's motives for patronizing scholarship were not as 'pure', as 'scientific' as they used to be considered is of little importance. In the next two centuries Alfonso was seen as 'the astrologer'. One work he had translated showed how, through consulting the stars, one can discover if a counsellor is loyal, if an affair will go ill or well. The *Libro de las cruces* shows how to form horoscopes and predict events of interest to kings. A chapter added by the Jewish translator to the original text described the planets dominating particular cities in the peninsula; this information indicated when one should attack a particular city or people. The *Lapidario* lists the secret virtues of stones and shows how they are connected with planets. Astrology also intervenes in the *Libro de ajedrez* (*Book of Chess*) and it is alluded to in Alfonso's historical and legal works. It has been said that astrology was Alfonso's 'principal preoccupation'. But it led the king 'to provide astronomers with a working library on the construction and use of the essential instruments of their science, so that they would not need to consult other works.' Alfonso intervened himself, planning his compilations and

[1] E. S. Procter, *Modern Language Review*, 40 (1945), 12; G. Menéndez Pidal, *BRAH* 150 (1962), 25-51.

having them revised. The *Alfonsine Tables*, for instance, are based on a work of the eleventh-century astronomer Al-Zarqālī but contain a long introduction and new observations made at Toledo in the 1260s. If no Arabic work on the construction of an astronomical instrument could be found Alfonso had one of his Jewish astronomers fill the gap.[1]

HISTORICAL WORKS

The translations of astronomical and astrological works produced for Alfonso date mainly from 1250 to 1259 though they were sometimes revised in later years. Alfonso's more original compilations belong to the second stage of scholarship at his court. The main legal works, the *Espéculo*, and at least the first *Partida*, date from the 1260s. The *Estoria de Espanna* (usually known today as the *Primera Crónica General*) was probably begun in 1270, the *Grande e general estoria* about 1272.

The first redaction of the whole of the *Primera Crónica* dates from 1274. The final version was only completed as far as *c.* 565 in Alfonso's reign. The final version of the whole *Crónica*—like that of the *Partidas*—was made under Alfonso XI. The main outlines were laid down by Alfonso X though the last chapters (from 1243) seem to have been written after his death. The text of the *General estoria*, as we have it, was completed during his reign.

Alfonso turned aside from the more restricted *Primera Crónica* to the *General estoria*. He intended to take the history of mankind from the Creation to his own reign. The work got no further than the Virgin Mary. But the part completed is four times longer than the *Primera Crónica*. Alfonso confined himself to peoples in touch with Israel, especially Egypt, Greece, and Rome. The scholars working for him were probably those who had begun the *Primera Crónica*. Many of the same sources, Ovid, Lucan, Statius, Suetonius, were drawn on for both works. A wider range of sources was used, however, for the *General estoria*.

The basis was the Vulgate Bible. Most extra-Biblical insertions

[1] Carreras Artau, *Filosofía*, i. 15 f.; Alfonso el Sabio, *Libro de las Cruzes*, ed. L. A. Kåsten and L. B. Kiddle (Madrid, 1961), especially pp. 160 ff.; Aly Aben Ragel, op. cit.; A. Steiger, *Revista del Instituto Egipcio de Estudios Islámicos en Madrid*, 3 (1955), 93–109, at 96; A. G. Solalinde, *RFE* 2 (1915), 283–88; 13 (1926), 350–6; Procter, loc. cit., pp. 12–29, at 18.

were taken from the late twelfth-century *Historia scholastica* of the Parisian master Petrus Comestor but Alfonso gave far greater space to secular history and attempted to synchronize Biblical and non-Biblical history. His main aim was to bring out the moral lessons of scripture by glossing it with all the sources available, which include Muslim and rabbinical texts as well as Spanish historians and French vernacular *romans*.[1]

The *Primera Crónica General*, or *Estoria de Espanna*, surpasses its contemporary rivals 'by its selection of sources and the plan that it follows'. Like the *General estoria* the *Crónica*'s use of Greek and Muslim sources distinguishes it from contemporary historical works written outside Spain; its use of epic vernacular poems can be paralleled in Catalan chronicles but not in the rest of western Europe. Alfonso's vision embraced the whole past of the Iberian peninsula, Muslim as well as Christian, in one chronological framework.[2]

THE CASTILIAN COURT AND LITERATURE 1284–1325

In the fifteenth century Fernán Pérez de Guzmán wrote of Alfonso X: 'Although he sleeps he lives through his *Tablas* of astrology. He orders and guides our memories with laws. He delights us with histories and adorns us with philosophy.' It would have been difficult to find anything resembling this to say of Alfonso's two immediate successors. Sancho IV appears to have had little interest in culture. No payments for literary work are recorded in his (quite considerable) surviving accounts. This hiatus in literary patronage continued under Fernando IV. Sancho assisted a school at Alcalá de Henares but one cannot trace the university, which flourished there later, back to his time. No universities were in fact founded in Castile–León from the time of Alfonso X, the real founder of the University of

[1] For the legislative works see above, p. 298, notes 1–2. D. Catalán Menéndez Pidal, *De Alfonso X al Conde de Barcelos* (Madrid, 1962), pp. 19–203; Alfonso el Sabio, ed. A. G. Solalinde, *General estoria*, i (Madrid, 1930), pp. ix-xxiii; idem, *RFE* 21 (1934), 1–28; M. R. Lida de Malkiel, *Romance Philology*, 12 (1958–9), 111–42; D. Catalán, *Hispanic Review*, 33 (1965), 310–12; L. B. Kiddle, ibid. 4 (1936), 264–71; 6 (1938), 120–32; M. Morreale, in *The Cambridge History of the Bible*, ii (Cambridge, 1969), 470–3.

[2] R. Menéndez Pidal, *Estudios literarios*, 7th edn. (Buenos Aires, 1952), p. 165; idem, *Primera Crónica General de España*, i (Madrid, 1955), p. xxxvi; D. Catalán, *Romania*, 84 (1963), 354–75; C. E. Dubler, *Vox Romanicum*, 12 (1951–2), 120–80; Procter, *Alfonso X*, pp. 78–112.

Salamanca and creator of schools in Seville and Murcia, until the Catholic Kings; six universities were founded in the Crown of Aragon in these two centuries. Alfonso XI took up the centralizing ideas of Alfonso X and had a number of works interrupted by Alfonso's death completed, but his patronage of learning was on a far less ambitious scale. The stimulus had been provided, however, and court patronage was now less necessary. Don Juan Manuel in prose, the Archpriest of Hita in verse, developed Castilian in vastly different ways, but Alfonso X had given them models they could use. The moralist of the *Partidas* and the historical works lies behind Don Juan's didactic works; Alfonso's poems, with their range from devout to obscene, behind the Archpriest. Neither Don Juan nor the Archpriest could have written as they did without Alfonso's example.

Outside Castile Alfonso's historical works were known in Portugal. Fragments survive of a translation of the *General estoria* into Portuguese. The comparative brevity and particular interest of the *Primera Crónica General* gave it greater popularity. Some six continuations, abbreviations, or re-editions are known before 1344. The Portuguese court took up the work. King Dinis (1279–1325) had it translated, perhaps at the instance of his illegitimate son, Count Pedro of Barcelos. Alfonso's historical work deeply influenced the Portuguese *Cronica geral* of 1344, which was compiled by Count Pedro. It thus stands at the origin of late-medieval Portuguese as well as Castilian historiography. A résumé of Alfonso's *Primera Crónica* was even used by the leading historian of Muslim Granada, Ibn al-Khaṭīb. The *Partidas* and the astronomical works were used and imitated by Pere III of Aragon (1336–87), the monarch who most closely resembles Alfonso in his interest in learning in the century after Alfonso's death.[1]

[1] Fernán Pérez de Guzmán, *Loores de los claros varones de España*, 341 (*NBAE* xix. 744); M. Martins, *Estudos de literatura medieval* (Braga, 1956), pp. 94–100; L. F. Lindley Cintra, *Cronica Geral de Espanha de 1344*, i (Lisbon, 1951); R. Menéndez Pidal, *BRAH* 136 (1955), 131–97; D. Catalán, *De Alfonso X*, pp. 291–411; idem (ed.), *Crónica de 1344 que ordenó el Conde de Barcelos don Pedro Alfonso*, i (Madrid, 1971); M. M. Antuña, *Al-Andalus*, 1 (1933), 107–54; Catalán, in *Mélanges R. Lejeune*, i (Gembloux, 1969), 423–41.

PART III

THE STRUGGLE FOR HEGEMONY
1325–1410

I

Alfonso XI of Castile and the Struggle for the Straits of Gibraltar (1325–1350)

THE BEGINNING OF THE REIGN: THE STRUGGLE WITH THE NOBILITY

THERE were strong similarities between the internal political situation in the three major Christian kingdoms of the peninsula in the first half of the fourteenth century. Dinis of Portugal, Alfonso XI of Castile, and Pere III of Catalonia–Aragon were confronted with attempts by the leading nobility (especially the king's closer relations)to control the government. In general the kings were victorious but in Castile the conflict revived and continued intermittently until the accession of the Catholic Kings in 1475. In Catalonia–Aragon the *tertius gaudens*, the lower nobility and the towns of Catalonia, were to replace the king's relations as his main opponents.

In Castile the situation during the minority of Alfonso XI (1312–25) was chaotic. The contrast with the Catalan expansion into the Mediterranean (Sardinia was occupied in 1323–6) and with the apparent calm of Portugal under Dinis was striking.

According to the main source for the reign, the *Crónica de Alfonso XI*: 'All the *ricos omes* and *caballeros* lived from plundering the land and the "tutors" [regents] allowed this so as to have their support [against each other]'. Each city was divided into factions which (once dominant) oppressed the rest of the population. At least one tutor was ready to abandon royal rights to get control of a town. Towns independent of tutors were ruled by local tyrants, who took over the royal revenues. In some towns there were revolts by the artisans. It was impossible to travel except in large armed companies.[1]

[1] *Crónica de Alfonso XI*, 37, 24 (*BAE* lxvi. 197, 190). See also above, Part II, Ch. II, pp. 315 f.

This picture may be designed to cast Alfonso XI's achievements into higher relief but it is probably substantially true. Where the *Crónica* (apparently written for Alfonso's son Enrique II in the 1370s) appears to romanticize is when it presents a picture of the boy king assuming power (at fourteen) in 1325 and immediately setting out to remedy the country's ills.

Alfonso certainly possessed the great physical energy he needed as king. He was passionately fond of jousting and hunting, and, when not at war, was engaged in one or other of these sports. He was also to display considerable mental energy but in his early years he was largely guided by two lesser nobles, Alvar Núñez de Osorio and Garcilaso de la Vega.[1]

It was difficult for the most energetic king to reduce rebellious nobles. One strong castle, well defended, could hold out a month or more. There were many castles and it was not easy to keep a royal army together. When Alfonso XI besieged a great noble, Don Juan Núñez, in Lerma, the castle was victualled by nobles in the royal army, 'for there was no man [among the nobility] who did not have brothers or cousins or someone to whom he was greatly indebted in Lerma'.[2]

Given the situation, Alfonso's advisers, and later the king himself, proceeded by a mixture of terror and intrigue. In 1325 Alfonso was confronted with the united opposition of two former regents. Don Juan Manuel was temporarily conciliated by the king's marriage (later annulled) to his daughter and the governorship of Andalusia. Don Juan, son of the Infante Don Juan, was lured to Toro by promises, trapped, and murdered. The Crown occupied his lordship of Vizcaya. Later Alfonso had his now too powerful ex-favourite Alvar Núñez murdered since it was the only way to dispose of him. Posthumous judgements of high treason followed. Equally bloody methods were used to impress on rebellious townsmen the error of their ways.

These methods, together with the knowledge of when it was necessary to forgive the most persistent rebels, served Alfonso well, but his success in achieving internal order was principally

[1] *Crónica*, 38 f., 141, 263 (pp. 198 f., 266, 338). Cp. A. Giménez Soler, *Don Juan Manuel* (Saragossa, 1932), p. 539.

[2] *Crónica*, 134, 158 (pp. 262, 276). See above, Part I, Ch. II, pp. 313 f.

due to his being able to divert rebellious energies to the struggle over the Straits of Gibraltar.[1]

THE STRUGGLE WITH ISLAM

The emirate of Granada had profited from the chaos of Castile during Alfonso's minority. In 1319 two of Alfonso's earlier 'tutors' were killed when attacking Granada. The Granadan counter-offensive took Baeza in 1324, Martos in 1325. In 1331 a raid from Granada penetrated across Murcia to Elche in the Crown of Aragon and brought back, 1,500 prisoners and 3,000 cattle. By this time, however, increasing Castilian pressure had made clear to Granada that she had to choose between submission to Castile or appeal to Islamic North Africa. She chose the second alternative.[2]

THE BANŪ MARĪN

The Banū Marīn (Merinids) of Morocco had intervened repeatedly in Spain in earlier reigns. They were to appear again, for the last time, under the great Emir Abū al-Ḥasan (1331–51). Ibn Khaldūn remarks: 'The strength of the Muslims became again equal to that of the Christians . . . When [Abū al-Ḥasan] desired to wage the Holy War his fleet was as well equipped and numerous as that of the Christians.' Although Abū al-Ḥasan's main interests were in North Africa (he conquered Tlemcen—central Algeria today—in 1337, Tunis ten years later), he felt 'an extreme passion for the Holy War'. For two decades his power menaced Spain.[3]

The first round of the struggle went to Islam when Gibraltar (taken by Castile in 1309) fell to Morocco in 1333. The *Crónica de Alfonso XI* blames the former governor of Andalusia, Don Juan Manuel, for failing to save Gibraltar. The *Crónica* ignores the earlier injuries inflicted by Alfonso on Don Juan and the warnings he sent the king of the danger to Gibraltar, but it does

[1] *Crónica*, 41, 48, 74 ff. (pp. 199 f., 202 f., 219). On Segovia, 49 (pp. 203 f.). For Alfonso's clemency, 172 (p. 283).

[2] A. Giménez Soler, *La Corona de Aragón y Granada* (Barcelona, 1908), pp. 198 f., 252; Ibn al-Khaṭīb, cited by L. Seco de Lucena Paredes, *Al-Andalus*, 21 (1956), 288 f.

[3] See above, Part II, Ch. II, pp. 324–9. Ibn Khaldūn, *The Muqaddimah*, 3, 32, transl. F. Rosenthal (Princeton, 1967), ii. 45 f.; idem, *Histoire des berbères*, transl. Slane, iv. 217.

appear that Alfonso was virtually alone in his attempt to recover the fortress. It was almost impossible to wage war in the south while half Castile was in revolt, and while even the Master of a Military Order founded to fight Islam could ally with Granada. In 1334 one of the frontier commanders observed: 'Because of the discord between them the Moors lost the land and now by the same discord [between Christians] they hope to recover it.'[1]

Alfonso was obliged to make and renew truces with Granada and Morocco. When the truce expired in 1339 both sides were ready. By now Alfonso's power was more assured. Don Juan Manuel was too old to lead a new revolt. His noble allies had been defeated or killed and his intrigues with Aragon and Portugal had failed. Galleys sent by Pere III of Catalonia–Aragon were to contribute decisively to Alfonso's ultimate victory over Islam. Pere's father, Alfons III (1327–36), had promised assistance which—together with a proposed international crusade—had never materialized, in part because of the unwelcoming and suspicious attitude of Castile. Pere III (1336–87), though at first allying with Don Juan, was soon to act in union with Castile; he realized that the Merinid danger threatened him also. In 1337 Pere was already organizing the defence of his shores, attacked by Merinid galleys. After an attempt to make a separate peace with Morocco had failed Pere turned to a closer alliance with Castile. In 1339 the Catalan fleet reached the Straits. Alfonso XI needed Catalan help so badly that he was even prepared to pay for it.[2]

In 1339 the main struggle began with a surprise attack at dawn by Castilians on a raiding force led by Abū Mālik, Abū al-Ḥasan's son, who was killed in the fray. A Christian poet imagined Abū al-Ḥasan's vow of vengeance: 'I will pass the sea and take vengeance. I will not return until I have taken five kings . . . I will gain Castile and crush Christendom and be crowned in Toledo.' The poet also imagined a letter from an eastern caliph telling the Merinids to 'conquer the frontier, Castile, León, Navarre and Portugal, Catalonia and Aragon,

[1] *Crónica de Alfonso XI*, 107, 202 (*BAE* lxvi. 241 f., 303); Giménez Soler, *Don Juan*, pp. 600, 613.

[2] *Don Juan*, pp. 575 f., 621–31; idem, *La Corona*, pp. 251, 263; J. Miret y Sans, *AIEC* 2 (1908), 270, 296 ff., F. Sevillano Colom, *EHMed* 3 (1970), 55–74.

Britain and Rome', to 'reconquer Europe for our law'. Sixty thousand horsemen, 30,000 archers, with Turkish bows, and infantry covering the sands of Ceuta were said to be on the march. The *Crónica* varies between 53,000 and 70,000 horse and 400,000 and 700,000 foot. The report that troops from 'the Sultan of Babylon' had joined the expedition also appears in a letter of Pere III to the pope.[1] These reports, though containing vastly swollen figures, indicate the scale of the threat posed to Castile.

In April 1340 the Castilian fleet (most of the Catalan galleys had been temporarily withdrawn) was almost destroyed by the Moroccans. It took Alfonso XI months to collect a new fleet, consisting largely of Genoese galleys. In August Abū al-Ḥasan crossed from Morocco to Algeciras, where he was joined by Yūsuf I of Granada. In September the combined Islamic armies laid siege to Tarifa, which seemed likely to fall. If it did fall Castile would have lost the most important conquest it had made from Islam since 1248, and control of the Straits would have passed to Morocco, which already held Gibraltar and Algeciras.

According to the *Crónica*, some of Alfonso XI's advisers held that he should not risk battle against vastly superior forces and should surrender Tarifa in return for a truce. However, it was decided to advance by land. Supplies were scarce. Alfonso's financial troubles were constant and appear in the expedients he resorted to, including pawning the crown jewels. It was calculated that if Tarifa was not relieved the Christian army could remain outside its walls for four days only. The besiegers were also short of food since their communications with Morocco had been cut by the reconstituted Christian fleet but (on about 10 October) twelve of the fifteen Castilian galleys patrolling the Straits were lost in a storm.

Hearing of Alfonso's approach Abū al-Ḥasan moved his army to a defensive position near the sea, intended to bar the approach to Tarifa. On 29 October the Christians reached the Peña valley, crossed by the rivers Jara and Salado. They were led by Afonso IV of Portugal, with some 1,000 knights, and by

[1] *Poema de Alfonso XI*, vv. 908 ff., 929 ff., 939, 958 f. (*BAE* lvii. 504 ff.); *Crónica*, 239, 250 (*BAE* lxvi. 316, 324); Pere III's letter in *EEMCA*, 2 (1946), 57 ff.; J. A. Robson, *English Historical Review*, 74 (1959), 399 f.

Alfonso XI, with 8,000 horse and 12,000 foot. The veteran rebels Don Juan Manuel and Don Juan Núñez, the city militias of the south, Basque, Leonese, and Asturian troops were present. There are no reliable figures for the Muslims, who were certainly far more numerous. Huici suggests 60,000 Moroccans and 7,000 Granadans. The Muslims were superior as archers, but in a pitched battle their lighter horses and arms placed them at a disadvantage. They could not resist a determined charge of mailed horse. The Christian infantry were also well armed and contributed to the victory of 30 October.

During the previous night 1,000 horse and 4,000 foot had been introduced into Tarifa. No one dared to inform Abū al-Ḥasan of this move. The king of Castile advanced, with a papal banner, indicating that the war was a crusade, against the Merinids; the king of Portugal against the forces of Granada. The Castilians took the fords of the Salado but most of them dispersed to loot the Merinid royal tents and kill the emir's wives. For a time a renewed Merinid attack on Alfonso XI seemed likely to succeed, but at this point the troops in Tarifa launched a surprise attack on the Muslim rear. The Muslims' attempt to change front in mid-battle led to confusion and rout. The Portuguese, who had been fighting the Granadans all day, were cheered, according to a Portuguese source, by the arrival of a Relic of the True Cross; according to a Muslim chronicle they were rescued by Castilian infantry.

Abū al-Ḥasan escaped to Algeciras and from there, the same night, to Morocco. The Christians claimed that 400,000 Muslims had been slain for a Christian loss of only twenty horsemen. Musa II of Tlemcen noted that the battle of the Salado 'humbled the head of Islam and filled the idolaters with joy'. The *Crónica de Alfonso XI* considered the battle the greatest Christian victory ever won over Islam in Spain. The *Poema de Alfonso XI* compared the victors to the heroes of the *Song of Roland*. Forgetting the Portuguese on land and the Catalans at sea, both sources give the glory entirely to Castile. A Portuguese bishop saw God as the head of Alfonso's army. He urged him to go on to take Africa, which by right was his. The victory was celebrated in rhymed inscriptions. Its fame travelled rapidly through Europe.[1]

[1] A. Huici Miranda, *Las grandes batallas de la reconquista* (Madrid, 1956), pp.

THE CAPTURE OF ALGECIRAS

The battle did not end the struggle for the Straits of Gibraltar. This was decided by the capture of Algeciras, which took place four years later, in 1344. The victory of the Salado was principally important because of the vast booty gained by Alfonso XI. All the enemy spoils were reserved for him. Those who tried to conceal their loot were pursued by the Crown even outside Castile. The plunder of 1340 made it possible for Alfonso to hire over fifty Genoese galleys and so to begin the siege of Algeciras in 1342. During the almost two years' siege Catalan squadrons (usually ten but sometimes twenty galleys which might remain over a year at a time in the Straits) took such an effective part that Pere III could tell the pope that, without his ships, 'Algeciras would not have been taken'.[1]

The Castilian–Catalan command of the Straits, though not complete, prevented large-scale reinforcements and provisions from reaching Algeciras from Morocco. However, the conquest of the city was a formidable task. In June 1342 the Catalan consul at Seville reported that Alfonso's land forces then moving against Algeciras consisted only of the Military Orders, the royal household, and some town militias. It took eight months before the city was completely encircled. Alfonso had to go armed night and day, both against would-be assassins, and so as to be ready to enforce the night blockade. After almost a year of the siege many of the king's advisers favoured its abandonment, in return for tribute from Granada. In May 1343 the blockade seemed about to dissolve with the withdrawal of the Catalan galleys. Alfonso's persistence won its reward. The siege of Algeciras drew the attention of Christian Europe. Don Juan Manuel and other nobles, the king of Navarre, leading barons from Catalonia, Gascony, and England, arrived to take part. These foreign guests vastly impressed Muslim envoys with their strange heraldry, but most of them did not endure the hardships of the siege to the end. Algeciras was surrendered by

[1] H. Grassotti, *CHE* 39–40 (1964), 119–32; Giménez Soler, *La Corona*, pp. 273 ff.; *CDIACA* vii. 160 ff., 184 f.

331–87; *Crónica*, 243, 247, 251 f. (pp. 319, 322, 325–9); *Poema*, v. 1739 (p. 529); Alvaro Peláez, *Speculum regum* (1341), in R. Scholz, *Unbekannte kirchenpolitische Streitschriften*, ii (Rome, 1914), 514 ff.

treaty on 26 March 1344. Granada was granted a ten years' truce, on payment of twice its earlier tribute.[1]

THE END OF THE REIGN

The *Crónica de Alfonso XI* virtually ends with the capture of Algeciras. Our information on Alfonso's last years is fragmentary. From 1343 to 1349 he appears to have been partly occupied with diplomatic negotiations with France and England. These are also the years of the internal reforms which will be noticed below. In 1349 Alfonso again turned to the Straits. The capture of Gibraltar would have completed the defence of Tarifa and the conquest of Algeciras. Conditions were more favourable than in 1342–4. The Merinids, who still held Gibraltar, were engaged in civil war, and no help came from Morocco. Catalan galleys and troops again arrived to assist Castile. But 1349 was also the year of the Black Death. The plague struck the besieging army. Alfonso refused to withdraw. He died on Good Friday, 27 March 1350. The siege was at once raised.[2]

In a contemporary letter Ibn al-Khaṭīb declares that Gibraltar was about to be taken by the infidel. Only Alfonso's death preserved Islam in Spain. Alfonso's achievement had been considerable. Granada was to survive until 1492. At times it played a role in Castilian politics but it did not possess enough force to become a major threat. The Merinids had presented this threat. They had raised western Islam to a height from which it overshadowed Spain. But, like the Almohads before them, their empire was too vast to last. It crumbled within a year, undermined by revolts by local princes and by descendants of Abū al-Ḥasan. The one-time ruler of North Africa died in 1351, virtually abandoned, in the mountains of Morocco. After his death, Ibn Khaldūn declares, 'the naval strength of the Muslims declined once more . . . The Muslims came to be strangers to the Mediterranean'. The European side

[1] *Crónica*, 269–336 (pp. 343–90); L. d'Arienzo, *Carte reali diplomatiche di Pietro IV il Ceremonioso* (Padua, 1970), pp. 72 f.; *EEMCA* 2 (1946), 67; Giménez Soler, *Don Juan*, p. 642.

[2] G. Daumet, *Étude sur l'alliance de la France et de la Castille au XIVe et au XVe siècles* (Paris, 1898), pp. 2–18; idem, *Bulletin hispanique*, 17 (1915), 1–14; P. E. Russell, *AEM* 2 (1965), 301–32; *Crónica*, 338 f. (pp. 390 ff.); Giménez Soler, *La Corona*, pp. 291 f.

of the Straits of Gibraltar was not entirely in Christian hands, but control over the Straits had passed from Islam.[1]

INTERNAL REFORMS

In his last decades Alfonso XI undertook a number of administrative reforms, designed to make the Crown's hard-won victory over the nobility permanent. These reforms represented a return to the centralizing policy of Alfonso X, which had hardly been applied. Alfonso X had granted his *Fuero Real* to Madrid in 1262 but the more traditional *Fuero Viejo* was observed there until 1339, when Alfonso XI reimposed the *Fuero Real*. Alfonso X had prescribed the use of travelling royal judges, sent out on tours of inspection. Alfonso XI revived the use of these judges.

It was essential to maintain control over the main cities. One of the easiest ways to do this was to restrict the governing municipal body (*cabildo*) to a small group of local nobles and citizens; this group was far easier to manipulate than a large open assembly. In Seville the *cabildo* was restricted in 1337 to twenty-four, in Murcia to thirteen men, appointed by the king and changed by him whenever he so chose. The city officials were also appointed by the Crown. The same tendency towards a 'closed' *cabildo* is found in Don Juan Manuel's *Ordinances* for his town of Peñafiel (1345).[2]

In 1346–7, in successive meetings of Cortes, Alfonso promulgated laws regulating justice for all Castile–León. The *Ordenamiento* of 1348, published in the Cortes of Alcalá, summed up Alfonso's views. Local customs (*fueros*) were regarded as mere supplements to the new law. The *Ordenamiento* dictated judicial procedure according to Roman law. So as to prevent private war all castles were taken under the protection of the Crown. An attempt was made to establish a regular paid army. A vassal's failure to appear in arms when summoned, properly

[1] Ibn al-Khaṭīb, transl. M. Gaspar y Remiro, in *Revista del Centro de Estudios Históricos de Granada y su reino*, 4 (1914), 223–7; also transl. Casiri, *Bibliotheca Arabico-Hispana Escurialensis*, ii (Madrid, 1770), 303; Ibn Khaldūn, *Muqaddimah* (cited, p. 339, n. 3).

[2] *Documentos del Archivo General de la Villa de Madrid*, ed. T. Domingo Palacio, i (Madrid, 1888), 85–91, 253–5. See R. Gibert, *El concejo de Madrid*, i (Madrid, 1949), 22 ff., 104, 123–37. R. Carande, *AHDE* 2 (1925), 282 ff.; J. Torres Fontes, *AHDE* 23 (1953), 139–59; *CHE* 25–6 (1957), 251–67; Giménez Soler, *Don Juan*, p. 656.

equipped and accompanied, made him liable to penalties ranging from the loss of his pay to exile and death. In all this Alfonso XI followed the ideas of Alfonso X, whose *Partidas* were now proclaimed as supplementing royal and local laws. The *Ordenamiento de Alcalá* was often cited as authoritative by later kings.[1]

As in earlier reigns, royal revenues were administered by Jews. Alfonso XI's main financial ministers were Joseph Halevi (Don Yuçaf of Écija) and Don Samuel ibn Wakal. In 1342 the *alcabala* was reimposed as a general sales tax of 5 per cent on all transactions.

A more significant example of Alfonso's policy is his treatment of the Mesta. In 1273 Alfonso X had granted the Mesta powers as a general body, regulating the activities of all sheep- and cattle-owners and notably the vast annual migrations of sheep from south to north and back again. The intervening reigns had seen a strong reaction by the towns, who resented the loss of taxes on sheep passing through their lands. Alfonso XI revived the Mesta's powers, making it an instrument for the exaction of royal rights and the restriction of local taxes. While acting with moderation, and refusing to make a clear sweep of town claims, he effectively protected the countrywide shepherds' organization and so advanced royal authority yet again.[2]

[1] *El Ordenamiento de Leyes que D. Alfonso XI hizo en las Cortes de Alcalá* . . . (Madrid, 1774), pp. 68, 70, 79–86.

[2] *Crónica*, 39, 82, 96 (pp. 199, 224, 230 f.); A. Ballesteros, *Sefarad*, 6 (1946), 253–87; Baer, *History* i. 325 ff.; S. de Moxó, *La Alcabala* (Madrid, 1963), pp. 22 f., 27; J. Klein, *The Mesta* (Cambridge, Mass., 1920), pp. 186–92, 310 f.

II

Pere III of Catalonia–Aragon: an Attempted Mediterranean Empire: Majorca and Sardinia (1336–1356)

IN the late thirteenth and early fourteenth centuries the Catalan-Aragonese confederation had attained a strong economic position in the western Mediterranean. Its territorial acquisitions had also been considerable. They had included the Balearic Islands (1229–35), Sicily (1282), and, in the 1320s, Sardinia.[1] By the accession of Pere III in 1336 all these possessions either had become independent or were in danger of being lost.

The Balearics formed part of the kingdom of Majorca, created in 1276. Sicily had been independent since 1295. Both these kingdoms were ruled by junior branches of the Catalan dynasty, the House of Barcelona. The king of Majorca was a vassal of Catalonia–Aragon. But these ties did not secure Catalan control over the lesser kingdoms. In any crisis Majorcan rulers turned to France for protection against their too-grasping relatives. Catalan relations with Sicily were more cordial but the two countries pursued distinct, at times divergent, policies. In Sardinia rebellion had broken out within a few years of its conquest. The struggle with the native Sards and their Genoese allies was to continue for over a century. The island was often all but lost to Catalonia.

Pere III (1336–87) was the first Catalan ruler to see a comprehensive interrelationship between Sicily, Sardinia, Majorca, and Catalonia, and the first to attempt to make this relationship a reality, to create any kind of 'Mediterranean Empire'.[2] His long reign was largely devoted to the integration of his ancestors' conquests under Catalan rule. He himself conquered Majorca and spent years and vast treasure in Sardinia. His

[1] See above, Part II, Ch. I.
[2] ibid. p. 271.

plans for the acquisition of Sicily were realized by his son Martí I.[1]

Pere III inherited a federation—the kingdoms of Aragon and Valencia, the principality of Catalonia, the subordinate quasi-colony of Sardinia—of which the economic heart was Catalonia and the effective capital Barcelona. The Catalan economy was still vigorous. After 1350 it was affected by the crises that afflicted the whole Mediterranean world but, for another century, Barcelona continued to be a leading economic centre.[2]

The alliance of Crown and merchants profited both parties. The urban patricians and merchants of Barcelona were almost always the strongest supporters of Pere's Mediterranean policy, whether it was directed against Majorca or Genoa; they were to aid him when he was in danger of being defeated by the nobility of Aragon in 1347–8. On the other hand Pere authorized changes in Catalan maritime law which produced the *Libre del Consolat del Mar* in its final form. He also gave the 'Consulate of the Sea' (*Consolat del Mar*), which existed in all major ports, and was controlled by merchants, power over all commercial cases.[3]

PERE'S CHARACTER

Pere III's share in revising maritime law is typical of his character in general. Not in the least an original mind, he was a pre-eminent organizer. He regulated the royal court, reorganized the Chancery, Archives, and Library, and founded two universities. The Catalan translations he had made included astronomical tables, the Koran, texts of Maimonides. He encouraged the composition of original works, from poems and chronicles to encyclopedias and maps. He rebuilt his palaces at Barcelona and Saragossa, expanded the docks at Barcelona, and began the Lonja there. The walls of Valencia, the royal tombs of Poblet arose at his wish.[4]

This crowned administrator was a man of extreme passion. The great sixteenth-century historian, Zurita, saw Pere as ruled

[1] Below, vol. ii, Part II, Ch. I.

[2] Above, Part II, Ch. I, pp. 271 ff.; also Vol. ii, Part I, Ch. I.

[3] A. García Sanz, *BSCC* 35 (1959), 189–94; idem, *VIII CHCA* ii, 1, pp. 257–69. See also Capmany, ii. 211 f.

[4] Riquer, ii. 339.

by a perverse hatred of his own relatives: 'His nature was so perverse and inclined to evil that in nothing did he distinguish himself so much as in persecuting his own blood.' Pere's upbringing was not calculated to produce a balanced temperament. He grew up believing that his Castilian step-mother, Queen Leonor, had not only taken large parts of his domain for her children (as she had) but had tried to poison him. At one point he nearly fled to France for safety. Pere's consequent hostility to his relatives was natural but it almost caused war with Castile in 1336 and was probably a cause of the later Castilian war. Pere's violent nature also appears in the punishment inflicted in 1348 on some Valencian rebels who were killed by molten lead from the bell which had called them together being poured down their throats. In general Pere took every crisis to its most extreme conclusions. Soldevila remarks that many conflicts of his reign could have been avoided but for Pere's attitude.[1]

Pere is far better known to us than most medieval kings. He appears very clearly in his *Chronicle*, in his speeches to the Corts, and in his letters. A seven-months child, he sought to make up for his short height with magnificent robes, a majestic deportment, and the rigorous ceremonial with which he hedged himself round. His determination to assert his divine mission explains the obstinacy with which (at sixteen) he insisted on crowning himself in Saragossa, rather than be crowned by the archbishop (one of his main supporters). When Pere deliberately descended to the popular level, dancing with the people of newly conquered Perpignan, he did so partly to win them over but also, perhaps, because he needed to relax the violent tension at which he normally lived.[2]

Belief in his divine mission made Pere insert in his *Chronicle* the deaths he had ordered, 'by which We did justice'. He wished even his defeats to be recounted since they displayed his diligence in combating disaster. He saw himself as David delivered from Saul and Absalom (his relatives); as Lot he was saved from the five hostile kings (in Pere's case Castile, Portugal, Navarre, England, and Granada). He laid less stress on

[1] Zurita, *Anales*, viii. 5; Pere III, *Crónica*, i. 51; iv. 60, ed. Pagès, pp. 63 f., 285. See R. d'Abadal, *HE* xiv, pp. xcv–cvii, Soldevila, *Història de Catalunya*, p. 449.

[2] *Crònica*, ii. 10 f., 34; iii. 199 (pp. 75 f., 95 f., 232 f.).

human advisers than on divine aid. Three advisers, in particular, were important to Pere.

PERE'S ADVISERS

His uncle, the Infant Pere, was probably largely responsible for turning Pere III to Catalonia (his youth was spent in Aragon), and to Catalan traditions. Pere's uncle was behind the king's first (and only unqualified) success, the conquest of Majorca in 1343. Until the Infant became a Franciscan in 1358 he was important in Pere's counsels. In 1364 he helped to bring about Cabrera's downfall and to prepare Enrique of Trastámara's invasion of Castile in 1366.

Bernat de Cabrera, Pere's chief minister from 1347 to 1364, attempted, in contrast to the Infant Pere, to create an authoritarian government. His use of royal power to further his own interests helps to explain his hostility to Castile, but he served Pere III well; the latter finally recognized his error in allowing Cabrera's destruction. Cabrera's downfall was partly brought about by Pere's third queen, Elionor of Sicily, whom he married in 1349 and who died in 1375. Elionor always sought to direct Pere's policy towards the acquisition of Sicily, after Cabrera's fall with some success. She was as hostile to Enrique of Trastámara as was Cabrera. Apart from these leading figures Pere was also influenced by many other contending factions, among whom the Aragonese nobles, who favoured Enrique and his pretensions to Castile, stood out against the Catalans, more interested in Mediterranean than in land expansion.[1] Pere himself determined the main lines of his policies.

PERE'S AIMS: INTERNAL: A NEW ALFONSO X

In Pere III one can see a conscious attempt to emulate the earlier court of Alfonso X of Castile (1252–84). Pere's interest in Alfonso appears in the Catalan translations he had made of the *Partidas* and of the *General estoria*. He carried Alfonso's work further. The *Tablas Alfonsíes* contained serious errors. Pere had

[1] Rubió, *Documents*, i. 263 f.; *Crònica*, Prol. (pp. 5 f.); Gubern, in *Pere III, Epistolari*, i. 40–7; R. d'Abadal, *HE* xiv, pp. lxiii-lxvii; *CDIACA* xxxiv. 236–75, 480–91. On the Infant Pere, A. M. de Barcelona, in *Estudis franciscans*, 11–15 (1913–15). S. Sobrequés i Vidal, *Els barons de Catalunya* (Barcelona, 1961), pp. 163–70; U. Deibel, *La Reyna Elionor de Sicilia* (in *Sobiranes de Catalunya*) (Barcelona, 1928).

his astronomers make new observations and construct new tables in Hebrew, Latin, and Catalan, adapted to the meridian of Barcelona, as well as an enormous celestial sphere which Pere kept in his library. The Jew Isaac Nafuci of Majorca made clocks, quadrants, and astrolabes for him. As with Alfonso X, Pere's aim was to be able to make astrological forecasts. Pere's son Joan I was perhaps more interested than his father in nautical discoveries and instruments.[1]

Pere's creation (in the 1350s) of two new universities, Perpignan and Huesca, emulated Alfonso X's interest in Salamanca, though Pere's foundations did not endure. Pere's patronage of Catalan literature paralleled that of Alfonso in Castilian, though Pere as royal patron should also be compared here to his younger contemporary Charles V of France (1364–80). Pere had his notaries and secretaries, friars and Jews, execute many translations from Castilian, French, Provençal, Latin, Arabic, and Hebrew. As was the case with Alfonso X and Castilian, these translations greatly expanded the literary, scientific, and theological range of Catalan.

LAW

There was always a specific aim behind the translations and the original works ordered by Pere III. Alfonso X's *Partidas* provided a vernacular model for the systematic application of Roman law. Pere ordered the *Partidas* to be translated so that 'We might ordain similar laws which could properly be called Ours'. *Partida* II. xviii, 18, in particular, provided a law governing the holding of royal castles, which made it possible for the king to demand them from his vassals whenever he pleased. Traditional Catalan law on the subject made it far more difficult to remove an unsatisfactory castellan. The adoption of the *Partidas* was part of Pere's attempt to centralize his kingdom and make royal authority more effective.[2]

POETRY

Pere's original works had the same aims as the translations he sponsored. Pere took a considerable interest in troubadour

[1] A. Rubió, *EUC* 8 (1914), 219–47; J. Mª. Millás, *VII CHCA* iii. 318. See above, Part II, Ch. II, p. 330. Rubió, *Documents* ii. 128, 149.

[2] Rubió, *Documents* ii, pp. lxvi f.; i, pp. xxx ff., 208 f.; R. d'Abadal, *Dels visigots als catalans*, ii (Barcelona, 1970), 335–79, from *EUC* vi-vii (1912–13).

poetry. In 1338 he promoted the first Catalan poetic competition (*Jocs Florals*), an imitation of the Consistory at Toulouse, founded in 1323. Pere's sons patronized similar meetings at Barcelona. Pere himself wrote poems in Catalanized Provençal, at times intended to stir up patriotic feeling. This effort to save troubadour poetry failed. An essentially courtier lyric could not live in a bourgeois world unless a new content was infused into it, as in Italy. More interesting to us are the historical works produced under Pere's direction.[1]

HISTORY

Pere's interest in history appears from 1339, when he was nineteen. He collected the chronicles of Castile, Navarre, and Portugal, France, Hungary, Dacia, Norway, and Sicily. His library left to Poblet was largely historical in content. He ordered the redaction of a compendium of universal history, another of (translated) *Chronicles of Sicily*, and a *Chronicle of the Kings of Aragon and the Counts of Barcelona* (often known as the *Chronicle of San Juan de la Peña*). This last work was written in the three official languages of the Crown of Aragon, Latin, Catalan, and Aragonese. It was intended as an introduction to the *Chronicle* of Pere's own reign. The latter was written by a team of collaborators under Pere's close supervision. Begun before 1349 it reached 1369.[2]

Pere was the theologian of his own acts. The *Chronicle of San Juan de la Peña* outlined a glorious ancestry to rival that of the kings of Castile. His own *Chronicle* provided proof of God's blessing on Pere's mission as heir of the kings of Aragon and counts of Barcelona. Pere used his *Chronicle* as he did oratory, poetry, official documents (a main source of the *Chronicle*), and sculpture, to enhance the glory of his dynasty in the eyes of the Catalan bourgeoisie on whom he increasingly depended.[3]

[1] Riquer, i. 565–72.

[2] E. González Hurtebise, *Revista de bibliografia catalana*, 4 (1904), 188–214; J. Massó Torrents, *Revue hispanique*, 15 (1906), 554–79; Riquer, i. 480–501; J. Rubió, *HGLH* i. 708 ff.

[3] Massó, p. 546; Rubió, *Documents* i. 124, 153, 192; ii, pp. xxxiii ff.; A. Durán and J. Ainaud de Lasarte in *Ars Hispaniae*, viii. 214 ff.; *Epistolari*, ed. Gubern, i. 142 f.; *Parlaments a les Corts Catalanes*, ed. R. Albert and J. Gassiot, p. 24; *Crònica*, i. 40 (p. 52).

PERE'S EXTERNAL AIMS

Pere's external aims have already been alluded to. They were largely the same as those of his predecessors. The reintegration of Majorca within the Crown of Aragon had been pursued by almost every ruler since the separation of 1276. The acquisition of Sardinia had been begun by Jaume II. The main differences between Pere's policy and that of his predecessors were the virtual abandonment of the attempt to expand by land against Castile (though when war began Pere sought hard for territorial concessions), and the passion with which Mediterranean expansion was pursued through the Venetian alliance and consequent war with Genoa. Behind this policy was a political vision of the Mediterranean world which saw the necessity of dominating the western half of that inland sea.[1]

Pere's interests extended to the Catalan duchy of Athens (only directly attached to him from 1380), to Catalan bishops in Morocco, to the Canaries, and to the Holy Places of Jerusalem, but his central concern was for the western Mediterranean. Compared with this, trade—and, even more, political relations—with Egypt or the Christian East were peripheral. Only once, in 1351, did the Venetian alliance take Catalan galleys as far as the Bosphorus. Pere imitated his predecessors in seeking tribute from the North African States. He failed to obtain it, except, in 1360, from Tunis, a very small amount, which was not in fact paid. After 1348 Sicily was racked by civil war between the 'Catalan' and 'Latin' parties. Pere observed neutrality; he was sufficiently occupied with Genoa.[2]

PERE'S INSTITUTIONAL REFORMS

Pere III devoted much attention to improving the royal administration. He made increasing use of Roman law and lawyers trained in it and of the system of *familiares*, privileged persons, clerics, Jews, some lay officials and non-nobles, directly attached to him. In 1336–96, under Pere and Joan I, some 1,000 *familiares* were named.

[1] V. Salavert y Roca, *IV CHCA* i. 213, n. 37 (Pere to his heir, 1380).

[2] Rubió, *Documents*, ii, p. xvi. For Egypt, etc. see A. López de Meneses, *CHE* 29–30 (1959), 293–337. On North Africa, C.-E. Dufourcq, *BRABL* 19 (1946), 83–6; 21 (1948), 101 f., 104 f.; *Miscelánea de textos medievales*, ii (Barcelona, 1974), esp. 99, 137.

In 1344 Pere issued very detailed *Ordinances* for the royal household and Chancery. They made great use of the *Palatine Laws* of Jaume III of Majorca, whom Pere had just dethroned, but are closer to reality than Jaume's laws, for instance over the Chancery. This was administered according to Pere's *Ordinances*, with a high ecclesiastic as Chancellor, a lay lawyer as Vice-chancellor, acting as head of the royal court, and (from 1354) a protonotary, in command of twelve royal secretaries. The first protonotary, Mateu Adriá, also served as ambassador and counsellor and translated the *Partidas* and *Palatine Laws* into Catalan. Great precautions were taken to safeguard the content, style, and authenticity of royal documents. These regulations helped to produce a remarkable group of trained administrators who often also figure in Catalan literature.[1]

The first royal archivist was appointed in 1346. His task was not only to copy, catalogue, and preserve documents but to discover precedents for actions the Crown wished to take. Pere was largely responsible for the preservation of one of the finest royal Archives in Europe, that of Barcelona.[2]

In 1354 Bernat de Cabrera issued *Ordinances* on the naval forces of the Crown. In 1359 further *Ordinances* appeared governing the hierarchy of command and prescribing the careful recording of each expedition. In 1358 *Ordinances* dealt with the office of *Maestre Racional*, the financial official who normally accompanied the king on his journeys. A close control over payments and accounts rendered by subordinate officials was attempted. The mere order of the king himself was not sufficient authority on which to accept an account.[3]

By these series of *Ordinances* Pere sought to strengthen the central organs of administration, which could help him to hold his disparate realms together, and to counteract their constant tendency to move apart. But the strongest link between Aragon, Catalonia, and Valencia was the royal dynasty. Hence the means already noted by which attention was focused on the

[1] J. Vincke, *AEM* 1 (1964), 333–51; F. Sevillano Colom, *AHDE* 20 (1950), 137–241; idem, *VIII CHCA* ii. 2, pp. 103–18 (Mateu Adriá).

[2] Rubió, *Documents* i. 137, 139, 221; J. Rubió, in *Cuadernos de Arqueología e Historia de la Ciudad* (Barcelona), 12 (1968), 133–8.

[3] *Ordenanzas de las armadas navales*, ed. A. de Capmany (Madrid, 1787); *CDIACA* vi. 327–40. The *Ordinacions* for the Maestre Racional are in ACA, Real Patrimonio, reg. 781, fols. 280–7.

dynasty and on Pere's person, continually glorified in chronicles, oratory, and art.

LIMITATIONS ON ROYAL POWER: THE NOBILITY

When Pere III sought to implement his programme of Mediterranean advance and internal reform he was faced with opposition from several quarters. In Catalonia the nobility was far weaker than it had been a century before. Only one of the ancient independent counties (Pallars) survived, largely because it was loyal to the Crown. The lesser noble houses had become Crown servants. In 1347–8 Pere was opposed by most of the nobility of Aragon and Valencia but, with Catalan help, he was able to overcome it. The nobility preserved, however, their feudal jurisdiction unimpaired.[1]

THE CHURCH

Opposition between Church and Crown grew fiercer under Pere III. Pere had a papal official who had excommunicated him taken to the top of a high tower and suspended by his feet until he decided whether he preferred to be let go or to raise the excommunication. On another occasion Pere personally threatened with death a cleric trying to enforce debts to the papacy. Papal processes and Bulls were publicly burnt.

Pere insisted on control over church appointments. He objected violently in 1344 when the see of Saragossa was given to a pope's nephew, 'a person not bound to Us by natural duty'. After 1350 almost no foreign name appeared among the bishops of Pere's realms. Sardinian sees were reserved for Catalans and Aragonese. The Military Orders were useful to Pere. In 1342 they contributed 215 knights to defend Valencia against invasion. Constant royal pressure prevented any independent action on the part of the Orders. Their commanders became royal servants.

The papacy complained continually of royal attacks on clerical privileges. These privileges did not protect clerics accused of murder. A concord in 1372 stipulated that the king would not 'destroy bishops' castles and goods', though if prelates 'impeded'

[1] Sobrequés, op. cit., pp. 73–100, 113–16, 120–4. See below, pp. 370 f. R. d'Abadal, in *HE* xiv, pp. lvii, lxxvii-lxxx.

royal jurisdiction he might 'defend his rights'. During the Papal Schism, which began in 1378, Pere used his neutrality ('indifference') to take over papal revenues.

Although Pere III never challenged the theoretical papal position he believed firmly in his duty to see to the religion of his subjects. Much as Charlemagne six centuries before, Pere ordered his people to commit to memory the main prayers of the Church and invited them to take part in the Jubilee pilgrimage to Rome in 1350, so as to return better Christians and subjects. Pere's *Ordinances* regulated the office of Royal Almoner (a Cistercian of Poblet). Every day the king had thirteen poor persons fed at his table and kissed their hands. Alms were distributed as dowries to deserving girls (and ex-prostitutes), to the sick and blind, to ex-slaves, pensioners, Religious Orders, pilgrims, and foreigners, from nobles to hermits.[1]

THE CORTS OF CATALONIA

Very real limitations on Pere's policy were provided by the towns of Catalonia, represented in Corts. The towns would normally support Pere against papal exactions but joined with the Church and nobility to preserve their own privileges. During the crisis caused by the Black Death Pere could not simply issue an edict regulating prices and wages (as the king of Castile could do). He had to tell his officials to negotiate its acceptance with the Catalan towns and to ask prelates and nobles to promulgate it 'in *their* jurisdiction'.

There were eighteen general meetings of the Catalan Corts during Pere's fifty-year reign, apart from thirteen *Parlaments*, usually confined to one estate. A number of these general meetings lasted two or more years. There were also at least three joint meetings in Monzón of the three Cortes of the federation. Owing to the constant wars with Genoa and Castile, the Crown's financial demands on the Corts increased and the latter's hold over policy tightened correspondingly. From 1359 the permanent *Diputació* of the Corts controlled the raising and,

[1] J. Vincke, *VII CHCA* i. 267–85; idem, *Documenta*, pp. 409, 478–87; *CDIACA* vi. 254 f.; H. Kern, *VIII CHCA* ii. 1, pp. 71–83; F. J. Miquel Rosell, *Regesta de letras pontificias* (Madrid, 1948), pp. 328 ff.; Tejada y Ramiro, iii. 597–600; A. Altisent, *L'Almoina Reial a la Cort de Pere el Cerimoniós* [1378–85] (Poblet, 1969). On the Orders, A. Luttrell, *VIII CHCA* ii. 2, pp. 67–77.

to a large extent, the use of the revenues on which the Crown was dependent.[1]

LIMITED NAVAL STRENGTH

The limitations of royal power were made very clear by war with Castile (1356–66). They already appear, however, in the naval campaigns of Pere's first decade. As a land power Catalonia–Aragon could not challenge Castile or France. The famous light infantry which had defeated the French in the 1280s, the *almogàvers*, appear only after 1344 in one document of 1354. Possibly the Black Death of 1347–50 had depopulated the mountainous regions where they were recruited. As Pere III saw with exceptional clarity, Catalonia's future was in the Mediterranean. What forces did she possess at sea?

One must not confuse promises with performance. In 1337 Pere proposed to arm sixty new galleys (forty heavy, twenty light) against the Merinids of Morocco who threatened to invade the peninsula. In fact he dispatched eleven galleys in 1339 to the Straits of Gibraltar in the summer, four in the winter. In 1340 thirteen light galleys were sent, in 1341–2 (after the defeat of the Castilian fleet) twenty, but Castile paid for twelve galleys for three months. In 1342–3 only ten galleys were sent. These galleys were largely equipped in Valencia though Barcelona contributed ten in 1341, five in 1342. In 1343 Barcelona sent twenty-two galleys (instead of a proposed thirty) against Majorca.

In these years the largest war fleet Pere could raise was thirty-two galleys in 1343 (twenty-two against Majorca, ten in the Straits). Pere planned to mortgage Crown rights to raise this fleet but it was not very large. In 1340 in the Straits, forty-four Moroccan galleys and thirty-five armed ships defeated thirty-two Christian galleys and nineteen ships. If forty Genoese galleys had joined the Moroccans (as was rumoured they would do) the Castilians and Catalans would have been totally outclassed. The Catalan fleet was the only one in Spain or Portugal built and manned by natives of the peninsula (Castile and Portugal were dependent on Genoa for their ships and commanders). It could remain a year at sea in the Straits of Gibraltar.

[1] Abadal, loc. cit., p. lxxxiv; *Ordenanzas de las armadas navales*, pp. 115–23. See below, pp. 382 ff.

But it was too small, as later years were to confirm, to compete easily with any first-class sea power, Genoa, Morocco, or Castile (under Genoese direction).[1]

The acquisition of Majorca in 1343 promised increased naval strength. In 1323 Majorca had sent twenty galleys to Sardinia, in 1341 eight to the Straits (more had been promised but not sent). Pere III enlarged the docks for galleys in Majorca as well as Barcelona. But in the 1350s Majorca (particularly hard hit by the Black Death) could only provide a few warships and financial aid; it figures far less thereafter in naval history.[2]

In 1351–2 the Catalan fleet sent to the Bosphorus consisted of twenty-five galleys (eight had been bought from Marseille); in 1353 the fleet sent to Sardinia of forty-six galleys and eleven ships. This was the greatest fleet Pere sent to sea. Like the fleet of 1351–2 it was largely financed by Venice. With twenty Venetian galleys it defeated fifty-five Genoese galleys and five ships. In 1356 Pere lent France fifteen galleys. In 1359 Pere could muster only ten galleys to defend Barcelona itself against a much larger Castilian fleet.[3]

THE INHERITANCE OF ALFONS III (1327–1336)

Pere's father, Alfons III, left him a difficult inheritance. Alfons's conquest of Sardinia during his father, Jaume II's, reign had given him greater prestige when he became king than the young Alfonso XI of Castile possessed. He had remarkable physical courage and a facile sympathy for his subjects. His character was diagnosed by Jaume II, who advised him to be 'firm in justice' and 'temperate with his gifts'. After his second marriage in 1329 Alfons fell under the spell of the Castilian Queen Leonor. Since dividing his kingdoms was barred by law, Leonor had her elder son Ferran given Tortosa and enormous lands, including Alicante and Játiva, 'the keys of all our king-

[1] The last reference to the *almogàvers* (see above, Part II, Ch. I, p. 242) in L. d'Arienzo, *Carte reali diplomatiche di Pietro IV il Ceremonioso* (Padua, 1970), pp. 242 f. On the fleets 1337–44 J. A. Robson, *English Historical Review*, 74 (1959), 386–408. For 1343 see *CDIACA* xxxi. 166 ff.

[2] F. Sevillano Colom, in *Historia de Mallorca*, iv (Palma, 1971), 445, 514–18; A. Santamaría, *AEM* 5 (1968), 501–7.

[3] Pere III, *Crònica*, ed. Pagès, v. 9 and 19 f.; vi. 22 (pp. 297, 302 ff., 351). See, however, Rubió, *Diplomatari*, pp. 265 f.; Capmany, ii. 258–61; G. Meloni, *Genova e Aragona*, i (Padua, 1971), 78, 117, 121, 161, 165. See below, Ch. III, p. 384, n. 1.

doms', according to her step-son Pere III. Constitutionally ill, Alfons died at only thirty-seven.[1]

PERE'S EARLY YEARS

Pere became king at sixteen. As heir to the throne he had protested to the pope against new donations to his half-brothers. In the first year of his reign (1336) he almost broke with Castile by his refusal to confirm the inheritance left his step-mother and her sons. Castilian pressure and the refusal of Aragonese nobles to attack Queen Leonor's main supporter, one of their number, forced Pere to return the lands he had taken. The common danger from Morocco enforced alliance with Castile. Pere's half-brothers were to trouble him until they died but the first major crisis came over Majorca.[2]

MAJORCA

Jaume I's bequest of a separate kingdom (the Balearics, Rousillon, Cerdagne, and Montpellier) to his second surviving son in 1276 had caused trouble ever since. Jaume II of Majorca was forced into a vassal relationship to his elder brother, Pere II, in 1279; he sided with France against Pere in 1285. In retaliation Majorca was seized by Catalonia–Aragon and only relinquished, at papal insistence, in 1298. Jaume II of Aragon tried to get it back by legal means in 1324. Alfons III proved more cordial; he married his daughter to the young Jaume III of Majorca. Pere III was less patient. Jealous of Jaume III's independence, of his ties with France and influence at the papal court of Avignon, he was always ready to consider himself insulted by him, and to use any pretext to dispossess him.[3]

THE CONQUEST OF MAJORCA

The pretext soon appeared. Jaume III was foolish enough to anger France, his one possible protector against Pere. In April 1342 he summoned Pere, as his overlord, to support in arms his jurisdiction in Montpellier. Pere allowed Jaume to become committed to war with France but avoided his request for help by summoning Jaume to Corts in Barcelona a month earlier, on

[1] F. Valls-Taberner, *Obras selectas*, iv (Barcelona, 1961), 309–11; Pere, *Crònica*, i. 46 (p. 58).

[2] Zurita, *Anales* vii. 23, 32, 40.

[3] *Crònica*, ii. 37 (p. 101). See Zurita, *Anales* vii. 55.

25 March, to answer framed-up charges. Given the imminent danger of war with France Jaume could not come. He was now technically at fault. Pere's lawyers began to prepare their case. In May Jaume made peace with France but she was too occupied with England to assist him. In July 1342 Jaume arrived in Barcelona, on a safe-conduct. Pere later accused him of trying to kidnap him and carry him off to Majorca until he had released Jaume from vassalage and given him a large part of Catalonia. Pere's story of this plot is unconvincing. It would have been insane of Jaume to attempt to kidnap Pere when four Catalan galleys were watching his own fleet. The only independent witnesses mentioned were dead when the *Chronicle* was written. However, the plot was a mainstay of the *Process* against Jaume. It also gave Pere an excuse to seize his sister, Jaume's wife, and keep her in Barcelona (according to Jaume his wife preferred to remain there).[1]

Jaume's seizure of all Pere's subjects in his lands and their goods provided Pere with a further excuse to attack him. On 21 February 1343, without waiting for the end of the legal process, Pere declared Jaume deprived of the kingdom of Majorca and the other fiefs he held from him. On 25 May the Catalan fleet (116 sail, including twenty-two galleys) reached Majorca. The landing was effected with very slight loss. On 28 May Jaume III left the island, on 31 May Pere entered its capital, the City of Majorca. The conquest of Jaume's other lands, Roussillon and Cerdagne, took another year. Papal and French diplomacy failed to save Jaume. Persuaded to surrender to Pere on 15 July 1344, Jaume soon discovered that Pere's 'mercy and grace' would reduce him to a minor noble. Jaume could not accept this. Escaping from Catalonia he fought on until he was killed in 1349, during his attempt to recover Majorca.[2]

CAUSES BEHIND THE CONQUEST

Historians usually see the creation of the kingdom of Majorca by Jaume I as a grave error and that kingdom as doomed from the beginning. From the Catalan point of view the new kingdom was certainly an error. The existence of a separate Majorca was

[1] *Crònica*, iii. 11–19 (pp. 113–25). See *Proceso contra . . . Jaime III* (*CDIACA* xxx. 274 f., 351; xxix. 60, 84). On this see Zurita, *Anales* vii. 59 ff.

[2] *Crònica*, iii. 20–35, 54–185 (pp. 126–43, 156–223).

highly prejudicial to Catalan interests. It does not follow that the kingdom was not viable politically. Despite the division by sea between the Balearics and the mainland territories and the continual hostility of the elder branch of the House of Barcelona, the kingdom of Majorca survived from 1276 to 1344. The spiritual vitality of the kingdom in art and literature was matched by its economic importance. The resistance of the subjects of Jaume III of Majorca in 1343–9 to the crushing force brought against them by Pere III also attests their appreciation of their independent status.

THE MAJORCAN ECONOMY

Ramon Muntaner, who knew the Mediterranean well, claimed that the inhabitants of independent Majorca were among the most prosperous in the world. In 1310 its king struck gold coins, thirty-six years before Catalonia–Aragon did so (at Perpignan, in the territories of Majorca, after its conquest). Majorca thus preceded Catalonia in adhering to the 'gold standard' of Genoa, Florence, Venice, and France (Majorcan gold coins imitated the French in type).[1]

CARTOGRAPHY

From Ramon Lull (1232–1316) onward there is no break in the line of Majorcan writers, friars and laymen, poets and moralists, alchemists and cartographers. Majorcan importance in cartography is generally recognized. Some Majorcan maps extended farther than the Italians (probably their first masters and their only rivals) to reach Scandinavia and even China. Majorcan maps (the earliest known is dated 1339) 'are not merely navigation charts but give information of value to sailors, merchants, scholars, and curious amateurs'. Later Majorcan cartographers worked in Barcelona—for the Crown and for Italian patrons—and in Portugal.[2]

JEWS AND MUSLIMS

The leading Majorcan cartographers were Jews or, later, *conversos*, forced converts to Christianity. Jewish and Muslim merchants played a far more important role in the Majorcan

[1] Muntaner, *Crònica*, c. 8; F. Mateu y Llopis, *BSAL* 30 (1947–52), 95–120.

[2] A. Rubió, *EUC* 3 (1909), 396 f.; L. Bagrow, *History of Cartography*, ed. R. A. Skelton (London, 1964), pp. 65 f.

economy than they did in Barcelona. In 1315 it was stated that foreign Jews were drawn to Majorca by the privileges available to them there. Majorcan Jews' links with North Africa were recognized as 'very necessary' to the island. Majorcan Muslims also contributed, on a lesser scale, to the North African trade. Over a hundred African Muslim merchants were resident in Majorca in 1331.[1]

MAJORCAN TRADE: DIFFUSION

The geographical situation of Majorca gave it an advantage over Barcelona. Its merchants, ably assisted by their independent kings, exploited this advantage to the full. In 1302–43 Majorcan consulates are documented in ten ports in North Africa, in Seville, Málaga, Granada, Naples, Pisa, Genoa, Constantinople, and Bruges.

Majorcans smuggled goods from Alexandria, plundered the Greek islands, and acquired slaves in Crete. The Majorcan Crown sent alum to Flanders in 1324. In 1342 Jaume III licensed an expedition to the Canaries. These distant enterprises were less important, however, than trade with southern France, Italy, and North Africa.[2]

Majorca had been linked with Marseille and Montpellier (which was under the Majorcan Crown) from the Christian Conquest of 1229, with Genoa and Pisa before that time. Majorca was a vital stage between Europe and North Africa, between the Mediterranean and the Atlantic. Italians forbidden to trade in Barcelona in 1325 naturally turned to Majorca, Pisans and Genoese became 'citizens of Majorca'. They helped to establish Majorcan trading colonies along the African coast from Morocco to Tunis; 261 Majorcan merchants are documented as trading with North Africa in 1308–31, as against only 212 Catalans.[3]

[1] A. Morel-Fatio. *Revue des études juives*, 4 (1882), 49, 53 f.; G. Llabres and F. Fita, *BRAH* 36 (1900), 128, 187–91, 199; Dufourcq, p. 35; idem, *MÂ* 71 (1965), 492; idem, *AEM* 7 (1970–1), 59 f., 64 f.

[2] Sevillano Colom, op. cit., pp. 500 ff.; Dufourcq, pp. 554 ff. On the slave-trade, Verlinden, i. 395, and Rubió, *Diplomatari*, pp. 174, 202–5; Dufourcq, *MÂ* 71 (1965), 489 f. E. Serra i Rafòls, *EUC* 22 (1936), 207–28; Sevillano, *BSCC* 46 (1970), 359 ff.; idem, *Anuario de estudios atlánticos*, 18 (1972), 27–57.

[3] E. Baratier, in *Histoire du commerce de Marseille*, ed. G. Rambert, ii (Paris, 1951) 124–33; Dufourcq, pp. 61, n. 5, 596–604. For Pisa, T. Antoni, *Bollettino storico pisano*, 39 (1970), 31–40.

Majorcan port registers survive for five years from 1321 to 1340. The number of foreign ships visiting Majorca ranges from 444 (1332) to 617 (1340). They came from, and went to, France, Spain, Portugal, Italy, Crete, and North Africa. The island functioned as a vital centre of exchange. Ships from Marseille could find there pepper, Greek wine, cheese, wax, alum, paper, leather, the products of North Africa, as well as of the eastern Mediterranean. Majorca sent iron to Constantinople, fish to Genoa, salt to Venice. In 1314 one Majorcan ship going to Bone carried 'oil from Seville, figs from Murviedro and Murcia, Calabrian cotton, Damascene glass, cloth from Perpignan and Sicilian cheese', as well as antimony, saffron, tin, almonds, plants, wine, shoes, and armour (prohibited as an export to North Africa).[1]

MAJORCA AS ECONOMIC RIVAL TO BARCELONA

Professor Dufourcq has estimated that the value of the merchandise passing through Majorca in 1300–43 may have amounted to over half the value of the trade of Barcelona. After a period of depression there was a revival in 1339–42, the years that preceded the extinction of Majorcan independence by Pere III. Pere's conquest of Majorca was naturally supported by the merchants of Barcelona, who could not afford to allow so much trade to escape them.

In 1320 King Sancho of Majorca had noted 'the great envy that all men feel towards [Majorcan merchants]'. This 'envy' appears in the continual attempts of the rulers of Catalonia–Aragon to thwart Majorcan economic expansion. Majorca was expected to follow the Catalan line. It did not do so. Majorcan rulers obtained the same privileges for their subjects as Catalans enjoyed abroad, set up independent consulates (against Catalan opposition), traded with States with which the Crown of Aragon was at war, and established custom barriers against Barcelona. Pere III's renewal of all Barcelona's privileges in the Balearics on the eve of his expedition of 1343 was a natural counter-move. In return, Barcelona contributed some 70,000

[1] M. Durliat and J. Pons i Marquès, *VI CHCA*, pp. 345–63; R. Pernoud, in *Histoire . . . Marseille*, i (1949), 179 f.; F. Sevillano Colom, *Navegaciones mediterráneas Mallorca* (Bari, 1969), esp. p. 22.

lb. (about 50 per cent of the total contributions of the Catalan cities) to the conquest of Majorca.[1]

MAJORCA'S INDEPENDENT POLICY

Under Jaume III Majorca adopted a still more independent policy. In 1339 Jaume concluded a treaty with Abū al-Ḥasan, the formidable ruler of Morocco, who was about to invade Spain in force. Jaume sent only eight galleys to the Straits of Gibraltar in 1341, after years of appeals and orders from his feudal overlord, Pere III, for twenty galleys or more.[2]

An independent Majorca menaced Catalan communications with North Africa, Sicily, and the new Catalan colony, Sardinia. In the 1340s Sardinia was still a lucrative source of salt, silver, and grain for Catalonia. If Pere was to hold Sardinia he needed to hold Majorca too.

The legal *Process* against Jaume III accused him of allying with the enemies of Catalonia–Aragon, France, Castile, Pisa, Genoa, and Morocco. There was some substance to these accusations. Jaume's treaty with Morocco and relations with France have already been mentioned. The close commercial ties between Majorca and Italy could become political alliances. Jaume was in touch with Naples and its possessions in Provence, which included Marseille. In 1343 Jaume tried to hire galleys from Marseille against Pere III. In 1349 he succeeded in doing so. This year his troops were largely Genoese. In 1342 Sicily refused to help Pere against Majorca. Naples threatened to intervene to save Jaume. The papacy, under French influence, repeatedly attempted to save him. This foreign interest in keeping Majorca independent attests its general recognition as a viable separate state; it also helps to explain Pere's determination to bring this independence to an end.[3]

[1] Dufourcq, pp. 67, 419–27, 563 f.; Durliat and Pons, pp. 358 f., 363. J. Vich and J. Muntaner, *Documenta regni Majoricarum* (Palma, 1945), pp. 99 f.; Capmany, ii. 111, 135, 227 f.; A. Gímenez Soler, *BRABL* 5 (1909–10), 195, n. 1; *Cortes de Cataluña*, i. 2, pp. 431 f.; A. Santamaría, *AEM* 7 (1970–1), 181 ff.; J. Sobrequés Callicó, *VIII CHCA* iii (1973), 291–302.

[2] *BSAL* 15 (1914–15), 317 f.; F. Sevillano Colom, *EHMed* 3 (1970), 55–74. For Abū al-Ḥasan see above, Ch. I, pp. 339 ff.

[2] *Proceso*, in *CDIACA* xxx. 235; Baratier, op. cit.; Arienzo, op. cit., pp. 78, 82 f.; Miquel Rosell, op. cit., pp. 291, 297–317.

MAJORCAN RESISTANCE TO PERE III

In 1343 Pere told the Majorcans he had conquered that he had come 'as the doctor who heals the sick', to remedy Jaume's misgovernment. Jaume had raised heavy taxes—partly to defend Majorca against Pere. The latter lowered taxes both on Christians and Jews. Majorcan trade continued after 1343 but it did not rise to the level it had enjoyed before the conquest.[1]

The period 1343–9 was especially troubled. Jaume III was still alive and, first from Perpignan, later from Montpellier, he continually sought to recover Majorca. Armed resistance in the island ceased, at latest, by April 1344, but the plots of Jaume's adherents in Majorca and Roussillon continued, as did their torment, executions, and exile. In 1347 Pere himself made the remarkable admission that 'the majority of Roussillon . . . and all the other land we have taken from [Jaume] love and desire him'. The long list of exiled Majorcans included lawyers, citizens, merchants, and even a vegetable seller. Jaume's 'underground' agents included a cathedral canon, a barber, and a weaver. Pere's 'Reformer' was accused of depopulating Majorca by his severity.[2]

Reports from Majorca to Pere III give a day-by-day account of the rumours preceding Jaume's expedition to Majorca in 1349. The Black Death the previous year must have killed many of Jaume's supporters but Pere's governor believed that, on landing, Jaume would be joined at once by most men outside the City (today Palma) and very soon by the City itself. The population was therefore herded into the City and the town of Inca to prevent their assisting Jaume. Only the chance arrival of troops going to Sardinia defeated Jaume. He was killed in battle at Lluchmayor on 25 October. Pere was unwilling to let his conquered cousin rest in his former island. Afraid of a cult rising round Jaume's body he ordered it to be transported to Valencia. Jaume's children (Pere's nephews) were imprisoned, Jaume's son—Jaume 'IV' of Majorca—until 1362, when he

[1] *Crònica*, 47 (p. 149); *Proceso*, in *CDIACA* xxx. 317; Llabrés and Fita, loc. cit., pp. 207, 274; Villanueva, xxi. 189; Sevillano, op. cit. (p. 363, n. 1).

[2] *Proceso*, in *CDIACA* xxxi. 369, 383 ff.; *Crònica*, iii. 207, iv. 12 (pp. 236, 247); J. Vich y Salom, *Aspectos históricos de la Casa Real de Mallorca* (Palma, 1948), pp. 13 f.; A. Campaner, *Cronicón mayoricense* (Palma, 1881), pp. 57–61, 96; Vich and Muntaner, op. cit., pp. 189, 202–10, 214, 240, etc.

escaped from the iron cage in which he was shut up in Barcelona. He was to trouble Pere until his death in 1375.[1]

SARDINIA

Within a year of the Catalan victory over Pisa in 1324 and the occupation of the main Sardinian cities trouble began with the Sards themselves.[2] Much of Pere III's energies were spent on Sardinia. The roots of the internal trouble were the oppressive behaviour of the Catalan officials and settlers, and the relationship between the Crown and the Judges of Arborea, who held almost a third of the island. Internal revolt was kept alive by external Genoese aid.

REBELLION: INTERNAL CAUSES

In 1400 the representatives of the Catalan towns recognized the damage done by Catalan officials. They complained to the king of 'the great and absolute power given the governors of Sardinia . . . The governors have persecuted, afflicted, and greatly harmed many inhabitants, so that it was and is the common view that the rebellion began with the behaviour of these governors'. From 1326 the almost annual dispatch of one 'Reformer' after another revealed the Crown's suspicion of its local officials.

The relationship between the Judges of Arborea and the Crown of Catalonia–Aragon was based on mutual misunderstanding. The Judges, the leading native noble dynasty, had hoped to rule Sardinia under nominal Catalan suzerainty. When they found they were treated as vassals on a level with others a clash was inevitable. It came with the accession of Mariano IV of Arborea in 1346. Pere III adopted the same tactics towards Mariano as he had employed (very successfully) against Jaume III of Majorca. He tried to provoke Mariano into a rebellion which would justify confiscating his possessions. Mariano had no wish to become king of Sardinia but to control it as its virtually independent governor. He served the Catalans against other rebels but received no reward. When Pere used Mariano's brother against him he rebelled in 1353.[3]

[1] Campaner, pp. 97, 104–7; C. A. Willemsen, *SFG*, i. 5 (1935), 240–96.

[2] See above Part II, Ch. I, p. 266.

[3] *Cortes de Cataluña*, iv. 379; A. Boscolo, *VII CHCA* i. 216 f., 221 ff.; E. Putzulu, *Archivio storico sardo*, xxv, 1–2 (1957), 83 ff., 95 f.; ibid. xxviii (1962), 129–59.

Before Mariano's rebellion the Crown was already in financial trouble. In 1344 it was stated that 'all the revenues and rights in the island [were] so exhausted' that they could not pay for its administration and defence. But, until the Black Death and the rebellion, Sardinian wheat and salt exports could still normally cover the Crown's local needs and support the Catalan merchants who monopolized the export trade. In about 1345 a plan was submitted by a Catalan official to the Crown. It was proposed to eliminate all the old lords of Sardinia, including the Judge of Arborea, and replace them by Catalans who would live on their fiefs and control the island. Although the plan is anonymous it reveals that the fears that drove Mariano to rebellion had some foundation.[1]

EXTERNAL INTERFERENCE: GENOA

Genoa had never accepted the Catalan conquest of Sardinia. In 1325–6 Genoa allied with her ancient enemy Pisa to attack the Catalans. Genoese ships raided the Catalan coast and shipping. It was the beginning of a hundred years' war at sea between Genoa and Barcelona. In 1330–6, with little help from the Crown, Barcelona maintained the naval war. Formal peace did not end privateers' activities. In 1343–9 Genoa assisted Jaume III of Majorca against Pere III.[2]

In Sardinia itself the situation was relatively favourable as long as the alliance with the Judges of Arborea continued. But, as the Catalan grip on the island tightened, discontent grew. In 1338 a royal order forbade any non-Catalan or Aragonese sleeping inside the castle of Cagliari. In 1342 ecclesiastical posts were virtually reserved for non-Sards. In 1346 the governor of Sardinia recommended the confiscation of the extensive lands held by the Genoese Doria family, to prevent their transferring them to the city of Genoa. The Doria moved first, however. In 1347 they rebelled (supported by Genoa) and attacked Sassari. Sassari was saved by Mariano of Arborea but again besieged in 1349.[3]

At this point the Genoese–Catalan struggle became involved

[1] M. Costa, *HV* i. 395–415; B. R. Motzo, in *Studi storici in onore di F. Loddo Canepa*, i (Florence, 1959), 165–80.

[2] M. Mitjá, *VI CHCA*, pp. 447–59; J. Broussolle, *EHMod*, 5 (1955), 23–6; J. Mutgé, *AEM* 2 (1965), 229–56.

[3] D'Arienzo, op. cit., pp. 21, 71, 114, 170 f.; Meloni, op. cit., pp. 27, 42 f., 45 f.

with the perennial Venetian–Genoese conflict. Pere had been looking for Italian allies since 1346. A Venetian–Catalan alliance, signed on 16 January 1351, established mutual assistance against Genoa. Pere originally intended to confine his attention to the western Mediterranean, while leaving the East to Venice. He was obliged to intervene in the East by force of circumstances. The shrunken Byzantine empire soon joined the alliance. On 13 February 1352 the allied Venetian–Catalan–Byzantine fleet won a Pyrrhic victory over the Genoese in the Bosphorus. At least half of the twenty-five Catalan galleys were lost.[1]

From now on, reverting to his original plan, Pere III prosecuted the war only in the western Mediterranean. On 27 August 1353 Bernat de Cabrera, with Venetian aid, won a resounding victory off Sardinia, capturing thirty-three Genoese galleys. This victory was nullified, however, by the rebellion of Mariano of Arborea. In 1354–5 Pere himself was obliged to lead a large-scale expedition (about 100 sail) to Sardinia. The city of Alghero was taken on 9 November after four months' siege. It was repopulated by Catalans; Catalan is spoken there today by their descendants. Pere's army was weakened by malaria. He complained bitterly of continual desertions and found it impossible to obtain reinforcements. Pere was forced to make peace at Sanluri (11 July 1355) with Mariano, on terms very favourable to the latter. He had little choice. Venice had made a separate peace with Genoa. Pere was on his own. The Sardinian Parliament he called in 1355 to muster strength to resist Mariano's demands proved a dismal failure. The greater Sardinian nobles did not attend.

Pere states in his *Chronicle* that he had set Sardinia at peace. This was either propaganda or self-delusion. By 1356 Mariano was complaining that the virtual political autonomy granted him in 1355 was not observed by Catalan officials. In 1358 he was again in revolt. War with Genoa in Sardinia became henceforth war with the Sardinians.[2]

[1] Pere III, *Crònica*, v. 2–11 (pp. 291–8); Meloni, pp. 65 f., 108 ff., 115 f. Idem, in *Medioevo, eta'moderna* (Cagliari, 1972), pp. 103–17; M. Blason-Berton, *AEM* 5 (1968), 237–63; A. Luttrell, in *Martínez Ferrando, Archivero* (Barcelona, 1968), pp. 265–77.

[2] Meloni, pp. 136, 151–214; *Crònica*, v. 20, 30–41 (pp. 302–20); Pere III, *Epistolari*, i. 113–21; D'Arienzo, pp. 251 f., 318; eadem, in *Medioevo, eta' moderna.*

CORSICA

In 1297 Pere III's grandfather, Jaume II, had received from the papacy the title of King of Sardinia and Corsica. No serious attempt was made to acquire Corsica—where Genoese influence matched that of Pisa in Sardinia—before Pere III. In 1348 Pere was disposed to invade Corsica if sufficient local assistance was available. In 1351 he was tiying to extort Bonifacio and other places in Corsica from Genoa by treaty but in 1358 he promised Genoa to abandon his Corsican claims. During the war with Castile (1356–66) Pere could hardly deal with native Sardinian rebels, let alone with Corsicans. A fragile peace with Genoa lasted until 1373.[1]

INTERNAL REVOLT: THE UNIONS OF ARAGON AND VALENCIA (1347–1348)

Shortly after the Catalan conquest of the kingdom of Majorca (1343–4), and before the main struggle with Genoa over Sardinia (1351–3), Pere III encountered internal rebellion in Aragon and Valencia.

The heart of the rebellion was in Aragon. In 1283 the Aragonese nobles had become virtually independent of the Crown. In 1301 Jaume II secured the legal condemnation of some leading nobles. The Justicia of Aragon, chosen from the lower nobility, was to hold the balance between the Crown and the great barons. The latter resented Pere's attempt to increase royal power and seized any chance to extend their influence to Valencia. The Aragonese were suspicious of the new group of advisers Pere had recruited from Majorca, men imbued with the autocratic teachings of Roman Law. Pere's *Ordinances* of 1344 appeared the programme for a restructured, more centralized monarchy.[2]

The pretext for revolt was provided by the question of succession to the throne. Pere as yet only had daughters. In 1346 he sought to assure the succession of his eldest daughter

[1] G. Sorgia, *Studi sardi*, 20 (1966–7), 181–89.

[2] *CDIACA* xxxviii. 190, 206; Zurita, *Anales* v. 51. See above, p. 354, notes 1, 3.

pp. 121–47; A. Giménez Soler, *BRABL* 5 (1909–10), 88–93; G. Meloni, *Studi sardi*, 20 (1966–7), 285–98; Putzulu, loc. cit., pp. 97 f. See below, Vol. ii, Part II, Ch. I.

Constanza instead of his undependable brother Jaume. Jaume at once found allies in the nobles of Aragon. The Aragonese *Unión*, dormant since 1301, was revived and soon included all but two nobles and four towns of Aragon. A Valencian *Unión* arose in imitation.

For a time rebellion triumphed. In the Cortes of Saragossa (August–October 1347) Pere was obliged to yield to all the Aragonese *Unión*'s demands. Pere was saved by the intrigues of Bernat de Cabrera, who now became his chief minister. Cabrera succeeded in dividing the *Unión* by promising rewards to a number of its noble leaders. But the death of Jaume in Barcelona in November merely meant his replacement as rebel leader by Pere's more formidable half-brother Ferran, who could count on Castilian support. The Valencian *Unión* had already defeated their royalist opponents. In February 1348 civil war had spread over Aragon. Pere was forced to recognize Ferran as his heir and to enter Valencia on 1 April. He remained there 'as a prisoner' until 11 June, when the Black Death's arrival gave him an excuse to leave the city.

The loyalty of Catalonia (secured by Cabrera), negotiations with Alfonso XI of Castile, and the military victory of Lope de Luna at Epila on 21 July over the Infant Ferran and the Aragonese Unionists changed the situation. On 14 October there followed a meeting of the Aragonese Cortes in the Dominican convent in Saragossa, at which Pere, as he told his uncle, personally cut to pieces the privileges of the *Unión*, smashed its seal and bulls with a mace, and, together with the Cortes, 'wept' the death of the *Unión*, as its documents went up in smoke. After the surrender of Valencia on 10 December Pere ordered a similar destruction of the records of the Valencian *Unión*, again before the local Corts.[1]

These symbolic gestures, together with a few executions, satisfied Pere. Pere's triumph was very far from absolute. He was aware that he had not only been opposed by leading nobles but by 'many knights and lawyers and merchants and artisans' in Valencia and elsewhere. He had triumphed over one group of nobles, with the help of another faction—whose leaders,

[1] J. Caruana Gómez de Barreda, *EEMCA* 3 (1947–8), 485, 494; Zurita, *Anales* viii. 7–33; Pere III, *Epistolari*, pp. 90–101; M. Dualde Serrano, *EEMCA* 2 (1946), 295–377; Abadal, *HE* xiv, pp. xcix f.

especially Luna, received rewards. There were no more armed rebellions against Pere, but he was obliged to respect the rights of his subjects. The main Aragonese privileges were confirmed and extended. The Justicia of Aragon was now appointed by the king, but his authority, as a shield against royal oppression, grew. In 1371 the Justicia was declared judge in all cases to which the Crown was party.[1]

PERE'S FIRST TWO DECADES

The first two decades of Pere's reign were the happiest. The conquest of Majorca was his greatest achievement. A serious rebellion in two of the main territories of the confederation had been defeated. Catalan fleets had defended the Straits of Gibraltar against the Merinids and had triumphed in the Bosphorus and off Sardinia against the Genoese. But Pere's external victories and internal successes sprang principally from Catalonia. Could Catalonia stand the strain of war on two fronts, not only against Genoa but also against Castile? And if it could do so would its Corts not exact a heavy price in political power from Pere and his Crown?

[1] Pere, *Crònica*, iv. 43 (p. 272); Abadal, pp. clxxxii f.; A. Marichalar and C. Manrique, *Historia de la legislación y recitaciones del derecho civil de España*, v (Madrid, 1862), 115–24, 134 f.

III

Pedro I of Castile: an Attempted Peninsular Empire (1350–1369)

DURING his reign and soon after his death Pedro I of Castile was subjected to a flood of misrepresentation, legend, and hostile propaganda. The efficacy of this propaganda is shown by the fact that he is commonly known today as Pedro the Cruel, when contemporary rulers as deserving of the epithet have escaped or survived it.

ANTI-PETRINE PROPAGANDA

Several distinct elements were fused in anti-Petrine propaganda. In a 'vision' Alfonso X was supposed to have learnt that his descendants would cease to reign in the fourth generation (represented by Pedro) after him. This 'vision' was perhaps invented by the circle round Don Juan Manuel, before Pedro's accession. It appears in a number of anti-Petrine texts, together with pseudo-prophecies attributed to Merlin. These 'prophecies', translated into Catalan by 1377, present Pedro I as 'a perfect example of cruelty', who 'plunders his land and waters it with blood . . . a destroyer of his nobility', while Pedro's bastard brother and successor, Enrique II of Trastámara, is represented as a crusader, whose followers will be richly rewarded in this world and the next.[1]

In 1377 Pedro I was safely dead. While he was still alive he had been attacked in a series of ballads, sufficiently popular in form to be sung in his enemies' camps. These ballads countered the fact of Enrique's illegitimacy by alleging that Pedro ('Pero Gil') was not the son of Alfonso XI. The ballads also accused Pedro of murdering his half-brother Fadrique, his cousin, the Infant Joan of Aragon, and his French queen, Blanche. These

[1] P. Bohigas, *RFE* 25 (1941), 383–98; idem, *BBC* 8 (1928–32), 261–70. See also García de Eugui, *Crónica general de España*, in *Anales de la Universidad de Chile*, 122 (1908), 490 f.

accusations 'answered perfectly the political needs' of the climatic years of the civil war, 1366–9. What made their effect lasting was their use by Pedro López de Ayala.

Ayala's *Chronicle* of Pedro's reign remains our main source. Ayala deserted Pedro for Enrique of Trastámara. Perhaps his greatest service to the Trastámaras was with his pen. His use of the anti-Petrine ballads canonized propaganda as history. Ayala's literary skill cannot clear him here of the charge of 'political journalism'. He also made use of the 'Merlin' prophesies. Ballads and 'prophesies', together with skilful innuendo, give us the king whom Ayala presented as Pedro the Cruel.[1]

Since Pedro sought to conquer and annex the Crown of Aragon, it is natural that a Catalan such as Eiximenis should have compared the king to the cruellest contemporary Italian tyrant, and seen his death as deserved as theirs. Given the favour Enrique II enjoyed in France and at the papal court of Avignon, it is also not surprising to find Pedro represented as a Jew and heretic in French and papal chronicles. The same hostile picture appears in the Florentine Matteo Villani. By the fifteenth century the same view was accepted in Castile itself. Even a chronicle written for the descendant of one of Pedro's last loyal followers sees him as ruined by a Jewish adviser and by his mistress María de Padilla, as struck down by God for 'the blood of the innocent he had shed'.[2]

PEDRO'S CHARACTER

Pedro's government was, a Muslim contemporary said, 'hard and tyrannical'; in this he was not exceptional for his age. Pedro's father Alfonso XI, his half-brother Enrique II, and his contemporaries, Pere III of Catalonia–Aragon and Pedro I of Portugal, were all as capable of summary executions as Pedro of Castile. Pedro's use of Jewish advisers and Muslim troops was

[1] W. J. Entwistle, *Modern Language Review*, 25 (1930), 306–26; idem, *European Balladry* (Oxford, 1951), pp. 157–60; J. Catalina García, *Castilla y León*, i (Madrid, 1891), 2, n. 1. See also the *Cuarta Crónica General* (*CDIHE* cvi. 77, 82, etc.).

[2] Eiximenis, *Crestià*, iii. 116, cited A. Ivars, *AIA* 20 (1923), 223; *Chronique latine de Guillaume de Nangis*, ed. H. Géraud, ii (Paris, 1843), 368 ff.; S. Baluze, *Vitae Paparum Avenionensium*, ed. G. Mollat, i (Paris, 1914), 311–13, 359 f., 411 f.; Villani, *Cronica*, i. 41, iv. 18, viii. 81 f., ed. F. G. Dragomanni (Milan, 1848), v. 49 f., 320 f., vi. 158 f.; Gutierre Diez de Games, *El Victorial*, ed. Carriazo, 10–15 (pp. 48–57); R. Delachenal, *Histoire de Charles V*, iii (Paris, 1916), 247 ff.

part of the traditional Castilian policy of *convivencia*. Because it was not understood beyond the Pyrenees it does not prove that he was irreligious. Pedro was also unfortunate in being uninterested in the cult of chivalry embodied by the Black Prince and admired by Ayala.[1]

HIS AIMS

Pedro's policy was largely modelled on Alfonso XI's. He sought to unite Castile internally under strong centralized rule and to expand its frontiers. Going further than his father, he sought to control the whole peninsula and almost succeeded in doing so. Troops from Granada, Navarre, and Portugal fought for him against Catalonia–Aragon. He brought Vizcaya under direct royal control. His vast conquests in Aragon and Valencia were baptized 'New Castile', and he was seen as the future 'emperor of Spain'. The Trastámaras later pursued the same aim of peninsular hegemony by force and by marriage alliances; Pedro had already attempted a marriage alliance with Portugal.

Pedro's internal policy was based on control of the cities by the restricted municipal councils created by Alfonso XI, the control of the Military Orders and the great sees, the use of Genoese and Jewish experts, and dominance over the nobility. Much of this policy was successful. Pedro was supported by the main cities in Galicia, Castile, and Andalusia, and by the Basque ports. His failure was due to the noble opposition, led by his illegitimate half-brothers, and to his choice of an external enemy. Alfonso XI had succeeded in using the nobility in the struggle over the Straits of Gibraltar. Pedro may have seen the war with Aragon as serving the same purpose. However, Pere III of Aragon was far more successful in using the internal opposition in Castile and in drawing support from elsewhere (France) than Granada had been with Morocco. Religion was used by Alfonso. It was used against Pedro. Instead of leading a holy war, as Alfonso had done, Pedro became the target of a papal crusade.[2]

Pedro's nobles proved undependable because they saw that

[1] Ibn Khaldūn, apud R. Dozy, *Recherches sur l'histoire et la littérature de l'Espagne pendant le moyen âge*, 3rd edn. (Paris, 1881), p. 110; P. E. Russell, *The English Intervention in Spain and Portugal* (Oxford, 1955), pp. 16–22.

[2] C. Viñas, *Hispania*, 1. 4 (1940–1), 93–101; 5, pp. 45–71; J. Torres Fontes, *CHE*, 25–26 (1957), 251–78; Pere III, *Crònica*, vi. 52 (ed. Pagès, p. 386).

the king was intent on depriving them of any power. Pedro's use of low-born advisers was not new but it was more systematic than before. It was noted as a cardinal error by a relatively friendly Portuguese contemporary, who sees Pedro as 'putting himself in the power of men as vile as descendants of boatmen, falconers, and crossbowmen'. By 1364, if not before, Pedro could no longer depend on his nobles to command his armies. It was this that repeatedly prevented his complete victory over Pere III.[1]

After 1353, when Pedro was eighteen, he had no dominant minister. He was obliged to defend himself against the constant attempts of his half-brothers to dethrone him. In 1366 Pedro explained to Edward III of England that his brother Enrique 'calls me cruel and tyrannical because I have punished those who refused to obey me and who committed great crimes against my subjects.' Throughout his reign Pedro displayed remarkable astuteness in dividing his enemies; he showed foresight in his alliance with England in 1362. As a military strategist, in his war with Aragon, he was superb. As the reign advanced other characteristics appeared. Pedro's violence reached new heights in his mutilation of prisoners in 1362 and his massacre of the crews of four or five Catalan galleys in 1365. His greed appears in his refusal to use the great treasure he had accumulated to buy off the mercenary companies invading Castile in 1366. Much (not all) of the evidence for Pedro's failings in these years comes from a hostile source, Ayala, but it is clear that Pedro reacted with increasing violence as disloyalty around him grew.[2]

PEDRO'S EARLY YEARS: AS HEIR

Pedro was the second (and only surviving) son of Alfonso XI and Queen María of Portugal. Born on 30 August 1334, he was fifteen at his father's death. During his years as heir Pedro and his mother had lived in the shadows, Alfonso's mistress, Leonor de Guzmán, and her children in the limelight of power. Doña

[1] E. S. Procter, *English Historical Review*, 55 (1940), 209 f., 213 ff.; *Os Livros de Linhagens*, in *Portugaliae Mon. Hist., Scriptores*, i. 278; Pere III, *Crònica*, loc. cit.; Ayala, *Crónica de Pedro I*, año XVI, 3 (*BAE* lxvi. 535).

[2] Russell, pp. 38, 1–4; Ayala, año XIV, 6, año XVI, 1, año XVII, 1 (pp. 527 f., 534, 537). See *CDIACA* xl. 159 f.; xxxii. 329, 353, 381; L. V. Díaz Martín, *Itinerario de Pedro I*, p. 404 (doc. 866).

Leonor lived openly with Alfonso and enjoyed enormous influence. Her second surviving son Fadrique was made Master of Santiago at the age of ten, and a relative became Master of Alcántara. In 1345 Don Juan Manuel told Pere III that Alfonso had given everything he could 'except the Crown' to his bastard sons. In 1348 Alfonso proposed that his eldest bastard Enrique of Trastámara, already lord of Asturias, should marry the elder daughter of Pere, and should be king of Murcia, and his illegitimate daughter should marry Pere himself. It is against this background that one should see Pedro's accession when his father unexpectedly died in 1350. In a double sense Alfonso was responsible for his son's troubles. His harsh, authoritarian government was inevitably followed by a reaction from the nobility while the appanages granted his bastard sons made them the natural leaders of the resulting discontent.[1]

AS KING

In 1350 the nobility failed to unite. Queen María and her cousin Juan Alfonso de Albuquerque assumed control in Pedro's name. Doña Leonor was soon arrested and Enrique, failing to hold Algeciras against Pedro, fled to Asturias. The murder of Doña Leonor in 1351, ordered by Queen María, seemed less important than the Cortes of Valladolid. This meeting reinforced royal authority by setting up a rudimentary police system throughout the country. It passed measures to protect the Jews and internal and foreign trade. A treaty between England and the Basque ports received Pedro's confirmation. Ordinances attempted to meet the situation caused by the Black Death and to control wages and prices.[2]

Trouble began with Pedro's marriage in 1353 to a French princess, Blanche of Bourbon. France had promised a vast dowry in order to secure Castile's aid against England. This dowry was never paid. Pedro had been forced into the marriage by Albuquerque (María de Padilla was already his mistress and he may have been secretly married to her). The discovery that no dowry would be forthcoming probably explains his immediate abandonment of Blanche and his rejection of Albuquerque.

[1] A. Giménez Soler, *Don Juan Manuel* (Saragossa, 1932), pp. 645, 652 f. See also C. da Silva Tarouca, *Crónica dos sete primeiros reis de Portugal*, ii. 169.

[2] *Cortes de León*, ii. 1–144. See below, Vol. ii, Part I, Ch. I.

However, this step gave Pedro's nobles a pretext for protest. In 1354 Pope Innocent VI, who found it hard to collect papal revenues from Castile, openly invited Albuquerque and Pedro's bastard brothers to force the king to return to Blanche.

THE REVOLT OF THE NOBILITY

Pedro had been prepared to work with his half-brothers until they betrayed him by joining Albuquerque. Even his mother joined the rebels. They came to include a large part of the kingdom, which felt that the personal power of the king needed control. But the rebel leaders were themselves simply actuated by a quest for power. At one point (1354) Pedro was their prisoner, in Toro, but they could not decide what to do with him. He found it easy to turn his cousins, the Infants Ferran and Joan of Aragon, against his half-brothers. By 1356 the revolt was crushed but Pedro was not secure. He had pardoned his brothers; they seized the first opportunity to rebel again. Enrique, exiled to France, was at once in touch with the mercenary companies, the French court, and the papacy at Avignon, the three forces which were to aid him to victory in the end.[1]

THE WAR BETWEEN CASTILE AND CATALONIA–ARAGON

The war between Castile and the Crown of Aragon (1356–66) filled most of Pedro I's reign and eventually determined his fall. The war also revealed the decline of Catalonia–Aragon, which appeared irremediably inferior in power to Castile. The struggle between the peninsular powers drew Castile into the main power conflict of western Europe, the Hundred Years War between France and England.

ITS CAUSES

Seen from one side the war was the decisive phase in the rise of Castile to hegemony in the peninsula, from the other it was the last effort of Catalonia–Aragon to balance Castilian power.

The war grew directly out of frontier questions. In 1304 the

[1] J. B. Sitges, *Las mujeres del Rey Don Pedro I de Castilla* (Madrid, 1910), pp. 335–82; J. Zunzunegui, *Bulas y cartas secretas de Inocencio VI (1352–1362)* (Rome, 1970), pp. 104, 126 f., 305, 471; L. Suárez, *HE* xiv. 29–38.

Peace of Agreda had divided the old Muslim kingdom of Murcia, giving Aragon Alicante and Orihuela, Castile the rest. Castile had never completely acquiesced in this settlement. The second marriage of Alfons III of Aragon to a Castilian princess (Alfonso XI's sister Leonor, Pedro I's aunt), and the appanages granted her sons, Ferran and Joan, in the disputed area, gave Castile the chance to reopen the question. In 1347 Pere III of Aragon was warned that Alfonso XI was about to attack him. In 1347–8 Alfonso intervened to assist Ferran and the *Unión* of nobles of Aragon and Valencia against Pere. Pedro I, in his turn, supported his first cousin Ferran, who repeatedly attempted to invade Aragon or Valencia. A treaty (October 1352) was no more than a truce. In 1355 Ferran transferred his castles of Alicante and Orihuela to Pedro I as pledges of loyalty. Pere III could not agree to give them up. Throughout the war this question was to prove one of the main obstacles to a settlement.[1]

Other areas of friction between Castile and Catalonia–Aragon existed in the presence of Castilian exiles in Aragon and in the naval war between Catalonia and Genoa which began in 1351. The Catalans had defeated Genoa in sea battles but Genoese corsairs and their Castilian allies preyed on Catalan shipping. Reprisals followed which culminated in the seizure of ships with Genoese goods by a Catalan squadron off San Lúcar de Barrameda, despite the protests of Pedro I, who was present. Pedro's letter of 8 August 1356, demanding redress, was rejected by Pere III on 4 September. The war had already begun. Castilian galleys had attacked the Balearics and Castilian troops had crossed the Valencian frontier. Pere III opened negotiations on 20 August with Enrique of Trastámara, whom he intended to use against Pedro. If Pedro was primarily responsible for the beginning of hostilities Pere had no hesitation in accepting the challenge. His projects soon included the large-scale acquisition of land from Castile. He told the count of Foix that he would have 3,000–4,000 horse, against Pedro I's 2,000.[2]

[1] J. Camarena Mahiques, *VIII CHCA* i. 3–24. For the *Unión* see Ch. II above, pp. 369 f. Zurita, *Anales* viii. 6, 20, 33, 41, 47, 49; ix. 1; A. López de Meneses, *EEMCA* 8 (1967), 232–36.

[2] For the Genoese war, Ch. II above, pp. 367 f. Pere III, *Crònica*, vi. 3 f. (pp. 326–35); Sitges, pp. 157 f. Instructions to envoys to the count of Foix (25 Aug. 1356) in ACA, reg. 1293, fol. 44; see fol. 43^{v}.

COURSE OF THE WAR

This estimate was to prove wildly optimistic. From the beginning Castile appeared more powerful than its enemy. In March 1357 Tarazona in Aragon fell in one day to Pedro. A truce negotiated by a papal legate spared Pere further reverses. Pedro's breach of the truce did not produce a definite rift between him and the papacy. Pere drew nearer to France, Castile to England. Until 1362 there was no decisive victory on land. In 1358 Pedro was occupied with internal treason, in 1359 with his impressive though unsuccessful naval expedition against Barcelona. The failure in 1360 of Enrique of Trastámara's invasion of Castile showed that no general rebellion was likely. Pedro agreed to peace in 1361 so as to overthrow Pere III's possible ally in Granada and restore Muḥammad V. In 1362–3 Pedro launched lightning attacks on Aragon and Valencia. In July 1363 Pere III had to accept the peace of Murviedro, which included the incorporation of half Aragon into Castile. The failure to implement this peace was probably due to divided counsels among Pere's advisers.

When the war was renewed Pere III turned even more urgently than before to France and the mercenary Companies in that country, at present unemployed. The Companies' services were contracted at a vast cost. Their entry into the war gave it a new character. The peninsula was now directly involved in the conflict between France and England.[1]

THE WAR OF SUCCESSION IN CASTILE

Since 1325, at least, France and England had competed to attract Castile. Only the death of the English princess to whom Pedro was affianced when heir to the throne prevented an English alliance in 1348. In the negotiations renewed in 1358 it was principally England that was interested, and particularly the Black Prince (Edward, Prince of Wales), who ruled the English possessions in France (in the peace of 1362 England acquired almost half French territory). The Anglo-Castilian alliance of 1362 made France Pedro's inevitable enemy. In

[1] Pere III, *Epistolari*, ed. Gubern, i. 155 f.; Suárez, *HE* xiv. 48–98. On Murviedro see Russell, op. cit., pp. 29 f.

1363 Enrique was first formally recognized (in a secret treaty between him and Pere III) as claimant to Castile—the alternative claimant, the Infant Ferran, was soon after eliminated by Pere. The leader of the Companies in their invasion of Castile in 1366 was the famous French commander, Bertrand Du Guesclin, though his subordinates included a number of English and Gascon adventurers. The expedition was financed by France, the papacy (still officially on excellent terms with Pedro), and Pere III. It was presented by France and the papacy as a crusade against Granada. The real aim was to remove the Companies from France and to use them to overthrow Pedro and replace him with Enrique, who was pledged to transfer a sixth of Castile to Pere III and to assist France in her projected *revanche* against England.[1]

The first part of this plan was accomplished rapidly. From March to May 1366 the Companies drove Pedro to retreat first from Burgos, then from Toledo, and finally from Seville. Enrique (II) was crowned king at Burgos on 5 April and entered Seville by 12 June. Pedro had been outflanked strategically by the Companies' rapid advance through Navarre to Burgos. Burgos and other towns wished to defend Pedro's cause but he was betrayed by his nobles, who were probably influenced by the far superior equipment of the Companies and by their large numbers.

Pedro decided that he could defeat Enrique only by using the same type of professional soldiers as his brother had employed. On 1 August Pedro arrived in English-held Gascony to ask his English allies (especially the Black Prince) to restore him to the throne. The Black Prince was prepared to do so, at a price. In the Treaty of Libourne (23 September) and later Pedro was obliged to promise vast sums for the expenses of the expedition. Vizcaya and other Basque ports were to be transferred to England while Charles II of Navarre, in return for free passage through his lands, was to receive the whole of Guipúzcoa and a series of fortresses along the Ebro. The regions Pedro was

[1] For 1325 see D. W. Lomax, *AEM*, 7 (1970–1), 105 f.; for the 1340s P. E. Russell, *AEM* 2 (1965), 301–32; idem, *English Intervention*, pp. 35 ff.; Delachenal, *Charles V*, iii. 269–302. For the 'crusade' see *Life of the Black Prince by the Herald of Sir John Chandos*, ed. M. K. Pope and E. C. Lodge (Oxford, 1910), pp. 51 f.; also Froissart, c. 229.

promising away contained the main ports in Castile. The fact that France never made similar demands on Enrique helps to explain the success of French policy.[1]

In February 1367 Pedro I, escorted by the Black Prince and some 10,000 English and Gascon troops, crossed the Pyrenees. On 3 April the invading army soundly defeated Enrique at Nájera. The English archers, who 'shot thicker than rain falls in winter', were particularly effective against their new opponents, who were also disunited. Enrique fled through Aragon to France. Pedro's victory seemed decisive. However, he was unable to pay his English allies the money he owed them, though he imposed unpopular taxes to try to do so. Pedro also refused to hand over the lands the prince unrealistically claimed from him. Castilian finances were shattered by the successive demands of Pedro, Enrique, and again Pedro. Pedro was not allowed to execute or imprison his leading enemies captured at Nájera. Their ransoms were too valuable. They were soon free again to continue the war. In August 1367 the Black Prince withdrew in disgust from Spain; he had already begun to negotiate with Pere III the division of Castile between England, Aragon, Navarre, and Portugal, once both Pedro and Enrique had been eliminated.

In September Enrique was again in Castile. This time, however, he had no large foreign mercenary force at his command. The civil war entered a period of stalemate. In general Pedro controlled Andalusia and Galicia, Enrique Castile, and León, but few cities supported Enrique until they were forced into submission. In order to get Du Guesclin's military help Enrique agreed (20 November 1368) to commit Castilian naval strength permanently to France against England. The Black Prince did nothing to counter this. On 14 March 1369 Pedro I was defeated by Enrique and his French mercenaries at Montiel. On 23 March he was betrayed by Du Guesclin, who had promised to help him escape from Montiel castle, and murdered by his half-brother, 'knight and servant of Jesus Christ', as he now entitled himself. Enrique was at last free of his rival but it was to take him several more years to overcome Pedro's supporters. Two more decades would pass before the marriage of

[1] Russell, *Intervention*, pp. 45–68; J. Valdeón Baruque, *Enrique II de Castilla* (Valladolid, 1966), pp. 104–9.

his grandson to Pedro's granddaughter ended the dynatsic struggle.[1]

RESULTS OF THE STRUGGLE

Pedro I was overthrown by French aid. His three successors were to act as dependent allies of France. Castilian naval intervention assured French victory over England. In return England invaded Castile and sustained Portugal's struggle against Castilian hegemony. This unprofitable involvement of Castile in the Hundred Years War was one result of the war between Castile and Aragon which had developed into the Castilian war of succession. The other main result of this conflict was a crucial weakening of Catalonia–Aragon and particularly of its monarchy.

THE FAILURE OF THE CROWN OF ARAGON

Given the difference in population between Catalonia–Aragon and Castile (perhaps one million, as compared to six or seven million), Pere III may be praised for ending the war with no territorial losses. But Pere had failed to gain any of his objectives. Pere obtained vast concessions of territory (Murcia and the whole eastern-frontier zone of Castile) from his half-brother, the Infant Ferran, and later from Enrique of Trastámara, but these concessions remained waste paper. After his victory Enrique refused to fulfil his promises. Pere's negotiations with the Black Prince, Navarre, Portugal, Granada, and Morocco proved equally fruitless.[2] Pere III overthrew his rival Pedro I, only to find the pretender he had helped to the throne equally dangerous. And Pedro had not been defeated by Catalonia–Aragon itself (Pedro enjoyed constant military superiority) but by internal factions in Castile, assisted by professional mercenaries from France. This result had been brought about at a vast cost. The war crippled the Aragonese monarchy financially. Its power largely passed to the separate representative assemblies (Corts or Cortes) of Catalonia, Valencia, and Aragon.

[1] Russell, pp. 83–148; *Life of the Black Prince*, p. 103; E. Deprez, *Revue historique*, 136 (1921), 37–59; Zurita, *Anales* ix. 69; Valdeón, pp. 169–78; Sitges, pp. 455–68; Catalina García, i. 416.

[2] See below, Ch. IV, pp. 397 f.

FINANCIAL DÉBÂCLE

In 1356 when the war with Castile began, Pere III had no financial reserves. Pedro I had vast resources. He could mobilize troops rapidly and pay them regularly. Pere was dependent on grants from his Corts. These took time to summon and, even during a foreign invasion, insisted on the redress of grievances before voting money (for a specified purpose, sometimes restricted to defence of their local area). The grant took months to collect. If Pere raised an army he could not keep it long in the field. He was forced to reduce his soldiers' pay and to pay them irregularly. Pere had to rely largely on loans from his cities and on expedients such as pawning his plate and jewels, counterfeiting French and Castilian coinage, and seizing church plate and the revenues of clergy absent at the papal court. The last measure almost provoked a head-on conflict with the papacy. Pere also had to sell so many royal rights and revenues that by 1382 he was overwhelmed with debts.[1]

MILITARY INFERIORITY

It was with great difficulty and delays, by taxing the local towns, Jews, Muslims, salt mines, etc., that Pere was able to finance a defensive war, and pay the garrisons holding the frontier castiles in Aragon. To raise cavalry which could take the offensive required a grant from the Corts. In 1364–5 the Catalan Corts voted customs dues and taxes on virtually every product, as well as on every home. The sum voted only supported 1,500 horsemen (only half of them fully armed) and some galleys for two years. In 1360 the Cortes of Aragon voted money for 1,000 horse. In 1359 Valencia was supporting 500, Majorca 300. Pere III's armies probably never numbered 3,000 horse at one place. Of these 1,000 were usually Castilian émigrés. Pedro I's armies were generally over twice as large as Pere's. Hence his ability to execute rapid strategic movements and to garrison many conquered towns. In 1363 Pere was ready to abandon large regions of Aragon and Valencia to obtain

[1] J.-L. Martín, *AEM* 3 (1966), 515 ff.; idem, *VIII CHCA* ii. 2, pp. 79–90; J. Miret, *MÂ* 29 (1917–18), 73 f.; idem, *Revue hispanique*, 13 (1905), 102 f.; J. Coroleu, *Documents historichs catalans del s. XIV* (Barcelona, 1889), pp. 59 f.; J. Vives, *SFG*, i. 3 (1931), 129–40. For Pedro cp. Díaz Martín, docs. 762, 792, 848, 859, 907, etc.

peace. Pedro's military superiority was only reversed by the entry of the mercenary Companies into the war in 1366. (In 1370 Pere stated that men-at-arms must henceforth possess the plate armour of the Companies.) Traditional Catalan superiority at sea was also challenged by Castile. In 1359 Pedro I's naval attack on Barcelona failed but his fleet (twenty-eight galleys, eighty ships, with three galleys from Granada and ten from Portugal) was not defeated by Pere's forty galleys, which could not long keep the seas. In 1364 there were only nineteen Catalan as against thirty Castilian galleys. It was very difficult to find Catalan crews and rowers.[1]

Pere III realized his financial and military weakness. From the beginning he relied principally on Castilian exiles and political alliances. As Abadal remarks he forgot that diplomacy in the end is no substitute for power. If Pere had achieved his territorial ambitions Castilian hegemony might have been prevented by the combined action of the other peninsular kingdoms. As it was the war meant the end of Catalan–Aragonese attempts to expand by land. Internally it transferred power over finance to the regional assemblies of the Crown.[2]

[1] A. Gutiérrez de Velasco, *Hispania*, 19 (1959), 3–43; idem, in *J. Zurita, Cuadernos de Historia*, 10–11 (1960), 75, 83, n. 58, 86, n. 64; *Cortes de Cataluña*, ii. 254–305; iii. 63–6. Martín, loc. cit., Abadal, *HE* xiv, pp. clxvii-clxxviii.

[2] Abadal, pp. cxl-cxliv. For Pere's attempts to secure Muslim mercenaries from North Africa see C.-E. Dufourcq, in *Miscelánea de textos medievales*, ii (Barcelona, 1974), 75, 79.

IV

The Vicissitudes of Castilian Hegemony: Castile, Portugal, and Granada (1369-1410)

ENRIQUE II of Trastámara ascended the throne during a civil war which tore Castile apart, at the price of making it a French military protectorate. The climax of the struggle was Enrique's murder of his half-brother, the legitimate Pedro I. Despite these beginnings the first rulers of the new dynasty, Enrique II (1369–79), Juan I (1379–90), and Enrique III (1390–1406), carried out valuable experiments in government, though there were also negative developments.

The new monarchy was institutional rather than personal. Enrique II, his son, and grandson attempted to use both the higher and lower nobility—which Pedro I had tried to eliminate as a political force—and the Cortes. This body, which Pedro had largely ceased to consult, met each year or, at least, every two years, from 1369 to 1396. Royal institutions, the Council, the Chancery, the Audiencia or central court of appeal, the Household, were all reformed or created. Military organization improved under the pressure of defeat. Clergy trained at the papal court at Avignon attempted, though without much success, to reform the secular clergy. Some important monastic Orders entered Castile for the first time while new Orders were created there.

The other side of Trastámara rule, the same drive for peninsular hegemony which had ruined Pedro I, emerged very clearly under Juan I. Pero López de Ayala, in his *Rimado* (after 1385), depicts an exhausted country, plundered by unpaid soldiery and newly ennobled beggars on horseback. While the Cortes issued laws which became dead letters after three months, and the town representatives clamoured for peace, Juan I drifted from one war to another until his campaigns to annex Portugal ended in the tremendous military bankruptcy of Aljubarrota.[1]

[1] See Menéndez Pelayo, *Antología*, i. 365.

In 1391, during the minority of Enrique III, Castile saw the first serious attacks on its Jewish communities. The weak Crown attempted to prevent the pogroms but it was partly responsible for them. In the civil war of 1366–9 Enrique II had opened the gate to anti-Semitism, and his policy of co-operation with the Cortes and the Church made it impossible to return wholeheartedly to the earlier tradition of *convivencia*.[1]

The first Trastámaras had no easy task. The plague which had ravaged Europe in 1348–51 returned in 1362–3, 1374, and 1384. Some regions were depopulated. A vast inflation produced a rise in prices and wages of about 100 per cent in 1351–69. Widespread unemployment provided ready recruits for banditry and for anti-Jewish propaganda. The civil war worsened conditions for the towns, which lost ground, both with regard to the Crown and the nobility.[2]

THE END OF THE CIVIL WAR

The death of Pedro I in March 1369 did not end the civil war. Enrique II did not control Galicia, the Basque country, Toledo, or most of Andalusia. He had to conquer these regions from Pedro's supporters while at the same time defending himself against neighbouring powers. Navarre, Portugal, and Catalonia–Aragon were all hostile to Enrique. They all sought, as did England—which ruled half France from Bordeaux—to profit from the chaos to annex what they could of Castile. Enrique's only ally was France. French mercenaries carried Enrique to victory in 1366 and 1369 but they could not remain for ever, however highly they were rewarded.

In 1369–71 Enrique II passed from a highly unstable position to relative security which his son would attempt to convert into predominance over the Iberian peninsula. This transformation was due to the inability of Enrique's enemies to act together. Catalonia–Aragon was exhausted by the war with Castile. Its ruler, Pere III, endeavoured to isolate Enrique diplomatically. He was reluctant to fight. England put forward claims but was soon occupied by renewed war with France. Navarre was only interested in the border cities she had gained. Muḥammad V of

[1] See Vol. ii, Part I, Ch. IV.

[2] J. Valdeón Baruque, *Enrique II de Castilla* (Valladolid, 1966), pp. 33–69, 77–81. For 1384 see *CDIHE* cvi. 102.

Granada (1354–91) announced the conquest of Algeciras in 1369 in a letter to Mecca; it is still recorded in an inscription in the Alhambra. But the city was not held but destroyed and abandoned. The conquest of Algeciras in 1344, which secured Castile's control of the Straits of Gibraltar, was not reversed. In 1370, at a time when Enrique was in great difficulties, Muḥammad agreed to a long truce which gave him the opportunity to turn towards Morocco, whose policy he came to control.[1]

The first serious rival to Enrique for the Castilian throne was Fernando of Portugal (1367–83). Portugal's long immunity from war had made her rich. In Fernando's reign 400–500 ships were often anchored off Lisbon. Fernando had inherited a great treasure which he poured into war with Castile. 'It seemed to him a little thing that all Castile should be his in a short time.' His claims were accepted by Catalonia–Aragon, and by most of Pedro's supporters. Fernando repeatedly occupied Galicia, and his naval blockade of Seville lasted over a year, but his troops were unable to confront Enrique's French mercenaries. The breaking of the blockade and papal intervention persuaded Fernando to make peace on 31 March 1371. The fall of the remaining Petrist strongholds soon followed. By November Navarre and Catalonia–Aragon also abandoned the struggle.[2]

CASTILE AGAINST ENGLAND

Enrique's throne was not secure, however. In September 1371 John, duke of Lancaster, a younger son of Edward III of England and his new representative in France, married Doña Constanza, the elder surviving daughter of Pedro I by María de Padilla, whose children had been twice recognized as legitimate by the Castilian Cortes in 1362–3; their legitimacy was not challenged by the Trastámaras. This marriage gave Enrique a new rival for Castile, more formidable than Fernando of Portugal, since he was supported by England, which despaired of breaking Enrique's alliance with France. On 10 July 1372 Lancaster and Portugal signed a treaty against Enrique, the first of a series of Anglo-Portuguese alliances designed to

[1] M. Gaspar y Remiro, *Revista del Centro de Estudios Históricos de Granada y su Reino*, 4 (1914), 294–365; 5 (1915), 1–8; M. A. Ladero Quesada, *Granada*, pp. 97 ff.

[2] F. Lopes, *Crónica de D. Fernando*, prol., c. 26, ed. Arnaut, pp. 4 f., 77; P. E. Russell, *The English Intervention in Spain and Portugal*, pp. 149–64; Valdeón, pp. 203–69. But see, for 1376, *Miscelánea de textos medievales*, ii. 128.

counter-balance Castile and France, but in 1372–3 the Castilian invasion of Portugal was so rapid and successful that no English aid could arrive in time. Although Fernando's renunciation of the English alliance was not sincere—he used the interval of peace to prepare for another war by fortifying his cities, improving his armed forces, and encouraging ship-building—Portugal was temporarily out of action.[1]

In 1372 the French support for Enrique which had twice given him Castile at last began to pay. In June twelve Castilian galleys, under a Genoese admiral, destroyed a large English fleet taking reinforcements to La Rochelle. A reinforced Castilian fleet enabled the French to capture the city. While Lancaster's plans to invade Castile by land failed to mature, and Enrique's incursion into Gascony proved a fiasco, Castilian galleys carried out repeated and very destructive raids on the English coasts and ravaged English shipping. Meanwhile the English possessions in France fell, one after the other. French gains from the Castilian alliance are clearer than the profit to Castile, as distinct from Castile's ruler, whose throne was still supported, in 1373, by 1,000 French men-at-arms. Castile's gains were largely commercial and maritime. Castilian colonies of merchants along the French coasts profited from freedom from taxes on their goods. In Flanders English wool was replaced as the major import by Castilian. The Basque ports were interested in trade with Bruges and in the privileges they obtained at the reconquered La Rochelle, in Normandy and Brittany. Castilian shipping prospered as Castile's sailors came to control the English channel.[2]

ENRIQUE II'S INTERNAL POLICY

Enrique II's rising against his brother Pedro I began as a revolt of the nobility. In 1366 he claimed he had come 'to place all and each in his degree and state and liberties'. As against the legitimist supporters of Pedro's daughters he exalted his supposedly free election by the people. Despite this propaganda Enrique—apart from his French troops—drew his support almost exclusively from nobles impatient of Pedro's refusal to grant them what they wanted. In 1367 Enrique told the Cortes that 'God

[1] Russell, pp. 165–203.
[2] Russell, pp. 204–47; Suárez, *HE* xiv. 160–66, 185–88.

willed us to come to raise up the houses of the good men [nobles] of Castile which were till now depressed'. Enrique frequently summoned the towns to Cortes but the nobility and the Church were the bases of his power and it was they which received the richest rewards.

THE NOBILITY: MERCEDES

In April 1366, as soon as he held one major city, Burgos, Enrique began to make lavish grants (*mercedes*)—lordships in land, towns, etc., often with full rights of jurisdiction—to his noble supporters. Many more *mercedes* were conceded in 1369–71. The civil war had destroyed the old higher nobility. Enrique sought to fill the vacuum. Three main groups benefited: the new king's relatives, foreign mercenary commanders and lesser nobles. Only one foreign commander remained in Castile; the rest soon sold their lands. Enrique's illegitimate sons and nephews were richly endowed. Loyal lesser nobles, mainly from the northern periphery, Navarre, Alava, the Rioja, León, received extensive lands in Old and New Castile, in Andalusia, or in rebellious Galicia or Asturias. On a lower level Enrique would grant jurisdiction over a small town in the beneficiary's own region. His aim was to procure a solid political basis for his regime, reinforcing and counterbalancing a group of titled royal princes by a class of untitled noble royal servants, who occupied the principal Crown offices. Enrique granted both groups *mayorazgos* (entails), which guaranteed the transmission of a grantee's lands intact to one male heir. The king believed that this system would enable his nobles to serve the Crown more effectively than if their lands were to be dispersed between their children.[1]

RESULTS

Enrique's *mercedes* were naturally welcome to the nobility, who contrasted his 'largesse' with Pedro's 'covetousness'; his monarchy seemed to them 'more humane and temperate'. However, his policy weakened the Crown. Many of the lands granted away had been confiscated from Pedro I's supporters but others were originally Crown lands. The grants of jurisdiction

[1] *Cartulario del Infantado de Covarrubias*, ed. L. Serrano (Madrid 1907), p. 217; Valdeón, pp. 96–100, *Cortes de Leõn*, ii, 162.

contained in the *mercedes* meant that the Crown no longer effectively controlled large areas of the country. By 1373 the Cortes were complaining of the abuses of justice by the new lords. By 1371 the Crown's revenues were also diminished, not least by the alienation of royal taxes in many lordships. The *mayorazgos* helped to create a closed aristocracy of a few strong lineages. Enrique's hope, expressed in his will (1374) that many *mayorazgos* would revert to the Crown for lack of direct heirs, proved illusory. The policy initiated by Enrique and continued by his successors ensured the dominance of the social, economic, and political scene for centuries by the Ayalas, Manriques, Velascos, Mendozas, and another ten or twelve families.[1]

THE CHURCH

Enrique also rewarded the ecclesiastical magnates who had assisted him. The Military Orders received large *mercedes*, the archbishoprics of Toledo and Santiago (a frontier region), and the see of Burgos notable grants. Favoured religious houses, such as the Dominicans of Palencia, also benefited. Enrique sought to protect the Church against royal officials, lay nobles, and towns. In return for all this the Castilian Church 'baptized' the Trastámara usurpation as a crusade against an impious Jew-loving tyrant.

THE TOWNS

During the civil war and in his attempt to reconstruct the monarchy Enrique relied mainly on the nobility and the Church. In his first meetings of Cortes (1367–71) both these estates were present in force. The third estate, the towns, were, as usual, represented but they received soft answers, the superior estates *mercedes*. Nobles and churchmen did not trouble to attend later Cortes. The towns' representatives repeated demands for representation in the Royal Council received little satisfaction. Enrique granted some local exemptions from taxes. He gave way (1371) to the demand that the Jews should be forced to wear distinctive dress but insisted on the payment of debts to them. He continued to employ Jewish financiers.[2]

[1] Valdeón, pp. 117–26, 274–305; idem, *Hispania*, 28 (1968), 38–55. Noble reactions: Pedro Ferrús, in *Cancionero de Baena*, 304, ed. Azáceta, ii. 657, 661; Fernán Pérez de Guzmán, *NBAE* xix. 747 f. *Cortes de León*, ii. 208, 262 f., 266 f.

[2] Valdeón, *Enrique II*, pp. 297 f., 307–34; *Cortes*, ii. 144–55, 183, 203–16, 244–49.

'ECONOMIC POLICY'

Enrique's interventions in economic life were as blundering as those of most medieval rulers. In 1369 he debased the coinage so as to pay his mercenary troops. Naturally, prices and wages soared. Enrique endeavoured to hold inflation down by an *Ordinance* which he had to withdraw a year later (1370). In 1370 he devalued his new coinage to a third of its nominal worth. By 1373 the situation improved. Other measures, such as the prohibition of the export of foodstuffs, were more valuable as popular concessions than they were successful.

ROYAL INCOME

The loss of royal revenue incurred by the *mercedes* was only partly compensated for by the now general levy of the *alcabala* (a 10 per cent sales-tax), by the increased levies from the Mesta of the sheep-owners, and from the Jews.[1]

ROYAL INSTITUTIONS

Enrique based his monarchy on his subjects' self-interest, on the nobility, the Church, to a lesser extent cities and Jews. He hedged it round with new or reformed institutions. In 1371, at Toro, he published *Ordinances* on the Chancery and the Royal Court of Appeal (*Audiencia*). The composition of these bodies was regularized. They became more professional. The *Audiencia* was intended to administer law based on Alfonso X's *Partidas*, according to the Roman legal ideas of the judges, trained in Bologna, who also dominated the Royal Council. By the end of Enrique's reign a fiscal clearing-house, the *Casa de Cuentas*, existed within the Household. Jews still acted as Treasurer and rented out the royal revenues but the *contadores* controlling the *Casa* and the inferior tax-gatherers were Christians. They were charged with recording the ingress and egress of moneys and probably with establishing a rudimentary budget. The Crown was owed about 9,000,000 maravedis—much of this debt going back years; the existence of this new central fiscal office implied a striking advance for the monarchy.

Enrique had begun as a typical noble rebel. After his triumph

[1] *Cortes*, ii. 172–80, 186 f., 204 f.; Valdeón, pp. 334–50; idem, in *Homenaje al profesor Alarcos* (Valladolid, 1965–7), ii. 829–45.

over internal opposition (1369–71) his grants to the nobility became more sparing. At Toro he returned to the centralizing ideas of his father, Alfonso XI, and even of his brother Pedro I. Enrique and his successors were to pursue these ideas more indirectly than their predecessors, hampered by the increased power they had given to the nobility.[1]

THE ADVANCE OF CASTILIAN HEGEMONY IN THE PENINSULA: ENRIQUE II

Alfonso XI's and Pedro I's policy was based on two main aims, the establishment of a stable and centralized monarchy in Castile, and the hegemony of Castile in the peninsula. Enrique II could not have forgotten the sight of his brother Pedro's armies besieging Valencia. During his exile he had sought to intermarry his bastard line with the House of Barcelona. In 1371 he proposed his daughter as a bride to Fernando of Portugal. Hegemony through intermarriage was to be one of the main tactics of the Trastámaras though they were prepared to use force if necessary. The seignorial regime established in Castile by Enrique also played a role in Trastámara attempts to unite the peninsula. While it attracted the nobility of the lower Duero and of Aragon it repelled the mercantile interests of Lisbon and Barcelona. Diverse reactions within Portugal and Catalonia–Aragon to the 'new model' Trastámara monarchy help to explain the course of the struggle with Portugal in the 1380s, the Compromise of Caspe in 1410–12. In the 1380s the Portuguese nobility failed to carry the day for Castile, in 1410–12 the Catalan bourgeois proved too divided to resist the Castilian claimant to the throne, who was supported by the Aragonese nobility.[2]

In 1373 Enrique's bastard son, Fadrique, was betrothed to the heiress to Portugal, Beatriz; in 1375 Elionor of Aragon married Juan, the heir to Castile, and Leonor of Castile Carlos, heir to Navarre. The initiative was due in each case to Enrique. Both Portugal and Aragon only agreed when the failure of England to intervene left them exposed to Castilian invasion. Renewed negotiations between Navarre, Aragon, and England,

[1] *Cortes*, ii. 188–192, 217–43; Suárez, *HE* xiv. 151; Valdeón, pp. 355–63; idem, *Hispania*, 26 (1966), 99–134.

[2] Pere III, *Crònica*, vi. 41, ed. Pagès, pp. 371 ff., etc.; Suárez, pp. 180 f.

and scanty English troops failed to save Navarre from military defeat by Castile in 1378–9; in the Peace of Briones it became a Castilian protectorate. The direct way from English-held Gascony to Castile was barred. In 1379 Joan, the heir to Catalonia–Aragon, married a French princess. His pro-French and pro-Castilian policy continually undermined the Anglo-Aragonese alliance his father Pere III wished for and removed a major problem for Castile.[1]

Enrique II died in May 1379. In ten years he had saved Castile from the imminent danger of division among its enemies. It was again, as it had been under Pedro I, the dominant power in the peninsula. Lancaster and his wife continued to claim the Castilian throne, but the only ally they could now use, Portugal, was tied by alliance to the Trastámaras.

JUAN I (1379–1390)

On his deathbed Enrique told his heir, Juan I, to cling always to the French alliance. Juan was to follow this advice. In most ways Juan was a pale imitation of his father. Prim and pious, emotional and introspective, lacking Enrique's cruelty but also his energy, Juan carried his father's policies to disastrous extremes. In his internal policy Juan favoured the Church against both Jews and nobles. Clerics were among his principal advisers and he relied on them against his rebellious relations. The reign saw a considerable advance of new or reformed religious orders.[2]

Juan's first years saw a further series of Castilian triumphs. The naval war with England continued. Castilian galleys ascended the Thames and burnt Gravesend. Their co-operation with French troops in suppressing a rebellion in Flanders was rewarded by further privileges there. The attempt of Fernando of Portugal to free himself from Castile by again allying with Lancaster brought a second Portuguese defeat (1379–82). This was followed in May 1383 by the marriage of Juan I himself to the Portuguese heiress Beatriz. Juan's first wife had recently died. Her two sons were heirs to Castile. A Castilian protectorate

[1] Russell, pp. 249–96.

[2] Ayala, *Crónica de Enrique II*, año XIV, 3 (*BAE* lxviii. 37, also 42). On Juan I: F. Lopes, *Crónica de D. Fernando*, 155, 169 (pp. 429 f., 465); Suárez, p. 203; Russell, p. 280. For Juan and the Church see e.g. P. Floriano Llorente, *El Libro Becerro de la Catedral de Oviedo* (Oviedo, 1963), pp. 102–6, 132–41, 174–9.

over Portugal, rather than a union of Crowns, was stipulated, after Fernando's death, with the Portuguese queen mother, Leonor, acting as regent. It seems unlikely that Juan I meant to keep to these conditions. In any case control over Portugal would completely exclude England (and his rival Lancaster) from the peninsula. In 1383 the House of Commons forced the English government to attempt to make peace with the Trastámaras. This favourable situation was only changed by the Portuguese crisis.[1]

THE PORTUGUESE CRISIS (1383–1385)

Fernando died on 22 October 1383. The queen mother, though much disliked because she was known to be under the influence of Castilian émigrés, was duly proclaimed as regent on behalf of Beatriz. The major crisis which followed was precipitated by Juan I's insistence that his wife should be at once proclaimed queen, and by his sending orders directly to a number of towns. Before Juan could advance into Portugal the queen mother's Castilian lover Andéiro had been murdered (6 December) and the Lisbon mob had risen. Queen Leonor soon withdrew to Santarem and appealed to Juan I for help. He had entered Portugal on 13 December, against the advice of most of his Council.

Andéiro's murderer, Dom João, Master of the Military Order of Aviz, a bastard half-brother of the dead King Fernando, could not conceive of resisting Castile. His flight to England was only prevented by the urgent pleas of the mob and the advice of a mysterious hermit recently arrived from Jerusalem. In January 1384 João was acting as 'Ruler and Defender' of Portugal in the name of another (legitimized) son of Pedro I, the Infante João, whom Juan I had just imprisoned. It was only gradually that Dom João supplanted his half-brother and was acclaimed king.

JOÃO I: HIS SUPPORTERS

In 1383 the future João I of Portugal was a mediocre young man of twenty-five, hesitant and violent by turn about, his piety the one feature of his character his advocates felt safe to stress. His success was due to the unpopularity of the legitimate heiress

[1] Russell, pp. 296–355; Suárez, pp. 230–6.

Queen Beatriz, because of her Castilian marriage; to the absence of other candidates; to his advisers; and to the support he received from the cities of Lisbon and Oporto. In December 1383 he was mainly supported by the craftsmen of Lisbon. The richer citizens who ruled Lisbon were only brought over by threats from a crowd of artisans. In return for their support the craftsmen's representatives received (1 April 1384) the right to intervene in the election of city magistrates and in the imposition of taxes.

The rich of Lisbon were more important, however, to João. It was they who financed the resistance to Castile. In return, in 1384 and 1385, Lisbon received a series of privileges, which defended its merchants from foreign competition within Portugal, exempted them from all internal customs dues, and freed the city from most taxes due to the Crown. These privileges were granted to the oligarchical council which continued to rule Lisbon.

Peasant revolts swept the countryside. The nobles who supported João (the majority at first opposed him) required and obtained from him a guarantee and increase of their privileges before they formally recognized him as regent. There was no lasting social revolution. The main cities acquired greater independence of the Crown but the nobility did not disappear. The war with Castile soon became a national religious struggle, in which an archbishop could arm galleys and small armies triumph under the banner of the Cross. The fact that Portugal (and England) supported one of the two contending popes in the Great Schism (1378–1416), while Castile supported the other, lent an added religious dimension to the struggle.[1] Juan I had expected a rapid take-over. He was to be disappointed. In January 1384 Juan induced Queen Leonor to give up the regency to him. Most fortresses north of the Tagus supported him. João's repeated attempts to secure help from England failed to produce any troops until early 1385. Juan's siege of Lisbon lasted from May to September 1384. By then the besieged were starving. They were only saved by the plague

[1] Russell, pp. 357–62; F. Lopes, *Crónica de D. João I*, i. 17–24, 191, 88, 110, ed. Braamcamp Freire, 33–43, 369, 147, 186; S. Dias Arnaut, *A crise nacional dos fins do século XIV*, i (Coimbra, 1960); M. Caetano, 'O Concelho de Lisboa na crise de 1383–1385', *Academia portuguesa de história, Anais*, ser. II, 4 (1953), 175–247.

which struck the Castilian army but spared the town. Juan's obstinacy in continuing the siege cost him over 2,000 men-at-arms and his best commanders. The Portuguese saw themselves delivered by a miracle. As the Castilians withdrew Dom João sent his troops, new apostles, 'to preach throughout the kingdom the Portuguese Gospel'. But these expeditions were generally unsuccessful. Juan had left Castilian garrisons in many towns and was planning a new invasion.[1]

By the time that this invasion materialized Dom João had been acclaimed as king on 6 April 1385 at the Cortes of Coimbra, his spokesman declaring that Juan I, as a supporter of an anti-pope, was a heretic and that 'election belongs freely to the people'. In March some English troops had reached Lisbon. However the Portuguese were mainly dependent on themselves. Juan I had secured some French mercenaries and five Catalan galleys. His treasury was already empty in 1383. A series of forced loans and heavy taxes were barely able to meet the cost of his massive preparations.[2]

ALJUBARROTA

Juan was determined to risk everything on one battle. He did so at Aljubarrota on 14 August. He probably had 5,000 men-at-arms (over 1,000 French and many Portuguese), 2,000 light horse (some of them Mudejars), and over 10,000 bowmen and other infantry. The Portuguese numbered 2,000–3,000 men-at-arms and several thousand foot. There were about 700 English and Gascons, including some 300 archers. The battle lasted less than an hour. The Castilians were tired from a twenty-kilometre march. They were launched by young and untried leaders at a strong defensive position. The Castilians and their allies who had survived the crossfire of the English archers (each archer could fire at least ten arrows a minute) were confronted with a rough palisade and ditch. Attempts to turn the flank of this position met a complex of wolf-traps and trenches. It is not surprising that the result was as complete a Franco-Castilian defeat as Nájera had been in 1367. Juan's generals and almost

[1] Russell, pp. 362–73; Lopes, *D. João*, i. 159 (p. 299).

[2] Lopes, i. 185, 188 (pp. 352, 362); M. Caetano, 'As Cortes de 1385', *Revista portuguesa de história*, 5 (1951), 5–86; L. Suárez, *AEM* 2 (1965), 375; Russell, pp. 373–80.

all the Portuguese nobles with him were among the 2,500 men-at-arms killed.

RESULTS OF ALJUBARROTA

The battle saved Portuguese independence. To the great fifteenth-century Portuguese historian Fernão Lopes a new age of the world had begun. This vision had solid foundations. Independent of Castile, Portugal could expand outside the peninsula. In the 1390s the trade of Lisbon was already gravitating towards the North Sea.

Juan I fled by sea to Seville. Most of the places held by Castile in Portugal soon surrendered. The news reached the aged Ibn Khaldūn in Cairo. In the peninsula it delighted the opponents of the Trastámaras. In England it decided Lancaster to try again for the Castilian crown. Two weeks after Aljubarrota Juan I announced that he would avenge his defeat. João of Portugal knew that Castile would have French assistance. He invited Lancaster to assert his claims. By December 1385 the English Parliament had voted the necessary funds. The Anglo-Portuguese Treaty of Windsor followed in May 1386. The terms guaranteed the presence of Portuguese galleys to protect the English coasts against Castilian attack. In return Portugal secured the promise of military aid and commercial privileges.[1]

In December 1385 Juan I appealed to the Castilian Cortes. A new Council representing the three estates was set up and 'the first serious attempt made to give the Crown a semi-permanent army'. The Cortes voted 10,000,000 maravedis. In 1386–8 they were to meet every year and to vote other very large sums. In return the Crown was obliged to make substantial concessions. Juan also found it necessary to multiply donations to his noble supporters and to reward the friendship of Navarre by returning the castles taken in 1379. Even with these concessions he could only maintain a defensive war. In March 1386 Juan ordered the concentration of all provisions in walled fortresses. He also attempted to arrange peace by a large payment and by a royal marriage. This was to be the final solution of the

[1] Russell, pp. 380–403, 414 ff., 568 f.; Ayala, *Crónica de Juan I*, año VII, 14 (*BAE* lxviii. 103 f.); S. Dias Arnaut, *Revista portuguesa de história*, 10 (1962), 467–99; Russell, ibid., pp. 419–33; A. do Paço, *Bulletin des études portugaises*, N.S., 24 (1963), 11–24; Lopes, i. 163 (p. 308); F. Melis, *Aspetti della vita economica medievale*, i (Siena, 1962), 276; R. Dozy, *Recherches*, 3rd edn., i. 112.

dynastic quarrel but it was not adopted until Lancaster had tried military invasion.

On 25 July 1386 the English expedition of about 7,000 men reached La Coruña. This force could probably have defeated Juan whose troops were dispersed and only numbered 3,000 men-at-arms, 1,000 of whom were French. But Lancaster had come too late in the year to be able to do more than conquer most of Galicia before winter set in. Lancaster had to turn to Portugal. In November, in return for Philippa, Lancaster's daughter by his first marriage, and for the promise to cede a strip of territory 80 km. wide along the western frontier of Castile, João promised military aid. By this promise Lancaster had given Juan I the means of rallying Castilian opinion to his side. Juan's speech to the Castilian Cortes in November reveals considerable internal discontent. To counter this the king announced that Lancaster was planning to divide Castile between the rebellious Portuguese, Aragon and Navarre. Muslim Granada was perhaps added for good measure but Lancaster was indeed negotiating with Pere III of Aragon who had refused to assist Castile against England. Pere's death on 5 January 1387 improved the situation for Juan. Pere's heir, Joan I (1387–95) was far less independent of Castile than Pere had been.[1]

By 1387 delays, the plague, and the garrisons left in Galicia had reduced Lancaster's field army to some 1,500 men. João's troops numbered some 9,000. Together the allies probably outnumbered Juan I's men-at-arms (half of them French) but their joint invasion of Léon (March–May 1387) proved a complete fiasco. Juan's troops avoided battle and no important towns fell or surrendered voluntarily. But Juan was ready for peace. To recover Galicia, dismiss his unpaid French allies, isolate Portugal, and end the dynastic feud it was worth while to agree to more generous terms than Juan had offered before the invasion. In the Treaty of Bayonne (July 1388) Lancaster received very large sums, including an annual pension. His daughter Catalina, Pedro I's granddaughter, married Enrique, Juan's heir and the grandson of Pedro's murderer, Enrique II. While Lancaster 'lined his own nest with Castilian bullion' he abandoned not only his claim to Castile but his Portuguese ally and

[1] Russell, pp. 403–48; Suárez, pp. 260–70; Floriano Llorente, op. cit., pp. 102–6; *Cortes de León*, ii. 314–35, 349–55.

the interests of his own country. Castile remained tied to France. Castilian galleys continued to harry the English coasts until the truce of 1389 between France and England (renewed in 1394).

Juan I was forced to agree to a separate truce with Portugal. His intention to conquer it was unchanged but his unexpected death on 9 October 1390, leaving as heir a child of eleven, enforced a more lasting peace. Although Castilian participation in the Hundred Years War greatly diminished after 1389 the Franco-Castilian alliance was renewed by Enrique III and his successor. Since England could not upset the French 'political protectorate over Castile' it was necessary to cultivate the alliance with Portugal. This alliance was strengthened by Lancaster's daughter Philippa, João I's queen (d. 1415). It was she who linked Portugal and England at a time when Castile was culturally, as well as politically, a province of France.[1]

INTERNAL REFORMS

In his last years Juan I attempted to strengthen his weakened authority by a series of administrative reforms. Some of these were propaganda measures, designed to placate the discontent expressed in Cortes by the third estate, and did not endure. The (theoretical) representatives of the cities' place in the Royal Council only lasted two years. In 1387 they were replaced by professional lawyers. The site and jurisdiction of the Royal Appeal Court (the *Audiencia*) were defined more precisely in 1387 and 1390. The *Hermandades* (Brotherhoods) of 1387 provided local police forces prized by the Cortes which extended throughout the country.

Juan I favoured attempts to reform the life of the secular clergy. These were not very effective. The Church was largely absorbed in ancient rivalries over jurisdiction with towns and nobles. One result of church reform was increasing anti-Judaism.

CORTES

In 1385–90 the Crown presented very heavy and repeated financial demands to the Cortes. The cities' representatives underwent a rapid education in political bargaining. They demanded concessions in return for tax grants. In 1387 they

[1] Russell, pp. 449–554 (quotations from pp. 524, 539).

claimed the right to inspect the royal accounts, in 1388 to limit the amount voted and to control its collection and its use. Juan I was barely able to neutralize the cities by adding enough nobles, exempt from taxes, to the commission. In 1390 Juan failed to obtain a regular income, which would have enabled him to accumulate money for a new war with Portugal. A military reform was projected, which would permanently assure the Crown 4,000 men-at-arms, 1,500 light horse, and 1,000 mounted archers. This reform was modified by Juan's concessions but it pointed to the future.[1]

THE MINORITY OF ENRIQUE III

During the minority of Enrique III of Castile (1390–3) the higher nobility, created by his father and grandfather, in its internecine struggles almost overthrew the throne. In 1390 the king was eleven. His relations (the legitimate and illegitimate descendants of Enrique II), the archbishops of Toledo and Santiago, the masters of the Military Orders, fought for power. The Cortes of Madrid (1391) imposed a Council of regency too large to act effectively in a crisis. A contemporary poem remarks that 'even a Master of Theology could not describe the chaos in the court'.

MASSACRES OF THE JEWS

The elements hostile to the Jews, the urban middle class, the city mob, and the more fanatical clergy, seized their chance. There had been massacres of Jews during the civil wars of the 1350s and 1360s. Now they recurred on a far larger scale. In November 1390 several Jewish communities were attacked in Andalusia. The main storm broke in Seville on 4 June 1391. During the next two months pogroms spread not only throughout Castile (Old Castile was less severely afflicted than Andalusia) but also the Crown of Aragon. The Jews of Castile had been one of the main supports of the monarchy. The massacre or forced conversion of a large proportion of them created vast problems for the future. The remaining Jews were to be again persecuted, and there now also existed a powerful class of Jewish *conversos* to Christianity, a provocation to Jews and Christians.

[1] Suárez, pp. 287–300; Ayala, *Juan I*, año XII, 5–6 (pp. 130–3).

Those responsible for the pogroms were hardly punished. Bloodshed in Seville and Murcia between rival noble clans, a separatist movement in Guipúzcoa in the north, were further proof of the powerlessness of the Crown.[1]

The Cortes of Burgos (1391–2) appeared to control the situation. Their very success against the king's relatives proved fatal. The advocates of a strong monarchy took care to avoid giving the representatives of the cities the chance to act again as arbiters of power. It was not the third estate but the lesser nobility who profited from the mediocrity of the royal princes. The archbishop of Santiago, Don Juan García Manrique, promoted the rise of the Manriques, Stúñigas, Ayalas, Dávalos; the rival archbishop of Toledo, Don Pedro Tenorio, that of the Mendozas, Velascos, Guzmanes, and Manueles. The official declaration (2 August 1393) that Enrique III was of age made little change in the situation. The Cortes of 1393 accepted the Crown's raising taxes without a previous vote, without a serious protest. From now on they were on the defensive.

DISAPPEARANCE OF THE ROYAL PRINCES

1394–5 saw the destruction of the power of the royal princes. Foolish enough to reject the enormous offers made them and then to fail to unite in arms, they were overcome with little difficulty, imprisoned for life, exiled, or allowed to vegetate in obscurity. The incorporation of the Marquesado of Villena in the Crown (1394–8) provided a colophon to the conflict with the princes. Alfonso de Aragón's services to earlier Trastámaras profited him little. His elimination from Castilian politics removed Aragonese infiltration across the frontier.[2]

The Crown had triumphed, and with it its servants, the lesser nobility. As the two contending archbishops disappeared from the scene there remained Enrique III and a small group of office-holders, notably the Constable (commanding the army), Ruy López Dávalos, Juan Hurtado de Mendoza, who ruled the Royal Household as Majordomo, and Diego López de Stúñiga, the *Justicia Mayor*.

[1] Suárez, *HE* xiv. 304–12; *Cancionero de Baena*, 57, ed. Azáceta, i. 128.

[2] Suárez, xiv. 316–40. On the Marquesado E. Mitre Fernández, *Murgetana*, 30 (1969), 55–62.

ENRIQUE III: PERSONAL REIGN

We possess a contemporary description of Enrique III, revealing in its lack of admiration. From the age of seventeen or eighteen Enrique was constantly ill. His manner was harsh and cold. He did not conform to the norm of the medieval ruler; he was not concerned to appear a constant fount of largesse. He chose his counsellors with care, favouring friars, prelates, and lawyers, and accumulated considerable treasure.

EXTERNAL POLICY, TRADE

Enrique was also unconventional in being uninterested in war. His war with Portugal was a minor affair; it was not begun by him. Although the war made clear that Castile was again able to defeat Portugal the result was the effective concession of Portuguese independence. Following the lead of its constant ally France, Castile sought a lasting peace with England and the end of the Papal Schism. Castilians enjoyed a virtual monopoly of trade with Flanders. In 1397–8 Enrique signed edicts encouraging native shipping. In 1405, as a reprisal for English piracy, Castilian galleys attacked Cornwall.

Basque ships appeared more often in the Mediterranean, bringing silk from Constantinople, or transporting Catalan and Genoese goods from Barcelona or Valencia. In 1404 royal galleys quartered the western Mediterranean searching for Berber and Catalan pirates. Castilian diplomatic interests extended to the East. In 1402 Enrique sent ambassadors to observe the struggle between Tamerlane and the Turks. His later relations with Tamerlane took a Castilian mission to Central Asia.[1]

INTERNAL POLICY: THE CORTES

Enrique's relative freedom from foreign wars made him far more independent than his two predecessors had been of the Cortes, which were not summoned between 1396 and 1401.

[1] Fernán Pérez de Guzmán, *Generaciones y semblanzas*, ed. R. B. Tate (London, 1965), pp. 5–8; Suárez, xiv. 347–72, xv. 41–3; idem, *Relaciones entre Portugal y Castilla* (Madrid, 1960), pp. 17–37, 71–179; Rubió, *Diplomatari*, pp. 559–61; *Cortes de Cataluña*, iv. 369; J. Day, *Les Douanes de Gênes, 1376–1377* (Paris, 1963), ii. 689; M. Del Treppo, *Rivista storica italiana*, 70 (1958), 51; Ruy González de Clavijo, *Embassy to Tamerlane*, transl. G. Le Strange (London, 1928), pp. 24 f.

When they met they were treated as an appropriate background for the ratification of treaties and for decisions with regard to the Schism. The protests of the cities' representatives against royal officials and unequal taxation were unsuccessful. Their only success was the passage of laws against the Jews (1405).[1]

THE RISE OF THE LESSER NOBILITY

Enrique III—or rather his servants—had destroyed the higher nobility, the royal princes, enriched by his grandfather, Enrique II. Enrique III did not attempt—as Pedro I had done —to do without any nobility at all. He redistributed many lands recovered from the princes. The bishopric of Oviedo, held by a leading royal servant, received the lands of one bastard princeling. Portuguese émigré nobles were rewarded with some of those of another. Families of lesser nobles from the northern periphery of Castile had begun their rise under Enrique II. His *mercedes* (grants of lordships, with jurisdiction, royal taxes, etc., often secured by a *mayorazgo* or entail) had been increased by purchases, exchanges, and intermarriage. Enrique III conceded more lordships and *mayorazgos* (some of which could now descend through daughters as well as sons). After 1397 few of these grants were to Castilians. Royal generosity to the Portuguese émigrés, the Acuñas, Pachecos, and Pimentels, was meant to secure allies against Portugal. It founded some of the greatest and most troublesome Castilian noble dynasties. Leading families profited greatly from the possession of offices at court. The Mendozas appear to have become (in two generations) hereditary *Mayordomos*, the Velascos hereditary *Camareros* (Chamberlains). The main governorships (*adelantados*), Galicia, León, Castile, soon became hereditary. A man such as the constable, Ruy López Dávalos, could use his power at court to become governor of Murcia, and the governorship to acquire lands locally.

The Crown tried to control appointments as Master of the Military Orders, and to defend bishoprics and monasteries against both nobles and royal officials. There were signs of danger, however. By 1406 several noble 'leagues' had tried to bring pressure on the king. About twelve powerful lineages had

[1] Suárez, xiv. 341 f., 361 ff., 373; *Cortes de León*, ii. 544–54.

emerged. Through intermarriage their lands could range from Galicia to Andalusia. Their position was not immovable. They still needed the monarchy, especially court offices. The long minority of Enrique's heir, Juan II, would cement their power. Under Enrique III one noble, Diego Hurtado de Mendoza, controlled the whole province of Santander and lands round the mountain passes of the central Sierras. He named the representatives Guadalajara sent to Cortes. He was also admiral of Castile. But the position he had acquired almost collapsed at his death. His widow was forced to pay large sums to the *Camarero Mayor* to secure her children's inheritance.[1]

ENRIQUE'S ATTEMPTS TO CONTROL THE NOBILITY

Enrique III attempted to control the rising nobility. In 1398 he reaffirmed the duty of all nobles to contribute to all royal and municipal taxes, except for the *servicio de la moneda*, voted by Cortes. He also dictated rigid norms defining who could enjoy the privileges of *hidalguía*. He made more use than his predecessors of royal officials known as *corregidores*. Fifty years later Enrique was seen as placing '*corregidores* in the whole kingdom, from Seville to Vizcaya'. Enrique's use of *corregidores* was more limited than this but it illuminates his policy and the difficulties it met with.

Corregidores, with extensive powers to reform local administration and to judge civil and criminal cases, were appointed, officially, to end noble feuds and maintain order. In some cases they were intended to combat the local monopoly of power by a lay or ecclesiastical lord, at other times to reinforce a lord's control over his locality.

Enrique employed *corregidores* mainly in Andalusia, the Basque provinces, and Galicia, regions particularly hard to control by normal methods. A fair proportion of his appointments went to men from outside the region in question. Enrique's *corregidores* proved ineffective against a royal servant as important as Diego Hurtado de Mendoza. In 1400, when Don Diego was discharging his office as admiral in the Mediterranean, Enrique sent a *corregidor* to Guadalajara to take from him the municipal offices. In 1401 the admiral returned and

[1] See above, p. 390, n. 1. Mitre, *Evolución de la nobleza en Castilla bajo Enrique III* (Valladolid, 1968).

the *corregidor* was recalled. In 1402 another *corregidor* was ordered by Enrique not to interfere with the admiral's jurisdiction in Asturias. On other occasions the Crown granted privileged abbots, bishops, and lay nobles the right to appoint *corregidores* themselves to enforce their control of their lordships.

Corregidores represent an attempt by the Crown to control its kingdoms. They were also used, at this stage, as a weapon by powerful centrifugal forces. The one element which always suffered from *corregidores* was the cities. Their independence was diminished by any outside official, whether his appointment was royal or noble in origin. The cities' protests against *corregidores* appear in the meetings of Cortes from 1401 onwards. The Crown refused to abandon them, however.[1]

END OF ENRIQUE'S REIGN

Enrique III's first and only son, the future Juan II, was born on 6 March 1405. After a long illness the king died eighteen months later, on 25 December 1406. The Cortes had just voted the large sum of 45,000,000 maravedis for war with Granada. Which side was responsible for this war? In 1404 Carlos III of Navarre had warned Muḥammad VII of Granada that Enrique would attack him, as part of his plan to seize on 'all the neighbouring kingdoms'. Such a plan was in the Trastámara tradition but there is no solid evidence for Enrique's aggressive designs. Muḥammad began the attack in 1405. Enrique was disposed to sign a new truce (6 October 1406). But Muḥammad was feigning. The same month he again invaded Castile. War was now inevitable.

THE REGENCY OF FERNANDO DE ANTEQUERA

The Cortes were presided over by Enrique's brother, Fernando. It was he who demanded support for a vast army to crush Granada. When Enrique died funds were available and the one possible leader was Fernando. Enrique's will left, as joint regents for his infant heir, his wife, Queen Catalina, and Fernando, while separate tutors were appointed for the king's education. Within a year, using the pretext of the war, Fernando

[1] Ibid., pp. 120 ff., 168 f.; idem, *La extensión del regimen de corregidores en el reinado de Enrique III de Castilla* (Valladolid, 1969); Garcí Sánchez (of Seville), in *Anales de la Universidad Hispalense*, 14 (1953), 25.

had assumed effective control. The provinces of Castile were divided between him and the queen. In this division Fernando received all the southern provinces. He already had, by inheritance and marriage, personal domains in the north stretching from Portugal to Navarre and including major economic centres such as Medina del Campo. These lands, which formed the largest collection of lordships in Castile, remained under his jurisdiction.

In 1406 Fernando was twenty-six years old. His contemporaries stress his prudence and caution. He had chosen his collaborators and was planning the advancement of his sons, Alfonso, Juan, Enrique, Sancho. Alfonso was betrothed to Enrique III's elder daughter María. If the child king Juan II died Alfonso would inherit Castile. Negotiations for Juan's marriage to the heiress of Navarre were underway. It seems that during his brother's last illness Fernando was offered the Castilian throne. He preferred to maintain his nephew while he used his regency to promote his sons' position in the peninsula and to make them indispensable to the Castilian monarchy.

WAR WITH GRANADA

The immediate future was that of war with Granada. Fernando controlled the spending of the money voted for the war. Contemporary critics recognized that Fernando 'grew great with the war'. It gave him his fame as 'a paladin of Christendom'—symbolized by the sobriquet 'de Antequera'—and permanent control of Castilian power. Fame and power together were to give him the Crown of Catalonia–Aragon in 1412, in the 'Compromiso de Caspe'.[1]

Since 1370 Granada had enjoyed peace with Castile, broken only by frontier raids. Truces were renewed regularly, in return for heavy tribute. When war began again in 1407 Granada found it impossible to obtain aid from Aragon, as she had done in the past, and hard to obtain it from Morocco. In 1407 the destruction of the Moroccan fleet bringing 800 horse and large supplies of money and provisions cut off aid from North Africa.

Granada was principally assisted by the venality and in-

[1] E. Mitre, in *Homenaje al prof. Alarcos*, ii. pp. 733–9; i. dem, *Evolución*, pp201–22; I. I. Macdonald, *Don Fernando de Antequera* (Oxford, 1948), pp. 25–33; J. Torres Fontes, *AEM* 1 (1964), 375–83; Pérez de Guzmán, p. 9; Suárez, *HE* xv. 33.

trigues of the Castilian nobility and by Fernando's inexperience. No clear general plan is visible in Fernando's first campaign (1407). This was followed by a two years' truce, due to power struggles within Castile.

The only real gains made were in 1410. In this year Fernando, after a siege lasting five months, captured the city of Antequera, with, a foreign eye-witness stated, 'the help of certain great siege-engines'. It was the most important Christian victory in Spain since the battle of the Salado (1340). It bestowed on Fernando the glory he needed. It had required an elaborate effort which was not to be repeated until the 1450s. Fernando refused to grant a long truce or to allow trade relations. Granada's vassalage to Castile was underlined. Fernando's immediate involvement with the Aragonese succession prevented him from following up this success.[1]

INTERNAL POLICY

By September 1408 Fernando had overcome the attempts of Queen Catalina and her supporters to dispute his authority. His triumph assured a peaceful minority for Juan II. Although Fernando took care to correct local abuses, his efforts to further royal centralization were minimal compared to those of Enrique III. He prevented the anti-Jewish and Mudejar laws promulgated by the queen in 1408 being applied in his provinces. Fernando was less concerned to strengthen the Crown's position than to tighten his own grip on Castilian policy. When, in 1410, the Aragonese succession became a possibility he was supported as candidate by the queen and by all Castile. He had used his few years well. In 1408 he had made one of his sons, Sancho, Master of Alcántara, in 1409 another son, Enrique, Master of Santiago. As both were under age Fernando himself controlled the considerable military and financial resources of two of the three Castilian Military Orders. Fernando's vast lands were divided, after he became king of Aragon, between his second son Juan, who later married the heiress to Navarre, and his third son, Enrique. His heir, Alfonso, married Juan II's sister, María, Enrique another sister, Catalina. His daughters

[1] L. Suárez, *Juan II y la frontera de Granada* (Valladolid, 1954), pp. 5–15, 34 ff.; Torres Fontes, *MEAH* 14 (1965), 137–67; Macdonald, pp. 43–73, 103–32; *Voyages et ambasades de Messire Guillebert de Lannoy* (Mons, 1840), p. 8.

became queens of Castile and Portugal. Until his death in 1416, even as king of Aragon, Fernando ruled Castile as regent. If Fernando's children had remained united they would have controlled almost the whole peninsula. As it was, the period when he ruled, first Castile and then both kingdoms, was remembered as an island of peace in Castilian history, in strong contrast to the two long reigns that followed (1416–74).[1]

[1] Torres Fontes, *AEM* 1 (1964), 384–88, 402–19; Macdonald, pp. 73–103. M. A. Ladero Quesada, *Andalucia en el siglo XV* (Madrid, 1973), pp. 100 f.

Select Bibliography

GENERAL

Bibliographical Guides

For Portugal there is the very valuable work of A. H. de Oliveira Marques, *Guia do estudante de história medieval portuguesa* (Lisbon, 1964). No similar work exists for Spain. See also the *Dicionário de história de Portugal*, ed. J. Serrão, 4 vols. (Lisbon, 1963–71), of which the same could be said. B. Sánchez Alonso, *Fuentes de la historia española e hispanoamericana*, 3rd ed. (Madrid, 1952), is difficult to use. One can consult the unfinished work of R. Foulché-Delbosc and L. Barrau-Dihigo, *Manuel de l'hispanisant*, 2 vols. (New York, 1920–5, repr. 1959). The sections on 'Medieval Spanish, Catalan, and Portuguese Literatures', in *The Medieval Literature of Western Europe. A Review of Research, mainly 1930–1960*, ed. John H. Fisher (New York, 1966), pp. 331–79, are useful but less critical. C.-E. Dufourcq and J. Gautier-Dalché, 'Histoire de l'Espagne au Moyen Âge (1948–1969)', *Revue historique*, 245 (1971), 127–68, 443–82, 247 (1972), 367–402, is very valuable. A lengthy, though not entirely accurate, bibliography for 1252–1410, with some indication of manuscript sources, by R. Altamira, in the *Cambridge Medieval History*, vii (Cambridge, 1932), 919–31, is more useful for Castile than for the Crown of Aragon.

Up to 1952 the best historical bibliographies are contained in *AST*, from 1953 in *IHE*; from 1964, see also *AEM*. The following historical periodicals are indispensable (see also List of Abbreviations): *Al-Andalus* (Madrid 1933–) (the main review for Spanish Islamic Studies); *AST* (Barcelona, 1926–) (with *Hispania Sacra*, the foremost review for church history) *AHDE* (Madrid, 1924–); *Arbor* (Madrid, 1944–); *BRABL; BRAH; Bulletin hispanique* (Bordeaux, 1899–); *CHE* (Buenos Aires, 1944–); *EUC; ER; Hispania* (Madrid, 1940–); *Hispania Sacra* (Madrid, 1949–); *RABM; Sefarad* (Madrid, 1941–) (invaluable for Spanish Judaism).

Archives

L. Sánchez Belda, *Bibliografía de archivos españoles y de archivística* (Madrid, 1963). See also idem, *Guia del Archivo Histórico Nacional* [Madrid] (Madrid, 1960). J. E. Martínez Ferrando, *Archivo General de la Corona de Aragón* [Barcelona] (Madrid, 1958). V. Rau, *Arquivos de Portugal: Lisboa* (Lisbon, Luso-American Educational Commission, 1961). In general, far richer archival sources exist for the

Crown of Aragon than for other kingdoms (see below, especially under Part II, Chs. I and II).

Literary sources

J. Simón Díaz, *Bibliografía de la literatura hispánica*, 2nd edn., (10 vols. Madrid, 1960–72). M. C. Díaz, *Index scriptorum latinorum medii aevi hispanorum* (Madrid, 1959), to 1350, registers works and many manuscripts. See also I. Rodríguez, 'Literatura latina hispana del 711 hasta Trento', *Repertorio de historia de las ciencias eclesiásticas en España*, ii (Salamanca, 1971), 99–123 (esp. 114–20); ibid. i (1967), 225–342 (about 160 authors writing in Latin, Castilian, and Catalan, from 1200 to 1511). F. Pons Boigues, *Ensayo bio-bibliográfico sobre los historiadores y geógrafos arábigo-españoles* (Madrid, 1898, repr. 1972), badly needs to be brought up to date. For historians see B. Sánchez Alonso, *Historia de la historiografía española*, i (Madrid, 1941).

Introductory Works

Luís Suárez Fernández, *Historia de España, Edad Media* (Madrid, 1970) [to 1504], is an excellent statement of the results of modern research, better on Castile (the author's special interest) than on the Crown of Aragon, and on political than on economic, social, and religious history. Has the unusual merit of considering Portugal to be part of the peninsula. Chapters 22–48 (pp. 275–682) concern the centuries discussed in these volumes. J. A. García de Cortázar, *La época medieval* (Historia de España Alfaguara, ii) (Madrid, 1973), complements Suárez's work, by insisting on non-political themes (though he virtually omits Portugal). Chs. 4–7 (pp. 177–495) deal in part with our period, although they begin far earlier in time. Both these works have select critical bibliographies but no notes. It is, therefore, difficult to find the basis for particular statements. F. Soldevila, *Historia de España*, vols. i–ii, 2nd edn. (Barcelona, 1961–2) provides a Catalan point of view, to compare with the Castilian emphasis found in the older histories of A. Ballesteros y Beretta and others. The volumes of the *Historia de España*, ed. by R. Menéndez Pidal, destined to cover the period 1038–1350, have not yet appeared.

In English the essays collected by P. E. Russell, *Spain, a Companion to Spanish Studies* (London, 1973) (stronger on literature than on other subjects) and A. D. Deyermond, *A Literary History of Spain, The Middle Ages* (London, 1971), are useful.

Regional Histories

Castile. A useful brief introduction by J. Valdeón, *El reino de Castilla en la edad media* (Bilbao, 1968). See also Suárez, above.

Crown of Aragon. For Aragon proper J. Mª. Lacarra, in *Aragón, cuatro ensayos*, i (Saragossa, 1960), 203–304, is excellent but hard to find and has no notes (new revd. edn., *Aragón en el pasado* (Madrid, 1972)). F. Soldevila, *Història de Catalunya*, 2nd edn. (Barcelona, 1963), carefully revd. and documented (1st edn. 1934–5).

There is no similar work for *Valencia*, though J. Reglá, *Aproximació a la història del país Valencià* (Valencia, 1968), is a good sketch of problems. The *Història del país Valencià* has so far only reached the Islamic period (i, Barcelona, 1965). The *Historia de Mallorca*, ed. J. Mascaró Pasarius, of which vols. iii and iv (of six) have appeared (Palma, 1970–1) is very uneven but contains valuable contributions by A. Santamaría and F. Sevillano.

Granada. M. A. Ladero Quesada, *Granada, historia de un país islámico (1232–1571)* (Madrid, 1969), a valuable, though brief sketch. The last of Muḥammad 'Abd Allāh 'Inan (Enan)'s volumes on Islamic Spain, *The End of the Moorish Empire in Spain and the History of the Moriscos*, 2nd edn. (Cairo, 1958), is unfortunately only available in Arabic. For R. Arié, *L'Espagne musulmane au temps des naṣrides (1232–1492)* (Paris, 1973), see the review by P. Chalmeta, *Hispania*, 33 (1973), 677–82. C. Torres Delgado, *El antiguo reino nazarí de Granada (1232–1340)* (Granada, 1974) is more detailed but adds little except with regard to frontier fortifications.

Navarre. J. Mª. Lacarra, *Historia política del reino de Navarra hasta su incorporación a Castilla*, 3 vols. (Pamplona, 1972–3, not available until 1974) will change our picture of Navarrese history in the earlier period, but perhaps not in that dealt with here.

Portugal. A. H. de Oliveira Marques, *History of Portugal*, 2 vols. (New York–London, 1972), is the first reliable work to appear in English. Vol. i, pp. 73–216, covers, briefly, the period discussed here. There is an excellent critical bibliography.

Literature

There is a succinct account of Castilian literature by Juan Luis Alborg, *Historia de la literatura española*, i (Madrid, 1966, or revised reprint) and a much fuller history in the uneven *HGLH* i–iii (1949–53). The sections on 'Literatura Catalana' by J. Rubió Balaguer in this work are excellent. A very full and valuable account of Catalan literature to the seventeenth century by M. de Riquer, *Història de la literatura catalana*, 3 vols. (Barcelona, 1964). The classic works of Menéndez y Pelayo, *Antología* and *Orígenes*, are still unsurpassed. For Portuguese literature A. J. Saraiva and O. Lopes, *História de literatura portuguesa*, 5th edn. (Lisbon, n. d. [1967?]), has not replaced the more perceptive M. Rodrigues Lapa, *Lições de literatura portuguesa época medieval*, 6th edn. (Coimbra, 1966). For introductory works on the economy, law, religion, art, etc. see below, under the separate chapters.

PART I: THE IBERIAN PENINSULA, 1200–1350

CHAPTER II: ECONOMY AND SOCIETY

I. *Primary Sources*

The disproportion between the rich archival resources of the Crown of Aragon and the poverty of Castile is almost as marked in economic and social as in political history (for the latter see below, under Part II, Ch. II). The municipal and notarial archives of Seville, for instance, in the fourteenth century are very imperfect compared to those of Barcelona. See R. Carande, *AHDE* 2 (1925), 240, 361; F. Pérez-Embid, *MÂ* 75 (1969), 265.

For the *repopulation*, see for Andalusia, J. González, *Repartimiento de Sevilla*, 2 vols. (Madrid, 1951), and J. Torres Fontes, *Repartimiento de Murcia* (Madrid, 1960). See also idem, *Colección de documentos para la historia del reino de Murcia*; i, *Documentos de Alfonso X el Sabio* (Murcia, 1963); ii, *Documentos del siglo XIII* [1223–1305] (Murcia, 1969); iii, *Fueros y privilegios de Alfonso X el Sabio* (Murcia, 1973). For Majorca and Valencia the texts of the *Repartiments* ed. by P. de Bofarull y Mascaró, *CDIACA* xi (Barcelona, 1856), are less satisfactory. The best account of the *Repartiment* of Majorca is in J. Mª. Quadrado, *Historia de la conquista de Mallorca* (Palma, 1850), pp. 432–535.

For medieval *trade* we now have the excellent collection of customs tariffs, with detailed commentary, of M. Gual Camarena, *Vocabulario del comercio medieval, colección de aranceles aduaneros de la Corona de Aragón (siglos XIII y XIV)* (Tarragona, 1968). For other source-collections for Catalan trade see below, under Part II, Ch. I.

Society. Alfonso X, *Cántigas de Santa María*, best ed. by W. Mettmann, 4 vols. (Coimbra, 1959–72), is as valuable a source as his legal collections (see Part II, Ch. II, above), of which *Las Siete Partidas*, consulted in the standard, though unsatisfactory edn. of Madrid, 1807 (repr. 1972) is the most important. J. Guerrero Lovillo, *Las Cántigas, estudio arqueológico de sus miniaturas* (Madrid, 1949), reproduces all the illustrations. The best recent study of the miniatures is by G. Menéndez Pidal, *BRAH* 150 (1962), 25–51. For further bibliography on Alfonso X and on Ramon Lull and Juan Manuel see below, Ch. VI. The best collections of documents on royal courts of the period are, for Castile, M. Gaibrois de Ballesteros, *Historia del reinado de Sancho IV de Castilla*, 3 vols. (Madrid, 1922–8), and, for the Crown of Aragon, in F. Soldevila, *Pere el Gran*, I, *L'Infant*, 3 parts (Barcelona, 1950–3), and J. E. Martínez Ferrando, *Jaime II de Aragón, su vida familiar*, 2 vols. (Barcelona, 1948) (esp. vol. ii).

Urban problems in the Crown of Aragon can be studied through the regulations of the Mustaçaf. See F. Sevillano Colom, *Valencia urbana medieval a través del oficio de Mustaçaf* (Valencia, 1957); A. Pons,

Libre del Mostassaf de Mallorca (Mallorca, 1949), and through Catalan town ordinances, many of which were published by F. Carreras y Candi, in *BRABL* 11–12 (1923–6). Other important legal collections for this period are *Los fueros de Aragón*, ed. G. Tilander (Lund, 1937); the *Furs de Valencià*, ed. G. Colon and A. Garcia (Barcelona, 1970) (Latin version, *Fori antiqui Valentiae*, ed. M. Dualde Serrano (Madrid, 1950–67), and the *Libre de les costums generals de Tortosa*, ed. B. Oliver (Madrid, 1881), and the *Fuero general de Navarra*, ed. P. Ilarregui and S. Lapuerta (Pamplona, 1869). For the Crown of Aragon, and especially for Catalonia, see also Rubió, *Documents*, and Segura, *Aplech*.

II. *Secondary Works, General*

For the geographical background see J. M. Houston, *The Western Mediterranean World, an Introduction to its regional landscapes* (London, 1964), Part II, 'The Iberian Peninsula'. The economic history of Spain was first approached from a modern point of view by J. Vicens Vives (d. 1960). His *Manual de historia económica de España*, 4th edn. (Barcelona, 1965), transl. as *An economic history of Spain* (Princeton, 1969), will long remain valuable, provided that the hypotheses with which it abounds are not treated as dogmas. S. Sobrequés Vidal, 'La época del patriciado urbano', in *Historia de España y América*, ed. Vicens Vives, ii (Barcelona, 1961), 8–406 (identical with the 1st edn., entitled *Historia social y económica . . .*), covers the period to 1474. It is a very useful work but its lack of notes makes it hard to check any statement and the bibliography is totally inadequate and occasionally misleading. The review by C. Viñas y Mey, *Arbor*, 43 (1959), 33–57, 202–76, of vols. i–ii of the work, correctly points out that it is stronger on economic than social history and that it is not based on primary sources but on a selection of secondary works. The statistics given are not always reliable. There is a notable bias in favour of Catalonia. The new *Historia económica y social de España*, to be published by the Cajos de Ahorros de España, will contain a volume on the Middle Ages by J. M[a]. Lacarra. A. H. de Oliveira Marques, *A sociedade medieval portuguesa* (Lisbon, 1964), transl. as *Daily Life in Portugal in the Late Middle Ages* (Madison, Wisconsin, 1971), is valuable though, here again, it is sometimes difficult to check particular statements. Rubió's *Vida* is invaluable.

On *repopulation* there is a valuable collection of essays, *La reconquista española y la repoblación del país* (Saragossa, 1951). See also C. J. Bishko, 'The Castilian as Plainsman: The Medieval Ranching Frontier in La Mancha and Extremadura', *The New World looks at its History*, ed. A. R. Lewis and T. F. McGann (Austin, Texas, 1963), pp. 47–69 (transl. into Spanish in *HV* i. 201–18), and, for Murcia, J.

Torres Fontes, *Repartimiento de la huerta y campo de Murcia en el siglo XIII* (Murcia, 1971). The articles by R. Pastor de Togneri, *CHE* 43–4 (1967), 88–118, and by L. C. Kofman and M. I. Carzolio, *CHE* 47–8 (1968), 136–70, are of interest for the growth of population in Castile–León from the tenth to the thirteenth (in the first case to the fourteenth) century.

On *agrarian history* see the bibliography (1940–61) by E. Giralt y Raventós, *IHE*, 5 (1959), pp. ix–lxxix. See J. A. García de Cortázar y Ruiz de Aguirre, *El dominio del monasterio de San Millán de la Cogolla (siglos X a XIII)*, (Salamanca, 1969), pp. 36ff. M. Gual Camerena has provided the first thorough investigation of salt in medieval Spain, in *HV* i (1965), 483–97, and of the textile industry in *AEM* 4 (1967), 109–68. The classic work on sheep-farming in Castile remains J. Klein, *The Mesta, a Study in Spanish Economic History 1273–1836* (Cambridge, Mass., 1920, Spanish transl., Madrid, 1936). R. Pastor de Togneri, *Moneda y crédito*, 112 (1970), 47–69, has shed new light on the period before the Mesta was created.

For Catalan *maritime trade* see below, under Part II, Ch. I. There is very little of value for Castile in this period, other than R. Carande, 'Sevilla, fortaleza y mercado', *AHDE* 2 (1925), 233–401 (repr. separately, 1972), though see M. del C. Carlé, 'Mercaderes en Castilla', *CHE* 21–2 (1954), 146–328. The best study of *piracy* is by J. Mª. Ramos y Loscertales, *El cautiverio en la Corona de Aragón durante los siglos XIII, XIV y XV* (Saragossa, 1915). The I Congreso Internacional de Historia Mediterránea (Palma, December, 1973) included a series of important reports on *war at sea*. The following should be cited: Ch.-E. Dufourcq, 'Chrétiens et maghribins, durant les derniers siècles du moyen âge'; C. Torres, 'El Mediterráneo Nazarí: Diplomacía y piratería (siglos XIII–XIV)'; M. Mollat, 'Essai d'orientation pour l'étude de la guerre de course et la piraterie (XIIIe–XVe siècles)'; H. Bresc, 'Course et piraterie en Sicile (1250–1450)'. On general economic developments see the report by A. Boscolo at the same Congress, whose proceedings will be published in Barcelona.

There are few monographs of value on the *nobility* in this period. On the *lower nobility*, in Castile, see C. Pescador, 'La caballería popular en León y Castilla', *CHE* 33–4 (1961), esp. 197–209; 35–6 (1962), 56–201; 37–8 (1963), 88–198; 39–40 (1964), 169–260. M. del C. Carlé, 'Infanzones e hidalgos', *CHE* 33–4 (1961), 56–100, mainly concerns the period before 1250. S. Sobrequés i Vidal, *Els barons de Catalunya* (Barcelona, 1957), is valuable. See also E. Lourie, 'A Society organized for War: Medieval Spain', *Past and Present* 35, (1966), 54–76.

On the *bourgeoisie* see L. García de Valdeavellano, *Sobre los burgos y los burgueses de la España medieval* (Madrid, 1969). M. del C. Carlé, *Del concejo medieval castellano-leonés* (Buenos Aires, 1968), is less valuable for our period (see p. 73, n.1.). For the office of the Mustaçaf see the works of Sevillano and Pons cited under Primary Sources and, below, under Ch. V. F. Sevillano Colom has provided an excellent synthesis, 'De la institución del Mustaçaf de Barcelona, de Mallorca y de Valencia', *AHDE* 23 (1953), 525–38.

There are no detailed studies of the peasantry of value for the period 1200–1350. On slavery the standard work, by Ch. Verlinden, *L'Esclavage dans l'Europe médiévale*, I (Bruges, 1955).

CHAPTERS III–IV: THE CHURCH, LAW, ROYAL AND LOCAL INSTITUTIONS

Much recent work is inventoried and discussed in *Repertorio de historia de las ciencias eclesiásticas en España*, Salamanca, Instituto de Historia de la Teología Española, i (1967), ii (1971). See also the new *Diccionario de historia eclesiástica de España* (Madrid), of which vols. i–iii (A-RU) appeared in 1972–3.

P. Linehan, *The Spanish Church and the Papacy in the thirteenth century* (Cambridge, 1971), provides an up-to-date discussion of the peninsular Church, based on research in all the archives available, with special emphasis on Castile. R. I. Burns, *The Crusader Kingdom of Valencia, reconstruction on a thirteenth century frontier*, 2 vols. (Cambridge Mass., 1967), is an excellent detailed study of the setting up of the diocese of Valencia.

Problems of Church and State are dealt with by J. Vincke, *Staat und Kirche in Katalonien und Aragon während des Mittelalters* (Münster i. W., 1931). Vincke has also published a valuable collection of 669 documents (mainly post-1300) on this subject: *Documenta selecta mutuas civitatis Arago-Cathalaunicae et ecclesiae relationes illustrantia* (Barcelona, 1936). See also F. J. Miquel Rosell, *Regesta de letras pontificias del Archivo de la Corona de Aragón* (Madrid, 1948) (762 documents, only 54 of which are post-1400).

The dioceses most fully studied are those of Santiago and Pamplona. On the former we have the monumental work of A. López Ferreiro, *Historia de la Santa A. M. Iglesia de Santiago de Compostela*, 11 vols. (Santiago). Vol. V (1902) concerns the thirteenth century, vol. vi (1903) the fourteenth. Drawing on local and Vatican archives J. Goñi Gaztambide has described the bishops of Pamplona in *Principe de Viana*, 18 (1957) (thirteenth) and 23 (1962) (fourteenth century). A study of a leading bishop and jurist, Vidal de Canellas, by A. Durán Gudiol, *EEMCA* 9 (1973), 267–369. See also J. F. Rivera Recio, *Los arzobispos de Toledo en la baja edad media* (Toledo,

1969), and L. McCrank, 'Restoration and Re-Conquest in Medieval Catalonia: The Church and Principality of Tarragona, 971–1177', unpublished Ph.D. dissertation, University of Virginia, 1974.

The main collection of late-medieval Spanish church councils remains the unsatisfactory J. Tejada, vols. iii–vi (1851–9). There is also no satisfactory account of Spanish universities (see Ch. III, p. 99 n. 1, and R. Gibert, *Bibliografía sobre universidades hispánicas* (Granada, [1970]). Twelfth and thirteenth-century Iberian canonists are listed by A. García, *Repertorio de historia de las ciencias eclesiásticas en España*, i (1967), 409–17; idem, *AHDE* 36 (1966), 575–92. For early lawyers in Portugal see M. J. Brito de Almeida Costa, *Bracara Augusta*, 14–15 (1963), 340–57. Educational deficiencies among the clergy are discussed by P. A. Linehan, in *El Cardenal Albornoz y el colegio de España*, ii (Bologna, 1972), 261–74.

Military Orders

D. Lomax, *La Orden de Santiago (1170–1275)* (Madrid, 1965) (a volume on the later history of the Order is in preparation). A. J. Forey, *The Templars in the 'Corona de Aragón'* (London, 1973). Both these books are very well documented. A. Luttrell is preparing a similar work on the Hospital in the Crown of Aragon, and J. F. O'Callaghan on the Order of Calatrava. The more restricted studies of M[a]. L. Ledesma Rubio, *La encomienda de Zaragoza de la Orden de San Juan de Jerusalén en los siglos XII y XIII* (Saragossa, 1967), and S. García Larragueta, *El gran priorado de Navarra de la Orden de San Juan de Jerusalén; siglos XII–XIII*, 2 vols. (Pamplona, 1957), should also be cited. For Montesa see O'Callaghan, in *Miscelánea de textos medievales*, i (Barcelona, 1972), 213–51.

Monasticism

We do not have satisfactory histories of most of the leading monasteries, still less of convents of women, or of friars in Spain. J. Pérez de Urbel, *Los monjes españoles en la edad media*, ii (Madrid, 1934), is very brief for this period. For Catalan monasticism see M. M. Riu, *AEM* 7 (1970–1), 593–613. The *I Col. loqui d'història del monaquisme català*, 2 vols. (Santes Creus, 1967–9), contains valuable studies, as does the *II Col. loqui* (Poblet, 1972). On economic aspects of Poblet see L. McCrank, in *Analecta Cisterciensia*, 29 (1973), 57–78, and in *Cistercian Studies*, 2 (1974). For Castile we now possess two important works: J. A. García de Cortázar, *El dominio del monasterio de San Millán de la Cogolla* (Salamanca, 1969), and S. Moreta Velayos, *El monasterio de San Pedro de Cardeña* (Salamanca, 1971). On Oña (1011–1399) see M. Bonaudo de Magnani, *CHE* 51–2 (1970), 42–122. Inevitably, these authors concentrate on the economic aspect of the monasteries they study. See also J. García González, *Vida económica de los monasterios benedictinos en el siglo XIV* (Valladolid, 1972). The history of monastic spirituality—and of popular religion—remains as yet unwritten. For pilgrimage to Santiago see López Ferreiro, op. cit., and the work by L. Vázquez de Parga, *et al.*, *Las peregrinaciones a Santiago de Compostela*, 3 vols. (Madrid, 1948–9).

Royal and Local institutions, Law

R. Gibert, *Historia general del derecho español* (Granada, 1968), and L. García de Valdeavellano, *Curso de historia de las instituciones españolas de los orígenes al final de la edad media* (Madrid, 1968, 3rd edn., revd., 1973), are useful.

The bibliography missing in Gibert's book is supplied by the author's contribution to *Introduction bibliographique à l'histoire du droit et à l'ethnologie juridique*, ed. J. Gilissen (Brussels, 1963). Compare M. Caetano, *Lições de história do direito português* (Coimbra, 1962). H. da Gama Barros, *História da administracão pública em Portugal nos séculos XII a XV*, 2nd edn., 11 vols. (Lisbon, 1945–50), is a mine of valuable information, to which there is no Spanish parallel. On the Cortes see the articles cited in Ch. III p. 101, n. 2, p. 104, n. 2, for feudalism, p. 106, n. 1. H. Grassotti, *Las instituciones feudo-vasalláticas en León y Castilla*, 2 vols. (Spoleto, 1969), goes to about 1350 but is mainly useful for the earlier Middle Ages. J. Mª. García Marín, *El oficio público en Castilla durante la baja edad media* (Seville, 1974), is more theoretical than practical in his approach. For Navarre see P. E. Schramm, 'Der König von Navarra (1035–1512)', *Zeitschrift der Savigny-Stiftung für Rechtsgeschichte*, 78, 1; Germ. Abteil. (1951), 110–210, and the works of Lacarra, cited on pp. 102 and 103, and in the General Bibliography. For feudalism see Valdeavellano (p. 106, n. 1), and, for Portugal, Ch. Verlinden, 'Quelques aspects de l'histoire de la tenure au Portugal', *Recueils de la Société Jean Bodin*, *3* (Brussels, 1938), 231–43.

CHAPTER V: THE PENINSULA A LAND OF THREE RELIGIONS

Relations with Islamic Countries. There is no work on the relations of Castile with Islamic countries to compare with Dufourcq (1966) on the Crown of Aragon and North Africa, or with Giménez Soler on the same Crown and Granada. See also below, under Part II, Ch. I; the reports by Dufourcq and Torres cited above, under II; and R. I. Burns, 'Renegades, Adventurers, and Sharp Businessmen: the thirteenth century Spaniard in the cause of Islam', *Catholic Historical Review*, 58 (1972), 341–66.

A land of three religions. The pioneer work of A. Castro, of which the most recent version in English is *The Spaniards, an introduction* (Los

Angeles, 1971), is still best consulted in *La realidad histórica de España* (Mexico, 1954) (the revd. later editions are incomplete).

An age of optimism. On Ramon Lull see R. Sugranyes de Franch, *R. Lulle, docteur des missions* (Schöneck-Beckenried, 1954), and my *Ramon Lull and Lullism in fourteenth-century France* (Oxford, 1971), esp. Chs. I and VI. There is no similar study of Don Juan Manuel (see below, under Ch. VI), nor is there a satisfactory work on the general subject of *convivencia* and intolerance.

Jews and Mudejars. Far more work has been done on Jews than on Mudejars. The classic work by J. Amador de los Rios, *Historia social, política y religiosa de los Judios de España y Portugal* (Madrid, 1875, repr. 1960) has been virtually superseded by Y. F. Baer, *History* (1961–6), based on his earlier collections of documents (*Die Juden*, 1929–36). Many studies of local Jewries in *Sefarad.* For León see Rodriguez Fernández (cited p. 170, n. 1), for Perpignan, Emery (p. 172, n. 1). More general works of great value are F. Cantera, *Sinagogas españolas* (Madrid, 1955), and Cantera and Millás Vallicrosa, *Las inscripciones hebraicas de España* (Madrid, 1956). There is a useful catalogue of Castilian legislation against the Jews by P. León Tello, in *Fourth World Congress of Jewish Studies*, ii (Jerusalem, 1968), 55–63.

No work on the Mudejars exists to compare with Baer's on the Jews. Francisco Fernández y González, *Estado social y político de los Mudejares de Castilla* . . . (Madrid, 1866), is useful but out of date. Florencio Janer, *Condición social de los Moriscos de España* . . . (Madrid, 1857), has little on the Mudejars. Isidro de las Cagigas, *Los Mudejares* (Madrid, 1948–9), 2 vols. (often cited) is useless. L. Torres Balbas, *Algunos aspectos del mudejarismo urbano medieval* (Madrid, 1954), a distilled version of many years' work, is of great value, not only for art history. Other monographs are cited in the notes. More work has been done on the Mudejars of Valencia than on any other region, particularly by M. Gual y Camarena and F. A. Roca Traver (see p. 184, n. 1), and, in America, by Fr. Robert I. Burns and Thomas F. Glick. For the former see p. 178, n. 2. A sequel, *Medieval Colonialism: Postcrusade Exploitation of Islamic Valencia*, a study of the financial exploitation of the Mudejars, will also be published by Princeton. Fr. Burns's other recent studies include: 'Islam [as an Established Religion] in the Kingdom of Valencia', in *Studies in Mediaevalia and Americana, Essays in Honor of William Lyle Davis, S.J.* (Spokane, 1973), pp. 1–34; 'Spanish Islam in Transition: Acculturative Survival and its Price in the Christian Kingdom of Valencia', in *Islam and Cultural Change in the Middle Ages*, ed. S. Vryonis, Jr. (Berkeley and Los Angeles, 1974); 'The Muslim in the Christian

Feudal Order', in *Studies in Medieval Culture*, 5–6 (1973). For Professor Glick's works see below. For the Crown of Aragon in general see E. Lourie, 'Christian Attitudes towards the Mudéjars in the Reign of Alfonso III of Aragon (1285–91)', unpublished D. Phil. thesis, Oxford, 1967. John Boswell has completed a dissertation at Harvard under my direction on the Mudejars of the same Crown under Pere III (1356–66 especially). An exceptional case of a Mudejar lordship surviving to 1318 has been studied by P. Guichard, *MCV* 9 (1973), 283–344 (Crevillente, between Valencia and Murcia).

Institutions. See P. Chalmeta, 'La Ḥisba en Ifriquiya et al-Andalus', *Les Cahiers de Tunisie*, 18 (1970), 87–105; idem, 'La figura del almotacén en los fueros y su semejanza con el zabazoque hispano-musulmán', *Revista de la Universidad de Madrid*, 19 (1970), 145–67; and now his major work, *El 'Señor del Zoco' en España, edades media y moderna* (Madrid, 1973); T. F. Glick, 'Muḥtasib and Mustasaf: A Case Study of Institutional Diffusion', *Viator*, 2 (1971), 59–81, and the same author's fundamental work, cited p. 189, n. 1, also above, under Ch. II, p. 415.

Art. There is an excellent introductory work by B. Bevan, *History of Spanish Architecture* (London, 1939). G. E. Street, *Some Account of Gothic Architecture in Spain* (London, 1865), is still invaluable. The standard collective history in the *Ars Hispaniae* (Madrid, Plus-Ultra). The relevant volumes are IV, 'Arte almohade, arte nazarí, arte mudéjar', by L. Torres Balbas (1949); VII, 'Arquitectura gótica' by Torres Balbas (1952); VIII, 'Escultura gótica', by A. Durán Sanpere and J. Ainaud de Lasarte (1956); IX, 'Pintura gótica', by J. Gudiol Ricart (1955); XVIII, 'Miniatura', by J. Domínguez Bordona (1962). See also Marqués de Lozoya, *Historia del arte hispánico*, ii–iii (Barcelona, 1934–40); C. R. Post, *A History of Spanish Painting*, 14 vols. (Cambridge, Mass., 1930–66). Other works are cited in the notes. See also P. Héliot's general survey, 'Les Débuts de l'architecture gothique dans le Midi de la France, l'Espagne et le Portugal', *AEM* 8 (1972–3), 105–41. Much information can be found in the two series: *Guías artísticas de España*, ed. J. Gudiol Ricart (Barcelona, Aries), and *Los monumentos cardinales de España* (Madrid, Plus-Ultra).

Literature. See the works cited above, under General Bibliography (p. 410), and, for translations also, below under Part II, Ch. II. For Catalonia see also A. Cardoner i Planas, *Història de la medicina a la Corona d'Aragó (1162–1479)* (Barcelona, 1971), esp. pp. 35–61, and the valuable list of Catalan Jews writing in Hebrew by J. Riera i Sans, in *Miscellanea Barcinonensia*, 13 (1974), 33–47.

CHAPTER VI. SOME FIGURES OF THE AGE

Bibliography on Alfonso X in the works of Ballesteros and Procter cited on pp. 216 and 218, and in the notes and Bibliography to Part II, Ch. II below. For works on Ramon Lull see my *Ramon Lull* (cited Ch. V above), pp. xvii f. Don Juan Manuel's works were edited by P. de Gayangos (*BAE* li (Madrid, 1860)), except for his *Libro de la caza*, ed. G. Baist (Halle, 1880), and again by J. Mª. Castro y Calvo (Barcelona, 1947). Castro and M. de Riquer published the first volume of a new complete edition in 'Clásicos Hispánicos' (Barcelona, 1955). It contains the *Libro del cavellero et del escudero*, the *Libro de las armas*, the *Libro enfenido* (or *Libro de los castigos*). J. Mª. Blecua edited the *Libro infinido* and the *Tractado de la Asunción* (Granada, 1952). See p. 225, n. 1.

There are no satisfactory general studies of Don Juan Manuel. A. Giménez Soler, *Don Juan Manuel* (Saragossa, 1932) (see G. Sachs, *RFE* 20 (1933), 185–7) is mainly useful for political history and, even here, should be treated with precaution. The bibliography on the Archpriest of Hita is vast. See now the *Actas del I Congreso Internacional sobre el Arcipreste de Hita*, ed. M. Criado de Val (Barcelona, 1973). The best editions are those of Criado de Val and E. W. Naylor (Madrid, 1965) (palaeographical): of J. Corominas (Madrid, 1967), and that of R. S. Willis (Princeton, 1972) (with an excellent English translation).

PART II: CASTILE AND CATALONIA–ARAGON 1225–1330

CHAPTER I: CATALONIA-ARAGON: A MEDITERRANEAN EMPIRE (1229–1327)?

I. *Primary Sources*

Our sources for the thirteenth- and fourteenth-century history of the federation of Catalonia–Aragon are far superior to those we possess for Castile, Portugal, or Granada. The archives of Catalonia, Valencia, and Majorca, and, most of all, the Archivo de la Corona de Aragón in Barcelona, are incomparably richer than contemporary Castilian archives. For the thirteenth century and the first quarter of the fourteenth these archives have been fairly well explored, at least from the point of view of political history. There also exist, for Catalonia–Aragon in this age, a series of chronicles which are among the most impressive of the Middle Ages. In Castile, from the time the *Primera Crónica General* comes to an end about 1250 until Ayala's chronicles begin in 1350, there is nothing to compare with this series. The first Portuguese historian of comparable penetration and style does not appear until Fernão Lopes in the fifteenth century. The works of the last outstanding historian of Islamic Spain,

Ibn al-Khaṭīb (d. 1374) have not yet been fully published: what has appeared so far does not promise great revelations.

A. *Chronicles* For the *Libre dels feyts* of Jaume I, and the *Crònica* of Ramon Muntaner, two of the three main Catalan chronicles for the century, I have used F. Soldevila, *Les Quatre Gran Cròniques* (Barcelona, 1971). The relationship between the Catalan text of Jaume I and the Latin of Pere Marsili, *Liber Gestarum*, published in part by J. Mª. Quadrado, *Historia de la conquista de Mallorca* (Palma, 1850), has not yet been clarified. For the third main Catalan chronicle, Bernat Desclot, *Crònica* (also in Soldevila) I use the critical edition by M. Coll i Alentorn, 5 vols. (*ENC* A 62–4, 66, 69–70) (Barcelona, 1949–51), while awaiting that of J. Rubió i Balaguer. The *Gesta Comitum Barcinonensium*, ed. L. Barrau-Dihigo and J. Massó Torrents (Cròniques Catalanes, ii) (Barcelona, 1925), is also important. The three former chronicles are all translated into English (in every case from somewhat unsatisfactory editions), as *The Chronicle of James I, King of Aragon*, trans. J. Forster, 2 vols. (London, 1883); *Chronicle of the Reign of King Pedro III of Aragon*, transl. F. L. Critchlow, 2 vols. (Princeton, 1928–34); and *The Chronicle of Muntaner*, transl. Lady Goodenough (Hakluyt Society), 2 vols. (London, 1920–1). See R. Sablonier, *Krieg und Kriegertum in der Crònica des Ramon Muntaner* (Berne, 1971).

B. *Documents* Basic collections are, for Jaume I, Huici, *Colección*; for Pere II, Carini, *Archivi*, and *De rebus*; for Jaume II, Finke, *Acta*, and 'Nachträge zu dem Acta Aragonensia', in *SFG* i, 4 (1933). See also G. La Mantia, *Codice diplomatico dei re aragonesi di Sicilia*, 2 vols. [1282–92] (Palermo, 1917–56); V. Salavert y Roca, *Cerdeña y la expansión mediterránea de la Corona de Aragón, 1297–1314*, 2 vols. (Madrid, 1956) (vol. ii); J. Reglá Campistol, *Francia, la Corona de Aragón y la frontera pirenaica*, 2 vols. (Madrid, 1951) (vol. ii). For maritime trade, apart from Capmany (new edn., 1961–3), see P. Voltes Bou, 'Repertorio de documentos referentes a los cónsules de Ultramar de Barcelona', *Estudios y documentos del Instituto Municipal de Historia de Barcelona*, 13 (1964), 21–166, and J. Mª. Madurell Marimón and A. García Sanz, *Comandas comerciales barcelonesas de la baja edad media* (Barcelona, 1973) (255 documents, 1236–1501). See also Martínez Ferrando, *Jaime II*, and Soldevila, *Pere el Gran*, cited under II. For royal finances see below, II, Institutions. Fundamental reference works for 1233–91: J. E. Martínez Ferrando, *Archivo de la Corona de Aragón, catálogo de la documentación relativa al antiguo reino de Valencia*, i, *Jaime I el Conquistador*, ii, *Pedro el Grande*, 2 vols. (Madrid, 1934), and the continuation by R. Gallofre Guinovart, *Documentos del reinado de Alfonso III de Aragón . . .* (Valencia,

1968). A *Diplomatarium regni Valenciae, regnante Iacobo primo*, in 5 vols., is in progress. Vol. I, ed. Robert I. Burns, is almost ready. For legislation see the *Cortes de Cataluña*, I. 1 (1896). The records of the Cortes of Aragon and Navarre are not published. See J. Mª. Lacarra, *AEM* 7 (1970), 645–52; for Valencia (1238–1410), see S. Romeu Alfaro, *AHDE* 40 (1970), 581–607. For cultural history, in the broadest sense, see Rubió, *Documents*.

II. *Secondary Works*

Jeronimo Zurita, *Anales de la Corona de Aragón*, 4 vols. (Saragossa, 1610), remains fundamental. The new edition, with notes (Valencia, 1967–) has only reached Book III (to 1276). I cite by book and chapter. F. Soldevila, *Història de Catalunya*, 2nd edn. (Barcelona, 1963), is invaluable. Many of the problems referred to are discussed in greater detail in my *The Problem of a Catalan Mediterranean Empire 1229–1327*, to appear as a supplement to the *English Historical Review* (Longmans, 1975).

A. *The rulers* *Jaume I* (1213–76). Apart from Jaume's *Libre dels feyts* and Huici, the fundamental work is J. Miret i Sans, *Itinerari de Jaume I 'el Conqueridor'* (Barcelona, 1918). The most recent historian of Jaume I is F. Soldevila, *Els primers temps de Jaume I* [1208–29] (Barcelona, 1968). Two other works by Soldevila cover the whole reign, *Els grans reis del segle XIII: Jaume I, Pere el Gran* (Barcelona, 1955), and the more popular *Vida de Jaume I el Conqueridor*, 2nd edn. (Barcelona, 1969). See also the older works of Ch. de Tourtoulon, *Études sur la Maison de Barcelone, Jacme 1er le Conquérant, roi d'Aragon . . .*, 2 vols (Montpellier, 1863–7) (Spanish transl., Valencia, 1874), and F. D. Swift, *The Life and Times of James the First, the Conqueror* (Oxford, 1894).

Pere II (1276–85). F. Soldevila's monumental work, *Pere el Gran*, had only reached 1278 when its author died (Primera Part, l'Infant, 3 parts; Segona Part, El Regnat fins a l'any 1282, part 1 [to 1278] (Barcelona, 1950–62). Soldevila provided less detailed coverage in *Els grans reis* (cited above) and *Vida de Pere el Gran i d'Alfons el Liberal* (Barcelona, 1963).

Alfons II (1285–91), and *Jaume II* (1291–1327). *Els descendents de Pere el Gran* by S. Sobrequés, J.-E. Martínez Ferrando and E. Bagué (Barcelona, 1954), covers these two reigns in outline and that of Alfons III (1327–36). Martínez Ferrando, *Jaime II de Aragón, su vida familiar*, 2 vols. (Barcelona, 1948) (vol. ii of documents). See also Klüpfel (cited, p. 258, n. 1).

B. '*Mediterranean Empire*', *Trade*. The work by J. Lee Shneidman, *The Rise of the Aragonese-Catalan Empire, 1200–1350*, 2 vols. (New

York, 1970), can be ignored. See my review in *Speculum*, 47 (1972), 345–53, and, in general, my work, *The Problem*, cited above. L. Nicolau d'Olwer, *L'espansió de Catalunya en la Mediterrània oriental* (Barcelona, 1926), is very readable and solidly based on contemporary sources. For general discussions see Y. Renouard, *VII CHCA* (1962), i. 231–64; F. Giunta and A. Boscolo, ibid., pp. 187–228.

On *Sicily* see F. Giunta, *Aragonesi e catalani nel mediterraneo*, ii (Palermo, 1959); see also his *Uomini e cose del medioevo mediterraneo* (Palermo, 1965), pp. 131–65. For the 'Sicilian Vespers' and the sequel, the classic work of M. Amari, *La guerra del Vespro Siciliano*, 9th edn., 3 vols. (Milan, 1886); O. Cartellieri, *Peter von Aragon und die sizilianische Vesper* (Heidelberg, 1904); and the important articles by H. Wieruszowski, *BRAH* 107 (1935), 547–602; *Archivio storico italiano*, 96 (1938), 141–62, 200–17; *SFG* 5 (1935), 230–9 (restated in *Quellen und Forschungen aus italienischen Archiven und Bibliotheken*, 37 (1957), 136–91). Sir Steven Runciman, *The Sicilian Vespers* (Cambridge, 1958), adds little to earlier studies and is, at times, misleading.

On *Sardinia:* C. Manca, *Fonti e orientamenti per la storia economica della Sardegna aragonese* (Padua, 1967) (catalogues the sources for the 14th cent. in the Archivo de la Corona de Aragón). Idem, *Aspetti dell'espansione economica catalano-aragonese nel mediterraneo occidentale. Il commercio internazionale del sale* (Milan, 1966). Salavert (cited above, under I) covers the preparations for the conquest very thoroughly; A. Arribas Palau, *La conquista de Cerdeña por Jaime II de Aragón* (Barcelona, 1952), the actual conquest.

The Islamic world: Granada, North Africa, the East. A Giménez Soler, *La Corona de Aragón y Granada*, in *BRABL* 3–4 (1905–7). I cite the separate edition (Barcelona, 1908). Idem, *El sitio de Almeria en 1309* (Barcelona, 1904). On North Africa there is the fundamental work of Dufourcq, *L'Espagne catalane* (1966). Since this appeared A. Masía de Ros, *La Corona de Aragón y los estados del Norte de Africa, política de Jaime II y Alfonso IV en Egipto, Ifriquía, y Tremecén* (Barcelona, 1951), is mainly of value for relations with Egypt. On this see also A. S. Atiya, *Egypt and Aragon, embassies and diplomatic correspondence between 1300 and 1330 A.D.* (Leipzig, 1938), who publishes some of the same documents as M. A. Alarcón y Santón and R. García de Linares, *Los documentos árabes diplomáticos del Archivo de la Corona de Aragón* (Madrid, 1940), but the latter publication also includes Arabic documents from the rulers of Granada and North Africa.

For the *Catalan Company* see now A. E. Laiou, *Constantinople and the Latins, the Foreign Policy of Andronicus II, 1282–1328* (Cambridge,

Mass., 1972), pp. 131–242, also K. M. Setton, *The Catalan Domination of Athens, 1311–1388* (Cambridge, Mass., 1948).

C. *Institutions* 1. Royal institutions *Administration, in general. The* only thorough study we have is that of L. Klüpfel, *Verwaltungsgeschichte des Königreichs Aragon zu Ende des 13. Jahrhunderts* (Berlin, 1915) (based on records for Alfons II, 1285–91). For Jewish administrators in the previous reign see D. Romano, *Los funcionarios judíos de Pedro el Grande de Aragón* (Barcelona, 1970), for *familiares*, H. Schadek, *SFG* i. 26 (1971), 201–348, 27 (1972), 264–78.

Finances. Only a beginning has been made with publishing royal accounts. *CDIACA* xxxix (1871), contains information for 1294 and 1315. E. González Hurtebise edited *Libros de tesorería de la Casa Real de Aragón*, i, *Reinado de Jaime II, 1302–04* (Barcelona, 1911). This series should be continued.

Chancery. F. Sevillano Colom, 'De la cancillería de la Corona de Aragón', *Martínez Ferrando, Archivero* (Barcelona, 1968), pp. 451–80. A. M. Aragó and J. Trenchs, 'Los Registros de Cancillería de la Corona de Aragón (Jaime I y Pedro II), y los Registros Pontificios', *Annali della Scuola Speciale per Archivisti e Bibliotecari dell'Università di Roma*, 12 (1972), 26–39. F. C. Casula, *La Cancilleria di Alfonso III il Benigno, re d'Aragona (1327–1336)* (Padua, 1967).

Local administration. J. Lalinde Abadía, *La jurisdicción real inferior en Cataluña* (Barcelona, 1966). F. A. Roca Traver, *El Justicia de Valencia, 1238–1321* (Valencia, 1970). L. Piles Ros, *Estudio documental sobre el Bayle General de Valencia. su autoridad y jurisdicción* (Valencia, 1970) (more important for the 15th cent.).

2. *Municipal, local institutions, Cortes* J. Mª. Font Rius, *Orígenes del regimen municipal de Cataluña* (Madrid, 1946). On the Aragonese *Unión* the thesis of L. González Antón, *Aportación al estudio de las uniones aragonesas y de las Cortes del Reino, 1283–1301*, about to appear, contains important unpublished documents. On the Cortes all we have is E. S. Procter, 'The Development of the Catalan "Corts" in the thirteenth century', *EUC* 22 (1936), 525–46.

3. *Economic, maritime institutions* R. S. Smith, *The Spanish Guild Merchant, A History of the Consulado, 1250–1700* (Durham, N. C., 1940). Usher's work (cited p. 272, n. 2) is more valuable for the period from 1350 onwards. The *Libro del Consulado del Mar*, ed. A. de Capmany y de Monpalau, Estudio preliminar by J. Mª. Font Rius (Barcelona, 1965). See A. García Sanz, 'Estudios sobre los orígenes del derecho marítimo hispano-mediterráneo', *AHDE* 39 (1969), 213–316, who is preparing a critical edn. of the *Libro*, and his introduction to the work cited above, under 1 B Documents.

CHAPTER II: CASTILE: 1252–1325

I. *Primary Sources*

The sources we possess for the political history of Castile and Granada are far inferior to those available for the history of the Crown of Aragon. There is no central royal Castilian archive to compare with that in Barcelona; the ACA there often supplies vital documents for Castilian history also. Royal registers were kept in Castile, as in Aragon, but only a few fragments survive, for 1283–6 (Gaibrois, *Sancho IV*, i), and many isolated royal letters. The oldest Castilian registers preserved entire date from 1467. See F. Arribas Arranz, *BRAH* 162 (1968), 171–200. Apart from the ACA, other archives, the Public Record Office in London, the Archives Nationales in Paris, and the Vatican Archives, can only partially fill these gaps. There are no surviving archives from Granada before the Christian conquest of 1492.

Castilian chronicles for the period cannot, again, compare with Catalan sources. The *Crónicas* of Alfonso X, Sancho IV, and Fernando IV were all probably composed by one author who apparently wrote under Fernando's son, Alfonso XI, and was a royal official. He appears to have used earlier accounts for some episodes of the reign of Alfonso X such as the magnates' revolt of the 1270s (Chs. 20–58), but in general the *Crónica de Alfonso X* is of little value. The later *Crónicas* improve as they near the time of writing but they are all incomplete and need correction from documentary sources which are often unavailable. They are also heavily biased in favour of Queen María of Molina, the widow of Sancho IV, who is the heroine of the whole work. Hence the author attempts to justify Sancho's revolt against his father Alfonso; he does so by suppressing a number of facts.

There also exists a short *Crónica* by Jofre de Loaisa, archdeacon of Toledo (d. *c.* 1310), written in Castilian but only preserved in a Latin version. This work (covering 1248–1305) fills in certain gaps in the royal *Crónicas*. Jofre writes from much the same point of view as the latter (he is equally anti-Aragonese, for instance) but he is somewhat more critical of Sancho IV.

The most important Muslim chronicles of the period are those of Ibn al-Khaṭīb (d. 1374), for many years a leading statesman of Granada, and of Ibn Khaldūn (1332–1406). These are valuable for the internal history of Granada and for its relations with Castile.

A. *Chronicles* 1. Castilian. *Crónicas de Alfonso X, Sancho IV, Fernando IV*. In *BAE* lxvi. 3–170. Index to the three *Crónicas*, with bibliography of manuscripts etc., by C. Mª. del Rivero, *Hispania*, 2

(1942), 163–235, 323–406, 557–618. *Crónica de Alfonso XI*: see below, under Part III, Ch. I. Jofre de Loaisa, *Crónica*, in *Bibliothèque de l'École des Chartes*, 39 (1898), 325–78. Repr., ed. A. Ubieto (Valencia, 1971).

2. Muslim. Ibn al-Khaṭīb, *Kitāb a'māl al-a'lām* (History of Muslim Spain), ed. E. Lévi-Provençal (Rabat, 1934; 2nd edn. Beirut, 1956), partly trans. W. Hoenerbach, *Islamische Geschichte Spaniens* (Zurich–Stuttgart, 1970) (711–1240). The later part (to 1368) is not translated. Idem, *Ihata Fi Tarij Garnata* (on the History of Granada), partly transl. (into Latin) in M. Casiri, *Bibliotheca arabico-hispana Escurialiensis*, ii (Madrid, 1770), 249–319. On Ibn al-Khaṭīb see Muḥammad Abd'Allah Enan, *Lisan ud-din Ibn-ul Khaṭīb* (Cairo, 1968) (in Arabic).

Kitāb al-Ibar, transl. as Ibn Khaldūn, *Histoire des berbères*, by Baron de Slane, 4 vols. (Algiers, 1852–6). Idem. *Histoire des Benou 'l-Ahmar, rois de Grenade*, transl. Gaudefroy-Demombynes, *Journal asiatique*, 9e série, 12 (1898), 309–40, 407–62.

Other Muslim chronicles are sometimes useful, notably: Ibn Abī Zar 'al-Fāsī, *Rawd al-Qirtās*, transl. A. Huici, 2 vols. (Valencia, 1964) (to 1326); Ibn Idārī, *Al-Bayān al-Mugrib*: the section on the Almohads ed. Huici, *Colección de crónicas árabes de la reconquista*, ii–iii (Tetuán, 1953–4) (to 1268).

3. Portuguese. *Crónica dos sete primeiros reis de Portugal*, ed. C. da Silva Tarouca, 3 vols. (Lisbon, 1952–4) (to Alfonso IV, 1325–57). Perhaps largely written by Fernão Lopes (15th cent.).

B. *Documents* 'Documentos de la época de D. Alfonso el Sabio' (1246–84), *MHE* 1 (1851), 1–344; 2 (1851), 1–135. 'Documentos de la época de D. Sancho el Bravo' (1291), *MHE* 3 (1852), 423–68. See also above, under Part I, Ch. II, I, and below, under II, Gaibrois de Ballesteros. A. Benavides, *Memorias de Fernando IV de Castilla*, 2 vols. (Madrid, 1860) (vol. ii). *Cortes de León*, i, 54–372. 'Las Cortes de 1252', ed. A. Ballesteros, 'Anales de la Junta para ampliación de estudios', 3. 3 (1911), 109–41. A. Giménez Soler, *Don Juan Manuel, biografía y estudio crítico* (Saragossa, 1932), contains an important collection of documents (pp. 221–708), dating from 1252 to 1348, not always accurately transcribed. See also A. Canellas López, *BRAH* 145 (1959), 231–86 (documents from the Biblioteca del Cabildo, Saragossa), and L. González Antón, in *Suma de estudios en homenaje al Dr. A. Canellas López* (Saragossa, 1969), pp. 563–84 (an agreement of 1315).

II. *Secondary Works*

A. *General* There is no reliable detailed account of the period. The useful survey of problems by J. Gautier-Dalché, *AEM* 7

(1970–1), 239–52, covers only the first half of the fourteenth century.

For Alfonso X, A. Ballesteros Beretta, *Alfonso X el Sabio* (Barcelona, 1963), has virtually replaced the Marqués de Mondejar, *Memorias históricas del rei D. Alfonso el Sabio, i observaciones a su chronica* (Madrid, 1777). Ballesteros's book is the work of a lifetime and is of great value, though, because of its posthumous publication, many documents are carelessly transcribed and need to be checked with the original sources.

M. Gaibrois de Ballesteros, *Historia del reinado de Sancho IV de Castilla*, 3 vols. (Madrid, 1922–8), is concerned only with political history but the documents in i (especially royal accounts of the 1290s) and in iii are of great importance for religious, social, and economic history.

There is no useful modern account of either the reign of Fernando IV or the minority of Alfonso XI. For the period 1300–3 see M. Gaibrois y Riaño de Ballesteros, *Un episodio de la vida de María de Molina* (Madrid, 1935).

B. *Institutions* J. Klein, *The Mesta* (cited above, p. 289). There is no satisfactory work on the Castilian navy. C. Fernández Duro, *La marina de Castilla* (Madrid, 1895), needs to be replaced by a modern study. J. González, 'Origen de la Marina real de Castilla', *RABM* 54 (1948), 229–53, is useful for the background.

Finances. No general work, though the material exists in Gaibrois, *Sancho IV*, etc. S. de Moxó, *La Alcabala: sobre sus orígenes, concepto y naturaleza* (Madrid, 1963), is useful. See also idem, 'Los Cuadernos de Alcabalas, orígenes de la legislación tributaria castellana', *AHDE* 39 (1969), 317–450, and E. Benito Ruano, 'La alcabalina', in *León y su historia*, i (León, 1969), 283–99. (See below under Cortes.)

Administration. Chancery. For Alfonso X, E. S. Procter, in *Oxford Essays in Medieval History presented to H. E. Salter* (Oxford, 1934), pp. 104–21; for Sancho IV, L. Sánchez Belda, *AHDE* 21–2 (1951–2), 171–223.

Local Administration. A. Sinués Ruiz, *El Merino* (Saragossa, 1954). E. S. Procter, *The Judicial Use of Pesquisa in León and Castile, 1157–1369* (London, 1966). On the *Hermandades* (p. 303, n. 1) see now E. Benito Ruano, *Hermandades en Asturias durante la edad media* (Oviedo, 1972); C. González Minguez, *Contribución al estudio de las Hermandades en el reinado de Fernando IV de Castilla* (Vitoria, 1974), and the more general work of A. Álvarez de Morales, *Las Hermandades, expresión del movimiento comunitario en España* (Valladolid, 1974).

Cortes. The most extensive recent discussion of the Castilian Cortes (see p. 306, n. 1) is that of J. M. Pérez-Prendes y Muñoz de

Arracó, *Revista de estudios políticos*, 126 (1962), 321–429. For some criticism of Pérez-Prendes see J. Valdeón, *AEM* 7 (1970–1), 634–37. See also J. F. O'Callaghan, 'The Cortes and Royal Taxation during the Reign of Alfonso X of Castile', *Traditio*, 27 (1971), 379–98.

Nobility. S. de Moxó, 'La nobleza castellano-leonesa en la edad media', *Hispania*, 30 (1970), 5–68, esp. 30–49.

C. *Granada* See above, under General Bibliography (p. 411).

D. *The Court and Learning: Alfonso X* Bibliography assembled by G. H. London, *Boletín de filología española*, 2, 6 (April 1960), 18–31 (some 260 items), a supplement to J. A. Sánchez Pérez, in *Anales de la Universidad de Madrid*, Letras, 2 (1933), 186–214, 289–311, and in his *Alfonso X, el Sabio* (Madrid, 1944). The most valuable introduction is that of E. S. Procter, *Alfonso X of Castile* (Oxford, 1951). For Alfonso's political ideas see J. A. Maravall (cited p. 298, n. 2); for his scientific works D. Romano, 'Le opere scientifiche di Alfonso X e l'intervento degli ebrei', *Accademia Nazionale dei Lincei, Atti dei Convegni*, 13 (Rome, 1971), 677–711, is fundamental. On the historical works the studies of D. Catalán Menéndez Pidal (cited pp. 332 f.) have carried further the researches of his grandfather. See now F. Rico, *Alfonso el Sabio y la 'General estoria'* (Barcelona, 1974). One should also cite M. C. Díaz y Díaz, 'La obra de Bernardo de Brihuega, colaborador de Alfonso X', in *Acta Salmanticensia*, 16 (Salamanca, 1962), 145–61. See also above, Part I, Ch. VI, p. 221, n. 1.

PART III: THE STRUGGLE FOR HEGEMONY 1325–1410

CHAPTER I: ALFONSO XI OF CASTILE AND THE STRUGGLE FOR THE STRAITS OF GIBRALTAR

I. *Primary Sources*

A. *Chronicles* 1. Castilian. *Crónica de Alfonso XI*. In *BAE* lxvi, 173–392. On this work, perhaps written at the request of Enrique II in the 1370s, and the fuller (unpublished) *Gran Crónica* see the studies by D. Catalán Menéndez Pidal, *BRAH* 154 (1964), 79–126, 156 (1965), 55–87; *AEM* 2 (1965), 257–99. The author's most recent view is that the *Gran Crónica* is an interpolated version of the *Crónica*, which uses the *Poema de Alfonso XI* by Rodrigo Yáñez (in *BAE* lvii. 477–551, and ed. Yo ten Cate (Madrid, 1956). See also Catalán, *BRAH* 13, (1952), 247–66; *BRAE* 48 (1968), 189–236.

2. Muslim. See above, Bibliography for Part II, Ch. II. Several other chronicles are useful for the Merinids in Spain; one, the work by a contemporary, Abū'Abd Allāh Muḥammad ibn Marzūq, *Al-Musnad aṣ-sāhīh al-Ḥasan . . .* (*The True and Beautiful Collection on*

the Memorable Deeds of our Lord al-Ḥasan), partly ed. and transl. by E. Lévi-Provençal, *Hésperis*, 5 (1925), 1–82, is disappointing in this respect. See the discussion of sources in Huici (cited below, II).

3. Portuguese. Rui de Pina, *Crónica do Rei D. Afonso IV*, ed. C. da Silva-Tarouca, *Crónica dos sete primeiros reis de Portugal*, ii (Lisbon, 1952). A late source incorporating earlier material, much less favourable to Alfonso XI than his *Crónica*.

B. *Documents* The Archivo de la Corona de Aragón in Barcelona has again provided most of the documents published on this reign, and especially on the struggle for the Straits. See *CDIACA* vii (1851), 75–189 (1337–45). A. Giménez Soler, *La Corona de Aragón y Granada* (Barcelona, 1908). A. Canellas López, *EEMCA* 2 (1946), 7–73 (documents of 1300–86 but the majority 1333–44) uses the Archivo Municipal of Saragossa. See also Robson and Sevillano, cited under II, and Giménez Soler, *Don Juan Manuel* (cited above, under Part II, Ch. II).

Cortes de León, i, 372–637. For the *Ordenamiento de Alcalá* see the edition by J. de Asso y del Rio and M. de Manuel y Rodríguez (Madrid, 1774) (facs. edn. Valencia, 1960).

II. *Secondary Works*

The reign of Alfonso XI has not been discussed in detail by any modern historian. Of A. Ballesteros Beretta's unpublished 'Historia de Alfonso XI', only one article has appeared in *BRAH* 124 (1949), 11–58, on the first year of Alfonso's personal reign (1325).

For the *struggle over the straits* see J. A. Robson, *English Historical Review*, 74 (1959), 386–408, and F. Sevillano Colom, *EHMed* 3 (1970), 55–74. Both authors use the ACA and Sevillano Majorcan archives as well. There is an excellent account of the Battle of the Salado in A. Huici Miranda, *Las grandes batallas de la reconquista* (Madrid, 1956).

On Alfonso XI's *internal reforms* the article of J. Torres Fontes, on the administration of Murcia, *AHDE* 23 (1953), 139–59, and that of J. I. Ruiz de la Peña on León, in *León y su historia*, i (León, 1969), 301–16.

CHAPTER II: PERE III OF CATALONIA–ARAGON: AN ATTEMPTED MEDITERRANEAN EMPIRE

I. *Primary Sources*

A. *Chronicles* Pere III's own *Crònica* (1319–82) is critically edited by A. Pagès (Toulouse, 1942). See the review by M. Coll, *ER* 1 (1947–8), 254–7. The only translation available is the unsatisfactory Spanish version by A. de Bofarull (Barcelona, 1850). An English transl. by Mary Hillgarth will appear shortly. The text of Pagès is included, with notes, in F. Soldevila, *Les Quatre Gran Cròniques* (Barcelona, 1971).

The *Crònica dels reys d'Aragó e comtes de Barcelona* was published by A. J. Soberanas Lleó (Barcelona, 1961) (*Crònica general de Pere III*). The text, also known as *Crónica de San Juan de la Peña*, exists in Latin, ed. A. Ubieto (Valencia, 1961) and in Aragonese, ed., with the Latin, by T. Ximénez de Embrun, *Historia de la Corona de Aragón* (Saragossa, 1876). Pere's historical works are well discussed by Riquer, i, 480–501. See also J. Rubió, *EUC* 21 (1936), 343–55.

B. *Documents* 1. Cultural and internal Rubió, *Documents*, is indispensable. The publication of Pere's more personal letters, Pere III, *Epistolari*, ed. R. Gubern, with a valuable introduction, has only attained one volume (to 1361, Barcelona, 1955). A useful small collection is that of C. Sánchez-Cutillas, *Lletres closes de Pere el Cerimoniós endreçades al Consell de Valencia* (Barcelona, 1967). J. Mª. Millás Vallicrosa provided an admirable edition, in Hebrew, Catalan, and Latin, of *Las tablas astronómicas del rey Don Pedro el Ceremonioso* (Madrid, 1962). See also J. Mª. Madurell Marimón, *Hispania*, 24 (1964), 581–98. Pere's *Ordinacions* are in *CDIACA* v (1850). A new edition, with a detailed comparison with Jaume III of Majorca's *Leges Palatinae*, is needed. Further ordinances are cited on p. 354, n. 3.

The Corts of Catalonia (only, see above, p. 422) under Pere appear in *Cortes de Cataluña*, i. 2–iv (1896–1901).

2. External a. Majorca. Pere's legal case is contained in the *Proceso contra el rey de Mallorca, D. Jaime III*, 3 vols., *CDIACA* xxix-xxxi (1866). See also Lecoy de la Marche (cited below, under II). Majorcan sources are used in A. Campaner, *Cronicón mayoricense* (Palma, 1881), and, more fully, by J. Vich and J. Muntaner, *Documenta regni Majoricarum* (Palma, 1945). B. Font, *BSAL* 32 (1964), 253–60, publishes a list of payments for the campaign of 1349.

b. Sardinia. Much recent work has been done on Sardinia under Pere. A. Boscolo provides a statement of the resources in the ACA in *Archivio storico sardo*, 29 (1964), 391–97. See also J. Mateu Ibars, 'Fondos archivísticos sardos para el estudio de la gobernación del reino en el siglo XIV', *Martínez Ferrando, Archivero* (Barcelona, 1968), pp. 323–50. Two important collections of documents have been published recently by the University of Cagliari: F. Casula, *Carte reali e diplomatiche di Alfonso III, il Benigno, re d'Aragona, riguardanti l'Italia* (Padua, 1970), and Luisa d'Arienzo, *Carte reali diplomatiche di Pietro IV, il Ceremonioso, re d'Aragona, riguardanti l'Italia* (= *CDIACA* xlv) (Padua, 1970), who registers 882 documents mostly before 1362, the majority concerning Sardinia, though the papacy also appears frequently. Some years earlier E. Putzulu published, from Sardinian sources, '"Cartulari de Arborea" Raccolta di documenti diplomatici inediti sulle relazioni tra il Giudicati d'Arborea e i Re d'Aragona (1328–1430)', *Archivio storico sardo*, 25, 1–2 (1957), 71–170. See now J. Trenchs and R. Saínz de la Maza, *Documentos pontificios sobre Cerdeña de la época de Alfonso el Benigno (1327–1336)* (Barcelona, 1974).

Some of these collections help to document the expedition to the Bosphorus in 1351–2. See also for this, *MHE* 2 (1851), 249–389.

II. *Secondary Works*

A. General and biographical Given the richness of the documentary sources the absence of much modern research into Pere's reign is surprising. The best general account remains Zurita, *Anales*, Books VII–X. R. Tasis [i Marca], *La vida del Rei En Pere III* (Barcelona, 1954), is a modern presentation, without references, based on Pere's *Crònica*. The same author's *Pere el Ceremoniós i els seus fills* (Barcelona, 1957), is an abbreviated (annotated) version of the earlier work. The most valuable general discussion is that of R. d'Abadal i de Vinyals, 'Pedro el Ceremonioso y los comienzos de la decadencia política de Cataluña', *HE* xiv (1966), pp. ix-cciii (published in Catalan with notes, *Pere el Cerimoniós*, Barcelona, 1972). The account by Juan Reglá Campistol of Pere's reign in 'La Corona de Aragón (1336–1410)', ibid., pp. 439–527, is disappointing.

As Abadal observes (p. cxiii) the question of Pere's cultural formation is still unresolved. For the general cultural background A. Rubió, *EUC* 8 (1914), 213–47, is excellent.

B. Institutions Karl Schwarz, *Aragonische Hofordnungen im 13. u. 14. Jahrhundert* (Berlin–Leipzig, 1913), studies the *Ordinacions* (see, however, above, under I. B). J. Lalinde Abadía has a general discussion of 'Las instituciones de la Corona de Aragón en el siglo XIV', *VIII CHCA* ii, 2, pp. 9–52. F. Sevillano Colom, 'Apuntes para el estudio de la Cancillería de Pedro IV el Ceremonioso', *AHDE* 20 (1950), 137–241, is fundamental. (See also the works cited above under Part II, Ch. I, II, C 1.) For Pere's naval forces see J. A. Robson, 'The Catalan fleet and Moorish Sea-Power (1337–1344)', *English Historical Review*, 74 (1959), 386–408, an inquiry which should be carried into later decades.

C. External Expansion 1. Majorca. The main work remains A. Lecoy de la Marche, *Les Relations politiques de la France avec le royaume de Majorque*, 2 vols. (Paris, 1892), esp. vol. ii (with many documents). J. Rey Pastor and E. García Camarero, *La cartografía mallorquina* (Madrid, 1960), catalogue the surviving Majorcan maps. There is an excellent discussion of Majorcan trade by F. Sevillano Colom in *Historia de Mallorca*, ed. J. Mascaró Pasarius, IV (Palma, 1971), 431–520. See also p. 363, n. 1. The conquest itself is described by C. A. Willemsen, 'Der Untergang des Königreiches Mallorka und das Ende der mallorkinischen Dynastie', *SFG* i, 5 (1935), 240–96, and 'Jakob II, von Mallorka und Peter IV, von Aragon (1336–1349)', ibid. 8 (1940), 81–198.

2. Sardinia, Corsica, North Africa. A general account of Pere and Sardinia has yet to be drawn from the documentary collections cited above. G. Meloni, *Genova e Aragona all'epoca di Pietro il Cerimonioso*, i (1336–54) (Padua, 1971), is an excellent military and diplomatic history. For one aspect see E. Putzulu, 'L'ufficio di Maestro Razionale del regno di Sardegna', *Martínez Ferrando, Archivero* (Barcelona, 1968), pp. 409–30, esp. 414–19. On Corsica see G. Sorgia, 'Corsica, Genova e Aragona nel basso medioevo', *Studi sardi*, 20 (1966–7), 167–239 (to 1481), and in *VIII CHCA* iii (1973), 101–13 (Pere III). For North Africa see Ch. E. Dufourcq, 'Chrétiens et maghribins durant les derniers siècles du Moyen Âge', to appear in the Actas del I Congreso Internacional de Historia Mediterránea (Palma, 1973); his analysis of the evidence for 1360–86 in *Miscelánea de textos medievales*, ii (1974), 65–166. The general accounts of Pere's policy by J. Camarena Mahiques and V. Salavert Roca, in *VIII CHCA* iii, are disappointing. See below, Vol. ii, Part II, Ch. I, and the accompanying Bibliography.

CHAPTER III: PEDRO I OF CASTILE: AN ATTEMPTED PENINSULAR EMPIRE (1350–1369)

I. *Primary Sources*

A. *Chronicles* 1. Castilian. The standard account of the reigns of Pedro I, Enrique II, and Juan I is that by Pero López de Ayala (d. 1407). Ayala's *Crónica de Pedro I* was written after Pedro's fall and has to be used with caution (see also Vol. ii, Part I, Ch. VII). Ayala's chronicles are contained in *BAE* lxvi and lxviii, which reprints, with some errors, E. de Llaguno Amirola's edition of 1779–80. A new edition is needed. Ayala's younger contemporary writing under Enrique III, Juan Rodríguez de Cuenca, *Sumario de los reyes de España*, ed. Llaguno (Madrid, 1781, repr. Valencia, 1971, with indices) adds very little. P. E. Russell edits 'The *Memorias* of Fernán Álvarez de Albornoz' in *Hispanic Studies in honour of I.*

González Llubera, ed. F. Pierce (Oxford, 1959), pp. 319–30. This short work is well informed and corrects Ayala's chronology.

2. Muslim. Ibn al-Khaṭīb, 'Correspondencia diplomática entre Granada y Fez, siglo XIV', ed. and transl. M. Gaspar y Remiro, *Revista del Centro de Estudios Históricos de Granada y su reino*, 2 (1912)–5 (1915)—letters written in the name of Yūsuf I and Muḥammad V of Granada (1352–69). A chapter of Ibn al-Khaṭīb, *Nufādat al-yirāb fi ulālat al-igtuāb*, on the events of 1359–62, ed. A. Mujtār al-'Abbādī in *Revista del Instituto de estudios islámicos en Madrid*, 7–8 (1959–60), 43–73 (Arabic section; Spanish summary, pp. 199–202).

3. French, English, etc. The most reliable contemporary account of the war of succession is the *Life of the Black Prince by the Herald of Sir John Chandos*, ed. M. K. Pope and E. C. Lodge (Oxford, 1910). Froissart's account is second-hand and very unreliable. Some other sources are cited on p. 373, n. 2.

B. *Documents* The paucity of documents for general Castilian history before the Catholic Monarchs is particularly marked for Pedro I's reign. Many documents issued by him appear to have been deliberately destroyed though see Catalina García (cited below, under II A). No records of Cortes are preserved after 1351, though several meetings are recorded. The Archivo Municipal of Murcia is an exception. It was put to good use by F. Cascales, *Discursos históricos de la muy noble y muy leal ciudad de Murcia y su reino* (Murcia, 1621, 3rd edn., 1874), and again, in our day, by J. Torres Fontes. Thus, while Pere III of Catalonia's attempt to produce official history can be corrected from his own ACA, it is impossible to correct Ayala in this way. See, below, *ADDENDA* on p. 436.

The Valencian archives and the ACA can be used. The *Colección de documentos inéditos del Archivo General del Reino de Valencia*, ed. J. Casañ y Alegre, i [*unicum*] (Valencia, 1894), contains the agreements between Pere III and Enrique de Trastámara from 1356 to 1366. See also Sánchez-Cutillas (cited above, under Ch. II, I B). Some information can be extracted from the *Proceso contra Bernardo de Cabrera* [1364–66], 3 vols. (*CDIACA* xxxii–xxxiv, 1867–8). Other important documents for 1365–7 from the ACA, ed. J. Miret i Sans, 'Négotiations de Pierre IV d'Aragon avec la cour de France', *Revue hispanique*, 13 (1905), 76–135.

II. *Secondary Works*

A. General and Biographical The political history of Castile in this period is discussed in detail in J. Catalina García, *Castilla y León durante los reinados de Pedro I, Enrique II, Juan I y Enrique III*, 2 vols. (Madrid, 1891) (ends in 1390). Vol. I contains a valuable list of 361 documents issued by Pedro I. This work is not replaced by L. Suárez Fernández's more modern synthesis, 'Castilla (1350–1406)', in *HE* xiv (1966), 3–378.

There is a dearth of good biographies of Pedro. Prosper Merimée, *Histoire de Don Pèdre 1er, roi de Castille* (Paris, 1848), often reprinted and translated, is still a readable presentation of Ayala's *Crónica*, with some useful additional material. J. B. Sitges, *Las mujeres de Don Pedro I de Castilla* (Madrid, 1910), is the best later study. There is a study of one region by A. Rodríguez González, 'Pedro I de Castilla y Galicia', *Boletín de la Universidad Compostelana*, 64 (1956), 241–76. For an account of Doña Leonor de Guzmán at the beginning of the reign see A. Ballesteros-Beretta, *BRAH* 100 (1932), 624–36. Pedro's legend is elucidated by P. Bohigas's studies (cited p. 372, n. 1).

B. Pedro's policy and ideas B. F. Taggie, 'The Castilian Foreign Policy during the Reign of Pedro I, 1350–69', unpublished Ph.D. dissertation, Michigan State, 1973. For his administration see J. Torres Fontes, *CHE* 25–6 (1957), 251–67 (the Murcian evidence). Pedro's general ideas and those of his opponents are discussed by J. Gimeno Casalduero, *La imagen del monarca en la Castilla del siglo XIV* (Madrid, 1972).

C. War with Aragon, War of Succession The articles of A. Gutiérrez de Velasco, based on the ACA, are useful. Taken in the order of the chronology of the war with Aragon they appeared in *J. Zurita, cuadernos de historia*, 10–11 (1960), 69–98 [1357]; ibid. 14–15 (1963), 7–30 [1358–62]; ibid. 12–13 (1961), 7–39 [1362–67]; 'Los ingleses en España', *EEMCA* 4 (1951), 215–319 [1367 onwards]. One should also consult J. B. Sitges, *La muerte de Don Bernardo de Cabrera* (Madrid, 1911). The fundamental work for the war of succession in Castile is P. E. Russell, *The English Intervention in Spain and Portugal in the time of Edward III and Richard II* (Oxford, 1955). A valuable earlier account in R. Delachenal, *Histoire de Charles V*, iii (Paris, 1916), 239–490.

The results of the wars for the Crown of Aragon have been investigated by J.-L. Martín, 'Nacionalización de la sal y aranceles extraordinarios en Cataluña (1357–67)', *AEM* 3 (1966), 515–24; idem, 'Las Cortes catalanas en la guerra castellano-aragonesa (1356–65)', *VIII CHCA* ii, 2 pp. 79–90; and by Gutiérrez de Velasco, 'La financiación aragonesa de la "Guerra de los dos Pedros"', *Hispania*, 19 (1959), 3–43. For the war see also the thesis of John Boswell, cited above, under Part I, Ch. V (Mudejars).

CHAPTER IV: THE VICISSITUDES OF CASTILIAN HEGEMONY: CASTILE, PORTUGAL, AND GRANADA (1369–1410)

I. *Primary Sources*

A. Chronicles 1. Castilian. Ayala's chronicles (see above, Ch. III) extend into the reign of Enrique III (to 1396). They are particularly valuable for the reign of Juan I. Leonor López de Córdoba, *Relación escrita para sus descendientes, CDIHE* lxxxi, 35–44, is an account, written many years later, of the siege of Carmona (1370–1) by the daughter of a leading loyalist to Pedro I.

2. Muslim. See Ibn al-Khaṭīb, cited under Ch. III, above.

3. Portuguese. The chronicles of Fernão Lopes, esp. his *Crónica de D. Fernando*, ed. S. Dias Arnaut (Porto, 1966), and his *Crónica de D. João I*, Part I ed. A. Braamcamp Freire (Lisbon, 1915), II ed. W. J. Entwistle (1968), are of great interest. Fernão Lopes is later in date than Ayala (he wrote perhaps from 1418 to *c.* 1460) and uses him extensively but also corrects him, partly from documents, though he is also a fervent nationalist. See P. E. Russell, *As fontes de Fernão Lopes* (Coimbra, 1941), and in *Revista Portuguesa de História* 10 (1962), 430–2.

B. Documents J. Valdeón Baruque edits 'Un cuaderno de cuentas de Enrique II' [1379], *Hispania*, 26 (1966), 99–134, and is preparing a documentary collection for Enrique's reign. L. Suárez Fernández has in preparation a documentary collection for Juan I.

II. *Secondary Works*

A. General and biographical See the general works listed above, under Ch. III, II A. J. Valdeón Baruque, *Enrique II de Castilla y la consolidación del regimen (1366–1371)* (Valladolid, 1966), with a useful, though incomplete, bibliography. See the revew by J. R. L. Highfield, *English Historical Review*, 82 (1967), 789–91. L. Suárez Fernández, *Juan I de Castilla (1379–1390)* (Madrid, 1955), is the first draft (at times with greater detail) of his relevant chapters in *HE* xiv. There is, as yet, no general study, in detail, of Enrique III.

B. Internal policies For Enrique II, Valdeón, op. cit.; on the *mercedes*, idem, in *Hispania*, 28 (1968), 38–55. E. Mitre Fernández's studies on the reign of Enrique III are also of great value. See especially his *Evolución de la nobleza en Castilla bajo Enrique III, 1396–1406* (Valladolid, 1968), and *La extensión del regimen de corregidores . . .* (Valladolid, 1969), also *Asturiensia Medievalia*, ii (1975), 177–237.

C. Foreign Relations The most valuable study continues to be Russell's (cited above, under Ch. III, II C). For *Granada* see A. Mujtār al-'Abbādī, *El reino de Granada en la época de Muhammad V*,

Madrid, 1973. For the conflict with Portugal there is no satisfactory work. S. Dias Arnaut's massive *A crise nacional dos fins do século XIV*, I, *A sucessão de D. Fernando* (Coimbra, 1960), studies only the beginning of the crisis. See Suárez's review, in *Hispania*, 22 (1962), 629–31, and his own interpretation, in *AEM* 2 (1965), 359–76. See also M. Caetano's articles, cited on pp. 395–6, and, for the influence of the papal schism, A. Brásio, in *Bracara Augusta*, 14–15 (1963), 118–36.

ADDENDA

Part I, Ch. II. *Agrarian history* (p. 414). For salt in Asturias see *Asturiensia Medievalia*, i (Oviedo, 1972), 11–155. For the *bourgeoisie* (p. 415) in Oviedo see *ibid.*, ii (1975), 107–76.

Part I, Chs. III-IV. *Monasticism* (p. 417). The accounts of nine monasteries (in 1338), contained in García González's book, are excellently analysed by S. Moreta, *Rentas monásticas de Castilla: problemas de método* (Salamanca, 1974).

Part II, Ch. II. *Local administration* (p. 427). See G. Martínez Díez, *Alava medieval*, ii (Vitoria, 1974).

Part III, Ch. II (p. 432). *Sardinia.* On Catalan relations with Genoa, Pisa and Sardinia see the contributions of G. Meloni, M. Tangheroni, and C. P. Kyrris, to *Atti del 1º Congresso storico Liguria-Catalogna* (Bordighera, 1974).

Part III, Ch. III. *Documents* (p. 433). L. V. Díaz Martín, *Itinerario de Pedro I de Castilla* (Valladolid, 1975), registers 1,012 dated documents but the majority are of very limited interest and over half belong to 1350–52.

Index

* References included here to modern authors are mainly to the Bibliography.